THE 1979 PITTSBURGH PIRATES

Edited by Bill Nowlin and Gregory H. Wolf
Associate editors Russ Lake and Len Levin

Society for American Baseball Research, Inc.
Phoenix, AZ

When Pops Led the Family: The 1979 Pittsburgh Pirates
Edited by Bill Nowlin and Gregory H. Wolf
Associate editors Russ Lake and Len Levin

Copyright © 2016 Society for American Baseball Research, Inc.
All rights reserved. Reproduction in whole or in part without permission is prohibited.

ISBN 978-1-943816-35-4
Ebook ISBN 978-1-943816-34-7

Cover and book design: Gilly Rosenthol

All photographs courtesy of the Pittsburgh Pirates, except as noted.
The photographs of Joe Coleman (p. 58), Gary Hargis (p. 88), and Alberto Lois (p. 113)
are courtesy of the National Baseball Hall of Fame.
Cover photos courtesy of the National Baseball Hall of Fame.

Society for American Baseball Research
Cronkite School at ASU
555 N. Central Ave. #416
Phoenix, AZ 85004

Phone: (602) 496-1460
Web: www.sabr.org
Facebook: Society for American Baseball Research
Twitter: @SABR

Table of Contents

Introduction 1
Three Rivers Stadium, by Chip Greene..3

PLAYERS
How the Pirates Were Put Together, by Rod Nelson.................................12
Matt Alexander, by Rory Costello..15
Dale Berra, by Bob Hurte...23
Jim Bibby, by Rory Costello...27
Bert Blyleven, by Gregory H. Wolf..34
Doe Boyland, by Rory Costello..44
John Candelaria, by Steve West..51
Joe Coleman, by Gregory H. Wolf...57
Mike Easler, by Clayton Trutor..64
Dock Ellis, by Paul Geisler...69
Tim Foli, by Norm King...76
Phil Garner, by Norm King...82
Gary Hargis, by Michael Jaffe..87
Grant Jackson, by Maxwell Kates..90
Bruce Kison, by Gregory H. Wolf..98
Lee Lacy, by Gregory H. Wolf..105
Alberto Lois, by Tom Crist...112
Bill Madlock, by Norm King..115
John Milner, by Jon Springer..122
Omar Moreno, by Norm King...127
Steve Nicosia, by Phillip Bolda...133
Ed Ott, by Bob Hurte...138
Dave Parker, by J. G. Preston..143
Rick Rhoden, by Paul Hofmann..153
Dave Roberts, by Gregory H. Wolf...159
Bill Robinson, by Alan Cohen...165
Don Robinson, by Thomas E. Kern...173
Enrique Romo, by Rory Costello...179
Jim Rooker, by Rich Shook...187
Manny Sanguillen, by Bob Hurte..193

Willie Stargell, by James Forr...201

Rennie Stennett, by Joseph Wancho...208

Frank Taveras, by Rory Costello..213

Kent Tekulve, by Bob Hurte...219

Ed Whitson, by Michael Huber...224

Chuck Tanner and the Bullpen, by Rory Costello...229

MANAGER AND COACHING STAFF

Chuck Tanner, by Dan Fields...229

Harvey Haddix, by Mark Miller...238

Joe Lonnett, by David E. Skelton...245

Al Monchak, by Carole J. Olshavsky..250

Bob Skinner, by Joseph Wancho...254

FRONT OFFICE

Harding "Pete" Peterson, by Rich Puerzer..259

John W. Galbreath, by Warren Corbett..263

THE REGULAR SEASON REVIEW AND SELECT GAME ACCOUNTS

1979 Pirates Game-by-Game Timeline, by Richard Riis...269

May 9, 1979, by Frederick C. Bush..289

May 25, 1979, by Matthew Silverman..292

June 1, 1979, but Eric Robinson...295

June 3, 1979, by Gregory H. Wolf..298

July 21, 1979, by Rock Hoffman...301

August 19, 1979, by Gregory H. Wolf..303

August 25, 1979, by Nick Waddell...305

September 23, 1979, by Gregory H. Wolf...308

September 30, 1979, by Gregory H. Wolf...311

THE POST-SEASON

The National League Championship Series, by Thomas E. Schott..313

The 1979 Baltimore Orioles, by Gordon Gattie...320

The 1979 World Series, by Frederick C. Bush..325

STATISTICS AND MORE

"We Are Family"—the song, by David E. Skelton...346

By the Numbers, by Dan Fields...348

Contributors..357

When Pops Led the Family: The 1979 Pittsburgh Pirates
An Introduction

THE 1979 PIRATES WERE A TESTIMONY to teamwork, a team in the purest sense of the word, in a sport that cherishes, indeed exalts, individual greatness and personal accomplishments. They became the first team in major-league history to win the World Series without having a pitcher who won at least 15 games or a batter who drove in at least 100 runs in the same season. The squad was a perfect blend of veterans, youngsters, and role players, all of whom seemed sincerely to have fun playing and, importantly, winning. Its diverse, divergent personalities, from Pops, Mad Dog, Scrap Iron, and the Cobra to the Candy Man and the Hammer, were held together as a family by skipper Chuck Tanner.

Resiliency, inextinguishable spirit, trust in one another, selflessness, confidence, and unparalleled pride were trademarks of the 1979 Pirates. The club was expected to challenge for its sixth NL East division title of the decade—and first in four years—in 1979. The previous season the Pirates had overcome an 11½-game deficit to the Philadelphia Phillies on August 12, only to lose the division crown in the next to last game of the season. But when the 1979 Pirates got off to a horrible start, losers of 18 of their first 30 games, critics dismissed them as too old. Willie Stargell, the team's 39-year-old graybeard and unequivocal vocal leader, refused to take the sportswriters' bait. Instead, he suggested that that Pirates public-address announcer play the disco hit "We Are Family" by Sister Sledge. That song defined the team, and collectively the Pirates continued to believe in themselves.

In a season of many turning points, one of the biggest occurred on June 28 when the Pirates acquired disgruntled, former two-time batting champion Bill Madlock from the San Francisco Giants. Madlock was installed at third base, moving Phil Garner to second, his natural position, and the Bucs took off. From July 2 to August 16, the Pirates won 33 of 48 games, transforming a 6½-game deficit into a four-game lead. The Pirates showed what kind of family they were in the final two frenetic weeks of the season when they fell out of first place on September 20, replaced by the surging Montreal Expos, winners of 26 of their previous 34 games. Ten days later, the Pirates captured the division crown on the last day of the season, led by NL Co-MVP Stargell's team-high 32nd home run.

The 1979 Pirates were anything but a lucky team that got hot at the end of the season to snare an unexpected crown. They were good! The club won 98 games, its most since the 1909 team posted 110 wins and won the World Series. If anything the '79 Pirates were a balanced team that led the league in scoring and finished second in home runs and batting average; however, only one member of the team was named to the All-Star squad—the enigmatic Dave Parker, the reigning two-time NL batting champ, who finished with a career-best 109 runs scored and batted .310. The pitching staff, typically derided for its lack of a bona-fide ace, boasted six hurlers who won at least 10 games, led by John Candelaria's 14, Brice Kison's 13, and Bert Blyleven's 12. But the key to the staff was a trio of relievers, Kent Tekulve, Enrique Romo, and Grant Jackson, who combined for 250 appearances and logged in excess of 350 innings.

After steamrolling the Cincinnati Reds in the NLCS, the Pirates fell behind the favored Baltimore Orioles three games to one in the World Series. With their backs to the proverbial wall, the Pirates yet again demonstrated their resiliency by winning the final three games, the latter two on the road, outscoring the Orioles 15-2 in those games, to capture their second title of the decade.

WHEN POPS LED THE FAMILY

The 1979 World Series champion Pirates are one of the most memorable teams in baseball history and helped define an era. One look at their pillbox caps, adorned with stars distributed by Stargell, or their typically garish uniforms, complete with striking yellow jerseys often worn with the same-color pants, and the viewer is transported back to the Steel City at the close of the '70s. *When Pops Led the Family* celebrates this team and its cast of characters. Included are stories about all of the players, members of the coaching staff, and the front office, an in-depth season summary, and detailed game accounts from some of the most pivotal games of the season and all of the postseason games. Essays on Three Rivers Stadium, Tanner's use of his bullpen, and the "We Are Family" song help round out the volume.

When Pops Led the Family features contributions from 39 members of the Society for American Baseball Research (SABR). These volunteers are united by a passion for researching and writing about baseball history. We thank all of them for their contributions, meticulous research, cooperation through the revising and editing process, and finally their patience. Also deserving the utmost praise and thanks are Russ Lake, fact-checker, and Len Levin, copy editor. This book was originally conceived by George Skornickel and would not have been possible without the generous support of the staff and Board of Directors of SABR, SABR Publications Director Cecilia Tan, and designer Gilly Rosenthol (Rosenthol Design).

Special thanks to the Pittsburgh Pirates Baseball Club, and the team's Bree Main and Samantha Lynn for providing many photos for this book. The Pirates' support of SABR's nonprofit mission is greatly appreciated. We also thank John Horne of the National Baseball Hall of Fame for supplying additional photos.

- Bill Nowlin and Gregory H. Wolf, editors

Three Rivers Stadium

By Chip Greene

THREE RIVERS STADIUM; IF IT WASN'T THE most picturesque coliseum in American sports history, it was perhaps one of the most perfectly named.

In southwestern Pennsylvania, Pittsburgh, the county seat of Allegheny County, lies partly in a hilly region known as the Golden Triangle, the location of the city's business district. For those unfamiliar with the region, one look at a map and it's immediately apparent where the area derives its name from. Flowing diagonally from northeast of the city to southwest is the Allegheny River. Meandering gracefully from the southeast to the northwest is the Monongahela River. At the confluence of those two waterways, the point of the triangle, is formed the Ohio River; and it's there, where the three rivers converge, across the Allegheny River from the Golden Triangle, on the riverbank known as the north shore, that Pittsburgh's sports fans gathered for 31 years at Three Rivers Stadium to watch their favorite baseball team, the Pirates.

It is a riverbank steeped in local lore. During the region's formative years, as the French and British vied for supremacy amid the native American Indians (Three Rivers Stadium was built on a Delaware Indian burial ground), each nation erected enclosures for protection, Fort Duquesne by the French; and Fort Pitt by the British. As those two world powers battled for local sovereignty, George Washington engaged in several military campaigns on the north shore, attempting to take possession of Fort Duquesne.

Three Rivers Stadium wasn't the first ballpark to occupy the shoreline; in fact, it was merely the latest in a line of stadiums which had once stood upon the same site. In 1882 the Alleghenys,[1] a founding member of the American Association, began play on the north shore at Exposition Park, in what would be the first incarnation of a structure known by that name. Exposition Park I remained intact for just one season. By opening day of 1883, flooding along the shore had forced hasty construction of a second version of Exposition Park, in roughly the same location, but on higher yet overlapping ground. The Alleghenys took up residence in that ballpark too, but for only a single season, as for the next six years the team called nearby Recreation Park its home. It was only a matter of time, however, before they once again occupied the Exposition Park grounds.

The year 1887 brought to the region a change in the baseball landscape. That season the Alleghenys not only joined the National League, but they also adopted as their identity the city across the river. For the first time, the team playing at Recreation Park was known not just as the Alleghenys, but as the *Pittsburgh* Alleghenys. If they were rarely very good on the field, at least they were major league.

If the lineage of today's Pittsburgh Pirates[2] can be traced to that first Alleghenys team playing at the first Exposition Park on the north shore, then Opening Day 1891 marks the date when all of the attributes of one of baseball's most historic franchises were finally in place. On April 22, 1891, the Pittsburgh Pirates lost their season's opener, 7-6, to the Chicago Colts, at the Pirates brand-new stadium, again named Exposition Park (III). It was the third and ultimately final version, which stood atop the previous two incarnations. It was to remain the team's home for the next 18 seasons. That span, though, was dwarfed by the Pirates' stay at their next ballpark. To get there, the team left the north shore and moved across the river to the heart of the Golden Triangle.

Little need be said about Forbes Field; much has been written about one of the legendary ballparks in baseball history. Besides, this essay is about Three Rivers Stadium, not Forbes Field. Suffice it to say that once the Pirates moved into their new state-of-the-art, concrete and steel coliseum in June 1909, they stayed in that ballpark in the Oakland neighborhood of Pittsburgh for the next 61 years, and won three World Series. By the 1950s, however, with the Forbes Field infrastructure beginning to crumble and the ballpark showing its age, a search was on for a new facility that would propel the Pirates into the modern era. Once again, attention turned back to the north shore.

Revitalization

Over the several generations that the Pirates called Forbes Field their home, the riverfront where once had stood the three versions of Exposition Park had become a sprawling industrial area, which by the early 1950s was severely in need of an architectural makeover. With the concurrent aging of Forbes Field, the need was acute for a new ballpark that could house not only the Pirates, but also the city's football team, the Steelers. Planning for a multipurpose municipal ballpark had begun as early as 1948, when the first proposal was submitted to the city; but it wasn't until the '50s that substantive efforts to address the ballpark issue took shape. It was then that the city decided to revitalize the north shore. Baseball, it was determined, would return to the riverfront, at the site where it had all begun, the site where the three rivers met.

Officially, that site for what was initially to be called Pittsburgh Stadium was chosen in 1958.[3] Completion was estimated for some time in the early 1960s. Once built, the plan was for the ballpark to be the crown jewel in a complex that would include hotels, restaurants, and a riverfront park. In original conception the ballpark was to be round, with an open end facing south, toward the skyline of downtown Pittsburgh. Some designs, however, envisioned a bit more extravagance. Rather than a ballpark that would stand on the waterfront, one particularly grandiose design proposed a "Stadium Over the Monongahela" that would be built completely *over* the water.[4] In that, a massive span would replace the existing Smithfield Street Bridge, and the ballpark would be built atop the span, with two parking lots below. The entire structure would stand above the river, "with plenty of room for boats to pass beneath."[5] The prohibitive cost alone of such a project probably ensured that such a proposal was never even considered.

With the ballpark's location chosen, it took five years before work got under way to clear the land for eventual construction. That began in 1963. However, political squabbles and labor disputes further delayed the project. One key milestone, though, eventually served as the catalyst to begin building the ballpark, In 1958, work had begun on the Fort Duquesne Bridge, which would span the Allegheny River and

connect the downtown with the north shore. The bridge's main span was completed in 1963, yet, due to "red tape and governmental disagreement,"[6] overall completion languished for several more years, during which time the project became known as the "Bridge to Nowhere."[7] (The roadway ended 90 feet short of the shoreline.) In 1968, however, the last piece was finally put in place, and the bridge was completed. Accordingly, on April 25, 1968, ground was broken on the long-delayed Pittsburgh Stadium. After a decade of waiting, construction of the Pirates' new home was begun.

Three Rivers Stadium

Construction was scheduled to take two years; if all went according to plan, it would be ready for the start of the 1970 season. All didn't go according to plan, however. On Opening Day, April 7, 1970, the Pirates lost to the New York Mets, 5-3, at Forbes Field. Soon, a revised completion date of May 29 was reported, but that, too, proved inaccurate, as the lights had yet to be put into place. Meanwhile, on June 28, the Pirates hosted the Chicago Cubs for a doubleheader at Forbes Field.[8] The next day the Pirates were to embark on a 14-game road trip. Hopes were high throughout Pittsburgh that the Pirates' next homestand would take place in their shiny new arena.

So it did. It hadn't always been apparent, though, what name would be given to that new arena. While it had taken more than the projected two years to build the new ballpark, it took nearly as long to reach consensus on a new name. After much deliberation, the agreed-upon name was the uniquely descriptive Three Rivers Stadium.[9] It was as apropos of its time as it was of its location.

The decades of the 1960s and '70s became the era of the multipurpose stadium. In addition to Pittsburgh's quest to provide a single home for both its baseball and football teams, similar stadiums with comparable intent had also recently been constructed in Washington, New York (Queens), Houston, Atlanta, St. Louis, and Cincinnati, with Philadelphia forthcoming. Architecturally there was little to tell one of these stadiums apart from another: They were round, multi-tiered, symmetrical structures designed to accommodate the playing fields of two entirely different sports with entirely different dimensions. By design, such requirements left little room for creativity. In identity, these stadiums came to be called "cookie cutter."

Sitting almost exactly on the site of Exposition Park, Three Rivers Stadium never fulfilled the elaborate plans for the north shore that had been imagined back in 1958. The adjoining hotels and shops were never built; nor was the beatific open end of the ballpark with its proposed magnificent view of the Pittsburgh skyline. Instead, cost constraints dictated that the city got what it paid for: At a cost of $55 million, the architectural triumvirate of Deeter, Ritchey, Sippel; Michael Baker Jr.; and Osborn Engineering provided a functional, multipurpose stadium that seated 47,971 fans for baseball and 59,000 for football. Around a circular bowl, five tiers of red and yellow seats enclosed the stadium. (Over the years, numbers were painted on the right-field seats to designate where Willie Stargell's home runs landed.) Converting the stadium for the Steelers' occupancy in the fall included moving two banks of 4,000 seats along the first and third base lines to become 8,000 seats on the 50-yard line. The main scoreboard was located over the outfield fence in center field; this was replaced in 1984 by a $5 million video scoreboard placed below the stadium's rim in center field. For Pirates fans, it was to be an antiseptic, manufactured environment, far removed from the cozy confines of beloved Forbes Field, right down to the artificial, plastic Tartan Turf upon which the modern game of baseball was to be played. (In 1983 the original Tartan Turf was replaced by Astroturf.)

Three Rivers Stadium was not without its elegance, though. High atop the stadium, providing a birds-eye view of the field, was the luxurious Allegheny Club, a restaurant that accommodated 300 people for the field view and 400 in the main dining area. In an effort to maintain the team's link to its past, moved from Forbes Field and displayed in the restaurant were an 8-by-12-foot section of the old ballpark's left-field brick wall (on which the 406-foot marker had been visible), over which Bill Mazeroski hit his Game Seven World

Series-winning home run in 1960; a plaque showing where Babe Ruth's 714th home run had landed in Forbes Field; and 12 Romanesque window frames from the Pirates' iconic former home. Additionally, an 18-foot, 1,800-pound statue of Pirates legend Honus Wagner that had stood behind the left-field wall at Forbes Field was moved outside the new stadium, to be joined in 1994 by another in honor of Roberto Clemente. All ensured that as the Pirates moved into the future, their past would never be forgotten.

On the Field

In the 31 years that Three Rivers Stadium stood on the north shore, the Pirates won two World Series and witnessed several historic accomplishments by some of baseball's most legendary players. Following are some of the stadium's most memorable events.

July 16, 1970: The first game

After their doubleheader sweep of the Cubs at Forbes Field, the Pirates' road trip had been a tremendous success, as they posted a 10-4 record. Returning home for the opener at Three Rivers Stadium, they held first place in the National League East, 1½ games ahead of the New York Mets. The Pirates' opponents on this clear evening were the West Division-leading Cincinnati Reds, winners of three in a row.

A crowd of 48,846, the largest ever to attend a baseball game in Pittsburgh, was on hand to witness the festivities. Among the VIPs in attendance were Pittsburgh Mayor Peter Flaherty and Pirates part-owner and vice president Bing Crosby. Bandleader and singer Billy Eckstine, a Pittsburgh native, sang the National Anthem, and Pirates Hall of Famer Pie Traynor threw out the first pitch.

The conditions were perfect for Three Rivers' inaugural game. Although the day had begun with cloudy skies and light rain, by afternoon the skies had brightened and at game time a full moon bathed the stadium. In the bottom of the first inning, Richie Hebner got the first hit, an infield single, and he scored the first run on Al Oliver's double. Pittsburgh starter Dock Ellis protected the lead until the top of the fifth, when the Reds' Tony Perez blasted the stadium's first home run, his 30th, a two-run shot, to put Cincinnati in front. The Pirates' Willie Stargell evened the score in the bottom of the sixth with a solo homer, but in the top of the ninth, the Reds' Lee May singled home Perez from second base to give Cincinnati a 3-2 victory, the only blemish on an otherwise perfect evening.[10]

August 14, 1971: The first Three Rivers Stadium no-hitter

It had been a long time since fans had witnessed a no-hitter in Pittsburgh. On September 20, 1907, at Exposition Park, Pirates right-hander Nick Maddox, in the midst of a fabulous rookie season, tossed what until the night of August 14, 1971, was Pittsburgh's only no-hitter when he beat the Brooklyn Superbas, 2-1. During the 61 years that baseball was played at Forbes Field, no pitcher had ever thrown a hitless gem. On this night, however, one of the greatest hurlers in baseball history threw his only no-hit game.

Over the course of a career that would eventually earn his enshrinement in the baseball Hall of Fame, Cardinals hurler Bob Gibson had twice thrown one-hitters. Until this night, though, he had never thrown a no-hitter. Ten days before, against the Giants in San Francisco, Gibson had won his 200th game in a gutsy complete-game, seven-hit performance. On this Saturday night, he was demonstrably better, even dominant. Until the seventh inning the Pirates never came close to recording a hit. Then in the seventh, with one out, Milt May blasted a drive deep toward the 390-foot mark in left-center field. Running full speed, the Cardinals' Jose Cruz, losing his hat in the process, chased down the ball and caught it on the warning track. That was the Pirates' lone threat as Willie Stargell was called out on strikes to end the game. Gibson allowed just four baserunners while fanning 10 as he throttled the Pirates, 11-0.

October 13, 1971: The first World Series night game

In their second season playing at Three Rivers Stadium, the Pirates played for baseball's championship. There had been 67 previous World Series, and all had one thing in common: Every game had been played during the day. That changed on the evening of October 13, 1971. After opening the Series in Baltimore, where the Pirates dropped two daytime games to the Orioles, the Series moved to Pittsburgh for the next three games. On Tuesday afternoon, October 12, the Pirates, behind a three-run homer from Bob Robertson and a stellar complete-game three-hitter by Steve Blass, downed the Orioles 5-1. On Wednesday evening, the two teams met in Game Four for the first night game in World Series history.

It couldn't have started worse for Pittsburgh. Against the Pirates' left-handed starter, Luke Walker, in the top of the first inning the Orioles' first three batters singled; then a passed ball by Pirates catcher Manny Sanguillen allowed the first run. After an intentional walk to Orioles slugger Frank Robinson, Walker gave up consecutive sacrifice flies, and six batters into the game, Baltimore led 3-0. But they'd not score again in this contest.

With the Orioles' Davey Johnson due up, Pirates manager Danny Murtaugh summoned from the bullpen 21-year-old rookie right-hander Bruce Kison, who, over the next 6⅓ innings allowed just one hit and no runs. (He hit three batters.) By the third inning the Pirates had tied the game, 3-3, and in the seventh, pinch-hitting for Kison, Milt May singled home the eventual winning run, to tie the Series at two games apiece.

After surprise starter Nelson Briles fired a two-hit shutout against the Orioles the next afternoon, again at Three Rivers Stadium, the Series returned to Baltimore and went to a seventh game. Finally, on Sunday afternoon, October 17, the Pirates defeated the Orioles 2-1, and won the franchise's fourth world championship.

September 30, 1972: Roberto Clemente's 3,000th hit

To those readers who were born in the 1960s and came of age in the '70s, it's perhaps natural to associate Roberto Clemente's career with Three Rivers Stadium. In actuality, though, Clemente spent just 2½ of his 18 seasons playing on the north shore; moreover, due to injuries, he played a total of just 136 games at Three Rivers before his untimely death on December 31, 1972. In light of Clemente's tragic loss, one of those games provided one of baseball's most singular and poignant moments.

At the conclusion of the 1971 season, in which he had produced his third consecutive .340-plus batting average, Clemente had amassed 2,882 hits, leaving him just 118 shy of joining the rarefied 3,000-hit club. With injuries limiting the superstar to playing just 102 games in 1972, on Thursday night, September 28, in Philadelphia he collected hit number 2,999, a leadoff single to right field in the fourth inning, then asked to be removed for a pinch-hitter in the sixth inning. Clemente wanted to get his 3,000th hit before the home fans.

On Friday night, September 29, at Three Rivers Stadium, the Mets' Tom Seaver shut out the Pirates on two hits. Clemente went 0-for-4. The next afternoon, with only 13,117 fans in attendance, the Pirates faced Mets left-hander Jon Matlack. In his first at-bat against Matlack, Clemente struck out. Then, leading off the Pirates' fourth inning, Clemente lashed a double to the wall in left-center field for his 3,000th hit, just the 11th man at that point to join the exclusive fraternity. The crowd arose as one and provided Clemente a heartfelt standing ovation. Perched on second base, Clemente doffed his cap and soaked in the adulation. Umpire Doug Harvey handed Clemente the ball from the historic hit. Finally, an inning later, the Mets' Willie Mays, a fellow member of the 3,000-hit club, visited Clemente in the Pirates dugout and offered his congratulations.

As the Pirates removed Clemente from the starting lineup of the team's final three games in preparation for the playoffs, the double became Clemente's final regular-season hit.

July 23, 1974: Three Rivers' first All-Star Game

In 1974 the All-Star Game came to Pittsburgh. Only twice before had the city hosted baseball's annual event; the first time was July 11, 1944, with the National League victorious by a 7-1 score. The classic also came in 1959, when two All-Star games were played, and

Forbes Field hosted the first. The National League won that day, July 7, 5-4.

On this night in 1974 a sellout crowd of 50,706 was on hand. After Pirates owner John Galbreath threw out the first pitch, the National League, which had won 10 of the previous 11 contests, again got the better of the American League, winning 7-2. For the Nationals, the Cardinals' Reggie Smith hit a solo home run, the Dodgers' Steve Garvey was named the game's MVP, and reliever Ken Brett, the Pirates' lone representative, was the winning pitcher.

It was the third win in a row for the National League, and advanced the circuit's record in All-Star Games to 26-18-1.

August 9, 1976: The first no-hitter by a Pirate at Three Rivers Stadium

It couldn't have been a more perfect giveaway. On August 9, 1976, in recognition of the Pirates' newest star, 6-foot, 7-inch, 22-year-old left-handed pitcher John Candelaria, whose nickname was, naturally, Candyman, the team gave away candy bars to all 9,860 attendees that night. Indeed, they were in for a treat.

A Pirate hadn't pitched a no-hitter since Dock Ellis, at San Diego, in 1970. Bob Gibson, the future Hall of Famer who'd thrown the first no-hitter at Three Rivers, was in attendance as part of ABC's *Monday Night Baseball* TV broadcast team. This night the Pirates faced the Los Angeles Dodgers. The Dodgers were in for a quick but futile evening, as Candelaria was totally dominant. In the third inning, by virtue of two errors and a walk, Los Angeles loaded the bases with two outs, but Candelaria escaped harm when he got Bill Russell to ground out. Other than that, offered Candelaria afterward, "It was (Ted) Sizemore's line drive to Taveras in the sixth inning. A foot either way and it's a base hit."[11]

In the end Candelaria retired the Dodgers in order in every inning except that dicey third, and struck out seven. Although he claimed later that "I knew I had it from the first inning," still, against Russell with two outs in the ninth, "I thought Russell's fly [to shallow center field] was gonna drop in at first. I thought 'what a way to lose it.'"[12] However, center fielder Al Oliver raced in and caught the ball one-handed, brushing against shortstop Frank Taveras, and the no-hitter was preserved.

THE 1979 PITTSBURGH PIRATES

In the locker room after the game, the players laid towels from the door of the clubhouse to Candelaria's locker. On the towels were candy bars. As the team celebrated, Oliver presented Candelaria with the game ball.

October 14, 1979: Pirates win World Series Game Five to save the Series

There couldn't have been much optimism in Pittsburgh the afternoon of October 14, 1979 … other than, perhaps, among Pirates manager Chuck Tanner, starting pitcher Jim Rooker, and Rooker's teammates. With the Pirates in the World Series against the Baltimore Orioles, in a rematch of their 1971 encounter, the Orioles had taken a three-games-to-one lead, and had only to win Game Five to avenge their 1971 loss. For Baltimore, 23-game winner Mike Flanagan, the eventual American League Cy Young Award winner, would take the mound. Opposing him was Rooker, a 37-year-old left-hander whose fastball rarely touched 90 mph and who had won all of four games during the regular season. Of such matchups, however, are Series victories often made.

With Rooker's aged arm rarely able to get batters out with speed, "The book on Rooker is that he's a breaking ball pitcher," explained his catcher, Steve Nicosia, after the Pirates had defeated the Orioles, 7-1, behind five strong innings by Rooker. "He doesn't usually throw the ball by guys. He spots his fastball. Today they were looking for offspeed stuff and he was busting the fastball. The next thing you know they were 0-2. … That was the best fastball he's had all year."[13]

Indeed, as the Orioles flailed at inside fastballs, Rooker allowed just three hits in his five innings. In the bottom of the fifth, with Baltimore ahead 1-0, Rooker was lifted for a pinch-hitter. As the Pirates scored seven runs over the next three innings, right-hander Bert Blyleven shut out the Orioles over the next four innings to preserve Rooker's performance, and the Pirates went on to win and extend the Series. When they returned to Baltimore and took the next two games, Pittsburgh rejoiced in the Pirates' second world championship of the decade.

September 27, 1992: Pirates defeat Mets to win third consecutive division title

Since the beginning of divisional play in 1969, only two National League teams had won three consecutive division titles: the Pirates in 1970-72, and the Philadelphia Phillies in 1976-78. Now, having won division titles in both 1990 and '91, the Pirates sought to be the first team to twice win three in a row.

If excitement was in the air for the Pirates, it was most likely a muted enthusiasm. In the previous two years the team had celebrated divisional titles only to lose in the NLCS, to the eventual World Series champion Reds in 1990, and to the Atlanta Braves in 1991. Still, 1992 was a new year, with new opportunities for victory, and as the Pirates took the field against the New York Mets, they were determined to once again clinch the National League East crown.

On this Sunday afternoon at Three Rivers Stadium, few pitchers were better prepared mentally to take the mound in a pressure situation than was veteran left-handed starter Danny Jackson, who had won World Series titles with the Kansas City Royals in 1985 and the Cincinnati Reds in 1990. So it was that Jackson threw seven-plus strong innings, allowing New York just six hits and one run, and the Pirates clinched the title with a 4-2 win. This time, though, there was little celebration in the clubhouse, for the team knew how much work remained; and alas, for the third consecutive season, the Pirates were beaten in the NLCS, once again by the Braves.

It would be 21 years before Pittsburgh celebrated another trip to postseason action.

The Final Game

By the 2000 season the Pirates had largely fallen into disrepair, much as had Three Rivers Stadium; and as the team on the field ceased to be competitive, the fans stayed away. In 1994, the ballpark hosted its second All-Star Game, for which new blue seats were added in the lower deck. However, by the mid-1990s many upper-deck seats were routinely covered by huge canvas tarpaulins that bore Pittsburgh's championship logos. (In a summary of the Pirates final game at Three Rivers, it would later be written that the ballpark had "lost favor because it had poor sight lines, lacked swanky luxury boxes and had tens of thousands of empty seats for many baseball games."[14]) Eventually, as both the Pirates and Steelers sought ways to generate extra revenue, it was determined that separate stadiums would be built on each side of Three Rivers Stadium, the new facilities to be named Heinz Field (for the Steelers) and PNC Park (for the Pirates). They were to be ready for occupancy by their respective 2001 seasons.

On October 1, 2000, the Pirates played their final game at Three Rivers Stadium. They went into the game with a record of 69-92, which placed them fifth of six teams in the National League's Central Division. Their opponents were the Chicago Cubs, who stood five games behind the Pirates, in last place.

For the record, the Pirates lost that day to the Cubs, 10-9, coincidentally the same score by which Bill Mazeroski's home run had won the World Series for the Pirates at Forbes Field in 1960. Before 55,351 fans (ironically a Three Rivers record for baseball attendance), the Pirates' John Wehner, a Pittsburgh native who as a boy had attended Pirates games at the ballpark, hit his fourth and last career home run, the final home run to go over the wall at Three Rivers Stadium. For his fifth-inning two-run blast, the fans gave him a standing ovation.

Much of that applause was undoubtedly in recognition of the ending of an era.

The Ending

February 11, 2001, was a frigid morning in Pittsburgh, with the temperature in the teens. Despite the cold, thousands of people from all over the Golden Triangle gathered to witness the demolition of Three Rivers Stadium. The previous week, explosives experts from Controlled Demolition Inc., which had charge of the implosion, had packed the stadium with 4,800 pounds of dynamite that would level the iconic arena. Earlier, the Carnegie Science Center had held a raffle to select the person who would win the honor of pushing the button that would detonate the charge. A stadium employee named Elizabeth King won the raffle, and at 7:58 A.M., she and her 16-year-old son, Joseph, pushed the button. Within seconds the western wall collapsed into a cloud of dust, and in 19 seconds Three Rivers Stadium had been reduced to an 8,000-ton pile of concrete and scrap metal. Beneath the rubble lay nearly 31 years of Pittsburgh's sports memories.[15]

Today the spot where Three Rivers Stadium stood is commemorated by a Pennsylvania Historical and Museum Commission marker, placed there on November 26, 2007, at Art Rooney Avenue, near North Shore Drive. (The locations of Forbes Field and Exposition Park are also commemorated with historical markers.) Only the stadium's Gate D marker remains as a memorial to the history that was created along the bank of the Allegheny River, near the site where the three rivers meet.

SOURCES

In addition to the sources cited in the Notes, the author consulted the following.

Mulligan, Stephen. *Were You There? Over 300 Wonderful, Weird and Wacky Moments from Pittsburgh's Three Rivers Stadium* (Pittsburgh: RoseDog Books, 2013), 51.

popularpittsburgh.com/baseballhistory/.

ballparksofbaseball.com/past/ThreeRiversStadium.htm.

ballparks.com/baseball/national/3river.htm.

3riversstadium.com/about/history.html.

pittsburghsteelers.co.uk/steelers/trs/three%20rivers%20page1.htm.

pahighways.com/features/threeriversstadium.html.

NOTES

1 Before 1907, when Pittsburgh annexed the region, the area that included the north shore was a separate city known as Allegheny City. For the first five years of the team's existence, the Alleghenys were known simply by that name. It wasn't until the team joined the National League that it became known as the Pittsburgh Alleghenys.

2 As to the team's new nickname, after a convoluted series of maneuvers involving the Alleghenys, the Burghers, a team in the newly formed Players League, and both the American Association and National League, the Alleghenys were accused by the American Association's Philadelphia Athletics of "pirating" one of their players; hence, the Pittsburgh team changed their name to the Pirates.

3 brooklineconnection.com/history/Facts/ThreeRivers.html.

THE 1979 PITTSBURGH PIRATES

4   Phillip J. Lowry, *Green Cathedrals: The Ultimate Celebration of Major League and Negro League Ballparks* (New York: Walker Publishing Co. 2006), 192.

5   Ibid.

6   newsinteractive.post-gazette.com/thedigs/2013/07/24/pittsburghs-bridge-to-nowhere/.

7   Ibid.

8   Sixty-one years earlier, the Cubs had been the Pirates' opponent the day Forbes Field opened, June 30, 1909, so it was perhaps fitting that the Cubs were also the Pirates' opponent in the ballpark's final game. On this day the Pirates swept the Cubs in what turned out to be the final major-league games played at the venerable ballpark in the Oakland neighborhood.

9   brooklineconnection.com/history/Facts/ThreeRivers.html.

10 As the first Pirate to hit a home run in the new stadium, Stargell won a $1,000 prize that had been donated by a local lumber company.

11 United Press International, *Bucks County* (Pennsylvania) *Courier Times,* August 10, 1976.

12 Ibid.

13 *Lancaster* (Pennsylvania) *Daily Intelligencer,* October 15, 1979.

14 Associated Press, *Titusville* (Pennsylvania) *Herald,* October 2, 2000.

15 *Altoona* (Pennsylvania) *Mirror,* August 12, 2001.

How the Pirates Were Put Together

By Rod Nelson

Amateur Signings and Draft Picks

DATE	PLAYER	TRANSACTION	CREDITS
August 7, 1958	Willie Stargell	SIGNED by the PIRATES as an AMATEUR FREE AGENT.	[Bob Zuk, Scout; Rex Bowen, Scouting Director]
January 8, 1968	Frank Taveras	SIGNED by the PIRATES as an AMATEUR FREE AGENT.	[Antonio Bojos and Howie Haak, Scouts; Rex Bowen, Scouting Director]
June 7, 1968	Bruce Kison	DRAFTED by the PIRATES in the 14th ROUND of the 1968 AMATEUR DRAFT.	[Edward "Babe" Barberis, Scout; Rex Bowen, Scouting Director]
February 12, 1969	Rennie Stennett	SIGNED by the PIRATES as an AMATEUR FREE AGENT.	[C. Herbert Raybourn and Howie Haak, Scouts; Harding "Pete" Peterson, Scouting Director]
March 30, 1969	Omar Moreno	SIGNED by the PIRATES as an AMATEUR FREE AGENT.	[C. Herbert Raybourn and Howie Haak, Scouts; Harding "Pete" Peterson, Scouting Director]
July 16, 1969	Kent Tekulve	SIGNED by the PIRATES as an AMATEUR FREE AGENT.	[Richard Coury and Joe Consoli, Scouts; Harding "Pete" Peterson, Scouting Director]
June 4, 1970	Dave Parker	DRAFTED by the PIRATES in the 14th ROUND of the 1970 AMATEUR DRAFT.	[Jim Maxwell, Ken Beardslee and Syd Thrift, Scouts; Harding "Pete" Peterson, Scouting Director]
June 4, 1970	Ed Ott	DRAFTED by the PIRATES in the 23rd ROUND of the 1970 AMATEUR DRAFT.	[Joe Consoli, Scout; Harding "Pete" Peterson, Scouting Director]
June 6, 1972	John Candelaria	DRAFTED by the PIRATES in the 2nd ROUND of the 1972 AMATEUR DRAFT.	[Howie Haak and Danny Murtaugh, Scouts; Harding "Pete" Peterson, Scouting Director]
June 5, 1973	Steve Nicosia	DRAFTED by the PIRATES in the 1st ROUND (24th pick) of the 1973 AMATEUR DRAFT.	[Fred Hannum, Max Macon and Howie Haak, Scouts; Harding "Pete" Peterson, Scouting Director]
March 12, 1974	Alberto Lois	SIGNED by the PIRATES as an AMATEUR FREE AGENT.	[Howie Haak, Scout; Harding "Pete" Peterson, Scouting Director]
June 5, 1974	Gary Hargis	DRAFTED by the PIRATES in the 2nd ROUND of the 1974 AMATEUR DRAFT.	[Deni Pacini, Scout; Harding "Pete" Peterson, Scouting Director]
June 5, 1974	Ed Whitson	DRAFTED by the PIRATES in the 6th ROUND of the 1974 AMATEUR DRAFT.	[Ken Beardslee, Scout; Harding "Pete" Peterson, Scouting Director]
June 3, 1975	Dale Berra	DRAFTED by the PIRATES in the 1st ROUND (20th pick) of the 1975 AMATEUR DRAFT.	[Howie Haak and Gene Baker, Scouts; Harding "Pete" Peterson, Scouting Director]
June 3, 1975	Don Robinson	DRAFTED by the PIRATES in the 3rd ROUND of the 1975 AMATEUR DRAFT.	[Murray Cook, Scout; Harding "Pete" Peterson, Scouting Director]
June 8, 1976	Doe Boyland	DRAFTED by the PIRATES in the 2nd ROUND of the 1976 AMATEUR DRAFT.	[Jim Maxwell, Scout; Harding "Pete" Peterson, Scouting Director]

Trades and Free Agent Signings

DATE	PLAYER	TRANSACTION	CREDITS
October 25, 1972	Jim Rooker	TRADED by the Kansas City Royals to the PIRATES for Gene Garber.	
April 5, 1975	Bill Robinson	TRADED by the Philadelphia Phillies to the PIRATES for Wayne Simpson.	[Joe Brown, General Manager]
December 7, 1976	Grant Jackson	TRADED by the Seattle Mariners to the PIRATES for Craig Reynolds and Jimmy Sexton.	[Joe Brown, General Manager]
March 15, 1977	Phil Garner	TRADED by the Oakland Athletics with Chris Batton and Tommy Helms to the PIRATES for Tony Armas, Doug Bair, Dave Giusti, Rick Langford, Doc Medich and Mitchell Page.	[Harding "Pete" Peterson / Joseph O'Toole, Co-General Managers]
December 8, 1977	Bert Blyleven	TRADED as part of a 4-team trade by the Texas Rangers to the PIRATES. The Atlanta Braves sent Willie Montanez to the New York Mets. The Texas Rangers sent Tommy Boggs, Adrian Devine and Eddie Miller to the Atlanta Braves. The Texas Rangers sent a player to be named later and Tom Grieve to the New York Mets. The PIRATES sent Nelson Norman and Al Oliver to the Texas Rangers. The New York Mets sent Jon Matlack to the Texas Rangers. The New York Mets sent John Milner to the PIRATES. The Texas Rangers sent Ken Henderson (March 15, 1978) to the New York Mets to complete the trade.	[Harding "Pete" Peterson / Joseph O'Toole, Co-General Managers]
December 8, 1977	John Milner	TRADED as part of a 4-team trade by the New York Mets to the PIRATES. The Atlanta Braves sent Willie Montanez to the New York Mets. The Texas Rangers sent Tommy Boggs, Adrian Devine and Eddie Miller to the Atlanta Braves. The Texas Rangers sent a player to be named later and Tom Grieve to the New York Mets. The Texas Rangers sent Bert Blyleven to the PIRATES. The PIRATES sent Nelson Norman and Al Oliver to the Texas Rangers. The New York Mets sent Jon Matlack to the Texas Rangers. The Texas Rangers sent Ken Henderson (March 15, 1978) to the New York Mets to complete the trade.	[Harding "Pete" Peterson / Joseph O'Toole, Co-General Managers]
March 15, 1978	Jim Bibby	SIGNED as a FREE AGENT with the PIRATES.	[Harding "Pete" Peterson / Joseph O'Toole, Co-General Managers]

April 4, 1978	Manny Sanguillen	TRADED by the Oakland Athletics to the PIRATES for a player to be named later, Miguel Dilone and Elias Sosa. The PIRATES sent Mike Edwards (April 7, 1978) to the Oakland Athletics to complete the trade. (Originally SIGNED by the PIRATES October 2, 1964 as an AMATUER FREE AGENT)	[Harding "Pete" Peterson / Joseph O'Toole, Co-General Managers; Original Signing by C. Herbert Raybourn and Howie Haak, Scouts; Robert Clements, Farm Director]
September 1, 1978	Matt Alexander	SIGNED as a FREE AGENT with the PIRATES.	[Harding "Pete" Peterson / Joseph O'Toole, Co-General Managers]
December 5, 1978	Enrique Romo	TRADED by the Seattle Mariners with Rick Jones and Tom McMillan to the PIRATES for Odell Jones, Mario Mendoza and Rafael Vasquez.	[Harding "Pete" Peterson / Joseph O'Toole, Co-General Managers]
January 19, 1979	Lee Lacy	SIGNED as a FREE AGENT with the PIRATES.	[Harding "Pete" Peterson, General Manager]
March 15, 1979	Mike Easler	TRADED by the Boston Red Sox to the PIRATES for George Hill (minors), Martin Rivas (minors) and cash.	[Harding "Pete" Peterson, General Manager]
April 7, 1979	Rick Rhoden	TRADED by the Los Angeles Dodgers to the PIRATES for Jerry Reuss.	[Harding "Pete" Peterson, General Manager]
April 19, 1979	Tim Foli	TRADED by the New York Mets with Greg Field (minors) to the PIRATES for Frank Taveras.	[Harding "Pete" Peterson, General Manager]
May 8, 1979	Joe Coleman	SIGNED as a FREE AGENT with the PIRATES.	[Harding "Pete" Peterson, General Manager]
June 28, 1979	Bill Madlock	TRADED by the San Francisco Giants with Lenny Randle and Dave Roberts to the PIRATES for Fred Breining, Al Holland and Ed Whitson.	[Harding "Pete" Peterson, General Manager]
June 28, 1979	Dave Roberts	TRADED by the San Francisco Giants with Bill Madlock and Lenny Randle to the PIRATES for Fred Breining, Al Holland and Ed Whitson.	[Harding "Pete" Peterson, General Manager]
September 21, 1979	Dock Ellis	PURCHASED by the PIRATES from the New York Mets. (Originally SIGNED by the PIRATES January 14, 1964 as an AMATEUR FREE AGENT)	[Harding "Pete" Peterson, Gen Mgr; Original Signing by Chet Brewer, Scout; Robert Clements, Farm Director]

*compiled by Rod Nelson, SABR Scouts Committee; Transactions data courtesy of Retrosheet

Matt Alexander

By Rory Costello

MATT "THE SCAT" ALEXANDER HOLDS an odd distinction: He is the foremost pinch-running specialist in major-league history. Over parts of nine seasons (1973-81), he played in 374 games — yet amassed only 195 plate appearances. A favorite of manager Chuck Tanner, Alexander won a World Series ring with the 1979 Pittsburgh Pirates. Along with his speed and snappy nickname, this man brought a sense of fun and enjoyment that fit right in with the "Fam-a-lee."

Matt could handle the bat and almost any position. However, he was in the field in just 138 games, while pinch-running some 271 times. In that role, he holds the major-league records not only for appearances but also for stolen bases (91) and runs scored (89). Unfortunately for him, he was pigeonholed. Pittsburgh sportswriter Phil Musick got Alexander's views on this subject in spring training 1979.

"No one's ever given me the time to show what I can do," he says, a lean, tightly-muscled sprinter's body slipping into uniform. "What people don't understand is that it's never a lack of opportunity, just time. I could hit .260 if I played every day up here. Maybe .270, .280 with a good hitting instructor. But a lot of the time, when a player's called up, it's those first few weeks that count. If you don't get in the lineup, you become an extra man the rest of your career."[1]

Although Alexander was an observer most of the time, he turned this position to his advantage. "It taught me a lot about the game," he said in an interview with the author in 2009. "All aspects: hitting, fielding, staying focused, paying attention. I got so I could tell when I was going to be used. A couple of times, I got caught off guard in early innings, but it would always be a situation where it was important to the game."[2]

Matthew Alexander Jr. was born in Shreveport, Louisiana, on January 30, 1947. He was the baby among four children. Along with his older brother, Lloyd Joiner, and sister, Barbara McMillian, he also had a half-sister, Mathis Lee Robinson. Matthew Sr. worked in construction as a cement finisher, while mother Gertrude Wooten Alexander worked in private homes.

"Sonny" came to baseball at an early age. "I always loved the game from childhood," he remembered. "I was swinging a stick or bat from the time I was 4 years old. We used to play a game called 'straight base' as kids — it was home and just one other base in a straight line. Then when I was older, in downtown Shreveport, we used to play baseball on Sundays."

"My stepdad used to take me to the Shreveport Sports games on Saturdays and Sundays. Back then, blacks had to enter at the side [at the stadium then known as Texas League Park]." In 1957, the African-American citizens of Shreveport launched a boycott against the Sports franchise and the state of Louisiana's recently imposed ban on interracial sports. In response to plunging attendance (among both black and white fans), Sports owner Bonneau Peters — who had openly stated that no black would ever play on his team[3] — sold the club after that season.[4] Alexander, who was then only 10, does not remember the boycott — but he does remember Peters' statement. "I had a vision that one day I'd play at that field," he said, "and I did, with Midland in 1972. It was a dream come true."

At Bethune High School, Matt made the all-city basketball team as a guard. "I was short but quick. I averaged 14 points a game and I was the captain. I played football too, I was a running back and quarterback, but I was too small." Despite his speed, Alexander never ran track except to satisfy a phys ed requirement. One surprising note is that in all his years as an athlete, nobody ever clocked him with a stopwatch.

At that time, Matt was a pitcher in baseball. "I always had a strong arm," he said. Bethune won the Louisiana State AAA championship during his senior year, and one of Matt's two playoff wins came against his future teammate with the Oakland A's, Vida Blue of DeSoto High in Mansfield. When they met again

WHEN POPS LED THE FAMILY

in 1975, "Vida would bring it up, but I didn't. I wasn't a guy to rub things in. I liked to stay calm and collected."

Matt earned a scholarship to Grambling State University, a historically black institution about 65 miles east of Shreveport. Although best known for its football program, Grambling has produced 12 big-league baseball players over the years. Tommie Agee and Ralph Garr were the most successful of these men; Alexander was a year behind Garr. Another big-league outfielder who played for the Tigers, fellow Shreveport native John Jeter, inspired Matt to follow him. "I had other scholarships, including Southern University, but I always wanted Grambling. It was down the road and I could come home weekends."

A profound influence on Matt and many other Grambling alumni was Ralph Waldo Emerson "Prez" Jones, who served the university for 51 years (1926-1977). Jones was Grambling's president for the last 41 years of that time; he formed the baseball and football teams and was baseball coach throughout his tenure. "I want to really thank him," Alexander said. "He was good — really good. He had his own way of teaching you about the game, and he gave me a chance to further my education."

Longtime Pirates scout Lenny Yochim, a New Orleans native who would later help save Matt's career, also tipped his cap to Jones. "I enjoyed scouting Grambling," Yochim said. "[Jones] had clout, his players were sharp, humble, courteous, attentive, well schooled in baseball and obedient to their leader. His teams conducted infield drills that would outshine major-league clubs. When they were finished a scout could leave there satisfied he saw what a player could do. Does he have arm strength, body control, agility, quick reflexes, can he come in on a slow hit ball and make the body control play, catching the ball on the run and throwing with accuracy. The coach was well respected in baseball and as a person."[5]

Matt, who had switched to the infield, made the Southwest Athletic Conference's all-conference team twice in three years. He hit .377 in both 1967 and 1968. "I'm glad I didn't pitch," he said in 2009. "We had guys who could really throw." One was Jophery Brown, who pitched one game for the Cubs in 1968 and then went to Hollywood as a bit-part actor and top stuntman. "We didn't realize how good we were — we just went out and played. Scouts came out, and then we'd realize. There was a lot of good raw talent. Six guys signed off the '67 team."

"I didn't know Ralph Garr before Grambling, but I got to know him real well. He was the first player I met who could talk trash and then go out and back it up on the field. He taught me a lot about confidence."

During the summer of '67, Alexander played for the Liberal (Kansas) Beejays in the Jayhawk League. This summer collegiate baseball league boasts a high caliber of play; since their inception in 1955, the BeeJays alone have sent 165 alumni to the majors, as of 2008.

On June 7, 1968, after Matt's junior year, the Chicago Cubs selected him in the second round of the amateur draft. The scout who recommended him was legendary Negro Leaguer Buck O'Neil, who found a lot of young African-American talent in the Deep South for the Cubs. "He'd call you 'lad,'" Matt remembered. "He had a really deep voice. He was the 'cleanest' man I've ever seen — he could really dress! He always looked sharp and wore nice shoes. If he wore sandals, those were some sandals."

"Buck told me, 'Keep on playing hard,' and I did. The draft, that just shocked me. I thought I'd be drafted, but low. I was parking cars in Shreveport when a friend told me I went in the second round. I quit the job right on the spot and ran home. All I could think was, 'I'm in the game. I'm going to get some money!'"

Matt signed on July 9 after some negotiating. "Ralph Rickey, the top pick, got $50,000, and I held out for $30,000. The Cubs offered $20,000 because there was a question on my arm. I'd gotten hurt and wasn't showing velocity. Buck needed to work me out again. I wouldn't sign until I got $25,000." Within the week after signing, he married Rose Marie Williams, whom he had met at Grambling, where she worked in the cafeteria. "We were engaged at that time. Once I knew I had money and could support her, we went ahead."

Alexander then reported to rookie ball with the Caldwell (Idaho) Cubs in the Pioneer League. His respectable showing (.261 average, one homer, 10 RBIs) won him a berth on the league's All-Star team at second base. Matt then had to weigh a tradeoff. "I went back to Grambling for one semester in the fall of 1968, but I never graduated. At first, I thought going back to school was a good thing, and it was, but I missed Instructional League. Another guy Buck signed kept playing and made Double-A the next spring [rising to the majors the same year]. That was Oscar Gamble."

Alexander was promoted to the Class-A Midwest League in 1969. With the Quincy Cubs, the switch-hitter hit .274 with 8 home runs and 32 RBIs and then jumped to the San Antonio Missions in the Double-A Texas League (.303-1-13).[6] It appeared that he was moving briskly up the ladder with the Cubs, but then he missed two full seasons in military service.

"When I left college, my draft status changed to 1A. I was drafted in the Army, but George Freese [then a Cubs scout] knew some people in the Navy. I was told to go volunteer, then they'll work it out so I could get in Special Services and play some ball." In both 1970 and 1971, Alexander was with the Hawaii SubPac Raiders, a Navy team out of Pearl Harbor. Among other opponents, the Raiders traveled to Fairbanks to face the Alaska Goldpanners.

When asked if his time in the service threw a wrench in his pro career, he said, "It slowed me down, I was going at a good pace. But I look back and I'm glad. I matured as a man and got to travel."

After his discharge, the Cubs sent Alexander to the Arizona Instructional League in 1971 and invited him to spring training with the big club in 1972. He made it to the last round of cuts. His initial assignment was Triple-A Wichita, but before playing a game there, he went back to Double-A. He spent the entire season with the Midland Cubs (.270-5-45) and then played winter ball for the first time. He went to Ciudad Obregón, Mexico, in La Liga Mexicana del Pacífico (LMP).

The manager of the Obregón Yaquis in the winter of 1972-73 was Dave García, then a coach with the San Diego Padres. "Obregón needed speed," Alexander recalled. "Dave García looked in the Texas League stats and saw me leading the league in steals." The Yaquis were league champions that winter, led by the native-born Romo brothers, Enrique — Matt's future teammate with the '79 Pirates — and Vicente. Other big leaguers on the squad included Johnny Grubb, Derrel Thomas, and Dave Hilton from the Padres system, as well as veteran Jim Campanis. The Yaquis went on to compete in the Caribbean Series in Venezuela, but went just 1-5; Alexander collected 6 hits in 27 at-bats.

Alexander followed up with a promising season at Wichita in 1973 (.309-2-51). On August 23, he made his big-league debut at Wrigley Field. It was a sign of things to come — he pinch-ran for Ron Santo in the 10th inning and scored the tying run as the Cubs pulled out a 4-3 win.

With Ciudad Obregón once more in the winter of 1973-74 (.245-2-19), Alexander got to play in another Caribbean Series. Mexico fielded two teams in the tourney that year, as the second-place Yaquis replaced Venezuela, whose players were striking. Alexander went 7-for-27 as his team split its six games. He followed up by making the Chicago roster out of spring training in 1974. In the middle of May, after

Bill Madlock had sprained an ankle, Alexander got a trial of roughly three weeks as the Cubs' starting third baseman, including several games as the leadoff man. When Madlock returned, though, Alexander (who was also slowed by a pulled leg muscle) was left with spot duty. The Cubs sent him down to Wichita in late July and outrighted him there after the season. (He recalled playing in Mexico again that winter, but there may be a gap in the records.)

On April 28, 1975, the Cubs traded Alexander to the Oakland A's for pitcher Howell "Buddy" Copeland in a minor-league deal. Oakland was about to end its experiment with track star Herb Washington as pinch-runner deluxe. Despite his world-class speed, Washington did not know or have instincts for the game, and he was simply too limited. The club needed a true ballplayer to fill the specialist role — in fact, it added two. Reggie Jackson said, "We've got these two new guys — Alexander and [Don] Hopkins — and they can do other things, plus they run the bases better than Washington." Even A's owner Charlie Finley, the original proponent of "designated runners," concurred. "We've got to have pinch-runners who can steal bases and also do other things."[7]

Somehow manager Alvin Dark found a way to get Hopkins into 82 games and Alexander into 63 that season. Between them, they totaled 19 plate appearances. Unfortunately, Alexander suffered a shattered eye socket in early June from a batting-practice grounder, but he won the respect of his teammates as the more complete player. "He's the best," said Gene Tenace. "Definitely. The other two can't compare with him."[8]

When the A's met the Red Sox in the playoffs, however, they kept both Hopkins and Alexander on the roster. Hopkins got the lone pinch-running appearance that Dark found necessary.

Alexander also acquired his nickname — "The Scat" — courtesy of Oakland announcer Monte Moore. "At first, I didn't understand it," he remarked. "But it stuck, and I thought it was perfect."

In 1976, the A's — under new manager Chuck Tanner — stole 341 bases, a record in the post-Deadball era. They kept two specialist runners. Hopkins was sent down, though; former Expo and Cardinal Larry Lintz took his place. Alexander remained with Oakland the entire season, while Lintz played briefly at Triple A. Alexander did not lack confidence: In 1976, he once challenged Thurman Munson, "You better make a perfect throw," but the Yankees' captain gunned him down. Perhaps the missing edge was his golf spikes, which he had worn throughout 1975 and early '76, until Rangers manager Frank Lucchesi blew the whistle.

"I'd say, 'You better get ready' as a psych game with the catchers," Alexander recalled. "The best I faced was Jim Sundberg. He was quick and had a strong, accurate arm. He could throw it in a small square box over second base. Outside that box, it was going to be tight, but I'd usually win. Who was going to make a mistake? That's who'd lose." It was like a chess match. Along with Sundberg, Alexander put Steve Yeager and Gary Carter in his top three opposing catchers. "Munson had a quick release, but he would often throw sidearm, so his ball would tail."

The A's roster showed much the same pattern in 1977, although Lintz was sent down for a longer stretch in midseason. Over those two years, the two men played in vastly more games than they had plate appearances. However, one of Charlie Finley's odder experiments took place on a road trip from May 23 through June 2, 1977. Finley and new manager Jack McKeon (who would be fired on June 10) had Alexander lead off eight games and listed him as the starting shortstop. Yet each time they pulled Matt after his first at-bat for Rob Picciolo.

"Charlie Finley had some brilliant ideas," said Alexander. "He made the lineup out himself every day. Alvin Dark and them just wrote the lineup down. The idea with me was to try to produce a run in the very first inning. I would look to get on base any way I could, then play my role without wasting a player."

"There was a lot of pressure in Oakland. You [as a pinch-runner] had to go on the first or second pitch or get fined. But I'll tell you what Finley was doing, he was giving the batter more of a chance to hit."

Alexander stole a major-league career-high 26 bases in 1977, though he was caught 14 times, and also batted .238. "When I hit, Finley thought I'd put pressure on him to start! He told me not to get ideas." Alexander didn't make waves — "I'd seen him release guys on the spot. There was one guy who hurt his Achilles playing flag football, and when Finley found out, he was gone. I also remember John Jeter fell short [getting released by the Indians in 1975] because he was talking trash about not getting playing time for Frank Robinson."

Back in Mexico during the winters, Alexander was the Liga Mexicana del Pacífico's top base stealer in both 1976-77 (17 for the Guaymas Ostioneros) and 1977-78 (20 for the Hermosillo Naranjeros). In February 1978, though, he came down with a case of hepatitis in Mexico. "It wasn't the contagious kind. I was taking medications for an ailment I had, and my liver reacted badly to the chemical toxin." He never made it to spring training, and on March 31, Finley — in a move that could well have been illegal — released him.

He returned home, attended barber college "with a little money from the GI Bill," and played with a local team called the Shreveport All-Stars on Sundays. "He thought about needing just 24 more days in the major leagues to get his pension, and how there aren't any pensions for barbers."[9]

"The phone hadn't rung in early August, so Alexander did something uncharacteristic. He got impatient and called Pirates scout Lenny Yochim. The word got to Chuck Tanner [who had become Pittsburgh's manager in 1977]."[10]

Lenny Yochim expanded: "I asked him if he was in playing shape and he said yes. I asked him if he was in running shape and he said yes. I asked him to be honest with me because he would have to come off the bench running. In all probability he wouldn't be asked to pinch-hit. He assured me he was ready. Matthew was a good person and I trusted him in what he gave me.

"I told him to call Chuck Tanner. I told him that Chuck liked what he could do to help the club and that our club didn't have anyone to fill the role as an extra as well as Matt. Matthew was very instrumental in the success of the Pirates in 1979. He called Chuck and they connected. I sure was happy for Matthew."[11]

Alexander responded, "I'm still grateful to know Lenny." He remembered, "I got called in for a workout [at Three Rivers Stadium], and I was running from pole to pole." There wasn't going to be a spot right away, but on September 1, when the rosters expanded, the Pirates added the free agent as Tanner had promised. On September 21, Alexander showed how he could influence a game. In the top of the 14th inning against the Cubs at Wrigley Field, he stole second and scored as Dave Rader's throw went into center field and center fielder Bobby Murcer's throw hit him in the back as he took third. "'I'm still a little peaked [from the illness] but I can do the job. It's not how fast you run. It's how you do the job,' said Alexander."[12]

"I was just grateful for the pension time," Alexander said in 2009, "but it turned out to be so much more. Pittsburgh was the best highlight of my life and career. With the Cubs, I couldn't see the whole picture. I was lost. I think I was hid because if I was in the minors somebody else would have wanted me. With the A's, I was wanted, but there was pressure. With Pittsburgh, it was, 'We respect your talent. You're a ballplayer.' It was a joy, a relaxation. It brought the best out of me."

In 1979, Alexander spent a couple of stretches at Double-A Buffalo. The Pirates faced some temporary roster needs, and as the 25th man, he was "on the bubble." In fact, he was outrighted to Buffalo in July. He had to pass through irrevocable waivers in August before the Pirates could recall him. There was a good explanation, though. "Chuck didn't send me to the Triple-A club, which was Portland, because he didn't want to make me move my family across the country. They kept me close, they knew they were bringing me back."

Alexander occasionally spelled center fielder Omar Moreno, who was early in a streak of 503 consecutive games played, as well as Dave Parker in right. He went 7-for-13 (.538), which partly offset his 1-for-30 showing with Oakland in 1976. That fall, *Time* magazine described the intangible spirit Matt brought to the club:

"He developed baseball's equivalent to spiking a football: Whenever he reached home plate, he would turn around and dance across it backward.

"Each time he earned applause from his teammates and an understanding smile from Tanner. 'Just because you play baseball for a living doesn't mean it has to be a job,' he says. 'You ought to have fun playing in the big leagues just like you did when you were a little kid, because the more you enjoy it, the better you play.'"[13]

Everything broke right for the Pirates that year. Alexander recalled how the manager won games with some unorthodox tactical maneuvers. He pointed to a game at Three Rivers Stadium on August 5. Steve Nicosia had gone 4-for-4 that afternoon, but Tanner lifted him for pinch-hitter John Milner with the score tied 8-8, the bases loaded, and two out in the ninth inning. Phillies manager Danny Ozark then pulled righty Rawly Eastwick in favor of southpaw Tug McGraw. Even so, Tanner stuck with the lefty Milner. Chuck kept his reasons close to the vest with the newspapers, but as Alexander told it in retrospect, the skipper knew that McGraw's screwball would break away from "The Hammer." Milner then won the game with a grand slam as McGraw eschewed his out pitch for a fastball.

Alexander made one appearance in the National League Championship Series against the Reds. Running for Tim Foli in Game One, he scored the go-ahead run in the 11th inning as the Pirates won, 5-2. An Associated Press photo shows him leaping with joy as Willie "Pops" Stargell's three-run homer off Tom Hume left Riverfront Stadium.

Rain postponed the start of the 1979 World Series, but Alexander put the skills he'd learned the previous year to use. "Matt Alexander, the Pirates' running specialist, was ... engrossed in his role as resident barber, cutting the hair and trimming the beards of Dave Parker, John Milner, Bill Madlock, Manny Sanguillén, and Mike Easler."[14] A UPI photo captured Alexander wielding his electric clipper as Parker relaxed with a cloth around his neck.

Alexander also appeared just once in the World Series; Orioles catcher Rick Dempsey caught him stealing in the ninth inning of Game Two. The *Pittsburgh Post-Gazette* noted, "You could almost hear Matt Alexander turn feverish for another chance to try. ...'Dempsey was the first catcher to throw me out this year. I was going against the elements. It was raining and the basepaths were wet. I do respect Dempsey, but it will only be after this Series that I can say whether he's good, average, or great.'"[15] Alexander stayed in to play left field for the remaining half-inning of the game but saw no further action after that.

In 2004, Chuck Tanner looked back on his champion club after a quarter-century. He said, "We had 25 MVPs on the team because everyone contributed to the cause."[16] There were many different sides to that team, and one of them was spiritual. Catcher Manny Sanguillén said, "I think our club has the most Christians." Alexander added, "We act like fools but we worship together and play ball together."[17]

Alexander, who attends the club's reunions every five years, emphasized the family atmosphere as he reminisced 30 years later. "It was guys who hung out together, guys that could communicate together. It was wild and crazy, like a zoo. You had to be there. But when it was time to go play, it was serious business. And when we won, it was such a release of pressure."

He also provided insight on the leadership of captain Willie Stargell — "a great person," said Alexander, and it's not a word he throws around lightly. "I caught him on the downside, he had bad knees and couldn't run so good. I helped him stretch his hamstrings and back, I used to sit on his back. But his presence made you feel good. He could talk to you and you would listen. He was funny. He showed us what it was like to play hurt. And he could still hit. The sound of the ball off his bat, it was like a shotgun."

"Pops" would also award stars to deserving players to affix to the old-timey pillbox caps the team wore in those days. "You'd be looking forward to getting a star. You had to earn it, do something *real* good. I got a few, for stealing 'the money base.'" That wasn't the only reward Alexander got from Stargell. "One time in L.A., we went to this little town, and there was a tailor shop. He told me to pick out a suit, any fabric. It was a $600 suit back then. I still got it!"

Alexander was with another Liga Mexicana del Pacífico champion in the winter of 1979-80, Hermosillo. He played only 15 games that winter, though, as he injured a hamstring. He remained with the Pirates throughout the 1980 season, maintaining both his specialty roles: pinch-runner and clubhouse barber. "Alexander charges $5, $10, and $15 for haircuts. 'The price depends on the size of the head and how much hair the player has.'"[18] At the end of the year, Pittsburgh sent him to Triple-A Portland, which he accepted, although he had a right to refuse the assignment.

In 1979, he had stated, "Young guys coming up need to play. I wouldn't want to block a young guy's chance to get to the major leagues."[19] Two years later, though, it was different. "Being a champion and having a ring," said Alexander in 2009, "it was taking a step back. But I knew I was a professional, I knew I needed to make a living. I got my pension time and I got my ring, and I wasn't playing a major role." Alexander got into 27 games at Portland, which also used mainly veterans such as Rusty Torres and Dave Augustine. He returned to Pittsburgh for part of May and September 1981.

That winter he played ball in a new nation: Venezuela. In 31 games with Navegantes del Magallanes, he stole 15 bases while batting .230 with one home run and 9 RBIs. "It was tough," he said, "a better league than Mexico, a higher level of competition. I didn't play well, and they released me. They are serious there. But I'm still glad I went."

At the end of spring training in 1982, on March 29, the Pirates sold Alexander's contract to the Mexico City Tigres. He remained there for the next two seasons, setting a league record in steals with 73 in 1983 (since surpassed) while batting .312. "Mexico City also had a nice park, like the big leagues, and drew well," he says. Even so, he wound up leaving after the '83 season, for a most unusual reason.

"We made the playoffs, but the owner's son, who ran the club, got killed in a helicopter crash. The owner [Alejo Peralta] was superstitious and thought all the Americans his son [Eduardo] had brought in were bad luck. He got rid of the imports."

Alexander split 1984 between Veracruz and Toluca and then retired before the 1985 season. "I was kind of burned out," he said in 2009. "I was trying to pay on both ends, home and Mexico, and the money's not that great. I was 38, it's hot, and I like to play hard. And even though we had a custom bus with six or seven beds, there was the travel. It took a toll. I had an offer with the Mexico City Reds, but I turned it down."

In 1986, he noted some other pros and cons of playing in Mexico. Positive memories included "breaking the record, learning Spanish and learning to live in another culture." On the flip side, he observed, "Make sure you get everything in your contract, and be sure the contract terms are understood by everyone."[20]

Alexander "was offered a coaching position in Mexico, but turned it down in order to continue his search for a position as an instructor, coach, or minor-league manager with a major-league organization."[21] He had shown initiative in this area with the A's, helping Vida Blue with his pickoff motion and Mitchell Page with stealing bases. "I never got one [a coaching spot]," he said. "I think I went the wrong way — I tried the front door. I sent a résumé to all the organizations and thought I'd get a bite. But I never heard anything. In baseball, it's who you know."

After retiring from baseball, Alexander returned to Shreveport. In 1989, at age 42, he came back for one appearance with the Winter Haven Super Sox of the short-lived Senior Professional Baseball Association. True to form, he scored as a pinch-runner. "The Senior League was amazing because guys could still play!" He recalled. "I worked out at second base, but turning a double play in practice, I came down wrong and pulled a calf muscle. It never got right. I went home for a month and then they called me back, but I hurt it again. So I never got a chance to do much."

"I worked odds and ends for several years, and then I got a job at Libbey Glass in Shreveport in 1992. I stayed there 15 years and then retired. In 2008, I got a job driving a van for the handicapped, dropping them off to medical appointments and things like that. I'll have to quit that when I start drawing Social Security, though."

Matt and Rose Marie were divorced around 1990; they had two children, Yolanda and Matthew III. Matt married Andrea Faultry in 2002 and has two stepsons named Kiera and Cameron.

Alexander remained involved with baseball in Shreveport after his playing days ended. In recent years, he served as an assistant coach at Huntington

High, where Albert Belle starred in the 1980s. He has also been coaching American Legion ball in his local district. When asked about the declining trend among African-Americans in baseball, he offered a varied analysis.

"It's a combination. There are so many other avenues, basketball and football. And computers — the kids are getting soft. They don't want to go out when it's hot and play hard, which is what I did when there weren't as many things to do. The kids who do play, they're not getting good instruction in the fundamentals. Now colleges are looking for five-star players who can do everything already, not kids who have to learn — and who have fear." Finally, he noted, "There's no more sandlot ball on Sundays, like blacks used to play."

In 1995, the Southwest Athletic Conference inducted Matt Alexander into its Hall of Fame. It didn't work out that way in the majors, but this good-humored man said he believes that life unfolds as it does for a reason. He summed up his career this way: "I scuffled for it, but I wound up in the right place at the right time. In baseball, somebody's got to like you. Another thing: You got to produce."

Grateful acknowledgment to Matt Alexander for his memories (telephone interviews, June 28 and July 19, 2009). Thanks also to SABR members Lenny Yochim; Cliff Blau, whose research provided additional information (notably from the National Baseball Hall of Fame's clippings file); and Alfonso Tusa (Venezuelan winter statistics). Further thanks to Alfonso Araujo (Mexican winter statistics).

SOURCES

Blau, Clifford. "Leg Men." *Baseball Research Journal*, Society for American Baseball Research, 2009.

www.retrosheet.org

Professional Baseball Players Database V6.0

Treto Cisneros, Pedro, Editor, *Enciclopedia del Béisbol Mexicano*. Mexico City, Mexico: Revistas Deportivas, S.A. de C.V., 1998.

Araujo Bojórquez, Alfonso. *Series del Caribe: Narraciones y estadísticas, 1949-2001*. Colegio de Bachilleres del Estado de Sinaloa, 2002.

www.paperofrecord.com (various pieces of information from *The Sporting News*)

NOTES

1. Phil Musick. "Alexander Hangs On By Strand of Hair." *Pittsburgh Post-Gazette*, March 16, 1979.
2. Matt Alexander interviews with author, June 28 and July 19, 2009. All direct quotations by Alexander and not otherwise attributed come from these interviews.
3. Ed Mickelson. *Out of the Park* (Jefferson, North Carolina: McFarland & Co., 2007), 130.
4. Bruce Adelson. *Brushing Back Jim Crow* (Charlottesville, Virginia: University of Virginia Press, 1999), 207.
5. E-mail from Lenny Yochim to Rory Costello, July 5, 2009.
6. Had Alexander joined the Missions earlier in the year, he could have realized his dream of playing in Shreveport three years before he finally did.
7. Ron Bergman. "Loss of Catfish Hastened Herbie's Farewell," *The Sporting News*, May 24, 1975: 13.
8. Ron Bergman, Ron. "Mercury Matt Spurts Into Hearts of A's," *The Sporting News*, September 20, 1975: 7.
9. Musick, op. cit.
10. Phil Musick. "Speedy Trip Up for Alexander," *Pittsburgh Post-Gazette*, September 22, 1978.
11. E-mail from Lenny Yochim to Rory Costello, July 5, 2009.
12. Howard Ulman. "Wild Pegs Give Bucs Win," Associated Press, September 22, 1978.
13. "The Full-Tilt Boogie Buccaneers," *Time*, October 15, 1979.
14. Murray Chass. "Series Opener Is Postponed by Rain," *New York Times*, October 10, 1979: B5.
15. "Series Notebook." *Pittsburgh Post-Gazette*, October 13, 1979: 7.
16. Joe O'Loughlin. "Where are they now? Former manager Chuck Tanner," *Baseball Digest*, November 2004.
17. Milton Richman. "Pirates considered 'crazy,'" United Press International, October 10, 1979.
18. Charley Feeney. "'New' Law Gaining Respect of Pirates," *The Sporting News*, April 5, 1980: 46.
19. Musick, "Alexander Hangs On By Strand of Hair."
20. Al Doyle. "The Mexican League: Survivor in a Troubled Economy," *Baseball Digest*, March 1986: 76.
21. Ibid.

Dale Berra

By Bob Hurte

ON OCTOBER 8, 1956, A PREGNANT Carmen Berra sat in the Yankee Stadium stands for the fifth game of the World Series. When public-address announcer Bob Sheppard introduced pinch-hitter Dale Mitchell of the Brooklyn Dodgers, she thought how Dale might be a name for her unborn child, especially since it could be used for either a boy or a girl. When Dale Mitchell struck out to finish the only perfect game in World Series history, she exclaimed to those around her, "Dale is going to be my baby's name!"[1]

On December 13, 1956, Carmen and Yogi Berra became the proud parents of Dale Anthony Berra.

Dale grew up in Montclair, New Jersey, with a legendary surname. He admitted that sometimes he took being the son of a Yankee legend for granted. He was always around baseball his whole childhood, never realizing that his experiences might be a dream for others his age. When he was a teenager, his father was a New York Mets coach and then their manager, which meant Dale spent a lot of time in Shea Stadium. At times he was the team's batboy.

Athletics and the Berra family were synonymous. Dale's older brother, Larry, was a catcher in the low minors in 1971 and 1972; his other brother, Tim, played a season as a wide receiver/kick returner for the 1974 Baltimore Colts.[2]

Yogi supported him, never pushed him toward an athletic career. Berra remembered asking his father to play catch with him. Yogi's typical response would be, "That's what you have brothers for."[3]

Dale Berra was a three-sport star at Montclair High School. He earned 11 varsity letters in football, hockey, and baseball. But he did not want a fuss made over his name: "I was just plain Dale."[4]

Dale was a first-round draft pick by the Pittsburgh Pirates (20th overall) in 1975. He felt there was more pressure being a first-round pick than there was being Yogi's son.

Dale broke in with the Niagara Falls Pirates of the Class-A short season New York-Penn League in 1975. His manager was Glenn Ezell. Berra was the only nonpitcher on the roster to reach the major leagues. (Future major-league pitchers Bryan Clark and Al Holland were on the team.) He hit .257 with three home runs.

In 1976 Berra played for the Charleston (South Carolina) Patriots in the Class-A Western Carolinas League. His manager, Mike Ryan, was a catcher for 11 years for the Boston Red Sox, Philadelphia Phillies, and the Pirates. Berra felt Ryan instilled a strong work ethic in his players; he expected them to play hurt.[5] Berra played in all 139 games, batting .298 with 16 home runs, and in 1977 he moved up to the Columbus Clippers of the Triple-A International League, where he batted .290 with 18 home runs.

On August 21 of that season, in a game against the San Francisco Giants at Three Rivers Stadium, Pirates second baseman Rennie Stennett, running from first base on a groundball by Ed Ott, slid hard into second, and broke his leg, and was lost for the season. The Pirates immediately called up Berra from Columbus.[6] "I felt I was ready," Berra said. "At the time, I was the best player they had at Triple A."[7]

Berra made his major-league debut the next night, playing third base against the San Diego Padres. To accommodate him, Phil Garner moved from third to second.[8] Berra batted sixth and went hitless in three at-bats as the Padres' Bob Shirley beat Jim Rooker, 1-0.

Berra was adequate in the field but he batted just .175 during his short stay with Pirates. One of his seven hits was a game-winning single in the 11th inning against the Philadelphia Phillies on September 6. Berra was only 20 years old, and he felt that the experience was a lot of fun. Since it was a big jump from playing at Columbus, Berra returned there for more Triple-A seasoning in 1978. He was called back to the Pirates in late July. Before leaving for Pittsburgh, Berra was the top vote-getter for the International League's All-Star Game. He had been playing shortstop for the Clippers, and was batting .280 with 18 home runs and 63 RBIs when called up.

Big-league reality intruded. Berra was 0-for-24 upon his return to Pittsburgh and batted .207 in 56 games. He hit his first major-league home run off Tom Dixon of the Houston Astros in the fourth inning of a 7-6 victory on August 20. His fourth homer of the season was a three-run game winner off Gene Garber to beat the Atlanta Braves on September 3. On September 28 the Pirates were 3½ games behind the Phillies before hosting Philadelphia for the last four games of the regular season. They swept a twi-night doubleheader to cut their deficit to 1½ games but they lost the third game of the series, 10-8, and their postseason hopes were extinguished when a ninth-inning rally fell short. Pittsburgh won the final game of the season, 5-3, and Berra hit a home run in his last at-bat of the season. Berra finished his season in Pittsburgh with 6 home runs, 14 RBIs, and a .207 average in 56 games. The Pirates finished second in the National League East, 1½ games behind the Phillies.

The Pirates wanted Berra to learn how to play the outfield at Bayamon in Puerto Rico's winter league. He did not last long; he quit, returning home to Montclair. General manager Harding Peterson was not upset, saying, "We had to persuade him to go in the first place. He wasn't happy and he said he couldn't put his mind on baseball under those circumstances if he remained, it may have done more harm than good."[9]

Berra opened the 1979 season in Pittsburgh, but when the team traded for two-time NL batting champion Bill Madlock on June 28, Berra, hitting just .196 with one home run, was optioned to Triple A, this time the Portland Beavers of the Pacific Coast League. He spent July and August playing there batting .324 in 56 games.

When Pittsburgh shortstop Tim Foli needed a rest, Berra was brought back on August 26. The Pirates wanted him eligible for the possible postseason. He flew to Los Angeles where the Pirates were playing. "As soon as I got off the plane, there was a message for me to call (Peterson). He said that he was sorry, but he could not call me up until the end of the Triple-A season." The problem was red tape involving player recalls.[10] When Berra's call-up was finally approved, he played in 10 of the remaining 30 games at shortstop to give Foli a breather. He hit a two-run homer in his first game back, in a 5-3 victory over the San Francisco Giants on September 1. The Pirates went on to win 20 of their final 30 games and capture the NL East division title by two games over the Montreal Expos.

Although Berra was ineligible for postseason play, he was invited to sit in Pittsburgh's dugout in the NLCS against the Cincinnati Reds, and the World Series against the Baltimore Orioles. However, Frank Cashen of the commissioner's office stepped in and rescinded his bench-seat invitation for the World Series, along with that of Joe Coleman. Cashen told them, "You might pass on information that could influence the outcome of a game."[11] Berra's teammates voted him a full share of the team's World Series earnings and a ring.

Berra remained in Pittsburgh for the 1980 and '81 seasons as a utility infielder. The limited playing time thwarted his hitting consistency and effectiveness. In 1980 he played in 93 games, hitting six home runs, driving in 31 runs while batting .220. Then in the 1981 strike-shortened season, he played in 81 games and batted .241 with 2 home runs and 27 RBIs.

After Pittsburgh traded Foli to the California Angels for utilityman Brian Harper in December 1981, Berra was the Pirates' starting shortstop in 1982. He batted .263 with 61 RBIs and tied Atlanta's Rafael Ramirez for the most home runs by a National League shortstop (10). His partner in the middle of the infield was rookie Johnny Ray.

During the early stages of the season, fans started booing Berra for mistakes in the field. But his play steadied and he succeeded in turning the fans' boos into cheers. Berra attributed his turnaround to manager Chuck Tanner. He played eight years for Tanner and said Chuck was the best manager he ever played for, with his ability to instill confidence in his players. "Even if you struck out three times with the bases loaded or made an error to lose a game, he'd pat you on the back and say, 'Hey, there aren't many guys in the world who can make an error and lose a major-league baseball game. You're good enough to be in a position to do that."[12]

Berra put up similar offensive numbers in 1983—10 home runs, 52 RBIs, and a .251 batting average. Pittsburgh ended up in second place in the NL East, six games behind the Phillies. But in 1984 Berra's offense took a slide and the fans began to demonstrate their disfavor, so forcefully that it essentially forced the Pirates to move him out of town. After the 1984 season, the team realized the need for a power-hitting outfielder and Berra's job was in jeopardy.

On December 20, 1984, the Pirates traded Berra, pitcher Alfonso Pulido, and minor-league outfielder Jay Buhner to the New York Yankees for outfielder Steve Kemp, former Pittsburgh shortstop Tim Foli, and cash.[13] Yogi and Dale became the second father-son manager-player combination in major-league baseball history after Connie and Earle Mack of the Philadelphia Athletics.

With the Yankees, Dale would compete with Mike Pagliarulo for the third-base job. "At the ballpark, he's just another player to me. If he can play, he plays. If he doesn't, he sits," Yogi said.[14]

Dale grasped the chance to show his father what he could do. That chance did not last long. Yogi was fired after the first 16 games, and replaced by Billy Martin. Dale played in only 10 games for his father. After Yogi was fired, Dale's performance dipped. He batted .229 and .231 with a total of three home runs during less than two seasons in New York.

Around this time the biggest blight to Dale Berra's career occurred. At the end of the 1985 season, he testified in federal court that he used cocaine from January 1979 into 1984. Berra was the fourth player to testify the he bought the drug from Curtis Strong, a 38-year-old caterer who was charged with 16 counts of cocaine distribution. The players who testified were granted immunity from prosecution.[15]

Looking back on his major-league career, especially 1983 and 1984, Berra said he should have improved progressively. Instead, he regressed. "I made some bad choices and bad judgments and it cost me my career!" he said.[16]

The Yankees released Berra, on July 27, 1986. He signed with the Houston Astros a week later. Yogi was an Astros coach at the time. Dale played for Houston's Triple-A team in Tucson for the remainder of 1986, and until mid-August 1987. He then appeared in 19 games with the Astros, batting .178, and was released on October 13, 1987. Berra took one more shot at the game, during the 1988 season with Rochester of the Triple-A International League, but batted just .181 in 69 games for the Baltimore Orioles' affiliate. Berra's 11-year career in the majors was over. His career statistics included 49 home runs, 278 RBIs, and a batting average of .236.

In 2016 Berra was living in Montclair with his wife, Jane, and their three daughters. He and his brothers, Larry and Tim, operate a family business called LTD (the first letter of their names). They handled Yogi's affairs until he died on September 22, 2015. "We've taken agents out of dad's life. We're the third party," Dale said before Yogi's death. "Anything that dad does is done through our company. We control his autograph shows, corporate appearances, and functions. It's all Yogi's stuff."

The brothers' company was also responsible for the Yogi Berra Museum, on the Montclair University campus, a celebration of Yogi's illustrious career.[17] Yogi Berra Stadium is its neighbor, where the independent minor-league New Jersey Jackals play. Dale said he has been clean and sober for over 20 years.

Dale never felt he needed to measure up to his father's career; not to be as good as him was not an insult. But in describing them both, he came up with a "Yogi-ism" of his own: "Our similarities are different."[18]

SOURCES

In addition to the sources reflected in the Notes, the author also consulted:

Appel, Marty. *Pinstripe Empire: The New York Yankees From Before the Babe to After the Boss* (New York: Bloomsbury USA, 2012).

Skirboll, Aaron. *The Pittsburgh Cocaine Seven: How a Ragtag Group of Fans Took the Fall for Major League Baseball* (Chicago: Chicago Review Press, 2010).

NOTES

1 Dale Berra, telephone interview, January 9, 2016.

2 *The Sporting News*, August 9, 1982.

3 Doug Kennedy, "Son of a Legend," *Pittsburgh Sports Report*, pittsburghsportsreport.com/2009-Issues/psr0905/09050116.html.

4 Ken Rodriguez, "Like Father, Like Some Sons: M's Griffey an Exception Rather Than Rule of Success," Knight Ridder News Service, July 4, 1990.

5 Dale Berra, telephone interview.

6 Stephen Mulligan, *Were You There? Over 300 Wonderful, Weird, and Wacky Moments from Pittsburgh's Three Rivers Stadium* (Pittsburgh: Rose Dog Books, 2013), 87.

7 "Son of a Legend."

8 *The Sporting News*, September 3, 1977.

9 Charley Feeney, "Decision on Pirate Infield Hinges on Stennett's Ankle," *The Sporting News*, December 30, 1978: 40.

10 Vic Debs, *That Was Part of Baseball Then* (Jefferson, North Carolina: McFarland, 2002), 52.

11 Dick Young, "Young Ideas," *The Sporting News*, October 27, 1979: 16.

12 Debs, 53.

13 Moss Klein, "Pirates Send Yogi's Son to the Yankees," *Newark Star Ledger*, January 7, 1985: 40.

14 Ibid.

15 Michael Goodwin, "Dale Berra Admits Cocaine Use," *New York Times*, September 10, 1985.

16 Dale Berra, telephone interview.

17 "Son of a Legend."

18 *Sports Illustrated*, August 9, 1982

Jim Bibby

By Rory Costello

EVERYTHING ABOUT JIM BIBBY WAS BIG. His frame: 6'5" and 235 pounds, with "legs like oak trees."[1] His hands: he could fit eight baseballs in his right hand—palm down—one more even than Sandy Koufax and Johnny Bench.[2] His fastball: "vicious…serious heat… would scare the bejesus out of most batters."[3] His appetite: as his older brother Fred said, "Jim's the only guy I've ever known who has to have two plates in front of him. One for meat, one for greens."[4] And most of all, his heart—so many fond memories flowed in after he died in 2010.

The burly righthander didn't make it to the majors until he was nearly 28. He was wild, and it took him time and effort to harness his ability. His development was also delayed because he missed three full seasons in the minors—two in Vietnam and one after a back operation. Yet eventually he won 111 games as a big-leaguer (against 101 losses). He was an important part of the staff for the World Series champions of 1979, the Pittsburgh Pirates "Fam-a-lee." He followed up with his career year in 1980, at the age of 35.

After his big-league career ended in 1984, Bibby spent 16 years as a minor-league pitching coach—15 of them in Lynchburg, Virginia, the area where he lived much of his life. He also pitched in the Senior Professional Baseball Association in 1990. Upon his death, the Lynchburg Hillcats issued a statement saying, "Bibby was a foundation for baseball in the Lynchburg area, an institution in the Carolina League and his #26 is the only retired number in Lynchburg baseball history. Anyone who knew Bibby would tell you, you could not find a more jovial soul."[5]

James Blair Bibby was born on October 29, 1944 in Franklinton, North Carolina. This small town is in Franklin County, in the north-central part of the Tar Heel State. Jim was one of three brothers in a family headed by Charlie Bibby and his wife, Evelyn Stallings Bibby. After Frederick and James came Henry Bibby, who went on to fame in basketball. In college at UCLA, under the great coach John Wooden, Henry was the point guard for three straight NCAA championship teams from 1970 to 1972. As a rookie in the NBA, he was a reserve for the New York Knicks, who won the 1973 championship. His playing days ended in 1981 after nine seasons, and he then went on to a long career as a coach. Henry Bibby's son Mike played in the NBA from 1998 through 2012.

In 1981, Rick Telander of *Sports Illustrated* wrote an in-depth feature about Jim and Henry, providing much detail about their early lives and subsequent careers. They and Fred grew up on a farm in Franklinton.[6] Bibby described it in his own words the previous year, talking with Dan Donovan of *The Pittsburgh Press*. "My dad owns his own farm and it's 150 acres. The three boys, we all had a lot of work to do with the tobacco, corn, cotton, the animals. There was no need to lift weights. Farm work's terrible—I hate it—but we were never poor. We had everything we wanted—we never had to make ends meet. We had everything you buy at the store now, only it was better.

"We always had time to play baseball and basketball. Some of the other kids didn't have time because of all the work we had to do. But whenever it was time to play baseball, my dad would always say, 'Go ahead.'"[7]

Jim went to Franklinton High School, which "wasn't big enough to field a football team," he told Donovan. "We graduated 26 people my senior year. We had all the grades, elementary school through senior high, in one building. We were small, but we always had good sports teams in both baseball and basketball."[8]

Bibby then followed brother Fred to Fayetteville State University in North Carolina, about 90 miles from home. Fred was a basketball star at FSU, eventually becoming a member of its athletic Hall of Fame. He helped Jim obtain a basketball scholarship too.[9] Yet while Jim had great size, his true talent was not on the hardwood. As Henry Bibby told Rick Telander

in 1981, "Jim was a hot dog, the 11th man. He'd get in a game, look up in the stands, score two points and think it was a big deal."[10]

During the 1965 summer break from FSU, Bibby was told about a New York Mets tryout camp near his home town. He got to throw only a few pitches before the rain came and he was sent home. Yet later he got a call to come to the club's rookie-league team in Marion, Virginia, where he signed for no bonus but started his career.[11] That team included another fireballing righty, Nolan Ryan. "I just threw one fastball after another and I was always wild," said Bibby in 1981. "Neither one of us knew a damn thing about baseball. We were both ungodly wild."[12] In 13 games that season, Bibby walked 27 batters in 24 innings, fueling an 11.25 ERA.

At the end of Bibby's first pro season, the U.S. Army drafted him and shipped him to Vietnam, where he served as a truck driver. Returning in 1967 to Fort Lee, Virginia, he picked up with his second love, basketball, playing on the post team with NBA star Lou Hudson. Discharged in January 1968, Bibby returned to baseball with the Mets' Carolina League team (Class-A) in Raleigh-Durham. In 23 games (19 starts), he posted a 7-7 record and improving his control to a degree (74 walks in 131 innings). He had 118 strikeouts and a 2.82 ERA.

Bibby's showing with Raleigh-Durham was impressive enough for him to attend spring training with the big club in 1969. He impressed manager Gil Hodges and pitching coach Rube Walker with his strength, staying power, and stuff. Walker also thought that control would come over time. Jim himself said, "I don't really know how good I am—or if I'm any good at all. I've never pitched against really tough competition."[13]

The Mets assigned their prospect to Double-A Memphis. After a 3-5 start, he finished 10-6 with a 3.32 ERA for the Blues, striking out 115 and walking 57 in 122 innings. As he had hoped in camp, the hot streak won him promotion to the Mets' top farm club, Tidewater in the International League, in July 1969. He went 4-4, 3.48 in 11 starts for the Tides, who won the IL regular-season pennant but then lost in the first round of playoffs to Columbus.

The Mets then called up Bibby, and though he didn't get to appear in a game for the eventual World Series champions, he was part of the celebration as the team clinched the National League East. Video footage shows an exuberant Jim and teammate Amos Otis up on the interview platform along with Mets broadcaster Lindsey Nelson. Bibby remained with the club as a batting-practice pitcher while they beat Atlanta in the playoffs. For his services, he received $100.[14]

During spring training with the Mets in 1970, Bibby's "back, weakened by a congenital bone spur, gave out one day as he was covering first base."[15] The injury was initially reported as a "strain" or "sprain" but it was a lot more serious. Spinal fusion surgery was required, and "he was given a 50-50 chance of playing again."[16]

After his surgery, Bibby missed the entire 1970 season with the Mets. Rehabilitation and hard work enabled him to come back strong with Tidewater in 1971 with 15 wins and 6 losses (and an ERA of 4.04 due to 109 walks in 176 innings). That August, *The Sporting News* featured Bibby as he hoped for another call-up to the majors. He said, "I wonder what more the Mets want me to do or show. I feel I've proved myself down here, and remember I've already had my share of waiting."17

Although the Mets did recall Bibby again that September, he never did get into a game with them. On October 18, 1971, he was traded to the St. Louis Cardinals in an eight-player trade, which was dismissed at the time as a minor deal. Out of all the players involved, in retrospect Bibby clearly had the most upside. Perhaps the Mets — at that time viewed as a pitching-rich organization — thought they could afford to deal a player who was nearly 27, unproven and with control problems. At the time, beat writer Jack Lang said, "The sale of Jim Bibby came as no surprise. The big guy throws hard but that's about all."18

Yet as Lang pointed out that November — even before the Mets made the infamous Nolan Ryan trade — the club's pitching depth was not actually that great. Jerry Koosman was then battling injuries and Jon Matlack was the lone prime prospect.19 One wonders if Bibby was included in the trade over the objections of Whitey Herzog, then the farm director for New York.

In the winter of 1971-1972, Bibby played his only season of winter ball in Puerto Rico. He spent most of the 1972 season with the Cardinals' top farm club, Tulsa, Oklahoma in the American Association. He had a very good year, going 13-9 with a 3.09 ERA, while striking out 208 (and walking just 76) in 195 innings. The Cardinals called him up after the rosters expanded in September, and he made six starts, winning his debut — which was actually his least impressive performance — but losing his last three.

The Cardinals used Bibby just six times with poor results in the early part of the 1973 season before dealing him to the Texas Rangers on June 6 for Mike Nagy and John Wockenfuss. Whitey Herzog, who had become the manager in Texas after leaving the Mets organization, was instrumental in the deal. In his fifth outing for the Rangers, Bibby threw a one-hit shutout at home against Kansas City. The only hit was a sixth-inning double off the wall by Fran Healy. Herzog said after the game, "I've known Bibby for four or five years and he has never lacked talent. I thought he was a good risk when I picked him up. I didn't give up anything and I was desperate for pitching help."20

Yet the righty's best outing of the year was a no-hitter (the first in Rangers history) in Oakland on July 30. Bibby threw 148 pitches in his gem, nearly all fastballs, as he struck out 13 and walked six. "You couldn't dig in against him because he was wild," said Reggie Jackson. "He's close to Nolan Ryan." Sal Bando concurred, saying, "That's the first time I've seen Bibby and I hope it's the last." A's manager Dick Williams added, "Damn he was quick. He was conveniently wild. He did a heck of a job. I can't get upset."21

The last out was a looper into right center, which Texas beat writer Mike Shropshire called "a ball that I had seen the Rangers misplay with numbing frequency." Yet while Vic Harris did ram into second baseman Dave Nelson, Nelson hung on to preserve the no-hitter. Catcher Dick Billings said, "The big guy was absolutely unbelievable. I don't think there is a man in baseball who could have touched some of those pitches. I've never seen smoke like that."22

Bibby — who was known for sweating buckets when he pitched — said afterward, "I bet I lost ten pounds by the time it was over. But I'm gonna get it all back in the clubhouse with some of that good cold beer and I'm ready for it right now."23 As another reward, club owner Bob Short gave him a $5,000 raise on the spot.

The big man finished the season at 9-10, 3.24 for the Rangers, a dreadful club that got Whitey Herzog fired in early September. In 1974, Billy Martin (who had taken over as skipper) lifted the Rangers to second place. Bibby posted a 19-19 record in 41 starts, though his 4.74 ERA was a sign of inconsistency — he still didn't have much besides his fastball. Author Joe Posnanski broke down the extremes of hot and cold in his Bibby retrospective of February 2010. "In his 19 victories, he had a 2.50 ERA and the league hit .194 against him. In his 19 losses, he had a 9.23 ERA and the league hit .359 against him."24

Posnanski added, "The rest of his career was not quite so up and down, not quite the same blend of brilliant and disastrous. But Jim Bibby always seemed to carry a part of 1974 with him. It seemed like most days when he went out there to pitch, a team would say 'Oh man, we don't stand a chance tonight.' Trouble is, you never knew which team."[25]

Bibby's social awareness was on display in a July 1975 article in *Texas Monthly*. Writer Paul Burka, who followed the Rangers for a week earlier that season, got into a conversation with Jim on a bus ride. "Baseball, Bibby said, is a white man's game—not on the playing field, but in the stands. Black people don't come to the ballpark, and it bothers him." They went on to exchange various theories about how this came to be.[26]

After a 2-6, 5.00 start, Bibby was traded that June (along with Jackie Brown, Rick Waits and $100,000) to the Cleveland Indians for Gaylord Perry. As the *Cleveland Indians Encyclopedia* noted, "The financially strapped Indians. . .also cleared the air in the clubhouse, as Perry did not get along with manager Frank Robinson."[27]

During his two-plus seasons with the Indians—who were then actually mediocre, not terrible on the field—Bibby won 30 and lost 29 with a 3.36 ERA. He was a swingman, starting 61 games and relieving in 34 others. Indians pitching coach Harvey Haddix helped him greatly with his delivery. As Haddix told Rick Telander, "It's very hard for a big man to be coordinated. Jim was never in control of himself. For someone like Jim, with hands that size. . .well, it's like you or me trying to throw a golf ball accurately."[28]

Joe Posnanski said, "Bibby pitched his guts out for the Indians, especially in '77. I loved Bibby. Big, wild, overpowering, frustrating, scary, larger than life."[29] In August 2011 Posnanski also told another funny anecdote that he heard from Duane Kuiper, Bibby's Cleveland teammate. Kuiper was furious with Rod Carew of the Twins after Carew had slashed him while breaking up a double play. "Don't worry," Bibby said. "I'll get him for you." However, the opportunity did not arise until years later—in an exhibition game in Japan. Bibby drilled Carew in the ribs with his fastball, flexed, and said, "That was for Duane Kuiper."[30]

Bibby's time as an Indian was also productive off the field. He went back to school at Lynchburg College and obtained a degree in physical education, graduating with the class of 1977.

Bibby left Cleveland for the same reason he arrived. The *Indians Encyclopedia* said, "Lack of ready cash also cost the Indians the service of Jim Bibby, which was then unfairly blamed on [general manager Phil] Seghi. Because the team was late in paying Bibby a $10,000 incentive bonus he'd won in 1977, he was declared a free agent and was lost to the Tribe."[31] Cleveland sportswriter Terry Pluto added, "Bibby had to continually bug the front office for the bonus he was owed from the 1976 season, so this time he was really running out of patience."[32]

On March 15, 1978, nine days after arbitrator Alexander Porter upheld Bibby's breach of contract grievance, the pitcher signed with the Pittsburgh Pirates. He had other offers, but even though the money in Pittsburgh wasn't the best—an estimated $700,000 over an unspecified multi-year contract—he liked the Pirates because they were not too far from his home in Virginia. He also rightly noted, "The team has good potential and can go places."[33]

Manager Chuck Tanner continued to use Bibby as a swingman. In 1978, he started 14 games out of 34 appearances, and in 1979 he started 17 games and relieved in the same number. Harvey Haddix had come over from Cleveland starting in 1979 and he helped keep Bibby's delivery smooth. Haddix said, "If he hadn't wanted it real bad, he'd have been a goner. You don't hang on in the big leagues because you look good in uniform."[34] Bibby was 12-4 with a 2.81 ERA for the '79 champions. He also hit two of his five career home runs that year; Big Jim hit only .148 in the big leagues, but as *The Pirates Encyclopedia* put it, he could drive a ball a long way when he connected.[35]

The "Fam-a-lee" clubhouse was a boisterous place, and as Rick Telander observed, Bibby "fit in nicely, giving and taking insults with the best." He'd also shown his fun-loving side in Texas, where he used the stage name "Fontay O'Rooney."[36] Yet he was also a serious man who sincerely cared about his teammates' personal well-being.[37]

In the playoffs against Cincinnati, Bibby started one game. He then started two more in the World Series against the Orioles, including Game Seven. He had no decisions but pitched effectively, allowing just four earned runs in 17 1/3 innings.

That was the only time Bibby ever got to the postseason, though. The Pirates fell back to third in the NL East in 1980 — despite his best year ever. Moving back into the starting rotation (he relieved just once all year), he tied his career high with in wins with 19, and since he lost just 6, his .760 winning percentage led the NL. Jim was named to the All-Star team for the only time in his career; he finished in third in the voting for the Cy Young Award (behind Steve Carlton and Jerry Reuss). "I'm not raring back and throwing hard all the time," he said that May. "I only do it when I have to."[38]

The 1981 season featured another of Bibby's most brilliant performances — he thought it surpassed his no-hitter. On May 19, he threw his other big-league one-hitter, and it was nearly a perfect game. At Three Rivers Stadium against Atlanta, Terry Harper's bloop single to right led off the game — but after that, not another Brave reached base. "I was more consistent tonight than in my no-hitter," said Bibby, who threw just 93 pitches that night.[39]

However, Bibby's year was interrupted not only by baseball's strike but also by injury. He made only four starts after the strike ended. He underwent surgery for a slight tear in his rotator cuff on April 21, 1982 — bone fragments were also removed from his shoulder. He missed the entire season, though he was able to throw on the sidelines in September. In January 1983, he expressed optimism about his comeback.[40] As it turned out, though, he had a poor year: 5-12, 6.69 in just 78 innings pitched. He got into the seventh inning in just two of his starts. As Chuck Tanner noted that May, "Bibby was throwing hard. It was just a matter of location."[41]

In November 1983, the Pirates allowed Bibby to become a free agent. He signed with the Rangers in early February 1984, again sounding upbeat. "I feel that I'm 100 percent right now. I don't know if I'm going to throw as hard as I did when I was a rookie in Texas but I'm more of a pitcher now. I have a repertoire of pitches that I can put over the plate. I felt good physically last year. My mechanics were a little off."[42]

Bibby made the club out of spring training, but relieved in just eight games before Texas released him on June 1. Eight days later, he signed as a free agent with the St. Louis organization. He appeared in two games for Louisville, their top farm club, but even though he allowed just two hits in five innings and did not give up any runs, the Cardinals released him on July 1. The U.S. Olympic squad had also hit him hard in a game on June 17. "I saw a lot of good players on that team," said Jim.[43] The hitters included Mark McGwire, Will Clark, Barry Larkin, and B.J. Surhoff.

That wasn't quite Bibby's last professional action on the mound, though. During the fall and winter of 1989-90, when the Senior Professional Baseball Association held its only full season, he joined the Winter Haven Super Sox. He pitched 54 2/3 innings in 11 games, going 2-4 with a 4.12 ERA.

In July 1984, Bibby went directly into coaching, starting with the Durham Bulls in North Carolina. He learned of a vacancy for the 1985 season in Lynchburg, near his home in Madison Heights, Virginia, which he pursued. He thus could enjoy full-time family life while still working and giving to his love, baseball. From 1985 through 1999, he was pitching coach for Lynchburg. The franchise was affiliated with the Mets (1985-87), Red Sox (1988-94), and thereafter the Pirates. Among the notable future major-leaguers he coached were Aaron Sele, Kris Benson, and Francisco Rodriguez. In 2002, after Lynchburg retired his number, he said, "When I see guys make it to the bigs and have success there, that's more gratifying to me than anything else."[44]

In 2000, Bibby stepped up to Pittsburgh's top affiliate, Nashville in the Pacific Coast League. After that season, his contract was not renewed, he underwent double knee replacement surgery, and so retired. Though his knees weren't up to throwing BP and hitting fungoes after more than 30 years on the field, he still often got out to games in Lynchburg.[45]

Among his other leisure pursuits, golf was Bibby's favorite. In October 2011, his wife Jackie (they were married in 1968) and daughters Tanya and Tamara staged the first Jim Bibby Golf Classic at his club, Colonial Hills Golf Course in Forest, Virginia. The tournament was under the aegis of the James "Jim" Bibby Memorial Foundation, the non-profit organization that his family created "to continue Jim's initiatives for supporting organizations and programs promoting fitness and health and wellness." Proceeds of the tournament went to benefit two of his favorite causes, the YMCA of Central Virginia and the Children's Miracle Network.[46]

Bibby was a longstanding member of First Baptist Church of Coolwell in Amherst. He was also active in his community. In addition to serving on the board of the Lynchburg YMCA and acting as an ambassador for the Children's Miracle Network, he was an advocate for the Sickle Cell Foundation. He was also a loyal supporter of both the Jerry Lewis Labor Day Telethons and the American Cancer Society's Relay For Life.[47]

After battling bone cancer, Jim Bibby died on February 16, 2010. At his memorial service, his friend Susan Landergan, CEO of the Lynchburg YMCA, said, "Big heart, big body, big talent, big personality, big hands, big humor, big hugs. Bibby lived life big."[48]

Special thanks to Tamara and Jackie Bibby for their help and input.

SOURCES

www.baseball-reference.com

www.retrosheet.org

www.lynchburg.edu

NOTES

1. Mike Shropshire, *Seasons in Hell* (New York: Dutton Books, 1996), 39.
2. Rick Telander, "He's Not Hot Stuff, He's My Brother," *Sports Illustrated*, March 2, 1981. "For the Record," *Sports Illustrated*, March 1, 2010.
3. Shropshire, op. cit., loc. cit.
4. Telander, op. cit.
5. "Lynchburg Legend Jim Bibby Dies at 65." Lynchburg Hillcats website, February 17, 2010 (http://lynchburg.hillcats.milb.com/news/article.jsp?ymd=20100217&content_id=8086010&vkey=news_t481&fext=.jsp&sid=t481)
6. Telander, op. cit.
7. Dan Donovan, "Pirates' Bibby Becoming BIG Factor," *Pittsburgh Press*, May 15, 1980: C-1.
8. Ibid.
9. An article in the *Fayetteville Observer*, published shortly after Jim Bibby's death alludes to the pitcher's purported baseball career at Fayetteville State University. However, the Bibby family regards this account as inaccurate. See Sammy Batten, "Jim Bibby (1944-2010)," February 19, 2010.
10. Telander, op. cit.
11. The scout was Bill Herring, a North Carolinian who had pitched and managed in various minor leagues in the area.
12. Telander, op. cit.
13. Fred Girard, "Rookie Bibby Makes Pitch For Mets Job," *St. Petersburg Times*, March 4, 1969: 3-C.
14. "Pennant Playoffs Sweetened World Series Pot," *The Sporting News*, November 29, 1969: 34.
15. Telander, op. cit.
16. Telander, op. cit.
17. George McClelland, "Bibby Impatiently Awaits Mets' Next Distress Signal," *The Sporting News*, August 7, 1971: 43.
18. Jack Lang, "Mets Dump Ex-Heroes, Seek Slugger," *The Sporting News*, November 6, 1971: 50.
19. Jack Lang, "Met Rep as Pitcher-Rich Club Just Doesn't Tally." *The Sporting News*, November 13, 1971: 45.
20. Fred Rothenberg, "Bibby Pitches 1-Hitter," Associated Press, June 30, 1973.
21. "No-Hitter Bibby 'Close to Ryan,'" Associated Press, August 1, 1973. "Bibby was also once a Met," Associated Press, July 31, 1973.
22. Shropshire, op. cit.: 106.
23. Ibid., loc. cit.
24. Joe Posnanski, "The Biggest Pitcher I Ever Saw," *Sports Illustrated*, February 18, 2010.
25. Ibid.
26. Paul Burka, "If It's Tuesday, This Must Be Oakland," *Texas Monthly*, July 1975: 88.
27. Russell Schneider, *The Cleveland Indians Encyclopedia* (Champaign, Illinois: Sports Publishing LLC, 2004), 235.
28. Telander, op. cit.
29. Posnanski, op. cit.
30. Joe Posnanski, "That Was for Duane Kuiper," Joe Posnanski's "Curiously Long Posts" blog on the *Sports Illustrated* website (http://joeposnanski.si.com/2011/08/18/that-was-for-duane-kuiper/). This game probably took place in November 1979, as part of an All-Star series between the National League and American League. A combined American squad also faced Japanese players in two games.
31. Schneider, op. cit.: 380.
32. Terry Pluto, *The Curse of Rocky Colavito* (New York: Simon & Schuster, 1994), 195.

33 Charley Feeney, "Bibby, at Start, Booked for Buccos' Bullpen," *The Sporting News*, April 1, 1978: 45.

34 Telander, op. cit.

35 David Finoli and Bill Rainer, *The Pirates Encyclopedia* (Champaign, Illinois: Sports Publishing LLC, 2003), 363.

36 Shropshire, op. cit.: 39.

37 Telander, op. cit.

38 Donovan, op. cit.

39 Charley Feeney, "Harper's Leadoff Single Ruins Bid at Perfect Game," *Pittsburgh Post-Gazette*, May 20, 1981: 17.

40 Charley Feeney, "Bibby Feels He's Set for Comeback," *The Sporting News*, January 24, 1983: 40.

41 Charley Feeney, "McWilliams Adds Strength, Deception," *The Sporting News*, May 16, 1983: 18.

42 Jim Reeves, "Bibby, 39, Rejoins Rangers," *The Sporting News*, February 20, 1984: 42.

43 "Olympians Impress Bibby," *The Sporting News*, July 9, 1984: 37.

44 Lisa Winston, "Longtime Player and Coach Honored," *USA Today Baseball Weekly*, July 10, 2002.

45 Ibid.

46 Press release for Jim Bibby Memorial Golf Classic, July 7, 2011.

47 "James Blair 'Jim' Bibby," *Lynchburg News & Advance*, February 19, 2010.

48 Dave Thompson, "Mourners Remember Jim Bibby's Big Personality, Care for Community," *Lynchburg News & Advance*, February 21, 2010.

Bert Blyleven

By Gregory H. Wolf

BERT BLYLEVEN'S CAREER STATISTICS speak for themselves: 287 victories, 4,970 innings pitched, 3,701 strikeouts, and 60 shutouts accumulated over the course of 22 seasons in the big leagues (1970-1990, 1992). However, some sportswriters questioned whether the Dutch-born right-hander, whose curveball was regarded as the era's finest, was Hall of Fame material when he retired. In his most productive campaigns, Blyleven was overshadowed by Jim Palmer, Tom Seaver, Catfish Hunter, and Nolan Ryan while toiling for small-market and primarily mediocre teams in Minnesota, Pittsburgh, and Cleveland. Critics pointed unfairly to Blyleven's 250 losses and an unfounded reputation for losing big games as reasons for his Hall-unworthiness, while overlooking his championship with the Pirates in 1979 and the Twins in 1987. Blyleven's oft-times prickly relationship with his teammates, managers, and sportswriters didn't help his cause. In his first year of eligibility for the Hall of Fame, in 1998, Blyleven garnered only 17.5 percent of the necessary 75 percent of the vote required for enshrinement. Over the course of the next 13 years the case for Blyleven grew, as advanced statistical metrics, such as WAR (wins above replacement), ERA+ (ERA adjusted to a player's ballpark and league), FIP (fielding independent pitching), and a rejection of won-loss records in favor of hits, strikeouts, and walks per nine innings, offered new lenses to analyze a pitcher's effectiveness.[1] These modern metrics revealed Blyleven as not just one of the best pitchers of his generation, but also one of the best in baseball history. In 2011 Blyleven was elected to the Hall of Fame with 79.7 percent of the vote.

In his Hall of Fame induction speech, Blyleven attributed his "stubbornness and determination" throughout his big-league career to his immigrant parents, who fled war-torn Europe in search of a better life.[2] Netherlands natives Johannes Cornelius and Jannigje Blijleven married when the country was under Nazi occupation. Three years after the birth of their third child, Rik Aalbert, on April 6, 1951, the Blijlevens emigrated from Zeist, Netherlands, to Saskatoon, (Saskatchewan) Canada, and eventually settled in Garden Grove in Southern California in 1957. With their names anglicized, Joe and Jenny Blyleven raised their family which grew to seven children (four girls and three boys) with Dutch values of diligence, integrity, and commitment in a household of limited means.

Bert began playing baseball at the age of 9, having been introduced to the game by his father, a carpenter by trade, who became a fan of the American pastime by listening to Dodgers games on the radio. The youngster was quickly converted from catcher to pitcher when the coach discovered the strength of the right-hander's arm. After that conversion, Blyleven's father built a pitcher's mound in their backyard so Bert could practice. Bert described his parents as his "mentors," who were regulars at his games, where the elder Blyleven often drew the ire of umpires and spectators for his constant arguing of balls and strikes.[3] Well aware of Sandy Koufax's chronic arm pain, Joe forbade Bert to throw the curveball until he was about 14 years old, leaving his son to envision Dodgers broadcaster Vin Scully vividly describe Koufax's devastating pitch.

The 6-foot-3, 160-pound Blyleven began to attract big-league scouts by the end of his junior year at Santiago High School in Garden Grove and in the local American Legion league. The author of at least two no-hitters and a 21-strikeout performance in his prep career, Blyleven earned all-league honors as a senior in 1969, and participated in several contests showcasing promising prospects in Southern California. The Minnesota Twins selected Blyleven in the third round with the 55th overall pick in the 1969 amateur draft. Team scouts Jesse Flores Sr. and Dick Wiencek offered an estimated $15,000 bonus and signed the 18-year-old hurler at the Blyleven residence.

According to Blyleven, Flores told the elder Blyleven that Bert would be in the majors in less than two years. Flores's bold prediction was off by about a year. Just weeks after graduating from high school, Bert commenced his 24-year career in professional baseball by progressing rapidly through the Twins' affiliate in the Rookie Gulf Coast League and wining all five of his decisions for the Orlando Twins in the Class-A Florida State League. That fall he exceeded expectations by emerging as the best pitcher (7-0, 1.50 ERA) in the Florida Instructional League, where he was selected as an all-star by both scouts and managers.

Just 18 years old, Blyleven participated in the Twins' spring training as a nonroster invitee in Orlando in 1970. "I fell in love with him right away," said Minnesota skipper Bill Rigney, who recognized that the youngster with just 25 starts in his first season of pro ball needed more seasoning.[4] Blyleven was assigned to the Evansville (Indiana) Triplets in the Triple-A American Association, but his tenure in Triple A lasted only seven starts, one of which was a sparkling 10-inning complete-game shutout with 17 strikeouts against Iowa on May 15, 1970.

When their right-handed starter Luis Tiant, who was 6-0 at the time, was sidelined with a fractured right shoulder in late May, the Twins promoted Blyleven. Team scout Early Wynn thought the teenager was ready for prime time. "With his live fastball and marvelous coordination," said the former 300-game winner, "[Blyleven] reminds me of Herb Score."[5] On June 5, 1970, Blyleven debuted against the Washington Senators at RFK Stadium. The youngest player in the majors, as well as the first in major-league history to be born in the Netherlands, the 19-year-old hurler surrendered a home run on a 3-and-2 fastball to the first batter he faced, Lee Maye, but settled down to yield just five hits while striking out seven in seven innings to earn the victory, 2-1. Pitching consistently for the AL West Division champions, Blyleven fanned 12 in a complete-game victory over the Milwaukee Brewers on August 4 to set a new Twins record for strikeouts by a rookie, and tied an AL record by whiffing the first six California Angels batters he faced in a 5-1 loss on September. "His curveball," said Blyleven's batterymate George Mitterwald, "is, well, fantastic."[6]

Blyleven finished with a 10-9 record, becoming just the 25th pitcher to reach double digits in victories as a teenager, and posted a 3.18 ERA in 164 innings. *The Sporting News* named him the AL Rookie Pitcher of the Year. Despite AP reports that Blyleven would start in the best-of-five ALCS versus the Baltimore Orioles, Rigney chose a different young hurler, Tom Hall (11-6), with only 11 starting assignments for the season, to make a crucial postseason start after Cy Young Award winner Jim Perry (24-12) lost Game One.[7] In relief of veteran starter Jim Kaat, who was on the ropes in the third inning of Game Three, Blyleven tossed two innings in Baltimore, yielding two hits and an unearned run in the Twins' third straight loss, which eliminated Minnesota from the postseason.

Essentially a two-pitch hurler (curveball and fastball) thus far in his career, Blyleven developed an offspeed pitch during spring training in 1971, and the results were immediate. He blanked Milwaukee

on four hits in his first start, followed by a three-hit shutout at Kansas City five days later. "I'm holding the ball differently and it's moving in on the hitters," said Blyleven. "When I throw the fastball I hold the ball the same way I do on a changeup."⁸ Minnesota beat reporter Bob Fowler also noticed another change in the 20-year-old "man-child."⁹ Blyleven had packed on an estimated 20 pounds to his frame; at 210 pounds Blyleven seemed stronger and more durable. "He's the most coachable pitcher I've ever handled," said pitching coach Marv Grissom, who lauded Blyleven's unparalleled work ethic.¹⁰

On a staff that finished 11th of the 12 teams in ERA (3.81) in 1971, Blyleven emerged as the club's best pitcher, overtaking graybeards Perry (35 years old) and Kaat (32), yet his record stood at a misleading 10-15 after a 6-3 loss in Baltimore on August 22. In 12 of those losses, Blyleven received only three or fewer runs of support from an otherwise above-average offense, and thus acquired the reputation as a tough-luck loser that stuck with him for the remainder of his career.

While the Twins stumbled to a disappointing fifth-place finish (74-86), Blyleven concluded his first full campaign on a tear, winning six straight decisions, including two shutouts and a 10-inning scoreless no-decision, and carving out a 1.69 ERA in 69⅓ innings. He finished fourth in the AL in strikeouts (224) and fifth in ERA (2.81), and led the circuit in strikeouts-to-walks ratio (3.80).

Blyleven's biggest moment of 1971 was probably when he married Patricia Ann Whitehead in July. They had four children, Todd, Tim, Kimberly, and Tom. Todd followed his father's footsteps. In 1990 he was drafted out of Villa Park High School by the California Angels in the 39th round, and in 1991 he was selected out of Cypress College by the Los Angeles Dodgers in the 90th round. The big (6-foot-5) right-handed pitcher spent his five-year professional career primarily in the low minors for three organizations.

In 1972 Blyleven picked up where he had left off the previous season, winning his first four decisions to set a new Twins record with 10 consecutive victories, as the club got off to a hot start and occupied first place as late as May 20. But those successes proved to be short-lived. The team took a nosedive in June. Rigney was fired on July 5 and postseason aspirations faded quickly. Blyleven slumped, too, losing 12 of 15 decisions to fall to 10-15 on August 19. "I was throwing across my body," said Blyleven of his pitching woes. "I was landing on the heel on my left foot."¹¹ Working closely with new skipper Frank Quilici and pitching coach Al Worthington to improve his mechanics, Blyleven found his groove over the last five weeks of the season, posting a 1.45 ERA in his final nine starts covering 74⅔ innings. Despite a team-record 2.84 ERA, the Twins finished in third place (77-77). Blyleven's 17-17 record failed to tell the story of his success. The Twins scored three runs or less in all but one of his losses. He posted a robust 2.73 ERA in 287⅓ innings, and once again ranked fourth in punchouts (228).

The unequivocal ace of the staff, Blyleven got off to a rough start in 1973, losing six of his first eight decisions with an ERA north of 4.00 as he struggled once again with pitching mechanics. "He wasn't following through," said pitching coach Worthington. "He was releasing the ball too soon."¹² With the aid of film (a novelty at the time), Blyleven adjusted, and subsequently won 10 of his next 14 starts and posted a 1.48 ERA in 121 innings in one of the most dominating stretches in his career. Seven of those victories were shutouts, including the first of his five career one-hitters, against Kansas City on May 24. The spree of whitewashes cast the 22-year-old hurler with his trademark pronounced high leg lick and his tongue sticking out of his mouth into the national spotlight. "[Blyleven] makes the baseball dance and twist on the way to the plate," wrote the AP after his 4-0 victory over the Angels and their speedballer, Nolan Ryan, on June 29.¹³ "He is the best curveball pitcher I've ever seen," said Boston's DH, Orlando Cepeda, who had battled Koufax as a member of the Giants in the 1960s.¹⁴

Blyleven fashioned the best season ever by a Twins hurler, setting team records in shutouts (a major-league-leading 9), complete games (25), innings (325), and strikeouts (258), while winning 20 games and posting a career-low 2.52 ERA. Despite those gaudy numbers, he finished a distant seventh in Cy Young

Award voting, hurt by his 17 losses and playing for a third-place team that finished at 81-81, 13 games behind first-place Oakland. Sportswriters might have overlooked Blyleven, whose teammates scored three runs or fewer in 16 of his losses (28 total runs), but fellow pitchers did not. "The best pitcher in the league is Bert Blyleven," said Oakland ace Catfish Hunter. "He's got the best stuff."[15] By one contemporary metric (WAR), Blyleven was not just the best pitcher in the league, but the most valuable player.[16] His only blemish was his performance in the All-Star game in Kansas City, where he yielded two hits and walked two in just one inning and was charged with the loss.

Emboldened by his success, Blyleven demanded that the Twins double his salary in 1974, leading to tensions with club owner Calvin Griffith, who was notoriously tight-fisted and the last major-league owner who derived his income solely from the team. Though he received a substantial raise to a reported $55,000, Blyleven's relationship with the front office was in a free-fall. Playing through occasional lower back pain, Blyleven split his 34 decisions, finished a distant second once again to Ryan in strikeouts (249 to 367) and posted a stellar 2.66 ERA, but few saw him as the Twins finished last in attendance. Griffith rejected Kansas City's offer to buy the hurler for a million dollars, but Blyleven's days with the Twins nonetheless seemed numbered.

After losing a contentious salary arbitration, Blyleven received another blow when he came down with a sore shoulder to start the 1975 season. Eventually diagnosed with a torn muscle, the 24-year-old hurler landed on the 21-day DL in early June. Blyleven seemed as strong as ever upon his return, completing 15 of 22 starts with a sturdy 2.62 ERA. He pitched at least 10 innings on three occasions, including an 11-inning shutout with 13 strikeouts against Milwaukee at County Stadium on August 27. It was his 24th career shutout, breaking Kaat's team record. Described as "enigmatic" by the AP, Blyleven's stellar season (15-10, 3.00 ERA, 20 complete games, and 233 strikeouts) barely registered on the national radar for the fourth-place Twins, who once again finished last in attendance.[17] And for the second straight season, Blyleven failed to receive even one vote for the Cy Young Award.

With his frustrations mounting, Blyleven formally asked for a trade after the 1975 season. Firebrand Gene Mauch, hired to replace Quilici, did not take kindly to his outspoken hurler, deriding him as a "pattern pitcher" whom batters had long figured out.[18] Despite desperately needing a cash infusion for his club, Griffith refused to sell Blyleven and rejected multiple trade offers. It was a contentious time in baseball. Under the leadership of Marvin Miller, executive director of the Major League Baseball Players Association, pitchers Andy Messersmith of the Los Angeles Dodgers and Dave McNally of the Montreal Expos successfully challenged baseball's century-old reserve clause, effectively ushering in free agency with arbitrator Peter Seitz's ruling in December. Armed with this freedom, Blyleven, as well as many other big leaguers, decided to play out their option by not signing a contract for the 1976 season in order to become free agents.

With trade rumors swirling, Blyleven's seven-year tenure with the Twins came to a close after a forgettable outing on May 31 in front of 8,379 at Metropolitan Stadium. As Blyleven left the mound in the ninth inning of an eventual complete-game 3-2 loss to California, he gave the jeering and booing crowd a three-finger salute. "I couldn't care less about the fans," he said after the game.[19] AL President Lee MacPhail subsequently fined the hurler and ordered him to issue a public apology.[20] One day after his unsportsmanlike exit, Blyleven was traded along with infielder Danny Thompson to the Texas Rangers for shortstop Roy Smalley III (nephew of Mauch), pitchers Bill Singer and Jim Gideon, infielder Mike Cubbage, and an estimated $250,000. (Thompson, battling leukemia, died that December.)

In his debut with the Rangers on June 5 at Arlington Stadium, Blyleven tossed an 11-inning complete game with 10 punchouts, but lost 3-2 to Detroit's Mark "The Bird" Fidrych. After Blyleven was clobbered for 14 earned runs on 19 hits (including four home runs) in 15⅓ innings during his next two outings, critics lampooned the trade for a hurler who was not under contract and who was widely expected to play elsewhere the next season. Turning a deaf ear to criticism, Blyleven worked out his kinks with Texas pitching coach Sid Hudson, who suggested that he throw a sinker. On June 21 Blyleven tossed a sparkling 10-inning, one-hit shutout to beat Oakland, 1-0, pick up his first win with his new club, and reach the 100-victory plateau for his career. Five days later Blyleven hurled another 10-inning, 1-0 shutout, scattering 10 hits against Chicago. In his return to Minnesota on July 26, Blyleven took no pity on his former teammates and a small weeknight crowd at Metropolitan Stadium, blanking them on two hits. While Texas finished in fourth place in the AL West (76-86), Blyleven's cumulative 13-16 record overshadowed his 2.87 ERA in 297⅔ innings and 219 strikeouts.

Blyleven returned to the Rangers in 1977 on a one-year-contract in an injury-plagued season. A groin pull forced the 26-year-old pitcher to miss starts on at least three occasions, and Blyleven's campaign seemed to be over on September 6 after a "roughed-up" loss (five runs, six hits, three walks in 3⅔ innings) at Minnesota. Defying odds, he returned on September 22 to toss what proved to be his only no-hitter, a 6-0 victory with seven strikeouts and one walk over the Angels at Anaheim Stadium while facing just 28 batters. "I wasn't coming out," said the pitcher, whose groin tightened in the first inning, "even if I had to throw it underhanded."[21] In 30 starts, Blyleven (14-12) had a 2.72 ERA in 234⅔ innings.

Just about a month after Blyleven signed a six-year deal with the Rangers in the offseason, he was shipped on December 8 to the Pittsburgh Pirates in a rare four-team trade that also involved the New York Mets and Atlanta Braves.[22] Overall, 11 players (including Blyleven) changed addresses during the deal, which was consummated near the end of the winter meetings in Hawaii. Disappointed that he was not sent to a team in Southern California, where he and his family lived in the offseason, Blyleven did not seem overly excited to be headed to Pittsburgh, whose manager, Chuck Tanner, was known for having a quick hook with his starters. "I really don't care where I play," he said. "I'll pitch for Bert Blyleven and do the best I can."[23] Such comments did not endear the hurler to Pirates fans, who lost longtime favorite and All-Star outfielder Al Oliver to Texas in the swap. The optimistic Tanner waxed excitedly about Blyleven's pitching attributes and exclaimed, "Bert Blyleven is capable of winning 25 games!"[24]

In the context of his career, Blyleven's three-year tenure in Pittsburgh was underwhelming and marked by an increasingly acrimonious relationship with Tanner. Blyleven's first victory as a Pirate (an 11-inning, six-hit, 1-0 shutout of the Mets on April 26) was probably the highlight of the 1978 season, during which he went 14-10 (3.03 ERA) in 34 starts and was bothered by persistent shoulder pain.

No longer mentioned among the best pitchers in baseball, Blyleven got off to a horrendous beginning in 1979, winless in his first nine starts with an ERA of 5.17. Requiring regular cortisone shots in his ailing shoulder, Blyleven called the period the "most frustrating" in his life.[25] While the "We Are Family" Pirates coalesced into one of the most memorable and tight-knit teams in club history to win 98 games and capture the NL East Division crown, Blyleven was portrayed in the press as a "mystery man" who was more concerned with his own statistics than team success.[26] "It's tough pitching for Tanner," said Blyleven (12-5), who led the staff in starts (37) and innings (237⅓), but completed only four games. "[He] goes to the bullpen so often. ... I'm a competitor. I don't like to be taken out of the game."[27] Blyleven looked back on 20 no-decisions that he had when the regular season ended.

As the Pirates beat the Cincinnati Reds during a pair of anxious extra-inning affairs at Riverfront Stadium in the first two games of the best-of-five NLCS, Blyleven seemed frustrated with years of criticism that he lacked concentration and couldn't win the big game, calling his reputation a "bad rap."[28] He secured the Pirates' berth in the World Series and quieted critics, at least temporarily, with an eight-hit, complete-game victory, 7-1, on October 5 at Three Rivers Stadium.

With the Pirates down after they lost Game One of the World Series, Blyleven started Game Two against the Baltimore Orioles, scattering five hits and two runs in a six-inning no-decision in the Pirates' eventual 3-2 victory at Memorial Stadium. Blyleven's most important outing of the season, and of his career thus far, came in Game Five on October 14 in Pittsburgh, ironically in his first relief stint since his third season. With the Pirates facing a three-games-to-one disadvantage and trailing 1-0 in an elimination game, Blyleven took over for Jim Rooker to begin the sixth frame and tossed four scoreless innings, yielding three hits. The Pirates exploded for seven unanswered runs, making Blyleven the victor. Pittsburgh won the final two games in Baltimore to complete their comeback and win a dramatic World Series.

The nadir of Blyleven's career came the following spring when he walked out on the Pirates after an outing on April 29 versus Montreal when he was yanked with two on and two out during a shaky sixth inning. "It wasn't a snap decision," said Blyleven, who returned to California and demanded a trade. "I've been thinking about it for more than a year."[29] The hurler cited "nonsupport and lack of confidence from my manager" as reasons for his self-imposed retirement.[30] "I may seem strange, but for the first time in a long, long time, I feel happy."[31] While Blyleven was vilified nationally as an entitled millionaire who symbolized the fan's perception of all-that-was-wrong with the skyrocketing salaries in professional sports, his teammates were shocked. "I can't understand why he left," said Bill Madlock. I would respect him more if he left for personal reasons."[32] Blyleven ultimately returned, was reinstated on May 11, and was in the starting rotation two days later in San Francisco, where Tanner left him in for the whole contest of a 5-0 defeat. But the damage had been done. A pariah in the clubhouse, Blyleven lashed out at the media for what he perceived as unfair treatment, and went on a "silence kick," refusing to grant interviews to reporters.[33] The Pirates finally traded their disgruntled hurler (8-13, 3.82 ERA in 32 starts) along with Manny Sanguillen on December 9 to the Cleveland Indians for four marginal players (utilityman Gary Alexander and pitchers Victor Cruz, Bob Owchinko, and Rafael Vasquez.) The "checklist" end results from this transaction proved that "addition by subtraction" does not always work. In 1981 Alexander batted .213 in 51 plate appearances; Cruz was 1-1 in 22 relief outings; Owchinko was traded at the end of spring training to the Oakland A's for reliever Ernie Camacho; Vasquez, who was a highly thought of prospect within the Pirates organization in the late '70's, ended up 4-8 after being dispatched to Double-A Buffalo.[34]

Blyleven immediately propped up Cleveland's staff, which had produced the worst team ERA (4.68) among all 26 big-league teams in 1980. After losing on Opening Day, the 30-year-old hurler tossed six consecutive complete-game victories en route to a 7-4 record and 2.83 ERA before the 1981 season was interrupted for nearly two months by the players' strike. Snubbed for the All-Star Game, which kicked off the so-called second half of the season, on August 9 in Cleveland, Blyleven was widely praised by Indians skipper Dave Garcia as the "leader of the staff."[35] Known throughout his career for his offseason exercise regimen and stamina, Blyleven developed a sore elbow in September, prematurely ending his season with an 11-7 record and a sparkling 2.88 ERA in 159⅓ innings. Few outside of Cleveland took note of Blyleven's stunning renaissance. While Milwaukee's newly acquired reliever Rollie Fingers won the Cy Young Award, Blyleven was the easily the most valuable pitcher in the AL, according to one contemporary metric (WAR), but did not receive a single vote for the coveted award.

After he missed most of spring training in 1982, Blyleven's career seemed in jeopardy when he was diagnosed with a torn muscle in his right elbow after making just four starts. He underwent surgery performed by renowned surgeon Dr. Frank Jobe, and missed the rest of the season.

According to Cleveland sportswriter Terry Pluto, many wondered if Blyleven would ever pitch again. His return in 1983 was further complicated by a fracture of his left elbow suffered in an apparent fall at his home in California.[36] But with Dutch perseverance, Blyleven, described as the "most encouraging development" of spring training, made an unexpected recovery.[37] He pitched steadily yet unspectacularly in the first half of the season before shoulder and elbow miseries landed him on the DL three separate times in the second half of the season, once again raising doubts about his future.[38]

Blyleven's return to pitching prominence was one of the feel-good stories of the 1984 season. He did not make a start for almost four weeks after he stepped on a ball in the outfield while shagging batting-practice flies in Milwaukee in mid-May and fractured his foot. Still, Blyleven went 19-7 and posted a stellar 2.87 ERA in 245 innings for the last-place Indians and new manager Pat Corrales. In Blyleven's seven losses, his teammates managed to score a total of six runs. Praised by *The Sporting News* as the "best pitcher in the American League," Blyleven increasingly relied on his curveball, sinker, slider, and changeup to augment his fastball.[39] "I think all the injuries in the last two years have forced me to become a better pitcher," said Blyleven, who finished third in voting for the Cy Young Award.[40] The 15-year veteran had lost none of his competitive spirit. "I get enjoyment from striking out a guy and making him look bad," admitted Blyleven bluntly. He then added, in sabermetric-like language, "I've always been a strikeout pitcher. It's the best way to get rid of the hitter. If he doesn't make contact, there can be no chance for a mistake."[41]

But by his fifth start in 1985, Blyleven was at a boiling point. Frustrated that he had not been traded despite his public demands since the previous spring, Blyleven was struggling with an ERA just over 5.00. He blew his top on April 28 after allowing three home runs in an exasperating outing at Baltimore by making an obscene gesture to the jeering crowd at Memorial Stadium when he was removed from the game in the bottom of the eighth. Reprimanded by AL President Bobby Brown, Blyleven subsequently reeled off three shutouts in his next six starts, then commenced a string of 10 consecutive complete games from June 6 through July 24. Named to the AL All-Star team for the second and last time, Blyleven struggled (three hits and two earned runs in two innings), but received a hearty welcome on July 16 from the sellout crowd at the Metrodome, the Twins' domed stadium in downtown Minneapolis. Blyleven, whom Cleveland had placed on waivers after the June 15 trading deadline, was later claimed by Minnesota, which acquired the 34-year-old hurler on August 1, along with a player to be named later (pitcher Rich Yett), in exchange for three prospects, infielder Jay Bell, pitcher Curt Wardle, and minor-league outfielder Jim Weaver. Blyleven made a smooth transition to the Twins, posting an 8-5 record and completing nine of his 14 starts. Finishing a distant third once again in the Cy Young Award voting, Blyleven (17-16 record, 3.16 ERA) led the AL in starts (37), shutouts (5), and strikeouts (206), while pacing the majors in complete games (24) and innings (293⅔). As of 2016, the latter two figures have not been matched by any big leaguer.

Blyleven's post-surgery renaissance continued in his first full season in 1986 after his return to the Twins. "Bert's delivery always has been smooth, loose, a lot of leg drive, everything going forward at the same time," said skipper Ray Miller.[42] On August 1 Blyleven tossed an overpowering two-hitter against the Oakland A's, striking out a career-high 15, including the 3,000th in his career, to become the 10th major leaguer to reach that milestone.[43] He reached another, albeit infamous milestone on September 29 when he yielded his 47th home run of the season, to Jay Bell (who was making his major-league debut and hit the first pitch Blyleven threw to him) in a victory over Cleveland at the Metrodome to break Robin Roberts' record set in 1956 for the most gopher balls in a season. "I don't like this ballpark," said Blyleven, who ultimately surrendered 50 round-trippers in '86 with 31 of those blasts coming at the Metrodome. "I'm a fastball pitcher and the ball carries here."[44] The baseball really carried in the Metrodome on September 13 when Blyleven allowed five home runs in 5⅓ innings to Texas. Blyleven (17-14, 4.01 ERA) fanned 215 and led the AL in innings (271⅔).

Led by a quartet of young sluggers (Kirby Puckett, Kent Hrbek, Gary Gaetti, and Tom Brunansky), the Twins (85-77) captured the AL West crown in 1987. In the postseason, Blyleven (15-12, 4.01 ERA in 267 innings) put to rest any suggestion that he could not win the big game. In the best-of-seven ALCS he defeated the heavily favored Detroit Tigers (98-64) twice, including the Game Five clincher in Tiger Stadium. He ran his postseason winning streak to five games in

Game Two of the World Series against the St. Louis Cardinals, scattering six hits and yielding two runs in seven innings in an 8-4 victory at the Metrodome with the partisan home crowd cheering loudly while waving "Homer Hankies." "When you put fifty-five thousand screaming people in here, it's something," said Blyleven, soaking in every moment. "The best thing to do is just not think."[45] Though he picked up the loss, 4-2, in Game Five at Busch Stadium in St. Louis (seven hits, three runs, two earned in six innings), the Twins defeated the Cardinals in Games Six and Seven when they returned to the fever-pitched decibels of the Metrodome to capture their first championship since the franchise relocated from Washington, DC, after the 1960 season.

Blyleven's second stint with the Twins ended after the 1988 season when he was traded to the California Angels for two prospects (first baseman Paul Sorrento and reliever Mike Cook) with limited big-league experience; both teams also tossed in a minor leaguer. Blyleven had struggled in 1988, notching just 10 victories and was bothered by a bruised right thumb. He also led the majors in two dubious categories: the highest ERA among starters (5.43) and losses (17, tied with Atlanta's Tom Glavine).

"I've dreamt about this since I was growing up," said Blyleven about pitching in Anaheim in front of friends and family in 1989.[46] In what sportswriter Tim Harrigan of the AP called a "brilliant year," the 38-year-old Blyleven resurrected yet again his career, posting a 17-5 record with a 2.73 ERA in 241 innings to finish fourth in the Cy Young Award balloting for the third-place Angels.[47] In his last start of the campaign, he tossed his AL-best fifth shutout, and the 60th of his career, blanking Kansas City on seven hits. Blyleven attributed his success to his slider, which tended to ride in on left-handed hitters, as well as excellent command of his low-and-outside fastball.[48] He walked a career-low 1.6 batters per nine innings.

Plagued by shoulder pain in 1990, Blyleven (8-7, 5.24 ERA) was forced to end his season prematurely when he was diagnosed with a torn muscle after a start on August 10. After an arthroscopic procedure in October, Blyleven reported to spring training in 1991. But when his pain resurfaced, he was once again examined by the Angels' orthopedic surgeon, Dr. Lewis Slocum, who discovered a serious tear in his rotator cuff.[49] Ten days after his 40th birthday, Blyleven had his second shoulder operation in less than eight months, and subsequently missed the entire 1991 season.

Few sportswriters thought the 41-year-old hurler could return to baseball in 1992. But as he had done so many times in his career, Blyleven proved his critics wrong. On May 19 he took the mound for the first time in more than 21 months and tossed six innings, yielding eight hits and three runs to the New York Yankees. Granted free agency after the 1992 season, Blyleven had no plans to retire. Despite losing seven of his last eight decisions, he pitched noticeably better over his final 12 starts with the Angels, finishing with an 8-12 record.

Only 13 victories shy of the magical 300 mark, Blyleven signed an incentive-laden contact with the Twins in 1993. He was roughed up in spring training and did not make the Opening Day roster. He subsequently announced his retirement, bringing his big-league career to an end. His name is displayed prominently among the career leaders in many pitching categories, including wins (287, 27th), losses (250, 10th), starts (685, 11th), innings (4,970, 14th), strikeouts (3,701, 5th), and shutouts (60, 9th). Blyleven accumulated 96.5 WAR (11th among pitchers), ahead of Christy Mathewson, Gaylord Perry, Warren Spahn, Steve Carlton, and Nolan Ryan.

Blyleven was also considered one of the baseball's best and most notorious pranksters, famous for his "hot foot."

Blyleven's name is synonymous with Twins baseball even though he played half of his career with other teams. In 1996 he was named color commentator for Twins television broadcasts, developing a style that matched his personality on the field. Known for his insightful analysis, occasional controversial comments, and unequivocal "homer" support of the club, the still brash Blyleven began his 21st season as commentator in 2016. Blyleven was elected to the Twins Hall of Fame in 2002, and had his number 28 retired by the club in 2011. His close association with the Twins was forever cemented when he chose to be portrayed wearing a Twins cap on his Hall of Fame plaque upon his election to that shrine in 2011. He also served as pitching coach for the Dutch national baseball team in 2009 and 2013 in the World Baseball Classic.

As of 2016, Blyleven lived with his second wife, Gayle, in Fort Myers, Florida, and the Twin Cities.

SOURCES

In addition to the sources cited in the Notes, the author also accessed Blyleven's player file and questionnaire from the National Baseball Hall of Fame, the Encyclopedia of Minor League Baseball, Retrosheet.org, Baseball-Reference.com, Bill Lee's *The Baseball Necrology*, the SABR Minor Leagues Database, accessed online at Baseball-Reference.com, *The Sporting News* archive via Paper of Record, and Ancestry.com.

NOTES

1 With the rise of sabermetric analysis, WAR, ERA+ and FIP have become three of the most compelling metrics used to analyze a pitcher's value and effectiveness. WAR (Wins Above Replacement) attempts to measure a player's value in wins he provides the team in comparison to a replacement-level player. ERA+ (Adjusted ERA) adjusts a pitcher's ERA according to ballpark factors and the league average. FIP (Fielding Independent Pitching) attempts to measure a pitcher's effectiveness by removing fielding variables.

2 Bert Blyleven's Hall of Fame induction speech, July 24, 2011. Player's Hall of Fame file, Cooperstown, New York.

3 Ibid.

4 *The Sporting News*, July 4, 1970: 10.

5 *The Sporting News*, June 13, 1970: 39.

6 *The Sporting News* July 4, 1970: 10.

7 AP, "Blyleven earns playoff start," *Winona* (Minnesota) *Daily News*, October 1, 1970: 22.

8 Pat Thompson, "Blyleven 4 hits Brewers," *Winona* (Minnesota) *Daily News*, April 8, 1971: 2.

9 *The Sporting News*, May 1, 1971: 9.

10 Ibid.

11 *The Sporting News*, August 19, 1972: 15.

12 *The Sporting News*, June 9, 1973: 3.

13 AP, "Darwin's slam boosts Twins Over Angels, 4-0," *Winona* (Minnesota) *Daily News*, July 1, 1973: 18.

14 AP, "Blyleven logs 7th shutout, 12th win," *Winona* (Minnesota) *Daily News*, July 12, 1973: 16.

15 *The Sporting News*, December 8, 1973: 52.

16 Blyleven achieved a 9.9 WAR.

17 AP, "Blyleven, Twins Zip Yanks, 3-0," *Daily Journal* (Fergus Falls, Minnesota), July 22, 1975: 12.

18 AP, "Rangers Offer Three Players for Blyleven," *Daily Journal* (Fergus Falls, Minnesota), December 31, 1975: 13.

19 AP, "Blyleven Booed After 3-2 loss," *Daily Journal* (Fergus Falls, Minnesota), June 1, 1976: 9.

20 AP, "MacPhail Orders Public Apology by Blyleven," *Winona* (Minnesota) *Daily News*, June 3, 1976: 17.

21 *The Sporting News*, October 8, 1977:12.

22 A scorecard might have been needed to keep track of the 11 players who were involved in the rare four-team trade involving the Texas Rangers, Pittsburgh Pirates, Atlanta Braves, and New York Mets. Atlanta sent Willie Montanez to New York. Texas shipped Tommy Boggs, Adrian Devine, and Eddie Miller to Atlanta, and a player to be named later (Ken Henderson) and Tom Grieve to New York. Pittsburgh sent Nelson Norman and Al Oliver to Texas. New York sent Jon Matlack to Texas. New York sent John Milner to Pittsburgh. Blyleven was sent to Pittsburgh.

23 *The Sporting News*, December 24, 1977: 51.

24 Ibid.

25 Charley Feeney, "Blyleven Not Happy About Winless Start," *Pittsburgh Post Gazette*, May 15, 1979: 13.

26 *The Sporting News*, June 30, 1979: 24.

27 Charley Feeney, "It's Blyleven vs. LaCoss in Game 3," *Pittsburgh Post Gazette*, October 5, 1979: 9.

28 Ibid.

29 Charley Feeney, "Blyleven Walks Out, Wants Trade," *Pittsburgh Post-Gazette*, May 1, 1980: 9.

30 *The Sporting News*, May 17, 1980: 5.

31 Ibid.

32 Phil Axelrod, "Madlock Baffled by Blyleven's Departure," *Pittsburgh Post-Gazette*, May 2, 1980: 16.

33 *The Sporting News*, June 21, 1980: 33.

34 One of the worst trades in Pirates history.

35 *The Sporting News*, September 19, 1981: 21.

36 *The Sporting News*, April 4, 1983: 26.

37 Ibid.

38 Ibid.

39 *The Sporting News*, October 22, 1984: 14.

40 AP, "Cleveland's Blyleven Pushes for a Trade," *Des Moines* (Iowa) *Register*, September 11, 1984: 18.

41 AP, "Indians Hurler Blyleven focuses on Strikeouts at Expense of Shutouts," *Arizona Republic* (Phoenix), April 10, 1984: 44.

42 *The Sporting News*, March 31, 1986: 32.

43 Blyleven joined the following members of the 3,000-strikeout club with the date of their entry in parentheses: Walter Johnson (1923), Bob Gibson (1974), Gaylord Perry (1978), Nolan Ryan (1980), Tom Seaver (1981), Steve Carlton (1981), Ferguson Jenkins (1982), Don Sutton (1983), and Phil Niekro 1984.

44 AP, "Cleveland Rookie Helps Blyleven Secure Record," *Star-Democrat* (Easton, Maryland), October 1, 1986: 26.

45 AP, "Blyleven returns to roots, wins for Twins," *The Tennessean* (Nashville), October 19, 1987: 18.

46 AP, "Twins Deal Blyleven to California," *Star-Democrat* (Easton, Maryland), November 4, 1988: 9.

47 Tim Harrigan, AP, "The Big A. Blyleven back among best in the league," *Arizona Republic* (Phoenix), September 30, 1989: 38.

48 Dave Luecking, "His Biggest Prank. Blyleven Proves He's not Washed Up," *St. Louis Post-Dispatch*, August 27, 1989: 66.

49 Robyn Norwood, "Tour de Pain: At 40, Angels' Blyleven Is Given Little Chance to Pitch Again After Major Surgery—but He Has Pedaled that Route Before," *Los Angeles Times*, July 14, 1991.

Doe Boyland

By Rory Costello

DORIAN "DOE" BOYLAND WAS A GOOD prospect who never got a proper chance to show what he could do in the major leagues. The first baseman received three trials with the Pittsburgh Pirates — in 1978, 1979, and 1981. He got into a total of 21 games, but started none of them and played in the field in just one — all his other opportunities came as a pinch-hitter or pinch-runner. He got just two singles and a walk in 20 plate appearances.

For a time Boyland was touted as the heir to the great Willie Stargell in Pittsburgh. He wasn't a big power hitter — the most home runs he ever had in any season was 14 — but he hit for good average and stole an unusual number of bases for his size (6-feet-4 and 200 pounds) and position. He worked hard to become adept in the field — he had never played first base before turning professional. Yet even after Stargell entered his twilight as a player, the Pirates used other veterans instead. Boyland finally got a change of scenery in 1982, but could not break through in the San Francisco Giants organization either. He retired from pro baseball after that season.

Boyland then went on to huge success as a businessman. He founded his company, Boyland Auto Group, in 1987 and led it to the number-4 ranking on *Black Enterprise*'s auto dealers list for 2013. Brainpower, charisma, and determination were all big ingredients — yet he also gave credit to what he learned as a member of the 1979 World Series champion Pirates, especially from manager Chuck Tanner. In a 2011 promotional video, Boyland said, "I was very fortunate to be involved with the 1979 Pittsburgh Pirates.... I've got the [World Series] ring on right now. That was a dream in itself. I still get asked today, 'How was it?'

"But the one thing that was very helpful, in terms of not just making money, and people respecting what I've done, and having arrived as a baseball player ... Chuck Tanner was the eternal optimist. He could motivate a guy that was tired, hurt, injured, didn't feel like playing, to run through a brick wall. And not knowing at the time, I was picking all of that stuff up. So by the time it came that I was in the automobile industry and became a manager, I understood what motivation was all about."[1]

Dorian Scott Boyland was born on January 6, 1955, in Chicago. His parents were William and Alice (née Walker) Boyland.[2] He had one sibling, an older sister named Brenda. William and Alice were divorced when little Dorian was around 4 years old.[3] Alice, who worked as an accountant for retailer Montgomery Ward, then brought both children up by herself. She was a heroine to her son.[4]

In pursuit of better education for her children, Alice moved the family to the South Shore neighborhood of Chicago in 1962.[5] Dorian attended Isabelle O'Keeffe Elementary School and South Shore High, and his drive was evident from an early age. "As I was growing up, the only motivation I really had, that I could recall, was that I always wanted to do the right things. I wanted to get straight A's, I wanted to be the fastest guy in kickball, I wanted to be the last person out in dodgeball, I wanted my mom to say, 'Good job.' I wanted to be the best at whatever I was trying to accomplish."[6]

At one time in his youth, though, Boyland joined a gang. He talked about it with a group of 250 Chicago youngsters in 2010. "Seeing he was headed for trouble, his single mother sent him away to live with his grandmother. 'I learned a lot that summer, came back and made a different choice.'"[7] Throughout his life, this man never touched alcohol, tobacco, drugs, or even coffee.

Boyland won a scholarship to the University of Wisconsin at Oshkosh. His first love was basketball, and he later said that he chose UW-Oshkosh because of the head basketball coach, Robert White. In 2011 he called Coach White "a pioneer in recruiting minority players and diversifying the team," and talked of how the coach and his wife were another pair of parents to him.[8]

"Oshkosh had a good baseball team too," wrote *Pittsburgh Press* columnist Dan Donovan in 1978, "and since Boyland threw the ball pretty well, he volunteered to pitch." He had a strong freshman year on the mound, helping the Titans get to the 1973 NAIA College World Series.[9] One of his teammates was Jim Gantner, who went on to play 17 seasons in the majors with the Milwaukee Brewers. "The scouts came out to see him, and so they saw me too," said Boyland.[10]

Knee surgery after a basketball injury changed his priorities. "I lost some quickness," Boyland said. "I knew if I was going anywhere in sports, it would have to be in baseball."[11]

Over time in college, Boyland's bat got him into the everyday lineup. When he was not pitching, he played designated hitter and (on occasion) the outfield. As a senior in 1976, though his pitching record was so-so, Dorian was 29-for-95 (.305) with 6 homers and 26 RBIs.[12] Major-league scouting directors and coordinators named him to the second team of *The Sporting News* College All-America squad in 1976.[13]

That June Pittsburgh chose Boyland in the second round of the amateur draft. "I was not really surprised about being picked in the second round," he said, "because scouts had told me that I would be going in the first three rounds, and I had been contacted by the Pirates' chief scout [future general manager Harding "Pete" Peterson] this summer."[14]

Howie Haak, the Pirates' superscout, was surprised that Boyland was still available. He later said, "We knew he could run, and he had a good arm. We've found that most natural athletes can learn to hit. If they can't, you send them home."[15]

"I am really glad to be with the Pirates," Boyland also said, "because they like my hitting. They haven't said too much about pitching, because as a pitcher I would only get to bat every fourth day and they seem to want my bat in the order every day." The Oshkosh baseball coach, Russ Tiedemann, said, "Dorian is not a good cold-weather pitcher and pitching in Wisconsin in the spring has not been real good to him. He does have all the tools to make it in the big leagues, though."[16]

Murray Cook, then Pittsburgh's assistant farm director, liked Boyland's overall baseball abilities. "We think he is the type of player that can help us to a pennant. We just feel this way but have no guarantees. We do know he has the size, agility, and coordination of a baseball player. Boyland is also an outstanding runner with fine speed and an adequate arm, so he has the tools we look for. We want him to play every day at this point and do not plan on using him as a pitcher."[17]

Boyland reported to Salem (Virginia) of the Carolina League (Class-A), where he was made a first baseman, though he had never played there before. "That was my plight," he said. He was thrown in the deep end, with no instruction, and expected to cope. "I got there and the manager, Steve Demeter, told me, 'You're batting fourth and playing first base.'"[18]

"I didn't know how to field the ball at first base," he said in 1978. "And when I picked it up, I didn't know how to throw it. I looked pretty silly. I never knew there was so much involved in playing baseball."[19] He later added, "It really made me depressed."[20] In 71 total games, Boyland hit .269 with 3 homers and 31 RBIs. "I was hitting a buck-twenty or a buck-forty early on. If I hadn't been a second-round pick, they would probably have released me."[21]

Nonetheless, Boyland was invited to practice with the big leaguers in spring training 1977.[22] He stepped up to Double-A and hit very well for Shreveport in the Texas League: .330-11-60 in 119 games. He also stole 30 bases and got caught just six times. The first-base position belonged to him—even though, in his own words, "I still couldn't catch a cold there." (He committed 28 errors.)[23]

In the fall of 1977, the Pirates and New York Yankees fielded a combined entry in the Florida Instructional League.[24] "I was finally taught how to play first base—by the Yankees. Ed Napoleon took me out and put me through all kinds of drills. I learned how to grip the ball so it wouldn't move like it did when I was a pitcher. Gene Michael helped too." According to Boyland, the Yankees were interested in acquiring him (that December they lost Willie Upshaw to the Toronto Blue Jays in the Rule 5 draft).²⁵

Shortly after that, Boyland gained his first experience in winter ball. He joined Navegantes de Magallanes in the Venezuelan league. He got into 28 of the 70 games that season, because 34-year-old veteran Bob Oliver (the first baseman at Triple-A Columbus that year) was also with the Navigators. In just 98 at-bats, though, Boyland hit well: 5 homers, 24 RBIs, and a .337 average. One of his managers that season was Pirates first-base coach Alex "Al" Monchak. A number of other Pirates prospects were there too, such as pitchers Rod Scurry and Fred Breining, and infielder Gary Hargis. When asked about his experience in Venezuela, Boyland responded enthusiastically. "I loved it, loved it. I didn't stay in a hotel, I stayed with the people because I wanted to improve my Spanish. Still to this day it's one of my favorite places."²⁶

Boyland was again invited to work out with the Pirates in the spring of 1978. "Remember the name: Dorian Boyland," said beat writer Charley Feeney, mentioning for perhaps the first time that the young man was someday expected to replace Willie Stargell.²⁷ Stargell himself said, "You can see he's going to hit for a good average. He's got strong, quick wrists." But Dorian said, "I want to be [a] complete first baseman. … I want to bunt, steal bases, and hit for average as well as show power. I also want to be a good first baseman defensively."²⁸

Boyland moved up to Triple-A Columbus of the International League for the 1978 season—Bob Oliver was out of the Pirates organization—and had another good year (.291-12-61 in 113 games). He was rewarded with his first call-up to the majors that September.

His debut was bizarre and unique. During the first game of a doubleheader on September 4 at Pittsburgh's Three Rivers Stadium, Chuck Tanner sent Boyland in to pinch-hit for pitcher Ed Whitson. The score was tied 4-4 against the New York Mets with one out in the seventh inning, and Phil Garner was on first base. Pitcher Skip Lockwood had a 1-and-2 count on Boyland, but Lockwood had to come out of the game with a sore shoulder. Mets manager Joe Torre brought in a southpaw, Kevin Kobel, and Tanner sent righty Rennie Stennett in to hit for the lefty Boyland. Stennett promptly took strike three; by the rules, the strikeout was charged to Boyland.²⁹

"For many years I dreamed of what I might do in my first major-league at-bat," Boyland said. "I dreamed of hitting a grand-slam homer and even of striking out, but I never thought I'd strike out—and be watching from the dugout."³⁰

Sixteen days later, Boyland got his first base hit in the majors. It came at Wrigley Field in Chicago, playing for the first time in his hometown in a major-league uniform, with his mother, sister, and around 100 friends in the crowd.³¹ Tanner then put the steal on, although Pittsburgh was trailing 4-1 in the eighth inning. He kept it on, even though Frank Taveras fouled off four straight pitches. On the fifth attempt, Taveras lifted a short fly that Boyland thought was catchable, but Cubs shortstop Iván de Jesús didn't get to it. Doe headed for third base, but "'I missed second,' he said. 'I knew I missed it. I hoped they [the umpires] wouldn't notice. Manny Trillo called for the ball and appealed. They proved me wrong.'"³²

Boyland's lone outing in the field as a big leaguer came at Three Rivers on the last day of the season.

Willie Stargell—batting leadoff for one of just 15 times in his 21 years as a Pirate—opened the bottom of the first with a single. Boyland came in to run for him and played first base the rest of the way, getting his only RBI in the majors with his only other hit.

Boyland returned to Venezuela for the winter of 1978-79. He was not as successful this time (.268-0-18 in 30 games) and had to leave early after sustaining a wrist injury.[33] That problem wasn't serious, but a recurring hamstring problem plagued him in 1979. In spring training, the Pirates wanted Boyland to work in left field, since Stargell (who became the NL's co-MVP that season) was still the main man at first base. "A ball was going down the line and I broke for it. I felt something in my leg," Boyland recalled in 1980. He sat out the rest of spring training and was sent down to the Pirates' new Triple-A team, the Portland Beavers of the Pacific Coast League.[34]

"I'd finally become a real first baseman, and what happened? They sent me back to the outfield," said Boyland. "But here's my demise. When the Pirates sent me down, I was distraught. I said some unkind words to Chuck Tanner.[35]

With Portland, Boyland remained in left field—and pulled the hamstring again in his first game. He was out for a month, played again, and was hurt again.[36] All told, Boyland played in just 30 games for the Beavers, hitting just .245-2-12 in 102 at-bats.

Even so, when the rosters expanded that September, Boyland went back up to Pittsburgh. He pinch-hit three times, striking out twice, and also pinch-ran once. He was not eligible for the Pirates' successful postseason; he was one of the eight players who received a modest $250 cash grant when the team voted on World Series shares.

His leg did not bother Boyland while he was with Pittsburgh, but during winter ball in the Dominican Republic with Águilas Cibaeñas, the problem recurred after an opposing first baseman tripped him. "Now he has to prove he can play again," said Howie Haak.[37]

In the spring of 1980, the new heir apparent to Stargell at first base was a big Puerto Rican named Eddie Vargas. Vargas (who made the majors briefly with the Pirates in 1982 and 1984) was coming off a strong year in Single A and was headed for Double A. He was also four years younger than Boyland. "This year in spring training I'm more realistic," said Boyland. "I know I would only make the team in the event of a trade or an injury. If I don't make the team, I'll set my goals very high. If I have a good season in Portland, I can make the team next year or maybe someone else will want me."[38]

A little over a week later, the subject arose of what would happen if Stargell got hurt. Boyland responded, "It all depends on how serious an injury and how everybody else on the team is doing and the extent of the injury. Then they might say, 'Get Doe Boyland up here.'"[39] As it turned out, "Pops" was able to play in just 67 games in 1980—but Pittsburgh used John Milner and Bill Robinson at first base that year. Bill Madlock, Manny Sanguillen, and Kurt Bevacqua also filled in.

Meanwhile, Boyland spent the year at Portland. There had been talk that he would play left field, but he returned to first base, hitting .281-14-67 in 120 games. His leg was healthy again, as evidenced by 26 stolen bases. "And I played flawless defense," he added. "But you know how it is—you get labeled, and that's it."[40]

Despite his good year, Boyland saw no major-league action in 1980. "Everybody thought I was going up after September 1," he remarked the following spring, "But all I got was a plane ticket home to Chicago. And during the year I was very disappointed I didn't get called up. I was hitting about .340 and I was leading the team in home runs and stolen bases. I got so down I went into a tremendous slump for about a month and a half. There was no one for me to talk to and I let it bother me."[41] He put it even more strongly looking back in 2014: "I was done. I was through."

In the spring of 1981, after a winter in the Mexican Pacific League with Águilas de Mexicali, Boyland roomed with Mike Easler. "The Hit Man" knew first-hand about waiting years to get his chance to break through in the majors. "He's helped me accept my situation a little better," Boyland said. "Seeing what he went through to get here.... I know I just have to hang in there."[42]

Yet even though Boyland was hitting well in camp, general manager Pete Peterson told him that in all likelihood he was bound for Portland again. Stargell was still on the scene—"If Willie can get to the plate in a wheelchair, he's going to play," Boyland said.[43] Plus, shortly before the season started, Pittsburgh acquired Jason Thompson from the California Angels. Things might have turned out differently, though, had Commissioner Bowie Kuhn not prevented the Thompson trade from becoming a three-way deal with the Yankees. Jim Spencer, who had little left in the tank, would have wound up with the Pirates instead.

Boyland, who had welcomed the idea of a trade, still had confidence in his abilities. He said, "I think I can hit 20 home runs and steal 30 bases in the major leagues. That's pretty select company."[44] During 1981, though, he was hurt again and had to share time at Portland with Craig Cacek (four months older) and Bob Beall (who was turning 33—the Beavers roster had at least 10 players aged 30 and over that year). Boyland got into just 68 games, and though he hit .310, he had only 2 homers and 28 RBIs.

Despite his part-time status, Boyland made it back to Pittsburgh in September for the last time. He got into 11 games, going hitless with a walk in nine trips as a pinch-hitter and pinch-running twice.

Boyland played in seven games for Magallanes during the 1981-82 winter season. On December 11, 1981, he was dealt to the San Francisco Giants for veteran pitcher Tom Griffin. "I was out of options," he recalled, "so I thought they would finally keep me. So what did they do? They traded me."[45]

Boyland still held promise for at least one high authority—Frank Robinson, who was then the Giants' manager. Robinson called him a good young prospect (though Doe was about to turn 27) and said, "I saw Boyland when I was at Rochester in 1978 and he impressed me."[46]

It was much the same story with San Francisco, though. The Giants had two veteran first basemen in Enos Cabell and Dave Bergman. Then in late February 1982, they signed another veteran, switch-hitting Reggie Smith, as a free agent (the seven-time All-Star outfielder played first base only during his final season). "I remember Frank Robinson giving me the news," said Boyland.[47]

Shortly thereafter, Cabell was traded, and Boyland—a nonroster player—was given a chance to stick with the big club in spring training.[48] Yet Darrell Evans, who played first base a good deal, was on the team too. Boyland was ticketed for Triple-A Phoenix. There he played in 107 games, but the primary first baseman for that team was José Barrios—again, a younger player than Boyland (by two years). Boyland was in the lineup more often as a designated hitter, and his production was not high (.259-7-52 in 371 at-bats).

"I said to myself that year, 'Better find a new job.'"[49] After he quit, Boyland—with his degree in business administration and computer science—was mulling an offer from Intel Corp. to become a systems analyst. (The semiconductor company still has a major presence in Oregon.) The door to his true career then opened, though, thanks to Ron Tonkin, who was president and part-owner of the Portland Beavers—and a leading car dealer in the Portland area.

"He convinced me to come try the car business for 60 days, and if I didn't like it, I could go back to my other position," said Boyland in 2005. Thinking he would have a managerial position, he accepted—but when he got to the dealership, he found he was a rank-and-file salesman. Boyland added, "It was the best thing that ever happened to me."[50]

When the two-month trial period was up, Tonkin made Boyland an assistant manager. Within two years, they were partners, acquiring a Dodge dealership together; Boyland held a 30 percent stake. In 1987 he bought his own dealership, and over time he built it into a chain of Dodge, Ford, Nissan, Mercedes-Benz, Honda, and Hyundai agencies.[51] The jewel in the crown: Mercedes-Benz of South Orlando, which opened at a prime location in 2004. The Mercedes regional manager for the Southeast said of Boyland, "He has a knack for responding to market demands and understanding how markets change."[52] One of Boyland's partners put it this way: "Dorian is a very driven guy with vision. … He's got the moxie and savvy to put deals together."[53]

Boyland also based his business on knowing the numbers—something that dated back to early childhood—and fiscal prudence. From the beginning, he established a core value: ensuring satisfaction for his customers, employees, and manufacturers. He felt a strong sense of duty in setting a successful example for the minority community and helping the generations that followed his.[54]

Boyland emphasized the importance of connections with people in his foreword to the 2014 book *Networking for Black Professionals*. In addition to what he called "the 3 C's"—Competitive Edge, Confidence, and Competence—he said that talking to people daily and listening to them bred high customer satisfaction. He concluded with the encouraging words, "Don't let fear hold you back, take the ride and see where it leads you!"[55]

Boyland said he often saw players he faced—"Manny Trillo was just in the store last week"—and comrades from the 1979 Pirates. For example, "Lee Lacy was just here. Dave Parker comes down all the time."[56] Though his stay in the big leagues was brief, Dorian Boyland cherishes the many friendships he formed during his baseball career.

Grateful acknowledgment to Dorian Boyland for his memories (telephone interviews, May 5 and May 7, 2014) and to his sister Brenda Mitchell for the introduction.

SOURCES

Internet resources

purapelota.com (Venezuelan statistics).

blackenterprise.com.

NOTES

1. Boyland Auto Group—"Ride with a Winner" promotional video, 2011 (youtube.com/watch?v=fg2zO783P0c).
2. *Who's Who Among African-Americans* (Farmington, Michigan: Gale Group, 2002), 126. This reference gave Alice's maiden name as Jones, but according to her daughter, Brenda, it was Walker.
3. Telephone interview, Dorian Boyland with Rory Costello, May 7, 2014.
4. Lucia Reid, "The Midas Touch," *Onyx* (Orlando, Florida), July-August 2007, 23.
5. Reid, "The Midas Touch," 22.
6. "Ride with a Winner."
7. Maudlyne Ihejirika, "Success 'up to you,' teens told," *Chicago Sun-Times*, May 8, 2010.
8. "Coach White to be honored at men's basketball reunion," *UW Oshkosh Today* website, August 10, 2011.
9. The NAIA's freshman eligibility rules are different from those of other associations, such as the NCAA.
10. Telephone interview, Dorian Boyland with Rory Costello, May 5, 2014.
11. Dan Donovan, "Baskets to Bases: Boyland a Natural," *Pittsburgh Press*, March 2, 1978: A-7.
12. Dave Grey, "Boyland, Pascarella are high draft picks," *The Daily Northwestern*, (Neenah/Menasha, Wisconsin), June 9, 1976: 9.
13. Lou Pavlovich, "Bannister Chosen Player of Year on All-America Team," *The Sporting News*, July 31, 1976: 28.
14. Grey, "Boyland, Pascarella are high draft picks."
15. Donovan, "Baskets to Bases: Boyland a Natural."
16. Grey, "Boyland, Pascarella are high draft picks."
17. Ibid.
18. Telephone interview, Dorian Boyland with Rory Costello, May 5, 2014.
19. Donovan, "Baskets to Bases: Boyland a Natural."
20. Glenn Miller, "Waiting and Hoping," *St. Petersburg Independent*, March 20, 1980, 1-C.
21. Telephone interview, Dorian Boyland with Rory Costello, May 5, 2014.
22. Charley Feeney, "Bucs' Key Player: Versatile Robinson," *The Sporting News*, January 29, 1977: 46.
23. Telephone interview, Dorian Boyland with Rory Costello, May 5, 2014.
24. Don Greenberg, "He can go all the way—with experience," *St. Petersburg Times*, September 27, 1977: 4. Subject: Joe Lefebvre.
25. Telephone interview, Dorian Boyland with Rory Costello, May 5, 2014.
26. Telephone interviews, Dorian Boyland with Rory Costello, May 5 and May 7, 2014.
27. Charley Feeney, "Bucs to Lean Heavily on Toughy Duffy," *The Sporting News*, February 18, 1978: 50.
28. Donovan, "Baskets to Bases: Boyland a Natural."
29. Charley Feeney, "Pirates Trail by One After Sweep of Mets," *Pittsburgh Post-Gazette*, September 5, 1978: 13. This article says that Stennett swung and missed, but Boyland remembered that Rennie was caught looking.
30. Jerome Holtzman, "Some Free Advice," *The Sporting News*, October 7, 1978: 42.
31. Reid, "The Midas Touch," 23.
32. Miller, "Waiting and Hoping."
33. Dan Donovan, "Candelaria, Stennett Find Cure for Ailments in Winter Baseball," *Pittsburgh Press*, January 14, 1979: D-8.

34 Dan Donovan, "Another Turning Point for Boyland," *Pittsburgh Press*, March 11, 1980: D-1.

35 Telephone interview, Dorian Boyland with Rory Costello, May 5, 2014.

36 "Another Turning Point for Boyland."

37 Donovan, "Another Turning Point for Boyland."

38 Donovan, "Another Turning Point for Boyland."

39 Miller, "Waiting and Hoping."

40 Telephone interview, Dorian Boyland with Rory Costello, May 5, 2014.

41 Ron Cook, "Boyland weary of waiting to be Willie," *Beaver County* (Pennsylvania) *Times*, March 16, 1981: B1.

42 Ibid.

43 Dan Donovan, "Boyland Claims His Future Is Now," *Pittsburgh Press*, March 16, 1981, C-1.

44 Ibid.

45 Telephone interview, Dorian Boyland with Rory Costello, May 5, 2014.

46 Nick Peters, "Giants Under Fire for Peddling Griffin," *The Sporting News*, January 2, 1982: 41.

47 Telephone interview, Dorian Boyland with Rory Costello, May 5, 2014.

48 Nick Peters, "Robinson, Players Big on Confidence," *The Sporting News*, March 6, 1982: 36.

49 Telephone interview, Dorian Boyland with Rory Costello, May 5, 2014.

50 Christina Hildreth, "Grand slam performer," *Orlando Business Journal*, July 25, 2005.

51 Alan Hughes, "The Game Plan," *Black Enterprise*, April 1, 2012.

52 Hildreth, "Grand slam performer."

53 Hughes, "The Game Plan."

54 Reid, "The Midas Touch," 24-25. Ihejirika, "Success 'up to you,' teens told." Alan Hughes, "8 Steps to Keep Your Small Business on the Road to Success," *Black Enterprise*, March 25, 2013.

55 N. Renee Thompson, Michael Lawrence Faulkner, and Andrea Nierenberg, *Networking for Black Professionals* (Upper Saddle River, New Jersey: Pearson Education, Inc., 2014), vii-viii.

56 Telephone interview, Dorian Boyland with Rory Costello, May 5, 2014.

John Candelaria

By Steve West

YOU COULD SAY THAT JOHN Candelaria's story is a tale of heartbreak, or a tale of unfulfilled promise, or a tale of self-destruction, and you might be right every time. On the other hand, how unlucky can a person be if he managed to pitch in the major leagues for 19 seasons? The Candy Man would ignore all that talk about being star-crossed, and tell you that he spent his life the way he wanted, not how others thought he should. As he said several times during his career, "Life is to enjoy. It's a mystery to be lived, not a problem to be solved."[1]

John Robert Candelaria was born on November 6, 1953, in Brooklyn, New York, to Puerto Rican parents. His father, also named John, was born in Arecibo, Puerto Rico, in 1932, and his mother, the former Felicia Bauza, was born in Rio Piedras, Puerto Rico, in 1934. Both moved from Puerto Rico when they were children to New York, where they met and began a family. John had a brother, Michael, and two sisters, Maria and Dolores. As a child John learned to throw and catch from his father, who played amateur baseball in the New York area. His father saw his talent early: "This kid really has it," he told his family when John was just 5 years old.[2] But John's parents divorced and his father moved back to Puerto Rico when John was 6. His father worked as a car salesman, but John knew little of him once he left, relying instead on his mother, a homemaker, who would closely follow his career as an athlete.

Growing up in Brooklyn, John was a Yankees fan, although with money tight he didn't attend too many games. "I didn't go unless there was a doubleheader," he said. "I used to sit in the bleachers for 75 cents."[3] He played baseball at LaSalle High School, where he attracted attention from scouts during his freshman season, but he felt that he was being worn out by pitching so much, and so he quit baseball. He switched to basketball, where he became the school's all-time leading scorer and second all-time rebounder (to Lew Alcindor, later known as Kareem Abdul-Jabbar[4]), and his performances on the court attracted college scouts from across the country. He was selected to play for Puerto Rico in the 1972 Olympics, but suddenly decided that he would rather play baseball instead, believing that he could be in the major leagues in baseball before he would even be out of college if he were playing basketball.[5] Candelaria performed well enough in his return to baseball that he was scouted by Pittsburgh Pirates scout Dutch Deutsch,[6] who remembered him from his first year in high school, and was drafted in the second round of the 1972 draft by the Pirates. Candelaria was in Puerto Rico, preparing to play basketball in the Olympics, when Pirates officials arrived to sign him. They brought Roberto Clemente with them to act as translator, and Clemente told him in Spanish to reject their offer of $15,000, that he was worth much more.[7] He did, and Clemente's advice proved sound, as Candelaria eventually signed for $40,000.[8]

After signing with the Pirates Candelaria was sent to Charleston (South Carolina) of the Class-A Western Carolinas League for the remainder of the 1973 season, going 10-2 despite feeling the effects of not having pitched regularly for so long. In his best start he threw a one-hitter—allowing the hit to the opposing pitcher in the sixth inning. Moving to Salem (Virginia) of the Class-A Carolina League in 1974, he went 11-8, but suffered from back pain throughout the season. This injury would become a recurring motif during his career. Candelaria sometimes claimed that it began when he slipped on the mound during a start in 1974, but at other times he said it came from a childhood injury, and Pirates doctors even suggested the problem dated back to when he was born.[9] At various times he also said that an operation to fuse the bones in his spine might help with the pain he often felt while pitching, but that it would end his baseball career.[10]

After the 1974 season Candelaria went to Puerto Rico to play winter ball for Bayamon, and learned from the veteran players there. "They taught me to spot my pitches and to use my curveball with more success," he said.[11] He pitched winter ball in Puerto Rico for three seasons.

Candelaria had one start for Charleston (West Virginia) of the Triple-A International League at the end of the 1974 season, and was assigned there again in 1975. He broke out, running his record to 7-1 with a 1.77 ERA. "His control is super. ... He is throwing consistently harder than he did when I first saw him two years ago," Charleston manager Steve Demeter said.[12] When left-hander Ken Brett went on the disabled list the Pirates needed a starter, so Candelaria got the call and made his major-league debut on June 8 in Pittsburgh, in the first game of a doubleheader against the San Francisco Giants. He pitched six innings and impressed, even though he gave up all the runs in a 3-1 loss. He stayed in the rotation, and on June 20, before 47,867 at Shea Stadium, he pitched in New York for the first time, where with a large group of family and friends watching, Candelaria earned his first major-league win by throwing his first complete game to beat the New York Mets, 5-1. "It was something special. Something I'll always remember," he later said.[13]

Despite his early success, Candelaria knew he hadn't made the big time just yet. "I've got a lot to prove," he said.[14] But he pitched well enough to stay with the team, finishing 8-6 with a 2.76 ERA. He ended the season pitching in the playoffs, starting Game Three of the NLCS in Pittsburgh, which the Cincinnati Reds won in 10 innings to complete their sweep of the then best-of-five postseason series. Even so, Candelaria struck out 14 batters in 7⅔ innings, an NLCS record that was not surpassed until 1997. "He's 6-5 and he's all arms and legs," said Pete Rose, although Candelaria was actually 6-7 (and 210 pounds).[15] Rose also said that it was "the greatest pressure game I've seen any pitcher pitch."[16]

Returning with the Pirates in 1976, the 22-year-old Candelaria showed composure beyond his years as he pitched in the rotation all season. "He has all the tools. ... He knows what he is doing on the mound," said Pirates manager Danny Murtaugh.[17] "He is a finished major-league pitcher despite his youth."[18] He did get one relief appearance when on May 26 he threw three shutout innings to get his first career save. But his highlight came on August 9 at home against the Los Angeles Dodgers. That night the Pirates held "Candy Night" and handed out candy bars to the crowd of 9,860, honoring the player who was now nicknamed the Candy Man, after the popular Sammy Davis Jr. song. Candelaria responded to the honor by throwing a no-hitter to beat the Dodgers, 2-0. He was perfect for every inning except the third, when he walked a batter and two others reached on errors to load the bases, but he got out of the jam and sailed the rest of the way home. (Many years later Candelaria admitted that one winter he needed to work out, and the game ball from his no-hitter was the only ball he had, so he practiced with it against a concrete wall and destroyed it.[19])

In 1977 Candelaria was feeling much more comfortable as a major leaguer. He had bought a home in Monroeville, just east of Pittsburgh, and in March he signed a multiyear contract with the Pirates. Even though he had some shoulder problems during spring training, and was having more back pain after slipping on the mound in Montreal in July, he pitched the full season and pitched well. He capped off his season by winning his last four starts to finish at 20-5, the only time he would win 20 games in his career. He won the ERA title at 2.34 (best in the major leagues), although he only finished fifth in Cy Young Award voting, the only season he got any votes for that award. Candelaria was also selected for his only All-Star team in 1977. (He didn't get into the game.)

Candelaria came into spring training 21 pounds lighter in 1978, hoping it would help his back, but he ended up with other problems. A sore left elbow in August had him skipping a few turns through the rotation, and he ended the year at 12-11. In 1979 he had numerous little injuries, not only from the back pain, but from a minor automobile accident on July 31, and then late in the season he pulled a muscle in his ribcage. He had helped the team return to the postseason with his 14-9 record, and started Game One of the NLCS, giving up two runs in seven innings as the Pirates won, 5-2, in 11 innings, starting their three-game sweep of the Cincinnati Reds.

In the World Series Candelaria started Game Three against Baltimore and struggled after being staked to a 3-0 lead, giving up two runs in the third inning before a 67-minute rain delay, and when he returned after the delay he allowed all four batters he faced to reach base (one on an error) before being pulled and taking the loss. But the Pirates fought back from a three-games-to-one deficit, and Candelaria started Game Six, in which he controlled the Orioles batters. He threw six shutout innings, allowing just two runners to get as far as second base, before being lifted for a pinch-hitter. Kent Tekulve came in and closed out the final three innings, the pair combining on a shutout that tied the World Series. "It's a tribute to him that he can pitch in pain the way he did tonight," Tekulve said.[20] The next night the Pirates did it again, beating the Orioles, 4-1, to become world champions.

In 1980 Candelaria came back to earth, and despite throwing the most innings of his career (233⅓) he had his first losing record at 11-14, and his highest ERA to that point at 4.01. The 1981 season was much worse, though, when on May 10 he felt something in his arm when he threw a pitch in a cold and wet game in St. Louis. Initially diagnosed with a torn biceps tendon, Candelaria turned to Dr. Paul Bauer, an expert in body mechanics. Bauer said he did not have a torn tendon, but rather nerve problems in his shoulder, and said Candelaria needed rehab and changes in his pitching motion. Candelaria went along with this idea, missing the rest of the season while working in Bauer's lab in San Diego, watching himself pitch on videotape and adjusting the way he pitched. It all worked; he avoided surgery and came back feeling better than ever. "I believed in myself, but they're the ones who showed me what to do. Without them I don't think I'd be pitching today."[21]

Candelaria returned in 1982 and pitched well all season, although no longer able to go as long as he did earlier in his career. He had said earlier that "I'm not a nine-inning pitcher. The back just aches too much

for me to pitch nine innings."[22] Now it showed; he completed just six games in the next three seasons (he had completed 11 in 1976 alone). In those years he also talked more about long-term contracts, but enmity was growing between Candelaria and the Pirates front office. He would snipe about management, and they would snipe back, a pattern that continued for the rest of his time in Pittsburgh. (At one point he called the general manager an "idiot" and a "bozo.") He said he would never re-sign with the Pirates, although he suggested that the length of the contract would be the most important factor. Sure enough, he soon signed a new four-year contract with the Pirates, which made him happy again, at least for the short term.

Candelaria had a tumultuous personal life, making what might be considered poor choices numerous times. He had married and divorced twice in the 1970s. His first marriage was to a woman who had three children from her prior marriage. He successfully fought a paternity suit after blood tests proved a child was not his, and the papers for his second divorce were served between innings of a game he was pitching in Pittsburgh.[23] He finally settled down in his relationship with a flight attendant, Donna Hall, and the couple had two children, Amber born in 1982 and John in 1983. But tragedy soon struck, with John Jr. nearly drowning after falling in the family pool in Sarasota, Florida, on Christmas Day of 1984. The child spent months in the hospital and then at home, all the time in a coma, before he died in November 1985. Candelaria was naturally devastated, and spent most of the year with his mind on far more important things than baseball.

During that time Candelaria had problems on the field as well. He had bone chips removed from his elbow in October 1984, and the team decided in 1985 to move him from the rotation to the bullpen, in part due to the surgery and in part due to concerns over his mental condition while dealing with his son. Candelaria initially complained about the move, saying he wanted his contract renegotiated, but after having some success he reconsidered. "Relieving isn't as bad as I thought it would be … I'm more involved in the games than I used to be," he said.[24]

Candelaria was always considered an oddball, a player who may have been a little too crazy at times. "There's the starting pitcher for tonight, hat on backward, leaning out the window screaming at people, talking to the grass, thinking about the hitters," as a teammate once described a bus ride to the ballpark in New York. A more astute analysis of Candelaria's style might be the following: "He wasn't particularly sharp. He didn't do anything extremely well. But when it was all over, he was the winner. Typical."[25] When asked once what he would be doing if he wasn't playing baseball: "I'd probably be living in an apartment building in Brooklyn and working for UPS. That would be fun, too."[26] Fun seemed to be his style, with a live-and-let-live attitude to both life and baseball. "If I ever lose the boy in me, what's the sense? I plan to be doing silly things when I'm 50. I just want to be remembered as footloose and fancy free."[27]

Eventually the Pirates tired of Candelaria's antics and insults, and let it be known that they were ready to move him. Several teams were interested, and he was traded to the California Angels in August of 1985, along with pitcher Al Holland and outfielder George Hendrick, for outfielder Mike Brown and pitchers Pat Clements and Bob Kipper. Candelaria still took some parting shots at the Pirates, saying he had been mishandled by manager Chuck Tanner. "I never should have been in the bullpen there," he said.[28] Switched into the rotation for the division-leading Angels, he pitched well, going 7-3, but the Angels fell just one game short of the Kansas City Royals in the AL West at the end of the season.

In 1986 Candelaria had pain in his elbow in the spring, and managed just two innings in his first start before succumbing to the pain. Surgery to remove bone spurs put him out for three months, although he returned and did well, going 10-2 with a 2.55 ERA, the second lowest of his career. This time the Angels won their division, and Candelaria, with relief help from Donnie Moore, pitched well to win Game Three of the ALCS against the Boston Red Sox, giving up one run in seven innings. "I'm throwing it better than I have in seven or eight years. … I'm just trying to stay inside myself," he said.[29] But coming back in Game Seven, Candelaria had a rough outing, although badly hurt by his defense. He gave up three runs in the second and four in the fourth, when Jim Rice ended his misery with a three-run home run. All of the runs were unearned—both of those innings had begun with an error—but it made no difference as Roger Clemens and Calvin Schiraldi held the Angels batters down and the Red Sox easily won. After the season, Candelaria was named the AL Comeback Player of the Year by *The Sporting News*.

Perhaps due to his personal problems from the last few years coming back to haunt him, Candelaria struggled with injuries and off-field trouble during 1987. On April 17 he was arrested for DUI after running a stop sign ("It was my off day. … It's nobody's business but mine," he said, earning the ire of anti-drunk driving campaigners), and on May 14 he got a second DUI arrest.[30] The Angels put him on the disabled list the following day for personal reasons, but he returned just two weeks later. In late June they put him back on the DL and checked him into rehab, where he spent more than a month dealing with his problems. "A lot of people assume that since you play this game, you should be happy. Sometimes it's

THE 1979 PITTSBURGH PIRATES

not that way. We're all humans and we all have our problems - regardless," he said.[31] He returned to the team in early August, but they traded him to the New York Mets in mid-September for minor-league pitchers Shane Young and Jeff Richardson. The Mets, chasing the St. Louis Cardinals in the NL East for a playoff spot, had just lost starter Ron Darling to a torn ligament, and immediately traded for Candelaria, who went 2-0 in three starts but the team fell three games short anyway.

Candelaria signed with the New York Yankees as a free agent for 1988, saying that they had guaranteed him a spot in the rotation, something the Mets wouldn't do. "Every kid fantasizes about pitching for his hometown team," he said.[32] In a stunning attack on the Angels during spring training, he told a reporter that Don Sutton had set him up for his first DUI arrest the prior year, claiming that Sutton had called police on him because Sutton wanted his spot in the rotation ("He later told me it was out of concern for my well-being," Candelaria said.)[33] He also slammed Angels manager Gene Mauch, calling him a control freak and saying, "He isn't a very good manager, and I think he knew that I knew that."[34] Then he suggested that rehab was the team's idea, and he didn't want to do it but was forced to, before finally admitting that "I have no one to blame but myself for what was a very tough and frustrating year."[35] The Angels declined to respond to Candelaria, although they reminded reporters that his tirade was similar to when he left the Pirates.

Things didn't go much better with the Yankees, though, as Candelaria argued with manager Lou Piniella during the season and told reporters he wanted out. Even though he was pitching well with a 13-7 record, when he came down with knee pain in August, he was done for the season, although Yankees doctors suggested he should be able to play. He had surgery for cartilage damage in his knee in October, and although he started 1989 in the rotation he returned to the disabled list in May for more knee surgery, missing another three months. When he returned it was to the bullpen for a few weeks, before being traded once again, this time in late August to the Montreal Expos for third baseman Mike Blowers. The Expos were hoping to add veteran talent for the stretch run, and Candelaria spent the last month of the season in their bullpen. But the Expos chose not to go to salary arbitration with Candelaria, so he once again was a free agent at the end of the year.

Candelaria signed with the Minnesota Twins for 1990, spending almost all his time there in the bullpen, compiling a 3.39 ERA along the way. Traded in July to the Toronto Blue Jays for second baseman Nelson Liriano and outfielder Pedro Munoz, he was used out of the bullpen but also for a couple of spot starts, and struggled, going 0-3 with a 5.48 ERA as the Blue Jays finished two games behind the Boston Red Sox in the AL East.

Yet again a free agent, Candelaria signed with the Los Angeles Dodgers in 1991, his eighth team in six years. Happy to be close to the Orange County home his family had lived in since moving to the Angels in 1985, he took the role of left-handed reliever, pitching in 59 games, the highest total of his career, even though he threw only 33⅔ innings. He returned to the Dodgers in 1992 with the same role, and in 1993 went back to where it all began, signing a one-year contract with the Pirates to be their left-handed reliever. Initial reports of his new-found work ethic—"I've mellowed out a lot. Let's put it that way"[36]—were ruined by his arrest for DUI in Sarasota, Florida, during spring training. He stayed with the team, but struggled, and eventually was released by the Pirates in July with an 8.24 ERA. With minimal interest from other teams—and perhaps not much interest from Candelaria himself—at age 39 his career was over.

As his career came to an end, Candelaria was regularly asked to look back at what he had accomplished. Numerous writers had written about him over the years, and many had said that he was a classic example of wasted potential. The general idea was that he would prefer to sit in the clubhouse and smoke and drink coffee, rather than working out or getting ready for baseball, and this rankled Candelaria. He had after all won 55 more games than he lost (career record of 177-122), and wondered just what he had to do to be considered a success. "I have been successful, I am successful, and I will be successful. Who is to say who has potential and what somebody else's potential is?"[37]

Candelaria tried various things after he retired from baseball, including owning an advertising agency in Pittsburgh. Ultimately, though, he found he preferred solitude. "I am a loner. That's the way I like it. It's what I choose."[38] He moved several times, finally settling in North Carolina, where as of 2016 he lived quietly.

NOTES

1 Douglas S. Looney, "The Mad Hatter of Pittsburgh," *Sports Illustrated*, June 14, 1982.
2 Gene Wojciechowski, "It Took Him Tirade After Tirade to Obtain a Trade," *Los Angeles Times*, March 31, 1986.
3 Charley Feeney, "Candy Could Frost Bucco Cake With 20 Big Wins," *The Sporting News*, March 19, 1977: 40.
4 Charley Feeney, "Sweet-Throwing Candy Man Makes Bucco Mouths Water," *The Sporting News*, May 29, 1976: 16.
5 A.L. Hardman, "Candelaria's Proper Decisions Include 6-0 Charleston Start," *The Sporting News*, June 7, 1975: 36.
6 Michael I. Cohen, "Scouting Report," *The Sporting News*, August 2, 1975: 4.
7 Roy Blount Jr., "Another Keel Haul in the East," *Sports Illustrated*, July 14, 1975.
8 Charley Feeney, "Kid Candelaria Helps to Lift Shadows on Pirates' Mound," *The Sporting News*, July 12, 1975: 16.
9 Looney.
10 Charley Feeney, "Candy Man Can, And Does, Set Buc Mark," *The Sporting News*, August 28, 1976: 7.
11 Hardman.
12 Ibid.
13 Feeney, "Candy Man's Pitching Sweetens Bucco Outlook."
14 "Candelaria Keeps Cool," *The Sporting News*, August 16, 1975: 36.
15 Earl Lawson, "Reds' Playoff Sweep Dims Candelaria's Flame," *The Sporting News*, October 25, 1975: 13.
16 Looney.
17 Feeney, "Sweet-Throwing Candy Man Makes Bucco Mouths Water."
18 "Candy 'Poisons' Giants," *The Sporting News*, May 15, 1976: 32.
19 Bill Plaschke, "Dodgers: Memories Not Enough to Satisfy Candelaria," *Los Angeles Times*, March 6, 1991.
20 Lowell Reidenbaugh, "Candy Sweet Pitching in Pain," *The Sporting News*, November 3, 1979: 41.
21 Armen Keteyian, "To Save His Arm, a Pitcher Should Use His Head and Study Mechanics," *Sports Illustrated*, October 17, 1983.
22 Charley Feeney, "Nicosia Waits, Watches and Catches Pirate Eyes," *The Sporting News*, May 26, 1979: 12.
23 Looney, "The Mad Hatter of Pittsburgh."
24 Charley Feeney, "Candelaria Relieved He's Staying in Pen," *The Sporting News*, May 20, 1985: 18.
25 Looney,
26 Ibid.
27 Ibid.
28 Tim Rosaforte, "Can Vs. Candy Man: A Battle For Control," *Orlando Sun-Sentinel*, October 10, 1986.
29 Ibid.
30 Mike Penner, "Candelaria Arrested For Allegedly Driving Under the Influence," *Los Angeles Times*, April 18, 1987.
31 Mike Penner, "Candelaria Back With Angels, Set to Make New Start," *Los Angeles Times*, July 25, 1987.
32 Ross Newhan, "Angel Memories Still Trouble Candelaria," *Los Angeles Times*, March 1, 1988.
33 Ibid.
34 Ibid.
35 Ibid.
36 John Mehno, "Pittsburgh Pirates," *The Sporting News*, March 8, 1993.
37 Looney.
38 Wojciechowski.

Joe Coleman

By Gregory H. Wolf

THREE MONTHS REMOVED FROM HIGH school, hard-throwing right-hander Joe Coleman burst on the national scene by tossing a four-hit complete-game victory in his debut with the Washington Senators in 1965. Among the most durable pitchers of his day, Coleman averaged 15 wins and 252 innings over an eight-year span (1968-1975) for the Senators and Detroit Tigers. The two-time 20-game winner and one-time All-Star concluded his 15-year big-league career in 1979 as a member of the Pittsburgh Pirates.

Joseph Howard Coleman was destined to become a baseball player when he was born in the Richardson House wing of Boston Lying-in Hospital on February 3, 1947. His father, Joe (Joseph Patrick) Coleman, was a big-league pitcher and one-time All-Star who went 52-76 in parts of 10 seasons spanning the years 1942-1955, mainly with the Philadelphia A's, the Baltimore Orioles, and the Detroit Tigers. "I can remember a time that I sat on Mr. (Connie) Mack's knee for a picture," said Coleman about living a boy's dream on the field in Shibe Park, shortly before the historic ballpark was renamed Connie Mack Stadium. "After the games I used to run around the infield and slide into every base."[1] The youngster accompanied his father and mother, Barbara, to spring training, and often traveled with the team to visiting ballparks. By the time he was 7 years old and with his father's career winding down, young Joe knew that he wanted to become a baseball player.

The Colemans lived in Natick, a town of about 20,000 residents located 20 miles west of Boston. Joe got his first taste of organized baseball while attending Bennett-Hemenway Elementary and Wilson Junior High Schools. At Natick High School, the right-handed Joe developed into an overpowering, dominant pitcher, winning 24 of 28 decisions; he also played basketball. "My father never pushed me," said Joe of his interest in baseball. "He let me pitch. If I had a question, then he'd help me."[2] But father Joe, who opened a sporting goods store in Natick, took obvious delight in his son's success. "By his senior year," said the elder Coleman, "[scouts] were swarming all over the place."[3] Joe had begun attracting attention while participating in Ted Williams's baseball camp in Lakeville, Massachusetts, after his freshman through junior years, and had played in the Hearst Sandlot Classic game at Yankee Stadium in New York in 1964. As a senior in 1965, the 6-foot-3, 165-pound Coleman was considered one of the top pitchers in the country.

The Washington Senators, acting on the recommendations of team scouts Joe W. Lewis Sr. and Hal Keller, selected Coleman in the first round in the inaugural major league draft on June 8, 1965.[4] He was the third overall pick (following outfielder Rick Monday by the Kansas City Athletics and pitcher Les Rohr by the New York Mets) and the first draft choice to make it to the major leagues. Coleman signed what Washington sportswriter Bob Addie called the "biggest bonus in Washington history," a reported $75,000, with Senators general manager George Selkirk.[5]

Just weeks after graduating from high school, Coleman reported to the Class-A Burlington (North Carolina) Senators in the west division of the Carolina League. He struggled against competition that averaged four years older, winning just twice in 12 decisions and posting a 4.56 ERA in 75 innings for a last-place team. The Washington Senators, plodding through their fifth consecutive dismal season since entering the American League as an expansion team in 1961 and drawing less than 7,000 per game, made national headlines when they called up the 18-year-old Coleman in late September.

Coleman made an auspicious big-league debut on September 28 in D.C. Stadium by tossing a complete-game four-hitter, striking out three and pitching around four walks to defeat another highly touted teenager, 19-year-old Jim "Catfish" Hunter

of the Kansas City Athletics in the first game of a twilight-night doubleheader, 6-1. Coleman yielded back-to-back doubles with two outs in the ninth inning to lose his shutout bid. Five days later, he went the distance again, holding the Detroit Tigers to just five hits in a 3-2 victory in the nation's capital. He got additional work with the Senators coaching staff in the Florida Instructional League in the fall.

Coleman arrived at the Senators' spring training facility in Pompano Beach, Florida, in 1966 under the glare of media attention. His first camp, however, was a lesson in humility as he struggled and was assigned to the York (Pennsylvania) White Roses in the Double-A Eastern League. "I wasn't in shape [and] I came down a week late because we had a little contract dispute," said Coleman. "I was overweight, lazy, and had the wrong attitude."[6] On another last-place team, Coleman posted just seven wins, led the league in losses (19) and home runs allowed (17), and carved out a disappointing 3.75 ERA in 199 innings. Recalled by the Senators in September, Coleman made the most of his one start by tossing another complete game, a six-hitter to defeat his hometown Boston Red Sox, 3-2, in front of fewer than 500 spectators in D.C. Stadium on September 26 during the second game of a Monday afternoon doubleheader.

Regardless of Coleman's 9-29 record in the minors so far, the Senators saw him as their future ace. "I think better up here than in the minors. The extra pressure makes me think more," said Coleman, who landed a spot in starting rotation to begin the 1967 season.[7] In his debut, he tossed 137 pitches and came within one out of his fourth consecutive complete game, but settled for his fourth straight win, beating a still-struggling New York Yankees team, 10-4. Another complete-game victory over the Chicago White Sox followed before reality set in. Coleman lost six of his next eight decisions and his 3.06 ERA ballooned to 5.33. Disconcerting to manager Gil Hodges, known as a disciplinarian, was Coleman's spoiled-brat behavior, such as arguing balls and strikes with umpires and complaining when he was removed for a pinch-hitter. Despite winning four straight starts from July 13 through July 26, Coleman, struggling with an 8-9 record, was unexpectedly sent down to Double-A York in mid-August. "Coleman's demotion surprised everyone," wrote Bob Addie.[8] Although Hodges claimed publicly that he thought Coleman was losing his confidence, he intended the demotion to be a wake-up call for his young hurler. Coleman was mainly relegated to the far end of the bullpen following his recall on Labor Day after a very rough starting assignment lasting just one-third of an inning on September 11 and finishing a once promising season with a disappointing 4.63 ERA (second highest among AL pitchers with at least 100 innings).

But Coleman emerged as a solid starter in 1968, leading the Senators, now managed by Jim Lemon, in starts (33), innings (233), and complete games (12), and lowering his ERA more than a run to 3.27. He credited his success to the Washington coaching staff. "There are better teachers in the big leagues. … Guys like [pitching coach] Sid Hudson who has taught me how to pace myself."[9] Coleman also mastered the forkball, which he had been playing around with for several years. "I started throwing it consistently in 1968," he explained. "I saw some diagrams of how [Elroy Face] threw his forkball in *Sport Magazine*. But my father wouldn't let me throw any kind of breaking stuff when I was a kid."[10] Coleman won 12 games, but also lost a team-high 16 for the last-place club. "If I'd go out and lose a close ballgame," said Coleman, "I'd get upset and maybe throw my chair around the clubhouse. And the guys would get on to me."[11] Some teammates referred to him scornfully as "Boy Blunder" for his rookie-like mistakes and sore-loser sulking after poor outings.

At the baseball winter meetings in December 1968, Bob Short, treasurer of the Democratic National Committee and former owner of the Minneapolis Lakers of the National Basketball Association, purchased a controlling interest in the Senators. The following month he shocked the baseball world by luring Ted Williams out of retirement to pilot the club. Washington had not seen as much excitement and anticipation for Opening Day since the days of Walter Johnson. Described by Dick Couch of the AP as the "brightest young star" on the staff, Coleman tossed a complete-game victory in his season debut, but otherwise struggled through July 4, winning just four of 11 decisions and surrendering 19 gopher balls in 115⅔ innings.[12] Tabbed a disappointment by his manager, Coleman turned his season around by tossing three consecutive shutouts, surrendering just 11 hits while striking out 31, as part of a career-best streak of 32⅓ consecutive scoreless innings. The 22-year-old cut down on his home runs-allowed total and established himself as the ace of the staff, leading the club in starts (36), innings (247⅔), complete games (12), and shutouts (4), while finishing with a 12-13 record. "It was a matter of getting adjusted," replied Coleman when asked about his dramatic midseason transformation. "I was on my own more, called my own game, did more things on my own after Ted knew me."[13] Coleman's forkball, which batterymate Jim French called "the best in the league,"[14] kept hitters off balance and helped him strike out 182 (tied for fifth most in the AL); "I need to throw three-quarter. Then my ball stays down and does something," said a reflective Coleman, who also sported a robust 3.27 ERA.[15] The surprising club won 86 games, the most for a major-league baseball team in Washington, D.C., since the 1945 Senators won 87, and finished in fourth place in the AL East in the first year of division play.

Coleman began the 1970 season seemingly prepared to continue his second-half surge from 1969. A four-game winning streak improved his record to 5-3 and lowered his ERA to 3.05 on June 10. One of those wins (a complete-game, 3-1 five-hitter over the Cleveland Indians) occurred on May 19 with umpire Ed Runge at first base; coincidentally, he was also the first-base ump when Coleman's father (then with Baltimore) tossed a complete game to defeat the Washington Senators, 5-3, on that same date 16 years earlier. Coleman's season unexpectedly veered out of control following losses in five consecutive starts and he was ultimately banished to the bullpen in early July. "Coleman is not the pitcher we thought he would be," opined owner Bob Short.[16] He returned to the rotation on August 2 for the second game of a doubleheader with rumors of his imminent trade in the offseason. While the weak-hitting Senators fell to last place in the AL East, Coleman dropped to 8-12 with a 3.58 ERA and exceeded 200 innings pitched for the third consecutive season.

Coleman and Williams had a contentious relationship, to say the least. Williams's distrust (some would say dislike) of pitchers was well known from his playing days and things were no different during his tenure as skipper of the Senators. "What would you think of a guy who welcomed you to his camp by asking, 'What's dumber than a pitcher?' and answered his own question by saying "Two," said Coleman.[17] Williams's general lack of confidence in pitchers, his belief that they needed to last just five or six innings, and insistence that they throw sliders (a pitch that he had trouble with as a batter) further inflamed his relationship with Coleman. Miffed by "Teddy Ballgame's" constant public berating of Coleman, Washington beat reporter Merrell Whittlesey noted that "Williams has been gruff at times with the youngster who should be the Senators star pitcher."[18] Coleman steadfastly refused to throw a slider and began to tune out his manager. "I knew that if I threw the slider, I'd risk hurting my arm," Coleman told Ed Rumill of the *Christian Science*

Monitor. "No matter how I tried, I couldn't change Ted's mind. He didn't like my stubborn attitude."[19]

Just days after the 1970 regular season ended, Coleman, dependable starting shortstop Ed Brinkman, swingman hurler Jim Hannan, and third baseman Aurelio Rodriguez were shipped to the Detroit Tigers for troubled former 31-game winner Denny McLain (who had been recently reinstated by Commissioner Bowie Kuhn and pronounced "not mentally ill"[20]), utilityman Elliott Maddox, relief pitcher Norm McRae, and third-sacker Don Wert on October 9. The transaction is now considered among the most lopsided in baseball history, though at the time many thought McLain would return to the form that earned him two Cy Young Awards. The trade crippled the Senators franchise just prior to their last season in Washington and subsequent relocation to Texas). McLain went 10-22 in 1971 and was out of the big leagues a year later; McRae never appeared again in the majors; Wert played in only 20 games before being released before midseason; and Maddox had three mediocre seasons. Detroit sportswriter Watson Spoelstra excitedly called the trade the "steal of the year" for the Tigers who solidified three positions.[21] Coleman developed into one of the most dependable workhorses in the league; the durable Brinkman shored up the middle infield for four years; and Rodriguez held down the hot corner for the remainder of the decade. Both infielders won Gold Gloves.

Coleman, who married Deborah Fitch just days after his trade, was in need of a change of scenery. The incessant losing and constant bickering with Williams had eroded his confidence. He looked forward to playing for a club that "makes money and puts people in the stands."[22] He also anxiously anticipated pitching for new Tigers manager Billy Martin, whose successful yet controversial one season as big-league skipper, guiding the Minnesota Twins to the AL West crown in 1969 was well documented.

In spring training with the Tigers, Coleman got the scare of a lifetime when he was hit in the head by a line drive off the bat of the St. Louis Cardinals' Ted Simmons on March 27. "I never saw the ball coming," said Coleman. "I don't remember a thing until I was on the ground with people standing around me."[23] Rushed to the hospital, he was diagnosed with a nondepressed linear fracture in his skull. He was hospitalized for two weeks and placed on the 21-day disabled list, but made a miraculous and quick recovery. He debuted for Tigers on April 24, allowing two runs on five hits over five innings in a no-decision against the Oakland A's. "You don't how happy I am to be here," said a relieved Coleman.[24] Suffering from headaches and working his way into shape, Coleman found his groove beginning July 9 when he tossed 10 scoreless frames against the Senators during an 11-inning pitching duel with Pete Broberg and Casey Cox at RFK Stadium, winning 1-0 to start a personal six-game winning streak. He emerged as one of the hottest pitchers in baseball, going 13-3 over his final 20 starts, a majority of them on three days' rest. "Pitching under Billy Martin has made all the difference in the world," said Coleman. "He gave me a free rein with my pitches. He said 'You're a pro. You know what's best for you. You pitch that way.'"[25] That not-so-subtle dig at Ted Williams aside, Coleman exacted revenge again on his former club by whiffing a career-high 14 in a complete-game victory on September 15. For the second-place Tigers, Coleman finished with a 20-9 record and sported a 3.15 ERA in a career-high 286 innings while a teammate, southpaw Mickey Lolich, led the majors with 25 wins and 376 innings. Coleman also set career highs in strikeouts (236) and complete games (16).

Coleman won 62 games in his first three seasons with the Tigers (just one fewer than AL stalwarts Catfish Hunter, Jim Palmer, and Lolich, but well behind Wilbur Wood's 70); however, his name rarely cropped up in discussions about the best pitchers in the league and he was once described as baseball's "forgotten man."[26] Overshadowed by Lolich, Coleman was more relaxed with the Tigers, responded to the trust Martin had in him, and shed his "hot-head" temperament. "I regret that show of temper," said Coleman of his days with the Senators. "It was a reputation I built up and it was a reputation I didn't want. But at the time, I deserved it."[27] Being on a winning club with stars like Al Kaline, Bill Freehan and Norm Cash, who garnered most of the media attention, also helped. "I got more runs, better defense, and a better team effort behind me," said Coleman. "When you're playing for a loser, you play for yourself, because you know you're not going to win."[28]

Coleman's development into a complete pitcher fueled his success. He claimed that he mellowed and no longer just tried to "blow the ball by the hitter."[29] Coleman possessed a strong fastball and increasingly relied on his elusive side-arm sinker and side-arm curve, but his forkball was his "out" pitch. "I don't know where it's going," he said. "I just throw the ball down the middle of the plate and wait to see where it breaks."[30]

Detroit captured the AL East crown on the next-to-last day of the 1972 strike-shortened season after a grueling, hotly contested division race with the Boston Red Sox, Baltimore Orioles, and New York Yankees. The now portly Coleman was at his best over the last six weeks of the season when the club needed him the most. He went 7-3 in his final 11 starts, including a masterful, four-hit, 11-inning shutout of the Minnesota Twins in the second game of a doubleheader on August 27. He finished the season with 19 wins, a career-best 2.80 ERA, and 222 strikeouts in 280 innings. He was a hard-luck loser; the Tigers scored just 14 runs in his 14 losses. Coleman was named to his first and only All-Star team, but did not pitch.

In the only postseason appearance of his career, Coleman tossed a gem in Game Three of the ALCS. He blanked the Oakland A's on seven hits and struck out a then Championship Series-record 14 in the Tigers' 3-0 victory. However, the Tigers eventually lost the best-of-five series, three games to two.

Coleman emerged as the club's most consistent winner in 1973, collecting 15 victories by the All-Star break. However, Oakland's Dick Williams, manager of the AL All-Star squad, snubbed the hurler, drawing Martin's ire. The Tigers took over first place in early August before falling out of contention by losing 10 of 14 games. The team reached its nadir in now infamous episode on August 30 against the Cleveland Indians. Martin, incensed that the umpires had refused to take measures against Gaylord Perry and his alleged spitballs, ordered Coleman (in the midst of a seven-game losing streak) to throw the illegal pitch. Martin was suspended, and subsequently fired on September 2 in a move that shocked the team. Propelled by a five-game winning streak after the brouhaha, Coleman finished the season with a career-high 23 wins (15 losses), a 3.53 ERA, and 202 punchouts in 288⅓ innings.

Coleman logged in excess of 200 innings for last-place Tigers teams in 1974 and 1975, but his record fell to 14-12 and 10-18 and his ERA rose dramatically to 4.32 and 5.55 (easily the highest in baseball). The Tigers were miffed by Coleman's rapid decline and control problems (he issued a career-high 158 walks in 1974). I've never seen a pitcher at his age (27-28), who never has had any arm problems, have as much trouble as Joe has had for us the last two years," said manager Ralph Houk.[31] Coleman, who revealed that he had a painful "huge knot" in his shoulder in 1974, was equally frustrated. "At times, I didn't have any idea what I was doing out there," he said. "I was having an awful lot of trouble with my forkball … and it was always my out pitch."[32]

Coleman spent his last four years (1976-1979) in the major leagues with six different clubs. After 12 mostly ineffective starts for Detroit in 1976, he was sold to the Chicago Cubs in an early June waiver transaction. No longer possessing his heater, Coleman moved to the bullpen and appeared in a career-high 51 games between the two clubs. He was traded to the Oakland A's in spring training the following year for pitcher Jim Todd and enjoyed a rebirth of sorts (2.96 ERA in 127⅔ innings) as a reliever and occasional starter. Following stints with the A's, Toronto Blue Jays, and San Francisco Giants, the Pittsburgh Pirates signed him as a free agent on May 8, 1979, and assigned to their Triple-A affiliate in the Pacific Coast League, the Portland Beavers.

The Pirates called up Coleman after the All-Star break to shore up an already overworked bullpen facing a heavy schedule, including seven doubleheaders in three weeks. With the bullpen already overworked, Coleman took one for the team against the Cubs on August 7, tossing the final 5⅓ innings and yielding nine runs in a 15-2 laugher, in a game which Dave Parker called the "incident."[33] "Our bullpen was beat up, and Joe knew that," said Kent Tekulve. "Every inning, [Coleman is] getting more and more exhausted. He's throwing a ton of pitches, and it's hotter than heck. He's sweating buckets. He's got a towel over his head in the dugout. It got to the point where you were literally worried about him."[34] According to Pittsburgh sportswriter Joe Starkey, when an exhausted Coleman entered the dugout after the eighth inning, skipper Chuck Tanner said, "You just won the pennant for us!"[35] Coleman pitched otherwise reasonably well and remained on the roster for the rest of the regular season, but was dropped for the postseason. Players voted him a half-share of their World Series winnings.

Coleman, just 32 years old, drew his release from Pittsburgh in the offseason, bringing his 15-year major-league career to an end. His final tally showed 142 wins, 135 losses, and a 3.70 ERA in 2,569⅓ innings. He started in 340 of his 484 appearances, completing 94, and tossed 18 shutouts. Coleman was especially tough on All-Stars Jim Fregosi (5-for 46, .109), Thurman Munson (9-for-56, .161), and Robin Yount (5-for 31, .161), but encountered problems with light-hitting Ted Kubiak (10-for-25, .400), Jake Gibbs (11-for-28, .393), and Ed Herrmann (15-for-41, .366). Well respected by his teammates, Coleman also served as player representative for several teams.

After his release from the Pirates, Coleman began a long and successful coaching career. In 1980 he was named player-coach for the Spokane Indians, the Seattle Mariners' and later California Angels' Triple-A affiliate in the PCL, and held the position for three years; he also made at least 10 appearances per year for the team. A highly respected teacher and mentor for young hurlers, Coleman served as bullpen and pitching coach for the California/Anaheim Angels (1987-1990; 1996-1999), as well as roving pitching instructor (1995-1996). He was also the pitching coach for manager Joe Torre with the St. Louis Cardinals (1991-1994). Since 2000, Coleman has been the pitching coach for several minor-league teams: the Triple-A Durham (North Carolina) Bulls (2000-2006) in the International League, and two clubs in the Class-A+ (Advanced) Florida State League, the Lakeland Flying Tigers (2007-2011) and the Jupiter Hammerheads (2012-2014).

A baseball lifer, Coleman grew up in big-league parks and has spent most of the last 50 years in them as a player or coach. In 2010 he became part of the first family with three generations of big-league pitchers when his son, Casey, debuted with the Chicago Cubs. As of 2014, Coleman and his wife lived in Florida during the baseball season and in Tennessee in the offseason.

SOURCES

Joe Coleman player file at the National Baseball Hall of Fame, Cooperstown, New York.

Ancestry.com.

BaseballLibrary.com.

Baseball-Reference.com.

Retrosheet.com.

SABR.org.

NOTES

1 News Enterprise Association, "Jr's Career Began in Dugout on Mr. Mack's Knee," *The News* (Frederick, Maryland), August 24, 1964: 21.

2 *The Sporting News*, September 18, 1965: 39.

3 Jack Sheehan, "Ball Park Always 2nd Home To Nats' Coleman," June 1967: 4. (Player's Hall of Fame file, National Baseball Hall of Fame, Cooperstown, New York).

4 Joe Coleman provided the names of these two scouts in his SABR Scouts Committee questionnaire.

5 *The Sporting News*, July 10, 1965: 22.

6 Murray Chass (Associated Press), "Pitcher Averages Better In Major Than In Minor Leagues. How Come?" *The Daily Mail* (Hagerstown, Maryland), April 4, 1967: 12.

7 Ibid.

8 *The Sporting News*, September 2, 1967: 6.

9 Joe Sargis (Associated Press), "Coleman Learning How To Pace Self," *Ogden* (Utah) *Standard-Examiner*, April 23, 1968: 10 A.

10 Frank Barrett Jr., "Young Coleman had it when Red Sox did not," *Lowell* (Massachusetts) *Sun*, August 7, 1971: 5.

11 *The Sporting News*, June 3, 1973: 3.

12 Dick Couch (Associated Press), "Joe Coleman Demonstrates Effects of Ted's Theories," *Free Lance-Star* (Fredericksburg, Virginia), March 25, 1969: 10.

13 *The Sporting News*, February 7, 1970: 43.

14 *The Sporting News*, August 2, 1969: 8.

15 Lew Ferguson (Associated Press), "Joe Coleman Still Needs Curve Work, Says Ted Williams," *Free Lance-Star* (Fredericksburg, Virginia), June 5, 1969: 10.

16 *The Sporting News*, August 8, 1970: 28.

17 Morris Siegel, "Coleman hasn't forgotten his two seasons with Ted," *Washington Times*, March 17, 1992: D5.

18 *The Sporting News*, June 27, 1970: 22.

19 Ed Rumill, "Discards slider, Coleman gets free rein with Tigers," *Christian Science Monitor*, May 28, 1971.

20 Ira Miller (UPI), "Denny McLain Sent To Senators In Eight-Player Transaction," *Cumberland* (Maryland) *News*, October 10, 1970: 15.

21 *The Sporting News*, October 24, 1970: 11.

22 *The Sporting News*, February 6, 1971: 36.

23 *The Sporting News*, April 10, 1971: 26.

24 *The Sporting News*, May 15, 1971.

25 Rumill.

26 Fred McMane (UPI), "Joe Coleman Just Misses First No-Hitter," *Dubois County* (Jasper, Indiana) *Daily Herald*, April 12, 1974: 12.

27 *The Sporting News*, June 16, 1973: 3.

28 Larry Paladino, "Line Drive To Head Didn't Halt Joe Coleman," *Lakeland* (Florida) *Ledger*, March 28, 1972: 1B.

29 UPI, "Joe Coleman Mellows With Age," *Sarasota Herald-Tribune*, May 19, 1973: C1.

30 *The Sporting News*, August 7, 1971.

31 *The Sporting News*, June 26, 1976: 16.

32 *The Sporting News*, May 24, 1975: 11.

33 Joe Starkey, "The 1979 Pirates: Where are they now?", Tribune-Review (Pittsburgh, Pennsylvania), August 16, 2009, http://www.pittsburghlive.com/x/pittsburghtrib/sports/.

34 Ibid.

35 Ibid.

Mike Easler

By Clayton Trutor

MICHAEL ANTHONY EASLER PLAYED 14 major-league seasons between 1973 and 1987. A left-handed hitter and right-handed thrower, Easler was nicknamed "The Hit Man" and "Line Drive" for his prowess at the plate. He was also sometimes referred to as Easy in reference to his last name, his graceful hitting stroke, and his quiet demeanor.[1] The Hit Man was the most commonly used nickname for Easler and the one that he himself embraced during his career.

The 6-foot-1 Easler played outfield and first base, and, during his tenure in the American League, often was a designated hitter. Easler played for six teams: the Houston Astros (1973-1975), California Angels (1976), Pittsburgh Pirates (1977-1983), Boston Red Sox (1984-1985), New York Yankees (1986, 1987), and Philadelphia Phillies (1987). He was a .293 career hitter who hit over .300 four times. While a member of the Pirates, he was selected to the National League All-Star Team in 1981 and was a part-time player on the Pirates' World Series championship team of 1979. In 2004 Easler was inducted into the Cleveland Sports Hall of Fame. A 2014 Cleveland.com online poll ranked him the best baseball player to ever come out of Northeast Ohio.[2] After leaving the majors as a player, Easler played professional baseball in Japan, then started a successful career as a coach, particularly as a hitting instructor.

Easler was born on November 29, 1950, in Cleveland to James E. "Ted" and Willie Mae (Watkins) Easler. Ted Easler worked for the US Postal Service while his mother was a homemaker.[3] Mike attended high school at Benedictine, an all-male Catholic high school in Cleveland, starring on the perennially powerful Benedictine Bengals baseball teams of the late 1960s.[4] After graduating from high school in 1969, Easler was drafted by the Houston Astros in the 14th round of the June amateur draft. He signed with the Astros in exchange for $500 tuition money which enabled him to attend Cleveland State University during the offseason.[5]

Easler's decade-long minor-league odyssey began in Covington (Virginia) in the Appalachian League, the home of the Astros' rookie-league affiliate. In many respects, Easler's first year of professional baseball set the tone for his minor-league career. He excelled at the plate, leading the team in batting average at .319 while struggling in the field. Easler proceeded swiftly through the Astros' minor-league system, posting excellent power numbers and batting averages year after year while struggling defensively in the outfield. As the early 1970s turned into the mid-1970s, Easler proved to be stuck in Triple-A baseball, putting up excellent batting numbers year after year but receiving nothing more than September call-ups from the Astros.

The success Easler achieved as a major leaguer was a product not only of his talent, but of his extraordinary work ethic and attention to the details of the game. Throughout his decade of minor-league baseball, Easler spent the winters playing in Latin America, primarily in Puerto Rico and Venezuela. He was also a student of the game, willing to spend hours in the batting cage and working on his fielding to improve his game. In a 2011 interview with David Laurila at fangraphs.com, Easler described his hitting style as influenced by Reggie Jackson, Pete Rose, and Mike Schmidt. "I was an adequate hitter," he said, far too modestly, "…I studied it and that's how I became better, just by doing the little stuff, like extra work in the batting cage."[6]

Easler got his first shot at the major leagues in 1973 after splitting the season between the Astros' Double-A affiliate in Columbus (Georgia) and Triple-A Denver, posting a .297 batting average with 13 home runs and 58 RBIs in 96 games. He made his major-league debut for the Astros on September 5, 1973, against the Cincinnati Reds at the Astrodome. Pinch-hitting for catcher Skip Jutze in the ninth inning of a 9-3 Astros defeat, Easler grounded out to first in his only plate appearance. Easler went 0-for-7 in six games for the Astros during September 1973.

Easler returned to the Denver Bears in 1974 and he hit .283 with a team-leading 19 home runs with 63 RBIs. He got his second September call-up that season. Again, he struggled against major-league pitching. Easler went 1-for-15 with six strikeouts, serving exclusively as a pinch-hitter. He returned to the Denver Bears in 1974 and hit .283 with a team-leading 19 home runs and 63 RBIs. One of his late-season home runs for the Bears was struck at Lawrence Stadium in Wichita, Kansas. The ball traveled well over 400 feet, then bounced across McLean Boulevard before rolling into the Arkansas River. Following a strong spring training in 1975, Easler was placed on the Astros' Opening day Roster, but the player later known as the "Hit Man" struggled for the third time at the big-league level, going 0-for-5 in five April pinch-hitting appearances. Houston sent Easler back to Triple-A, now in Des Moines, Iowa, to regain confidence, which proved successful. "I was trying to pull everything for a long time after I came down from Houston," Easler said. "(Iowa manager Joe Sparks) pointed out that I was looping my swing upward. He got me swinging level and hitting straight away…"[7] His confidence regained, Easler had another outstanding season in Triple A in 1975, hitting .313 with 15 home runs and 69 RBIs.

On June 25, 1975, Easler was traded for the first time, sent to the St. Louis Cardinals for a player to be named later who turned out to be Mike Barlow, a right-handed pitcher. Easler spent the remainder of 1975 and the 1976 minor-league season with the Cardinals' American Association affiliate in Tulsa. "The Hit Man" continued to dominate Triple-A pitching in 1976, batting a league-leading .352 with 26 home runs and 77 RBIs. He finished second to Denver's Roger Freed in the race for American Association MVP. Despite his success at the highest level of the minors, Easler did not get a shot at the big leagues with the Cardinals in either 1975 or 1976. The Cardinals' strong outfield regulars, Lou Brock, Bake McBride, and Reggie Smith, and backups Willie Crawford, Jerry Mumphrey, and Mike Anderson, kept Easler off the 25-man roster.

On September 3, 1976, the Cardinals traded Easler to the California Angels for minor-league third baseman Ronnie Farkas. The Angels added Easler to their September roster. He was primarily a designated hitter and pinch-hitter. Easler got his most extensive major-league experience to that point, hitting .241 with 4 RBIs in 54 at-bats for the Angels.

On April 4, 1977, two days before Opening Day, the Angels traded Easler to the Pittsburgh Pirates for minor-league pitcher Randy Sealy. The Pirates designated Easler for assignment to Columbus of the International League, where he spent virtually all of the 1977 and 1978 seasons. Again, Easler excelled against Triple-A pitching, batting over .300 both years and hitting 18 home runs each season. Again, talent in his parent club's starting outfield, this time Al Oliver, Bill Robinson, Dave Parker, and Omar Moreno, kept him out of the majors. In a September 1977 call-up, Easler went 8-for-18. In 1978 he made no appearances for the Pirates. After the 1978 season, the Red Sox purchased Easler's contract, only to trade him back to Pittsburgh

for minor leaguers George Hill, Martin Rivas, and cash during the next year's spring training.

For the first time in 1979, Easler spent an entire season in the major leagues. Serving almost exclusively as a pinch-hitter, he had 62 plate appearances for the world champion Pirates. Easler had only three starts. In 54 at-bats, he batted .278 with a strong on-base percentage of .371, 2 home runs, and 11 RBIs. One of his home runs was a 13th-inning, game-winning shot off Skip Lockwood of the New York Mets on May 16 at Three Rivers Stadium. Easler made his only career playoff appearances for the 1979 Pirates, going 0-for-2 in three plate appearances during the NLCS and World Series.

In 1980 Easler became a regular in the Pirates' outfield. The left-handed-hitting Easler and right-hander Lee Lacy platooned in left field as a replacement for the aging Bill Robinson. Easler and Lacy excelled as a platoon during the 1980 season, proving to be one of the few bright spots on the disappointing Pirates club of that season, which finished third in the NL East. Easler hit .338 with 21 home runs and 74 RBIs in 393 at-bats. He hit for the cycle against Cincinnati on June 12 and was named National League Player of the Week for the week of June 15. On the other side of the platoon, Lacy hit .335 with 7 home runs and 33 RBIs in 278 at-bats. Both Easler and Lacy batted for significantly higher averages than 1980 NL batting champion Bill Buckner (.324), but neither managed the required number of plate appearances to qualify for the award.

In August 1980 *Sports Illustrated* profiled the Easler and Lacy platoon, lauding both longtime benchwarmers for excelling when they finally got the shot to play on a regular basis. Pirates manager Chuck Tanner said that "when (Lacy and Easler) share the position, we have the best left fielder in the league."[8] "If I worked real hard and had a good spring, I hoped Chuck would play me more," Easler said of the 1980 season. The article detailed Easler's decade of minor-league baseball, his season after season of hitting excellence and his struggles in the field. It described Easler's offseason jobs as a bellboy and assembly-line worker to support his family. "People see Mike Easler of the Pittsburgh Pirates and think that's just great, but they have no idea of what it took to get here," Easler said of himself.[9]

Easler began to take the lion's share of starts in left field for the Pirates during the 1981 season. Lacy became a part-time starter in left field and right field that year, spelling Easler in left and slugger Dave Parker in right. Easler continued to excel in the new situation, batting .286 with 7 home runs and 42 RBIs in the strike-shortened season. At the time the players' strike suspended play on June 12, Easler was batting .317. Based on his first-half performance, Easler was named as a reserve to the 1981 NL All-Star Team, which was to be played in his hometown of Cleveland. Easler feared that the game would be canceled because of the prolonged labor stoppage, but players and owners came to an agreement in early August, and the season proceeded, beginning with the All-Star Game in Cleveland.[10]

The 1981 All-Star Game was Easler's only All-Star appearance or selection to the team. He entered the game in the top of the sixth inning, replacing his Pirates teammate Dave Parker in right field. In the top of the eighth inning, he was walked by Milwaukee's Rollie Fingers and later scored on Mike Schmidt's home run. Easler grounded into a force out to end the top of the ninth against Toronto's Dave Stieb. The National League won its 10th straight All-Star Game, 5-4.

Easler continued to post strong offensive numbers in 1982 and 1983 for back-to-back 84-win Pirates teams. In 1982 he hit .276 with 15 home runs and 58 RBIs. In 1983 he hit .307 with 10 home runs and 54 RBIs. Easler remained a defensive liability, often facing late-game defensive replacements by manager Tanner. To open the 1983 season, Tanner benched Easler in favor of the speedier and more defensively proficient Lacy. Easler described the benching as the "low point of my baseball career."[11] His hitting soon won him a place back in the lineup.

After the 1983 season, the Pirates traded Easler back to the Red Sox for left-handed starting pitcher John Tudor. The change of venue helped Easler enjoy a career year in 1984. He hit .313 with 27 home runs and 91 RBIs for the 86-win Red Sox, who finished fourth in the AL East. No doubt Easler benefited from a Boston lineup with four other regulars who swatted at least 20 home runs each: Tony Armas (43), Dwight Evans (32), Jim Rice (28), and Rich Gedman (24). Designated hitting also benefited Easler, who appeared in 129 of his 156 games at DH. Easler finished tied for fifth in the American League with188 hits and seventh in slugging percentage with a .516 mark. "Basically, I was an inside-out hitter made for Fenway Park," Easler said of his hitting style. "I had my power to the opposite field. I could turn on the ball, but that wasn't my strength. My strength was actually finishing high and going the other way. Very similar to Prince Fielder. My swing was close to his."[12]

Like the rest of the Red Sox, Easler's power numbers dipped considerably in 1985. He hit .262 with 16 home runs and 74 RBIs in 155 games, primarily at designated hitter. After the season, the Red Sox and Yankees swapped designated hitters. Easler headed for the Bronx while Don Baylor was Fenway-bound. Easler had an excellent season for the 1986 Yankees, batting .302 with 14 home runs and 78 RBIs. After the season, the Yankees traded Easler and middle infielder Tom Barrett (brother of the Red Sox' Marty Barrett) to the Philadelphia Phillies for pitchers Jeff Knox and Charles Hudson. The Phillies used Easler part-time in left field, where he hit .282 in 33 games. The Yankees reacquired him in June for outfielder Keith Hughes and third baseman Shane Turner. Easler hit .281 for the Yankees in 65 games that season, splitting his time between the outfield and designated hitting. The Yankees released Easler after the 1987 season, which proved to be his last in the major leagues. Easler was a .293 career hitter with 118 home runs and 522 RBIs in 4,061 plate appearances.

Easler played parts of two seasons (1988-1989) for the Nippon Ham Fighters in the Pacific League of the Nippon Professional Baseball League. Working primarily as a DH, Easler hit .302 in two seasons with the Fighters. Easler played his final season of professional baseball in the fall of 1989 with the West Palm Beach Tropics of the Senior Professional Baseball Association. The "Hit Man" went out in style, batting .323 in 35 games for the Tropics.

Easler became a highly in-demand hitting instructor, on both the major- and minor-league levels. He was the hitting coach for the Milwaukee Brewers (1992), Boston Red Sox (1993), St. Louis Cardinals (1999-2001), and Los Angeles Dodgers (2008).

Easler's most famous prodigy as a hitting instructor was Boston's Mo Vaughn. After struggling in his rookie year for the Red Sox, Vaughn, under Easler's tutelage, became one of the American League's most feared hitters and, in 1995, won the Most Valuable Player Award. After Easler left the Red Sox organization, Vaughn hired him to work as his private hitting instructor for the remainder of his career.[13] Also was the hitting coach for the Double-A Jacksonville Suns (2006) and the Triple-A Las Vegas 51s (2007), both part of the Dodgers organization, as well as the Triple-A Buffalo Bisons, the New York Mets' International League affiliate (2011). Additionally, he has served as a roving, minor-league hitting instructor in the Dodgers and Mets organizations.

Between his stints as a hitting coach, Easler was a manager four times. In 1990 he managed the Miami Miracle of the Class-A Florida State League to a 44-93 record. In 1994, he managed the Caguas Criollos of the Puerto Rican Professional Baseball League for four games. A dispute over how to use the team's pitching staff with Red Sox pitching coach Al Nipper, who oversaw the Red Sox affiliated-team on behalf of the major-league organization, led to Easler's abrupt dismissal. During spring training in 1995, Easler was let go by the Red Sox for refusing to work with replacement personnel during the lengthy players' strike which had started on August 11, 1994. He returned to managing in 1998, leading the Nashua Pride of the independent Atlantic League to a impressive 59-41 record and a third-place finish. In 1999 Nashua fell to fourth place with a 52-67 record. Easler became the St. Louis Cardinals' hitting coach and served for three years (1999-2001). In 2004 he coached the Florence (Kentucky) Freedom of the independent Frontier League In 2004 Easler was replaced by Eddy Diaz as manager for the Triple-A Yucatan Leones of the

Mexican League, and later took the reins for the final 49 games of the Florence (Kentucky) Freedom of the independent Frontier League.

As of 2015 Easler and his wife, Brenda (Johnson) Easler, resided in Las Vegas, Nevada.[14] Brenda is the sister of 15-year major leaguer Cliff Johnson, a power-hitting first baseman and designated hitter who played for seven teams. Easler became a born-again Christian during his minor-league playing career and was ordained as a Baptist minister.[15]

SOURCES

Baseball-Almanac.com.

NOTES

1. Anthony Cotton, "Happy at Going Halfsies," *Sports Illustrated*, August 18, 1980. Accessed on November 17, 2014: si.com/vault/1980/08/18/824880/happy-at-going-halfsies-hard-hitting-lee-lacy-below-left-and-mike-easler-constitute-a-mutual-admiration-society-which-is-a-good-thing-because-they-often-share-leftfield-for-pittsburgh/.
2. "Which Baseball Player Is the Best to Come From This Area?" *Cleveland.com*, April 30, 2014. Accessed on November 14, 2014: highschoolsports.cleveland.com/news/article/-2891660188822200122/which-baseball-player-is-the-best-to-come-from-this-area-baseball-roundtable-for-april-30-2014-poll/.
3. Claire Smith, "Manager's Dream Is Lost in the Sun," *New York Times*, November 9, 1994; "Easler, Cleveland, Ohio: Deaths," Ancestry.com. Accessed on November 12, 2014: search.ancestrylibrary.com/cgi-bin/sse.dll?db=ohdeath93-98&rank=1&new=1&MSAV=0&gss=angs-d&gsln=easler&mswpn__ftp=Ohio%2c+USA&mswpn=38&mswpn_PInfo=5-%7c0%7c1652393%7c0%7c2%7c3247%7c38%7c0%7c0%7c0%7c0%7c&uidh=hsj&mswpn__ftp_x=1&mswpn_x=XO&gsln_x=XO&gl=&gst=&hc=20&fh=20&fsk=BEEeEuMIgAAWgwAeOWI-61-.
4. "Which Baseball Player Is the Best to Come From This Area?" *Cleveland.com*, April 30, 2014. Accessed on November 14, 2014: http://highschoolsports.cleveland.com/news/article/-2891660188822200122/which-baseball-player-is-the-best-to-come-from-this-area-baseball-roundtable-for-april-30-2014-poll/.
5. "Mike Easler," Baseball-Reference.com: BR Bullpen, February 16, 2013. Accessed on November 17, 2014: baseball-reference.com/bullpen/Mike_Easler.
6. David Laurila, "Q&A: Mike Easler—The Hit Man Talks Hitters," fangraphs.com, September 2, 2011. Accessed on November 12, 2014: fangraphs.com/blogs/qa-mike-easler-the-hit-man-talks-hitters/.
7. "American Association," *The Sporting News*, June 14, 1975: 36.
8. Anthony Cotton, "Happy at Going Halfsies," *Sports Illustrated*, August 18, 1980. Accessed on November 17, 2014: si.com/vault/1980/08/18/824880/happy-at-going-halfsies-hard-hitting-lee-lacy-below-left-and-mike-easler-constitute-a-mutual-admiration-society-which-is-a-good-thing-because-they-often-share-leftfield-for-pittsburgh/.
9. Ibid.
10. Charley Feeney, "Easler's Star is Sinking Fast," *The Sporting News*, July 11, 1981, 39.
11. "Bucs' Easler Miffed Over Bench Role," *The Sporting News*, April 18, 1983, 16.
12. David Laurila, "Q&A: Mike Easler The Hit Man Talks Hitters," fangraphs.com, September 2, 2011. Accessed on November 12, 2014: fangraphs.com/blogs/qa-mike-easler-the-hit-man-talks-hitters/.
13. Tim Kurkjian, "MO TOWN: The Momentum of Mo Vaughn and the Streaking Red Sox has Boston Dreaming Impossible Dreams," *Sports Illustrated*, August 2, 1993. Accessed on November 17, 2014: si.com/vault/1993/08/02/129043/mo-town-the-momentum-of-mo-vaughn-and-the-streaking-red-sox-has-boston-dreaming-impossible-dreams; David Siroty, *The Hit Men and the Kid Who Batted Ninth* (Lanham, Maryland: Diamond Communications, 2002), 161-162; David Laurila, "Q&A: Mike Easler The Hit Man Talks Hitters," fangraphs.com, September 2, 2011. Accessed on November 12, 2014: fangraphs.com/blogs/qa-mike-easler-the-hit-man-talks-hitters/.
14. "Obituary: Raymond Johnson," *San Antonio Express-News*, April 19, 2003. Accessed on November 17, 2014: legacy.com/obituaries/sanantonio/obituary.aspx?n=raymond-johnson&pid=164315725.
15. Claire Smith, "Manager's Dream Is Lost in the Sun," *New York Times*, November 9, 1994.

Dock Ellis

By Paul Geisler

ONE OF THE BEST PITCHERS OF THE 1970S, Dock Ellis feared success nearly as much as he feared failure. He both angered and amused. His antics cut across racial and cultural lines, as he challenged old prejudices and "normal" ways of doing things. Ellis pitched a no-hitter in 1970 and the next year led the Pirates with 19 victories, started the All-Star Game for the National League, and won the World Series. He served as player representative for the Pirates, Yankees, and Rangers, and even got one vote for the Hall of Fame, yet claims he never pitched a game in the major leagues without the assistance of alcohol or drugs.[1]

Known as Peanut, then later simply "The Nut," Dock Phillip Ellis Jr., was born on March 11, 1945, in Los Angeles. His father, known as Big Dock, worked in a post office and as a longshoreman, then went to school to learn shoe repair. His wife, Naomi, assisted him when they opened a shoe-repair shop and a dry-cleaner business.

Dock attended the predominantly white Gardena (California) High School in hopes of finding a better education but found a good dose of racial prejudice. To avoid suspension when he got caught drinking and smoking marijuana at school, he agreed to go out for baseball. But he found racial resistance there as well. He excelled at basketball, however, as the only black person on the team.

Big Dock died when Dock was 18, and Dock decided to focus solely on baseball. Playing mostly in the infield, he became a pitcher when one day he threw the ball from the outfield fence all the way over the backstop. A tall, lanky right-hander at 6-feet-3 and 195 pounds, he batted both ways and threw so hard his friends would stop playing catch with him.[2]

Ellis attended Los Angeles Harbor College in Wilmington, California, but spent most of his time playing baseball in Watts for former Negro Leagues pitcher Chet Brewer. Brewer scouted for the Pirates and tutored several future major leaguers, including Bob Watson, Bobby Tolan, and Enos Cabell. Fielding several offers, Ellis always wanted to sign with Pittsburgh, as he finally did in 1964, but saw his signing bonus reduced from $60,000 to $2,500 after his arrest for stealing a car.[3]

When Ellis started at the Pirates' Class-A team in Batavia, New York, he felt extreme pressure to succeed and became steadily involved in alcohol and drugs. Homesick and lonely, he went to a bar with teammates and ordered a beer, hoping to pass as 21. When the waitress informed him that the drinking age in New York was 19, he said, "Okay, take the beer back, and bring me some vodka stingers."[4]

Despite his fears, Ellis excelled, but he soon became addicted to stimulants like Benzedrine (bennies) and Dexamyl (greenies). "I was into the speed … because of the expectations … to hurry up and get to the big leagues," Ellis recounted. "I had a no-miss tag on me. 'It's impossible for this kid not to get to the big leagues.' That's a lot of stress."[5]

In 1965 Dock married his first wife, Paula Hartsfield, an accomplished athlete and the first black homecoming queen at Manchester High School They were 20 and 17, respectively. They had one daughter, Shangaleza, in 1969.

Ellis had an overall won-lost record of 41-31 during his first four minor-league seasons through 1967. On the brink of making the Pirates in March 1968. he felt emboldened: "I held out this spring because … I never did get a bonus, and I thought I was entitled to more money."[6]

He finally accepted his contract and joined the Columbus Jets, the Pirates' Triple-A affiliate. He made his major-league debut on June 18 at Pittsburgh in relief against the Los Angeles Dodgers, and got his first win, pitching the 10th inning and allowing one hit. Ellis made and won his first start on July 31 in the second game of a twi-night doubleheader at

Cincinnati's Crosley Field, and finished the year in the starting rotation. In 1969 Ellis continued as a starting pitcher. Although he lost 17 games, he completed over 200 innings with a 3.58 earned-run average.

On Wednesday, June 10, 1970, Pittsburgh lost a day game in San Francisco and flew to San Diego for four games. Ellis obtained permission to drive home Thursday, an offday, and planned to return Friday to pitch the first game of a doubleheader. He said he took LSD on the way and timed it to kick in about the time he reached Los Angeles. He stayed with friends and continued with vodka and more acid, then lost track of the days.

A friend's girlfriend woke him up at 2:00 P.M., saying "Dock, you have to pitch today in San Diego!"

"I don't pitch until Friday," he replied.

"It is Friday!" she said.

"O wow. What happened to yesterday?" said the confused pitcher.[7]

Ellis caught a flight at 3:00 P.M. and arrived at the misty, drizzly, half-empty ballpark at 4:30 for the 6:05 game. He remembered having a sense of euphoria, with the ball feeling sometimes big like a balloon, sometimes small like a golf ball. He saw a comet tail on his pitches and Richard Nixon umpiring behind the plate. He could not see the hitters well enough except to tell whether they were on the right or left side of the plate. Catcher Jerry May had his fingers wrapped with reflective tape to help.[8]

Rookie Dave Cash sat next to Ellis in the dugout and from the fifth inning kept reminding him that he had a "no-no" going. Nine innings, eight walks, and one hit batsman later, the weak-hitting Padres lost, 2-0, without producing a hit. Pirates second baseman Bill Mazeroski saved the no-hitter for the first out in the bottom of the seventh inning with a "fantastic backhanded grab" of a line drive from pinch-hitter Ramon Webster. "I didn't think I had a chance for it," said Mazeroski after the game. Ellis knew otherwise: "When Maz dove, I knew he'd grab it."[9]

Ellis insisted that he did not intend to take LSD before pitching. He lost track of time. Yet he did admit that he worried about how he would be able to pitch. He knew the effects of LSD would not wear off before the game, so he took some speed, "because it was a habit. It was natural to take stuff, forgetting that I had taken the acid."[10]

Ellis went on to pitch three more shutouts in 1970, then developed a sore arm in mid-August and missed over a month. He still led Pirates starting pitchers with 13 wins, as the team won its division but was swept in three games of the best-of-five NLCS by the Cincinnati Reds.

Still complaining about arm trouble in 1971, Ellis started the season strong. His record of 14 wins against only three losses with a 2.11 ERA by July 6 earned him his first and only All-Star Game selection. When he learned that pitcher Vida Blue would start the game for the American League, he challenged the racial preferences in baseball: "They'll never start one 'brother' against another 'brother.'" The manager of the National League All-Stars, Sparky Anderson, said he picked Ellis to start because of his excellent numbers and the fact that he had six days' rest.[11] Ellis claimed that he had intentionally used a form of reverse psychology to ensure the outcome. "I said they wouldn't do it, so they had to."[12]

Ellis fared well through the first two innings of the game, allowing just a single. Then Luis Aparicio led off the third inning with a single, and Reggie Jackson, pinch-hitting for Blue, blasted Ellis's pitch off the light tower in right-center field at Tiger Stadium. With two outs, Frank Robinson added another two-run homer. Norm Cash struck out to end Ellis's All-Star career. The AL went on to win, 6-4, hanging the loss on Ellis.

Later that season the Pirates made history on September 1 against the Philadelphia Phillies by starting an all-black lineup, using a combination of American and Latin players, with Ellis as the starting pitcher.

Although Ellis finished the rest of the season with a mediocre five wins and six losses and a 4.50 ERA, the Bucs went on to beat the San Francisco Giants three games to one in the NLCS. They won the World Series, defeating the Baltimore Orioles in seven games.

While in San Francisco for the first two games of the League Championship Series, Ellis complained about his bed being too short in the team hotel, the

Jack Tar. He insisted on a suite, volunteering to pay the extra, but there were none available. Ellis checked out and moved to the Hilton. He also complained during the World Series in Baltimore about the Lord Baltimore Hotel. He got a different room, then finally moved to another spot with two rooms adjoining. He called the Pittsburgh "Establishment" cheap and bush league.[13] In Ellis's only appearance in the World Series, the Baltimore fans booed him loudly and waved handkerchiefs at him when he left the field during the third inning of the first game.[14] Many thought the Pirates would surely trade him, with his sore arm and loud mouth, but he stayed with Pittsburgh the next four seasons.

Ellis started on Opening Day for the Pirates in 1972, but still felt some arm soreness and even threatened to retire by age 30. He almost found himself sitting out more time than expected after an encounter with a security officer at Riverfront Stadium in Cincinnati. When Ellis arrived at the stadium together with Willie Stargell and Rennie Stennett on May 5, the guard, David Hatter, asked them all for identification. When Ellis flashed his world championship ring, Hatter interpreted his raising his fist, along with his "vile language," as a confrontation, and sprayed the hurler with Mace, arrested him, and charged him with disorderly conduct.[15]

Ellis sued the Reds, and the Cincinnati team dropped all charges before the trial. Ellis and the Reds wrote Reds apologies to each other.

Pittsburgh general manager Joe Brown admitted that Ellis had no identification card at the time because the team had never issued any. Within three days of the incident, the Pirates issued pink identification cards to all the players, with their pictures on the back.[16]

In 1972 Ellis pitched in only 25 games, all starting assignments. With all the controversy and arm concerns, he nonetheless had a very good year, with 15 wins, 7 losses, and a 2.70 ERA. He posted his best WHIP (1.157) since his rookie season in 1968.

The Pirates won the NL Eastern Division for a third consecutive season, but lost the NLCS to the Reds in five games via dramatic walk-off fashion on a ninth-inning wild pitch. Ellis started the fourth game

with the Pirates up two games to one and looking to clinch another pennant, but he was touched for three unearned runs on three Pittsburgh errors in five innings, and took the loss.

Ellis formed a very close relationship with Roberto Clemente. They roomed together when Ellis first got to the Pirates, and Roberto helped the kid from "the Neighborhood" make some adjustments to life in the big-time baseball arena. Clemente's tragic death in late 1972 shocked and traumatized Ellis. He went on a violent rampage in his house, displacing his anger and grief on his wife, Paula. They soon divorced.

Ellis started the 1973 pretty smoothly, until a picture circulated through the newspapers showing him in the bullpen before a game in August wearing hair curlers under an oversized cap. He wore them only during pregame warm-ups, but Pirates manager Bill Virdon passed word to him to stop wearing them.[17] Ellis accused Commissioner Bowie Kuhn of sending the edict, hiding behind Virdon. "There are many black men who wear curlers to help their hair," he said. "Baseball is getting behind the times again."[18] Ellis admitted later to biographer Donald Hall that he never wore curlers around the house, only before games. "That's when I was throwing spitballs. When I had the curlers, my hair would be straight. Down the back. On the ends would be nothing but balls of sweat."[19]

Again, Ellis developed arm trouble toward the end of the season. He missed the first three weeks of September and feared missing a pay raise the next year, saying, "This is going to cost me money now."[20] He had knee surgery in October to repair injuries from a fall when he was 11 years old. His doctors hoped that the surgery could actually help some of his arm problems. Despite the health holdups, Ellis had been one of the sturdiest pitchers on the Pirates staff, both winning and losing more games (59-40) than any other Pittsburgh hurler from 1970 through 1973.[21]

One day in 1974, the intimidation that Ellis felt building up from Cincinnati's dominance drove him to seek his own form of revenge against them. His anger dated back to losing the 1972 playoffs to the Reds. "All I heard was their players talking about how the Pirates were dumb players, and that's why they beat us."[22] On May 1 Ellis took the mound at Three Rivers Stadium in Pittsburgh to face Pete Rose, the first player to bat. He hit Rose, then Joe Morgan, then Dan Driessen, loading the bases. He tried to hit the fourth batter, Tony Perez, but Perez dodged the pitches and took a walk, forcing Rose home from third. Pittsburgh manager Danny Murtaugh had seen enough and pulled Ellis out. No other pitcher had hit three consecutive batters since a hundred years before, when Emerson "Pink" Hawley of the 1894 St. Louis Browns hit three in the first inning.[23]

Ellis had a reasonably good year in 1974, with 12 victories and a 3.16 ERA, yet again did not finish September because of arm trouble. The Pirates finished first in the NL East Division, but Ellis did not pitch in their three-games-to-one NLCS loss to the Los Angeles Dodgers.

Ellis enjoyed doing imitations in the clubhouse. He would do other players and umpires, but especially loved doing Muhammad Ali. One day in 1975 the Champ himself wandered into the Pirates clubhouse. Ellis showed off his quick feet and his quick mouth. Then Ali thumped him with a strong left jab to Dock's chest, throwing him back almost off his feet. Nevertheless, Ellis still fashioned himself "the Muhammad Ali of baseball."[24]

Late in the 1975 season Ellis refused an assignment to the bullpen. When he announced that he would speak to the team, everyone expected an apology. Instead, they got a rant against manager Danny Murtaugh, for which Ellis earned a 30-day suspension. Some players said Ellis tried to speak constructively, but others heard his words very differently. With the help of lawyer/agent Tom Reich, who had helped him during the Macing incident, Ellis was reinstated retroactively after 14 days. He did not lose any pay but still suffered a hefty fine. Ellis reluctantly accepted the bullpen assignment, but the ever-present trade rumors began to sound a lot more realistic during the offseason.[25]

The trade finally came—on December 11, 1975, to the New York Yankees. The very unbalanced transaction sent pitcher Ken Brett and second baseman Willie Randolph to the Yankees for pitcher Doc Medich, with Ellis's name added as a "throw-in."

As he left Pittsburgh, Ellis professed his love for the Pirates. "When the Pirates first signed me in 1964, I was wild. I was called a militant, although I don't think it was so. Joe Brown tried to understand me, and he did. So did the people who own the Pirates—the Galbreaths." Ellis said he really wanted to play for Billy Martin and the Yankees, and promised to focus totally on baseball in 1976, but he added, "I'll always be a Pittsburgher. I like the people there. I like the Pirates, too."[26]

Ellis started very strong in New York in 1976. By mid-July he had an 11-4 record, with five complete games and a 3.14 ERA. He pitched well throughout the season and posted 17 victories, the second-highest in his career, while topping 200 innings for the first time since 1971.

A beanball battle raged between the Yankees and the Orioles that season. On July 27 Ellis hit Baltimore's Reggie Jackson on the side of the face, forcing the slugger to go to the hospital for x-rays and miss a few games until the swelling went down. Jackson had hit six home runs in six games. Later in the game,

Orioles pitcher Jim Palmer obviously retaliated by hitting Mickey Rivers.[27]

Many remembered Jackson's towering home run off Ellis in the 1971 All-Star Game, but Ellis insisted that the July 27 incident arose from Jackson's taunting from the dugout and in the on-deck circle immediately before his at-bat.

Ellis started and won Game Three of the ALCS against the Kansas City Royals, then lost his start in Game Three at Yankee Stadium in the World Series against the Reds, who took four straight from the Yankees. Ellis received recognition for his standout season, as *The Sporting News* named him and Tommy John of the Dodgers the Comeback Players of the Year for 1976.

Peaceful times did not last long in New York for Ellis as he expected better compensation for his work. Reminiscing about the trade that brought him to the Yankees, he said, "The Yankees got me at a fire sale, and now they don't want to give me any money."[28] He also had words of advice for Yankees owner George Steinbrenner. "I think he should stay up in his office, push his buttons, count his money, and stay out of the locker room."[29]

The Yankees now saw Ellis as expendable. In a move labeled as a trade of "headaches," they sent him to the Oakland Athletics on April 27, 1977, along with outfielder Larry Murray and infielder Marty Perez, for pitcher Mike Torrez. "It's not the idea that I'm happy to be leaving the Yankee organization. I wasn't being paid, so I have to leave," reflected Ellis. He said joining the A's team full of rookies "makes me feel young again. Hopefully, I will pitch like I'm younger."[30]

Ellis had a very rough beginning with Oakland, with no wins and three losses in his first four starts, and a 23.48 ERA. His next three went much better, with an ERA of 3.93, but he won only one against two losses. Three days before his turnaround he shaved his head, a major shift from his usual style and a marked contrast from his curlers days.[31]

While in Oakland Ellis pulled what he later called the craziest thing he ever did. "They wanted me to keep charts. I said, 'Bleep the charts,' and set 'em on fire. They thought the clubhouse in Cleveland was on fire. The alarm went off. The automatic sprinklers started."[32]

Ellis's Oakland days lasted only until June 15, when the Texas Rangers purchased his contract for $275,000. But before he left Oakland, he had played for his third manager of the season. Charlie Finley, owner of the Athletics, changed skippers on June 10 when he surprisingly replaced Jack McKeon with Bobby Winkles.[33]

Rangers owner Brad Corbett received a lot of criticism, from fans and media alike, for signing Ellis. "All I can tell you that he's done a magnificent job for us," reported Corbett. "Dock Ellis got a bad rap. I love him. He's fair. He calls it the way he sees it."[34]

In July 1977 Dock married Austine Washington. They had one son, Dock Phillip Ellis III, or Trey.

The Rangers also went through a series of managerial shifts in 1977, resulting in Ellis playing for seven skippers during the season, including Frank Lucchesi, Eddie Stanky (one game), Connie Ryan (six games), and Billy Hunter in Texas. His season turned out mildly successful, as he pitched over 200 innings again. He bounced back from the poor showings in Oakland to finish with 10 wins and 6 losses for the Rangers, and a 2.90 ERA.

Once again, as in Pittsburgh and New York, Ellis served as player representative with the Rangers. His outspokenness came out again during the 1978 season. Manager Billy Hunter prohibited players from drinking at the hotel bar and banned mixed drinks on all flights. During a confrontation about the liquor rules with Ellis on the team bus, Hunter told him to sit down and shut up. Then Hunter decided to drop all alcohol from the flights. Enraged, Ellis resigned as player representative, complaining not only about the unreasonable rules, but also about feeling belittled in front of the team. "My father as the last man who told me to [sit down and shut up]. And as far as I'm concerned, nobody else can."[35]

Fans and media again called for a trade, but owner Corbett sided with his player over his manager. Hunter turned down a five-year contract extension in mid-season, and Corbett fired him with one day left in the season.

Ellis started 1979 with the Rangers, but did not pitch well. On June 15 Corbett relented and traded him to the New York Mets for pitchers Mike Bruhert and Bob Myrick. In 27 games for the Rangers and Mets, Ellis had a 4-12 record and an ERA over 6.00. On September 21 Pittsburgh purchased his contract, and Ellis got his wish to "come back and die as a Pirate."[36] He started one game and pitched two in relief during the last week of the season.

Pittsburgh released Ellis to free agency on November 1. Once again he flew into a rage at home, devastated that the Pirates had let him go. He had focused his whole life, since his teen years, on pitching a baseball. He traumatized his wife, Austine, so much one day at home that when she could get out of the house, she went to a hospital and never got back with Ellis again.

Corbett had promised Ellis a job after baseball, and Ellis traveled the world doing "soft PR" at $50,000 a year promoting his former owner's plastic-pipe company.[37]

In the fall of 1980, realizing he had a problem, Ellis called former major leaguer Don Newcombe, who he knew worked with other addicts. Dock called his sister Sandra from the airport and asked her to bring a bottle of vodka. "It's going to be my very last," he said.[38] Newcombe helped Dock get into The Meadows, a substance-abuse clinic in Wickenburg, Arizona, where he stayed 45 days — two weeks longer than insurance allowed, too terrified to leave until he felt ready to cope.

Ellis dedicated much of the rest of his life to helping fellow addicts find a path to recovery. He actually started this work during his playing days when he visited inmates in Pittsburgh area prisons. His own conversion experience drove his passion to work with others.[39] He wanted to "go to where they're at," to meet them in the clubhouses and in the bars. "By the time they come for help, they're already locked up and in trouble with their families."[40]

Dock married a third time, to Jacquelyn, in 1985, then soon divorced, and shortly thereafter he married Hjordis, who was with him until he died in 2008.

Dock's son Trey remembered the sense of calling that his father felt, "that feeling he got knowing he was changing somebody's life."[41] Ellis never forgot his own struggles. "Continuous recovery! I'll be recovering until I die!"[42]

Ellis was diagnosed with cirrhosis of the liver in 2007, and hoped for a liver transplant. With no insurance, his family relied heavily on friends from his baseball career to help pay bills. Heart damage precluded any transplant, and he died on December 19, 2008, at the age of 63.

Around the time of the 1971 All-Star Game, Ellis received what he regarded as perhaps his most prized possession: a handwritten letter from Jackie Robinson. In it Jackie wrote: "Try to get more players to understand your view, and you will find great support. You have made a real contribution."[43]

Possibly the most underrated, unpopular, and misunderstood player ever, Dock Ellis redefined "success" as something other than putting up impressive numbers in the major leagues. He pioneered a path across racial and cultural divides, and found a way not only to live beyond his fears but also to walk alongside others who struggled as he did.

NOTES

1. Jeff Radice, director and producer, *No No: A Dockumentary*. 2014.
2. Ibid.
3. Keven McAlester, "High Times," *Houston Press*, June 23, 2005.
4. Jerry Crowe, "Dock Ellis: The Man Who Pitched a No-Hitter While Under the Influence of LSD Has Found a New Delivery: He Coordinates a Substance-Abuse Rehabilitation Program: Ellis: 'I Couldn't Pitch Without Pills,'" *Los Angeles Times*, June 30, 1985.
5. Ibid.
6. Les Biederman, "Blass Blossoms; Ellis Could Be Next to Thrive," *The Sporting News*, September 11, 1968.
7. Radice.
8. Espn.com, "OTL: The Long, Strange Trip of Dock Ellis," espn.go.com.
9. Charley Feeney, "Maz' Dive Buoys Dock in No-No Against Padres," *The Sporting News*, June 27, 1970.
10. Crowe.
11. "Pipeline Full of Chit-Chat," *The Sporting News*, July 31, 1971.

THE 1979 PITTSBURGH PIRATES

12 Donald Hall with Dock Ellis, *In the Country of Baseball* (New York: Simon and Schuster, 1989), 175.

13 Charley Feeney, "Bucs 'Stuck' with Ellis, Big Winner, Big Yelper," *The Sporting News,* October 23, 1971.

14 Lowell Reidenbaugh, "Orioles Find Way Back With McNally," *The Sporting News,* October 23, 1971.

15 Charley Feeney, "Drydock Beckons Bucs' Storm-Tossed Ellis," *The Sporting News,* May 20, 1972.

16 "Dock Gets Identity Card," *The Sporting News,* May 27, 1972.

17 Hall, 215.

18 Charley Feeney, "Even Hair Curlers Rear Ugly Head in Bucs' Domestic Life," *The Sporting News,* September 1, 1973.

19 Hall, 217.

20 "Pirate Ellis in Dry Dock Again," *The Sporting News,* September 22, 1973.

21 Charley Feeney, "Bucs' Moody Ellis Happy — Knee Sound after Surgery," *The Sporting News,* March 15, 1974.

22 Crowe.

23 "N.L. Flashes — Dock Makes History," *The Sporting News,* May 18, 1974.

24 Radice.

25 Charley Feeney, "Apologetic Dock Earns Return to Bucs," *The Sporting News,* September 13, 1975.

26 Charley Feeney, "Dock Dons Walking Shoes for Pirate Exodus," *The Sporting News,* December 20, 1975.

27 Jim Henneman, "Oriole Feathers Fly in Duster Fight," *The Sporting News,* August 14, 1976.

28 Dick Young, "Young Ideas," *The Sporting News,* April 16, 1977.

29 "Insiders Say," *The Sporting News,* April 30, 1977.

30 Tom Weir, "Trader Finley Swaps Headaches, Torrez for Ellis," *The Sporting News,* May 14, 1977.

31 Tom Weir, "Page Injury Dims One of A's Few Bright Spots," *The Sporting News,* June 18, 1977.

32 Crowe.

33 "Winkles Take Over as A's Skipper; McKeon Gets Axe," *Gadsden* (Alabama) *Times,* June 11, 1977.

34 Randy Galloway, "Betrayed Corbett Ready to Cash Ranger Chips," *The Sporting News,* July 23, 1977.

35 Randy Galloway, "Dock Protesting Dry Runs, Leaps Overboard," *The Sporting News,* June 17, 1978.

36 Radice.

37 Hall, 328.

38 Radice.

39 Hall, 336.

40 Radice.

41 "OTL: The Long, Strange Trip of Dock Ellis," ESPN.com, August 24, 2012.

42 Hall, 336

43 Radice.

Tim Foli

By Norm King

DID YOU KNOW THAT CRAZY HORSE had a World Series ring?

Wait a minute! How could the Oglala Sioux Indian chief who, along with Sitting Bull, routed General Custer at Little Bighorn, have a World Series ring? He never played baseball. True. But "Crazy Horse" was also the nickname given to Tim Foli, a talented but hot-tempered infielder who played 16 years in the majors for six teams, and won it all with the Pirates in 1979.

Timothy John Foli entered the world on December 6, 1950, in Culver City, California, one of four children (two sons and two daughters) born to Ernie and Lillian Kathleen (Deserf) Foli. When Ernie Sr. wasn't toiling in the real-estate business, he worked with his sons as they moved up the Little League ranks. Both boys were athletes; Tim's brother, Ernie Jr., was eight years older than Tim, and also played professional baseball. He got as high as the Triple-A level as an infielder in the Los Angeles Angels and Kansas City Athletics organizations.

Tim began playing in a park league at the age of 6 before moving on to the Canoga-Winnetka Little League from age 9 until he was 13. The competitive intensity and fire that marked his career was evident even then.

"Tim has played with intensity and competitiveness all his life and even when he was six years old in the park league he was always far advanced," said his Little League coach, Quentin Quick. "He simply has tremendous desire and talent to go with it."[1]

That desire and talent turned Foli into a three-sport athlete at Notre Dame High School in Sherman Oaks, California. In his senior year, he was chosen Southern Section 3-A player of the year in baseball, when he hit an incredible .562. He was also an elite basketball and football player and was offered a scholarship to play quarterback at the University of Southern California under legendary coach John McKay. New York Mets scout Harry Minor had other ideas, however, and convinced the "Amazin's" to select him number 1 overall in the 1968 amateur draft. A bonus ranging from $70,000 to $85,000, depending on the source, convinced Foli he should forgo college and devote himself to professional baseball.[2] His first stop was with the Marion (Virginia) Mets of the Rookie-level Appalachian League, where his intensity gained notice.

"There he batted .281 (with four home runs and 36 RBIs in 235 at-bats) and began to build the reputation, says Ed Kranepool of the Mets, 'of a guy who's so hyper that he brings his bat back to his hotel room,'" wrote Pat Jordan in *Sports Illustrated*. The Mets sent him to their Visalia club in the Class-A California League for 1969. He had an impressive year, batting .303 with 15 home runs and 62 RBIs, and he made the all-star team, but after one tough game on a very hot day in which he went 0-for-5, he slept at second base.

"So I got a blanket and a record player and found the coolest place available," Foli recalled. "I lay down along near shortstop and listened to music and thought about how I wouldn't go nothing-for-five again."[3]

The problem Foli had playing in the Mets' minor-league system, besides being too hard on himself, was that the parent club, just coming off its first world championship, already had two veteran major-league-caliber shortstops, Bud Harrelson and Al Weis. That didn't stop Foli, however, from wowing them at the Mets' 1970 spring-training camp.

"Foli, the 19-year-old shortstop from Culver City, California, is the talk of Florida," wrote Jack Lang in *The Sporting News*. "He draws raves everywhere he goes from players, managers, scouts and fans."[4]

As any thespian will tell you, rave reviews don't guarantee a long run on Broadway. Such was the case with Foli, who for all the talent he displayed still only had 163 games of professional experience behind him. Mets management decided he would benefit from another year in the minors and sent him to the Tidewater (Virginia) Tides of the Triple-A International League. Foli, understandably, reacted like the 19-year-old that he was.

"They tell me I'm only 19 and I've played only 163 games in the minors," he said, "but why should that make any difference if I can do the job? And I know I can do the job."[5]

Unfortunately, Foli couldn't do the job offensively at Triple-A the way he did the previous season, with a lower batting average and diminished home-run and RBI totals (.261, 6, 30). The Mets nonetheless called him up during the September pennant race, and he made his major-league debut on September 11, 1970, as a ninth-inning defensive replacement for Harrelson. He didn't get to bat in that game, which meant he managed to avoid facing future Hall of Famer Bob Gibson.

Foli made his first major-league start the next day against the Cardinals, but not at his customary position—he played third base instead. The Mets were in only their ninth year of existence that season, yet Foli was the 43rd man to play the hot corner for the franchise. (Rumor had it that number 44 was going to be the winner of a fan essay contest.) Foli went 2-for-4 with an RBI at the plate, and had two putouts and three assists in the field with no errors. That September he got into five games with four hits and an RBI.

Wayne Garrett was expected to be the third baseman for the 1971 season, having played 70 games at the position the previous year. But just as spring training began, Uncle Sam came calling and Garrett was drafted into the Army, giving Foli an opening to make the team. Foli took full advantage of the chance, worked hard in Florida, and came north with the team as the backup to the more experienced Bob Aspromonte, who had been acquired from the Atlanta Braves in December 1970.

It was during the 1971 season that Foli's teammates started calling him Crazy Horse because, in the politically incorrect spirit of the time, "he keeps wandering up and down the dugout like an Indian on the warpath waiting to get at the U.S. Cavalry."[6]

Of course, part of that intensity stemmed from his being only 20 years old. How else to explain a dugout incident with teammate Ed Kranepool during a May 26 game against the Phillies? As the Mets infield warmed up prior to the first inning, when first baseman Kranepool tossed a grounder to Foli at third, Foli's return throw was wide, forcing Kranepool to stretch for the toss. Kranepool wasn't pleased, and so threw grounders to every infielder except Foli for the rest of the warmup. A seething Foli charged Kranepool in the dugout when the half-inning was over, demanding to know why Kranepool stopped throwing to him. Yelling led to pushing which led to Kranepool giving Foli a smack in the snoot and it was all over.

"He was showing me up in front of my teammates," said Kranepool. "I couldn't let him do that."[7]

Temper tantrums aside, it seems that the Mets had trouble finding a spot for Foli that season, playing him at third, second, and short over 97 games; he even

played five innings in center field. At the plate he hit only .226 with 24 RBIs in 288 at-bats, not the kind of numbers that warrant a lot of playing time.

They also don't warrant a team tolerating somebody getting into scraps with teammates and coaches. As if fighting with Kranepool wasn't enough, Foli also duked it out with Mets coach Joe Pignatano during spring training in 1972 over a mix-up about hockey tickets for an East Coast League playoff game. It seems that some ducats were left for Pignatano and he arrived at the arena to find Foli and others sitting in his seats. A slight confrontation ensued, but the players got up and moved. Foli, not one to let a sleeping pout lie, walked into the coaches' dressing room the next morning to discuss the matter further. A couple of punches and a broken pair of glasses later, Foli was soon gone from the Mets. They shipped him off to Montreal along with first baseman Mike Jorgensen and outfielder Ken Singleton in return for right fielder Rusty Staub on April 5, 1972.

The trade was a boon to Foli's career because he got the playing time at shortstop in Montreal that he would not have had in New York behind Harrelson. It also allowed him to play for Gene Mauch, who saw in Foli a younger version of himself, temper and all.

"Foli would light a fire under that team [the Expos], Mauch assumed," wrote Jordan. "Mauch said he had taken to the young shortstop because 'there's no mystery to him' and because he bore a strong resemblance to a fiery shortstop of another generation—Mauch himself."[8]

Foli replaced incumbent number-one shortstop Bobby Wine and hit reasonably well considering that he played in an era when not much offense was expected from the position (the top 15 shortstops in 1972 totaled 65 home runs; in 2013, the top 15 hit 184).[9] He hit .241 with his first two major-league home runs and 35 RBIs. Foli also led the league in fines resulting from run-ins with umpires (four), and turned being a batboy into a hazardous occupation by flinging bats, gloves, helmets, and other paraphernalia.

Foli's 1973 season was marred by a horrific collision with Bob Watson of the Houston Astros on July 8 at Montreal's Jarry Park. Watson, who was on first as a result of a Foli error, was heading to second on a groundball by Doug Rader while Foli was making the pivot for a double play. Watson put up his forearm just as Foli lurched forward to complete the throw, and the two crashed into each other, with Foli getting the worst of it. Foli and the baseball went flying while his glasses also sailed through the air from the force of the impact. To add insult to his injury, Foli was charged with his second error of the frame as he lay prone on the infield, bleeding from the mouth. He was carried off the field on a stretcher with a broken jaw, and missed exactly one month, returning on August 8. Three days after his return, he was suspended for three games for bumping umpire Ken Burkhart earlier in the season. Despite the injury and suspension, his numbers were similar to those of the previous season. In 82 fewer at-bats, he hit .240 with 2 home runs and 36 RBIs.

Foli had a routine season in 1974 in which he hit .254 with no home runs and 39 RBIs, and had a huge dust-up with the Dodgers' Rick Auerbach on July 7. Auerbach slid into Foli while trying to break up a double play, precipitating a fight between the two of them and a bench-clearing brawl. The Dodgers were furious with Foli. LA second baseman Davey Lopes called him a dirty player who can dish it out but can't take it, while catcher Joe Ferguson referred to him as a cheap-shot artist.[10]

Other teams may have hated Foli, but Ginette Pélissier, a former bunny at the Montreal Playboy Club, showed she loved him by marrying him in December 1974. As of 2015, they were still married, with five children.

The bunny's husband played shortstop like Hall of Famer Rabbit Maranville in 1975, leading all National League shortstops in putouts (260), assists (497), and double plays turned (104). His offensive numbers remained meager (.238, 1, 29), but his pugnaciousness was in fine form. He got into a fight with the Cardinals' Reggie Smith on July 5 when he accused Smith of coming into second base too hard while trying to break up a double play, and earned a three-game suspension in September for arguing with the umpires after a game in which he had been thrown out for … arguing with the umpires.

Whether it was helpful or not, Foli's fiery playing style was one of the few bright spots on a truly dreadful 1976 Expos team that went 55-107. So was the unusual way in which he hit for the cycle, the first in the team's history, and a natural one to boot. An April 21 game against the Cubs at Wrigley Field was suspended by darkness after six innings, by which time Foli had singled, doubled, and tripled in that order. His home run came in the eighth inning when play resumed the following day. He went 4-for-5 with three RBIs as the Expos won, 12-6.[11] Foli's overall numbers were improved. His six home runs were a career high, and he hit .264 and had 54 RBIs, the most in his career to that point.

Even though he had good numbers in 1976, Foli's days in Montreal were numbered by 1977. Giants shortstop Chris Speier wanted out of San Francisco because he never knew week-to-week where or if he was going to play. He wanted to come to Montreal because he loved the city and saw the team as an up-and-coming contender. Expos GM Charlie Fox, Speier's first manager with the Giants, was glad to oblige, not just because he knew Speier, but saw him as a winner. Fox sent Foli to San Francisco on April 27, 1977, in an even-up deal for Speier.

"I think they are both good shortstops," said Fox. "But if you put them both in a room and told me I could have either one, I would take Speier because I think he can make us a winner sooner."[12]

Things got off to a rocky start for Foli in the Bay area. In his first game with the Giants he made an error on a groundball by Jose Cruz of the Houston Astros. The next batter was Bob Watson, who had broken Foli's jaw four years earlier. Watson didn't break any body parts this time, but did smack a home run that gave Houston a 2-0 lead on its way to a 3-1 win. That start was a sign of things to come for Foli, as he hit .221 for the year, the lowest batting average of his career to that point, with 4 home runs and 27 RBIs.

If reality television shows existed back then, Foli could have starred in one called "What Goes Around Comes Around." In December the Giants sold Foli back to the Mets, for whom he replaced Bud Harrelson as the team's starting shortstop. (These were not the Mets that Foli signed with in 1970. That team was coming off a World Series win, but the woeful 1977 edition lost 96 games.) Foli rebounded offensively in 1978, hitting .257, again with 27 RBIs but only one home run. That wasn't good enough for the Mets, who opted for more speed from the shortstop position, and traded Foli and minor-league pitcher Greg Field to Pittsburgh for their shortstop, Frank Taveras, on April 19, 1979. Taveras had led both leagues with 70 stolen bases in 1977, and followed that up with 46 thefts in 1978. Foli, meanwhile, would end up with 81 steals for his entire career. He also had, by joining the Pirates, a FAM-A-LEE!

The 1979 Pirates were a close-knit group that danced all the way to the World Series to the tune of their theme song, the Sister Sledge hit "We Are Family." Led by their captain, veteran slugger Willie Stargell, and right fielder Dave Parker, the Pirates led the league in runs scored (775). Foli caught the team's hitting bug by putting up the best offensive numbers of his career—he had a .288 batting average with 65 RBIs, and scored 70 times. He also did well in the postseason, batting .333 in both the three-game sweep of the Cincinnati Reds during the best-of-five NLCS and the World Series triumph in seven games over the Baltimore Orioles, going the entire postseason without striking out. Being with the Pirates seemed to steady Foli. He made a good keystone combination with second baseman Phil Garner, and he didn't fly off the handle as often.

"Tim is still quick to jaw with a teammate and therefore is not the most popular Pirate, but he's come a long way in keeping his Irish temper under control," wrote Mailand McIlroy in a Pittsburgh-area newspaper. "Because he has a lot to say, some of the other players call him "coach" in a rather irreverent tone."[13]

Being in a good space won't prevent injuries or work stoppages. Various ailments, including a leg infection resulting from being spiked early in the season, limited Foli to 127 games in 1980, while a players' strike restricted him to 86 games in 1981. His numbers for the two seasons returned to his normal levels after peaking in 1979 (.258 batting average, 3 home runs, 58 RBIs for the two seasons combined).

Even the best families have their breakups, and such was the case with Foli and the Pirates, who traded him to the California Angels for catcher/outfielder Brian Harper on December 11, 1981. In what would have been a sequel had the show "What Goes Around Comes Around" existed, Foli was reunited with his manager from the Montreal days, Gene Mauch. Unlike the Montreal situation, Mauch was in charge of a playoff-caliber team in 1982 that won the American League West Division before losing to the Milwaukee Brewers in the then-maximum of five games in the ALCS. Foli was a major contributor to the team's success, leading AL shortstops in fielding percentage (.985) and finishing sixth in assists. He led both leagues in sacrifice hits (26). He also set a league record with only 14 walks in 528 plate appearances. He had only 2 hits in 16 at-bats in the playoffs.

The last three years of Foli's major-league career saw vastly diminished playing time. In 1983 a bruised rotator cuff kept him out of the lineup from early August through the rest of the season. He couldn't avoid trouble while injured; in September, he was suspended, then reinstated and fined for changing from his uniform into street clothes during a rain delay in Chicago. The Angels traded Foli to the New York Yankees after the season for pitcher Curt Kaufman. He played in only 61 games with the Yankees in 1984 and demanded a trade after the season because he wasn't getting any playing time, not because of his relationship with George Steinbrenner. In fact, he liked "The Boss."

"[A] lot of people didn't like George," Foli said. "I liked George. He'll do whatever it takes to win and I like that."[14]

The Yankees traded Foli back to Pittsburgh along with outfielder Steve Kemp and cash for infielder Dale Berra, outfielder Jay Buhner, and pitcher Alfonso Pulido before the 1985 season. Foli played in only 19 games for the Pirates that year before they released him on June 17. He then played one game for the Miami Marlins of the Class-A Florida State League before calling it a career. In his last three major-league seasons, Foli played in 168 games and batted .247 with 2 home runs and 47 RBIs.

After his playing days, Foli stayed in baseball as a coach and manager. He coached with the minor-league Marlins in 1986, then spent two seasons coaching third base with the Texas Rangers. In the winter of 1987, he managed the Criollos de Caguas of the Puerto Rican League in the Caribbean Series, but was fired after the team lost two of its first three games (including one in which they committed eight errors). His replacement, Ramon Aviles, led Caguas to the title.

Foli also coached with the Brewers, Reds, Royals, Mets, and Washington Nationals. He has managed at the Triple-A level for the Nationals, where he skippered his son Daniel, a career minor-league pitcher, for one game in 2006. By 2010 Foli was the Nationals' head of player development and special adviser to general manager Mike Rizzo.

It also turned out that you can take the Foli out of the fight, but you can't take the fight out of the Foli, even after his playing days. On August 24, 1993, while coaching at first base with Milwaukee, Foli was ejected during the second game of a doubleheader for fighting with the opposing third-base coach, Tommie Reynolds, during a lengthy bench-clearing brawl between the Oakland Athletics and the Brewers. While with the Reds in 2001, he got into a fight with fellow coach Ron Oester after a game and required stitches for a cut to the head.

As of 2015, Foli lived in Ormond Beach, Florida, with Ginette. He became a born-again Christian while with the Pirates and has devoted time to speaking to Christian groups.

SOURCES

biography.com/.

baseball-reference.com.

Los Angeles Times.

New York Times.

sportscelebs.com/.

Reds.enquirer.com.

THE 1979 PITTSBURGH PIRATES

NOTES

1. Frank Mazzeo, Column, *Valley News* (Van Nuys, California), June 4, 1971.
2. A *Montreal Gazette* article from September 26, 1972, lists the bonus at $70,000, *Sports Illustrated* (June 9, 1975) lists it at $75,000, and the *Valley News* (June 4, 1971) said that the bonus was $85,000, plus $10,000 for college tuition.
3. Ian MacDonald, "Foli's temper improves along with his hitting, fielding," *Montreal Gazette*, September 26, 1972.
4. Jack Lang, "Foli Most Marvelous of New Mets," *The Sporting News*, April 4, 1970.
5. Lang, "Mets to Place More Emphasis on Offense to Repeat Title Bid," *The Sporting News*, April 11, 1970.
6. Lang, "Foli Making Mets' Mark as King of the Rednecks," *The Sporting News*, June 19, 1971.
7. Pat Jordan, *Sports Illustrated*, June 9, 1975.
8. Ibid.
9. The author was 15 years old and working on a cable television baseball show in the summer of 1972. He interviewed Bobby Wine at Jarry Park on July 9. Wine was cut from the team the next day.
10. Associated Press, "Dodgers fuming at Expos," *Bakersfield Californian*, July 8, 1974.
11. It was the only time all season that the Expos scored in double figures.
12. Ian MacDonald, "Speier 'Elated' Over Deal That Turns Him Into Expo," *The Sporting News*, May 14, 1977.
13. Mailand McIlroy, "Foli Has Become Glue For Pirates Infield," *Daily News* (Huntington, Mount Union, and Sexton, Pennsylvania), March 19, 1980.
14. Tim McDonald, "Tim Foli is now Mr. Calm," *St. Petersburg (Florida) Evening Independent*, April 2, 1985.

Phil Garner

By Norm King

WHAT DOES PHIL GARNER HAVE IN common with Sir Edmund Hillary and Neil Armstrong?

The answer is that all three performed feats never before achieved by humankind. Sir Edmund was the first person to reach the summit of Mount Everest. Neil Armstrong was the first person to set foot on the moon. And Phil Garner boldly went where no Houston Astros manager had gone before when he led the team to its first World Series appearance in 2005.

Of course, that was not the only achievement of Garner's baseball career, but certainly one of the most significant in a career that included a World Series ring and three All-Star appearances in a 16-year playing career.

Philip Mason Garner was born on April 30, 1949, in Jefferson City, Tennessee, to Drew and Mary Francis (Helton) Garner. Both his father and grandfather were Baptist ministers. He grew up in Rutledge, Tennessee, 15 miles from Jefferson City. As a teenager, he went to Bearden High School in Knoxville due to the quality of the school's athletics and, upon graduating, accepted a baseball scholarship at the University of Tennessee.

Garner had a successful career as a Volunteer, both academically and athletically. He was twice named All-Southeast Conference and led the NCAA in 1969 with a 0.36 home runs per game average, based on 12 homers in 33 games. He graduated with a bachelor's degree in business.

The Montreal Expos drafted Garner in the eighth round of the 1970 amateur draft. The Expos showed minimal interest in their pick, so he didn't sign with them and became available in the January 1971 secondary draft. This time the Oakland A's, a dynasty in the making, scooped up the third baseman in the first round (third overall), signed him, and sent him to their A-ball affiliate, the Burlington (Iowa) Bees in the Midwest League.

Garner made a seamless transition from college ball to the pros. In 116 games, he hit .278, smacked 11 home runs, and drove in 70 runs. On the defensive side, the hot corner was proving to be a bit too toasty, as he committed 29 errors and had a .918 fielding percentage.

Garner married his wife, Carol, in 1971. They went on to have three children, sons Eric and Ty, and daughter Bethany.

Garner's fine 1971 season earned him a promotion for 1972 to the Birmingham A's in the Double-A Southern League, where he continued battering opposition pitching despite being on a bad (49-90, 29 GB) team. In 71 games, Garner hit .280, with 12 homers and 40 RBIs. These numbers earned him a midseason trip back to Iowa, this time with the Triple-A Iowa Oaks of the American Association. He had more difficulty hitting at this level, as his .243 average in 70 games will attest. He hit nine home runs and had 22 RBIs. Defensively, Garner had better statistics at Triple-A than he did at Double-A. Handling virtually the same number of chances at each level, He had fewer errors at Triple-A.

The poorer offensive numbers at Iowa convinced Athletics management that Garner needed more seasoning, and they sent him to their new Triple-A affiliate, the Tucson Toros of the Pacific Coast League, in 1973. That season, he batted .289 with 14 home runs and 73 RBIs, but committed 35 errors and had a .913 fielding percentage. Defensive numbers notwithstanding, Garner received a September call-up to the A's, who were on their way to repeating as World Series champions. He appeared in nine games for Oakland, and went 0-for-5 at the plate with three strikeouts.

With Sal Bando as the team's regular third baseman, the A's weren't in any hurry to bring Garner up, so he returned to Tucson for another season in 1974. That season turned out to be frustrating for Garner. He was doing well in Tucson; he hit .330 in 96 games. However, in two stints with the parent club, he got into only 30 games, mainly as a defensive replacement. He hit a meager .179 in 28 at-bats and spent a lot of time on the bench.

With an incumbent at third and poor statistics to show for his time in the majors, Garner didn't have a lot to be optimistic about as spring training 1975 rolled around. Then, on March 6, 1975, the A's cut longtime second baseman Dick Green from their roster and Garner, who hadn't played second base since his university days five years earlier, was slotted into the position.

"I haven't seen anything look tough for him in the drills," said A's manager Alvin Dark. "We'll just have to see what happens when the buffaloes come toward him at second base."[1]

As it happened, Garner handled the buffaloes and any other wildlife that came his way quite well. By midseason it was clear that he could not only make the plays around second base, but that he was also a much better hitter than Green.

"I thought Phil would have trouble at the beginning of the season but he didn't," said Bando. "He's aggressive at the plate and in the field. He's a good ballplayer — a good, gutty ballplayer."[2]

The "good, gutty ballplayer" helped the A's overcome the loss of staff ace Catfish Hunter and win a fifth consecutive American League West title. Overall, Garner hit .246 with six home runs and 30 RBIs. Despite the plaudits he was receiving, he still had to improve on defense, as he led the league in errors with 26.

By 1976 A's owner Charlie Finley was in full dismantle mode as he began getting rid of the players from his dynasty teams. He traded Reggie Jackson, Ken Holtzman, and minor leaguer Bill VanBommell to Baltimore for Don Baylor, Mike Torrez, and Paul Mitchell. The A's nonetheless remained competitive, finishing in second place in the AL West with an 87-74 record under new manager Chuck Tanner. Garner's offensive numbers improved; he hit .261, with eight home runs and 74 runs batted in. He also displayed good speed by stealing 35 bases. His defense was a little better, as he cut his errors to 22, but that was still second-highest in the leagues. Overall, Garner played well enough to be selected to the American League All-Star team.

Finley continued divesting the A's of their good players prior to the 1977 season. Garner was fortunate to be one of them, as he was part of a trade that saw him go to the Pittsburgh Pirates with Chris Batton and Tommy Helms for Tony Armas, Doug Bair, Dave Giusti, Rick Langford, Doc Medich, and Mitchell Page. Garner contributed to the 96-66 Bucs, now led by Tanner, instead of languishing with the 63-98 A's. His numbers were similar to those of the previous season. He hit .260, showed more power with 17 home runs, drove in 77 runs, and stole 32 bases. He also showed flexibility on defense, for while he played primarily at third base (107 games), he also saw action at second base (50 games) and shortstop (12 games). None of his defensive statistics, good or bad, were among the league leaders.

Garner's offensive numbers dipped slightly in 1978. He hit .261, but his home runs (10), RBIs (66), and stolen bases (27) were all down from the previous season, although he had a career-high .441 slugging percentage. Two of those home runs made baseball history.

On September 14 Garner hit a grand slam, the first of his major-league career, in a 7-4 Pirate win over the St. Louis Cardinals. Having quickly acquired a taste for grand salami, he hit another one the very next night in a 6-1 win over the Montreal Expos. It marked only the second time in National League history, and the eighth time in major-league history, that a player hit grand slams in consecutive games. The only previous National Leaguer to do it was James Sheckard of the Brooklyn Dodgers in 1901.

"I feel good I did it," Garner said after the second one, "but I wasn't trying to do that … when I went up there. At the time I was just glad we got a four-run lead out of it."[3]

Defensively, Garner split his time primarily between second and third, playing at each position in 81 games (as well as playing shortstop in four games). Perhaps the shifting of positions hurt his defense, because he ended up fourth in the league in total errors commit-

WHEN POPS LED THE FAMILY

(The Pirates) took Garner, an All-Star second baseman in the American League and stationed him at third. But since then, because of various injuries, Garner has played third, shortstop and second base for the Pirates. He figures the switching does have a little effect on his overall performance, but dismisses (the effects) by saying it's the mark of a professional to adjust.[4]

Somebody in Pirates management must have agreed with the article, because the team allowed incumbent second baseman Rennie Stennett to leave via free agency after the 1979 season and handed Garner the keys to the keystone sack. In 1980 Garner played in 151 games at second base and responded with another All-Star season. His batting average dropped to .259 and his home run total dropped to five, but he drove in 58 runs and stole 32 bases. Despite not having to make the adjustments that come with switching positions, he led the National League in errors by a second basemen with 21, although he also led the league in assists (499) and double plays turned (116) at his position. He had a hit, scored a run, and stole a base in the All-Star Game as well.

ted, with 28. Garry Templeton of the Cardinals led the league with 40.

Even Pittsburghers who hate disco love the song "We Are Family"—the anthem of the 1979 Pirates that rode the team's atmosphere and Willie Stargell's leadership to a World Series victory over the Baltimore Orioles.

Garner had arrived in Oakland too late to participate in any of the A's' ring ceremonies, but he played an important role in Pittsburgh's drive to the title. He had career highs in batting average (.293), hits (161), and on-base percentage (.359), and tied his career high in slugging (.441).

Garner also performed well under playoff pressure. He got five hits in 12 at-bats in the National League Championship Series with a triple, a home run, an RBI, and four runs scored. He batted .500 in the World Series with 12 hits in 24 at-bats, five RBIs, and four runs scored.

An Associated Press article on Garner just before the 1979 season illustrated what kind of ballplayer he was.

Garner's 1981 season was an odd one. His offensive numbers dropped significantly that season, yet he made the All-Star team again. He also found himself with a new team; the Pirates traded him to Houston as he was about to become a free agent and contract negotiations with the Pirates were proving fruitless. Shoulder surgery in April 1981 had also hampered Garner defensively.

The Astros desperately needed help at second base. Incumbent Joe Morgan was injured, and the team had had more auditions than a Broadway chorus for an adequate replacement. Garner arrived on August 31, just in time to qualify for the Astros' post-season roster, in return for Johnny Ray and two players to be named later.

For the year, Garner hit only .248, with one home run and 26 RBIs. In the National League Division Series loss to Los Angeles, he had two singles in 18 at-bats.

Astros general manager Al Rosen was determined to sign Garner after the 1981 season and he succeeded, getting Garner's signature on a three-year, $1.85 million contract, plus a club option. Perhaps having the security of a contract helped Garner relax, because in 1982 he rebounded from his poor 1981 numbers. Playing primarily at second base, he hit .274 with 13 home runs and a career-high 83 RBIs. He stole 24 bases.

An oddity of his 1982 season was his performance against the Pirates. The Astros won nine of 12 games against the Bucs, and while Garner batted only .191, he made those hits count, by driving in 11 runs and having two game-winning hits.

The 1983 Astros overcame a 0-9 start to remain competitive in the National League West, finishing in third place with an 85-77 record, six games behind division champion Los Angeles. According to Garner, the team never let adversity stop them.

"These guys just don't face reality," Garner said. "When we were 0-9, these guys weren't thinking whether we would ever win a game. Everybody felt like we were fixing to run off a string of wins at any time."[5]

Garner's batting average for the year had fallen to .238, but he still had good production with 14 home runs and 79 RBIs. And while the hits didn't keep on coming, the errors did. Having returned to third base because incumbent Art Howe was out all season due to injury, Garner finished second in errors among National Leaguers at the position with 24.

It's hard to say whether Garner felt as if he was living in George Orwell's *1984* during the 1984 season, but he definitely wasn't happy. The scrappy player, who had earned the nickname Scrap Iron for being a tough, gritty, sometimes brawling ballplayer, spent the 1984 season either on the bench or platooning at third base with Denny Walling.

"You remember Phil Garner," wrote Bob Hertzel in the *Pittsburgh Press*. "'Scrap Iron' they called him when he was here (Pittsburgh). In Houston, though, it's been more like 'Scrap Heap.'"[6]

He wanted to be traded but wasn't, and spent the entire season in Houston. It didn't help that team owner John McMullen said that other teams weren't "beating the doors down to get Phil Garner."[7]

Not surprisingly, Garner's production fell as a result. His batting average was a respectable .278, in 128 games, but he hit only four home runs and had 45 RBIs.

Considering Garner's subpar numbers and what McMullen said, it's surprising that the Astros exercised their option on him for 1985, but they did. Originally the plan was to have Garner and Walling platoon again, but Walling got off to a blazing start, batting .382 in April and finishing the month with an 11-game hitting streak. Walling therefore was moved to first base and Garner became the everyday third baseman for all or part of 123 Astros games that year. At the plate he hit .268, with six home runs and 51 runs batted in. No longer the speedster he once was, he stole only four bases and was caught stealing four times.

During the 1986 season, Garner achieved a personal milestone and the Astros had a highly successful season. On June 14 he not only hit his 100th career home run, but he did it in style, belting a grand slam that proved the difference in a 7-3 victory over the Giants. It was his first grand slam since the back-to-back clouts in 1978. The achievement was a bright spot in a campaign in which Garner was reduced to a part-time role, playing in only 107 games, many of them as a pinch-hitter. In 347 at-bats (his lowest total since the strike-shortened 1981 season), he hit .265 with nine homers and 41 runs batted in. His 37-year-old legs managed to steal 12 bases as Astros manager Hal Lanier brought the speed game to the team's offense. That approach helped the Astros go 96-66 and win the National League West crown.

Houston played the New York Mets, a team that won 108 games, in the National League Championship Series, and put up a mighty struggle before losing the series in six games. Garner had two hits in nine at-bats during the series, with a double and two RBIs.

Garner's career wound down in 1987 and 1988. He was traded from the Astros to the Los Angeles Dodgers on June 19, 1987, and was a part-time player for both teams, hitting .206 for the season with five home runs and 23 RBIs. He signed with the San Francisco Giants for 1988 and although he didn't play much, he did live up to his Scrap Iron nickname. After having back surgery in April to repair two discs, he was able to come back when the Giants expanded their roster in September. He played his last game October 2, 1988, and got a base on balls as a pinch-hitter. It almost seems appropriate that Garner's last out came when he tried to steal second.

Garner wasn't unemployed very long. Art Howe hired him as a first-base coach when Howe became Astros manager for the 1989 season, and he stayed with the team for three years. He got his first managerial post with the Milwaukee Brewers in 1992 and guided them to a 92-70 record, four games behind the eventual world champion Toronto Blue Jays. Garner remained Brewers manager until August 1999, but never again achieved the same level of success that he had that first season. In fact, his Milwaukee teams never played .500 baseball after 1992. In eight years, his overall record was 563-617 (.477).

Garner took the helm of the Tigers in 2000, and after two losing seasons, he was fired six games into the 2002 campaign. His record in Detroit was 145-185 (.439).

In July 2004 Garner replaced Jimy Williams as manager of the Astros. Houston was only a .500 team under Williams at 44-44, but the team responded well under Garner, going 48-26 the rest of the way and finishing second in the NL Central with a 92-70 record, 13 games behind St. Louis. A seven-game winning streak to close out the regular season proved a harbinger of things to come. The Astros made the NL playoffs as the wild-card team, and after defeating the Braves in five games in the NLDS, they took the NLCS to seven games before losing to the Cardinals.

The Astros repeated as the National League wild-card team in 2005 with an 89-73 record. It was déjà vu all over again as they defeated the Braves three games to one in the NLDS, and once again faced the Cardinals, who had won 100 games, in the NLCS. This time they were not to be denied as Roy Oswalt, the series MVP, pitched seven strong innings in Game Six, leading the Astros to a 5-1 win and the franchise's first-ever trip to the World Series.

Unfortunately for Garner and the Astros, they were victims of destiny. Their opponents in the Series that year were the Chicago White Sox, who last appeared in the fall classic in 1959, three years before the Houston franchise had even played one game. The White Sox swept the Astros in four straight, to win their first championship since the doughboys went to fight in World War I in 1917.

After an 82-80 record in 2006, the Astros fired Garner during the 2007 season after he compiled a 58-73 record in 131 games. Garner then entered the oil and gas business before coming full circle and joining his first team, the Oakland A's, as a special adviser in 2011.

No scrap heap for Scrap Iron.

SOURCES

Baseball-reference.com

fs.ncaa.org

mapquest.ca

news.google.com

paperofrecord.hypernet.ca.

NOTES

1. Ron Bergman, "A's Ticket Greenhorn Gardner for Green's Job," *The Sporting News,* March 29, 1975.
2. Ron Bergman, "Garner Gleans 'Green' Laurels as A's Rookie," *The Sporting News,* July 26, 1975.
3. "Garner Makes Record Books," *Frederick* (Oklahoma) *Daily Leader,* September 17, 1978.
4. Associated Press, "Garner, Parker Keep Bucs On Their Toes," *Reading* (Pennsylvania) *Eagle,* April 4, 1979.
5. Associated Press, "Astros still fighting for pennant," *Bonham* (Texas) *Daily Favorite,* September 15, 1983.
6. Bob Hertzel, "Like old times as Garner comes through at Three Rivers," *Pittsburgh Press,* August 20, 1984.
7. Ibid.

Gary Hargis

By Michael Jaffe

IMMORTALIZED IN THE MOVIE *Field of Dreams*, Archibald "Moonlight" Graham stands as the embodiment of the soul of a baseball player. His dream to simply play in at least one major-league baseball game and forever etch his name into the annals of baseball history is one shared by baseball players and fans alike. Graham took over in right field for the New York Giants during the last two innings of a game against Brooklyn on June 29, 1905, and never played again in the major leagues. Gary Hargis stands as a modern-day Moonlight Graham, carving his name in the baseball annals forever in 1979.

Gary Lynn Hargis was born on November 2, 1956, in Minneapolis to Harold Lynn and Patricia Lorraine (Orbeck) Hargis. Harold was an Air Force veteran of the Korean War. The family moved in 1971 to Lompoc, California, where he worked as a safety specialist for several nuclear-reactor industry companies. Gary Hargis grew up with four sisters. He excelled in baseball at Cabrillo High School in Lompoc. In his senior season, the Cabrillo team went 22-6.

In the star-studded 1974 amateur draft, the Pittsburgh Pirates selected the 17-year-old infielder Hargis in the second round. (In the first round, a Cabrillo High teammate, outfielder Kevin Drake, was selected by the Houston Astros.)

After signing a contract for a bonus described as "enough to buy a new car,"[1] Hargis was assigned to the Gulf Coast League Pirates of the Rookie League where he played in one game with one plate appearance. Shortly he was re-assigned to the Niagara Falls Pirates of the short-season New York-Penn League. In 62 games, Hargis batted .295 with 2 homers and 28 RBIs at shortstop. He demonstrated good speed by stealing 20 bases in 23 attempts.

In 1975 Hargis was assigned to the Salem (Virginia) Pirates of the Class-A Carolina League, where he played in 134 games at shortstop and part of one contest at third base. Hargis hit .268 for Salem with 2 home runs, 53 RBIs, and 17 stolen bases. Hargis's fielding was the most telling line in his statistical summary, but not for a very impressive reason: He made 45 errors in 618 chances at shortstop.

The spring of 1976 saw Hargis moving up the minor-league ladder, playing for the Shreveport Captains of the Double-A Texas League. In 130 games playing second base and shortstop, he hit .272 with 3 home runs, 39 RBIs, and 19 stolen bases. He showed considerable improvement defensively, cutting his errors to 17 in 658 chances at the two middle-infield positions.

Hargis reached Triple A in 1977, playing for the Columbus Clippers of the International League. His hitting still showed he was a prototypical weak-hitting utility infielder: .252 in 104 games with 4 home runs and 52 RBIs. On July 24 Hargis notably hit two home runs including a grand slam for six RBIs in a 7-6 victory over Charleston. Not known for his power, Hargis commented, "That's the first time in my life I ever hit two homers in a game—except for Little League."[2] He made 17 errors in 412 chances, predominantly at shortstop, and stole 13 bases.

Hargis returned to Columbus for the 1978 season, and the second season at Triple A seemed to be good for him. Getting used to the pitching at that level, he responded with a .283 batting average, 10 home runs and 45 RBIs in 107 games played at second, third, and shortstop. He made 18 errors in 407 chances. On June 28 Hargis went 6-for-7 in a doubleheader against Rochester. He had lost his regular game bat and was forced to use his batting-practice bat, which was an ounce heavier. He was 6-for-6 in the twin bill until he lined out in his final at-bat of the night. After the season, because of a history of shoulder injuries, Hargis spent time in winter ball working on a low side-arm throwing motion.

In the spring of 1979 the Pirates took a long look at Hargis at their major-league camp. He played in 10 spring games at second base, third base, and shortstop, primarily as a backup to Rennie Stennett. That spring Hargis commented, "I feel like I've spent my time in Triple A. I'd rather sit on the bench in the major leagues than play another year in the minor leagues."[3]

That season the Pirates relocated their Triple-A affiliate to Portland of the Pacific Coast League. Hargis was assigned once more to Triple A. In the first inning of his first PCL game, he smacked a two run-homer in Portland's 5-4 win over Tacoma. For the season, he hit .277 with 5 home runs and 42 RBIs, and made 11 errors in 464 chances at second and short.

Although his 1979 minor-league numbers were not overwhelming, they were good enough for Hargis to get the call he'd been waiting for. When the rosters expanded in September, the Pittsburgh Pirates, fighting to make the playoffs, called up Hargis.

Hargis's only major-league game was a crucial one. On September 29 the Pirates faced the Chicago Cubs in Pittsburgh. The starting pitchers were Dennis Lamp for the Cubs and future Hall of Famer Bert Blyleven for the Pirates. The Pirates were in first place in the National League East entering the game with a 97-63 record and two games left to play. The Montreal Expos were two games behind the Pirates in the NL East Division with a 94-64 mark, and the Pirates' magic number to clinch a spot in the postseason stood at 2.

The Pirates staked Blyleven to an early lead when Willie Stargell hit a first-inning two-run single and Bill Madlock's sacrifice fly made it 3-0. The Cubs got a run in the fifth. Blyleven was lifted with two outs in the sixth inning after allowing the Cubs to take a 4-3 lead with two doubles, a single, and a walk. The Cubs scored twice more after Blyleven left, and with a 6-3 deficit it seemed that Pittsburgh was in deep trouble. But the resilient Pirates got a run back in the bottom of the sixth and two more to tie the game in the seventh.

The game went on to extra innings. The Cubs took the lead in the top of the 13th, scoring an unearned run on Stargell's throwing error. In the bottom of the 13th, with two outs, shortstop Tim Foli singled off Cubs pitcher Bill Caudill. Pirates manager Chuck Tanner sent Hargis in to run for Foli. The Expos had already defeated the Phillies by this time, so the magic number for the Pirates to clinch a playoff spot remained at 2. Dave Parker's infield hit put Hargis at second with Stargell coming up. Stargell would go on to share the NL MVP award with Keith Hernandez, but this day he struck out to end the game, stranding Hargis at second and Parker at first.

The next day the Pirates clinched the NL East crown as they defeated the Cubs, 5-3, and the Phillies downed the Expos, 2-0. The Pirates went on to sweep Cincinnati in the NLCS and win the World Series in seven games over the Baltimore Orioles. For his efforts, Hargis received a World Series share of $250.

After the 1979 season, Hargis spent time in the instructional league learning to play center field. His history of injuries and a questionable arm for playing shortstop prompted the move. Chuck Tanner had given Hargis high praise in the spring of 1979, saying, "He's a scrappy, tough kid who plays baseball hard. A Phil Garner type."[4]

But when the 1980 Pirates headed north from spring training, it was without Hargis, who was the final player cut from the roster. Sent back to Portland,

he played a few games at shortstop, second base, and third base, but most of his playing time was in the outfield. On May 1 in a 13-3 win over Ogden, Hargis made two outs in an 11-run first inning in which every other Portland player reached base at least once. "I just couldn't believe that I'd made two outs in an inning. I've never done that," Hargis said. "If I'd made all three, I'd never have taken the field on defense."[5] For the season, Hargis hit .278 with 5 home runs and 43 RBIs.

On February 28, 1981, Hargis married Brenda Beach of Santa Barbara, California. That season he split time between Portland and Buffalo of the Double-A Eastern League. Overall he played in 87 games as an infielder and outfielder, batting .272 with 2 home runs and 33 RBIs. It was his final season in Organized Baseball; he and his wife settled down in Southern California. His final minor-league statistics, embracing eight seasons during which he played in 812 games, were a respectable .273 batting average with 33 home runs and 335 RBIs. He stole 88 bases in 112 attempts and made 130 errors, the majority at shortstop.

One can't help but to compare Hargis's major-league career to Moonlight Graham's. Neither player had an official plate appearance but their names will forever be listed in baseball records as major-league players. Asked in 2005 about the comparisons, Hargis said, "You keep thinking, 'Just let me get in one game so my name can get into the book. When you do, it's just like the movie. Your eyes light up, you never want the night to end. You just want to play ball, like you did when you were a kid."[6]

Thanks to Bill Mortell for his assistance and research.

NOTES

1 Charley Feeney, "Playing Games," *Pittsburgh Post-Gazette*, March 8, 1977: 13.

2 "International League Index," *The Sporting News*, August 13, 1977: 33.

3 Ron Cook, "Bill Robinson Finds Bat," *Beaver County Times*, March 28, 1979: B1.

4 Phil Musick, "Scrappy Rookie Hargis Impresses Tanner," *Pittsburgh Post-Gazette*, March 14, 1979: 19.

5 "Portland's Parade," *The Sporting News*, May 24, 1980: 39.

6 AP, "'Moonlight' Graham's One-Game Career Brought Plenty of Fame," Lubbockonline.com, *Lubbock Avalanche Journal*, June 26, 2005.

Grant Jackson

By Maxwell Kates

HE PITCHED 18 SEASONS IN THE MAJOR leagues but for Grant Jackson, it all came down to one inning in the final game ever played in the 1970s. It was familiar territory for the left-hander. Eight years before, the Baltimore Orioles took a lead over the Pittsburgh Pirates in the 1971 World Series, which culminated with Game Seven at Memorial Stadium. Jim Palmer was still pitching for the Orioles, Earl Weaver managing, Frank Robinson back as a coach. In the opposing dugout, Willie Stargell, Manny Sanguillen, and Bruce Kison were holdovers from 1971. Jackson pitched in both contests but unlike any of the other players, he pitched in one Series for each side. He had appeared in relief for the Orioles in 1971. Now he was trying to win the World Series for "the 'Burgh."

The fourth son of Joseph and Luella Jackson's nine children, Grant Dwight Jackson was born on September 28, 1942, in Fostoria, Ohio. In 2005 he told reporter Ron Musselman of the *Toledo Blade* that he retained fond memories of his hometown:

"Fostoria was a great place to grow up. I still go back there quite a few times a year. I have two sisters that still live there. And I help out some with the high school baseball team. ... I enjoy working with the kids."[1] Jackson lettered in football, baseball, and track at Fostoria High School and once fanned 33 batters in a doubleheader at an American Legion tournament.[2] Times were tough, however, for the Jackson family, as they were living on the lower end of the socioeconomic scale:

Joseph Jackson died of a heart attack in 1960, at age 52.[3] Carlos Jackson, Grant's older brother and also his biology teacher, then assumed the role of paternal influence "My dad, Joe ... had the greatest influence on me when I was younger," Grant said. "Those two took me under their wing at a very young age and helped make sure I did things the right way. My dad taught me how to be a man early on ... to keep my nose clean and just keep working hard and things would work out."[4]

Jackson graduated from Fostoria High in 1961 but his grades were too low to qualify for a scholarship to Bowling Green State University.[5] That was when he decided to contact perhaps the most famous of Fostoria's 15,000 residents, Philadelphia Phillies scout Tony Lucadello.[6]

Lucadello was remembered as "a great judge of talent" in his 32 years as a scout for Philadelphia.[7] His pedigree included a virtual All-Star team of Midwestern athletes, including Alex Johnson, Mike Marshall, John Herrnstein, Toby Harrah, Mike Schmidt, and Mickey Morandini, along with Canadians John Upham and Fergie Jenkins.

Lucadello's signing of Jackson was representative of an era when high-school athletes did not retain agents or hold press conferences, but rather relied on the good word of professional organizations. In 1962, the 6-foot, 190-pound Jackson signed for $1,500.[8]

"I signed on a Thursday," Jackson recalled. "On Saturday, Ray Hayworth, who was scouting for the [Milwaukee] Braves, said he was prepared to give me $35,000. I had to tell him I'd already signed."[9] The family needed the money and Jackson could not afford the luxury of waiting two days for an offer he did not know would arrive. Years later, he admitted that "I wish then I could have called the Phillies back and told them I wasn't going to accept their offer."[10]

The 19-year-old Jackson began his professional career at Bakersfield of the then Class-C California League, posting a record of 4-5 (5.79 ERA) in 1962. The league was reclassified to Single A before the next season, and Jackson improved to 12-8 (3.89) in 1963. A Bakersfield teammate, infielder Lou Garvin, tagged him with the nickname Buck.

"I reminded him of a cowboy when I walked to the mound. You know, bow legged, pigeon toed, walking like I was ready to draw a gun."[11] Jackson rose quickly through the Phillies system, to Eugene, Chattanooga, and finally Arkansas (Little Rock), where in 1965 he posted a record of 9-11 with a 3.95 earned-run average.[12]

Fergie Jenkins told how it was for Northern blacks unfamiliar with the racial climate in Little Rock. "Things were tenser, more overt in Arkansas," he said. "One day we came out of the ballpark and found the car covered with signs and scrawls on the windows." The messages were full of obscenities and racial invective. Position players like Dick Allen took the most abuse and was, for example, booed mercilessly when he misjudged a fly ball that landed for a double. Allen admitted that "these country hicks are getting me down, I can't stand it."[13]

Jackson's tenure in Arkansas did not last long. He was called up to Philadelphia on September 1 when the rosters expanded and pitched in his first major-league game two days later in Cincinnati. His baptism at Crosley Field served as proof that he was now pitching in a higher league.

The Phillies were leading, 6-3, with two Reds runners on base and nobody out in the bottom of the fifth. Jackson was summoned to relieve Ray Culp, and struck out pinch-hitter Tony Perez and Deron Johnson on six pitches. Then he faced Frank Robinson. Ahead in the count 2-and-0, Robinson slammed the pitch over the emblematic Crosley Field scoreboard, into "Hudepohl Heaven" and toward Interstate 75, for a three-run homer. The Reds won 16-7 and Jackson was tagged with the loss.[14] Despite the unpleasant initiation by Frank Robinson, the Phillies management retained their confidence in Jackson's potential. He won his first game later in the month in relief, and struck out 11 Mets in nine innings while yielding one run during a no-decision start in the season finale. Pitching coach Al Widmar was convinced he was "headed for stardom."[15]

Jackson had two short relief outings in April 1966, and was returned to the Pacific Coast League after Philadelphia acquired a pair of veteran starting pitchers from the Chicago Cubs. Fortunately for him, the Phillies had moved their Triple-A affiliate from Little Rock to San Diego. He was recalled again in September, but did not appear in the final month for the fourth-place club. Still, in 1967 he was in the major leagues to stay. By now the Phillies were an aging team and Jackson had hoped there would be room in the rotation for a young left-hander to complement Jim Bunning, Chris Short, Larry Jackson, and Ray Culp. Jackson did not like relief work and, according to Allen Lewis of the *Philadelphia Inquirer*, he "seldom did well coming out of the bullpen."[16] At the end of the 1968 season, his lifetime record was 4-10. The National League expanded to include two new teams and Jackson was disappointed that neither San Diego nor Montreal claimed him in the expansion draft. He wanted the opportunity to prove himself as a starting pitcher and was not getting it in Philadelphia.

Gene Mauch was fired as the Phillies' skipper two months into the '68 campaign. Under new manager Bob Skinner, Jackson was able to correct his delivery and improve as a pitcher. Unlike many young pitchers, often accused of pitching too quickly, Jackson's workmanship was considered too slow and deliberate.

"We speeded him up on purpose," said Skinner. "We want him to pitch fast. Before when he took his time, he went through check points instead of falling into a rhythm."[17] Widmar agreed, observing that Jackson "was trying to make every pitch a masterpiece."[18] As the 1969 Phillies headed north from Clearwater, Jackson was penciled as the fifth starter in the rotation. The Phillies had quickly sunk to the bottom of the National League East but defeated Pittsburgh 8-1 on April 12 to notch their first win of the season, with Jackson on the mound. He saved two of his better starts for the Cardinals, the defending National League champions, yielding only an unearned run on April 25 and shutting out St. Louis on May 4. Skinner was pleased with his pupil's progress:

"He doesn't pitch any faster than Bob Gibson. It's just that he's taking a completely different approach to pitching. He's staying within himself." Widmar concurred that Jackson "changed his delivery, the way he grips the ball, and he's concentrating much better. We've got him throwing a fastball that sinks now."[19] Augmenting the sinking fastball in his repertoire were a slider, curveball, and changeup.[20] He called his predominant pitch "a jive fastball," which he described as "a fastball, hit it if you can catch up with it."[21]

Jackson's newfound poise earned him a berth as the Phillies' representative at the 1969 All-Star Game in Washington. In what would be the only All-Star selection of his career, Jackson did not appear in the NL's 9-3 victory at RFK Stadium. Despite a season record of 14-18, Jackson had earned the respect of both his coaches and his peers.

"He makes a lot of good pitches now and he doesn't waste any time," observed Phillies catcher Mike Ryan. "Get it and throw it, that's the way he likes to pitch. We used the simplest signs when he's pitching so as not to slow him down."[22] Jackson's personal life was developing as well. While playing winter baseball in Puerto Rico, he met and married his wife, Milagros. Grant and Milagros had three children and lived year-round in Puerto Rico for much of his playing career.

Entering the 1970 season, the Phillies were rebuilding with Frank Lucchesi now as their manager. Jackson's record in 1970 regressed to 5-15 with a 5.29 earned-run average. Frustrated at the lack of progress of his club, Jackson finally received his wish on December 16, 1970, when the Phillies traded him along with utilityman Jim Hutto and outfielder Sam Parrilla to the defending World Series champion Baltimore Orioles for outfielder and prized prospect Roger Freed. Never again would he post a losing record in the major leagues.

Jackson had hoped to join the Orioles rotation as the fifth starter but in a season when Dave McNally, Jim Palmer, Mike Cuellar, and Pat Dobson each won 20 games, he was limited to nine starts with the 1971 Orioles.[23] Under the tutelage of manager Earl Weaver and pitching coach George Bamberger, Jackson began to appreciate his role as a left-handed relief specialist.

"I like to start," he told Lou Hatter of the *Baltimore Sun*. "That's where the money is. ... On the other hand, working out of the bullpen you've got to have a whole lot of saves, keep the earned-run average low, and slip in a few wins to get a big contract."[24] Though he did not register any saves in 1971, Jackson posted a record of 4-3 with a 3.13 ERA as the Orioles secured their third consecutive berth in the World Series. He pitched two-thirds of an inning in Game Four; both the game and the Series were 4-3 losses to the Pittsburgh Pirates.

It was during the 1972 season that Jackson entered his prime. After the All-Star break he won one and saved four while surrendering only four earned runs in 17 appearances. His success continued into 1973, when his season totals were nine saves, a 1.90 earned-run average, and an undefeated record of 8-0.[25] As the Orioles hosted the Chicago White Sox on June 5, Jackson was credited with the decision in a comeback victory. The following night, Jackson got the save as the Orioles won again. Later that month, he contributed 5⅔ innings, allowing just one hit in a 16-inning marathon victory over the Texas Rangers. In this drawn-out affair, he retired the last 12 batters he faced. This outing occurred during a stretch in which Jackson hurled 14 straight scoreless innings bringing his ERA down to 1.19. From June 5 to 9, Jackson pitched in four of Baltimore's five games:

"When he pitched the fourth [time]," observed Bamberger, "I felt he threw the ball better than in any of the three previous games. ... That's what makes Buck such an ideal bullpen man."[26] Jackson credited an exercise regimen of running, shagging fly balls, and playing "flip" toward his success, adding, "Call the bullpen, I'm ready! Just give me the ball!"[27]

In 1974 Jackson contributed a 6-4 record with 12 saves as the Orioles made their fifth postseason appearance in six years. His teammates noted that he was beginning to believe in himself: "Just being able to throw strikes in any situation without being nervous is the key to relief pitching. I don't get upset easy. I try to keep everything easy. I don't feel any pressure going in there."[28]

In 1976 free agency arrived and rumors circulated that club owner Jerold Hoffberger was selling the Orioles. The order of the day was to cut payroll. Following his third consecutive subpar outing on June 13, Jackson had a 1-1 record with a 5.12 ERA for Baltimore. At the trading deadline on June 15, impending free-agent pitchers Doyle Alexander and Ken Holtzman were traded to the first-place New York Yankees for pitchers Rudy May, Tippy Martinez,

Scott McGregor, and Dave Pagan, and catcher Rick Dempsey. Joining Alexander and Holtzman in the Bronx were catcher Elrod Hendricks and pitcher Grant Jackson. Yankees owner George Steinbrenner was jubilant about the trade, conveying to manager Billy Martin that "this trade just won you a pennant" and "you now have the best team on paper, and now you're just a push-button manager."[29]

The 1976 Yankees did, in fact, win their first American League pennant since 1964. Jackson contributed a record of 6-0 with an earned-run average of 1.69.[30] But his postseason record was not up to his usual standards, as he surrendered five earned runs between the American League Championship Series and the World Series.

In November 1976 the Seattle Mariners "surprised everybody" by selecting Jackson in the expansion draft.[31] Jackson never pitched an inning for Seattle; he was traded to Pittsburgh in December. The Pirates had won division titles in five of the previous seven years which translated into only one world championship. Competing with the Steelers' NFL dynasty, the Pirates drew sparse crowds to cavernous Three Rivers Stadium. It was clear to new general manager Harding Peterson that second place was no longer good enough for the Pirates fans.

The Pirates boasted an abundant farm system that included Tony Armas, Al Holland, Rick Langford, Mitchell Page, Craig Reynolds, Jimmy Sexton, and Ed Whitson—players who would have kept the Pirates in contention well into the 1980s. Peterson had no objection to sacrificing the future in order to win immediately. The same day as the expansion draft, he dealt catcher Manny Sanguillen and $100,000 to the Oakland A's for manager Chuck Tanner. Slugging outfielder Richie Zisk was traded to the White Sox for Rich "Goose" Gossage and Terry Forster—relievers who had pitched for Tanner in Chicago. In March 1977, a nine-player deal with Oakland landed infielder Phil Garner, while Reynolds and Sexton were dispatched to Seattle for Jackson. Joining a lineup that boasted sluggers Willie Stargell, Al Oliver, Ed Ott, and Dave Parker along with speedsters Omar Moreno, Bill Robinson, and Frank Taveras, the Pirates in 1977

became known as "lumber and lightning." Stargell felt that Tanner's influence would bolster attendance and put the Pirates over the top in the standings:

"Chuck's optimistic outlook on life and enthusiastic personality bred life on our club. He was also a very innovative leader who rarely managed by the book. He created whatever results a situation necessitated, whatever way possible."[32]

Tanner allowed his pitchers to bat after they had entered the game as a reliever. As Jackson himself remembered, "I took pride in knowing how to play the game, not just pitch. When you run the bases, you've got to run with your eyes wide open so you can see what's going on around and you know what to do. If you know the game, then you know how to run the bases and you can help the team in another way."[33]

Clad in their new disco-influenced black and gold attire, the Pirates raced toward the divisional lead in April and May before settling once again for second place. As Jackson remembered, it was a special season when the Pirates "had the best bullpen in baseball. Remember Goose Gossage? Terry Forster? [Kent Tekulve] and myself? All of baseball was saying if you got past the fifth inning and we were winning, you lost."[34] Indeed, the Pirates and their bullpen were credited with 34 wins and 39 saves in 1977. However, for the second year in a row, they finished in second place behind Philadelphia.

With Forster's departure to the Los Angeles Dodgers as a free agent, Jackson became Chuck Tanner's left-handed specialist in the bullpen. The Pirates fine-tuned their roster by trading the popular veteran outfielder Oliver to the Texas Rangers for starting pitcher Bert Blyleven and first baseman-outfielder John Milner in a four-team transaction during the winter meetings in December 1977. Sanguillen was reacquired from Oakland while hard-throwing pitcher Don Robinson was promoted from the minor leagues. Despite another fine season by Jackson out of the bullpen, the Pirates finished once again in second place, once again behind Philadelphia. The fans responded by staying home as the Pirates drew fewer than one million in 1978.

Additional roster changes were in order for 1979. Pitcher Jerry Reuss was traded to the Los Angeles Dodgers for Rick Rhoden while Rhoden's teammate Lee Lacy joined him in Pittsburgh as a free agent. Meanwhile, reliever Enrique Romo was picked up in a deal with Seattle. Early in the season, the Pirates swapped shortstops with the Mets, sending Taveras to New York for Tim Foli. The Pirates responded by sinking to the bottom of their division, posting a 7-11 record by the end of April. What followed exemplified why Willie Stargell was the National League's co-Most Valuable Player in 1979, both on and off the field:

"I kicked all nonplaying personnel out of the clubhouse.... My speech was simple. I reminded the guys that our slow start in '78 had cost us the pennant. I told them to become more consistent—never too high, never too low. I told them to keep their minds in the gray area in between. Then I told them to just go out and play some good old country baseball, and most of all, to have fun."[35]

True to the message of their theme song, "We Are Family," the Pirates jelled as team with Stargell as the "Pops." They went on to win 16 of their next 26 and vaulted into the pennant race by mid-July. Grant Jackson remained confident that he could get anyone out, no matter which side of the plate they faced.[36] In 72 appearances, he went 8-5 with 14 saves and an earned-run average of 2.96.[37] Once the Pirates returned to contention, it was not the Phillies but the Montreal Expos who gave them the most trouble. Jackson proved central to a critical moment of the season for both clubs.

After the Pirates acquired Bill Madlock in a blockbuster deal with the San Francisco Giants, the Expos, in the words of general manager John McHale, "had to counter" by trading for Rusty Staub.[38] A folk hero in the early years of the franchise, Staub made his first plate appearance in Montreal as a pinch-hitter on July 27. A sellout crowd of 59,260 gave Staub the most raucous standing ovation ever awarded to an Expos player.[39] With the Pirates ahead 5-4, two outs and a runner on in the eighth inning of the first game of a twi-night doubleheader, Staub faced Jackson amid a backdrop of deafening noise. Proving his statement that nothing ever bothered him, Jackson enticed Staub to slap an easy popup to Dave Parker in right field to end the inning. Pittsburgh won three games out of four in Montreal, making a statement that their early-season futility was little more than an aberration.

Pittsburgh and Montreal continued to fight a tough battle until the final day of the season when the Jolly Roger was raised over Three Rivers Stadium. Tanner continued to rely heavily on relievers Jackson, Tekulve, and Romo during the postseason after they combined for 250 regular season appearances. The Pirates swept Cincinnati in the best-of-five NLCS, thanks in part to Jackson's perfect 10th inning in Game One. As the Pirates broke the tie in the bottom half of the inning, Jackson was credited with a 5-2 victory.[40] His biggest fan it, would seem, was closer Kent Tekulve, who credited Jackson with "doing a helluva job" all season, especially early on when the Rubber Band Man was struggling.[41]

The 1979 World Series would be Jackson's third of the decade, each with a different team. After Bruce Kison lit up the scoreboard with Orioles in Game One by surrendering five runs in the first inning, Jackson pitched a scoreless ninth as part of an impressive bullpen effort, albeit a losing one.[42] "We lost the first game in that Series 5-4 but we weren't worried. I remember breaking out the crabs and beer and partying to Sister Sledge.'"[43]

Jackson pitched again in Games Three and Four, extinguishing rallies both times before the Pirates received a double dose of "Oriole Magic." Baltimore was now one game away from winning the World Series. "Even after we got down 3-1 in the Series, it bothered our fans but it didn't bother us," Jackson said. "We knew we had a better team than the Orioles."[44]

When it mattered most, Jackson rose to the occasion. The Pirates were down 1-0 in Game Seven when he was summoned from the bullpen in the fifth inning to replace reliever Don Robinson. With two on and two outs, Jackson retired Al Bumbry on a foul pop to Madlock to end the scoring threat. In the sixth and seventh, Jackson retired every hitter he faced. Meanwhile, Willie Stargell did what team leaders are supposed to do in Game Seven of the World Series, as "Pops" put Pittsburgh ahead with a two-run homer in the sixth inning. The Pirates scored two insurance runs in the ninth as Tekulve earned a save in the bottom half of the inning. The Pirates were world champions.[45]

"Winning Game [Seven] of the 1979 World Series was my biggest thrill in baseball, no doubt. People from that era here in Pittsburgh still remember it like it was yesterday," Jackson said.[46] He credited the team for its collective success but believed that the championship would have remained elusive without its captain: "Willie Stargell was the star of our team. He was a great leader, on and off the field. He was one of the best players and best teammates I ever came into contact with. The day he died was one of the sorriest days of my life."[47]

For his part, Jackson was impeccable in relief during the '79 postseason. Winning two and losing none, he surrendered no runs and two hits in 6⅔ innings. The strongest accolades he earned were once again from Tekulve: "In 1979, this guy was my setup man, so they say. I didn't look at it that way. He was my co-closer. Setup guys don't save 14 games. ... When you're playing a major league baseball season, the whole idea when you go to spring training is you want to play in the last game of the season and you want to win that last game of the season because that means you are going to be the world champions. This guy won the last game of the season and made us world champions."[48]

Even during the offseason, the Pirates remained a "family." Jackson, by now living year-round in Pittsburgh, remembered attending Steelers games with Stargell, Parker, and Madlock in the offseason. "We'd sit up at the very top of the stadium. When it got too cold, we'd go down to the Allegheny Club and we'd sit in there with John Henry Johnson and just talk. The game would be over and we'd still be in there talking about things."[49]

The Pirates' celebration was short-lived. Despite a successful record of 8-4 on Jackson's part, the team fell to third place in 1980 before plummeting to last place in the second half of the strike-shortened 1981 season. Jackson was sent in a cash deal to the Expos as the rosters expanded in September.[50] Though he struggled in Montreal, he was rewarded by a Pittsburgh teammate once the season was over. After Bill Madlock won the batting title, "he gave [coach] Joe Lonnett and myself each $5,000 because we would throw extra batting practice for him all the time during the season."[51]

In March 1982, Jackson was traded once again, to the Kansas City Royals for Ken Phelps.[52] Posting a record of 3-1 with a 5.17 ERA in 20 appearances, Jackson was released at the All-Star break. He returned to Pittsburgh for one final game before retiring as a player. His career totals showed a record of 86-75 with 79 saves and an earned-run average of 3.46.[53]

The next chapter of Jackson's career consisted of two decades as a coach in the major and minor leagues. In 1983 he became the Pirates' bullpen coach, remaining as long as Chuck Tanner was the manager, until 1985. In 1994 he joined former Orioles teammate Davey Johnson in Cincinnati as the Reds bullpen coach. In between, he accepted minor-league assignments with the Cubs, Reds, and Orioles organizations. Asked if he tried to instill a philosophy among young pitchers, Jackson replied, "I tell them the good ones put into action what they have worked on and then make it work in games. I tell them to take some pride in what they do."[54]

Did Jackson ever consider managing? "No" was his quick reply. "When you do that, you get gray hair, you get fat, and you start smoking. Lloyd [McClendon] doesn't have any gray hair because he's smart. He cuts it all off so you can't tell."[55]

Following the 2002 season as pitching coach for the Triple-A Rochester Red Wings, Jackson decided to retire from baseball. In 2004 he was part of the inaugural class of the Fostoria High School Hall of Fame. By 2005 he had as many grandchildren as are needed to field a team.[56] The sandlot where he played as a child in Fostoria was renamed Grant Jackson Field in his honor. Not one to dwell on his individual accomplishments, Jackson said, "I would only focus on what the team did but if the team did well, then that meant everyone on the team was having some success. If someone asks me what my stats were, I tell them to talk to my wife. She knows all of that stuff much better than I do. All I know is, I signed my contract in 1962 and I retired in 2002. I had a lot of fun in between and it was all because of baseball."[57]

NOTES

1. Ron Musselman, "Baseball Very Good to Jackson," *Toledo Blade*, June 19, 2005.
2. Musselman.
3. "Seizure Fatal to Joseph Jackson," *Findlay* (Ohio) *Republican-Courier*, June 20, 1960: 15.
4. Ibid.
5. Musselman.
6. 1960 US Census.
7. Fergie Jenkins, and Lew Freedman, *Fergie: My Life from the Cubs to Cooperstown* (Chicago: Triumph Books, 2009), 34.
8. Allen Lewis, "Rookie Jackson Front Runner in Race for Phil Starter Berth," *The Sporting News*, April 9, 1966: 24.
9. Ibid.
10. Musselman.
11. Doug Brown, "Jackson a Stone Wall as Oriole Fireman," *The Sporting News*, January 18, 1975: 50.
12. Lewis, "Rookie Jackson."
13. Jenkins, 54-55.
14. Lewis, "Rookie Jackson."
15. Ibid.
16. Allen Lewis, "Speed-Up on Hill Puffs Out Jackson's Victory Bag," The Sporting News, May 24, 1969: 21.
17. Ibid.
18. Ibid.
19. Ibid.
20. Bill Ranier and David Finoli, *When the Bucs Won It All: The 1979 World Champion Pittsburgh Pirates* (Jefferson, North Carolina: McFarland, 2005), 175.
21. Brown.
22. Allen Lewis, "Speed-Up on Hill Puffs Out Jackson's Victory Bag."
23. Brown.
24. Lou Hatter, "Jackson Shelves Curve to Outflank Bird Foes," *The Sporting News*, July 7, 1973: 15.
25. Ranier, 174.
26. Hatter.
27. Ibid.
28. Brown.
29. Dan Epstein, *Stars and Strikes: Baseball and America in the Bicentennial Summer of '76* (New York: Thomas Dunne Books, 2014), 175.
30. Ranier, 175.
31. Jack Lang, "Youth Has Its Fling in A.L. Expansion Draft," *The Sporting News*, November 20, 1976: 34.
32. Willie Stargell and Tom Bird, *Willie Stargell: An Autobiography* (New York: Harper & Row, 1984), 180.
33. Rich Emert, "Where Are They Now? Grant Jackson," *Pittsburgh Post-Gazette*, August 29, 2002.
34. Mike Mastovich, "Talking Baseball: Ex-Big Leaguers Entertain AAABA Crowd," *Johnstown* (Pennsylvania) *Tribune-Democrat*, August 10, 2009.
35. Stargell, 192.
36. Lou Sahadi, *The Pirates* (Markham, Ontario: Fitzhenry & Whiteside Ltd., 1980), 129.
37. Ranier, 176.
38. Maxwell Kates, "The Expos Emerge," in *Elysian Fields Quarterly*, Vol. 23, No.4, 2006, Tom Goldstein, ed., 49.
39. Alain Usereau, *The Expos In Their Prime: The Short-Lived Glory of Montreal's Team, 1977-1984* (Jefferson, North Carolina: McFarland, 2013), 58.
40. Ranier, 176.
41. Sahadi, 129.
42. Ranier, 63.
43. Musselman.

THE 1979 PITTSBURGH PIRATES

44 Ibid.

45 Ranier, 83-87.

46 Musselman.

47 Ibid.

48 Mastovich.

49 Emert.

50 Usereau, 126.

51 Emert.

52 Usereau, 153.

53 Emert.

54 Ibid.

55 Ibid.

56 Musselman.

57 Ibid.

Bruce Kison

By Gregory H. Wolf

WHEN WILD-EYED ROOKIE RIGHT-HAND-ed pitcher Bruce Kison was thrust into relief with two outs in the first inning of Game Four of the 1971 World Series against the overwhelmingly favored Baltimore Orioles, the Pirates were in a three-run hole and in danger of losing their third game of the Series with just one victory. But with the largest crowd ever to watch a baseball game in Pittsburgh (51,378) crammed into Three Rivers Stadium to witness the first night game in World Series history, the calm and collected Kison tossed 6⅓ scoreless innings, yielding just one hit. He kept the Orioles off balance with inside fastballs and sliders from his whip-like side-arm delivery, but set a World Series record by hitting three batters. His command of the plate and aggressive play, including barreling into Orioles second baseman Davey Johnson attempting to break up a double play, inspired the Pirates, whose comeback gave Kison the victory, 4-3, and knotted the Series at two games apiece. Four days later the Pirates captured the title behind Steve Blass's pitching and Roberto Clemente's fielding and hitting. Said Orioles manager Earl Weaver after his team's disappointing defeat, "Kison turned the Series around."[1]

Seemingly destined for stardom after his performance in the 1971 World Series, Kison struggled with an array of serious elbow and shoulder problems, and never achieved the potential many predicted. Nonetheless he was a valuable and versatile starter and reliever for the strong Pittsburgh Pirates teams of the 1970s, including both World Series champions (1971 and 1979), and established a reputation as a dependable big-game pitcher despite pitching in chronic pain. Often praised for his "bulldog mentality," Kison won 115 games and logged 1,809⅔ innings with a 3.66 ERA in his 15-year major-league career spent with three teams.[2]

Bruce Eugene Kison was born on February 18, 1950, in Pasco, a fertile farming community on the Columbia River in southeastern Washington. His parents were Fred, a building supplier, and Bertha (Rogers) Kison, a homemaker. Bruce was introduced to baseball while attending Mark Twain elementary school, and by the age of 12 was an accomplished pitcher and outfielder. He suffered a fateful injury as a 14-year-old in a local Pony League game. "I used to throw almost completely overhand," explained Kison, "but I got hit in the crazy bone on a pickoff throw to first. [After that, it] hurt me to throw overhand, so I started throwing side-arm. I found out that my ball moved more that way."[3] Kison began attracting scouts in his last two years at Pasco High School, where he tossed three no-hitters. The Pittsburgh Pirates selected him in the 14th round of the major-league amateur draft in 1968.

Kison began his professional baseball career with the Pirates' rookie affiliate in the Gulf Coast League. "We had 30 pitchers, and there were supposed to be just 15 by the end of the season," he said of his arrival in Bradenton. "It was like a pressure cooker, everybody trying to cut each other's throat.... You learn to evaluate yourself and your talent honestly."[4] Kison found a trusted mentor in pitching coach Harvey Haddix, whom he once credited as his most influential teacher.[5] The following year Kison was the Geneva Pirates' top starter in the short-season Class-A New York-Penn League.

In 1970 the Pirates took the reins off their young, rail-thin hurler who packed only 175 pounds on his 6-foot-4 frame. Kison dominated competition in the Class-A Carolina League, posting an 0.82 ERA in 33 innings for the Salem (Virginia) Rebels, earning an early-season promotion to Waterbury (Connecticut) of the Double-A Eastern League. He tossed a two-hit shutout and a three-hitter in his first two starts, but soon began suffering from a sore arm that proved to be a career-long concern. Despite struggling with his control (once hitting seven batters in a game and 21 in just 130 innings), Kison went 10-4 with a 2.28 ERA for the league champions. The Pirates added him to their 40-man roster at the end of the season.

Kison participated his first big-league spring training in 1971, but with just 281 innings of minor-league ball under his belt, he was not expected to challenge for a roster position. Assigned to the Triple-A Charleston (West Virginia) Charlies, the elusive side-armer proved his big-league readiness by winning 10 of 12 starts and posting a 2.86 ERA in 85 innings, and was named to the International League's all-star team.

The Pirates called up Kison on June 30 to serve as a temporary replacement for rugged right-hander Bob Moose, who was serving a two-week stint in the Army Reserve. Kison followed his ho-hum debut on July 4 against the Chicago Cubs (four runs and four walks in a six-inning no-decision) with three impressive performances to secure his place on the staff. He earned his first win by limiting the reigning NL pennant-winning Cincinnati Reds to five hits over 7⅔ innings on July 8 and tossed a sparkling two-hit shutout against the San Diego Padres on July 23. While the Pirates rode on the backs of the league's most potent offense to the NL East title by seven games over the St. Louis Cardinals, Kison helped solidify a staff that lacked a classic ace. With 13 starts among his 18 appearances, Kison finished with a 6-5 record and a 3.40 ERA in 95⅓ innings.

Pirates fans and the local media embraced the youthful looking Kison and his energetic style of playing. "At 21, he looks like 15," wrote Pat Jordan in *Sports Illustrated*. "He has a gawky adolescent body, all arms and legs and little torso. His face is long and fine boned and dusted with peach-like fuzz."[6] He was appropriately nicknamed Baby Face and Stretch, and later in his career was known as Buster.

Kison surprised the baseball world with his unexpectedly strong postseason performances in the Pirates' march to the title in 1971. In Game Four of the then best-of-five NLCS, he relieved starter Steve Blass to begin the third inning with the score tied 5-5, and held the San Francisco Giants scoreless over 4⅔ innings to earn the 9-5 victory and clinch Pittsburgh's first pennant since 1960. "Chills went down my back," said a candid Kison after his thrilling feat. "If you don't go out to the mound scared, you better get out of the game."[7] His victory in Game Four of the World Series helped make him a fan favorite throughout the 1970s in the Steel City.

While his teammates celebrated their 2-1 World Series victory in the clubhouse after Game Seven, Kison made national headlines by rushing to his wedding. He and his best man, Bob Moose, were picked up by helicopter (arranged by Pirates radio announcer Bob Prince) at Memorial Stadium in Baltimore and flown to the airport, where they boarded a private Learjet bound for Pittsburgh.[8] Less than three hours after reaching the pinnacle of team success in baseball, Kison married Anna Marie Orlando of Verona, Pennsylvania. Together they raised two children.

Kison's career almost unraveled in the offseason. He tossed 92 innings for San Juan in the Dominican Winter League and came down with a "tired arm."[9] Ineffective during the Pirates' spring training, he was placed on the disabled list shortly before the first-ever players' strike (which lasted 13 days). Sportswriter Charley Feeney, who had considered him one of "the best young hurlers on the Bucs staff,"[10] reported that Kison shortarmed the ball and had difficulty dropping

down in his side-arm delivery.[11] "I hurt my arm in winter ball," explained Kison, who had tossed almost 300 innings in the minors, majors, and the Dominican Republic in about nine months. "No one ever knew what it was, but the trainers and the team physicians said to pitch through it and I'd be all right. Every time I pitched, I had pain."[12]

Kison labored through a pain-filled campaign in 1972. Despite Feeney's warning that Kison "has too much potential to be used both ways," the young hurler alternated between starts and relief outings and failed to establish a consistent rhythm for skipper Bill Virdon, who had succeeded the retired manager Danny Murtaugh.[13] Kison, the youngest member of the staff, went 9-7 and posted a 3.26 ERA in 152 innings for the NL East champions. He made two relief appearances and picked up a victory in Game Three of the NLCS before the Pirates suffered a dramatic walk-off loss in Game Five to the Reds.

Kison's shoulder pain failed to respond to rest during the offseason. He did not pitch in the exhibition season's Grapefruit League in 1973 and began the season on the disabled list. With his career in jeopardy, Kison reported to Triple-A Charleston. He struggled with his control, walking 82, hitting a league-high 14 batters, and throwing 11 wild pitches in just 114 innings, and also landed on the DL with shoulder tendinitis. He offered a sliver of hope in his September call-up to Pittsburgh by winning all three of his decisions and logging 43⅔ innings in seven starts.

In the offseason, Kison made two changes that helped resuscitate his career. Not willing to give up on the hurler, the Pirates sent Kison to work with team pitching guru (and coach) Don Osborn in the Florida Instructional League. Kison gradually altered his motion and began throwing from a three-quarters delivery in order to put less pressure on his shoulder and gain better control over his pitches. He also rejected a widely accepted notion at the time and began a weightlifting routine prescribed by Pirates trainer Tony Bartirome designed to strengthen the upper portion of his arm and shoulder.[14]

Kison, pain-free for the first time in three years, was back with the Pirates in 1974. Murtaugh, back in the Pittsburgh dugout yet again after Virdon's sudden dismissal in early September 1973, relegated Kison to the bullpen to start the season, ostensibly to protect his arm from the cold weather. Kison appeared in a career-high 40 games, but encountered a new impairment just as his shoulder seemed to feel stronger. He suffered from chronic blisters that developed on the middle finger of his right hand typically in the sixth inning of his starts.[15] He lasted eight innings or more just three times in his 16 starts. In an otherwise mediocre year, Kison won all three of his decisions in September, including a complete-game three-hitter to defeat the Cubs, 2-1, in his last appearance to conclude the season with a 9-8 record and 3.49 ERA in 129 innings. Surprisingly, Murtaugh tabbed Kison to start Game Three of the best-of-five NLCS in Los Angeles with Pittsburgh on the brink of elimination. In arguably the Pirates' only highlight in their four-game series loss, "Stretch" blanked the slugging Dodgers on two hits over 6⅔ innings to earn the victory, 7-0, despite issuing six walks. More impressively, he extended his scoreless-innings streak in the postseason to 20 over six appearances.

Kison enjoyed the most productive stretch of his big-league career between 1975 and 1977 and finally shed the label of a "sometimes" pitcher derived from his inconsistent use and injury-plagued career. His success was no doubt the result of the Pirates' decision to use him almost exclusively as a starter (he started 90 games in 97 appearances), thereby sparing him the wear and tear on his shoulder from constantly warming up in the bullpen. "I figure I've served my apprenticeship," said a more mature and self-confident Kison early in the 1975 season about having earned the right to start regularly, and he added that he never complained about his role on the team.[16]

Kison matched his total of complete games in the previous season by going the distance in his 1975 debut, holding the New York Mets to three hits and three runs (two earned) in a 5-3 win at Three Rivers Stadium. Over the first two months of the season, he emerged as a consistent and dependable winner, tossing a career-best three consecutive complete games (all victories), and beating the reigning NL champion

THE 1979 PITTSBURGH PIRATES

Dodgers twice in nine days in July to improve his record to 9-4. Even more encouraging was Kison's ability to go deep in games. But then the slugging Pirates scored just six times in his next six outings, and he lost a career-worst seven consecutive starts. Still, as the Pirates marched to their fifth NL East crown in six years, Kison was a solid third starter behind Jerry Reuss and Jim Rooker, finishing with a 12-11 record and 3.23 ERA in 192 innings. In the Pirates' three-game sweep at the hands of Cincinnati's Big Red Machine in the NLCS, Kison's string of consecutive scoreless innings in the postseason was halted at 20⅓ when he surrendered a run in two innings of relief in Game Two.

Kison got off to a rough start in 1976, the year the Pirates, along with several other teams, made a bold fashion statement by donning old-style "pillbox" caps with horizontal stripes to celebrate the centennial anniversary of the National League. With an ERA hovering around 6.00 after his first five starts, Kison made an adjustment that helped propel him to a career year. "I used to pitch from the third-base side of the rubber," he explained. "My fastball was tailing away from left-handed hitters. The good ones were taking the pitch because it wasn't a strike."[17] In what seemed like an annual occurrence, Kison pitched his best baseball near the end of the season. In a distant second place on August 24, 15½ games behind the Philadelphia Phillies, the Pirates went on an 18-4 tear to pull within three games of the division leaders. Kison won all four of his starts, allowing just four earned runs in 31 innings during that span. Kison typically worked with backup catcher Duffy Dyer, and credited his batterymate for his success, "I'll admit that Duffy helps me concentrate."[18] Although Pittsburgh stumbled down the stretch to finish in second place, Kison sent career highs in wins (14) and innings (193). For the second consecutive season, he ranked 15th in the NL in ERA (3.08), his career low.

A changing of the guard was marked in 1977 when Chuck Tanner replaced the thrice-retired and increasingly frail Murtaugh, who had died at the age of 59 on December 2, 1976, after suffering a severe stroke two days before. Kison, widely expected to duplicate his success from the previous season, slumped to a 9-10 record, and was plagued by a nagging groin injury and persistent blisters on his pitching hand. More disconcerting to the Pirates was his bloated ERA (4.90), the second highest in all of baseball. Pittsburgh's hopes to reclaim the NL East crown were dashed in a costly victory against the Philadelphia Phillies on July 8. Kison, after yielding a go-ahead two-run homer to Garry Maddox, drilled Mike Schmidt two batters later. In the ensuing bench-clearing brawl, Willie Stargell injured his elbow, and played in only eight more games all season.

Though not physically intimidating on the mound like a J.R. Richard of the Houston Astros, Kison had the reputation as a "brush-back" pitcher and was once dubbed "The Assassin" for dusting off hitters who crowded the plate. Joe Goddard of *The Sporting News* considered him and Jim Barr of the San Francisco Giants masters of the lost art of throwing high and tight, à la Don Drysdale and Bob Gibson.[19] Kison's approach to the plate led to several high-profile brawls, such as the one with Schmidt, and, after he moved to the AL in 1980, with Buddy Bell, Gary Gaetti, and George Bell.

Kison lost his position in the starting rotation in 1978 to offseason acquisition Bert Blyleven, who had been obtained from the Texas Rangers, and rookie Don Robinson, and started just 11 times among his 28 appearances, logging only 96 innings. With his role on the club in limbo and trade rumors swirling, Kison unexpectedly won a spot in the rotation in spring training in 1979 after the departure of left-handed veteran Jerry Reuss. Reuss had been sent to the Los Angeles Dodgers for pitcher Rick Rhoden, who subsequently went on the DL for the season after only one start. Then 36-year-old Jim Rooker was injured. In his season debut, Kison struck out a career-high 10 in 6⅓ innings in a no-decision against the Montreal Expos.

After a three-week stint in the bullpen, Kison returned to the rotation in dramatic fashion on June 3 by shutting out the San Diego Padres on one hit in the Steel City. Initially Robinson was scheduled to start the game that night, but he could not get loosened up. The customarily mild-mannered Kison drew hefty criticism for lashing out at the official scorers, Pittsburgh sportswriters Charley Feeney and Dan Donovan, who had ruled Barry Evans's two-out eighth-inning smash that bounced off third baseman Phil Garner's glove and continued down the line a double and not an error.[20] The incident led to Feeney's and Donovan's resignation as scorers and a new policy (initiated by the local papers) that Pittsburgh sports reporters would no longer serve as scorers. Kison pitched his best baseball over the last five weeks of the season, winning all five decisions and posting a stellar 1.74 ERA in 46⅔ innings. The normally weak-hitting pitcher began that stretch by belting his only grand slam among his three career home runs in his win over the Padres on August 26. But his most important victory came in the Pirates 163rd and final game of the season (an extra contest needed due to a May 25 tie with the Mets). He held the Cubs to just one run over six innings in front of 42,176 fans at Three Rivers Stadium to edge out the Montreal Expos by two games and clinch the club's sixth NL East crown of the decade. "This is the most emotional situation I've ever been in, because we had to work so hard to get there," said an elated Kison after the game. "Other years we ran away with it, but not this year. And it's even more meaningful because the last two years we played our hearts out and came up empty."[21]

The team's unheralded pitching staff proved to be one of its strengths. Eight hurlers logged at least 100 innings and six notched at least 10 wins. Kison finished second on the club in victories (13), trailing only John Candelaria's 14, while his 3.19 ERA (in 172⅓ innings) was the best among starters and good for 11th in the league.

After the Pirates' three-game sweep of the Cincinnati Reds in the NLCS, Kison endured a nightmare as the Game One starter in the World Series against the Baltimore Orioles. Complaining of numbness in his arm on a cold, 41-degree night at Memorial Stadium, he yielded three hits, issued two walks, and threw a wild pitch leading to five runs (four earned) and was lifted after registering just one out in Pittsburgh's 5-4 loss. He was scheduled to start Game Five but was replaced by Rooker because of continued arm discomfort.[22] The "We Are Family" Pirates, led by Willie Stargell, became the first NL team since the 1925 Pirates and just the fifth major-league team since 1900 to win the World Series after being down three games to one.

Kison opted for free agency in the offseason, and his nine-year tenure with the Pirates came to a close on November 16, 1979, when he signed a five-year contract reportedly worth approximately $2.5 million with the California Angels. Never a star for the "Lumber Company," Kison fared well in pressure-packed games, notching 24 of his 81 wins as a Pirate in September (against just nine losses).

Kison won only 29 games and logged just 451⅓ innings in his injury-plagued tenure with the Angels. After losing his first two starts in the AL, he blanked the Minnesota Twins on one hit, a double by Ken Landreaux with one out in the ninth inning of a 17-0 rout at Metropolitan Stadium. Criticized as a bust and hailed as a poster child of the dangers of free agency, a pain-ridden Kison was shelved for the remainder of the season after a July 14 loss with a 3-6 record and a 4.91 ERA in 73⅓ innings.

Kison was diagnosed with damage to the ulnar nerve in his right elbow and metacarpal tendon in his wrist. He underwent career-threatening surgery and subsequently reported that his hand was paralyzed and that he had no feeling in three of his fingers.[23] Reflective of his team-first attitude, Kison made news by offering the Angels a refund of his salary to compensate for the "troubles" he caused, but GM Buzzie Bavasi declined the offer.[24] After a grueling rehabilitation, Kison defied predictions that he would never pitch again by returning to the mound 13 months later in what sportswriter Peter Gammons considered a feel-good story of the year.[25] For the 1981 season, Kison was 1-1, with a 3.48 ERA in 44 innings pitched.

The ever-competitive Kison rekindled some of his magic in 1982. Unexpectedly securing a spot in the rotation, he went 6-2 in his first 12 starts before Texas Ranger Johnny Grubb's line drive off his shin on June 22 sent him to the bullpen for more than two months. Prior to the August 31 trade deadline, the Angels reportedly offered Kison to the New York

Yankees for left-handed veteran pitcher Tommy John. Back in the rotation in September, he won three consecutive starts to finish with a 10-5 record and 3.17 ERA in 142 innings for the AL West champions. In Game Two of the best-of-five ALCS, Kison tossed a complete-game five-hitter, striking out eight, to beat the Milwaukee Brewers, 4-2. Four days later, Kison started the decisive Game Five. Pitching on short rest, he held the potent offense of the "Brew Crew" to just three hits in five innings, departing with the lead, 3-2, but Milwaukee gained a 4-3 comeback win for the AL pennant.

In defiance of the odds, Kison got off to another fast, strong start in 1983, winning six of seven decisions in nine starts. He tied his career high with 10 strikeouts on April 16 and also tossed three consecutive complete games from May 11 through 22 (culminating with his eighth and final shutout) for just the second time in his career. But the story was too good to be true. He developed back pain that prematurely ended his season in order to undergo career-threatening surgery on a lumbar disc on his spine in September.

Few questioned Kison's toughness and commitment to the game. After yet another arduous rehabilitation, he returned to the mound 10 months later in 1984 and labored through 65⅓ innings (5.37 ERA) in his final season in California.

Kison finished his career with the Boston Red Sox in 1985. His importance to the club transcended his five wins and 92 innings. Manager John McNamara praised the 35-year-old Kison's positive influence on his young staff, which included five starters 27 or younger (Roger Clemens, Oil Can Boyd, Bruce Hurst, Al Nipper, and Bob Ojeda).

After years of battling injuries, Kison retired after the 1985 season when he was diagnosed with a torn rotator cuff.[26] "I think what I will miss most is the competiveness of the game," said Kison, who went 5-1 with an impressive 1.98 ERA in 36⅓ innings in the postseason. "I'll also miss the camaraderie of my teammates."[27]

A lifelong student of the game, Kison transitioned into coaching. He returned to the Pirates in 1987 as a minor-league roving pitching instructor, and served in that capacity until 1990. In 1991 he began a productive eight-year working relationship with the Kansas City Royals. After one year as a minor-league pitching instructor, he served as bullpen coach (in 1992) and pitching coach (1993-1998) on the parent club under managers Hal McRae, Bob Boone, and Tony Muser. After serving as the pitching coach under Ray Miller in 1999, Kison also scouted for the Baltimore Orioles for more than a decade.[28]

As of 2015, Kison lived with his wife, Anna, in Bradenton, Florida.

SOURCES

Ancestry.com.

BaseballLibrary.com.

Baseball-Reference.com.

Retrosheet.com.

SABR.org.

NOTES

1 *The Sporting News*, October 30, 1971: 3.

2 *The Sporting News*, May 31, 1975: 12.

3 Joe Donnelly, "Kison: Look Honey, If I'm Late …," October 14, 1971. Kison's player file at the National Baseball Hall of Fame, Cooperstown, New York.

4 Pat Jordan, "An Old Hand With a Prospect," *Sports Illustrated*, June 14, 1971. si.com/vault/1971/06/14/611598/an-old-hand-with-a-prospect.

5 Mark Cardon, "Knocking Off Birds Is a Hobby For Kison," *Sarasota Herald-Tribune*, February 20, 1972: 1C.

6 Pat Jordan, "End of Innocence," *Sports Illustrated*, April 10, 1972. http://www.si.com/vault/1972/04/10/613983/end-of-innocence

7 Associated Press, "Cool Kid In Control. Kison Hurls Pennant-Clinching Victory For Bucs," *Toledo* (Ohio) *Blade*, October 7, 1971: 46.

8 *The Sporting News*, October 30, 1971: 16.

9 *The Sporting News*, February 12, 1972.

10 *The Sporting News*, December 25, 1971: 28.

11 *The Sporting News*, April 29, 1972: 11.

12 Dennis Morabito, "Kison no dumbbell, that's why he's back," *Beaver County* (Pennsylvania) *Times*, June 3, 1975: B1.

13 *The Sporting News*, December 25, 1971: 28.

14 Morabito.

15 *The Sporting* News, April 12, 1975: 17.

16 *The Sporting News*, May 31, 1975: 12.

17 *The Sporting News*, July 3, 1926: 29.

18 *The Sporting News*, October 2, 1976: 9.

19 *The Sporting News*, July 29, 1978: 22.

20 Phil Axelrod, 'Bucs Breeze, 7-0, on Kison's One-Hitter," *Pittsburgh Post-Gazette*, June 4, 1979: 9.

21 Don Donovan, "'79 Pirates Gave It Their All And Then Some," *Pittsburgh Press*, October 1, 1979: B4.

22 *The Sporting News*, October 27, 1979: 12.

23 *The Sporting News*, August 29, 1981: 27.

24 Associated Press, "Ailing Kison Offers Refund," *Observer-Reporter* (Washington, Pennsylvania), July 17, 1980: D1.

25 *The Sporting News*, August 29, 1981: 27.

26 Bob Hertzell, "Torn Rotator Cuff Throws Kison Into New Pitching Assignment," *Pittsburgh Post-Gazette*, February, 5, 1987: D1.

27 Associated Press, "Kison decides to retire," *Lewistown* (Maine) *Daily Sun*, February 25, 1986: 17.

28 Dan Connolly, "Orioles will have two more scouts on pro assignments," *The Sun* (Baltimore), February 9, 2012. articles.baltimoresun.com/2012-02-09/sports/bal-orioles-will-have-two-more-scouts-on-pro-assignments-20120209_1_scouts-orioles-amateur-andy-macphail.

Lee Lacy

By Gregory H. Wolf

"I CAN PLAY THIS GAME," SAID LEE LACY confidently. "For hustle and determination, I won't take a back seat to anyone."[1] An All-Star at three different infield positions in the minors, the right-handed-hitting Lacy broke in with the Los Angeles Dodgers in 1972 and fashioned a 16-year big-league career spent primarily as a versatile utilityman and platoon player whose calling card was consistent line-drive hitting with an occasional pop, and plenty of speed. "I've always been able to hit all kinds of pitchers," said Lacy, whose most productive seasons were in his early 30s with the Pittsburgh Pirates. "Basically, I'm a bad-ball hitter, so it doesn't matter where you throw it. I don't pay a lot of attention to fundamentals. I just attack the ball."[2]

Leondaus "Lee" Lacy was born on April 10, 1948, in Longview, Texas, but grew up in Oakland, California, where his Lone Star State-born parents, Berry and Johnny Lee Lacy, had relocated by the early 1950s. The elder Lacy was a former semipro ballplayer in Texas and one-time teammate with future Dodgers All-Star infielder Charlie Neal. By all accounts, Lee was raised with a baseball in his hand and learned his trade as a youth on the sandlots of Oakland's west side. "They told me I was too skinny to play ball," recalled Lacy about trying out for a Babe Ruth league.[3] But the youngster was undeterred. With the encouragement from his father and neighbor Charlie Beamon, a former right-handed pitcher who had a cup of coffee with the Baltimore Orioles in 1958, Lacy stuck with baseball as a way to escape the poverty and social unrest of Oakland of the 1960s. He was a standout infielder at McClymonds High School, whose contributions of players to the ranks of professional sports are among the most impressive in the country. The list includes Frank Robinson, Ernie Lombardi, Vada Pinson, and Curt Flood in baseball, Bill Russell and Paul Silas in basketball, and many others since. After graduating from high school, Lacy played baseball for Laney College, a local community college, earning second-team all-Golden Gate Conference honors as a third baseman in 1969.[4] He also polished his skills in the semipro ranks with the Alameda Braves. Based on the recommendation of longtime team scout Bill Brenzel, the Dodgers selected Lacy in the second round with the 29th overall pick in the January 1969 amateur draft.

Lacy joined an organization whose farm system was the best in baseball and stacked with major-league talent. In his first season he batted .293 for the Ogden (Utah) Dodgers, earning a berth on the All-Star team of the short-season Rookie-class Pioneer League. "I was surprised that most of the players weren't superhuman at all, they were just like me, normal," said Lacy.[5] With sluggers Steve Garvey and Ron Cey tabbed as the heirs apparent to the hot corner on the big-league club, Lacy was moved to shortstop in the Arizona Instructional League. He struggled in the field (63 errors in 111 games) at his new position for Bakersfield in the Class-A California League in 1970, but was once again named an All-Star owing to his .301 batting average. While the Dodgers had at least four major-league shortstop prospects (Lacy, Bobby Valentine, Ivan De Jesus, and Tim Johnson), Bakersfield manager Don LeJohn praised Lacy for his "aggressiveness," noting that the 22-year-old "hustles so we like to think that his chances are good at making it."[6] The only question was at what position.

In 1971 Lacy got a taste of what the big leagues might be like by participating in spring training with Los Angeles at Dodgertown in Vero Beach, Florida. Lauded by skipper Walter Alston and praised by sportswriter Bill Fleishman as the "top rookie" in camp, Lacy was assigned to Albuquerque in the Double-A Dixie Association.[7] At 6-feet-1 and about 170 pounds, Lacy was quick and agile, characteristics the Dodgers thought could land him a spot in the big leagues as a second baseman. Moved to the keystone sack, Lacy seemed to find his home. More at ease in the field

(.967 fielding percentage), Lacy continued his steady hitting (.307 average), but with little power (.371 slugging percentage) to earn his third consecutive league All-Star berth, all at different infield positions. He was also named the second baseman on the Topps-National Association Double-A All-Star team.[8]

Lacy honed his craft at second base with Hermosillo in the Mexican Winter League in the offseason in preparation for Dodgers spring training in 1972. (In characteristic fashion, he also bashed pitchers south of the border, setting a league record with 11 straight hits.[9]) But the Dodgers had the luxury of depth. Lacy began the season back in Double A, with El Paso in the Texas League, while their top second-base prospect, the speedy Davey Lopes (a converted outfielder), remained in Triple A for the third straight season.

Lacy finally had some chips fall his way when he got off to a torrid start with El Paso in 1972, earning the Topps Double-A Player of the Month award in June, when he batted .389, lined 20 doubles and knocked in 26 runs.[10] Dodgers GM Al Campanis turned to the hot-hitting Lacy, and not Lopes, for a look-see to shore up a suddenly depleted infield. Garvey was bothered by nagging injuries, infielder Billy Grabarkewitz was out with a broken finger, and shortstop Bill Russell was called to complete a two-week stint in the Army Reserve. Lacy debuted on June 30, batting leadoff and playing second base, going 1-for-5 in an 8-4 loss to the San Francisco Giants at Candlestick Park. After a successful pinch hit on July 2, Lacy went on a roll, batting .407 (11-for-27, all singles) with six runs and four RBIs to share NL Player of the Week honors with Pittsburgh's Manny Sanguillen. Lacy went from a short-term fix to the starting second baseman, supplanting Valentine, who moved into a super-utility role. Described as "an excellent fielder, with good hands, arm and range," Lacy fielded just a few percentage points under the league average and batted a respectable .259 in an era where middle infielders weren't expected to contribute much offensively. His season abruptly ended in the second game of a doubleheader on September 4 when Cincinnati's Hal McRae took him out on an aggressive slide, resulting in a strained tendon in his knee. Lacy was still hobbling two months later when he was sent to the Arizona Instructional League to work with Russell, his double-play partner, who had been converted from an outfielder in light of shortstop Maury Wills's age.

Lacy began the 1973 season as the Dodgers' regular second baseman, but not for long. Batting a paltry .226 with just one double after 16 games, he was benched in favor of Lopes. The slap-hitting Lacy, who critics claimed lacked a natural position, found himself on a team with what emerged as the most stable infield in baseball history. The quartet of Garvey, Lopes, Russell, and Cey remained together through the 1981 season, by which time each had earned a combined 21 All-Star selections. Not just good, the quartet was also remarkably resilient and healthy. Occasionally spelling Lopes and pinch-hitting, Lacy hit a disappointing .207 and slugged an anemic .222 in his sophomore season. A rusty Lacy played winter ball in Puerto Rico for San Juan, skippered by former Dodgers great Jim Gilliam.

For the remainder of his tenure with the Dodgers, through 1978 (interrupted by a brief interlude with the Atlanta Braves), Lacy bided his time as a role player, making occasional starts at second base, all three outfield positions, and a few times at third base. In 1974 the Dodgers captured their first NL pennant since 1966, in the heyday of Sandy Koufax and Don Drysdale. Lacy played only 35 games in the field, including 17 starts at second base, and batted a respectable .282 in just 78 at-bats. In the postseason he had only one plate appearance, striking out in the fifth inning as a pinch-hitter against Catfish Hunter in Game Three of the Dodgers' eventual World Series loss to the Oakland A's in five games.

While manager Walter Alston lauded his bench players like Lacy, Tom Paciorek, and Rick Auerbach as one of the strengths of the club, Lacy made it known that he would play anywhere, including the outfield. "I'm not yelling about wanting to be traded or anything," said Lacy. "I just know I can play. I can always hit."[11] He got his chance when early-season injuries moved Lopes to the outfield and later in the season when left fielder Bill Buckner was sidelined with a badly sprained left ankle that eventually required season-ending surgery. On May 17 Lacy finally launched his first career home run, after 535 at-bats, a three-run shot off Pittsburgh's Jim Rooker. Three days later, he connected for his second one. He made history with his first career pinch-hit round-tripper, on July 23 against St. Louis, when he followed Willie Crawford's blast to become with Crawford just the sixth set of teammates to have pinch-hit homers in the same inning.[12] Lacy proved that he was a bona-fide hitter (.314 average and impressive .451 slugging percentage), but it was his fielding that turned heads. "[M]ost spectacular has been his throwing from the outfield," gushed sportswriter Gordon Verrell, noting that Lacy threw out seven runners in just 43 games in the outfield."[13] Widely seen as the center fielder of the future, replacing the achy-kneed Jim Wynn, Lacy impressed the Dodgers' brass in the Arizona Instructional League. "He gets rid of the ball very well, like an infielder does," opined Alston.[14] But just when Lacy had a starting position in his sights with the Dodger blue, he was traded, along with Wynn, Paciorek, and Jerry Royster, to the Atlanta Braves for left fielder Dusty Baker and utiltyman Ed Goodson on November 17.

Atlanta moved Lacy back to second base, but as fate would have it, the 28-year-old's stint as a starter for the Braves lasted only about 2½ months. On June 23 he was shipped back to the Dodgers, along with pitcher Elias Sosa for outspoken and disgruntled reliever Mike Marshall. "I'm a smarter hitter now from just playing," said Lacy, whose center-field spot had been taken by offseason acquisition Rick Monday. Making starts in all three outfield positions and pinch-hitting, Lacy finished with a .269 batting average.

With the advent of free agency in 1976 contributing to the rise of salaries across baseball, Lacy's frustration as a utility player mounted. "There's not much chance of getting the (financial) security I want the way I'm being used," said Lacy as the Dodgers marched toward another NL pennant in 1977. "I can't overly enjoy this season, although it's a winning situation."[15] The lack of playing time affected Lacy's hitting (.266 in just 169 at-bats). In Game One of the World Series against the New York Yankees, Lacy connected for the biggest hit of his career, lining a one-out pinch-hit single off reliever Sparky Lyle and driving in Dusty Baker to tie the game 3-3 in the top of the ninth during an eventual 12-inning New York victory, 4-3, at Yankee Stadium. With the Dodgers later down two games to one, first-year skipper Tommy Lasorda shuffled his outfield, moving Reggie Smith to center and installing Lacy in right field for Games Four and Five. In the latter game Lacy went 2-for-3 with a run and an RBI single in the Dodgers' 10-4 victory in Los Angeles. New York captured the title the next game, 8-4, when starting hurler Mike Torrez caught Lacy's pinch-hit bunt popup to record the final out, setting off a melee at Yankee Stadium in a game most remembered for Reggie Jackson's three home runs on three consecutive pitches.

In what seemed like an annual tradition, trade rumors swirled around Lacy in the offseason. This time sportswriters had him in a package deal to the San Diego Padres in exchange for Dave Winfield, but Lacy was still with the team when the season opened. Making starts at five positions and pinch-hitting regularly, the valuable utility player had his best season at the most opportune time. On May 17 he connected for a home run off Pittsburgh's Will McEnaney to set a major-league record with his third pinch-hit home run in as many at-bats. (In 1979 Del Unser tied the record.) Lacy batted only .261, but for the first time in his career, he showed power, clouting 13 home runs and 16 doubles in just 245 at-bats, good for a career-best .518 slugging percentage. Lacy's late-season slump continued into the postseason for the pennant winners. He managed only two hits in 14 at-bats with no runs and one RBI in four starts as DH in the World Series as the Dodgers once again fell to the Yankees in six games. Declared a free agent in the offseason, he signed a lucrative six-year deal with Pittsburgh for a reported $1.05 million.

Lacy's contradiction-filled tenure with the Pirates marked both the zenith and nadir of his career. He proved he could be a consistent .300 hitter while also revealing a flawed side as he was involved in the Pittsburgh drug trials that rocked baseball in 1985 and 1986. He achieved personal and team success, yet could not shed a new label as platoon player.

"I can play five different positions, all the outfield plus second and third," responded Lacy when asked why the Pirates signed him. "I can give them a pinch-hitter, I can hit with power and I know how to win."[16] The signing seemed odd, given that all three Pirates outfield positions were occupied by well established veterans: perennial All-Star and former MVP Dave Parker in right, Omar Moreno in center, and the dependable Bill Robinson in left. Nonetheless the signing was lauded by pundits. "He'll help (the Pirates) win a lot of games that won't show up in his personal stats," suggested Dick Young in *The Sporting News*.[17] At Pirates spring training in Bradenton, Florida, the 31-year-old Lacy explained his approach to a new chapter in his career. "I am the Pirates' utility player," he said. "I've got to work harder because of my versatility. I have to concentrate more, and I've got to keep myself in good physical shape."[18]

Manager Chuck Tanner expected Lacy to have a big role on the team; however, Lacy "rusted on the bench," wrote Pittsburgh sportswriter Charley Feeney.[19] Suffering from a sore heel early in the season and slowed by a bad back and viral infection at the end of one of the most exciting campaigns in Pirates history, Lacy made only 41 starts (38 in left field) and hit a disappointing .247 in 182 at-bats. For the third consecutive season, Lacy was on a pennant-winning club. After not playing in the Pirates' three-game sweep of the Cincinnati Reds in the best-of-five NLCS, Lacy made four pinch-hitting appearances in the World Series against the favored Baltimore Orioles, connecting for a single in Game Five of the "We Are Family" Pirates' eventual title after being down three games to one.

"I wouldn't say that it was a wasted year," responded Lacy when asked about his first season in the Steel City. "A lot of positive things happened. It was a year where I didn't have too many alternatives. I was labeled an outfielder, but there was little room to play in the outfield."[20] Lacy spent most of the 1980 season platooning in left field with left-handed slugger Mike Easler while Robinson moved to first with reigning NL co-MVP Willie Stargell hobbled by bad knees. Lacy got off to a hot start, keeping his batting average north of .400 through June 21 (42-for-103, .408), including three three-hit games and one four-hit game. On July 20 Lacy punctuated a successful late-game at-bat in the first game of a doubleheader against Los Angeles by going 5-for-5 in the second game, giving him seven consecutive hits (over three games), scoring three times and driving in two runs on "Willie Stargell Day" in front of a raucous crowd of 41,932 at Three Rivers Stadium. Before the celebrations honoring the Pirates' captain between games took place, an ugly incident marred the first game when Dave Parker was almost hit in the head by a battery thrown from the right-field stands, and was removed for his safety. While the Pirates finished a disappointing third (83-79) in the NL East, Lacy batted a career-best .335 and slugged .511 to form with Easler (.338/.583) a potent one-two punch in left field. That success didn't assuage Lacy's frustrations, though. "A good ballplayer is never satisfied. I'm a platoon ballplayer because they think of me as a platoon player," he said. "I've never considered myself a platoon ballplayer."[21]

The fifth work stoppage since Marvin Miller became head of the Major League Players Association in 1966 led to the cancellation of 713 games of the 1981 season from June 12 through August 10. The Pirates (46-56) had their first losing season since 1973, as injuries and growing dissent among players marred the forgettable campaign. On May 22 Lacy was almost hit by a bottle while playing left field at Three Rivers Stadium, but refused to press charges. "A person is going to have to do a lot more than that for me to file a complaint," he said. "I did some things when I was young that I shouldn't have."[22] While Lacy's batting average slipped to .268, he emerged as a threat on the basepaths, crediting pinch-runner Matt Alexander for teaching him how to take big leads.[23] After stealing 18 bases in the previous season, he swiped 24 in 27 attempts in 1981.

Lacy took some heat in the offseason when he referred to Dave Parker "as a bad person to have on this team."[24] Since signing the largest contract in Pirates history during the 1979 season, the enigmatic Parker had become a target for fans' frustrations with the team and with what many perceived as exorbitant player salaries while Pittsburgh was gripped by economic woes after the collapse of the steel industry. Seemingly discontent, Lacy also added a jab about Three Rivers Stadium: "I like the guys on the Pirates, but I wouldn't mind being traded. The field is very hard, the worst in the league."[25] The Pirates had no intention of moving Lacy, widely regarded as one of the best-hitting platoon and bench players in baseball.

While Lacy and Parker avoided one another in the clubhouse in spring training, the Pirates got off to a slow start in 1982 and finished in fourth place in the division despite leading the league in hitting (.273) and slugging (.408) and placing second in runs. Lacy, making 53 starts for the injured Parker in right field, batted .312 while setting new personal bests for hits (112), runs (66), and stolen bases (40). On May 14 it appeared as though Lacy had finally hit his first career grand slam. With the Bucs trailing Cincinnati, 7-5, at Three Rivers, Lacy launched an offering from Reds reliever Tom Hume over the right-field wall with the bases loaded. In his excitement, Lacy passed Moreno about halfway to second base, and the result was an automatic out. "I grabbed my head and stopped, but I was already past Omar, and it was too late," said Lacy, whom teammates razzed mercilessly for his baserunning blunder and three-run single. "It goes to show you what happens when you don't know your own power," he joked.[26] Lacy never hit a grand slam in the big leagues.

Making starts in all three outfield positions in 1983, Lacy batted over .300 for the third time in four seasons and stole 31 bases, but was criticized for his lack of production. He started out with a "real bang" batting leadoff in the season opener in St. Louis as he hit the first pitch of the game, thrown by Bob Forsch, for a home run, but he drove in only 13 runs in 288 at-bats while the Pirates duplicated their 84-78 record from the previous season, although finishing two positions higher, in second place.

The next three years were trying ones for Lacy. His name seemed to regularly grace the front pages of Pittsburgh's sports pages in the 1983-84 offseason. After rumors of Lacy's trade to San Francisco proved to be false, he figured prominently in a mini-scandal when team coach Joe Lonnett castigated his defense in a widely reported interview. "Lacy can't play center field. Man, he'd kill you in center," said the longtime coach, explaining why rookie Marvell Wynn took over for Moreno, who had departed via free agency. "Wherever you put [Lacy], he's going to hurt you."[27] Lonnett also criticized the play of outfielder Lee Mazzilli, infielder Jim Morrison, and first baseman Jason Thompson, but somehow weathered the storm by issuing a feeble public apology, and was with the team when the club opened spring training.

The first salvo in the eventual drug scandals that rocked baseball in 1985 and 1986 occurred during spring training in 1984. Sportswriter Dan Donovan of the *Pittsburgh Press* reported on March 21 that Lacy was involved in a contentious child-custody suit in Oakland.[28] According to that report, Cecelia Trainor Chapman had filed an affidavit claiming that Lacy was "dependent on cocaine" and was unsuited to have custody of their daughter, Jennifer. Lacy was raising the child with his wife, Suzanne (née Mitchell), whom he had married in San Diego in July 1979. Lacy emphatically denied the charge, claiming, "How could I play baseball at age 34 if I did that?"

Despite the off-field distraction that forced Lacy to occasionally miss games to tend to personal matters in California, he entered his contract season with a vengeance while the Pirates plunged to last place in the NL East for the first time since division play began in 1969. He started a career-high 116 games, including 86 in right field, where he platooned with weak-hitting Doug Frobel (.203), and led the team with a .321 batting average (second highest in the league, but well behind Tony Gwynn's .351) on a career-best 151 hits. Declaring free agency after the season, Lacy signed a three-year deal with the Baltimore Orioles in January 1985.

"I hit the ball all over and have occasional power down the lines," said the 37-year-old Lacy, whose 70 RBIs in 1984 were easily the best total of his career. "I'll chink it over the infield or beat out chops. I love to bunt. If I see crumbs in the third baseman's eyes, like he's been out too late the night before, I'll lay one down for a hit."[29] But before Lacy could showcase his hitting in the AL, he severely injured his thumb diving for a fly ball in an exhibition game on March 12. He required surgery and missed five weeks.

Lacy's spring training went from bad to worse when Dan Donovan published a bombshell article in the *Pittsburgh Press* on March 31, 1985.[30] He reported that no fewer than eight major-league players, among them Lacy, Keith Hernandez, Tim Raines, and Enos Cabell, had testified before a federal grand jury in Pittsburgh before spring training about the sale of cocaine, as part of an investigation targeting dealers and not players. The ensuing trial, which began in September 1985, made national headlines with testimony from seven players, including former Pirates Dave Parker and Dale Berra, about widespread cocaine use among major-league players in the previous five years, and even inside the clubhouse at Three Rivers Stadium. Lacy was sworn in to testify, but did not. The trial eventually resulted in the conviction of seven drug dealers. Commissioner Peter Ueberroth considered the episode closed on February 28, 1986, when he suspended 11 players (seven for one year, Parker and Berra among them; and four for 60 days, including Lacy);[31] however, players were permitted to play if they agreed to donate 10 and 5 percent, respectively, of their salary to antidrug programs; all players agreed to the stipulation.

The drug trials notwithstanding, Lacy was steady offensively, though far from spectacular in his first two seasons in Baltimore, but proved to be a liability in right field. In 1985 he walloped his first and only walk-off home run, connecting off the California Angels' Donnie Moore with one on and one out in ninth to give the Orioles a 7-5 win on June 3. At the end of the same month he commenced a personal-best 20-game hitting streak (38-for-84, .452) en route to 144 hits and a .293 average as the oldest starting outfielder in the league; only the Angels 39-year-old first baseman Rod Carew was an older starting position player in the AL. Lacy inherited that mantle the following season, scored a career-high 77 runs and batted .287. Among his 91 big-league home runs, three came on June 8, 1986, at Yankee Stadium when he went 4-for-6 and set personal bests with four runs scored and six RBIs in the Orioles 18-9 thrashing of New York. With his playing time reduced in 1987, Lacy was released by the Orioles near the end of spring training in 1988, and subsequently retired.

In 16 big-league seasons, Lacy batted .286 and collected 1,303 hits. In parts of four seasons in the minors, he hit .314. Lacy enjoyed great success against pitchers Rick Reuschel (14-for-29, .483), Jerry Koosman (16-for-41, .390) and Steve Carlton (33-for-88, .372), while having difficulty against Gene Garber (1-for-20, .050), Joe Niekro (5-for-38, .132), and Bob Shirley (6-for-37, .162). And Lacy always seemed to take his game to another level when playing the Dodgers, against whom he batted .348 (49-for-141), his highest average versus any team. In 1989 and 1990 Lacy played in the short-lived Senior Professional Baseball Association.

As of 2016 Lacy resided in metropolitan Los Angeles, where he has long been active in various community outreach and charity programs sponsored by the Los Angeles Dodgers Foundation. He has regularly served as a guest instructor at youth baseball campus and participated in events focusing on education and baseball opportunities for inner-city youth, such as Dodgers RBI (Reviving Baseball in Inner Cities). "I just want to play," Lacy once said.[32] That remark aptly serves as an epitaph for his baseball career and reflects his passion for the sport that he has worked diligently to advocate and teach to youngsters.

SOURCES

In addition to the sources noted in this biography, the author also accessed the *Encyclopedia of Minor League Baseball*, Retrosheet.org, Baseball-Reference.com, the SABR Minor Leagues Database, accessed online at Baseball-Reference.com, and *The Sporting News* archive via Paper of Record. Special thanks to Bill Mortell for his assistance with genealogical research.

NOTES

1 *The Sporting News*, June 27, 1981: 28.
2 *The Sporting News*, March 11, 1985: 6.
3 Fred Lewis, "Lee Lacy 'Too Skinny to Play Ball' Fattens Average on Caloop Hurlers," *Bakersfield Californian*, August 1, 1970: 11.
4 "All Conference Trio Honored," *The Times* (San Mateo, California), May 20, 1969: 30.
5 Lewis.
6 Ibid.
7 *The Sporting News*, April 17, 1971: 39.
8 *The Sporting News*, December 4, 1971: 39.
9 *The Sporting News*, January 29, 1972: 42.
10 *The Sporting News*, August 5, 1972: 26.
11 *The Sporting News*, June 21, 1975: 3.
12 Crawford and Lacy's feat also marked just the fifth time in big-league history that teammates hit back-to-back pinch-hit home runs.
13 *The Sporting News*, October 11, 1975: 8.
14 Ibid.
15 *The Sporting News*, June 25, 1977: 24.
16 Marino Parascenzo, "Versatile Lacy Joins Bucs," *Pittsburgh Post-Gazette*, January 20, 1979: 10.
17 *The Sporting News*, February 3, 1979: 2.
18 Dan Donovan, "Motto of New Pirate Lacy: Be Prepared," *Pittsburgh Press*, March 2, 1979: 24.
19 *The Sporting News*, December 22, 1979: 6.
20 Dan Donovan, "Lacy'll Be Hanged If He Doesn't Help," *Pittsburgh Press*, March 5, 1980: 64.
21 Dan Donovan, He's Platooned but Lacy's a Good Soldier," *Pittsburgh Press*, August 3, 1980: 3.
22 *The Sporting News*, June 20, 1981: 30.
23 *The Sporting News*, June 27, 1981: 28.
24 "Lacy Labels Parker 'Bad,'" *Pittsburgh Press*, October 26, 1981: 3.
25 Ibid.
26 Russ Frank, "Lacy's Slam That Wasn't Still Grand," *Pittsburgh Press*, May 15, 1982: 8.
27 *The Sporting News*, February 13, 1984: 46.
28 Dan Donovan, "Lacy Used Cocaine, Witnesses Say," *Pittsburgh Press*, March 21, 1984: 51.
29 *The Sporting News*, March 11, 1985: 8.
30 Dan Donovan, "Ex-Pirate Lacy Called as Witness in Drug Probe," *Pittsburgh Press*, March 31, 1985: B10.
31 Charley Feeney, "Commissioner Penalizes 11," *Pittsburgh Post-Gazette*, March 1, 1986: 19.
32 *The Sporting News*, June 21, 1975: 3.

Alberto Lois

By Tom Crist

ONCE CONSIDERED A PROSPECT WITH tremendous promise, Alberto Lois was an outfielder and pinch-runner for the Pittsburgh Pirates in 1978 and 1979. Lois had a strong arm and considerable speed, able to run 60 yards in 6.2 seconds by his own account.[1] At one point he even drew comparisons to a "young Roberto Clemente."[2] Despite his talents, Lois, who was frequently injured during his short career, played in only 14 major-league games. His big-league career totals featured one hit in four at-bats (a .250 batting average), six runs, and one stolen base in two attempts.

Alberto Lois Pie was born on May 6, 1956, in Hato Mayor del Rey, Dominican Republic, to Eligio and Lucio (Feliciano) Lois.[3] As an 18-year-old in 1974, Lois was signed by longtime Pirates scout Howie Haak and played outfield for the Charleston (South Carolina) Pirates of the Class-A Western Carolinas League. During the 1974 season, he hit .260 with 37 stolen bases in 49 attempts while playing in 119 games. Lois would not play more than 100 games in any other season in his career. He was a right-handed outfielder who stood 5-feet-9 and was listed with a playing weight of 175 pounds.

Over the 1975 and 1976 seasons, Lois proved to be a talented hitter, and he moved quickly through the minor leagues. In 1975, he hit .302 while playing in 83 games for the Salem (Virginia) Pirates of the Carolina League. The following season, Lois began the season in Double A with the Shreveport Captains of the Texas League and hit .323 in 65 games. He was promoted to Triple A, the Charleston (West Virginia) Charlies of the International League, where he continued to show promise, hitting .300 in 31 games. In 1977, after an organization move to Ohio, Lois hit .282 in 42 games while playing in Triple A for the Columbus Clippers. However, his playing time was limited during this season due to hamstring injuries.

Lois's frequent injuries raised eyebrows in the Pirates organization, some of whom began to consider him to be a "chronic malingerer."[4] It did not help matters that Lois reported late for spring training each year.[5] Some of his teammates expressed frustration with Lois, perceiving that he was not living up to his potential. According to Nelson Norman, who played with Lois in the Pirates' farm system, "[He] could flat-out play. Lois was so good that he could come to the park drunk (which he sometimes did), and still get two or three hits. It was such a waste."[6]

By 1978 Lois had recovered from his injuries, but he still spent most of this season in the minors, splitting time between Single-A Salem and Triple-A Columbus. In 49 games for Columbus, Lois had 46 hits (.254 average) with six home runs and 20 runs batted in. He had five stolen bases in eight attempts.

In September of the 1978 season, Lois was called up to the big leagues where the Pirates, led by manager Chuck Tanner, were chasing the Philadelphia Phillies for the National League East Division title. Lois made his big-league debut on September 8, when the Pirates took on the New York Mets at Shea Stadium. The Pirates came into the contest with a 74-65 record, 1½ games behind the first-place Phillies. The Mets were in sixth place at the time, with a record of 56-85. The game was tied 2-2 until the bottom of the eighth when Mets first baseman Willie Montanez hit a double that drove in left fielder Steve Henderson for the go-ahead run. With two outs in the Pirates' half of the ninth, catcher Manny Sanguillen drew a walk to give the Bucs a glimmer of hope. It also provided an opportunity for Lois, who replaced Sanguillen at first base, to make his first major-league appearance as a pinch-runner. The opportunity was lost when Mets reliever Dale Murray got the next batter, Frank Taveras, to ground out to short and end the game.

Over the final few weeks of the season, Lois's playing time was limited to just two more games.

THE 1979 PITTSBURGH PIRATES

However, Pittsburgh remained on the Phillies' heels for the division title. In the final series of the regular season, the Pirates, who were now 3½ games out of first, would play the Phillies in a four-game series at Three Rivers Stadium. With the NL East Division title on the line, the Pirates swept a Friday night doubleheader to keep their slim playoff hopes alive. They were off to a good start the next afternoon when Willie Stargell's first-inning grand slam gave them a 4-1 lead. However, the Pirates' pitching staff—which gave up two home runs to Phillies' starting pitcher Randy Lerch and another one to left fielder Greg Luzinski—were unable to hold the lead, eventually losing, 10-8. The Phillies victory gave them their third straight division title.

With the Pirates eliminated from postseason contention, Lois got his first (and only) major-league start on October 1, in the final game of the season, batting seventh and playing left field, before moving to center. In the second inning Lois hit a line drive off Phillies left-hander Jim Kaat that landed out of the reach of center fielder Lonnie Smith. Lois reached third base. The triple was the only hit of his major-league career. The next batter, infielder Mario Mendoza, popped out to Phillies second baseman Bud Harrelson to end the inning and strand Lois at third base. The Pirates went on to beat the Phillies, 5-3. Pittsburgh concluded the season with a second-place record of 88-73, 1½ games behind Philadelphia.

In 1979 Lois once again started the season in the minor leagues, where he played at both the Double-A and Triple-A levels. For the Buffalo Bisons of the Double-A Eastern League, he had 11 hits in 11 games (.275 average), one home run, and one run batted in. For the Portland Beavers of the Triple-A Pacific Coast League, he had four hits in five games (.444 average), including a triple.

Lois was called up by the Pirates in mid-August for a week and then in September. The Pirates were in another tight division race, this time with the Montreal Expos. Heading into their September 9 afternoon game with the last-place Mets at Shea Stadium, the Pirates had a record of 84-57 and a one-game lead over the Expos for first place in the National League East.

Lois pinch-ran in the eighth inning with Pittsburgh trailing, 4-3, and scored the go-ahead run on Bill Robinson's two-out single to third baseman Richie Hebner, to break a 4-4 tie. The Pirates went on to win, 6-5, and maintain their one-game lead over the Expos.

In 1979 Lois appeared in 11 games, all as a pinch-runner. On September 25 he displayed his speed during a pivotal game against the Expos at Three Rivers Stadium. Coming into the game the Expos held a half-game lead over the Pirates with less than a week remaining in the season. In the bottom of the sixth the Pirates led, 6-4. After three singles and a Montreal error increased their lead to 8-4, Lois ran for John Milner, who had reached first on an error. With Bill Madlock at the plate, Lois stole second, the only stolen base of his major-league career. He scored on Ed Ott's base hit, and the Bucs went on to win the game, 10-4, and take over first place in the division for good. Lois was not on the postseason roster as the Pirates eliminated Cincinnati in the NLCS and won the World Series over the Baltimore Orioles.

After the season Lois returned to the Dominican Republic to play in the Dominican Winter League. On January 5, 1980, he was involved in a calamitous highway accident that ended his playing career. After a birthday celebration, he was driving a truck filled with his friends — five in the back and three in front. Railroad tracks crossed the road, and a train was parked right in his path. According to Lois, "there was no signal, no light. There was nothing."[7]

The truck collided with the train, killing six of his passengers. Lois was thrown from the truck and was unconscious for six days. Years later, he said that if it were not for a quick left turn, he would not have survived the crash.[8] On May 2, 1980, the *Pittsburgh Post-Gazette* reported that team doctors, who had recently performed eye surgery on Lois, had suggested he would never play again.[9] He reportedly lost his eye.[10]

The Pirates released Lois on August 20, 1980. He struggled to find work in the Dominican Republic. In 2001 he worked for the Pirates as a trainer at a team facility in the Dominican Republic, but was let go the next year as part of organizational changes.[11]

Attempts through SABR's Juan Marichal Chapter to locate Lois in 2015 proved unsuccessful, though it was reported that he had 11 children, all of them daughters.[12]

Lois is remembered by many as a player who once had tremendous potential but whose career was tragically cut short by injury. Although Lois's major-league career was brief, he is in some rare company: He is one of only 16 major-league players since 1901 who finished their career with a triple as their only hit. Of these 16 players, only five — including Lois — were position players.[13]

NOTES

1 George Gedda, *Dominican Connection: Talent From the Tropics Changes Face of National Pastime* (New York: Eloquent Books, 2009), 117.

2 Clifford Blau, "Leg Men: Career Pinch-Runners in Major League Baseball," *The Baseball Research Journal*, Society for American Baseball Research, Volume 38, Number 1 (Summer 2009), 70-81.

3 SABR's Biographical Research Committee shows that Lois's birth name has also been listed as Alberto Louis Pie.

4 Baseball-Reference.com (August 10, 2012). "Alberto Lois — BR Bullpen." Available online: baseball-reference.com/bullpen/Alberto_Lois. Accessed July 21, 2014.

5 Blau, 80.

6 Gedda, 118.

7 Gedda, 117.

8 Ibid.

9 Dan Donovan. "Pirates Notes," *Pittsburgh Post-Gazette*, May 2, 1980: B-10.

10 Email from Julio Rodriguez to Bill Nowlin, June 20, 2015.

11 Gedda, 118.

12 Email from Julio Rodriguez to Bill Nowlin, June 20, 2015.

13 Baseball Reference.com "Play Index." Available online: baseball-reference.com/play-index/. Accessed September 23, 2014.

Bill Madlock

By Norm King

IF ONE HAD TO SUMMARIZE BILL Madlock's career in song, the best two numbers to choose would be Cole Porter's "Mad Dogs and Englishmen" and Duke Ellington's "It Don't Mean a Thing if You Ain't Got That Swing." The former because "Mad Dog" was his nickname, the latter because it took only one cut for a scout to see that Madlock did indeed have that swing. He also had a lot of intestinal fortitude, overcoming a difficult upbringing to become a four-time batting champion and the owner of a World Series ring.

Bill "Mad Dog" Madlock was born on January 2, 1951, in Memphis, Tennessee. His father had abandoned his mother, so she gave Madlock to her mother, Annie Polk, to raise when he was less than one month old. He and Annie moved to Decatur, Illinois, when he was 2, and his aunt and uncle, Sarah and Wardie Sain, helped bring him up.

Madlock was well "Iked" at Eisenhower High School in Decatur, earning nine sports letters. As an all-state halfback, he once scored five touchdowns in a game, each on a run of 50 yards or more. In basketball, he made the all-Capitol Conference second team. More than 100 colleges sent representatives to scout Madlock for a possible football scholarship, but simple self-preservation convinced him to focus on baseball.

"I didn't want to have 6-foot-5, 250-pound guys bearing down on me, so I decided to play baseball," he said.[1]

The year 1969 was eventful for Madlock. He married Cynthia Johnson while still in high school.[2] He was drafted in the 11th round of that year's amateur draft as a shortstop by the St. Louis Cardinals, but didn't sign because he thought his playing time would be limited with Dal Maxvill manning the position for the big club. He also enrolled at Southeastern Iowa Community College in Keokuk, Iowa, to hone his baseball skills. That summer, after rejecting the Cardinals, he was back playing in Decatur when legendary baseball scout Ellsworth Brown, who was working for the Washington Senators at the time, took a different route home one night, thus changing Madlock's life forever.[3]

"I'd been down in southern Illinois, and I was driving home to Beason," said Brown. "Usually I go to Lincoln and back down the highway. This time I took a back road from Decatur through Chestnut, and I saw a ballgame going on right there in Beason. Lincoln's Legion club was there against Decatur. It was the last inning. I saw this kid by the name of Bill Madlock swing one time, and I said, 'Boy, he's got that quick bat.' I went to Lincoln's coach, John West, and said, 'How'd that kid do the last time up?' West said, 'He reached that fence out there.'"[4]

Brown passed that information on to the Senators, who drafted Madlock in the fifth round of the 1970 January secondary draft. After signing him on May 25, Washington sent him to the Geneva Senators of the Class-A (short season) New York-Pennsylvania League, where he hit a modest .269 with 6 home runs and 29 RBIs in 66 games. Madlock's time in Geneva was stressful, because he had difficulty finding accommodation; no one wanted to rent to a black family. Nonetheless, the National Association of Baseball Writers voted him to the Class-A All-Star team as a shortstop. This feat was particularly impressive because the team included players from the Florida State, Carolina, and Western Carolina Leagues, as well as the New York-Pennsylvania League.

The Senators promoted Madlock to their Double-A affiliate, Pittsfield of the Eastern League, for 1971. He made an impression there early, securing the victory in the team's second game with a two-run homer in the top of the 11th inning. The home run atoned for two errors he made earlier in the game, but it was also a harbinger of a disappointing season, in which he hit .234 with 10 home runs and 37 runs batted in.

"I would not have bitched if they had released me then and there," said Madlock. "I was awful. I figured

the quickest way to the majors was to be an infielder who hit home runs, when actually that was the quickest way back to Decatur."5

Perhaps he was being tough on himself because he played and starred in the Eastern League All-Star game, going 3-for-5 with one RBI and three runs scored as he led his American Division team to a 5-2 win over the National Division All-Stars.

Madlock was also right in the middle of a disturbing incident near the end of the season. A huge brawl erupted in the seventh inning of an August 7 game between the Senators and the visiting Waterbury Pirates when Madlock proved he was no chicken by charging the mound after nearly getting beaned by pitcher Bob Cluck. What followed was a vintage NHL-style donnybrook that lasted almost half an hour, with some players bringing bats into the melee (The *Berkshire Eagle* said that nobody connected with them). Things got so out of hand that the ballpark announcer began playing the national anthem in an effort to restore order.

Madlock was suspended for the remainder of the season, but was reinstated after two weeks. Three other players, two from Waterbury and one from Pittsfield, were only suspended for three games each. Madlock returned with a flourish, going 3-for-5 in his first game back and making a great backhand stop at third base to prevent a hit.

The next rung on Madlock's climb to the majors was a mile high, when he began the 1972 season, with the Denver Bears of the Triple-A American Association. He didn't do well, playing only 26 games and hitting .213 with one homer and 9 RBIs before being sent back to Pittsfield. This move proved beneficial to Madlock's career because Pittsfield manager Joe Klein gave him the at-bats he needed to learn how to be more selective. Madlock played in only 42 games for Pittsfield that year, but his average exploded to .328 with 4 home runs and 26 RBIs.

That extra time in Pittsfield created a terror at the plate, as Madlock moved up in 1973 to the Texas Rangers' new Triple-A affiliate, the Spokane Indians of the Pacific Coast League.[6] He hammered PCL pitching to the tune of a .338 batting average, and showed substantially improved pop with 22 homers and 90 RBIs. The home-run total proved to be the highest of his career.

Those numbers demanded a call-up to the majors, and that's exactly what happened that September. Madlock made his major-league debut with the Rangers on September 7, going 2-for-3 with a walk and two runs scored while playing an errorless third base in a 10-8 win against the eventual world champion Oakland A's. His first home run came September 17 off Jim Kaat of the White Sox, a two-run shot in the first inning of a 10-3 win. Overall, Madlock hit a most promising .351 in 77 at-bats.

The 1973 Rangers had the worst record in the major leagues at 57-105. They scored the fewest runs (619) and had the highest team ERA (4.64) in the American League. Since they had to improve in every facet of the game, they flipped a coin and decided to start with pitching. To do that, they sent Madlock and utility player Vic Harris to the Chicago Cubs for future Hall of Famer Ferguson Jenkins on October 25, 1973. After six straight 20-win seasons, Jenkins had gone 14-16 for the Cubs in 1973 and was starting to get up there at age 30. Madlock, of course, was an untested rookie.

The trade worked out well for both teams. Jenkins won 25 games for Texas in 1974, while Madlock, hit .313 with 9 home runs and 54 RBIs for the Cubs, despite the pressure of following Cubs legend Ron Santo at the hot corner. Madlock also finished third in Rookie of the Year voting behind Bake McBride of St. Louis and Greg Gross of Houston.

He also got into a fight with Cardinals catcher Ted Simmons as a result of the antics of St. Louis relief pitcher Al "The Mad Hungarian" Hrabosky. Hrabosky was famous for psyching himself up and annoying batters by taking a ball, rubbing it vigorously while walking off the mound toward second base, talking to himself and/or the goulash gods, and then firing it into his glove before returning to the mound to pitch with steam snorting out of his nose.

In a September 22 game at Busch Stadium in St. Louis, Madlock led off the ninth inning with Hrabosky on the mound. After Hrabosky finished his behind-the-mound ritual and returned to the hill, Madlock stepped out of the batter's box. Home-plate umpire Shag Crawford told Hrabosky to pitch, which he did. Crawford called an automatic strike. Realizing what was happening, Madlock ran back to the plate just in time to duck a high hard one. As chaos ensued around home plate, Madlock and Simmons began jawing at each other and the fight was on. The dugouts emptied, but the dustup was over in a few minutes. Ironically, and perhaps appropriately, that was also the day that the Cardinals retired Dizzy Dean's number 17.

"Madlock came back to the plate and just stood there staring at me," said Simmons. "I asked him, 'What are you looking at?' and he said, 'Nuts to you.' "Then I went 'wham.'"[7]

Whether Madlock said "nuts to you" or something less printable is a mystery lost to the ages. What can't be refuted is the fact that he won his first batting title in 1975 with a .354 batting average, 182 hits, 7 home runs, and 64 RBIs, despite missing most of September with a bruised thumb. He also made his first All-Star team, which was no mean feat in an era that included Mike Schmidt and Ron Cey among National League third basemen. He showed that he earned the nomination by getting the game-winning hit, a bases-loaded two-run single in the ninth, as the National League defeated the American League 6-3 in the All-Star Game. He shared the outstanding-player award for the game with Mets pitcher Jon Matlack.

Madlock really blew it in September. Unfortunately, he overblew it, losing to Johnny Oates of the Phillies in the second round of the Joe Garagiola/Bazooka Bubble Gum Blowing contest. The competition was a light-hearted creation for the television show *The Baseball World of Joe Garagiola*, which included one representative of each team except the Detroit Tigers and Pittsburgh Pirates.[8] This was just one example of Madlock's lighter and community-oriented side. On September 28 of that year, for example, he and Cynthia were grand marshals for a bike-a-thon in Rolling Meadows, Illinois, to raise money for multiple-sclerosis programs.

This doesn't mean that Madlock no longer blew his stack. He was fined $100 for throwing his batting helmet during one August game, then another $100 for saying, "Nuts to you" or words to that effect to umpire Art Williams. In September he was fined $250 for lunging at umpire Jerry Dale after being called out on strikes.

The Bill Madlock Bicentennial Brouhaha occurred May 1, 1976, at Candlestick Park in San Francisco. It all started in the third inning when Giants pitcher Jim Barr brushed back Cubs left fielder Jose Cardenal, who was batting one spot ahead of Madlock. Umpire Paul Runge warned Barr, but Cardenal threw his batting helmet at the pitcher and got ejected for his trouble. Barr then plunked Madlock when he came to the plate and the fun ensued. Madlock headed toward the mound, followed by San Francisco catcher Marc Hill, who was trying to restrain him, but Bill managed to reach around Hill and slug Barr as the benches emptied. Madlock was thrown out of the game after order was restored, but Barr was not (in what may be poetic justice, the Giants won the game 3-1 but Barr did not get the victory). Madlock was fined $500.

By the end of June, Madlock was hitting .311, but already had two more home runs, nine, than he had in all of 1975. He attributed his lower batting average to the 17 games he missed during spring training when the owners locked the players out in a labor dispute.

"The thing that hurt was a lack of spring training," Madlock said. "Last year after spring training, the players were in shape, and even after an injury, you could get right back in the groove. That's not the way it has been this season, especially for me."[9]

Things turned around after the All-Star break. With the help of a 17-game hitting streak in August, Madlock won his second consecutive batting title with a .339 mark. He also had 174 hits, 15 home runs, 84 RBIs, and a .412 on-base percentage. And he won the title in style. On the last day of the season, he trailed Ken Griffey Sr. of the Cincinnati Reds by .0042 points, .3375 to .3333. Griffey began the Reds' last game of the season against the Braves on the bench to protect his lead. Madlock went into his last game guns ablazing, going 4-for-4 against the Expos to raise his average to .339. Griffey entered his game when he heard what Madlock was doing, but must have been scared hitless because he went 0-for-2 (striking out both times) and ended up with a .336 mark.

Winning the batting title in that fashion showed that Madlock had a good sense of timing. So did completing his contract just as Major League Baseball was entering the free-agency era. But since this was the Cubs, owner Phil Wrigley was unwilling to open up the coffers and offered Madlock no more than $110,000 for 1977, far below his market value.[10] The two sides couldn't agree on a contract, so Wrigley traded Madlock and infielder Rob Sperring to the San Francisco Giants for outfielder Bobby Murcer, third baseman Steve Ontiveros, and minor-league pitcher Andy Muhistock. In essence it was Madlock for Murcer, and while Murcer had good numbers with the Giants in 1976 (.259, 23 homers, and 90 RBIs), he was almost five years older than Madlock at 31. Anyway, Madlock ended up signing a five-year, $1.3 million contract in San Francisco.

The only batting statistic that went higher for Madlock in 1977 was the number of groundball double plays he hit into, a league-leading 25. He did hit .302 with 12 home runs and 46 RBIs, but these were not the numbers the Giants expected when they traded for him. He attributed the decline in average to playing half his games at Candlestick Park.

"I'm just not going to hit as well at Candlestick Park as I did at Wrigley Field," he said in a 1978 article. "A lot of balls I hit in the gap get held up by the wind at Candlestick, and you just don't feel as comfortable batting in cold, windy weather as you do when it's warm."[11]

Madlock's 1978 season confirmed that assertion, as he hit "only" .309, with 15 home runs and 44 RBIs. Madlock didn't waste time fighting with opponents that year. He decided to fight with a teammate instead, when he duked it out with pitcher John "The Count" Montefusco during spring training. On March 7 The Count was being interviewed when Madlock interrupted the proceedings. The two started at it before teammates separated the combatants.

Another cornerstone of Madlock's 1978 season, or keystone in this case, was his switch from third base to second, which allowed Darrell Evans to move from left field to the hot corner. Giants manager Joe Altobelli made the changes to improve team defense; the Giants were 11th in the league with 179 errors in 1977 (only the San Diego Padres made more). In 1978 the Giants had only 146 miscues and their record improved to 89-73 from 75-87.[12]

Madlock went from the agony to the ecstasy, from the ridiculous to the sublime in 1979. He arrived at spring training angry over an item in Dick Young's column in *The Sporting News* that said Giants owner Bob Lurie had accused Madlock of trying to sabotage the team's effort to sign free agent Rod Carew. Lurie denied making the statement, but Madlock was not mollified.

"Young wouldn't tell me where he got it from but he said it was 100 percent true," said Madlock. "He said he got it from a big man in San Francisco so I guess that means somebody in the front office."[13]

Madlock said in the same article that he might request a trade after the season, but judging by his play early on, it was a case of the sooner, the better. After 69 games, he was hitting .267, with 7 home runs and 41 RBIs.

Matters came to a head on June 26. Madlock hadn't been playing much in recent games, and during that time the grandmother who raised him passed away, so even though he was in the lineup that night against the Braves, he was a powder keg waiting to go off. In the sixth, after having avoided a few pitches aimed at his head earlier in the game, he threw an elbow at Braves reliever Bo McLaughlin and the donnybrook was on.

That was the last straw for the Giants, who engineered a six-player trade with the Pirates on June 28 in which they sent Madlock, utilityman Lenny Randle, and pitcher Dave Roberts to Pittsburgh for hurlers Ed Whitson, Fred Breining, and Al Holland.

Much has been said and written about how the 1979 Pirates were a family under the great leadership of National League co-MVP (with Keith Hernandez of the Cardinals) Willie Stargell. However, the Pirates would probably not have even won the East Division, let alone the World Series, without Madlock. Because of his grandmother's death and a rainout, Madlock didn't play his first game as a Pirate until July 2. Before that game, Pittsburgh had a 37-34 record and was tied with the Cubs and Philadelphia Phillies for second, 6½ games behind Montreal. The team went 61-30 the rest of the season on the road to the championship. Madlock, now back at third base, hit .328 the rest of the season (.298 overall), with an additional 7 home runs and 44 RBIs, plus .375 in the World Series.

"I think Bill Madlock was the best third baseman offensively and defensively in the major leagues last year," said Pirates skipper Chuck Tanner in 1980. "It's hard for a pitcher to go nine innings with a guy like him in our lineup."[14]

It's also hard for Madlock to go nine innings when he is suspended. And that's what he was after an incident in Montreal on May 1, 1980, when he began arguing a called third strike with home-plate umpire Jerry Crawford. Since Madlock's was the third out of the inning, a teammate brought him his glove so that he could take his place in the field. Madlock decided to use the glove to emphasize his point, right in Crawford's face. National League President Chub Feeney suspended Madlock for 15 days and fined him $5,000, but Madlock appealed the suspension. Feeney dawdled on ruling about the appeal, which ticked off the umpires, who threatened to eject Madlock from every game he played. Feeney finally upheld the suspension, which prompted Players Association President Marvin Miller to appeal that decision to Commissioner Bowie Kuhn.

The whole situation was on the verge of exploding into a real mess when Pirates owner John W. Galbreath met with Madlock and his attorney, Steve Greenberg, after which Madlock decided to serve his sentence.[15] He withdrew the appeal on June 6. The Pirates went 6-9 while he was gone.

The suspension was a regrettable part of a forgettable season for Madlock that included knee and thumb injuries in addition to the suspension. He hit .277 for the year, the lowest batting average of his major-league career to date, with 10 home runs and 53 RBIs.

Nobody could accuse Madlock of being a prognosticator. As a case in point, he said he didn't think he would win the batting title in 1981 during a spring-training interview.

"I can't get the batting title hitting down where I do in the lineup," he said. "How many people win a batting championship hitting fifth or sixth? Not too many."[16]

He nonetheless did win it, even though some luck was involved. Madlock played in only 82 of the team's 102 games, missing the last two weeks of the strike-shortened season with an injury. He wasn't even among the top 10 in hits, but his .341 average was the league's highest in that bizarre season. He also hit 6 home runs, had 45 RBIs, and was an All-Star.

The batting title wasn't the only good fortune that went Madlock's way in 1981. After the season he signed a six-year, multimillion-dollar contract, thus avoiding free agency. And he won the Roberto Clemente Award as voted on by the Pittsburgh chapter of the Baseball Writers Association of America as the Pirate who most exemplified the standards of excellence set by the Pirates legend.

Madlock got some media flak in 1982 for winning the 1981 batting title as he did, but one would think that a player who had already won two batting titles has earned a bit of slack. He responded to the comments and the pressure of a new contract by having arguably the best season of his career, combining average and power numbers as he never had before. His .319 batting average represented a drop from the previous season, but it was still second in the league behind Al Oliver of the Montreal Expos, who hit .331. He also hit home runs (19) and had a career high in RBIs (95), and his 181 hits were only one below his career high. He was in such a good frame of mind all season that he even defended the umpires after they received a letter from Feeney criticizing their performance.

"The umpiring has been outstanding," he said. "If I don't complain, nobody should complain."[17]

Once everybody regained consciousness after hearing those comments, the Pirates chose Madlock to replace Willie Stargell as captain for the 1983 season after Pops, retired at the end of the 1982 campaign. Madlock was also named to President Ronald Reagan's Council on Physical Fitness, which at the time was headed by former NFL coach George Allen.

He responded to the additional responsibility by winning his fourth batting title (.323 average) and playing in his third All-Star game. His power numbers were down from 1982, but still respectable (12 home runs, 68 RBIs). He did have injury problems, including a bout of phlebitis and a torn tendon in his left calf, but still managed to play in 130 games. Yet despite winning the batting title, Madlock wasn't happy with his season.

"This may have been my worst season," he said. "I was never able to do what comes natural to me."[18]

Age, injuries, and the loss of natural ability took its toll, because 1983 represented Madlock's last dominating season in baseball. He had a disastrous year in 1984, hitting only .253 with 4 homers and 44 RBIs, while missing a third of the season after arm surgery. In 1985, he signed a six-year contract at the beginning of July to stay with the Pirates, only to be traded to the Los Angeles Dodgers at the end of August for outfielders R.J. Reynolds and Cecil Espy, plus first baseman Sid Bream. Madlock hit .360 in 34 games as Los Angeles won the NL West Division. In the NLCS, he hit .333 with three home runs but the Dodgers lost the postseason series to the Cardinals, four games to two.

The injury bug followed Madlock to sunny California; he was on the disabled list twice in 1986 and played in only 108 games. The Dodgers released him on May 29, 1987, and the Detroit Tigers signed him as a free agent on June 5. He retired from the major leagues after the 1987 season with a career .305 average, 163 home runs, 860 RBIs, and four batting titles.

Madlock stayed in the game after his major-league career ended. He played in Japan in 1988, batting .263 with 19 home runs and 61 RBIs for the Lotte Orions of the Japan Pacific League. He stopped playing altogether after a 55-game stint in the short-lived Senior Professional Baseball Association in 1989.

Madlock's post-baseball life has been filled with ups and downs. He had difficulties with the Internal Revenue Service, caused, as it turned out, by his former attorney investing some of his money in sham tax-avoidance schemes. He was also arrested in 1995 for passing bad checks, fined $5,000, and ended up having to pay restitution and performing 200 hours of community service.

He still managed to find work in baseball, as a hitting coach with the Detroit Tigers in 2000-2001, and was named an assistant to the vice president of on-field operations in Commissioner Bud Selig's office in 2002. He also managed and coached in independent leagues. In 2003 Madlock returned to Keokuk, Iowa, to receive a Distinguished Alumni award from Southeastern Community College.

As of 2015, Madlock lived in Las Vegas, Nevada, and teaches youngsters how to hit at The Dugout batting cage.

SOURCES

In addition to the sources cited in the Notes, the author accessed the following:

Baseball-reference.com.

Berkshire Eagle (Pittsfield, Massachusetts).

THE 1979 PITTSBURGH PIRATES

Biographical Dictionary of American Sports (New York: Greenwood Press).

Chicago Sun-Times.

Daily Herald (Chicago).

Oneonta (New York) *Star.*

News/Journal (Chicago).

Oneonta (New York) *Star.*

Sfgate.com.

Southern Illinoisan (Carbondale, Illinois).

State Journal-Register (Springfield, Illinois).

that70scard.com/the-joe-garagiolabazooka-bubble-gum-blowing-contest/.

NOTES

1. Steve Wulf, "Glad Times for Mad Dog," *Sports Illustrated*, May 9, 1983.
2. Together they had four children, Sarah, Stephen, William, and Jeremy. They later divorced.
3. Brown was inducted into the Baseball Scouts Hall of Fame in 2005 after a career of more than 50 years. Among the players he discovered was Hall of Famer Kirby Puckett.
4. "Beason's Baseball King 'Brownie' Dies," *The Courier* (Lincoln, Illinois), January 22, 2009.
5. Wulf.
6. The Washington Senators moved to Texas after the 1971 season.
7. Paul LeBar, "Hrabosky's Ritual Sparks A Brawl," Mount *Vernon* (Illinois) *Register-News*, September 23, 1974.
8. Kurt Bevacqua of the Milwaukee Brewers blew the field away with an 18¼-inch bubble. People can see the complete contest bracket on card #564 of the 1975 Topps Bubble Gum baseball card series.
9. Joe Mooshil, "Cubs' Madlock Still Has Hopes for Batting Title," *The Sporting News*, June 29, 1976.
10. Joe Rudi, for example, hit .270 with 13 home runs and 94 RBIs and won a Gold Glove with the A's in 1976, then signed a five-year, $2,090,000 contract with the Angels.
11. Nick Peters, "Madlock's Bat Picks Up Speed on Road," *The Sporting News*, June 24, 1978.
12. They also went from seventh in runs allowed (711) to third (594), which was a factor in their improved record.
13. Associated Press, "Unhappy Madlock Speaks Out," *Santa Cruz* (California) *Sentinel*, March 6, 1979.
14. Mike Tully, "Mad Dog Just Fit Buc Plan," *The Daily News* (Huntington, Mount Union, and Saxton, Pennsylvania), March 25, 1980.
15. Steve Greenberg was Hank Greenberg's son.
16. United Press International, "Madlock Can't See Bat Title," April 2, 1981.
17. Associated Press, "Feeney Receives Complaints but Players Say Umps Have Improved," *Gettysburg* (Pennsylvania) *Times*, July 24, 1982.
18. Alan Robinson, "Madlock Wins Fourth Batting Title," United Press International, October 4, 1983.

John Milner

By Jon Springer

JOHN MILNER IDOLIZED HANK AARON, lockered next to Willie Mays, and on his best days could hit home runs with as much authority as either man. While injuries and inconsistency prevented Milner from becoming an elite slugger, he carved out a 12-year career for the Mets, Pirates, and Expos, helping each of those clubs reach postseason play. And though a quiet sort in his playing days, Milner's post-career testimony about drug use provided a direct and unflinching peek into the dark side of the game as it was played in the late 1970s and early '80s.

John David Milner was born on December 28, 1949, in Atlanta, the second of Johnny Sims and Addie Milner's three children. Addie raised the Milner children herself on modest wages as a domestic housekeeper and with the help of a large extended family around the Atlanta suburb of East Point, where they lived. (John Milner was an older cousin of Eddie Milner, who had a nine-year major-league career from 1980 to 1988 playing for Cincinnati and San Francisco.)

Like most African-American residents of East Point, the Milners lived in the East Washington community, a section of the city segregated under 1912 Jim Crow laws. The area was adjacent to steel mills and fertilizer plants that drew its early residents, mostly Southern farmers seeking steady work amid a declining agricultural economy.[1]

Segregation was a defining influence for residents of the area, who often found themselves struggling for the same access to services and benefits afforded wealthier white residents. In the 1950s and 1960s of Milner's youth, black children and teenagers of East Point were prohibited from participating in Little League baseball with white children. They instead participated in separate Pony Colts and Pony Leagues organized by a noted community activist, Oscar James "O.J." Hurd, and supported by contributions from a local grocery store. Such community sports programs kept kids off the streets, and fed the segregated South Fulton High School, which became known statewide for the successful teams and athletes it produced in the 1960s, including Charlie Greer, who became a defensive back for the NFL's Denver Broncos, and Don Adams, a small forward for NBA teams including the Atlanta Hawks and Detroit Pistons. Milner, who graduated from South Fulton in 1968, garnered All-State recognition as a halfback in football, a guard in basketball, and a baseball outfielder for the Mighty Lions.

Although Milner probably preferred playing basketball to any other sport, only baseball would provide him the opportunity to participate in professionally. And he wasn't sure that chance would come. Milner had already applied for work with the East Point sanitation department when a Mets scout, Julian Morgan, informed him he'd been selected by the club in the 14th round of the 1968 first-year player draft. Five years earlier, Morgan had signed Cleon Jones, who by then was rounding into the best offensive player the young Mets franchise ever produced. Within a few years, it looked as though Milner might be the next.

Listed at 6 feet and 185 pounds, Milner was a taut, muscular left-handed hitter and thrower. He had fast wrists and a distinct batting stance, keeping his legs close together and his upper body leaning aggressively toward the plate, becoming an attacking dead-pull hitter who could punish pitches left out over the plate. Although scouts invariably noted that Milner "likes to swing the bat," he was disciplined enough to amass more walks (504) than strikeouts (473) over nearly 4,000 big-league plate appearances. Milner was considered an average corner outfielder with average speed and a subpar arm, and was adequate at first base, where he appeared the most on the field during his professional career. When Gil Hodges was asked what position Milner played best, the Mets manager replied "at bat."[2]

THE 1979 PITTSBURGH PIRATES

Hodges made that remark only weeks before suffering a fatal heart attack that cast a pall over the 1972 spring training for the Mets. Until then the story of the spring had been Milner. Then 22 years old and in his first major-league camp, "The Hammer"—a nickname given to Milner because of his admiration for, and resemblance to, "Hammerin' Hank" Aaron—had earned the team's Johnny Murphy Award as the best rookie in camp and won a job as the team's regular left fielder.

Milner had made his major-league debut the previous season during a September 15, 1971, doubleheader at Shea Stadium against the Chicago Cubs. In the opener he grounded out as a pinch-hitter facing Bill Hands in his first big-league plate appearance, then started in left field in the second game and singled to right off Burt Hooton for his first major-league hit. Milner had been called up from the Tidewater (Virginia) Tides of the Triple-A International League, where he had slugged 19 home runs while batting .290. This solid production was on the heels of All-Star seasons for the Mets' farm clubs in Marion (Virginia) of the Rookie-level Appalachian League (1968), Visalia of the Class-A California League (1969), and Memphis of the Double-A Texas League (1970).

Milner ripped 17 home runs as a rookie—the most for a power-thirsty Mets team—and finished a distant third behind a teammate, starting pitcher Jon Matlack (the winner) and San Francisco Giants catcher Dave Rader in the '72 Rookie of the Year voting. Milner credited the coaching of Whitey Herzog, then the Mets' farm director, for helping to hone his hitting during stints in the Florida Instructional League in 1970 and 1971.

Milner's 23 home runs in 1973 and 20 in 1974 also led the Mets. But it wasn't long before the debate around Milner was about what he hadn't accomplished.

Most contemporary accounts describe Milner as intense and fiercely competitive, often manifesting itself in an angry disposition. "He could go three for four, including a home run, and the Mets could win by five runs, and yet, when he enters the locker room afterward, he is steaming mad," writer Dick Schaap observed in 1972.[3] Writers found him frosty

and uncooperative, and occasionally others did too. He was suspended for three games in 1973 for bumping third-base umpire Lee Weyer in an altercation over a disputed catch. He clashed frequently with Joe Frazier, who managed the Mets in 1976 and early 1977. Milner's tendency to miss games with recurring ailments—most often sore hamstrings—earned him a "goldbrick" tag, a rap Milner insisted was unfair.[4]

As might be expected having grown up in the segregated South, Milner was sensitive to race playing a role in such criticisms. When the veteran and former All-Star Cleon Jones fell out of favor and was released just after midseason by the stodgy Mets management in 1975, the inference that he was a bad influence on Milner seemed to doubly insult the younger player. "Why do people always say one player was bad influence on another because the player is black?" Milner said in 1976. "Cleon didn't hurt me. He helped me. Did they say Cleon was a bad influence when we won the pennant in '73?"[5]

Milner's sister, Sharon, said her brother's gruff exterior was his means of protecting himself and that he was fun-loving and generous among friends and family. On road trips to Atlanta, Milner loved having black teammates including Jones, Tommie Agee, and Gene Clines as guests at his family's home, where they would gather for meals prepared by his mother, Addie.

Milner stayed with the Mets through the 1977 season, and though he never blossomed into a star, there were several highlights along the way on both sides of the baseball. Milner snared Glenn Beckert's soft liner at Chicago to turn an unassisted double play that clinched an improbable NL East division title for the 1973 Mets. In Game Three of the best-of-five 1973 NLCS against the heavily favored Cincinnati Reds, he gloved a smash off the bat of Joe Morgan to begin a 3-6-3 double play that ended with fisticuffs between the Reds' Pete Rose and Mets shortstop Bud Harrelson before escalating into a bench-clearing event. In the deciding Game Five, Milner fielded a roller hit by Dan Driessen and flipped the ball to Tug McGraw covering first base for the final out. However, instead of reveling in their pennant-winning victory on the field, Milner and the rest of his teammates had to race for the safety of their clubhouse as an estimated 5,000 New York fans stormed the Shea Stadium playing field in a wild celebration. In the top of the 12th inning during Game Two of the World Series, Milner's hard-hit groundball with two outs was not handled by Oakland's second baseman, Mike Andrews (his first of two miscues in the inning), and the error paved the way for a Mets victory. The extra-inning loss raised the ire of A's owner Charlie Finley so much that he attempted to replace Andrews on Oakland's postseason roster afterward. In 1974 Milner hit a prodigious home run off the Dodgers' Andy Messersmith that smashed some lightbulbs halfway up Shea Stadium's massive scoreboard in right center, said to be one of the longest ever hit in that ballpark.[6] And he rebounded from a poor 1975 (.191 in 91 games) with what was his best major-league season to-date in 1976, hitting a then career-best .271 with 17 home runs, including three of his 10 career grand slams.

In December of 1977, the rebuilding Mets sent Milner to Pittsburgh as part of a complex four-team, 11-player deal involving the Mets, Pirates, Texas Rangers, and Atlanta Braves.

A fresh start in Pittsburgh seemed to do Milner good for the next two seasons. No longer the feature of the offense as he was at times in New York, Milner settled into a role as a part-time starter at first base and in the outfield, a good fit among a contending team with several African-American stars, including Dave Parker, Frank Taveras, Bill Robinson, Willie Stargell, and later Bill Madlock.

The Pirates finished a game and a half behind the Phillies in 1978 but there was no denying them in 1979, when the team, united behind the Sister Sledge song "We Are Family," edged the Montreal Expos by two games for the NL East Division title, dispatched Cincinnati in three games during in the best-of-five NLCS for the NL pennant, and fought back from a three-games-to-one deficit to stun the Baltimore Orioles in the World Series.

Milner was a productive member of that championship squad, cracking 16 home runs and driving in 60 runs in 386 plate appearances. He started 85 games, splitting left field with right-handed-hitting counterpart Robinson, and occasionally spelling Stargell at first base. The Pirates caught fire in August, sparked by a five-game weekend series sweep of the Phillies at Three Rivers Stadium. Milner delivered the signature moment with a walk-off grand slam off Phillies left-handed relief ace and former Mets' teammate Tug McGraw to win the fourth of those five "playoff atmosphere" games, 12-8—a comeback victory that regained first place for the Pirates from Montreal and keyed a decisive month during which they played .700 ball.

Milner was 3-for-9 with two walks, a double, two runs scored, and one RBI during the World Series.

Milner retained his role as a part-time starter on the 1980 Pirates, although he and the club regressed—Milner lost more than 100 points off his slugging percentage from 1979, and the Pirates dropped to third place in the division. Milner played less in the outfield as Mike Easler settled into an everyday role, although Stargell's knee woes provided Milner with more time at first base. Milner opted for free agency in late October, but re-signed with Pittsburgh three months later.

THE 1979 PITTSBURGH PIRATES

On August 20, 1981, the Pirates swapped Milner to the Montreal Expos for first baseman Willie Montanez shortly after games resumed following the nearly two-month player strike. It was the second time Milner was essentially traded for Montanez—the Mets had received Montanez from Atlanta as part of the four-team December 1977 trade. Although the latter swap was hardly consequential, it should be noted that the team trading for Milner came out ahead in both of those deals.

The Expos sought Milner's power to bolster a club contending for its first playoff appearance in the split-season competition (imposed after the strike) featuring an extra tier of postseason games. He started a handful of games at first base for the Expos but was relegated to pinch-hitting when the Expos installed rookie Tim Wallach in right field and moved Warren Cromartie to first base down the stretch. Montreal edged St. Louis by a half-game for the second half of the NL East crown, and defeated the Phillies three games to two in a special division series. The Expos lost in five games to the pitching-rich Los Angeles Dodgers in the NLCS. Though Milner played very sparingly in the postseason (one hit and one RBI in three plate appearances), 1981 was the third season in which he played a role for an NL East champion in a tight pennant chase.

Pinch-hitting almost exclusively in 1982, Milner was batting just .107 when the Expos released him in early July, and Pittsburgh re-signed him later that month. Milner contributed two pinch home runs for the 1982 Pirates, including his 10th career grand slam.

The Pirates invited the then 33-year-old Milner to training camp in 1983, but released him just prior to Opening Day, ending his career in the big leagues. But it wouldn't be the last time fans would hear his name.

Milner later revealed that he used cocaine over the last four years of his career, buying as much as seven grams a week and sharing it with his teammates on the Expos and Pirates.[7] The revelations came as part of testimony in a grand-jury investigation into a Pittsburgh-based drug ring and the subsequent trials and convictions of two dealers in 1985.

One of several players to testify at the trials, Milner gave particularly direct testimony, providing a glimpse inside baseball that many weren't ready to see. He described having made a drug deal in the Three Rivers Stadium clubhouse while a game was going on, and also said Willie Mays during his time with the Mets had "red juice"—amphetamines dissolved in a liquid—in his locker. Though Milner said he didn't see Mays take the drugs, he admitted helping himself to them.[8] Mays, by then a Hall of Famer, denied Milner's charges. It would be many years before the pervasiveness of amphetamine use that Milner described in 1985 would come into better perspective among fans of the game.

Milner returned to East Point after his baseball career and worked in construction with an uncle, his sister said. He was never married or had a family, but aspired to support youth sports as his mentors had. A smoker, Milner developed lung cancer that progressed rapidly, and he died on January 4, 2000, at Grady Memorial Hospital in Atlanta. He had just turned 50 years old.

In 2002 the East Point neighborhood sandlot where Milner played football as a youth was rechristened as part of an 18-acre regional sports park. The John D. Milner Athletic Complex hosts youth soccer, football, kickball, and baseball on four lighted fields.

SOURCES

In addition to the sources cited in the notes, the author interviewed Sharon Milner on August 23, 2014, and October 11, 2014, and consulted:

Silverman, Matthew, *Swinging 73: Baseball's Wildest Season* (Guilford, Connecticut: Lyons Press, 2013).

scouts.baseballhall.org/.

ultimatemets.com.

baseballreference.com.

NOTES

1. Herman "Skip" Mason Jr., *East Point, Georgia* (Charleston, South Carolina: Arcadia Publishing, 2001).
2. Jack Lang, "Can Milner make a 'hit' with Gil?" *Newark Star-Ledger*, March 24, 1972.
3. Dick Schaap, "What Comes After Dawn's Early Light?" *New York magazine*, June 26, 1972.

WHEN POPS LED THE FAMILY

4 Charley Feeney, "Pirates Acquit Milner On Goldbrick Charge," *The Sporting News*, September 2, 1978.

5 Augie Borgi, "Milner: Not Looking Back On Disastrous '75 Season," *New York Daily News*, March 23, 1976.

6 Associated Press, "Monster blow by Milner dims lights," August 13, 1974.

7 "Milner: 7 grams a week," *New York Daily News* (wire services), September 24, 1985.

8 Michael Goodwin, "Milner Tells Court of Buying Cocaine," *New York Times*, September 13, 1985.

Omar Moreno

By Norm King

IMAGINE YOU'RE PLAYING WORD AS-sociation with a baseball nut. Mention Commerce, Oklahoma, and the fan will respond, "Mickey Mantle!" Shout out Donora, Pennsylvania, and the fan will bellow out, "Stan Musial." And if your next term is Puerto Armuelles, the fan is likely to shout … "Say that again?"

Small though it may be, Puerto Armuelles, a town in the Panamanian province of Chiriqui, is the birthplace of one of the greatest basestealers of the 1970s and 1980s, Omar Moreno.

Omar Renan (Quintero) Moreno was born on October 24, 1952, one of 10 children born to Aurelio Moreno Murillo, a foreman for the United Fruit Company, and Lidia Quintero de Moreno, a homemaker. The young Moreno had baseball in his genes—his father was a catcher in his younger days—pitching and playing the outfield. He was also a track star, building up his speed and leg strength running along the beaches near his home; his specialties were the 100-meter dash and the high jump. His speed, more than his hitting ability, attracted the attention of Pittsburgh's head Latin American scout, Howie Haak in 1968, when Moreno was only 15. "He couldn't hit the ball out of the infield but he sure could run," Haak recalled.[1]

Pittsburgh's Panamanian scout, Herb Raybourn, who worked under Haak, got Moreno's parents to sign a contract on his behalf while Omar was representing his province at the Panamanian national highschool championships in the city of Chitre (Moreno went 7-for-10 in three games and led Chiriqui to its first championship).[2] Moreno received quite the surprise when he returned home from the tournament.

"And so my mom says to me: 'Did you know you're going to the U.S. with the Pittsburgh Pirates?'" said Moreno. "I was in shock. … I said: 'Me?'" The left-handed-batting and -throwing Moreno began his odyssey through the minor leagues with the Pirates' affiliate in the Rookie Class Gulf Coast League in 1969. At age 16, he was two years younger than his next oldest teammate, and had to make the language and cultural adjustments common to young players from Latin American countries. He acquitted himself adequately offensively, getting into 25 of the team's 54 games and batting .290 with no home runs, 4 RBIs, and 5 stolen bases.

Moreno, who was 6-feet-2 and weighed 180 pounds, had trouble getting beyond the lowest levels of the minors during his first few years as a professional, bouncing back and forth between the Gulf Coast League and the lower-level Class-A (short season), and mostly as a part-timer at that; he didn't play in more than 100 games in a season at one location until his fifth year in the minors, when he played in 136 games for the Salem (Virginia) Pirates of the Class-A Carolina League in 1973 at age 20. He had a solid season, batting .284 with 9 home runs and 56 RBIs, all the while blazing along the basepaths with 77 steals, a league record (he also played three games with the Charleston (West Virginia) Charlies of the Triple-A International League. Those numbers got him promoted to the Thetford Mines (Quebec) Pirates of the Double-A Eastern League in 1974, where he hit .300, with 7 home runs, 39 RBIs, and 67 stolen bases.

After starting the season in Thetford Mines, Moreno was called up to the Charlies again on June 11, which was a wild day to be sure. Moreno was informed that morning of his promotion, then spent the day traveling to Charleston, where he found out that he was starting in that night's matchup against the Pawtucket Red Sox. That game lasted 16 innings and did not finish until after midnight. If Moreno was tired after the game, he could at least take comfort in the fact that he scored the tying run as Charleston overcame a two-run deficit in the bottom of the 16th to win 10-9. After the game, Moreno and his teammates boarded a bus for the five-hour trip to Toledo,

Ohio, where they started a four-game series against the Mud Hens the next night.

Moreno played in 23 games for Charleston and was batting only .220 when he returned to Thetford Mines for the remainder of what turned out to be a very good season. He was chosen to play in the postseason Eastern League All-Star Game.

Moreno finally got his first cup of coffee with the Pirates in September 1975 after a full season at Charleston, where he hit .284, smacked 9 home runs, and drove in 51 runs. His stolen-base total, 39, was down significantly from recent seasons. On September 5 he got the call into the manager's office that all minor leaguers hope for, and was given a plane ticket to Montreal, where the Pirates were playing the Expos. He pinch-hit for Richie Hebner in the seventh inning of that night's game, working a walk from Steve Rogers. He made his first major-league start on September 24, playing left field against the Phillies. He didn't waste any time making his first major-league error, misplaying a bases-loaded single by Greg Luzinski in the top of the first that allowed "The Bull" to reach second. Moreno made up for the miscue in the bottom of the inning. Batting second in the order, he got his first major-league hit with a single to left off Larry Christenson, stole second, and scored on a single by Al Oliver. It was the only Pirates run in an 8-1 loss.

After his team finished 11th in the National League with 49 steals in 1975, Pirates manager Danny Murtaugh said that his 1976 team was going to run more and that the young speedsters in the minors had a very good chance of making the big club in spring training.[3] "For the Bucs to run more in '76, Murtaugh said, youngsters such as Omar Moreno, Tony Armas, and Craig Reynolds would have to make the club," wrote Dave Brown. "And they would have to see enough playing time to steal bases."[4]

By the time the season started, however, Murtaugh felt that Moreno and at least one of his fellow youngsters still needed some seasoning. "We have some speed," he said, but (Miguel Dilone and Omar Moreno) are a year away."[5]

Moreno began the 1976 season in Charleston. It was evident by early May that he was working hard on all aspects of his game, and that the effort was paying off. His manager, Tim Murtaugh (Danny's son), admired the Panamanian for his dedication and willingness to work hard to improve.

"He [Moreno] has a major league arm—it is strong and accurate—and he is an intelligent ballplayer," Murtaugh said. "The only problem he had at the start of his career came from his failure to understand English. It took him a little while to catch on to what we were trying to tell him.

"He has made himself what he is today by hard work and, as I say, complete dedication."[6]

That industriousness earned Moreno a brief call-up on June 20 when first baseman Bob Robertson went on the 15-day disabled list with torn ligaments in his ankle. Moreno appeared in six games and returned to Charleston on July 4 after Robertson's injury healed. Moreno made those six games count; he got noticed when he played, at least by the media.

"The Pirates brass does some funny things," wrote Charley Feeney. "Omar Moreno, a left-handed pinch-hitter with speed, was shipped to Charleston, and Bob Robertson, a right-handed hitter with no speed, was taken off the disabled list. The move did one thing. It strengthened the Charleston farm club."[7]

Maybe somebody was reading Feeney's article, because Moreno was called up again on August 10 after Pirates rookie catcher Ed Ott broke a bone in his right hand. That news came two days after Moreno was named to the International League All-Star team for his .315 batting average with 3 home runs, 36 RBIs, and 55 stolen bases. Moreno didn't play in that All-Star game because this time the ticket was one-way. His confidence helped make sure of that. A few days after being recalled by Pittsburgh, Moreno found himself playing center field in the Astrodome replacing veteran All-Star outfielder Al Oliver. After being troubled with dizziness, Oliver was hospitalized while the Pirates were in Houston, and subsequently missed three weeks of action. After tests, it was discovered that Oliver was suffering from an inner-ear infection.

"Moreno has confidence now," said Pirates general manager Joe Brown. "He feels he belongs, and this is important with any young player."[8]

Moreno hit .270 in 48 games for the Pirates in 1976, and one of his early thrills was his first big-league home run, on a lucky Friday, August 13, a ninth—inning solo shot against Joe Niekro of the Astros in Houston that added the final run in an 8-5 Pirates victory. It was the first of two homers he hit in limited playing time, to go along with 12 RBIs, a .270 average, and 15 stolen bases.

Chuck Tanner became the Pirates' manager in 1977, and like a kid with a chemistry set, had more speed to play with than his predecessor. The Pirates lineup, which included Moreno, holdovers Rennie Stennett and Frank Taveras, and new third baseman Phil Garner, turned the basepaths at Three Rivers Stadium into the Pittsburgh Motor Speedway, as the Bucs stole 260 bases as a team to lead the major leagues—the Astros were second with 187—with Moreno contributing 53 to the total.[9]

As good as that number was, Moreno's rookie season was a disappointment to the Pirates. They didn't expect huge numbers or much power from him, but his .240 batting average was below team expectations. Ever the optimist, Tanner expected great things from Moreno in the future: "Moreno hasn't even begun to realize his potential," Tanner said.[10]

Moreno got off to a good start at the plate in 1978 in part because he was more familiar with the strike zone and also because he stopped trying to pull the ball. "I try to hit everything on the ground and to left and left-center field," he said. "I've been staying away from bad pitches because I'm not trying to pull the ball."[11] That approach worked in the first month of the season—he had a .286 average on May 1, but a horrible slump that month (16-for-107, .150) dropped his average to .198 by May 31. He remained in the batting order due to his speed and defensive ability. He worked his average back up to .235, and more than doubled his walk total for the season, to 81 from 38 in 1976. His biggest achievement of the season was to lead the majors in stolen bases with a team-record 71; he also scored 95 runs.

The Pirates' brass still wanted Moreno to improve his hitting. Every "Tom and Dick" was trying to give him advice, which only increased his anxiety level, so after the season they sent him to see former Pirates skipper Harry "The Hat" Walker, who was coaching at the University of Alabama. Walker had a good reputation with the Pirates as a hitting instructor. The San Francisco Giants traded 25-year-old Matty Alou to Pittsburgh after he hit .231 in 1965. Under Walker's tutelage, Alou won the batting title in 1966 with a .342 average, and maintained that batting stroke the rest of his career, as his lifetime .307 mark will attest.

Walker focused on getting Moreno to swing down on the ball and put it on the ground more. Moreno proved to be a very good student, as he set career highs in 1979 in batting average (.282), runs (110), hits (196), home runs (8), and RBIs (69) He also won his second consecutive NL stolen-base crown (77 steals). Defensively, he also showed how his speed permitted him to reach a lot of fly balls, as he led the league in putouts by a center fielder with 489, significantly more than Gold Glove winner Gary Maddox of the Phillies, who nabbed 425. Moreno also showed that just because he could reach more balls, it didn't mean that he always caught them, as he led National League center fielders in errors with 13. The Pirates reached the

World Series that year, and Moreno showed he could produce in the clutch; his 11 hits in the fall classic were just one below the totals of Series co-leaders Garner and MVP Willie Stargell as the Pirates defeated the Baltimore Orioles in seven games. Six of those hits came in the last two games, to help the Bucs come back from a 3-1 deficit. Moreno caught the final out in Game Seven.[12]

The Pirates had won the National League East by two games over the Expos. That offseason, the Montreal brass decided to fight fire with fire, or, more precisely, speed with speed. They acquired basestealer extraordinaire Ron LeFlore from the Detroit Tigers. LeFlore and Moreno had a season-long race for the National League's basestealing crown in 1980. The competition went right to the wire, with LeFlore edging Moreno out by one, 97 steals to 96. Moreno's steal of second in the first inning of a 5-1 loss in Houston on August 20 was historic. It was his 70th steal of the year, making him the first player since 1900 to have three consecutive seasons with 70 or more steals.[13]

For all his basestealing wizardry, it seems that Moreno should have gone back to that cat called "The Hat" for a refresher; the lessons he applied so well in 1979 didn't carry over into 1980, as he hit only .249, with 2 home runs and 36 RBIs. The lower numbers were due to several factors. One was a midseason finger injury suffered when he jammed the little digit of his left hand while sliding into a base on a steal. The injury, although painful, still allowed him to play, but he had difficulty gripping the bat and couldn't bunt for base hits. Another, according to Moreno, was his dissatisfaction with his contract situation.

"I was mad about my contract and the front office," Moreno said. "I said okay to a one-year contract in spring training because (Pirates management) said we'd talk about a five-, six-year contract later. Then they changed their minds and say no."[14]

Tanner said that Moreno's defensive abilities were far more important than his offensive output. He had a one-of-a-kind defensive triple crown in 1980, leading National League center fielders in putouts (481), assists (15), and outs made (560). "The last thing you look at with Moreno is his hitting," Tanner said. "I played him every day when he hit .235 and I would today. He takes so many hits away with his glove."[15]

The distractions that reduced Moreno's offensive production in 1980 were dealt with in the offseason. He had surgery on his finger, and signed a one-year deal after playing without a contract the previous year. He was confident going into spring training for the 1981 season, and even predicted that he would hit .300. Early on it became evident that Moreno was not going to reach that goal; his average stood at .203 by May 17. He slowly started hitting again by that point, and by June 10, the date of the first in-season strike in baseball history, he was hitting .261. He began hitting when play resumed on August 10, and had his average up as high as .291 by September 20 before finishing with a .276 mark with 1 home run and 35 runs batted in after starting all of Pittsburgh's 103 games. His basestealing fell off significantly; his 39 thefts were second in the league, but far below the league-leading total of Expos rookie Tim Raines, who had 71.

Raines's overwhelming win in the stolen-base race caught Moreno flatfooted, so when spring training rolled around for 1982, Moreno promised to take back his title. "He [Raines] really surprised me last year," Moreno said. "I am going to do my best to steal over 85 bases. That's what's on my mind now."[16]

Tanner even planned to help Moreno reach his goal by having Mike Easler bat second in the order behind him. Tanner reasoned that Easler, being a good fastball hitter, would see a lot of slow stuff, which would make it easier for Moreno to get a good jump. It was a good idea in theory, but Easler's woeful .143 average after nine games didn't discourage pitchers from throwing him anything. Tanner dropped Easler to sixth in the order starting with game 10 and kept him in the lower part of the lineup for the rest of the season.

The failed experiment did not prevent Moreno from having a productive year on the basepaths, as he stole 60 bases, third in the National League behind Raines (78 steals) and Lonnie Smith of the Cardinals (68). At the plate he had a typical Moreno season, with a .245 batting average, 3 home runs, and 44 RBIs.

Moreno was obviously very busy during the baseball season. But he was also involved in the community as local honorary chairman of the National Hemophilia Foundation, a cause that was important to him because he has a nephew with the condition, On April 18, 1982, he allowed himself to be roasted by his teammates at a fundraising dinner for the organization. The zingers were mild — Kent Tekulve said that Panama "had big, ugly tigers. …Omar had to be fast or he was lunch" — but the event was a sign of how highly his fellow Pirates thought of him.[17]

Moreno was a free agent after the season, and although his agent, Tom Reich, negotiated with Pittsburgh, the two sides were unable to reach a deal. On December 10 he signed a five-year, $3.25 million contract with the Houston Astros. Interestingly, Pirates general manager Pete Peterson felt that Reich did not handle the negotiations well for his client, and that the Astros' offer was not significantly more over the life of the contract than what Pittsburgh was willing to pay.

"If the Houston figures are correct, and I see no reason to not to believe they are, Moreno left for only — and I stress only — $25,000 a year," Peterson said. "If he wasn't happy in Pittsburgh, will he be happier in Houston for $25,000 more a year?"[18]

That question, while rhetorical, proved to be prophetic. Houston signed Moreno to bolster an offense that scored 569 runs in 1982, 11th in the National League.[19] By the midway point of the 1983 season, the same batting numbers that were just fine in Pittsburgh weren't quite up to snuff in Houston. By July Astros manager Bob Lillis had decided to bench the left-handed-hitting Moreno against certain southpaw pitchers. This didn't sit well with Moreno, who never even bothered to look at the lineup card in Pittsburgh because it was a given that his name would be there. After watching two games from the visitors' dugout at Montreal's Olympic Stadium in late July, the normally quiet Moreno demanded to be traded. Ultimatums don't go over well with Houston fans, and many of the 18,781 at the Astrodome that evening booed him mercilessly when he returned to the Astros lineup on July 27. It was clear at this point that the situation was untenable, so on August 10 the Astros traded Moreno to the New York Yankees for switch-hitting outfielder Jerry Mumphrey. Moreno was happy with the deal. "The Yankees have a good chance to win the pennant and I can help them," he said.[20]

Moreno played regularly in center field with the Yankees, but batted primarily eighth or ninth. The Yankees finished in third place in the AL East with a 91-71 record, seven games behind the eventual world champion Baltimore Orioles. For the year, Moreno batted .244, with 1 home run and 42 RBIs. While his numbers at the plate were typical, his numbers on the basepaths were not. He stole 37 bases (30 with Houston, 7 with New York), which is a good total for most players, but for Moreno it was his lowest total since he became an everyday player in 1977.

It was clear to Moreno early in spring training that the 1984 season was not going to be fun, and that he might have made a mistake leaving Pittsburgh. One reason was that Yankees manager Billy Martin, who coveted the speed-and-defense playing style at which Moreno excelled, had been fired, and replaced by the long-ball-loving Yogi Berra.

"They [the Yankees] have enough power. But they don't believe in speed here," he said during spring training. "There was nothing like Pittsburgh for me."[21]

Moreno played in only 117 games in 1984, and in 11 of those he was a late-inning defensive replacement. A slow start — he was hitting .184 after 14 games — earned him a seat on the bench for 17 of 19 games in late April and early May, the longest stretch of inactivity in his career. For the year, he hit .259, with 4 home runs, 38 RBIs, and 20 steals.

The Yankees traded for speedy basestealing outfielder Rickey Henderson from the Oakland A's after the 1984 season, sending a not-subtle-in-the-least message to Moreno that he couldn't expect much playing time in an outfield of Henderson, Dave Winfield, and Ken Griffey Sr. in 1985. In fact, he got into only 34 games and was batting just .197 before the Yankees gave him his unconditional release on August 16.

After being inactive for two weeks, Moreno received a call from the eventual World Series champion Kansas City Royals. Their regular center fielder, Willie Wilson, had been hospitalized after a bad reaction to a penicillin injection administered by the Texas Rangers' team physician. On September 5, in just his second game with the Royals, Moreno had an inside-the-park home run in the first inning followed by a two-run triple in the eighth to spark Kansas City to a 4-1 victory over Milwaukee. During their five-game sweep of the Brewers, Moreno was 9-for-17 (.529) with two home runs and eight RBIs. He batted .243 in 24 games with the Royals, but was not on the postseason roster.

The Royals cut Moreno after the season, but early in 1986, the Atlanta Braves, with Moreno's old friend Tanner managing, signed him to a minor-league contract. Moreno played well enough during spring training to earn a roster spot, and went north with the big-league club. He served in a part-time role, primarily in right field, playing in 118 games, hitting .234 with 4 home runs and 27 RBIs. He stole 17 bases but was caught 16 times. The Braves released him after the season and his baseball career was over.

After finishing in baseball, Moreno and his family, consisting of wife Sandra, son Omar Jr., and daughter Leury, returned to Panama. For many years he and Sandra ran the Omar Moreno Foundation, which made it possible for poor children to play baseball. In 2009, new Panamanian President Ricardo Martinelli asked Moreno to serve as Secretary of Sport, where he represented Panama internationally and oversaw the country's athletic programs.

Upon finishing that assignment, Moreno continued working with underprivileged children in Latin America. His ability as an offensive catalyst for the Pirates earned him election into the Pennsylvania Sports Hall of Fame in 2015. As of 2016, he was also active in the Pirates' alumni association and served as a Pirates coach during spring training. He was also busy with two granddaughters, Gaby and Camila, who kept him wrapped around their fingers.[22]

SOURCES

In addition to the sources cited in the Notes, the author also used:

Charleston (West Virginia) Daily Mail.

McCollister, John. Tales From the 1979 Pittsburgh Pirates: Remembering The "Fam-a-lee" (Champaign, Illinois: Sports Publishing LLC, 2005).

Salina (Kansas) Journal.

Vivatropica.com.

NOTES

1. "Moreno Pirates' Quiet Thief," Spokane (Washington) Spokesman-Review, July 10, 1979: 23.
2. Raybourn had a very good eye for talent—he also signed Manny Sanguillen and Rennie Stennett for the Pirates and later signed Mariano Rivera for the New York Yankees.
3. The Mets were last with 32.
4. Dave Brown, "Bucs Optimistic but "Shortcomings" Remain," Somerset (Pennsylvania) Daily American, January 24, 1976: 9.
5. Jed Weisberger, "Bucs Face Crucial Year as Phils Pose Challenge," Indiana (Pennsylvana) Gazette, April 10, 1976: 38.
6. A.L. Hardman, "Fast-Moving Moreno Leads Speedy Trio at Charleston," The Sporting News, June 12, 1976: 43.
7. Charley Feeney, "Pirates, Phils Split—But Nothing Is Settled," Pittsburgh Post-Gazette, July 5, 1976.
8. Charley Feeney, "Moreno Gives 'Steal' to Pittsburgh," The Sporting News, September 4, 1976: 12.
9. Tavares led the league with 70 steals, while Garner had 32 and Stennett had 28.
10. "Bucs Reflect on 1977 Campaign," Uniontown (Pennsylvania) Morning Herald-Evening Standard October 5, 1977: 5.
11. Charley Feeney, "Waiter Moreno Not Looking for Tips," Pittsburgh Post-Gazette, May 5, 1978: 13.
12. One of Moreno's prized possessions was a loud whistle his wife, Sandra, blew frequently to encourage him during the Series.
13. An article in the August 19 edition of the Tyrone (Pennsylvania) Daily Herald ("Division leaders Pitts., Houston Battle Tonight": 7) noted that milestone. Moreno had 69 steals at the time.
14. Dan Donovan, "He's Omar The Thrillmaker," Pittsburgh Press, July 27, 1980: D-2.
15. Ibid.
16. Ralph Bernstein, "Moreno Eyes Thievery Title," Gettysburg (Pennsylvania) Times, March 25, 1982: 13.
17. Dan Donovan, "It's a Toast for Moreno," Pittsburgh Press, April 20, 1982: C-1.
18. Charley Feeney, "Moreno Jumps Pirates for Astros," Pittsburgh Post-Gazette, December 11, 1982: 9.
19. The Cincinnati Reds were last in the league with 545 runs scored.
20. "Moreno Dealt to Yankees," Pittsburgh Post-Gazette, August 11, 1983: 23.
21. Bob Smizik, "Homesick: Yankee Sub Moreno Wishes He Never Left Pirates," Pittsburgh Press, March 19, 1984: D-3.
22. Email to author from Leury Moreno, January 16, 2016.

Steve Nicosia

By Phillip Bolda

A FIRST-ROUND DRAFT PICK BY Pittsburgh in the 1973 amateur draft, Steve Nicosia made his major-league debut with the Pirates on July 8, 1978. Plagued by injuries throughout his eight-year career in the majors, Nicosia had a lifetime batting average of .248 and hit 11 home runs in 938 at-bats. Though he was mainly a backup catcher, he started in four games of the 1979 World Series, including the decisive Game Seven victory over the Baltimore Orioles.

Steven Richard Nicosia was born on August 6, 1955, in Paterson, New Jersey, to Berniero and Grace Cardinale Nicosia. He had two older siblings Nicholas and Lillian. His father, known as Jerry, did not graduate from high school, and Grace attended three years of high school. Jerry was a presser in a clothing shop, and Grace worked as a cleaner in a clothing shop.

The family moved south and Steve grew up in Florida, graduating from North Miami Beach High School, playing baseball, soccer, and football there,[1] and playing American Legion ball before catching the eyes of fabled Pirates scout Howie Haak. The Pirates made him a first-round draft pick in 1973. His father had died in August of 1972 at the age of 54.

Nicosia said he started playing baseball at the urging of his brother, Nicholas, who was eight years his senior. "My brother was always an inspiration and a mentor to me," Nicosia said in 2013. "He taught me everything I know, from the time I was 4 years old."[2] Nicosia also played soccer and football in high school.[3]

Nicosia was one of 15 players ("unheralded heroes") highlighted in former umpire Ron Luciano's book *The Fall of the Roman Umpire*. Nicosia said he briefly tried pitching as a high-school sophomore. He hit batters with his first two pitches, walked the next batter on four pitches, and gave up a grand slam on the next. "I could see I probably wasn't going to make the big leagues as a pitcher," the book quotes him as saying. "I couldn't even make the second inning." He transferred to North Miami Beach High School the next year and volunteered to catch, opening his path to pro baseball.[4]

Of his six years as a major-league platoon player or backup catcher, he said, "Unless you're crazy, life in the bullpen will make you crazy."[5]

When Howie Haak scouted Nicosia in Miami, he reported that the youngster had a "gun" for an arm. Haak was for 20 years a special-assignment scout for the Pirates, and his involvement carried great weight in Pittsburgh; he was the one who recommended that the Pirates draft Roberto Clemente out of the Dodgers farm system.

The first catcher ever taken by the Pirates in the first round of the amateur draft, Nicosia was one of 88 catchers chosen in the 1973 draft, only eight of whom made the majors—including Eddie Murray, selected by the Orioles as a catcher in the third round. Nicosia was the 24th overall draft pick, and Pirates farm director Harding Peterson said Haak rated him among the top six prospects in the country. "We were surprised that no one drafted Nicosia before us," Peterson said.[6]

Nicosia said he might have gone earlier in the draft if not for a pulled muscle in his right shoulder, which kept him out of his last eight high-school games. "My American Legion coach, Fred Hannum, was a Pirate bird dog, and I think he kept the club up on my condition,," Nicosia said.[7] Former Pirates manager Danny Murtaugh, who saw Nicosia catch in a high-school all-star game, agreed that he was ready for the first round of the draft.[8]

By the time the Pirates were in spring training in February 1975, Nicosia had been tabbed as a player to watch by Pittsburgh sportswriters. He was only 19 and "he has to watch his weight," but "someday he could replace Manny Sanguillen." It was noted that Nicosia had a "strong accurate arm" was a "fine defensive catcher" and "had the potential to become a first-rate big-league hitter."[9]

"I'm willing to pay the price to become a big leaguer," Nicosia was quoted as saying. "I just don't eat desserts and other fattening food."[10]

Beyond his weight, Nicosia also gained "the lazy tag," with several scouts reporting that he "needs a kick in the rump once in a while."[11]

The Pirates paid Nicosia a reported $50,000 bonus to sign. He quickly found a difference in becoming a professional ball player. "I had never played every day before," he said. "I got off to a good start, but after two weeks I got tired. I caught 30 straight games. My body couldn't cope with playing every day."[12]

At 17, Nicosia began his career at Charleston (South Carolina) of the Class-A Western Carolinas League followed by three end-of-season games with Sherbrooke (Quebec) of the Double-A Eastern League. He was the youngest player on the squad when he arrived in Charleston, joining Pirate prospects John Candelaria and Willie Randolph. Charleston's manager was former major-league infielder Chuck Cottier, whom Nicosia credited with teaching him more about baseball than he had ever learned before. Nicosia had 23 passed balls in 53 games and hit .230.

In 1974 Nicosia batted .304 for Salem of the Class-A Carolina League, with 9 triples, 15 home runs and 92 RBIs. He made the league all-star team at catcher. Stocked with talented young players, Salem won the Carolina League championship.

Johnny Lipon, his manager at Salem, and called Nicosia "the finest young catcher I've ever seen," noting that he had also been Ray Fosse's manager at Triple-A Portland in 1967.[13]

Nicosia played in the instructional league in the fall of 1974 and was in spring training with the Pirates in 1975, but was sent back to Double A, this time with the Shreveport Captains. He continued to improve defensively, leading Texas League catchers in fielding percentage. He hit .268 and was named an all-star.

Nicosia and Willie Randolph were among the Pirates' winter-league players in Venezuela in the fall of 1975, playing for Johnny Lipon and the Magallanes team. In the 1976 season he was in Triple A, with the Charleston (West Virginia) Charlies, where the 20-year-old batted .262. In the fall of 1976 he was back in Venezuela, making the league's all-star team along with Dave Parker, Mitchell Page and Ken Macha. After an impressive spring camp before the 1977 season, Nicosia played in only 25 games for the Triple-A Columbus (Ohio) Clippers before having knee surgery in July.

Nicosia had a break-through season with Columbus in 1978. His .322 batting average was second in the International League to teammate Mike Easler's .330. At season's end Nicosia went 0-for-5 in a brief stint with the Pirates.

Nicosia had spent 2½ years at Triple A before making his major-league debut. Reflecting after his career on his time in the minors, Nicosia said, "(T)he most surprising thing I learned in the minor leagues is how little I learned." He also quipped, "The best thing about looking back on the minor leagues is being able to look back on it."[14]

The 22-year-old Nicosia was brought up from Columbus on July 2, 1978, when right fielder Dave Parker went on the disabled list. He was returned to the Clippers on July 16 when Parker was activated, and was later called up in September. At this point he was out of minor-league options, seeming to assure him a place on the 25-man roster the next season.

The Pirates did indeed keep Nicosia on the roster in 1979, and he had a solid rookie season, platooning as the starting catcher with Ed Ott. He batted .288 in 70 games. His first major-league hit, on April 7 at Pittsburgh, was a home run off the Montreal Expos' Ross Grimsley. On August 5 he was involved in a game that became a hallmark of the team and of manager Chuck Tanner. Against the Philadelphia Phillies and Steve Carlton, Nicosia went 4-for-4 with two doubles, a homer and three runs scored. In the bottom of the ninth inning, with the score tied 8-8, two outs and the bases loaded, Tanner brought in left-handed pinch-hitter John Milner to bat for Nicosia. The Phillies countered with southpaw Tug McGraw. Milner hit a walk-off grand slam on McGraw's first pitch.

Nicosia didn't mind one bit, telling teammates on the bench, "What are the chances of a guy like me (a .248 career hitter) going 5-for-5?"[15] "That's the way Tanner plays the game, and we're in this as a team."[16]

Nicosia did not play in the Pirates' NLCS sweep of the Cincinnati Reds, but started four games in the World Series and was behind the plate when Kent Tekulve closed out the seventh and final game. Nicosia was only 1-for-16, but made key defensive plays, including tagging the Baltimore Orioles' Ken Singleton out at the plate in Game Three, preserving a 3-2 Pirates lead. He was praised for his pitch selection. "You've got to give a lot of credit to Nicosia," Jim Rooker said after his gutty pitching performance in Game Five. "He called for the fastball on the right-handed hitters and ran it in on them."[17]

Nicosia expressed a great deal of respect for Tanner. "Any time things were going bad, Stargell would say, 'We need to have a team party,'" Nicosia recalled in 2009. "We'd rent a suite on the road, on a day off, and have a big pool party, just have some alcohol and have a good time. Most managers might put a squelch on that, have their coaches try to make it not happen. Chuck would come down and have a beer, then leave us alone."[18]

A lasting of image of Nicosia after Game Seven was burned into the memories of Pirates fans. As Baltimore fans swarmed the field, several grabbed for souvenirs and focused on the catcher's mask. "Dad's whaling on this guy who's trying to steal his mask," his daughter Nikki said after seeing the game on DVD years later.[19]

Again playing as a platoon catcher for the 1980 Pirates, the 24-year-old hit just .216. On June 23 in St. Louis, he was embarrassed when he allowed a stolen base to 41-year-old pitcher Jim Kaat. Just before the 1981 season began, Ed Ott, Nicosia's platoon partner, was traded to the California Angels. Nicosia had been expected to become the starter but he got off to a slow start in April. Tony Peña was called up from Triple-A Portland, quickly became the starter, and held the role for the next six seasons. Nicosia batted .231 in the 102-game, strike-shortened season.

Nicosia built a reputation as a steady catcher who knew how to handle a pitcher. Bill James noted that in 1981 the Pirates had a better record with Nicosia in the lineup than with Peña (24-24 with Nicosia, 22-32 with Peña). The Pirates had finished 25-23 in the first "half" of the season, and 21-33 when they returned from the players strike.[20] Nicosia let it be known that he would prefer to be traded to a club that would play him 120 games in a season, but that he was not bitter about his situation in Pittsburgh. "I have an excellent relationship with Chuck Tanner," he said. "I will never forget what Chuck did in the 1979 World Series. I platooned and caught three of the first six games. I didn't hit a lick. When it came to the seventh game, left-hander Scott McGregor started for Baltimore. I wouldn't have blamed Chuck if he started Ott. But he stuck with me and winning that game will be something I'll cherish the rest of my life."[21]

Perhaps Nicosia's most impressive batting statistic, and one that clearly endeared him to Tanner and Pirates fans, was his success against the Phillies' ace, Steve Carlton. Nicosia hit .339 against Carlton in 60 plate appearances. He so often found his way into the lineup against Carlton that he ended with more than twice as many at-bats against Carlton than against any other pitcher.

Nicosia played in only 39 games for the 1982 Pirates. He was 26 years old and had already suffered through a variety of injuries, including having surgery on both knees.[22] After the season he was eligible for arbitration but settled on a contract before his case was heard.

After going just 6-for-46 or the 1983 Pirates, Nicosia was traded to the San Francisco Giants for former Pirates catcher Milt May and cash. Peña now dominated playing time, appearing behind the plate in 126 games while heading toward a career-high 149 for the season. The trade was completed in mid-August just after Nicosia ended a stint on the 15-day disabled list with tendinitis in his right shoulder.

In 1984 Nicosia had a chance to become the Giants' starting catcher but was slowed by an early injury to his wrist. By the end of May, Bob Brenly was getting most of the playing time. In his backup role, Nicosia hit .303 in 48 games. However his reputation as a pinch-hitter and as a tough player grew in his short stint with the Giants. In early June he got eight hits in consecutive at-bats over three games, setting a Giants record. On June 28 he homered off former teammate John Candelaria and then hit a walk-off double in the 11th inning to give the Giants a 4-3 win over his old team.[23] On July 18 he hit two triples in a game—one of 74 two-triple games by catchers since 1919.

The home run off Candelaria was Nicosia's last in the big leagues. In August he broke two ribs in a home-plate collision with Mike Scioscia of the Dodgers while trying to score from second base, knocking him out of regular action for six weeks. The next season he was a free agent and batted only .186 playing for first the Montreal Expos and then the Toronto Blue Jays. He became the first player released by both Canadian major-league teams in one year to end his career.

When he signed with the Expos, there was again talk of him becoming the everyday catcher. But Nicosia's picture in the *Montreal Gazette* was captioned "Steve Nicosia—Often Injured" and noted the he had "serious defensive problems"; at one point in the season he had allowed 27 consecutive runners to steal second.[24]

In 2009, at the time of the 30th anniversary of the 1979 Pirates championship, Nicosia was living in Georgia, working for a company that serviced Marriott Hotels.[25] He later moved to Plantation, Florida, and remained active with Pirates fantasy camps, reunions of the 1979 team and other appearances.[26] After years of injuries, he had knee-replacement surgery.

Nicosia and his wife, Pam, went to high school together. Their four daughters all took part in sports. Kim and Kelly attended Florida Atlantic University and Florida International University respectively, both playing softball on athletic scholarships. Nikki and Traci, twins, played softball at Michigan State. Nicosia coached all of his daughters at one time or another and also coached his grandson's Little League team. He was a volunteer leader with the Pembroke Pines, Florida, softball program,[27] "(I)t keeps me feeling young," he said. "It's been a real positive experience."[28]

NOTES

1 Bill Ranier and David Finoli, *When the Bucs Won It All: The 1979 World Champion Pittsburgh Pirates* (Jefferson, North Carolina: McFarland & Company, 2005).

2 Rachel Levitsky, "Where Are They Now?—Steve Nicosia," *Baseball Alumni News*, Summer 2013. mlbpaa.mlb.com/mlbpaa/downloads/summer_13_newsletter.pdf.

3 Ranier and Finoli.

4 Ron Luciano, *The Fall of the Roman Umpire* (New York: Bantam, 1986).

5 Rafi Kohan, "Three Days in the Bullpen," *Slate*, September 25, 2012. slate.com/articles/sports/sports_nut/2012/09/i_spent_three_days_in_a_baseball_bullpen_this_is_what_i_saw_.html.

6 Charley Feeney, "Remember Name ... It's Steve Nicosia," *Pittsburgh Post-Gazette*, February 27, 1975. news.google.com/newspapers?nid=1129&dat=19750227&id=tEENAAAAIBAJ&sjid=imoDAAAAIBAJ&pg=7128,3261290&hl=en.

7 Ibid.

8 Charley Feeney, "Pirates' Nicosia Isn't Lazy in Ambition," *The Sporting News*, March 31, 1979.

9 Charley Feeney, "Remember Name ... It's Steve Nicosia."

10 Ibid.

11 Charley Feeney, "Pirates' Nicosia Isn't Lazy in Ambition."

12 Ibid.

13 Ibid.

14 Luciano.

15 Joe Starkey, "The 1979 Pirates: A Testament to Teamwork," *Pittsburgh Tribune-Review*, August 16, 2009.

16 Charley Feeney, "Bucs Bet on Their Sweet Bibby," *The Sporting News*, August 25, 1979.

17 Ranier and David Finoli.

18 Starkey.

19 "Careers winding down for Nicosia, Green and White," *State Journal* (Lansing, Michigan), May 8, 2008. archive.lansingstatejournal.com/article/20080508/GW19/805080349/Careers-winding-down-Nicosias.

20 Bill James, *The Bill James Baseball Abstract* (New York: Ballantine Books, 1982).

21 Charley Feeney, "Nicosia Idle but Not Bitter," *The Sporting News*, June 21 1982.

22 Steve Halvonik, "Catcher," *Pittsburgh Press*, July 8, 1982.

23 United Press International, "Steve Nicosia, who earlier homered, hit a game winning double," June 29, 1984. upi.com/Archives/1984/06/29/Steve-Nicosia-who-earlier-homered-hit-a-game-winning-double/5152457329600/

24 Brian Kappler, *"Catcher Nicosia hopes to be No. 1 with the Expos," Montreal Gazette*, February 16 1985.

25 Starkey.

26 Peter Greenberg, "Is the Winning Streak Over? Pirates Fantasy Camp, Part 5," January 28, 2014.

27 Cynthia A. Thuma, *Sport Lauderdale; Big Names and Big Games; A Sports Enthusiast's Guide to Broward County, Florida* (Charleston, South Carolina: The History Press, 2007).

28 O.J. Callahan, "Nicosia Clan a Sports Dynasty," *Fort Lauderdale Sun-Sentinel,* May 7, 2000. articles.sun-sentinel.com/2000-05-07/community/0005040751_1_middle-school-athletics-twins-nikki.

Ed Ott

By Bob Hurte

AFTER THE 1974 SEASON, PITTSBURGH'S new general manager, Harding Peterson, approached Ed Ott to inform him that the Pirates would like him to become a catcher. Ott refused; he had spent the past three seasons learning how to be an outfielder.

Later that winter he announced to his wife: "You know what, Joanie? I just came up with three reasons why I should try catching."

"What?" replied Joanne Ott.

"Dave Parker, Al Oliver, and Richie Zisk!"[1]

Nathan Edward Ott was born on July 11, 1951, to Howard and Esther Ott in Muncy, Pennsylvania. Howard worked as a grinder at Sprout Waldron Manufacturing Company, while Esther was a seamstress. They had six children, four boys and two girls. Muncy is a historic town in Pennsylvania's upper Susquehanna Valley.

Ott played Little League and American Legion baseball. He was an all-star third baseman for his Legion team. When he was 13, his father had him play in a couple of semipro leagues against men in their 30s, one in the Muncy area and another an hour east in Wilkes-Barre.

Muncy High School, which is close to Williamsport, the home of the Little League World Series, had basketball, football, and wrestling teams, but no baseball team. Ott was considered one of the best all-around athletes in his high school's history. (He was the first to be inducted into the school's Hall of Fame.) Ott, a running back, lettered three years in football, and was selected to the league all-star team all three of his years on the varsity. In one game he scored all of his team's 32 points. He was also an excellent wrestler in the 165-pound weight class, and was the league champion his junior and senior years.[2]

Selected out of high school as a third baseman by the Pittsburgh Pirates in the 23rd round of the 1970 amateur draft, the 18-year-old Ott quickly learned that his days as an infielder were over. At the spring camp of Niagara Falls in the Class-A (short season) New York-Pennsylvania League, manager Irv Noren told him that he would be in the outfield. Ott informed his skipper that he had never been an outfielder. Noren's response: You are now. Ott played in 61 games for Niagara Falls, batting .291. That same season the Pirates moved Dave Parker, a catcher in high school to the outfield. Ott credited Tom Saffell, their manager at Monroe (North Carolina) of the Class-A Western Carolinas League in 1971, with teaching them how to play the game within the game. Ott batted .292 for Monroe in 1971, then hit .304 for Salem (Virginia) of the Class-A Carolina League in 1972. That was followed by a jump to Triple-A Charleston, where he toiled from 1973 to 1975 with brief call-ups to the Pirates in the latter two seasons.

Ott was beginning to feel comfortable in the outfield after his second year at Charleston, then one day Pirates scouting director Harding Peterson told him, "We'd like to set you at catcher." Ott's response was, "Absolutely not. I just got done learning how to play the outfield, and now you want me to play catcher?"[3] But after thinking about it during the offseason, and considering the team's outfield prospects, Ott decided to make the switch. He also reasoned that he had played all of the infield and outfield positions, and might be able to extend his career by being a utility player. "It took me two weeks to figure out that I needed to keep my eyes open when the batter swung," Ott said.[4]

Peterson wanted Ott to go back to Double A to learn how to play catcher, but Ott refused to go below Triple A. He had made himself a promise that anytime he went back a level, it was time to get out of baseball. Describing the challenges of catching at each level, Ott said that in Class-A it was like being a hockey goaltender because "half of those kids have no idea where their pitches were going." In Double A, you had to be "part catcher and part goalie." At least at

Triple A, there are ex-major leaguers and pitchers who were close to possessing big-league control. Of the 17 pitchers Ott caught for Charleston, 14 became or at one time were major leaguers. Ott played in 121 games in 1975, and he was behind the plate for all but seven of them. At the plate he hit 10 home runs and drove in 55 runs with a .285 batting average. Behind the plate was more challenging; his fielding average was .974 with 20 errors and 23 passed balls.

Ott made the Pirates roster as third-string catcher at spring training in 1976, though Pittsburgh management wished he had another year at Triple A. He spent most of the season warming up pitchers in the bullpen; he broke his right hand warming up Bob Moose and landed on the disabled list.[5] On September 23, 1976, Ott started his first game behind the plate. (Both Duffy Dyer and Manny Sanguillen were injured.) He had two hits, including an opposite-field double to drive in the tiebreaking run in the top of the 10th inning against the Chicago Cubs at Wrigley Field. He also made a nice tag play at the plate in the bottom of the ninth to prevent the Cubs from scoring the winning run.

Ott started four more games and finished with a .308 batting average. Then, on November 5 Sanguillen was included in an unusual deal that brought the Pirates a new manager, Chuck Tanner. When Pittsburgh signed Tanner from the Oakland Athletics, A's owner Charlie Finley demanded a front-line player and monetary compensation from the Pirates, which turned out to be Sanguillen and $100,000.

The 1977 season was Ott's breakout year. He split the catching duties with Dyer. Ott had a solid offensive year and even with his lack of experience, he was respectable behind the plate. Before the season baseball experts considered the Pirates catching to be a weak point. Ott was stronger offensively, Dyer better defensively. Ott's signature game was the second contest of a twilight-night doubleheader against the New York Mets on August 12 in Pittsburgh. At the start of the day, the Pirates were in third place, 3½ games behind the division-leading Philadelphia Phillies. The Pirates won the first game, and the second game was a see-saw affair for five innings. In the sixth, with one out and a runner on second, Ott was intentionally

walked. Mario Mendoza then hit a groundball to shortstop with all the makings of a double play.[6] But Ott went hard into second base in an effort to take out second baseman Felix Millan, and Millan had to hold the ball. Millan felt Ott came in a little too hard, and threw a right hook at Ott with the ball still clenched in his hand. Ott took exception to this and displayed his wrestling skills by hooking his arm under Millan's crotch, lifting him up before slamming him on the ground. Both benches cleared, but no additional punches were thrown.

Ott's response: "What was I supposed to do, stand there and let him hit me again?"[7]

Millan was taken off the field on a stretcher. He had a broken collarbone, and it was the end of his major-league career. Ott was ejected by home-plate umpire Ed Sudol. Dyer took over as the catcher, and singled home the winning run in the bottom of the 12th inning as Pittsburgh swept the twin bill. Ott bruised his right shoulder in the scuffle and missed three games. NL President Chub Feeney fined Ott $250, which the Pirates catcher initially refused to pay.

Most big-league players sided with Ott, feeling it was a good baseball play. Chuck Tanner felt that Millan got what he deserved.[8] Pirates' coach Jose Pagan, a friend of Millan's, expressed the Mets second basemen's sentiments, saying, "Felix asked me to tell Ott that he was sorry because he lost his head for a fraction of a second and there were no hard feelings."[9]

After the altercation, the Pirates won 27 of their last 44 games, including 11 of the final 12. But the Phillies were also hot and the Pirates never moved out of second place, finishing five games behind Philadelphia.

The Pirates appeared to have a successful partnership of Dyer and Ott behind the plate in place for the 1978 season. But just before Opening Day, the Pirates traded three players to Oakland to bring Sanguillen back. Ott and Dyer were not happy about it. The trade might have been motivated by Dyer starting the season on the disabled list after breaking his thumb on March 17.

The return of Sanguillen did not affect Ott and Dyer's playing time greatly. While Manny appeared in 85 games, most were at first base; only 18 were behind the plate. Ott had another solid offensive season. While catching in 97 games, he batted .269, hit 9 homers, and drove in 38 runs. Dyer played in 55 games. The Pirates came closer to the Phillies, but again finished second, by only 1½ games.

Ott felt that the Pirates' 1979 world championship season was his finest major-league season, and the game on August 11 that season the best game of his career. Played at Veterans Stadium in Philadelphia before a national TV audience, it was a pivotal game for the Pirates against the Phillies, and went a long way defining the "We Are Family" moniker with an exclamation mark, the game that cemented the team's character. The Pirates resided in first place, 1½ games ahead of the Montreal Expos. After four innings, Pittsburgh was losing, 8-0. A TV shot of their dugout, showed a dejected group of players. Many of them were embarrassed and staring at their feet.

Ott said, "We were down 8-0, it was me, Garner, Madlock and Bill Robinson, and we were sitting side by side on the bench watching us get our butts kicked."[10]

This is when Willie Stargell walked over to them. He stood there with a bat on his shoulder. Ott felt that Willie was the heart of the team. He said, "Without your heart beating, you are nothing, you are dead. … He led us by example. There are 8 million people out there watching us on TV. We are not this bad a ballclub. Let's go out and show them what the Pirates are really made of!"

They looked at one another and together said, "Let's go!"[11]

In the fifth the Pirates began to chip away at the deficit with a five-run inning. In the seventh they scored four more runs and took the lead, led 9-8. Then with two outs in the eighth, Stargell singled, Milner doubled, and Madlock was walked intentionally, bringing up Ott with the bases loaded.

Since the Phillies' left-handed relief ace, Tug McGraw, was on the mound, Ott looked back into the dugout thinking that manager Tanner would send up a right-handed pinch-hitter.

"All I saw Tanner do was clap his hands and shout at me, 'Go get 'em!'"[12]

Ott obliged his manager. He smacked a hanging curveball long and deep to left field. Left fielder Greg Luzinski helplessly watched the ball disappear over the wall. It was the only grand slam of Ott's career, and it gave the Pirates a five-run lead.

The Pirates went on to win, 14-11. Ott was 4-for-5 with two runs scored and five RBIs. At the end of the regular season, the Pirates claimed the NL East Division by two games over the Expos. Ott started all three National League Championship Series games and was 3-for-13 as Pittsburgh swept the Cincinnati Reds. In the World Series, against the Baltimore Orioles, Ott scored the winning run in the ninth inning of Game Two, reaching on an infield hit and eventually coming home on a hit by Sanguillen. The Pirates came back from a three-games-to-one deficit and won the World Series. Ott went 4-for-12 and drove in three runs.

Ott and Steve Nicosia handled the bulk of the catching duties in 1979. Ott had 103 starts and Nicosia

55. Their performance was solid both defensively and offensively. Ott batted .273 and made four errors, while Nicosia batted .288 with three errors.

"I expect our catching to get better, because Ed Ott and Steve Nicosia improved so much last year," said Tanner in March 1980. "Ott didn't start catching until a few years ago, and Nicosia was a rookie last year."[13]

The two catchers were content with the platoon plan. They tried to make each other better. "We try to help each other," said Ott. "It's tough enough in this game without having problems with teammates."[14]

Ott had another solid season in 1980, batting .260, hitting 8 homers, and driving in 41 runs, but Nicosia's batting statistics fell dramatically to .216, one homer, and 22 RBIs.

At spring training in 1981, the Pirates were in an unusual position; they had four quality catchers. Besides the established duo of Ott and Nicosia, there were two young farmhands, Tony Peña and Junior Ortiz. Nicosia was going into his second year, and Ott would be able to become a free agent after the 1981 season.

The Pirates needed a power hitter, and on April 1 they traded Ott and pitcher Mickey Mahler to the California Angels for left-handed-hitting first baseman Jason Thompson. Ott played in 75 games for the Angels, hitting two homers and batting .217 during the strike-shortened season. It turned out to be Ott's last season. He battled arm problems. The game against the Texas Rangers on October 2 was his last major-league appearance. Ott underwent rotator cuff surgery and sat out the 1982 season. He appeared briefly as a first baseman in the Angels minor-league organization in 1983 and 1984 before retiring as a player.

Ott managed Pirates farm teams in 1985-86, managed in the independent minor leagues for three seasons, and was a coach for the Houston Astros under former Pirates teammate Art Howe from 1989 to 1993. As a manager, he expected a level of effort and hustle from his players. A prime example occurred in 1985 while he managed the Prince William (Virginia) Pirates of the Class-A Carolina League. One day his 20-year-old center fielder attempted a diving catch and missed. He got up and nonchalantly jogged to get the ball. Ott realized that he needed to nip this in the bud and went out to pitching mound. When the umpire informed him that he did not have anyone in the bullpen, he replied that he was replacing his center fielder. He pulled the player and together they walked back to the dugout.

The young player was Barry Bonds.

Said Ott, "He wasn't happy, but said when they got in the dugout, 'Mr. Ott, that will never happen again.'"[15]

Ott received phone calls from Pirates management about the incident, Bonds was a blue-chip prospect, but while he and Bonds never became close friends, they established a mutual respect.

Ott finally retired from baseball after the 2014 season. As of 2016 he lived in Forrest, Virginia, and spent his time fishing while his wife trained horses. During his first year of retirement, he admitted, "I had the shortest grass in all of Virginia!"[16]

SOURCES

In addition to the sources cited in the Notes, the author also consulted the following:

Donovan, Dan. "Whew, It's Over! Bucs Are Champs," in Peterson, Richard, ed., *The Pirates Reader* (Pittsburgh: University of Pittsburgh Press, 2003), 263-264.

Finoli, David, and Bill Ranier. *The Pittsburgh Pirates Encyclopedia* (Champaign, Illinois: Sports Publishing, 2003).

"Bucs Claim Two More Amidst Ott-Millan Bout," *Indiana* (Pennsylvania) *Evening Gazette*, August 13, 1977.

"World Series Champion Ed Ott Returns to Jackals Coaching Staff," Jackals Media Service, February 9, 2001.

NOTES

1 Ed Ott, telephone interview with author, January 18, 2016.

2 "Muncy High School Athletic Hall of Fame, Ed Ott—Class of 1970," muncysd.schoolwires.com.

3 Ed Ott interview.

4 Ibid.

5 "Bucs' Tekulve Chills HR Bats," *The Sporting News*, August 28, 1976: 18.

6 Michael Lecolant, "This Day in Mets History: 1977—Felix Millan's MLB Career Slammed to the Ground by Pittsburgh's Ed Ott," August 12, 1977, risingapple.com.

7 *The Sporting News*, September 10, 1977: 17.

8 *The Sporting News*, September 10, 1977: 9.

9   Ibid.

10 Ed Ott interview.

11 Ed Ott interview.

12 John McCollister, *Tales From the 1979 Pittsburgh Pirates: Remembering the "Fam-a-lee"* (Champaign, Illinois: Sports Publishing, 2005), 10.

13 "Pirate Attitude Is Key—Tanner," *The Sporting News*, March 8, 1980: 22.

14 "Ott, Nicosia Accept Platoon Plan," *The Sporting News*, July 19, 1980: 28.

15 Rich Emert, "Ott Is an Ambassador to Coaching in Minors," *Pittsburgh Post-Gazette*, August 25, 2005.

16 Ed Ott interview.

Dave Parker

By J.G. Preston

HOW YOU REMEMBER DAVE PARKER depends largely on what you remember him for.

Do you remember him as one of the best players in the major leagues in the last half of the 1970s? The man who was the National League's Most Valuable Player in 1978 and MVP of the All-Star Game in 1979? The man who played a key role on the Pittsburgh Pirates' 1979 World Series champions?

Or do you remember him as the overweight, injury-prone drug user who was the target of anger and resentment from Pittsburgh fans in the early 1980s when his production dropped off after he signed what was at the time the most lucrative contract in baseball history? The man who testified at a high-profile 1985 trial in federal court about his cocaine use and as a result was sued by the Pirates for fraud?

Parker's final totals after 19 seasons in the big leagues are impressive: 339 home runs, 1,493 RBIs, 2,712 hits, and a .290 batting average. He finished in the top five in the MVP voting five times (and got votes in four other seasons), played in six All-Star Games and was on the roster for another (and wasn't selected for the game in his MVP year due to injury) and was a regular in the lineup for two World Series winners. It's a resume similar to that of Jim Rice, Parker's American League counterpart for MVP honors in 1978. But while Rice was elected to the Hall of Fame, Parker never received as much as 25 percent of the vote in his 15 years on the ballot (Rice never received *less* than 29 percent), perhaps because the memories of the cocaine years and the perception of squandered talent were too much for some voters to overcome.

David Gene Parker was a big man with a big personality. ("There's only one thing bigger than me, and that's my ego," Parker told *Sports Illustrated* in 1979.[1]) He grew to be 6-feet-5 and was listed in his younger days at 225 pounds, although he was considerably heavier in the early 1980s. He was big from the beginning, weighing 11 pounds 14 ounces when he was born on June 9, 1951, in Grenada, Mississippi, one of six children of Richard and Dannie Mae Parker.[2]

Both parents were athletic. "My mother had a cannon for an arm," Parker said. "My dad never got to play organized ball. But he'd *crush* that ball. And he could run like a scalded rabbit. He beat me in a footrace one day after work—in his workboots, carrying his lunch bucket."[3]

In 1956 the Parkers moved to Cincinnati, where Richard worked at Lunkenheimer Valve Company and Dannie Mae worked as a maid. The family settled on Poplar Street, a short walk from Crosley Field, home of the Cincinnati Reds. Parker made that walk frequently in his youth. "Frank Robinson and Vada Pinson would come out and there I'd be, waiting for them," Parker remembered. "And believe it or not, they were always nice to me. They'd come out and give me a glove or a ball." As a teenager Parker worked as a vendor at the ballpark.[4]

Parker attended Courter Technical High School, where he was a standout in football, basketball, and baseball.[5] "Football was my first love," Parker confessed. "I loved it because it's a contact game. I liked to run over people."[6] As a junior in 1968 Parker earned first team all-Public High School League honors as a running back.[7] More than 60 college football programs, including many of the major powers of the day, contacted him. But an injury to his left knee in the first quarter of the first game of his high-school senior year in 1969 ended his dream of playing college football. He underwent surgery the day after Thanksgiving and sat out his senior season of baseball.[8]

As a junior Parker had led his Courter Tech team in batting average, home runs, and runs batted in.[9] His primary position was catcher, but he also did some pitching. And he played some outfield for a Cincinnati team sponsored by Wilson Freight that appeared in the Connie Mack World Series in August 1969.[10]

WHEN POPS LED THE FAMILY

Parker was on the radar of major-league scouts. Harding "Pete" Peterson, then the Pirates scouting director, first saw him at a tryout camp in Columbus, Ohio, before the June 1970 amateur draft. "He was one of 10 or 12 players we were looking at," Peterson recalled. "I didn't think he was the best of the group. I liked an outfielder named Bill Flowers. Remember him?" (Flowers was a Courter Tech classmate of Parker. Cleveland selected Flowers in the second round of the June 1970 draft and he played eight seasons in the minors but never got beyond Triple A.)

The Pirates drafted Parker in the 14th round, making him the 332nd player chosen.[11] Parker insisted he "would have been picked in the first or second round" had it not been for the knee injury,[12] but others disagreed; *Sports Illustrated* wrote in 1979: "Actually, say Peterson [then the Pirates' executive vice president] and scout Howie Haak, Parker, who then seemed incapable of hitting a ball in the air, just didn't look like all that much of a prospect. Furthermore, because he had a history of wrangling with coaches, he was dismissed by some scouts as a 'militant.' 'The Reds had been watching him all along,' says Haak. 'They laughed at us when we took him.'"[13]

Parker was listed as a catcher-outfielder on *The Sporting News*' list of draftees,[14] but that changed when Parker joined the Pirates' rookie league team in Bradenton, Florida. "The first day I reported, I was told to find a fielder's glove," he said. "That was the end of my career as a catcher."[15]

Playing the outfield for the Pirates' team in the rookie-level Gulf Coast League in 1970, Parker tied for the league lead in home runs and total bases and was named the league's most valuable player.[16] "That's when I realized I could do it," he said. "I was a 14th-round draft choice, but when I got with other kids from all over the United States and some foreign countries and stood out, I realized I must be pretty good."[17]

The Pirates were impressed enough to promote Parker—still only 19 years old—all the way to Double-A to start the 1971 season. But Parker struggled with Waterbury (Connecticut) in the Eastern League, hitting just .228 with no homers in 30 games before being demoted. "I was the youngest guy there and I tried too hard to prove myself," he said.[18]

After being sent to Monroe (North Carolina) of the Class-A Western Carolinas League, Parker re-established himself as a top prospect, batting .358.[19] Then in 1972 he earned player-of-the-year honors at Salem (Virginia) in the Class-A-Carolina League, leading the league in batting average, RBIs, runs scored, hits, doubles, stolen bases, outfield putouts, and outfield assists while missing the home run title by one.

In 1973 the Pirates promoted Parker to Charleston (West Virginia) of the Triple-A International League, where he got off to a blazing start. On July 10 Pirates outfielder Gene Clines tore ligaments in his right ankle going into second base in San Diego.[20] Parker, who was leading the International League with a .317 batting average, was called up to replace him, and on July 12—barely a month past his 22nd birthday—he made his major-league debut as the Pirates' right fielder and leadoff hitter. (Parker's first three starts came in the leadoff spot; he never hit in that position in the order again in any of his 2,331 subsequent starts.)

Parker hit .354 in September to finish the season with a .288 mark. But the left-handed hitter was used strictly as a platoon player; all of his 31 starts came against right-handed pitchers and he had just 10 plate appearances against lefties. In 1974 Parker was on the disabled list most of June and July with a hamstring injury. He finished the year with a .282 batting average but just four home runs in 220 at-bats, and again he saw limited action against lefties (three starts and 27 plate appearances).

But in 1975 Pirates manager Danny Murtaugh took the platoon restriction off Parker and, given the chance to play every day, Parker became a star. Over the next five seasons (1975-79) his batting average was .308 or better every year and he averaged 23 home runs, 98 RBIs, 95 runs scored, and 17 stolen bases per season. (He also proved Murtaugh was right to stop platooning him; Parker hit .300 or better against lefties for four straight years, 1976-79, and actually had a better batting average against left-handers than right-handers in 1976 and 1977.)

During that five-year span Parker led the National League in batting average twice (.338 in 1977 and .334 in 1978) and slugging percentage twice (1975 and 1978), was named to *The Sporting News'* postseason National League all-star team three times (1975, 1977, 1978) and won three Gold Glove awards for fielding excellence (1977-79). In 1977 he had 26 assists, still (through 2015) the most for any major-league outfielder in a season since another Pirate right fielder, Roberto Clemente, had 27 in 1961.[21]

Widely known by his nickname, "Cobra," given to him early in his Pirates career by team trainer Tony Bartirome,[22] Parker was a loud and lively presence in what was the loudest and liveliest clubhouse in the major leagues. "If you first meet me in the clubhouse, you'd say I'm very insulting," he noted. "Loud. Maybe you'd even think in terms of a bully."[23] But his taunts had a purpose. "I'm a motivator. I'll point out guys' faults. I'll tell a guy he's pulling out, that he couldn't hit a balloon. He thinks to himself, 'I'll show that turkey.' It makes him better."[24]

Phil Garner, Parker's teammate from 1977 to 1981, agreed. "If you feel down, sorry for yourself, he gets the spark going in you. Dave's found that picking on someone makes guys rally round, laugh. Suddenly, they're ready. It's group therapy."[25]

"It didn't matter where you were born, your ethnic heritage, religious background, marital status," said Jerry Reuss, a teammate of Parker's from 1974 to 1978. "Dave was an equal-opportunity offender. Nothing was sacred. Nor was it personal. But it was a daily comedy routine."[26]

On June 30, 1978, at Pittsburgh's Three Rivers Stadium, Parker attempted to score the tying run in the bottom of the ninth after Bill Robinson flied out to right field. Parker dived head-first into Mets catcher John Stearns, a former college football player, who was knocked on his back but held onto Joel Youngblood's throw to retire Parker and end the game.[27] "That was like the Pennsylvania Railroad colliding with the B&O," Pirates manager Chuck Tanner said afterward.[28]

Parker took three stitches over his left eyelid after the game. The next day his eye was swollen nearly shut, and it was determined that he had fractured his left cheekbone, but he agitated Tanner to put him in the lineup anyway. "I'm the toughest man in the world," he insisted two days after the injury. "I can see, so I can play."

"If I put his name in the lineup, I'm sure he'd play. But there's no way," Tanner responded. "There isn't a player alive who plays the game the way Dave Parker does. Every game is the seventh game of the World Series to him. There isn't a player alive who can do the things on the field that Parker can do. None."[29]

Parker went on the disabled list (and as a result was not selected to play in the All-Star Game), and when he returned to action July 16 he was wearing a hockey goalie mask to protect his face. Because he had trouble seeing some pitches wearing the mask, he went back to wearing a conventional batting helmet at the plate, but when he reached base he would switch to a batting helmet with a football facemask attached that he continued wearing into the 1979 season.[30]

Parker struggled at the plate when he came back from the injury, at one point going into an 0-for-24 slump. But he rallied to play the best baseball of his career down the stretch, batting .381 in August and .412

after September 1 to win National League Player of the Month honors in consecutive months. He finished the season with a major-league-best .334 batting average plus 30 home runs and 117 RBIs while leading the league in total bases, despite missing 13 games due to the injury. He won Most Valuable Player honors, receiving 21 of the 24 first-place votes.

After the 1976 season Parker signed a three-year contract calling for salaries of $175,000 in 1977, $200,000 in 1978, and $225,000 in 1979. He almost immediately regretted it, as he saw other players get bigger deals. "Putting my salary up against them is putting me up against guys who couldn't carry my bat to the plate," he said. "I feel I'm one of the best talents in baseball and I want to be paid like one of the best."[31] After his MVP season in 1978, Parker and his agent, Tom Reich, began negotiating a new long-term contract with the Pirates, with the threat that Parker might leave as a free agent when his existing contract expired at the end of the 1979 season.[32] There were reports that Parker was asking for $1 million a year—something no baseball player had ever received.[33]

On January 26, 1979, the Pirates announced they had signed Parker to a five-year contract that would begin in 1979 (replacing his existing agreement). While the terms aside from the length were not disclosed, it was immediately, and for years afterward, referred to as baseball's first million-dollar-a-year contract.[34] But while the contract was designed to pay Parker at least $7.75 million, the money would be paid out over 30 years, and he would not receive $1 million in any year he played.

His base salary was a mere $300,000 a year for each of the five seasons (1979-83). There was also a $325,000 bonus when the contract was approved and another $300,000 in 1980. Most of the money would come in deferred payments, beginning with a $1 million lump sum in January 1988, followed by 222 monthly payments of $20,833.33 each (a rate of $250,000 a year) beginning in January 1989. The contract also included a number of incentive bonuses, for which Parker eventually received $65,000.[35]

It was a contract that changed the way fans looked at Parker and would come to haunt him over the next five years. "I think it took away from people looking at me as Dave Parker, hustling ballplayer, and turned it into Dave Parker, million-dollar man."[36] And Parker found that that dollar figure was something Pittsburgh fans couldn't relate to. "Basically this is a coal-mining, steel-melting city," he said. "These people work hard for their money and it's hard for them to imagine making this type of money playing games."[37]

Parker was named the most valuable player in the 1979 All-Star Game at Seattle's Kingdome, not for his bat but for his arm. In the seventh inning, with the AL leading 6-5, Parker overran leadoff hitter Jim Rice's shallow fly ball, went back into the right-field corner to retrieve it after a high bounce, and retired Rice trying to advance to third base with a one-hop throw. Then in the eighth, with the game tied 6-6, Parker fielded Graig Nettles' hit in deep right field and threw home. The ball reached catcher Gary Carter shoulder-high on the fly, and Carter tagged out Brian Downing trying to score the go-ahead run.[38] The National League scored in the ninth and held on to win 7-6.

With Parker and 39-year-old first baseman Willie Stargell, the National League's co-Most Valuable Player, leading the way, the 1979 Pirates won 98 games and the National League East championship, after which they defeated the Cincinnati Reds in the National League Championship Series and the Baltimore Orioles in the World Series. Parker hit .365 in September and .341 in 10 postseason games, even though he was troubled by his left knee that was injured swinging at a pitch in late August, making it painful for him to try to pull the ball.[39] His 10th-inning single drove in the winning run in Game Two of the NLCS, and he was also credited with the game-winning RBI in Game Three of the NLCS and Game Six of the World Series.

Parker had what for any other player would have been considered an outstanding season. He finished second in the National League in total bases, third in doubles and tied for third in runs scored; ranked in the top 10 in batting average, on-base percentage, and slugging percentage; and won his third straight Gold Glove. But his batting average was "only" .310, more than 20 points below his league-leading marks of 1977 and '78, and his 94 RBIs were well short of the 117 he had the previous year. Some Pittsburgh fans felt that they should have gotten more in the wake of the big contract. "They said for a million dollars that was a bad year," Parker said. "The pressure was there, without a doubt."[40]

Things between Parker and Pittsburgh fans were so bad that he skipped the victory parade after the 1979 World Series. "Why should I? Where were they when I needed them?" Parker said.[41] And things would get much worse over the final four years of his contract.

The lowlight of 1980 came on July 20 when someone at Three Rivers Stadium threw a 9-volt battery at Parker while he was standing in right field during the first game of a doubleheader against the Dodgers. Parker immediately removed himself from the game and did not play the field in the second game. "I could hear it go by me," he said afterward. "It was too close for comfort. I wasn't going to stand there and give him another shot."[42] The next day, saying the battery incident was the "fourth or fifth" time he had been the target of a thrown object,[43] Parker asked to be traded, saying he had "reached the point of no return" with Pittsburgh fans.[44]

There were off-field problems in 1980 as well. A landscaper took him to court, claiming Parker owed $9,000 for work done on his home, and Pittsburgh National Bank sued him over missed payments on an $11,097 loan, neither of which Pittsburgh fans found appropriate for someone they thought was making $1 million a year.[45] And his common-law wife, Stella Miller Parker, sued for divorce, accusing him of adultery and "cruel and barbarous treatment."[46]

On the field, Parker's 1980 season was good enough—a .295 batting average, 17 home runs, and 79 RBIs—but in the context of his salary it seemed a big disappointment. He was limited to 139 games because of injuries that kept him from playing at full speed in many of the games he did play. In September *New York Times* reporter Jane Gross wrote that Parker's left knee was "so sore that he limped to the plate, looked like a lame horse on the base paths, and was forced to play deeper than usual in the field because he had trouble going back for the ball."[47]

"He plays a lot of times when he can hardly walk into the clubhouse," manager Chuck Tanner told Gross. "Every time I take him out of the lineup because he's hurting, he says he wants to play and I play him every time he asks."[48]

Parker had cartilage removed from his left knee after the season and recovered in time to start the 1981 campaign. But in a season that was interrupted by a nearly two-month players strike, he played just 67 games. He spent two weeks on the disabled list in May with a slight tear in his right Achilles tendon,[49] then missed time in late August and September with a painful thumb injury.[50] His batting average dropped to .258 and he hit only nine home runs, and his once-feared arm produced just one assist.

Parker's weight also became an issue. *Pittsburgh Post-Gazette* beat writer Charley Feeney wrote that it "might have gone higher than 260, but Parker insists [it] was never more than 245."[51] Either was well above what was considered Parker's normal playing weight of 230, and the extra weight wasn't doing his knees any good. "For the money Dave Parker makes," *Sporting News* columnist Bill Conlin wrote, "he owes Chuck Tanner, his teammates and Pirates fans more than first prize in a Goodyear blimp look-alike contest."[52]

Those Pirates fans were completely disenchanted with their "million-dollar-a-year" star. "How popular is Dave Parker in Pittsburgh?" Feeney wrote. "Let's put it this way: if Parker ran for mayor unopposed, he'd lose in a landslide."[53]

Somehow 1982 turned out even worse for Parker than 1981. He was out nearly six weeks in May and June with torn cartilage in his right wrist and spent another six weeks on the disabled list from late July until early September after he ruptured a ligament in his left thumb in a head-first slide.[54] He wound up playing only 73 games, with just six home runs.

Parker stayed off the disabled list in 1983 (although he later said he had a problem with his Achilles tendon all season[55]) and played 144 games. He went into the All-Star break with a .242 batting average and only three home runs, but the 32-year-old suddenly showed flashes of his old self in the second half, dropping his weight to 225 and hitting .305 with nine homers and

48 RBIs. Pirates fans forgave him enough to give him several standing ovations.[56] The comeback came at an opportune time, with Parker entering free agency for the first time after the season.

At that time free agents were subject to what was known as the "re-entry draft," in which teams drafted the right to negotiate with the player. There were no limits on the number of players a team could draft or on the number of teams that could draft a player. Dave Parker, former MVP and two-time batting champ, was drafted by only two teams: Seattle and his hometown Cincinnati Reds.[57]

And home was where Parker decided to go, in a move that reinvigorated his career. He signed a two-year contract with the Reds and celebrated his return to Cincinnati by marrying Kellye Crockett on Valentine's Day 1984. (The two were still married when this was written in 2015.)[58]

In 1984 Parker drove in 94 runs, his most since the Pirates' 1979 championship season, and hit .285. The Reds rewarded him with a three-year contract extension, and Parker rewarded them with one of his best seasons in 1985. He hit .312, his 34 home runs and 125 RBIs were career highs, he led the league in RBIs, total bases, and doubles, and he ranked second in hits and homers. He finished second in the Most Valuable Player voting to Willie McGee, who hit a league-leading .353 for the National League champion Cardinals.

The day before the 1985 All-Star Game, Parker won the first All-Star Home Run Derby, hitting six home runs at the Metrodome in Minneapolis. The event was organized as a team competition, and Parker's National League team lost to the American League team, 17-16.[59]

But Parker's on-field performance in 1985 was overshadowed by his testimony in a federal court drug trial in Pittsburgh in September. Granted immunity in exchange for his testimony against a man charged with distributing cocaine to professional baseball players, Parker said he first used cocaine while playing winter baseball in Venezuela in 1976 and had used the drug "with consistency" from 1979 until he quit late in the 1982 season because "my game was slipping. I felt it played a part in it."[60] He also named several other major-league players who he said had used the drug.

While Parker could not face criminal prosecution, his admission had financial consequences. On February 28, 1986, Baseball Commissioner Peter Ueberroth suspended Parker and six other players who had used cocaine and "in some fashion facilitated the distribution of drugs in baseball." The one-year suspensions were waived when the players agreed to contribute 10 percent of their 1986 salaries to programs to combat drug abuse, submit to drug tests for the rest of their careers, contribute up to 200 hours of community service and participate in antidrug programs established by baseball.[61]

Then in April the Pirates—under new ownership since Parker had played for them—sued Parker in an attempt to get out of making the more than $5 million in deferred payments called for under his 1979 contract. "He was using cocaine," Pirates president Malcolm Prine said. "That negatively affected his ability to perform. The Pittsburgh Pirates were deprived of that which he promised to provide."[62] The Pirates also claimed that Parker "failed to keep himself in good physical condition" under the terms of the uniform players' contract, "with his weight ballooning at times to in excess of 270 pounds, as a result of which he became injury-prone." ("That 270 pounds is in no medical records," Parker responded. "I'd like to see them prove that.")[63]

Parker and the Pirates reached a settlement in December 1988.[64] Terms were not announced, but Carl Barger, who was then the team president, said the team would pay "significantly less" than what was owed under the contract.[65]

Parker had another fine year for the Reds in 1986, playing every game and finishing fifth in the MVP voting. He led the league in total bases while hitting 31 homers and driving in 116 runs. In 1987 he drove in 97 runs, but his batting average dropped to a career low .253 (just .228 after the All-Star break), and after the season the Reds traded the 36-year-old to the Oakland Athletics for young pitchers Jose Rijo and Tim Birtsas.

Parker was in the A's 1988 lineup almost every day, either in left field or as the designated hitter, until he strained ligaments in his right thumb sliding into second base on July 3.[66] He returned to action in late August and was the regular DH after that, helping the A's win the American League pennant. He finished the year with modest numbers: a .257 batting average, 12 homers, and 55 RBIs in 101 games.

In 1989 Parker was used almost exclusively as a DH, and his bat helped the A's repeat as American League champions and sweep the San Francisco Giants in the earthquake-interrupted World Series. He led the team with 97 RBIs during the regular season and won the league's Designated Hitter of the Year award, then hit his first postseason home runs, two against Toronto in the American League Championship Series and one in Game One of the World Series. In the process Parker earned the respect of his teammates. "It's unbelievable how hard he works," Mark McGwire said. "He just lifts the whole ballclub up by his attitude. He is so well liked by everybody."[67]

The World Series marked the end of Parker's tenure in Oakland. He was a free agent after the season, and with the A's deciding not to offer a multi-year contract, he signed a two-year contract with Milwaukee.[68] He repeated as Designated Hitter of the Year with the Brewers, hitting .289 in 1990 with 21 homers and 92 RBIs. But the Brewers decided to get younger after the season, trading the 39-year-old Parker to the California Angels for 27-year-old outfielder Dante Bichette.

Parker struggled with the Angels in 1991, hitting just .232 with 11 homers in 119 games, and was released on September 7. A week later he was picked up by Toronto and hit .333 in 13 games to help the Blue Jays win the American League East, but because he joined the team after September 1 he was ineligible to play in the postseason.

While Parker was with the Angels, his teammate Dave Winfield encouraged him to consider buying fast-food franchises as a financial investment.[69] Parker and his wife bought a Popeye's fried-chicken franchise in Cincinnati, where they continued to make their home, and when he had no offers to continue his major-league playing career in 1992, Parker went home to help Kellye run the business and play in a local baseball league for men 35 and older.[70]

Parker got back into a major-league uniform in 1997, when Angels manager Terry Collins (who had been the second baseman on Parker's Carolina League team in 1972) hired him as first-base coach. "I really came back out just to be visible," said Parker, who was on the Hall of Fame ballot for the first time in 1997, "and I actually fell in love with coaching."[71] In 1998, given the chance to work for Tony LaRussa, his manager in Oakland, and become a hitting coach, Parker joined the St. Louis Cardinals coaching staff. But after that season Parker went home to Cincinnati, and as of 2015 had not had a full-time job in baseball since.

In August 2013 Parker revealed to Joe Starkey of the *Pittsburgh Tribune-Review* that he had been diagnosed with Parkinson's disease in February 2012.[72] Dave and Kellye sold their restaurants and started the Dave Parker 39 Foundation (39 being the uniform number Parker wore throughout his major-league career), "a non-profit organization focused on finding a cure for Parkinson's disease in our lifetime, and to make life better for those living with the disease today."[73]

In the most recent edition of his *Historical Baseball Abstract*, published in 2003, Bill James ranked Parker the 14th best right fielder in baseball history.[74] Of the 13 players ranked ahead of him, only Pete Rose, who is ineligible, is not in the Hall of Fame, and several players ranked behind him are in as well. Will a future Hall of Fame Veterans' Committee set aside Parker's cocaine use, look at his numbers and vote him in?

Regardless of whether Parker is ever selected for the Hall, he clearly qualifies on one count: Few players in the 1970s or '80s were as famous (even if he was at times infamous) as Dave Parker.

SOURCES

Special thanks to Michael Haupert, professor of economics at the University of Wisconsin-La Crosse, for providing a copy of Parker's official contract card, and to Bill Van Niekerken, library director for the *San Francisco Chronicle*, for providing articles from the *Chronicle*'s archive that are not available online.

David L. Snyder's article in the January 2012 *Albany* (New York) *Government Law Review*, "The Cobra's Contract: Revisiting Dave Parker's 1979 Contract With the Pittsburgh Pirates," is a comprehensive and fascinating look at the negotiations leading to Parker's historic contract with the Pirates and the team's lawsuit to dispute his deferred payments. The article is online at albanygovernmentlawreview.org/Articles/Vol05_1/5.1.188-Snyder.pdf.

Two good sources for information about the Pittsburgh cocaine trial of 1985 are Aaron Skirboll's book *The Pittsburgh Cocaine Seven: How a Ragtag Group of Fans Took the Fall for Major League Baseball* (Chicago: Chicago Review Press, 2010) and Steve Beitler's article "This Is Your Sport on Cocaine: The Pittsburgh Trials of 1985," published in the Society for American Baseball Research's *National Pastime 26* in 2006.

NOTES

1. Roy Blount, "A Loudmouth and His Loud Bat," *Sports Illustrated*, April 9, 1979.
2. Birth weight from Bernie Lincicome, "New Uniform Suits Parker Just Fine," *Chicago Tribune*, March 16, 1984: section 4, 1.
3. John Erardi, "Dave Parker a Hall of Fame Presence," *Cincinnati Enquirer*, August 6, 2014, cincinnati.com/story/sports/columnists/john-erardi/2014/08/06/erardi-dave-parker-hall-fame-presence/13697129/.
4. Bob Hertzel, "From Crosley to the Majors," *Cincinnati Enquirer*, March 15, 1973: 49.
5. Courter Tech shut down in 1974. Its former campus is now the home of Cincinnati State Technical and Community College, more commonly known as Cincinnati State. cincinnatistate.edu/about-cs/cincinnati-state-histor.
6. Charley Feeney, "On Playground or Battlefield, Parker Is BIG," *The Sporting News*, June 11, 1977: 3.
7. "Campbell Honored By PHSL," *Cincinnati Enquirer*, November 20, 1968: 24. Parker's exact statistics for the season are in question. In 1973, Bob Hertzel wrote in the *Cincinnati Enquirer* that Parker had 1,365 yards rushing in 10 games, a figure that was repeated in numerous other stories over the years. But when Parker was inducted to the Cincinnati Public Schools Hall of Fame in 2012, that organization said he "rushed for over 1,110 yards" and scored 68 points. That document is online at cps-k12.org/files/pdfs/Athl-HOF-12.pdf.
8. "Courter Is Minus Parker," *Cincinnati Enquirer*, November 18, 1969: 44. Parker actually did return to the football team before the season was over and was named second team all-PHSL before undergoing the operation.
9. cps-k12.org/files/pdfs/Athl-HOF-12.pdf.
10. "CM World Series Rosters," *Farmington* (New Mexico) *Daily Times*, August 15, 1969: 6. Other future major leaguers who played in the tournament included Rick Burleson, Steve Staggs, Mike Proly, Eric Raich, Tommy Bianco, Bob Kammeyer and Parker's Wilson Freight teammate Barry Bonnell. Rick Kehoe, later a National Hockey League star, played for the team from Windsor, Ontario, and Mack Brown, who coached the University of Texas football team to the 2005 national championship, played for the team from Nashville. Wilson Freight lost both its games in the tournament. Parker was not a member of the Wilson Freight team that won the Connie Mack World Series in 1968.
11. It was a horrible draft for the Pirates. Of the 13 players they selected before Parker, only John Caneira reached the majors, and he played only eight games. And of the 46 players they took after Parker, only 23rd-round pick Ed Ott played in the majors.
12. Charley Feeney, "On Playground or Battlefield, Parker Is BIG."
13. Roy Blount, "A Loudmouth and His Loud Bat." The Reds didn't do any better job drafting than the Pirates did in 1970. Of the 13 players Cincinnati selected before Parker was taken, only Ray Knight, Will McEnaney, and Tom Carroll reached the majors.
14. *The Sporting News*, June 20, 1970: 6.
15. Charley Feeney, "Danny Juggles Bucs, a Tribute to Parker's Bat," *The Sporting News*, May 4, 1974: 12.
16. His most valuable player award is mentioned in the *Pirates 1974 Press-TV-Radio Guide*: 34. Parker's high-school classmate Bill Flowers led the league in runs scored and stolen bases.
17. Bob Hertzel, "Reds Rained Out; Bucs' Parker Wants to Make It Big Without Tag of 'Another Clemente,'" *Cincinnati Enquirer*, May 1, 1974: 38.
18. Hertzel, "From Crosley to the Majors."
19. Parker didn't have enough plate appearances to qualify for the batting championship; the official league leader hit .343.
20. Charley Feeney, "Needless Slide May Put Clines on Shelf for '73," *The Sporting News*, July 28, 1973: 28.
21. Details of Parker's assists can be found at prestonjg.wordpress.com/2015/08/08/dave-parkers-remarkable-26-assists-in-1977/.
22. "[Pirates broadcaster] Bob Prince made it famous, but Tony Bartirome gave me the nickname," Parker said in 2012. blackandgoldworld.blogspot.com/2012/07/dave-parker-talks-coaching-hall-of-fame.html. Prince's Associated Press obituary and his biography included in the Society for American Baseball Research's Baseball Biography Project both credit Prince with the nickname.
23. Roy Blount, "A Loudmouth and His Loud Bat."
24. Ron Cook, "Dave Parker Deserves a Little Respect," *Beaver County* (Pennsylvania) *Times*, April 6, 1980: C-4.
25. Phil Musick, "'I'm Pursuing the Ultimate…,'" *Sport*, June 1979: 15.
26. Jerry Reuss, *Bring In the Right-Hander!: My Twenty-Two Years in the Major Leagues* (Lincoln, Nebraska: University of Nebraska Press, 2014).
27. Charley Feeney, "Fireworks Start in 9th as Mets Barely Nip Pirates," *Pittsburgh Post-Gazette*, July 1, 1978: 11.
28. Parton Keese, "4-Run Rally in 9th Beats Pirates, 6-5," *New York Times*, July 1, 1978.

29. Charley Feeney, "Parker Eyes Quick Return to Buc Lineup," *Pittsburgh Post-Gazette*, July 3, 1978: 11.

30. Paul Lukas, "Aggh! It's Dave Parker at the Plate!" sports.espn.go.com/espn/page2/story?page=lukas/080724.

31. Charley Feeney, "Parker's a Bitter Cookie ... Not Enough Sugar," *The Sporting News*, July 30, 1977: 9.

32. Charley Feeney, "Parker-Pirate Contract Duel Leaves Everybody Puzzled," *The Sporting News*, November 11, 1978: 44.

33. Jack Lang, "Parker Wins MVP as He Hits—Convincingly," *The Sporting News*, December 2, 1978: 59.

34. In a front-page story in the *Pittsburgh Post-Gazette* on January 27, Charley Feeney wrote that Parker "probably" received "a five-year package worth, including bonuses and fringe benefits, $5 million." The headline in the *New York Times* story of January 27 referred to a "$5 million contract," with Murray Chass calling it "a mammoth deal believed to be worth at least $5 million." Roy Blount, in his April 1979 *Sports Illustrated* cover story, wrote that the contract was "worth more than $1 million a year," and there are many such references after that. Parker even referred to himself as "the first million-dollar player" in a *Sport* magazine story in June 1979.

35. David L. Snyder, "The Cobra's Contract: Revisiting Dave Parker's 1979 Contract with the Pittsburgh Pirates," *Albany (New York) Government Law Review*, January 2012, Vol. 5, Issue 1, online at albanygovernmentlawreview.org/Articles/Vol05_1/5.1.188-Snyder.pdf. Snyder says the contract called for payments continuing into 2008, even though 222 monthly payments beginning in January 1989 would seem to end in 2007.

36. Jim O'Brien, "The Cobra Strikes Back: 'I'm the Best Player in Baseball,'" *Sport*, June 1981: 14.

37. Jim Murray, "Pirates' Dave Parker Is Earning His Keep and, at $10,000 Per Base Hit, Then Some," *Ottawa (Ontario) Citizen*, October 11, 1979: 25.

38. Dan Donovan, "All-Star MVP Parker Guns Down AL, 7-6," *Pittsburgh Press*, July 18, 1979: C-10. The throws can be seen at youtube.com/watch?v=RkCE6JHUb00.

39. Charley Feeney, "Next Spring Parker 'Can Talk Baseball,'" *The Sporting News*, November 24, 1979: 49.

40. Hal McCoy, "Parker: He's Worth Every Penny to Reds," *The Sporting News*, July 22, 1985: 21.

41. Phil Musick, "A Cobra Among the Cuties," *Pittsburgh Post-Gazette*, August 8, 1980: 13.

42. John Clayton, "Parker Feeling Mighty Low After Assault With Battery," *Pittsburgh Press*, July 21, 1980: B-5.

43. Dan Donovan, "Parker Still Shaken, Wants to Be Traded," *Pittsburgh Press*, July 22, 1980: C-6.

44. Norm Clarke, "Parker Demands Trade," *Sumter (South Carolina) Daily Item*, July 23, 1980: 1B.

45. Charley Feeney, "It's Open Season on Bucs' Parker," *The Sporting News*, August 23, 1980: 17.

46. Associated Press, "Parker's Wife Seeks Divorce," *Tuscaloosa (Alabama) News*, August 4, 1980: 13. Dave and Stella met in 1973, and her divorce petition claimed they were married by common law in April 1974. "Stella 'Parker' Now Tells Her Story of 'Divorce,'" *Jet*, September 25, 1980: 46. Parker was listed as married in the Pirates' 1978 media guide but was shown as single in 1979 and 1980, when apparently the couple lived apart. "She's an intelligent lady and I had considered marrying her," Parker said after the divorce filing. "But she became too confining so we had to part." Norman O. Unger, "Dave Parker Talks About Fears, the Heckling Fans, Lawsuit of 'Wife' and Woes of Fame," *Jet*, September 18, 1980: 54.

47. Jane Gross, "For Parker, a Season of Insult and Injury," *New York Times*, September 14, 1980.

48. Ibid.

49. "Dave Parker Becomes Latest Pirate Casualty," *The Sporting News*, May 30, 1981: 30.

50. Charley Feeney, "A Talented Moreno Deserves Applause," *The Sporting News*, September 26, 1981: 28.

51. Charley Feeney, "Parker Remains in Pirate Family," *The Sporting News*, December 26, 1981: 43.

52. Bill Conlin, "Dawson, Schmidt Hot MVP Rivals," *The Sporting News*, September 26, 1981: 25.

53. Charley Feeney, "Moreno to Ask Bucs for Five-Year Pact," *The Sporting News*, November 7, 1981: 20.

54. Charley Feeney, "Bucs Get 'Steal' in McWilliams," *The Sporting News*, August 16, 1982: 26; Charley Feeney, "Parker Has Surgery for Injured Thumb," *The Sporting News*, August 9, 1982: 15.

55. Dave Nightingale, "The Resurrection of Dave Parker," *The Sporting News*, March 24, 1986: 12.

56. Stan Isle, "Caught on the Fly," *The Sporting News*, August 22, 1983: 13.

57. Associated Press, "Formality Rules in Re-entry Draft," *Nevada (Missouri) Daily Mail*, November 8, 1983: 8.

58. United Press International, "Dave Parker gets married," *Ottawa (Ontario) Citizen*, February 16, 1984: 43.

59. Erik Malinowski, "Swing Away: The Untold Story of the First Home Run Derby," foxsports.com, July 10, 2014, foxsports.com/mlb/story/swing-away-the-untold-story-of-the-first-home-run-derby-071014.

60. Jan Ackerman and Carl Remensky, "Parker: Used Cocaine for 3 Years," *Pittsburgh Post-Gazette*, September 12, 1985: 1.

61. Michael Goodwin, "Baseball Orders Suspension of 11 Drug Users," *New York Times*, March 1, 1986.

62. Greg Hoard, "Pirates Seek to Stop Parker's Deferred Pay," *Cincinnati Enquirer*, April 22, 1986: C-1.

63 Ira Berkow, "The Dispute Over Parker's Contract," *New York Times*, April 26, 1986.

64 Associated Press, "Pirates Say They've Settled Drug Suit Against Parker," *Los Angeles Times*, December 13, 1988.

65 Bob Hertzel, "Pirates, Parker Reach Out-of-Court Settlement," *The Sporting News*, January 2, 1989: 52.

66 Kit Stier, "A's Loss of Parker a Bitter Pill," *The Sporting News*, July 18, 1988: 26.

67 David Bush, "Parker Gives A's Winning Look," *San Francisco Chronicle*, March 15, 1989: D1.

68 Ray Ratto, "Parker Signs With Brewers," *San Francisco Chronicle*, December 4, 1989: D1.

69 Jon Newberry, "Franchise Businesses Opening Doors of Opportunity," *Cincinnati Business Courier*, December 31, 2007. bizjournals.com/cincinnati/stories/2007/12/31/story4.html.

70 Elliott Teaford, "Competitive Spirit: Fire Still Burns Inside Bowa, Parker, Who Will Bring That Intensity to the Angels," *Los Angeles Times*, March 28, 1997.

71 Associated Press, "Coach Parker," *Southeast Missourian* (Cape Girardeau, Missouri), March 14, 1998: 3B.

72 Joe Starkey, "Ex-Pirates Slugger Parker Is Coping With Parkinson's," *Pittsburgh Tribune-Review*, August 5, 2013. triblive.com/sports/joestarkey/4480502-74/parker-parkinson-pirates#axzz3w2BUywTW.

73 daveparker39foundation.com/foundation.html.

74 Bill James, *The New Bill James Historical Baseball Abstract*, (New York: Free Press, 2003), 976.

Rick Rhoden

By Paul Hofmann

WHEN THE TOPIC OF DISCUSSION TURNS to great two-sport athletes who played major-league baseball during the last quarter of the 20th century, names like Bo Jackson, Deion Sanders, Brian Jordan, and Danny Ainge often come to mind. However, despite enjoying success in both baseball and golf, Rick Rhoden is often overlooked as two-sport standout. Rhoden is one of those rare two-sport athletes who excelled at an extremely high level on both on the pitcher's mound and the golf course. A scratch golfer during his baseball playing days, Rhoden pursued a professional golf career after a 16-year major-league career that saw him win 151 games for the Los Angeles Dodgers, Pittsburgh Pirates, New York Yankees, and Houston Astros.

Richard Alan Rhoden was born on May 16, 1953, in Boynton Beach, Florida. He was the younger of the two sons of Lloyd (Tom) Jefferson Rhoden Jr. and Ernestine Mathis Rhoden. Tom was one of the first firefighters for the City of Boynton Beach and an avid outdoorsman who loved hunting, a passion he passed down to both of his sons. Ernestine was a homemaker.

At the age of 8, Rhoden injured his right knee and an infection developed into osteomyelitis, a bone infection usually caused by infection in one part of the body that is transported through the bloodstream to a bone in a distant location. Among children and adolescents, the long bones of the legs and arms are most frequently affected.[1] In Rhoden's case, the ailment required him to have surgery to remove part of his knee and wear a leg brace until the age of 12.[2] But by the age of 14, Rhoden was beginning to show great promise as a baseball player. At Atlantic High School in Delray Beach, he struck out 20 batters in an eight-inning game and 19 in a seven-inning contest. On the American Legion sandlots he struck out 77 batters in 36 innings.[3]

After graduating from high school in 1971, Rhoden was selected by the Los Angeles Dodgers in the first round of the amateur draft, and signed with the Dodgers rather than attend college. The 6-3, 190-pound right-hander was touted to have a fastball that was to make Dodger fans "forget Sandy Koufax."[4] He was assigned to the Daytona Beach Dodgers of the Class-A Florida State League. In an abbreviated season, the 18-year-old Rhoden made 11 starts and posted a 4-6 record with a 3.98 ERA, five complete games and one shutout, a solid start for an 18-year-old fresh out of high school.

Climbing the ladder quickly, Rhoden followed his inaugural season with a combined 13-5 record at El Paso of the Double-A Texas League and Albuquerque of the Triple-A Pacific Coast League in 1972. He spent the entire 1973 season with Albuquerque and experienced a slight setback in his climb toward the majors. In 20 appearances, 19 as a starter, Rhoden was a modest 4-9 with a 4.50 ERA before arm miseries landed him on the shelf for the remainder of the season. He returned to Albuquerque in 1974 for what would be his final full season in the minors. Rhoden made 26 starts for the Dukes and finished the season with a 9-10 mark and 4.40 ERA before a midseason call-up to the Dodgers.

Rhoden made his major-league debut in Montreal on July 5, 1974, in the first game of a doubleheader. Coming on in relief with one out and runners on first and second in the bottom of the fourth inning, Rhoden gave up a two-run single to Bob Bailey before retiring the side. He was sent back to Albuquerque and was recalled by the eventual NL champion Dodgers in September. He made three more appearances for the Dodgers, including one on September 22 in which he earned his first major-league victory when he scattered three hits and yielded just one run in six innings of relief against the San Diego Padres.

The Dodgers broke spring training in 1975 with the 21-year-old Rhoden on the roster. He was used sparingly and pitched in only 26 games, 11 as a starter.

WHEN POPS LED THE FAMILY

On September 11 he tossed his first complete game, besting the Cincinnati Reds 5-2 at Dodger Stadium. He finished the year 3-3 with a 3.08 ERA in 99⅓ innings pitched.

Rhoden moved into the Dodgers starting rotation in 1976 and had a breakout season. He started 26 games and made it to the All-Star break with a perfect 8-0 record, and was named to the National League All-Star team. Rhoden didn't drop his first game of the year until August 6 and finished the season 12-3 with 10 complete games, three shutouts, and a 2.98 ERA. He pitched a scoreless eighth inning in the National League All-Stars' 4-1 victory in Philadelphia. (Rhoden was named to the NL All-Star team again in 1986, but did not pitch in the game.)

In 1977 Rhoden teamed up with Tommy John, Don Sutton, Burt Hooton, and Doug Rau to form one of the most formidable pitching rotations of the late 1970s. The five pitchers started 158 of the Dodgers' 162 games and accounted for nearly 78 percent of the National League champions' regular-season victories. The Dodgers and Rhoden got out of the gate quickly. On June 20 Rhoden became the National League's first 10-game winner. Relishing the outpouring of offensive support he received, Rhoden said after the June 20 game, "If they keep scoring like that for me, I ought to win 25 games."[5] In fact, he won only six more games that For the year, he made 31 starts and finished 16-10 with a 3.74 ERA. The Dodgers cruised to the NL West title by a wide margin, and faced the Philadelphia Phillies in the best-of-five League Championship Series.

Against the NL champion East Philadelphia Phillies, Rhoden came on in the bottom of the second inning of Game Three in relief of Hooton, who had surrendered three runs to put the Phillies up 3-2 and left the bases loaded. Rhoden retired Mike Schmidt on a foul popup and went on to pitch another four scoreless innings before leaving for a pinch-hitter. The Dodgers scored three runs in the ninth to win the game, 6-5, to go up two games to one in the series, and eventually advanced to the World Series against the New York Yankees.

Rhoden pitched twice in the World Series. In Game One he came on to start the 12th inning of a 3-3 game at Yankee Stadium. Willie Randolph greeted him with a double to deep left. The Dodgers intentionally walked Thurman Munson, then Paul Blair hit a walk-off single to left, tagging Rhoden with the loss. In Game Four at Dodger Stadium, he came on in relief of Doug Rau, who failed to retire a batter in the second. With one run already in and runners on second and third, Rhoden retired Graig Nettles on a run-scoring groundout before yielding a RBI single to Bucky Dent. Ron Guidry sacrificed, then Rhoden struck out Mickey Rivers to end the inning.

Rhoden helped his own cause when he ignited a third-inning rally with a ground-rule double to deep left off Guidry. Davey Lopes followed with a two-run home run to center to trim the Yankees' lead to 3-2. Rhoden held the Yankees in check until Reggie Jackson added an insurance run with a home run to left-center in the top of the sixth inning. Rhoden pitched seven innings of two-hit baseball while striking out five in the final World Series appearance of his career. The Yankees won the Series in six games.

THE 1979 PITTSBURGH PIRATES

Rhoden returned to the Dodgers rotation in 1978. However, after an up-and-down four months to start the season and the emergence of 21-year-old rookie Bob Welch, Rhoden was sent to the bullpen for six weeks in August and September. For the year, he appeared in 30 games, starting 23, and finished 10-8 with a 3.66 ERA.

The Dodgers won the NL Western Division title again and met the Phillies again in the NLCS. Rhoden's lone postseason appearance came in Game Four when he replaced Rau in the sixth inning with the score 2-2 and the Dodgers needing one more victory to win the pennant. Rhoden pitched well, going four innings and surrendering a single run on a seventh-inning home run by Bake McBride before being lifted for a pinch-hitter in the bottom of the ninth inning. The Dodgers pushed across the winning run in the bottom of the 10th and advanced to the World Series against the Yankees for the second consecutive year. Rhoden did not pitch in the Series.

With the emergence of Welch, Rhoden became expendable as the Dodgers sought to add the final pieces of the puzzle to win the World Series. Similarly, the Pittsburgh Pirates were looking to solidify the starting rotation of a star-studded club that was challenging the Phillies for supremacy in the NL East. On April 7, 1979, Rhoden was traded to the Pirates for left-handed pitcher Jerry Reuss. The Pirates were aware Rhoden was experiencing some arm troubles when they made the deal; in fact, he was not as healthy as the club thought. On May 8 Rhoden made his Pirates debut, starting against the Atlanta Braves. He yielded four runs in five innings, and after the game he was placed on the disabled list. The May 8 outing was Rhoden's only appearance for the 1979 World Champion Pirates. On June 28 he had season-ending shoulder surgery.

Still recovering from the shoulder surgery, Rhoden started the 1980 season with Portland of the Triple-A Pacific Coast League. He made 10 starts for the Beavers, going 6-3 with a 2.93 ERA. He showed that he was returning to his old form when he pitched an abbreviated seven-inning no-hitter on April 23. The Pirates recalled him in June and though he went 1-1 with an ERA of 6.00 in his first five starts, he finished strong, going 6-4 with a 3.17 ERA over his last 14 starts. All signs pointed to Rhoden being healthy and looking forward to a big year in 1981.

A traditionally fast starter, Rhoden won his first six decisions and finished the first half of the strike-shortened season of 1981 at 6-1. Notwithstanding his fast start, he was left off the NL All-Star team and when the regular season resumed he failed to recapture his early-season form. However, he did establish himself as an integral part of the rotation, leading the pitching staff in wins, starts, innings, complete games, and strikeouts during their 102-game year. He also cemented his reputation for giving his team a chance to win when he took the mound. Teammate Bill Madlock said, "When Rick Rhoden pitches, you know you are always in the game. He keeps you within striking distance. He does it better than anyone we have on our team."[6] Yankees third baseman Mike Pagliarulo echoed this sentiment six years later, saying, "(Rhoden) puts us in a position to win every time he goes out there."[7]

Rhoden entered 1982 with a career 13-0 record in the month of April. This year would be different. On April 15 Rhoden's older brother, Bill, 33 years old, was killed in a car accident in Charlotte, North Carolina. Despite learning of the tragedy hours before his scheduled start against the Montreal Expos that day, Rhoden took the mound and yielded only two earned runs in six innings. The 28-year-old Rhoden said, "It's the most difficult thing I've experienced in my life. It puts things in a different perspective. A lot of things you think are important, then something like this happens and suddenly they're not so important anymore."[8] Rhoden went on to have an inconsistent season. He didn't win his first game until May 5 and didn't get his ERA below 5.00 until July 28. While he pitched better toward the end of the season, he finished with an 11-14 record and a 4.14 ERA despite leading the team again in starts and innings pitched and tying Don Robinson for the team lead with six complete games.

The 1983 season was an amazingly consistent one for Rhoden, who improved on his 1982 ERA by more than a run. He recorded the only save of his major-league career on April 17, pitching three scoreless innings of one-hit ball against the Chicago Cubs as he combined with John Candelaria for a three-hit shutout. Rhoden finished with a 13-13 record and a 3.09 ERA. Again he led the Pirates in innings pitched, while his 35 starts tied Larry McWilliams for tops on the staff.

While the fortunes of the club went south and the Pirates fell into last place in the six-team NL East during the next three years, Rhoden remained an effective starter despite his requests to be traded after the 1985 season. From 1984 to 1986 he won 14, 10, and 15 games respectively and finished with a 2.72 ERA in 1984 and 2.84 and 1986. His 253⅔ innings pitched in 1986 were the most thrown by a Pirate in the decade and his 15 wins were the second highest victory total by a Bucs pitcher during the 1980s and Rhoden's most wins since 1977.

Rhoden entered the majors as a power pitcher, but after his shoulder troubles in 1979 he began to rely heavily on finesse and guile. He became a control pitcher who had great command of the ball and used craftiness and deception to work out of trouble. Consequently, he was often accused of scuffing the baseball during the latter part of his career. In 1987 American League President Bobby Brown said, "We think he's scuffing some balls but we have no proof because we haven't caught him in the act.[9] According to the BaseballPage.com website, former Dodgers teammate Don Sutton took credit for teaching Rhoden how to scuff the ball.[10] Rhoden, for his part, never confirmed or denied doctoring the baseball.

The accusation that Rhoden doctored the ball led to a bench-clearing brawl between the New York Mets and the Pirates in 1986. The incident occurred during the first game of a June 6 doubleheader between the two NL East foes in Pittsburgh. A fight broke out between Rhoden and former Pirates teammate Bill Robinson, the Mets' first-base coach, in the middle of the fifth inning with the Pirates leading, 2-1.[11] The Mets accused Rhoden of doctoring the baseball. Robinson kept telling the Mets hitters to ask home-plate umpire Billy Williams to check the ball.[12] In the top of the fifth, Gary Carter got into a long argument with Williams, and both managers showed up: Davey Johnson of the Mets to demand action and Jim Leyland of the Pirates to protect his pitcher.

Williams went to the mound to inspect Rhoden and found nothing. The alleged scuffed ball was tossed out of the game, but the Mets were not particularly pacified when Rhoden caught Carter looking on a breaking ball for strike three. Suddenly, as the Pirates were leaving the field, Rhoden began trading remarks with Robinson before the two exchanged blows as both benches and bullpens emptied to join the fray. Reflecting on the incident, Rhoden recalled it in a matter-of-fact manner, "He said something to me, and I said something back. I played with Bill. We've known each other for years, and things like that just happen in baseball."[13]

The Pirates finished in last place in the NL East in 1986 with a 64-98 record. While the team appeared headed in the right direction with an infusion of young talent, Rhoden continued to request a trade to a contending team. The request, according to his agent, was based largely on his desire to play in front of larger crowds and move beyond his recent divorce. On November 26, 1986, in an all-pitchers swap, the Pirates traded Rhoden, Pat Clements, and Cecilio Guante to the Yankees for Doug Drabek, Brian Fisher, and Logan Easley. Rhoden, as allowed because he was a 10-year major leaguer with five consecutive years with the Pirates, agreed to the trade only after the Yankees agreed to restructure his contract, guaranteeing the right hander $1.35 million.[14] Rhoden's 79 wins during the 1980s were 25 more than any other Pirate earned during the decade.[15]

In trading for Rhoden, the Yankees hoped they were acquiring a solid veteran who would fill a major hole in the rotation and help return the club to the top of the American League's Eastern Division. Despite having more than a decade of major-league experience under his belt, the 34-year-old Rhoden remained a student of the game and continued to use this to his advantage. Yankees catcher Rick Cerone tabbed Rhoden as "the most well prepared pitcher I've been around. He's observant. He asks questions. He studies the reports."[16]

Rhoden relished playing for a contender once again and raced out of the gate and notched 14 victories by early August. However, the Yankees' rotation had more holes than originally thought—Tommy John was 44 years old, Joe Niekro was 42, and 36-year-old Ron Guidry was winding down his career—and when Rhoden cooled off during the final seven weeks of the season, the Yankees slipped in the standings from leading their division to a fourth-place finish. Rhoden made 29 starts for the Yankees in 1987 and finished at 16-10 with a 3.86 ERA and a team-leading 107 strikeouts.

In his second season with the Yankees, Rhoden pitched an Opening Day three-hit shutout over the defending World Series champion Minnesota Twins. It was the 17th and final shutout of his career. Rhoden started 30 games that season and finished 12-12 with a 4.29 ERA. His 197 innings pitched led the Yankees.

Always a decent hitter, Rhoden made baseball history on June 11, 1988, when he became the first pitcher to start a game as a designated hitter since the inception of the designated-hitter rule in 1973.[17] (Pitchers Fergie Jenkins, Ken Holtzman, and Ken Brett had batted in lieu of a designated hitter, but did not start as DH's.) Rhoden made two plate appearances that day, less than 24 hours after dropping a 5-3 decision to the Orioles the evening before. He grounded out to third to lead off the bottom of the third and hit a sacrifice fly in the fourth. With the Yankees leading 8-3 in the fifth, Yankees manager Billy Martin lifted Rhoden in favor of pinch-hitter Jose Cruz.

After the season the Yankees traded Rhoden to the Houston Astros for minor-league pitchers Pedro DeLeon and Mike Hook and outfielder John Fishel. The Astros hoped Rhoden would fill the void created by the free-agency departure of Nolan Ryan. Rhoden started seven of the Astros' first 27 games in 1989, going 0-2 with a 4.08 ERA. On May 4 he was put on the disabled list after being diagnosed with bursitis in his rib cage.[18] After a rehab stint with Class-A Osceola, he returned to the Astros' active roster on July 25. In the final 13 appearances of his career, Rhoden tossed only 61⅓ innings, finishing the season at 2-6 with a 4.28 ERA. After the season the Astros released him.

A three-time Silver Slugger award winner (1984-86), Rhoden hit .308 in 1976, .375 in 1980, and .333 in 1984 and at one point during the summer of 1984 he hit safely in 11 straight games, the sixth-longest hitting streak by pitcher since 1920.[19] During the streak he got 16 hits in 32 at-bats. For his career he hit .238 with 9 home runs and 75 RBIs in 761 at-bats. The lanky right-hander was no less skillful with the glove. Eight times he either led or tied for the league lead in fielding with a 1.000 percentage and, at the time of his retirement, his career .989 fielding percentage ranked third among pitchers who tossed 1,500 or more innings. It has been suggested that if not for his childhood battle with osteomyelitis, which hampered his running even as an adult, he might have made the majors as a position player.

Rhoden didn't really embrace the game of golf until he became a major league. While he was with the Pirates he became an avid golfer, often playing with team equipment manager Kent Biggerstaff and team physician Jack Failia. He began to take the game more seriously after retiring in 1989. After his 41st-place finish in the 2006 US Senior Open, Rhoden said, "I never thought about professional golf [most of my life]. I stumbled into that celebrity tour when it was starting up right when I got out of baseball. I had never played in a golf tournament before those."[20]

A dominant player on the Celebrity Players Tour, Rhoden was a perennial tournament favorite at the American Century Championship in Lake Tahoe. He won the American Century Championship a record eight times (including back-to-back titles in 2008 and 2009), finished second five times, and third three times. He had 18 top-five finishes, and 22 top-10 finishes in the tournament and won more than 50 Celebrity Players Tour events.[21] As of 2016 he was celebrity golf's all-time winner and money leader, earning more than $1 million in his career.[22] Rhoden also played in 34 tournaments on the PGA Champions (seniors) Tour and qualified for the US Senior Open. In 34 starts on the Champions Tour between 2002 and 2009, he made the cut 30 times and had three top-10 finishes with career earnings of $342,428.[23] As of 2016 Rhoden was active in the athlete and celebrity marketing industry, making guest appearances and endorsements.

Despite being little more than a footnote to the 1979 Pittsburgh Pirates world championship season, Rhoden was one of the primary figures who bridged the Pirates of the 1970s with the Pittsburgh teams of the early 1990s. A top-of-the-rotation performer for the Pirates of the early to mid-1980s, Rhoden was also one of the most accomplished two-sport athletes in recent decades.

NOTES

1. webmd.com/a-to-z-guides/osteomyelitis-10585.
2. thebaseballpage.com/players/rhoden01/bio.
3. Ron Rapoport, "Rhoden's Blazer Cuts Path to Dodgers," *The Sporting News*, December 15, 1973.
4. Ibid.
5. Dodgers' Rhoden Roughs Up Cards," *Southeast Missourian*, June 21, 1977.
6. Ron Cook, "Pirates' Rick Rhoden Just Keeps Hanging in There," *Beaver County Times*, June 9, 1981.
7. Bill Utterback, "Rhoden Has Ball Playing on Winner," *Pittsburgh Press*, August 7. 1987.
8. "Rhoden Hurls Despite Death of His Brother," *Gettysburg (Pennsylvania) Times*, April 16, 1982.
9. David Fink, "Rhoden Ready to Be a Star in Yankees' Constellation," *Pittsburgh Post-Gazette*, July 6, 1987.
10. thebaseballpage.com/players/rhoden01/bio.
11. Joseph Durso, "Brawl Mars Split by Mets," *New York Times*, June 7, 1986.
12. Remembering Mets History (1986): The Bill Robinson—Rick Rhoden Brawl, centerfieldmaz.com/2014/06/remembering-mets-history-1986-bill.html.
13. Durso.
14. Murray Chass, "Yanks Get Rhoden for $1.35 Million," *New York Times*, November 27, 1986. nytimes.com/1986/11/27/sports/yanks-get-rhoden-for-1.35-million.html.
15. thebaseballpage.com/players/rhoden01/bio.
16. Utterback.
17. Joe Sexton, "Baseball; Rhoden Pitches In: A Designated Hitter," *New York Times*, June 12, 1988. nytimes.com/1988/06/12/sports/baseball-rhoden-pitches-in-a-designated-hitter.html.
18. Allen Wilson, "Rhoden Struggles in Osceola for Return to Houston," *Orlando Sentinel*, July 20, 1989. articles.orlandosentinel.com/1989-07-20/news/8907203346_1_rhoden-astros-boynton-beach.
19. Best Hitting Streaks by Pitchers Since 1920, baseball-reference.com/blog/archives/9814.
20. Shelly Anderson. "Rhoden Too Good for Celebrity Tour," *Pittsburgh Post-Gazette*, July 13, 2006.
21. tahoecelebritygolf.com/player_bios/Rhoden-Rick.html.
22. Scott Sonner, "Rhoden Wins Record 8th Celebrity Title," *Arizona Republic*, July 19, 2009. archive.azcentral.com/arizonarepublic/sports/articles/2009/07/19/20090719spt-tahoecelbs.html.
23. thepgatour.com.

Dave Roberts

By Gregory H. Wolf

THE HISTORY OF BASEBALL IS FILLED WITH highly touted pitchers who blow out elbows, injure shoulders, hurt backs, and damage knees throwing a baseball 60 feet 6 inches from an elevated mound to home plate, and never make it to the big leagues. Southpaw Dave Roberts appeared to be one of those pitchers whose major-league ambitions seemed to be derailed by injuries and chronic pain before it started.[1] Plagued by asthma as a child, Roberts endured an elbow operation and severe shoulder bursitis before debuting with the expansion San Diego Padres in 1969. Roberts, who also was waived twice in the minors, transformed himself from a hard-tossing hurler to a crafty control pitcher to win 103 games and log 2,099 innings in a 13-year (1969-1981) big-league career, most notably with the Padres, Houston Astros, and the 1979 World Series champion Pittsburgh Pirates. "I know I have limited ability," said the soft-spoken and refreshingly humble Roberts. "I try to stay within my capabilities. I don't try to throw all fastballs or I'd be a loser for sure. I try to keep the ball down and keep the batters off balance. I'm a finesse type of pitcher."[2]

David Arthur Roberts was born on September 11, 1944, in the small town of Gallipolis, Ohio, nestled on the Ohio River in the southeastern part of the state.[3] After attending George Washington elementary school, he began high school at Gallia Academy, and in 1963 graduated from Central High School in Columbus, Ohio, where his parents had relocated. Attracted to baseball as a child, Roberts progressed through Little League, Pony League, and Babe Ruth League, but did not attract much attention as a pitcher on Central's baseball team. Tall (6-feet-3) and sturdy (195 pounds), Roberts was also an excellent basketball player, earning All-Columbus honors. The hard-throwing southpaw's performance in the 1963 American Legion state playoffs and subsequent selection to the All-Ohio Legion team caught the eyes of big-league scouts from the California Angels, Philadelphia Phillies, Pittsburgh Pirates, and the San Francisco Giants. After the tournament, Roberts signed with the Phillies on the recommendation of legendary team scout Tony Lucadello, whose signees included future Cy Young Award winners Fergie Jenkins and Mike Marshall, and MVP Mike Schmidt.

Roberts began a frustrating, injury-filled six-year journey through the minor leagues in 1963 before he appeared as a midseason call-up with the expansion San Diego Padres, his fourth major-league organization. However, his career in Organized Baseball got off to a blazing start; he led the Class-A Western Carolina League in ERA (1.79) and won nine of 12 decisions for the Spartanburg (South Carolina) Phillies. Roberts was invited to Philadelphia's spring training in 1964, but despite his promising future, the parent club gambled by not protecting him as stipulated by the first-year player rule in effect.[4] Consequently, the Pittsburgh Pirates acquired Roberts off waivers for $8,000.

The Pirates thought they had a diamond in the rough in the 19-year-old fastballer. Roberts pitched almost year-round for the next three seasons, which may have contributed to his subsequent arm miseries. In his first full season of professional baseball, he posted a combined 8-10 record (3.96 ERA in 159 innings) for two teams in North Carolina, the Single-A Kinston Eagles (Carolina League) and Double-A Asheville Tourists (Southern League), in 1964. Roberts was clobbered in four starts (10.12 ERA) while pitching for his hometown Triple-A Columbus Jets of the International League to start the 1965 season, but he was sent back to Asheville and rebounded with a 9-8 record and a robust 2.93 ERA in 132 innings for the Tourists. After both seasons he got additional work in the Florida Instructional League. The promising lefty enjoyed a breakout season with the Tourists in 1966, ranking among the league leaders in wins (14), innings (190), strikeouts (157), and ERA (2.61), and earning a spot on the Southern League's all-star team.

Notwithstanding Roberts's accomplishments, the Pirates, like the Phillies three seasons earlier, had failed to protect the young pitcher. The Kansas City Athletics, in need of strong arms, took him in the Rule 5 draft in November 1966. Looking forward to pitching in an organization where his chances of making the big-league roster seemed encouraging, Roberts reported to the A's spring training coming off a commanding performance in the Dominican Winter League, where he posted a stellar 2.17 ERA in 108 innings and led Aguilas to the championship. However, his world came crashing down when he heard something "snap" in his left arm in an exhibition game against the Baltimore Orioles.[5] Incapable of pitching and in agonizing pain, Roberts found his career in jeopardy. The A's returned him to the Pirates organization for half of the draft price.

Roberts was diagnosed with damage to the ulnar nerve in his left elbow requiring surgery. He missed about three months, but the operation had a career-lasting effect. "I had to change from a fastball pitcher to a control pitcher," said Roberts.[6] He hurled only 62 innings for the Columbus Jets in 1967 while relying on his breaking ball and offspeed pitches.

In 1968 Roberts bounced back from his operation and enjoyed his thus far best year of baseball at the most opportune time. En route to leading manager Johnny Pesky's Jets to the International League championship series, Roberts paced the league in wins (18) and was named the pitcher of the year. Topps named him the national Triple-A hurler of the year.

In yet another unexpected twist on Roberts's path to the big leagues, the San Diego Padres chose him with their 39th pick in the expansion draft on October 14, 1968. "I had mixed feelings when San Diego drafted me," said Roberts, "because I had been told at Pittsburgh that I was going to be protected. … I couldn't figure it out. But I knew I was going to a club where I would get a chance."[7]

On the verge of realizing his boyhood dream, Roberts came down with piercing pain in his shoulder during spring training with the Padres in 1969. "My shoulder hurt so bad," he explained, that "I couldn't even toss the ball 15 feet in a game of pepper."[8] Failing to respond to sound treatment, cortisone shots, and other medications, Roberts feared for his career. "It seemed like every time I reported to a major-league training camp, I came up with a sore arm," Roberts said several years later with a note of frustration. "And every time I told anyone about it, I was sent out."[9]

A dejected Roberts was assigned to the Elmira (New York) Pioneers in the Double-A Eastern League, where he managed to win seven of 12 decisions and log 121 innings before earning a call-up to the Padres in early July. In his debut in the first game of a doubleheader on July 6 against the Houston Astros, Roberts scattered six hits and two walks over 7⅓ innings, yielding just one earned run but was collared with the 3-2 loss. Pummeled in his next three starts, Roberts was shunted to the bullpen and finished the season with a miserable 4.81 ERA in 48⅔ innings and an 0-3 record.

Roberts realized that his big-league career would be short-lived if his still chronically aching shoulder did not improve. Apparently learning a lesson from his previous experiences, he kept his injury and pain a secret from the team. ("You certainly aren't going to bite the hand that feeds you," he said.[10])

A devout man, Roberts contemplated quitting baseball in 1969, but turned to religion for a source of guidance and support. "I went to my priest in Columbus … and told him I knew people usually came to prayer as a last resort. He told me to pray and have faith but not to expect that anything would happen suddenly," said Roberts.[11] Whether it was a miracle, the effects of positive thinking, or the result of medication and treatment, Roberts reported to spring training with the Padres in 1970 completely pain-free. For the remainder of his playing career, he was known as a man of faith and nominated on multiple occasions for the Danny Thompson Memorial Award given annually to a player with exemplary Christian spirit in baseball. He also served as chapel leader on several teams.

In his 1970 debut, Roberts served notice that his shoulder was fine by limiting the Los Angeles Dodgers to just one hit in 7⅔ innings of scoreless relief to earn his first big-league win. By mid-June he moved into the starting rotation of the pitching-starved Padres. He lost 10 consecutive decisions for the offensively challenged team, before stringing together a team-record 28⅓ scoreless innings in September. The stretch included consecutive shutouts over the Dodgers (and a career-high 10 strikeouts) and the Atlanta Braves, both on the road. "He could have been 14-8," said Padres pitching coach Roger Craig of Roberts, who finished as the club's most consistent pitcher with an 8-14 record and 3.81 ERA in 181 innings. "He knows he can pitch in the majors."[12]

Roberts's 1971 season was as impressive as it was unlikely. Described as "brilliant" by *The Sporting News*, Roberts won 14 games and posted the second-lowest ERA in the NL (2.10) while logging a career-high 269⅔ innings.[13] He attributed his early-season success to a slider that he learned from a teammate, southpaw Dick Kelley. "It's my 'out' pitch now and has made me a complete pitcher," said Roberts, who garnered the praise of teammates and opponents.[14] Pete Rose of the Cincinnati Reds called Roberts the "best NL southpaw" after the crafty lefty tossed a complete-game five-hitter to subdue the reigning NL pennant winners, 5-1, on July 29.[15] Roberts garnered national exposure in a classic pitchers' duel with the New York Mets' Tom Seaver on August 11. While Seaver departed after hurling 10 scoreless frames and whiffing 14, Roberts tossed a career-best 12-inning complete game to shut out the Mets, 1-0. In the pitchers' rematch 10 days later, Roberts held the Mets to three hits but lost a heartbreaker when Cleon Jones belted a solo home run with two outs in the ninth inning for New York's 2-1 walk-off win. Described by Padres beat writer Paul Cour as the "hard luck player of the year," Roberts lost 17 games for the NL's worst team (61-100), but received only 22 runs of support in those games, including five shutouts. "The hardest thing in becoming a pitcher is gaining confidence," said a reflective Roberts of his unexpected success. "It took me a few years to get [it]."[16]

In a move widely criticized by the Southern California press, the Padres shipped Roberts to the Houston Astros on December 3 for three prospects,

pitchers Bill Greif and Mark Schaeffer, and light-hitting infielder Derrel Thomas. With the addition of Roberts, Houston's staff was expected to be among the best in the league and boasted hard-throwing workhorses Larry Dierker and Don Wilson. Pitching coach Jim Owens praised the team's prized acquisition: "[Roberts] moves the ball in and out as well as anyone we have. He doesn't have one great pitch, but he has four real good ones. He has a good fastball—not a great one—but a good one. He has a good changeup and a screwball. And he has that quick slider. He has the real short one. Not many pitchers can throw that short slider."[17] Widely tabbed as a possible 20-game winner, Roberts tossed several gems, such as three impressive shutouts (one of which was against his nemesis Seaver and the Mets) and a 10-inning complete-game victory over his former team, the Padres; however, his season was marked by inconsistency. "I know they are expecting a lot from me," said Roberts. "You try not to feel it and tell yourself it doesn't affect you, but really you know." Relegated to the bullpen for the final three weeks of the season, Roberts finished with a winning record (12-7) for the third-place club, but his ERA (4.50) and hits per nine innings (10.6) were the highest in the major leagues among qualifying pitchers.

Roberts rebounded in 1973, leading the Astros in wins (17) and ERA (2.85), and set a new team record with six shutouts for manager Leo Durocher, who reinstituted a four-man rotation in his first full season as the Astros' skipper. "I'd say it [the shutout record] was kind of a fluke," said the ever modest Roberts, a contact pitcher who yielded 9.5 hits per nine innings (seventh-highest in the NL). "But they [the defense] know the ball is going to be hit. I work fast and the defense stays alert."[18] With Roberts, Jerry Reuss, Don Wilson, and Ken Forsch, the fourth-place Astros (82-80 in the NL West) joined the Dodgers and Giants as the only NL teams that season boasting four starters who logged in excess of 200 innings.

Many Astros players were happy to see the cantankerous Durocher leave after the 1973 season, but Roberts was not among them. He voiced his displeasure when his former Padres pilot and new Astros skipper Preston Gomez decided to go with an increasingly common five-man rotation. "I throw too hard when my arm is rested," said Roberts, who was concerned about overthrowing and reinjuring his arm. "I've got to be tired and then the ball moves around."[19] Roberts made more news at the plate than on mound in the first month of the season, knocking in eight runs in his first six starts. Adept with the bat, Roberts once served as "designated pinch-hitter" for Elmira in the minor leagues, and batted a respectable .194 (103-for-531) in his big-league career. On August 24 Roberts tossed the only one-hitter in his career, defeating the Philadelphia Phillies, 1-0, at the Astrodome. The shutout, his second consecutive, concluded a stretch of 26⅔ scoreless innings. Mired in fourth place, the Astros accelerated their youth movement in the latter half of September. The 29-year-old Roberts (who finished with a 10-12 record and 3.40 ERA in 204 innings) was relegated to the bullpen. The Astros finished in fourth place (81-81 in the NL West) and once again had four hurlers who logged in excess of 200 innings (Roberts, Dierker, Reuss, and Tom Griffin).

After an offseason filled with rumors about his expendability or conversion to a reliever, Roberts reported to spring training in 1975 with his role on the team undefined. With no other viable southpaw starter, Gomez scrapped his plan of sending Roberts to the bullpen, but Roberts's frustrations mounted. After two poor starts, Roberts went AWOL on May 9 in Montreal, drawing a suspension and a fine. "This is not a spur-of-the-moment decision," said a discouraged Roberts. "This has been building up for years."[20] Roberts returned to the team five days later in Chicago, but never found his rhythm for the NL's worst team (64-97). His record dipped to 8-14 and his ERA rose to 4.27 (sixth-highest in the NL) in 198⅓ innings. Preston Gomez had been fired as Houston's manager in mid-August and replaced with Bill Virdon, who had just been released as manager of the New York Yankees. With just three appearances in September, Roberts anticipated being traded. On December 6 he was sent to the Detroit Tigers in a seven-player deal. Roberts, pitcher Jim Crawford, and catcher Milt May were swapped for catcher Terry Humphrey, outfielder Leon Roberts, and pitchers Mark Lemongello and Gene Pentz.

Roberts's first season in Detroit was a memorable one despite the team's 74-87 record. While teammate Mark "The Bird" Fidrych captured the hearts and imagination of baseball fans across America with his antics on the mound, not to mention his superlative pitching, Roberts got off to a surprisingly good start. Replacing Tigers legend Mickey Lolich, who had been traded to the New York Mets in the offseason, Roberts tossed three complete games of three hits or less in his first eight starts, matching his career total from the previous seven years in the NL. He blanked the California Angels in Anaheim on two hits in his AL debut on April 17, and tossed another two-hitter 11 days later in his home debut in Tiger Stadium on the corner of Trumbull and Michigan Avenues, defeating the A's 8-1 (the run was unearned). The venerable ballpark, with its natural grass, seemed ideally suited to Roberts's sinkerball. Pitching consistently all season and battling severe knee pain in September, Roberts logged a team-high 252 innings, completed a career-best 18 games, matched his career high with 36 starts, while winning 16 games (losing 17) and posting a 4.00 ERA.

In the offseason Roberts was diagnosed with an arthritic right knee and underwent surgery to repair damaged tendons.[21] His career, however, was irrevocably changed. Bothered by knee pain during his follow-through, the 32-year-old Roberts struggled in 1977, going 4-10 with a 5.15 ERA in 22 starts before the Tigers placed him on waivers. He was purchased by the Chicago Cubs on July 30, 1977, concluding a disappointing season with a 5-11 record and 4.59 ERA in 182⅓ innings. After averaging 221 innings per season between 1970-1976, Roberts spent the final four seasons of his big-league career (1978-1981) as a journeyman reliever and spot starter playing for five different teams (Cubs, Giants, Pirates, Mariners, and Mets). Back with the Cubs in 1978, he began on the disabled list because of chronic back pain. The pitching-poor Cubs experimented with Roberts as a starter in 1978, but the ailing lefty's 5.25 ERA over 20 starts proved that he was no longer a viable option in the rotation.

Roberts was granted free agency in November 1978, but his recent history of injuries and his bloated ERA scared off suitors. He finally signed with the San Francisco Giants on February 22, 1979. Roberts was an unexpected surprise, appearing 26 times (all but one in relief) and posting a robust 2.57 ERA over 42 innings when he was involved in what *The Sporting News* called a "shocking trade."[22]

The Pittsburgh Pirates, laboring to stay a few games above .500 near the end of June, shipped three young hurlers to the Giants (Fred Breining, Al Holland, and Ed Whitson) in exchange for third baseman Bill Madlock, a two-time former NL batting champion. Roberts and utilityman Lenny Randle seemed to be last-minute toss-ins. While Madlock proved to be one of the catalysts in Pittsburgh's drive to the NL East crown, batting .328 in 85 games, Roberts turned out to be an important piece in the Pirates heavily used bullpen. The acquisition of Roberts, noted Pittsburgh beat reporter Charley Feeney, was "too good to be true."[23] Slotted for the inglorious task of long relief, Roberts won five games in his 18 relief appearances (he also made two ineffective starts) and logged 38⅔ innings. The most important of his victories was probably on August 25, when he held the Padres scoreless on four hits over the final four innings of the Pirates' 4-3 triumph in 19 innings. On September 11 Roberts celebrated his 35th birthday by tossing four innings of scoreless relief to earn his 100th victory, 7-3, against the St Louis Cardinals. "He took all those ugly innings. He took all those situations where we didn't have to work because he would," said a teammate, closer Kent Tekulve, years later. "He was extremely durable. He didn't care that he was the 10th guy on the staff. He didn't care that he was not getting the credit. He just wanted to win."[24]

After 11 years in the majors, Roberts finally got his one and only taste of the postseason with the "We Are Family" Pirates. He made his sole appearance in the playoffs during the ninth inning in Game Two of Pittsburgh's three-game sweep of the Cincinnati Reds in the then best-of-five NLCS, walking Joe Morgan on four pitches. Though Roberts was the only pitcher on the 10-man staff not to see action in Pirates' victory in seven games over the Baltimore Orioles in the World Series, Feeney called him a "big plus on the staff" for mentoring young hurlers and sacrificing personal gain for team success.[25] His teammates confirmed that praise by voting him a full share ($28,236.97) of World Series earnings even though he was with the team just over half the season.[26]

Just about 18 months after reaching the pinnacle of team success, Roberts was out of the big leagues. He relieved twice for the Pirates in 1980 before he was sold in a waiver transaction to the Seattle Mariners on April 24. After a brief stint with the Mets as a free agent in 1981, he was waived again. He subsequently signed with the Giants on June 15, three days after the beginning of the players' strike, which resulted in the cancellation of about 38 percent of the season. He accepted an assignment to the Giants' Triple-A affiliate in Phoenix of the Pacific Coast League, but retired after six appearances, and did not return to the big leagues.

Roberts went 103-125, tossed 20 shutouts, and carved out a 3.78 ERA in 2,099 innings in his 13-year big-league career pitching for eight teams. He also won 70 games and logged 1,014 innings in the minors. A classic contact and control pitcher, Roberts struck out only 957 and walked just 615 while appearing in 445 major-league contests.

Roberts pitched in an era when players needed to work in the offseason. He sold season tickets for the Padres and Astros, earned a real-estate license, and once owned a company, Raincheck, that installed underground sprinklers. After his playing career, he worked for the Allegany County (Maryland) Detention Center, and also served as an assistant baseball coach at Potomac State College (1996-1998), a two-year institution in West Virginia.

Dave Roberts died at the age of 64 on January 9, 2009, at his home in Short Gap, West Virginia. According to various reports, he had developed lung cancer, ostensibly from working as a boilermaker as a young man, which had exposed him to asbestos. He was survived by his second wife, Carol, three sons (Chris, Rick, and Kyle), two stepdaughters (Kristy and Melaney), and seven grandchildren.[27] He was buried in Frostburg Memorial Park in Maryland.

"Dave was a consummate pro," said longtime Astros executive Tal Smith upon learning of the pitcher's passing. "He'll really be remembered and missed for the leadership he provided and for being such a good guy."[28]

SOURCES

Dave Roberts player file at the National Baseball Hall of Fame, Cooperstown, New York.

Ancestry.com.

BaseballLibrary.com.

NOTES

1. What's in a name? As of 2015, there have been four players named Dave Roberts who have played in the big-leagues since 1962. Other than the pitcher profiled in his biography, there were two utility players and an outfielder.
2. *The Sporting News*, March 13, 1976: 38.
3. According to many sources, Roberts is considered Jewish; however, this claim seems to be incorrect. Roberts was born to a Jewish father and non-Jewish mother and raised by her and a non-Jewish stepfather. Even Reform Jewish congregations did not accept children of non-Jewish mothers; Orthodox and most Conservative congregations still do not today. Roberts was born as David Arthur Roth Jr., according to one source (Astro Databank, astro.com/astro-databank/Roberts, Dave).
4. Cliff Blau, "The Real First-Year Player Draft," *Baseball Research Journal* (Summer 2010), sabr.org/research/real-first-year-player-draft
5. *The Sporting News*, January 22, 1972: 40.
6. United Press International, "Pitcher Dave Roberts proves too much for Dodgers batters," *Redlands* (California) *Daily Facts*, April 11, 1970: 11.
7. John Wilson, "Inside Dave Roberts' Battle to Escape Oblivion," *Houston Chronicle*. In Dave Roberts's player file, in the National Baseball Hall of Fame and Museum.
8. Ron Roach (Associated Press), "Determination, prayer buoy Padres pitcher Dave Roberts," *Arizona Republic* (Phoenix), June 18, 1970: 132.
9. Ibid.
10. Ibid.
11. Wilson.
12. *The Sporting News*, January 16, 1971: 59.
13. *The Sporting News*, September 11, 1971: 16.
14. *The Sporting News*, May 29, 1971: 20.
15. Bob Rosenthal (Associated Press), "Rose Claims Padres' Dave Roberts Best NL Southpaw," *Pontiac* (Illinois) *Daily Leader*, July 30, 1971: 6.
16. *The Sporting News*, January 22, 1972: 40.
17. Wilson.
18. Michael A. Lutz (Associated Press), "Roberts Says Season Fluke," *Corsicana* (Texas) *Daily Sun*, September 27, 1973: 12.
19. *The Sporting News*, April 27, 1974: 30.
20. *The Sporting News*, May 24, 1975: 21.
21. Richard L. Dancz, "Healthy Roberts Sees Tigers' Rise," *Ludington* (Michigan) *Daily News*, February, 1, 1977: 5.
22. *The Sporting News*, July 14, 1979: 18.
23. *The Sporting News*, July 14, 1979: 40.
24. Jenifer Langosch, "Former hurler Roberts passes away," *MLB.com*. January 9, 2009. mlb.mlb.com/news/article.jsp?ymd=20090109&content_id=3738241&vkey=news_mlb&fext=.jsp&c_id=mlb.
25. *The Sporting News*, October 20, 1979: 22.
26. *The Sporting News*, December 22, 1979: 51.
27. Mike Mathews, "Former Major Leaguer, Coach Dies," *Cumberland* (Maryland) *Times-News*, January 9, 2009.
28. Ibid.

Bill Robinson

By Alan Cohen

IT WAS ONE WEEK INTO THE 1977 season. Jim Kaplan of *Sports Illustrated* alluded to 34-year-old Bill Robinson's frustrations in his 10th major-league season:

"No matter where he is playing—be it Cincinnati or New York or Los Angeles—he is sure to hear it. 'Weaser,' someone will call to him from the stands. 'Hey, Weaser.' And Bill Robinson of the Pirates will know someone from his hometown of Elizabeth, Pa., just outside Pittsburgh, is on hand. Why was he given the name? Robinson doesn't know. What does Weaser mean? That's also a mystery. The nickname is downright befuddling, which makes it especially appropriate for Robinson, a .300 hitter with power and a good glove who, confoundingly enough, cannot get a regular job. 'I am the No. 1 utility man in baseball,' he says joylessly."[1]

"But in the Panglossian (excessively optimistic) world of Pittsburgh's new manager, Chuck Tanner, Robinson occupies the best of all possible positions." "'People call him a super-sub,' says Tanner. 'I call him a super-regular. He's more valuable than most regulars, because he can play so many positions.'"[2]

"Robinson's pre-batting ritual includes a quick Lord's Prayer while he crosses himself several times. Then he rubs his forehead from eyebrows to hairline with the middle and index fingers of his right hand, a relaxation technique he picked up from a kinesiologist. Finally Robinson assumes an upright stance made all the more menacing by his 6'3", 200-pound frame[3] and lashes downward at the ball with a whippy 33-ounce bat. 'I try to make the top of the ball mine,' he says. 'I swing for grounders and line drives. After all, how often does a guy drop a fly? But the big thing is, I've learned to relax and meet the ball instead of trying to overpower it. I've eliminated the word "pressure" from my vocabulary.'"[4]

"'His attitude has changed completely,' says Del Unser of the Expos, a close friend and former teammate of Robinson's in Philadelphia. 'He was very high-strung with the Yankees [1967-69] and at times with the Phillies [1972-74]. Now he can wait out a pitcher and hit breaking stuff. I think if he hadn't had to break in as a Yankee, he'd have been where he is now five years ago.'"[5]

William Henry Robinson Jr., the first-base coach and hitting instructor for the 1986 New York Mets, was born on June 26, 1943, in McKeesport, Pennsylvania. His father, Bill Sr., was a steelworker. His mother, Millie Mae, was a cook in a restaurant, and when the scouts visited during Bill's senior year of high school, she made sure they were well fed.

Robinson starred in baseball (as a pitcher/outfielder) and basketball at Elizabeth-Forward High School in McKeesport and had a basketball scholarship offer from Bradley University. He chose baseball and was signed in June 1961, when he graduated from high school, by John O'Neil of the Braves for a figure between $12,000 and $16,000.

Robinson's career got off to a less than resounding start. His travels began in 1961 at Wellsville in the Class-D New York-Penn League. Although he batted only .239, he had 15 doubles in 67 games and was off to Dublin in the Georgia-Florida League for the 1962 season. While there, he experienced the racial segregation that was inherent in the South in those years, but did not let it affect his play on the field. From there, Robinson headed up the ladder. He batted .304 at Dublin and followed that up with a .316 at Waycross in the Class-A Georgia-Florida League the following season. At Waycross he had 10 home runs, a league-leading 132 hits and 10 triples, 62 RBIs, and 29 stolen bases. He topped the league with a .478 slugging percentage. The 1964 season found him at Yakima in the Class-A Northwest League, where he had his best season so far, banging 24 doubles and 18 homers with 81 RBIs en route to a .348 batting average in 104 games.

Robinson had married his childhood sweetheart, Mary Alice Moore, in December 1963. Bill III came along in 1964 and Kelly was born in 1969. The Robinsons eventually settled in Washington Township, New Jersey. Bill was active in his community and received the George Washington Carver Award for community service in 1978.[6]

Despite his achievements, Robinson gained the reputation as a worrier, as noted in a small piece in *The Sporting News* in 1965.[7] Robinson spent all of the 1965 season with the Atlanta Crackers, the Braves' Triple-A farm team. He got off to a great start with three hits in his first game and went 7-for-16 in his first four games. The accolades were flowing and Toledo's manager, Frank Verdi, considered him to be "the best looking rookie I have seen in the league this year."[8] For the season, he batted .268. In 1966 the Milwaukee Braves moved to Atlanta, and the Braves moved their Triple-A team to Richmond. Robinson responded to the move with a .312 batting average and career highs of 20 home runs and 79 RBIs. He was named to the International League All-Star team.

Robinson, then 23, was called up to the Braves at the end of the 1966 season and saw his first action on September 20. He ran for Henry Aaron and finished the game in right field. His first hit came on September 25. Starting the game in left field, he singled in the eighth inning off Pittsburgh's Al McBean, driving in a run. He was given another start in the season finale against Cincinnati and went 2-for-4, including his first major-league extra-base hit, an RBI triple. In his six games with the Braves, he went 3-for-11.

But the Braves were fully stocked with outfielders and traded Robinson to the New York Yankees for Clete Boyer. The aging Yankees had fallen on hard times, falling to sixth in 1965 and 10th in 1966. Roger Maris had been traded to St. Louis, and it was expected that Robinson would take over in right field.

Robinson was counted on to save the franchise, and things started off fairly well. As Robinson remembered it, "(W)e opened in Washington (on April 10), and I hit a home run my first time up in an 8-1 win. They said 'God's here.'"[9] The score was actually 8-0, with the win going to Mel Stottlemyre, who limited the Senators to two hits.

As Marty Appel notes in *Pinstripe Empire*, "Robinson was a personal favorite of (team president Mike) Burke's. He wanted him to succeed badly. He was tall and rangy, he was black, and he seemed like a good statement for a team 'moving in new directions.'"[10] Burke was alluding to the fact that since Jackie Robinson entered baseball in 1947, the Yankees had been very slow to integrate, with only one black player of note, Elston Howard, playing for the club during the first 20 years of integration.

But the rest of the 1967 season for Bill Robinson was a disappointment. He suffered a shoulder injury, which he tried to hide. The fans were tough on him. "The boos really tore me up when I was with the Yankees," he said in 1974. "All ballplayers hear them and I couldn't take it. I'd be across the George Washington Bridge and heading home (to New Jersey) before the people even got to the clubhouse. I just couldn't face it anymore."[11] He batted only .196 with seven homers and 29 RBIs in 116 games, as the Yankees placed ninth for their third consecutive lower division finish.

Looking back on his season, Robinson said, "I was pressing too hard. Every time I came up, I wanted to hit a home run to impress people. Finally it got to the point where I was holding the bat so tightly I couldn't even hit the ball."[12]

Postseason shoulder surgery repaired the injury, but Robinson continued to struggle. He batted .240 in 1968 and .171 in 1969. In 1970 he was sent down to Triple-A Syracuse and batted .258. In December the Yankees traded Robinson to the Chicago White Sox for pitcher Barry Moore.

Appel noted, "It would forever be a mystery as to what went wrong with Bill Robinson in New York, and why that promise was never fulfilled"[13] (until he shined for Philadelphia and Pittsburgh).

The White Sox sent Robinson to Triple-A Tucson (Pacific Coast League), where he batted .275 with 14 homers and 81 RBIs in 1971. Frustration set in when he was not called up to the White Sox, and he even thought about quitting. His hopes were renewed when

THE 1979 PITTSBURGH PIRATES

Chicago dealt him to the Philadelphia Phillies for minor-league catcher Jerry Rodriguez.

In 1972 Robinson was still in the PCL, this time with Eugene, and batted .304 with 20 homers and 66 RBIs in 66 games. That earned him a call-up to Philadelphia in June, and he saw his first action with the Phillies on June 24, doubling against the Expos in a pinch-hitting role. During his days in the minor leagues, he learned of what he came to call the Willie Davis theory, which goes as follows: "It's not my life, and it's not my wife, so why worry about it." Basically, he learned not to dwell over everything and only worry about items of the utmost personal importance. The theory stood him well as he embarked on the most productive years of his career. There would be bumps along the way, but, for the most part, Robinson took things in stride and learned to relax.

Robinson got into 82 games with the Phillies in 1972, batting .239, but was in the majors to stay.[14] Actually, when he came to spring training in 1973, he was still 52 days short of qualifying for the major-league pension plan. Job number one was just to make the team. He exceeded all expectations. New manager Danny Ozark inserted Bill into the lineup more regularly and he batted .288 with 25 home runs and 65 RBIs in 124 games. It appeared as though Robinson had it made. Manager Ozark remarked, "He gave it his all and produced. I understood the problems he had in New York. He wasn't sure of himself. Now he'd got the confidence. If he could go back 10 years, he would be another Aaron or Mays."[15]

No sooner was Robinson a regular than his bad luck returned. He had offseason surgery for bone chips in his left elbow and found that, despite his fine performance, he came to spring training in 1974 without a regular job. A somewhat overblown dispute with Ozark would ultimately result in his leaving the Phillies.

"I saw the lineup card without my name on it and took a swipe at it, not meaning to touch it," Robinson recalled. "But it came off, and Ozark was watching. He called me into his office, which he had a perfect right to do, and we both let off a lot of steam. When I

was leaving, I tried to close the door gently, but there was a breeze and it slammed."[16]

Robinson got into only 100 games with Philadelphia in 1974 and his average dropped to .236 with only 5 home runs and 21 RBIs. After the season, he was traded to Pittsburgh for pitcher Wayne Simpson, and with the Pirates he blossomed.

Robinson joined the Pirates in 1975 at the none-too-tender age of 32 and was the fourth outfielder behind Richie Zisk, Al Oliver, and Dave Parker. He batted .280 with 6 homers and 33 RBIs. He started 41 games for the Pirates and had 16 multiple-hit games. The Pirates won the National League East title before being swept by Cincinnati in the League Championship Series. Robinson went hitless in two at-bats in the LCS.

The following season, Robinson saw more action, with 416 at-bats in 121 games. His batting average soared to .303, his first time above .300. He was the Pirates' leading right-handed slugger and the team's most valuable player. He received the Roberto Clemente Memorial Award from the Pittsburgh sportswriters. He performed at five different positions and pinch-hit

.455.[17] His power numbers were solid (21 homers, 64 RBIs) and the best was yet to come.

Off this showing, Robinson was slated for third base in 1977, but once again he would be denied. The Pirates traded for Phil Garner. Instead of blowing up as he had in Philadelphia, he calmly talked out his disappointment with two friends from his minor-league days and his father. "They all told me the same things," Robinson said, "that I still had a job and that things could be worse. So I didn't do anything rash, and I'm glad. We got a heck of a third baseman in the deal, and because I had thought I would start, I had gotten into the best shape of my life mentally and physically."[18]

"It's true we led Bill to believe he'd be starting at third this season," said General Manager Pete Peterson, "but we couldn't resist picking up Phil Garner from the A's. He (Garner) plays third, and Willie Stargell plays first. We want to stick with Al Oliver in left and Dave Parker in right, and we feel Omar Moreno in center gives us the kind of outfield defense we haven't had since Roberto Clemente. Not that Bill isn't good defensively. He is, and he's our top sub at all five positions. He may not get 400 at-bats, but he'll get plenty with his versatility."[19]

It wasn't long before Robinson saw action, filling in for injured Pirates in the outfield and at first base. It was early on that the Pirate injury list started to grow, and Robinson was a disgruntled bench warmer for just the first four innings of the season. When Al Oliver was sidelined because the pain from a mouth ulcer became too acute, Robinson moved into the outfield. Two games later, Stargell began suffering, first from a strained right knee, then from dizzy spells, and Robinson was moved to first base. Through the first seven games of the season, he was hitting .348 and leading the Bucs with eight runs batted in. There was even talk in Pittsburgh that the Pirates would trade one of their regulars so that Robinson can have a spot to call his own in the lineup.[20]

Despite this early activity, he was hampered by muscle pulls in his legs and started only 19 games during the first two months of the season. Everyone seemed to have suggestions to get him going and, at the suggestion of teammate Rich Gossage, he took to wearing pantyhose beneath his uniform pants.[21] He took more than his share of kidding, but went onto start 32 consecutive games between May 31 and July 2, batting .339 over that stretch.

It got better. From July 21 through August 2, Robinson had a power surge. He had five homers, including grand slams on July 28 and July 30, and batted in 21 runs. His batting average during the 13 games was .390 and his slugging percentage was a hefty .712. But he did not forget that it had not always been so easy. He could relate to "the guys sitting on the bench, because I have been in their spot for a long, long time. The toughest part of coming off the bench is that you know eventually you're going back to the bench. That's tough for any athlete to take."[22]

On August 15 of that season, the Pirates issued a press release which highlighted his exploits from June 24 through August 2, a period during which he had eight game winning hits. It was also noted that through August 14, he had come to the plate 24 times with a runner on third with less than two out, and driven in the runner on 22 of those occasions.[23]

For the record, Bill Robinson in 1977, despite not being a "regular", played in 137 games, 127 as a starter. The versatile Robinson started 79 games at first base, 11 games at third base, 36 games in left field, and 1 game in center field. He came to the plate 544 times. He set career highs, batting .304 with 26 homers and 104 RBIs.

During the offseason, Al Oliver was traded and Bill Robinson, at age 35, became the everyday left fielder in 1978. However, his numbers dropped off significantly. He batted only .246 with 14 home runs and 80 RBIs. A thumb injury early in the season set him back and as he continued to fail to produce, he began to press. Manager Chuck Tanner and his teammates were in his corner. Tanner said, "You don't give up on his type. He's giving it all he has and one day he'll get it all back and he'll win plenty of games for us."[24]

Robinson didn't let his off year at the plate affect his fielding as he led National League left fielders with a .989 fielding percentage. He stole a career high 14 bases. He did have his moments during the season,

THE 1979 PITTSBURGH PIRATES

with a pair of two-home-run games against the Cubs at Wrigley Field.

And then came 1979. Robinson got his home-run swing back and slammed 24 along with 75 RBIs as the "We Are Family" Pirates won their division for the sixth time in 10 years, and the first time since 1975. Robinson appeared in a career record 148 games for Pittsburgh, again without a regular position or place in the lineup. He was platooned with John Milner, and when Willie Stargell needed a rest, the Pirates would play both Robinson and Milner, and they were up to the task.

Actually, the Pirates got off to a slow start in 1979. They were six games under .500 on May 16 before taking 16 of 21 games to move into third place, three games out of first. During that stretch, Robinson batted .322 with seven homers and 19 RBIs, including two homers in a win on June 6. As the Pirates righted their ship, Robinson said "It was just a case of putting it together. We know we have the talent here. We know we can win. We have all the ingredients of a winner and many of us are tired of finishing in second place."[25] But then, the team treaded water.

As late as July 8, they were in fourth place, seven games behind the league leaders. Then they took off. They won 16 of 21 to move into first place for the first time on July 28. It became a two-team race between the Pirates and the surprising Montreal Expos the rest of the season.

On the decisive last day of the campaign, the Pirates hosted the Chicago Cubs. Robinson came off the bench in the top of the sixth inning to replace Milner in left field. His first, and only, plate appearance was in the bottom of the seventh inning. He came to the plate with the bases loaded and two outs. He delivered a single, driving in two runs to give the Bucs a 5-2 lead. The final score was 5-3, and the victorious Pirates advanced to the postseason. They defeated the Reds in the NLCS to advance to the World Series against Baltimore. After going 0-for-3 in the LCS, Robinson went 5-for-19 in the World Series as the Pirates defeated the Orioles in seven games. Robinson had his first World Series ring, and a full World Series share worth $28,236.87.

During the offseason, the Pirates, looking to shore up their pitching, offered Robinson as trade bait, but there were no nibbles.[26] Injuries plagued Robinson in 1980, and he played in only 100 games, 74 as a starter. He batted .287 with 12 home runs and 36 RBIs. The following season, he saw even less action, batting .216 and playing in only 39 games. The Pirates finished third in 1980 with an 83-79 record and, in the strike-shortened 1981 season were 46-56.

By 1982 the Pirates were showing their age. Although they finished with a winning record of 84-78, some of their players, most notably Robinson (39) and Willie Stargell (42) were getting old. On June 15, 1982, Robinson and his .239 batting average were traded to the Phillies for Wayne Nordhagen. As Robinson parted with the Pirates, Stargell said, "Bill Robinson is one helluva man, nothing but a plus in anybody's life. He is a caring, concerned man."[27]

In the remaining months of 1982, Robinson played in 35 games for the Phillies, batting .261 (18-for-69). He saw his last action in 1983, getting into only 10 games, and was released on May 23. Teammate Mike Schmidt remembered back to 1972 when he was at Eugene, Oregon, his last stop in the minors, and was teamed with Robinson. Schmidt remembered that Robinson "respected me as a player, and knowing that made me feel good. He kind of took me under his wing.... (J)ust a good friend, a guy that had been there before.... Robbie is a credit to the game of baseball. I don't know how to put it any other way."[28] Robinson finished his 16-year major-league playing career with a .258 batting average, 166 home runs and 641 RBIs.

In his last weeks with the Phillies, Robinson took the time to counsel rookie pitcher Charles Hudson on the importance of relaxing, and learning to "alleviate pressure."[29] He would spend the better part of his remaining years instilling that lesson on a new generation of players.

In 1984 Robinson joined the New York Mets as hitting instructor and first-base coach, and "Uncle Bill" was with the Mets for six years during which time the team never finished lower than second place. Robinson got his second World Series ring in 1986, and was a valued instructor working with the likes of Darryl Strawberry, who became his special project.

Ron Darling was in his first full season with the Mets in 1984, and on August 7 pitched against the Cubs at Wrigley Field. By day's end, he would know first-hand the value of Bill Robinson to the New York Mets. Darling was pulled from the game not long after hitting Dave Owen of Chicago in the fifth inning. An irate Cubs fan threw a cup of beer at Darling as he left the field. Darling was about to go back on the field and pursue his attacker when Robinson grabbed hold of him and set him down. Robinson, of course, could display his temper, and was about to pursue the fan. He backed off when the fan was escorted from the premises by security guards. When Robinson returned to the dugout, he shot a knowing glance in Darling's direction, which the young pitcher took as a much needed sign of encouragement.[30]

Robinson looked for every edge for his players, and was quick to accuse Pirates pitcher Rich Rhoden of doctoring the ball in a game against the Mets on July 6, 1986, in Pittsburgh. He confronted Rhoden after the pitcher struck out Gary Carter to end the fifth inning. A shoving match ensued and, before long, the benches cleared. Robinson was fined $500, but his players knew where he stood.

During the stretch drive in 1986, Robinson made it a point to put a picture in Strawberry's locker of Darryl hitting a line drive, just to remind his star pupil how he looked when swinging well.[31] During the last 11 games of the regular season, Strawberry batted .306 with 6 home runs and 15 RBIs. During his six years working with Robinson, Strawberry averaged over 30 home runs per season.

During the 1986 World Series, Robinson spoke of the challenges he faced with the Mets and the approach he had taken. "I think that with these young kids, you've got to be more than a hitting instructor. I'm not their father but you've got to give them fatherly street advice. It certainly helps me, not only being black, but talking to all the guys it helps a lot that I have a son who is the same age as most of these guys. I respect them all and think they respect me. They're trying to get where I've been."[32] Bill's son at the time became very close with Strawberry and Gooden. Every time Gooden had an issue, he was able to come to Robinson, who was much more than a hitting instructor.

And on that magical (for the Mets) evening in October, Bill Robinson was standing in the first-base coaching box when, in that fateful bottom of the 10th inning of Game Six of the World Series, every player got the low two when he arrived at first base. The rallying cry was "Don't make the last out!"[33] And then, Mookie Wilson hit a groundball in the direction of first base. "It made three nice bounces. Bounce … bounce … bounce. And then it hit something and didn't come up again. That fourth bounce. It was just our year."[34] Wilson remembered that during that fateful bottom of the 10th inning, each of the Mets involved in the rally told Robinson that they were not determined to make the last out.[35]

The Mets were unable to build on the success of 1986, and in 1989 after finishing in second place, six games behind the division-winning Cubs, Robinson was fired. After spending two years with ESPN, in 1992 he took a managing job at Shreveport in the Double-A Texas League and led the Giants affiliate to the championship with a 77-59 record. He was frustrated at not being given an opportunity to rise higher, as he aspired to eventually get a major-league managing position. He did feel that race had something to do with his not moving higher, stating: "If (becoming a big league manager) doesn't happen, it won't surprise me. Whether it's prejudice, whether it's timing, or whatever, it's always excuses."[36]

Robinson's next stop was back with the Phillies, as a minor league hitting instructor in 1994, and as manager at Reading in the Eastern League in 1996. The following season he moved up to Triple-A Scranton-Wilkes-Barre as hitting instructor, and was inducted into the Pennsylvania Baseball Sports Hall of Fame.

Robinson was doing what he loved. In 1998 he said, "It's been fun, gratifying to help young kids. I had delusions of being a major-league manager, but I know that's not going to happen. Baseball doesn't owe me a thing. As long as I have a uniform on, I'm grateful. I've been successful. Maybe not in a material way, but I have the Lord on my side and my family. What more could a man ask?"[37]

In 1999 Robinson was back in the Yankees organization, working with the hitters at Triple-A Columbus. He was rewarded for his efforts with a World Series ring when the Yankees won the championship that year. He stayed with Columbus for three years before returning to the majors as the hitting instructor for the Montreal Expos in 2001.

Robinson was ecstatic about returning to the big leagues as a coach. "I had waited 12 years to get back to the major leagues. After I accepted (the offer from Expos manager Jeff Torborg), I walked out on Madison Avenue (in New York), raised my hands to the sky, and said, 'Thank God.'"[38]

In 2003 Robinson was with the Florida Marlins and returned to the World Series, facing the Yankees and winning his fourth World Series ring as the Marlins defeated the Yankees. George Vecsey of the *New York Times* perhaps summed things up the best: "Whether (the Marlins) know it or not, their paternal hitting coach is an inspiration for athletes — or anybody else who has a bad day or a bad couple of years. You can come back. You can go from failure to the World Series."[39]

Robinson died suddenly on July 29, 2007, in Las Vegas while working as a minor-league hitting coordinator for the Los Angeles Dodgers. He was survived by his wife, Mary Alice, and their two children. William III played three years of minor-league baseball before moving into broadcasting, and Kelley worked in the fashion industry.

SOURCES

In addition to the sources cited in the notes, the author also consulted:

Vecsey, George. "And Here's To You Mr. Robinson, My Friend," *New York Times*, August 2, 2007: D-1.

Baseball-Reference.com.

Robinson's file at the Baseball Hall of Fame library.

NOTES

1. Jim Kaplan, "He's an Irregular Regular," *Sports Illustrated*, April 25, 1977
2. Kaplan.
3. Baseball-reference.com lists Robinson at 6-feet-2 and 189 pounds.
4. Kaplan.
5. Kaplan.
6. Jack Chevalier, *Philadelphia Tribune*, September 19, 2003.
7. *The Sporting News*, May 1, 1965: 42.
8. Furman Bisher, "Robby Came for Cup of Coffee, Stayed to Feast with Crackers," *The Sporting News*, July 24, 1965: 37.
9. Sam Smith, "Bill Robinson, In Search of Confidence," *Black Sports*, September, 1974: 23.
10. Marty Appel, *Pinstripe Empire: The New York Yankees from Before the Babe to After the Boss* (New York: Bloomsbury, 2012), 368.
11. Smith, 31.
12. Neil Amdur, "Robinson of Yanks Is Relaxed for His Second Time Around," *New York Times*, April 8, 1968: 67.
13. Appel, 378.
14. Ed Rumill, "Phillies Robinson Glad He Didn't Quit," *Christian Science Monitor*, June 27, 1973.
15. Smith, 47.
16. Kaplan.
17. Kaplan.
18. Kaplan.
19. Kaplan
20. Kaplan
21. Charlie Feeney, "Robinson Snubbed as All-Star, Glistens as Buc," *The Sporting News*, June 25, 1977: 15
22. Charlie Feeney, "Lucky Bucs Find Robinson Can Do Job on Daily Basis, *The Sporting News*, August 13, 1977: 8.
23. Pittsburgh Pirates Press Release, August 15, 1977, in Robinson file at the Baseball Hall of Fame.
24. Charlie Feeney, "Bucs Waiting For Robinson to End Slump," *The Sporting News*, July 8, 1978: 28.
25. Feeney, "Bucs Cash in on Robinson's Waiting Game," *The Sporting News*, June 23, 1979: 17.
26. Charlie Feeney, "Bucs Get No Nibbles With Robinson as Bait," *The Sporting News*, December 22, 1979: 61.
27. Frank Dolson, "Baseball Can't Lose People Like Robinson," *Philadelphia Inquirer*, June 6, 1983: 7-C.
28. Dolson.
29. Dolson.
30. Ron Darling with Danie Paisner, *The Complete Game* (New York: Random House, 2009), 133-34.
31. Jim Naughton, *New York Daily News*, October 5, 1986.

32 Malcolm Moran, "Robinson and His Gifted Student," *New York Times*, October 23, 1986: B16.

33 Interview with Bill Robinson III, June 2015.

34 Vic Ziegel, "Robby Back Where He Belongs," *New York Daily News*, March 27, 1998.

35 Mookie Wilson (with Erik Sherman), *Mookie: Life, Baseball, and the '86 Mets*, (New York: Berkley Books, 2014), 6.

36 Taylor Batten, Associated Press, "Is There Racism in Baseball?" *Mobile* (Alabama) *Register*, July 22, 1992: 26.

37 Ziegel.

38 Jack Chevalier, *Philadelphia Tribune*, November 13, 2011: 2C

39 George Vecsey, "Ex-Yankee Robinson Returns as a Winner, *New York Times*, October 20, 2003: D-4.

Don Robinson

By Thomas E. Kern

IN THE EYES OF PITTSBURGH PIRATES fans, Don Robinson showed up right on time for a city and a team looking for homegrown talent to fill out the Pirates pitching staff and add a piece to a team capable of winning a pennant in the late 1970s. Had the Philadelphia Phillies selected Robinson in the 1975 draft as many (including Robinson himself) had thought they would, Robinson's career would have turned out differently. Thankfully for Pittsburghers, he began and spent most of his career as a Pirate, contributing to and embraced as the youngest member of the 1979 World Series family in only his second year as a major leaguer.

Born in Ashland, Kentucky, on June 8, 1957, the son of Donald and Priscilla Robinson, Donald Allen Robinson had his father to thank for his devotion to baseball. An interview with Robinson offered a firsthand perspective of a father helpful to his baseball upbringing.[1] His father's love for the game and his commitment to his son's baseball development showed through the early exposure to baseball that he gave his son via Little League and other opportunities. Robinson's height—he was a 6-foot-4 right-hander by the time he reached high school—did not hurt, either. As a freshman member of the Ceredo-Kenova High School (Kenova, West Virginia) varsity baseball team, he threw a no-hitter. By his senior year, he had begun drawing the attention of major-league scouts from a number of teams, including Cincinnati, Philadelphia, and Pittsburgh. Kenova is 10 miles west of Huntington, 140 miles east of Cincinnati's Crosley Field, so it was only natural that Robinson followed the Reds in his youth. He graduated in June 1975 in a class of 112. Alongside the attention to graduation that month was the baseball amateur draft that would lay the groundwork for Robinson's career.

The idea of Robinson's favorite team drafting him was appealing, but it was the Philadelphia Phillies that made the most noise before the draft about signing him as a number-one pick. Robinson was that good. His pitching command gave him a fastball and a curve that complemented each other well. And he could throw hard. That said, the Phillies ended up drafting three others in the first three rounds. None of the three would ever make the majors. The Pirates, drafting eight spots behind the Phillies, took shortstop Dale Berra in the first round and Jeffrey Pinkus, a high-school pitcher who never advanced beyond Class-A, in the next round before selecting Robinson in the third round.

"Howie Haak called me to ask if he could watch me throw," Robinson said. Haak was the Pittsburgh scout who had recommended that the Dodgers sign Roberto Clemente. He later was instrumental in the Pirates signing Omar Moreno, Manny Sanguillen, and Rennie Stennett, all of whom contributed to Pittsburgh's 1979 World Series success. "I threw 15, 20 pitches," said Robinson and Haak said, "That's all I need to see," he recalled.

Like a number of draft picks, once selected, the conversation shifted to signing a contract. "I held out for more money. Murray Cook [from the Pirates front office] offered me $10,000 and then $20,000. I wanted $30,000." Robinson ended up signing for $38,000 plus incentives and was assigned to the Pirates' Gulf Coast League affiliate in Bradenton, where he pitched in 10 games as a starter, hurling 66 innings with a 2.45 ERA. He then played in the 60-day instructional league until November. There he hurt his arm and as he readied for 1976, Robinson said, he knew "my arm was not right." In 1976, he was the Opening Day starter for the Charleston (South Carolina) Patriots of the Class-A Western Carolinas League, and pitched in 24 games with a 12-9 record before having elbow surgery to remove a bone spur in August. That autumn he was invited to play in the Puerto Rico winter league. When he got to Puerto Rico, he said, "I could not throw 80 miles an hour." But with the help of Doc

Ewell, Houston's trainer, Robinson "got on a rubber band program [using a band to strengthen the arm] and did rehab there for five weeks, getting my speed back up to 90 mph."

In 1977 Robinson was assigned to Shreveport of the Double-A Texas League, where he went 7-6, then made one appearance for Triple-A Columbus and got a victory by pitching five scoreless innings. After a successful stint in Puerto Rico, Robinson got an invitation to spring training in 1978. Robinson credited Larry Sherry, then a Pirates minor-league instructor, for teaching him a hard breaking ball that complemented his fastball.

"When spring training came in 1978, I thought I would make Triple A. I was on the 40-man roster," Robinson said. At 21, this was not a bad trajectory for a third-round draft pick out of high school. Sherry was the pitching coach for the Pirates and Jose Pagan, his winter-league manager, the first-base coach. They were invaluable to Robinson's chances for making the big-league club since both had worked with him in the minors. Robinson often threw in later innings during spring training and estimated that he saw about 18 or 19 innings of work.

Manager Chuck Tanner "loved me," Robinson said. "We need to make a trade and if we do, you will make the team," Chuck told him. And sure enough, a trade of relief pitcher Elias Sosa, outfielder Miguel Dilone, and infielder Mike Edwards to the Oakland A's to bring back a Pittsburgh icon, Manny Sanguillen opened a pitching spot on the 25-man roster. Reportedly, Tanner told the front office as the roster was being finalized, "If he doesn't go north with me, I resign." Robinson went north. His uniform number? Robinson said, "43 was given to me—young player—you don't say anything."

Tanner advised Robinson that he would pitch if the team were way ahead or way behind. However, this soon changed. After making his debut on April 10, pitching 4⅓ innings in relief of Jim Rooker in a blowout loss to the St. Louis Cardinals and giving up four runs, he made his first start against Rick Reuschel of the Cubs on April 16 in Chicago. He gave up three runs (one earned) in seven innings and lost. He won his first game (a 2-1 complete game) against the Mets in New York on April 25. Robinson went on to pitch in 35 games that year, all but three as a starter.

The Pirates were a great team to begin a career with—"they were all vets," Robinson said. "On a veteran staff, you learned a lot." And Tanner made it clear to the youngsters (Robinson was 21) that you could not question or get back at a vet. "They taught me so much," Robinson said. Among the major influences was Willie Stargell. Stargell told Robinson, "If you want to stay in the big leagues, you have to be able to learn how to deal with failure." For Robinson with his arm problems, this became good advice and a catalyst to his being able to pitch in the majors for 15 years.

"It was a great run in 1978; we almost caught the Phillies [finishing 1½ games back]," Robinson said. Had the Pirates swept the Phillies in the four-game series at the end of the season (they won three of four), they would have been a half-game ahead in the division with a makeup game at Cincinnati to determine if a one-game playoff against Philadelphia would be needed to break a tie in the NL East.

THE 1979 PITTSBURGH PIRATES

As a 21-year-old rookie that year, Robinson put up pretty impressive numbers. His 14 wins against 6 losses (.700) was the second best won-loss percentage to NL Cy Young Award winner Gaylord Perry, who finished at 21-6 (.778) for the Padres.

Robinson was named *The Sporting News* NL Rookie Pitcher of the Year and was third in overall NL Rookie of the Year voting behind Bob Horner of the Atlanta Braves and Ozzie Smith of the San Diego Padres. He finished eighth in the Cy Young Award vote and had established himself as a young presence for the Pirates' 1979 starting rotation in a year they hoped they would contend with the Phillies and the Expos for the National League East Division championship.

Early in 1979, Robinson said, "(M)y shoulder started bothering me. [In an April 24 night game in Cincinnati] during a rain delay I could not lift my arm." Robinson went on to finish the game with a 9-2 victory over Frank Pastore (the pitcher the Reds selected instead of Robinson in the 1975 draft). "I was in and out of the rotation during the year and at one point did not pitch for two weeks. At one point, because of my shoulder problems, Chuck put me in the bullpen. I was taking cortisone shots." Back in the rotation on September 17, before 54,609 at Stade Olympique in Montreal, Robinson pitched a 2-1 complete-game victory over All-Star hurler Steve Rogers to put the Pirates in first by one game over the Expos. He lost twice in the remaining two weeks of the campaign, both to the Cubs. On the last day of the season, September 30, Bruce Kison defeated the Cubs 5-3 in Pittsburgh to win the NL East Division by two games.

The Pirates used John Candelaria, Jim Bibby, and Bert Blyleven in the best-of-five National League Championship Series rotation and employed Robinson out of the bullpen. Robinson came out of the bullpen against the NL West champion Cincinnati Reds in the NLCS came at Riverfront Stadium in the bottom of the 11th inning of Game One after Willie Stargell had broken a 2-2 tie in the top of the inning with a three-run homer. Grant Jackson had got the first two outs, but then gave up a single to Dave Concepcion and walked George Foster. Robinson was warming in the bullpen. He said, "I was throwing 97 mph, but could not hit the catcher." Tanner called for Robinson, who walked Johnny Bench on a 3-and-2 count to load the bases and bring up Ray Knight, representing the winning run. Said Robinson, "Stargell comes in from first and said he would pitch." That broke the tension for Robinson, who struck out Knight on a 1-and-2 pitch in the dirt, with Ed Ott firing the ball to Stargell to save the game for Pittsburgh.

Robinson came into Game Two after Kent Tekulve blew a save opportunity by allowing back-to-back doubles in the ninth and Dave Roberts followed and walked the only batter he faced. With the score tied 2-2, and the winning run at second base, Robinson struck out Concepcion and induced Foster to ground out. The Pirates scored in the 10th when Dave Parker singled home Omar Moreno. Robinson closed out the game in the bottom of the 10th by striking out Bench and retiring Dan Driessen and Knight on fly balls. Then Blyleven pitched a 7-1 victory in front of 42,240 in Pittsburgh for a three-game sweep of the NLCS to secure the NL pennant.

In the World Series, against Baltimore, Robinson again worked out of the bullpen. Game One had a disastrous start by the Pirates with Kison giving up five runs (four earned) in one-third of an inning. Relievers Rooker, Enrique Romo, Robinson, and Jackson threw 7⅔ innings of scoreless ball, but the Pirates could not overcome the first inning and lost 5-4 in Baltimore. Robinson's relief stint of two hitless innings was his third postseason appearance. He pitched again the next night, taking over a 2-2 game in the bottom of the seventh, walking the bases full before striking out Ken Singleton to end the inning. He retired the Orioles in the bottom of the eighth after giving up a leadoff single to Eddie Murray by pitching around an error and the Pittsburgh infield turning a 6-4-5-4 double play to snuff out a Baltimore scoring chance. Robinson got the win as the Pirates scored in the top of the ninth on Sanguillen's single.

Robinson did not pitch in the Game Three loss to the Orioles, but got into Game Four with the Pirates up 6-3. He started the eighth, replacing Jackson, and recorded his worst performance of the postseason.

Two singles, a groundout, and a walk loaded the bases. Tanner pulled Robinson and brought in Tekulve, who allowed all three of the runners to score along with three of his own. The Pirates lost 9-6 to go down 3 games to 2, but won Game Five, 7-1, and Game Six, 4-0 behind Candelaria and Tekulve, and the Series was tied. Robinson did not pitch in Game Four or Five.

In the Game Seven clinching win for the Pirates, Robinson pitched in the fifth inning in relief of Jim Bibby with the Orioles leading 1-0. He gave up a single to Doug DeCinces and then got two fly-ball outs but walked the opposing pitcher, Scott McGregor, on a full count. Grant Jackson relieved and retired Al Bumbry on a foul popup to third base to retire the side. The Pirates iced the Series with a two-run homer by Stargell in the top of the sixth and two more runs in the ninth.

Reflecting on the 1979 season, Robinson said, "A classy team! How much fun!" And the stories were true, "the music was turned up sky high in the clubhouse. Stargell and his speeches! Dave Parker was so witty. Everybody got along; there was so much experience on the team. I learned how to play the game the right way."

In the nearly eight full years with the Pirates that followed from 1980 until the trade-deadline move that sent him to San Francisco on July 31, 1987, Robinson appeared in 279 games, 69 as a starter, winning 43 and losing 55 with 42 saves. His career shifted gears from the starting rotation to the bullpen in 1984.

Robinson had shoulder surgery after the World Series and started 1980 on the disabled list. He ended the year at 7-10, starting 24 games and pitching 160⅓ innings. He was limited to 16 games in 1981 due to shoulder problems, the near two-month players strike, and an injury to his pitching hand suffered when he was in a traffic accident in Pittsburgh while riding with teammate Jim Bibby in early August. His best year other than his rookie campaign came in 1982. Other than 1978, "this was my healthiest year," he said. It may have been due to his winter rehab, but whatever the reason, He pitched 227 innings, the second highest innings total in his career, and had a career-high 15 victories (the most wins on the Pirates) against 13 losses for a team that finished 84-78 in fourth place in the NL East.

Robinson was always a good hitter. In 1982 he had 85 at-bats and batted .282 with two homers, 24 hits, and 16 runs batted in. It was the year he earned his first of three Silver Slugger Awards. His secret? "I waited for breaking balls."

But in 1983 Robinson appeared in just nine games, in between lengthy periods on the disabled list with recurring shoulder issues; and that fall, he played in the Florida Instructional League as a right fielder, leading the league with 9 home runs and 35 RBIs and batting .313. This offseason adjustment positioned Robinson to shift from pitching to the outfield, but in discussions with Tanner, the decision for 1984 was to use him as the setup man for Tekulve. Healthy again that season, he led NL relievers in innings pitched (122) and had 10 saves along with 8.1 strikeouts per nine innings, the highest ratio of his career. After the season he received the Fred Hutchinson Award, given annually to an active major-league baseball player who "best exemplifies the fighting spirit and competitive desire of Fred Hutchinson, by persevering through adversity."

Robinson went through an ineffective 5-11 season in 1985 and in 1986 new manager Jim Leyland converted him to the club's closer. He pitched in 50 games for a team that won only 64, finishing last in the NL East. He saved 14 games. In 1987 he continued in the role of closer, saving 12 games before being traded to the Giants, for whom he saved another seven.

In the later years in Pittsburgh, Robinson became good friends with Leyland and was seen as one of the veterans. Leyland worked hard to motivate his players and was known for his dugout and clubhouse tirades. According to Robinson, "Leyland screamed and yelled in the dugout as result of bad play by the Pirates and later called me in to his office to ask, 'Was I pretty good?'"

The post-World Series years were not the best for the Pirates: An inadequate roster, ownership transition challenges, the Pittsburgh Drug trials in which a number of major-league players (Dave Parker among them) were charged with drug use; all made for an uncertain time in Pittsburgh that Leyland, along with a remade farm system and some good trades, eventually remedied for the Pirates. But not until after Robinson was traded.

As the 1987 season progressed, the likelihood intensified that Robinson would be dealt. "When I got traded (I wanted to go to the Reds), Jim Leyland called me in to his office before the trade deadline to say that I had been traded to Cincinnati," he said. After a moment, Leyland told him it was a joke. The trade instead was with San Francisco and in return for Robinson, the Giants sent Mackey Sasser and $50,000 to Pittsburgh.

"The difference between Pittsburgh and San Francisco was night and day," Robinson said. San Francisco was the classier team, treating the team well, flying charters, etc. The Giants needed his help in the bullpen to compete for the NL West title. In second place when he was acquired, the team made several other moves to bolster its lineup, including picking up pitcher Rick Reuschel from the Pirates. Managed by Roger Craig, the team won the NL West by six games but lost to the St. Louis Cardinals in seven games in the National League Championship Series.

Robinson joined the Giants on the road in Cincinnati for their August 1 matchup against the Reds. Warming up in the sixth inning to relieve Mike LaCoss, Robinson said, "I was nervous." He pitched 2⅔ innings, giving up four hits and a run in a 7-3 Giants win.

One 1987 game Robinson recalled fondly was on September 28 against the Padres in San Diego. Inheriting a 4-3 lead, he took the mound to start the bottom of the fifth inning. The Padres tied the game 4-4 in the bottom of the seventh on a triple by Benito Santiago and Robinson implored Craig to keep him in the game and let him lead off in the top of the eighth. Craig agreed and Robinson responded by hitting a homer off a breaking ball from Lance McCullers.

Craig kept Robinson in to finish the game. In the ninth, the Padres got Tony Gwynn to third with two outs. Up next was John Kruk who in four previous plate appearances had walked once and struck out twice with no hits. His walk and one of his strikeouts came from Robinson. "I threw a split fastball to him that did not split," Robinson said. "When I looked back (to follow the track of the long fly ball to left field) I saw Jeff Leonard on the warning track, looking as if the ball was going into the stands. Then he caught it. He was pulling my leg."

Robinson pitched three times during the NLCS against St. Louis, in Games Three, Six, and Seven. With the Giants ahead 4-2 in Game Three, he took the loss in relief after allowing an inherited runner to score as well as two of his own. Craig Lefferts allowed Robinson's remaining baserunner to score, leading to a 6-5 loss. In Game Six Robinson pitched two hitless innings, but the Cardinals won 1-0, having scored off Dave Dravecky in the bottom of the second. In Game Seven, the clincher for St. Louis, Robinson pitched a scoreless eighth and was one of seven Giants pitchers in a 6-0 loss.

Robinson made it to the postseason one more time. The Giants played the Chicago Cubs in the NLCS in 1989 and Robinson pitched in Game Three with the series tied at a game each. He won the game after entering in the top of the seventh inning and giving up a run that put the Cubs up by one, 4-3. Robby Thompson hit a two-run homer in the bottom of the inning that reclaimed the lead for the Giants. In the top of the eighth, Robinson got two outs but then right fielder Candy Maldonado made an error and Shawon Dunston singled. Lefferts got the last out of the inning and Steve Bedrosian held the Cubs in the ninth, giving Robinson the win. The Giants won the NLCS 4 games to 1 and moved on to face the Oakland Athletics in the Bay Bridge World Series, known for the 6.9 magnitude Loma Prieta Earthquake that hit the area on October 17 just as Game Three was to begin. The Giants were down two games to none at that time and the Series was postponed until October 27. Robinson started Game Four and pitched only 1⅔ innings, giving up four runs. The Giants battled back, but could not catch the A's, who won 9-6 for the sweep. Robinson took the Game Four loss.

Robinson's hitting prowess manifested itself in San Francisco, where he won his second and third Silver Sluggers in 1989 and 1990. From 1987 to 1991, Robinson was 42-33 (.560) during the 170 games in which he was both a starter and a closer for the Giants. His 3.56 bettered his 10-year composite 3.85 ERA in Pittsburgh. Reflecting on his time in San Francisco he said, "I loved to play at Candlestick. We had the advantage." Playing for Roger Craig was also enjoyable. Craig's stature and his experience as a former pitcher were appreciated by Robinson.

After the 1991 season, during which he split time almost evenly as a starter and reliever, Robinson signed with the California Angels for 1992, but after going on the disabled list in April, he was released in mid-May after pitching in only three games (all as a starter) with a 1-0 record. Robinson was signed by the Philadelphia Phillies on May 22, but his season was cut short after he went 1-4 in eight starts with a 6.18 ERA. Plagued by a bad arm, he averaged a little more than five innings a start and was released on July 16. His last decision came on July 12 against the Padres, when he pitched only 2⅓ innings, giving up six runs. With injuries shutting him down for the rest of the year, Robinson decided to retire. Although Phillies manager Jim Fregosi (he and Robinson had played together in Pittsburgh in 1978) wanted Robinson to return in 1993, it was not to be.

Why retire in 1992 at the age of 35? "It wasn't fun anymore what with my health issues," Robinson said. "My biggest regret was not being healthy all of the time. I was only healthy in 1978 and 1982." Named "The Caveman" by Giants teammate Mike Krukow for his physique and his ability to endure numerous surgeries and shots, Robinson said his career was a testimony as much to his stamina and persistence as his split fastball, deadly curve, and silver bat.[2]

Robinson's experiences in dealing with injuries were emblematic of a time when most teams did not have the resources for medical and training support for players year-round. "My best years were after winter rehab got me ready," he said.

Living in Bradenton, Florida, where the Pirates have held their spring training since 1969, Robinson as of 2016 was the pitching coach for the State College of Florida Manatees, located in Bradenton.

SOURCES

Finoli, David, and and Bill Ranier. *The Pittsburgh Pirates Encyclopedia* (Champaign, Illinois: Sports Publishing LLC, 2003).

Ranier, Bill, and David Finoli. *When the Bucs Won It All* (Jefferson, North Carolina: McFarland & Company, 2005).

NOTES

1 Unless otherwise noted, all quotations from Don Robinson are from the author's interview with him on July 6, 2015.

2 Don Robinson, written note, January 10, 2016.

Enrique Romo

By Rory Costello

PITCHING ISN'T JUST ABOUT THROWING hard. It's about contrast and ball movement, and Enrique Romo kept hitters off stride and guessing. He had a broad repertoire, featuring a screwball, which he delivered from various arm angles while constantly changing speeds. "He's the kind of pitcher you don't want to face even once in a game," said an opposing batter, Art Howe.[1] One wonders whether such a hurler would have been allowed to develop in the U.S.—especially in today's game, which emphasizes the radar gun, mechanics, and a repeatable delivery.

Romo learned the game in a different place, though—Mexico. After pitching professionally for 11 years in his homeland, he came to the major leagues in 1977 with an expansion club, the Seattle Mariners. The Pittsburgh Pirates obtained him in a trade after the 1978 season, and it was a good deal for them. When the Pirates won the World Series in 1979, one of their strengths was the bullpen. Romo was a key ingredient, appearing in 84 games, second most in the National League that year after teammate Kent Tekulve's 94. In 1980 pitching coach Harvey Haddix said, "I think he was the unsung hero of last year's team. The middle man seldom gets the credit he deserves because he doesn't get wins or saves. But a good one keeps you in a lot of games, and Romo has done a tremendous job."[2]

Actually, the 5-foot-11 righty won 10 games and saved five more in 1979, while losing just five and posting a 2.99 ERA. He had another good year with Pittsburgh in 1980, followed by two so-so seasons—and then his big-league career ended under a cloud in the spring of 1983. Decades later, Romo still refused to talk about this personal choice, and he had not taken part in any of the champion team's reunions.

Enrique Romo Navarro was born on July 15, 1947, in Santa Rosalía, a port town in the state of Baja California del Sur. His parents were Santos "Santurria" Romo Urías, a policeman, and Rosario Navarro. Enrique was one of nine children in the family. He had four brothers (Vicente, Eusebio, José María, and Ramón) and four sisters (María Guadalupe, Lidia, Mirsa, and Olga).[3]

Vicente Romo, four years older than Enrique, was also a professional pitcher. He played more than 20 years in Mexico and the U.S., including eight seasons in the majors (1968-74; 1982) for five teams. Vicente's nickname was "Huevo" (Egg) and so Enrique was sometimes called "Huevito." In 1992 Vicente became a member of the Mexican Baseball Hall of Fame. Enrique joined him in 2003, making them the first of just two pairs of brothers to be inducted there.[4] In addition, José María, an outfielder, was good enough to play six seasons in the Mexican League (1979-84).

In 1952, when Enrique was about 5 years old, his family moved to the city of Guaymas, a short boat trip across the Sea of Cortez in the state of Sonora.[5] The youth started to play baseball as an outfielder with a Mexican Little League team at the age of 12.[6] Starting when he was 16, he served a three-year tour of duty in the Mexican Navy. "If I didn't play baseball, I would still be in the Navy," he said in 1980. "But as a boy I always watched the baseball players. I wanted to be one, and my older brother Vicente did well."[7]

In 1966, 18-year-old Enrique became a professional ballplayer. He joined Puerto México of the Mexican Southeast League, a Class-A circuit. He also switched to pitching at that time, strongly influenced by Vicente.[8] In 22 games for the Porteños, he pitched 61 innings, winning one and losing two with a 3.10 ERA. Romo then gained his first experience in winter ball with the Guaymas Ostioneros of La Liga Sonora-Sinaloa (as the Mexican winter circuit was then known).

Back with Puerto México in the summer of 1967, Romo had marks of 4-5, 3.74, pitching 82 innings in 18 games. He made a great stride forward that winter, going 15-4 with a 1.53 ERA for Guaymas. That performance won him the Rookie of the Year Award, and the Oystermen became league champions.

In 1968 Romo stepped up to La Liga Mexicana de Béisbol, Mexico's top summer league. He pitched there for nine seasons: four with the Jalisco Charros (1968-71), one with the Gómez Palacio Algodoneros, or Cotton Growers (1972), and four with the Mexico City Rojos (1973-76). Overall, he posted a won-lost record of 109-74, with a 2.67 ERA. He was mainly a starting pitcher, relieving 87 times in 292 total appearances. He threw 91 complete games, including 23 shutouts. He struck out 1,047 batters and walked 415 in 1,565 innings.

Romo also remained a standout in Mexican winter ball (that league became known as La Liga Mexicana del Pacífico, or Mexican Pacific League, with the 1970-71 season). Across 13 winter seasons, he won 96 and lost 64 for Guaymas, the Mazatlán Venados, and the Ciudad Obregón Yaquis.[9] He pitched 1,346 innings in 243 games, striking out 844 and walking 381, and his ERA was 2.72. In the winter of 1974-75, Romo put up a 12-2 record for Ciudad Obregón, leading the LMP in winning percentage. He matched that feat the following winter, again going 12-2 for the Yaquis. In both seasons, he was named the LMP's Pitcher of the Year.

Romo forged a lasting reputation among Mexican aficionados. One of the nation's leading baseball historians, Jesús Alberto Rubio, expressed it in a sentence that would fit well on a plaque: "Feared by his opponents, respected by his colleagues, and admired by the fans who saw him pitch." Romo was a member of three champion teams in the Mexican summer league, all with Mexico City (1973, 1974, and 1976). He added three more titles in winter ball. In addition to Guaymas (1967-68), they were Ciudad Obregón (1972-73) and the Navojoa Mayos (1978-79). He, as well as Pirates teammate-to-be Mike Easler, joined the Mayos as a playoff reinforcement in 1979. (This is a common practice during postseason play in winter ball.)

In addition, Romo played in three Caribbean Series, in which the region's winter-ball champions square off in a round-robin tournament. Mexico was not part of the competition when it was revived in 1970, but joined the following year. In the 1973 edition, he helped Mexico gain its only victory against five losses, relieving his brother Vicente in the eighth inning. Al Hrabosky, then a St. Louis Cardinals farmhand, got the save. The following year, although Ciudad Obregón had finished in second place in the LMP, the Yaquis still went to the Caribbean Series (held in Mexico that year) as a replacement for the team from Venezuela, whose players were on strike. In 1979 Romo gave up a game-winning homer to Mitchell Page that decided the series in favor of Venezuela.

During the 1976 summer season with Mexico City, Romo took his game to a new level—20-4, 1.89, with 239 strikeouts in 233 innings. The key to his increased success was a new weapon. "After I learned the screwball," he said, "I didn't have much trouble with left-handers. Before, I did."[10] It's also most intriguing that Romo was an indirect influence on the star Mexican pitcher Fernando Valenzuela. The screwball was what made Valenzuela successful too, and he learned it from Bobby Castillo—who had picked up the pitch by watching Romo.[11]

Romo's performance did not go unnoticed north of the Rio Grande. Lou Gorman, who had become general manager of the newly formed Seattle Mariners, was seeking to acquire talent by other means than the expansion draft. Gorman had contacts in the Mexican League and was friendly with Ángel Vázquez, owner of the Mexico City Reds. In 1974, when Gorman was with the Kansas City Royals, he had purchased the contract of Aurelio "Señor Smoke" López from the Reds. For the past few seasons, he had noted Romo's performance with interest. He struck a deal with Vázquez for $75,000, far below the $175,000 Seattle had to pay for each player acquired in the expansion draft.[12]

Gorman envisaged Romo as either a starter or reliever for Seattle. When the 1977 season opened, Enrique was the number-two man in the rotation. He pitched well his first time out; in seven innings, he gave up just two runs on four hits, while striking out nine (which proved to be a big-league career high). That night at the Kingdome, however, Nolan Ryan fired a three-hit shutout for the California Angels. Thus, Romo took the loss. Five days later, he had another good outing. He left after seven innings with a 2-1 lead, but the bullpen couldn't hold it. Romo's third start, on April 17, was his last ever in the majors. He left after 1⅔ innings with a hamstring problem — something that had been bothering him since spring training — and went on the disabled list.[13]

Upon his return, Romo proved highly effective in relief. That July, Mariners manager Darrell Johnson said flatly, "Enrique Romo is the best reliever in the American League."[14] He finished with a club-high 16 saves in 55 bullpen outings, to go with an 8-10 won-lost record and 2.83 ERA. He struck out 105 in 114⅓ innings. Had Seattle been able to win more than 64 games that year, there would have been more saves.

With the Mariners in 1978, Romo did not have as good a year overall (11-7, 3.69, 10 saves in 56 games). "The ballclub was not good offensively and the defense was shaky," he later said. "A pitcher doesn't have a lot of confidence on the mound there."[15]

That December Seattle traded Romo along with Rick Jones and Tom McMillan to Pittsburgh in exchange for Odell Jones, Mario Mendoza, and Rafael Vásquez. Rick Jones, a lefty pitcher, never appeared in another big-league game, though he was called up in September 1979. Neither did McMillan, a shortstop. Nonetheless, Romo alone made the trade turn out well for the Pirates. Right-hander Odell Jones was a talented pitcher but didn't do much at the top level, though he appeared as late as 1988. Though Mendoza was a good-fielding shortstop, his infamously weak batting gave rise to the term "The Mendoza Line."

Pittsburgh had to sweeten the pot with Vásquez to get the deal done. At the time Pirates general manager Pete Peterson said, "We recognize that Vásquez is an outstanding prospect."[16] As it developed, though, the Dominican (just 20 at the time of the trade) pitched just nine games for the Mariners in 1979 and never made it back to the majors. Peterson continued, "We're thinking of next year and Romo fits into our plans." Chuck Tanner added, "Our top priority in trades was a quality pitcher. We have accomplished our objective." Tanner also wanted to provide support for Kent Tekulve, who had pitched 135⅓ innings in 91 games in 1978.[17]

"The trade surprised me," said Romo in February 1979, while at the Pirates training camp in Florida. "I didn't think Seattle would trade me. But I was happy to come here. I am glad to be with a team that can win it all." That accurate prediction was issued in Spanish; Romo's English was limited, and Manny Sanguillen served as his interpreter.[18]

Superscout Howie Haak observed, "With a screwball pitcher like Romo on our team, getting [another] left-hander is not as important. Sure we'd still like to have two left-handers and two right-handers [in the bullpen], but it's not a big thing anymore."[19] As it developed, though, Pittsburgh did address this need in June by obtaining Dave Roberts from San Francisco to support Grant Jackson.

In an April interview, Romo was prophetic again. He said, "We have a good team but there are a lot of tough teams in our division. The season has a long way to go and we may have to go down to the last days of the race to decide the winner." He also thought that from what he had seen to that point, the caliber of play was higher in the National League—"the thing I especially notice is that the batters as a whole are much more difficult to get out." Several other interpreters were on hand for that talk, including teammates Rennie Stennett and Frank Taveras. (The latter was soon to be traded.)[20]

Romo got off to a shaky start with Pittsburgh in 1979. "I think he prefers warmer weather," said Harvey Haddix that June. "I think he had trouble with the colder weather we had. He's getting the feel of things over here. He's with a new team, in a new league. It's all strange for him. I think it takes a guy like him extra time." Chuck Tanner agreed. "I think Romo wanted to do so well, he tried too hard," said the skipper. He's settled down and is a better pitcher now."[21]

Tanner also emphasized the importance of Romo's role. "With the injuries we've had, the middle job is important to us. Very often we have to pull a starter early because we don't want him to aggravate an injury."[22] Yet it's noteworthy that Romo also finished 25 games in 1979.

That August Romo confirmed that he'd had to adjust to the NL hitters and that the cold early-season weather had bothered him. "I'm pitching some of the best ball of my career now," he said. The main thrust of that interview, though, was his unhappiness in Pittsburgh and the U.S. in general. In addition to the language barrier, he thought that the Pirates fans were more demanding than those in Seattle—"Here, they expect me to be good every time out." It also emerged that he thought Seattle had been disloyal by trading him, the best pitcher the Mariners had—he saw favoritism toward Americans.[23]

Through Rennie Stennett, Romo said that he would play five years total in the majors, then go home to his cattle and pig ranch in Mexico. Money was one reason to be in El Norte—but national pride was another. "I wanted to prove people wrong," he said. "They think all Mexicans are bad, that they cause discipline problems or something like that. They always think of Mexicans as gangsters, as bandits." Yet he had to laugh when his teammates—posing as "The Enrique Romo Fan Club"—presented him with a portrait of Pancho Villa.[24] The picture came to adorn the clubhouse wall.[25]

One risks perpetuating Latino stereotypes, but Romo was a mercurial sort, as teammate Phil Garner told columnist Joe Starkey in 2011. Chuck Tanner had to be both tender and tough in handling the reliever. The skipper offered hugs of consolation on plane trips to California when a sobbing Romo couldn't visit Mexico because his wife had taken away his green card. Tanner also lifted Romo off the ground by the throat when the pitcher once pulled a knife in the clubhouse, warning him not to do it ever again.[26]

Romo did not play a major role in the 1979 postseason. He appeared twice in the National League Championship Series against Cincinnati. In Game One at Riverfront Stadium, with the score tied at 2-2 in the eighth inning, he put two runners on; Tekulve then entered and induced a double play. The next day, Romo again came on in the eighth, replacing Grant Jackson with one out and nobody on. He gave up two straight hits; once more Tekulve got him off the hook and held the 2-1 lead (though he blew the save in the ninth).

Jackson, who knew Spanish from winter ball, thought nerves were a factor in the playoffs. He chatted with Romo to settle him down and said, "He'll be OK in the [World] Series."[27] Romo was used just twice against Baltimore, though. In the sleety Game One at Memorial Stadium, with the Pirates trailing 5-1, he pitched a scoreless fifth inning despite walking two. In Game Three at Three Rivers Stadium, he replaced starter John Candelaria in the fourth inning after Kiko Garcia had cleared the bases with a triple. Romo proceeded to hit a batter and give up a single, enabling the Orioles to score two more runs and extend their lead to 7-3. He stayed in for 2⅔ more innings after that, allowing one more run on four hits.

Ahead of Game Seven, the Pittsburgh press indicated that Romo's arm was bothering him.[28] That may explain why he did not appear in the last four games of the Series. The dreadful baseball weather in Baltimore and Pittsburgh that October was also not to his liking. "I never felt the cold like I did in the World Series," he said the following April.[29]

Back in Mexico over the winter of 1979-80, Romo (who had previously cut back to playing just part of the LMP season) played first base in a recreational league once a week. He joked, "I hit .700, but I'm not after Willie Stargell's job." He also dropped 15 pounds through dedicated exercise, getting down to 185. In March 1980 he said, "I'm prepared for the cold this year. I know what to expect and I'm not going to let it bother me. I'm just looking forward to the season."[30] He appeared in 74 games that year, pitching 123⅔ innings and posting a 5-5 record with a 3.27 ERA and 11 saves.

Romo also felt more at ease in the clubhouse. Grant Jackson said, "He didn't know what to think about us last year. He didn't know if we were fooling around with him or not. Now, he does." Manny Sanguillen added, "He couldn't believe how crazy we are. Now, he's one of the biggest crazies here. He fits in."[31]

That September Harvey Haddix described Romo's repertoire and deliveries well. "He's got a couple of different screwballs, a curveball and a fastball. He changes speed on all of them. He has a little slider. He throws side-arm, three-quarters and overhand." Art Howe, then with the Houston Astros, also viewed Romo's fastball as underrated. "You've got to be thinking fastball and adjust to the speed of the ball. ... Some guys think he doesn't throw hard, but he can move it up there on you pretty good."[32] Over the years, rumors also persisted that Romo employed a spitball or greaseball.

The same month, Chuck Tanner pointed to another of Romo's skills. On September 10 at Busch Stadium in St. Louis, the pitcher helped himself after walking the leadoff man in the ninth inning, pouncing on a sacrifice bunt and getting the force at second. "He's the best fielding pitcher in the league," said Tanner. "He's quick as a cat. You can't teach things like that."[33]

Romo was an all-around player. He had 10 hits in 37 at-bats in the majors (.270). His best moment with the bat came a few weeks after Tanner singled out his fielding. On October 1 at Shea Stadium in New York, he hit a grand slam in the eighth inning off reliever Roy Lee Jackson.

Early in the 1981 season, Romo talked about working on something else that had bothered him from time to time: beefs with umpires. This arose in the ninth inning against Montreal as he struggled to complete a difficult three-inning save. "I went out there and calmed him down," said catcher Steve Nicosia. "I told him, 'Hey, that's over. The umpire missed a couple, but let's go on to the next pitch.' When Romo gets huffin' and puffin' out there, he's losing his concentration."[34]

Romo — who looked increasingly piratical, with a beard and longer hair — pitched in 33 games in 1981. He was 1-3 with a 4.54 ERA, though he did pick up nine saves. After the players strike ended in August, though, he appeared just nine times. He went on the 21-day disabled list in late August and returned for five appearances during the last two weeks of the season.

In spring training 1982, John Candelaria, Don Robinson, and Jim Bibby all had arm problems. Thus, Tanner thought about making Romo a starter once again, as he had also considered at one point in 1980. Enrique responded, "I'm ready. Baseball is baseball. You pitch two or three innings or you pitch nine innings. Either way, you still have to get them out."[35] It didn't happen then because Pittsburgh acquired Ross Baumgarten from the Chicago White Sox, but Tanner again mulled giving Romo a start in late May after pulling Eddie Solomon out of the rotation.

In the end, though, Romo stayed in the bullpen, pitching in 45 games. He won nine and lost three, but his ERA was 4.36 and he had just one save. Toward the end of the season, Tanner gave him a stiff fine — $5,000 and two days' pay (roughly $5,000 more) — for "breaking training."[36]

After the 1982 season ended, Romo never wore a big-league uniform again. He did not report to spring training; according to his agent, Seymour Goldstein, Romo "brooded all winter" because of the fine.[37] The pitcher didn't get sympathy from his teammates, though. Captain Bill Madlock said, "When you don't show up for a game, you should be fined, especially for anything that hurts your teammates." Kent Tekulve, the team's player representative to the union, added, "You have to have a fine. Docking a guy two days pay isn't enough. Heck, I could take my family on vacation in the middle of September if all it would cost me was two days' pay."[38]

Chuck Tanner—one of the most sympathetic leaders in baseball history—was fed up and didn't want Romo back. The Pirates tried unsuccessfully to trade their disgruntled reliever; meanwhile, starting on March 6 they began to fine him $500 a day. On March 16 the *Pittsburgh Press* reached Romo's wife, Ruth, at their home in the city of Torreón. She said that he was in training "in another city, not too far away." Seymour Goldstein, who'd been optimistic earlier that it would all work out, said, "I've washed my hands of the whole thing."[39]

Finally, toward the end of March, Pete Peterson received a telegram from Romo informing him that the pitcher had retired.[40] The team was thus able to put him on the voluntary retirement list; otherwise, he'd have had to go on the restricted list. If that had happened, Romo—who still had two years left on his contract, worth $700,000—could still have shown up and claimed a roster spot. As his wife said, though, "Enrique doesn't want to play for the Pirates any more. I don't think he will come back unless maybe next year he changes his mind."[41]

That never happened. There was talk that Romo was playing in an "outlaw" league at home; that was La Liga Nacional, which was started in 1981 by ANABE (Asociación Nacional de Beisbolistas), a Mexican players association. This circuit—founded in the wake of a strike—was better described by Jesús Rubio as "a great social movement." It faced strong opposition from the entrenched Liga Mexicana and folded during the 1986 season.[42] Romo was with the club called Tuzos de Zacatecas.[43] If ANABE's records still exist, they would be extremely difficult to find.

The most that Romo ever appears to have opened up about the mystery of his big-league retirement—and that's very little—was in a Mexican interview from 2007. He said, "It's something that I'm never going to tell anyone. I've been asked that many times, why, when I was of sound mind at age 35. But I never had a problem with anyone in the United States. I believe I could have played another four years because I was sound, I did good work and I never hurt my arm, but it's something I keep to myself. It's something that I decided, and at times I reproach myself, but I don't regret it because I am well with my family."[44] He and Ruth (maiden name Ortiz) had two children, a daughter named Mary Gladys and a son who was also named Enrique.

The remark about not having any problems in the U.S. is interesting in view of an unconfirmed allegation in the book *When the Bucs Won It All*. Authors Bill Ranier and David Finoli wrote, "There was a story that Romo had been having a relationship with a woman who was involved with a mob figure and was told not to return to Pittsburgh."[45] It's most unlikely, however, that this rumor could ever be verified.

When the Mexican Baseball Hall of Fame inducted Romo in 2003, he was visibly moved and delighted. He said, "I feel satisfied to have played six seasons in the major leagues, I made my best effort, and I believe that I represented Mexico well." At that time, Romo held a job in a lathe workshop in Torreón.[46]

In November 2010 the Ciudad Obregón Yaquis bestowed a unique honor on Vicente and Enrique Romo, retiring their uniform numbers simultaneously. The occasion had another twist—receiving Enrique's ceremonial pitch was his countryman Mario Mendoza Jr., whose father had been part of the trade that brought Romo to the Pirates. Mendoza Jr., who had also worn number 11 with the Yaquis, took the shirt off his back and gave it to Romo.

In his mid-60s, Enrique Romo remained active in baseball. In September 2012, he joined the "Super Master" team representing Laguna, the region that surrounds Torreón and its twin city Gómez Palacio. They played in the Independence Cup competition in Jalapa, in the state of Veracruz. Laguna won, with good pitching from Romo in the first game.[47] In December 2013 he traveled from Torreón to Guaymas to face Vicente in a "Legends of Baseball" game, which featured an active major leaguer in Luis Ayala and at least one other MLB vet, Sid Monge. Enrique's side won, 13-9, and he got credit for the victory. He had won all five matchups against Vicente during their professional careers, and before the game, he had joked, "I see it being difficult for him to beat me, if he could not at his best!"[48]

Continued thanks to Jesús Alberto Rubio in Mexico.

SOURCES

In addition to the sources cited in the Notes, the author also consulted the following:

Books

Treto Cisneros, Pedro, editor. *Enciclopedia del Béisbol Mexicano* (Mexico City: Revistas Deportivas, S.A. de C.V.: 11th edition), 2011.

Internet resources

baseball-reference.com.

retrosheet.org.

salondelafama.com.mx/.

comc.com.

youtube.com.

NOTES

1. Dan Donovan, "Unsung Romo's Saving Grace Guns Down Houston," *Pittsburgh Press*, September 4, 1980, C-1.
2. Donovan, "Unsung Romo's Saving Grace Guns Down Houston."
3. Gilberto Castro Meza, "Rinden merecido homenaje con una placa al Huevo Romo," *El Sudcaliforniano* (La Paz, Baja California del Sur, Mexico), December 20, 2010. Gilberto Castro Meza, "Montarán una plaza alusiva en la casa donde nació 'Huevo' Romo," *El Sudcaliforniano*, October 27, 2009.
4. The other, as of 2016, is Aurelio Rodríguez and his older brother Juan Francisco.
5. Yesenia Torrecillas, "Vicente 'Huevo' Romo: El Cy Young Mexicano," Pelotapimienta.mx, March 6, 2014 (pelotapimienta.mx/vicente-huevo-romo-el-cy-young-mexicano).
6. Fred Sigler, "Trade Break for Romo," *Observer-Reporter* (Washington, Pennsylvania), April 17, 1979, C-1.
7. Jack Gurnet, "Cards Stun Pirates 8-2," *Sarasota Herald-Tribune*, March 30, 1980, 1-C, 6-C.
8. Sigler.
9. Romo's Mexican Hall of Fame web page states that he also played for the Hermosillo Naranjeros in the LMP, but this has not been possible to verify. Detailed LMP records are hard to come by. As nearly as can be determined, Romo played for Guaymas from 1966-67 through 1968-69, for Mazatlán from 1969-70 through 1971-72, and for Ciudad Obregón from 1972-73 through 1978-1979.
10. Dan Donovan, "Romo May Solve Bucs' Lefty Reliever Problem," *Pittsburgh Press*, February 27, 1979, C-4.
11. Steve Wulf, "No Hideaway for Fernando," *Sports Illustrated*, March 23, 1981; Dan Donovan, "Did Bucs Wake Up on Wrong Side of Season?", *Pittsburgh Press*, June 11, 1981, C-1; Moisés Ramiro Segundo, "El artista del screwball," *El Universal* (Mexico City), January 7, 2003.
12. Lou Gorman, *High and Inside: My Life in the Front Offices of Baseball* (Jefferson, North Carolina: McFarland & Company, 2008), 153-154. Donovan, "Romo May Solve Bucs' Lefty Reliever Problem".
13. Raymond L. Andrews, "Johnson spells relief R-O-M-O," United Press International, May 24, 1977.
14. Hy Zimmerman, "Who's Finest A.L. Fireman? 'Romo!' the Mariners Shout," *The Sporting News*, July 30, 1977, 16.
15. Donovan, "Romo May Solve Bucs' Lefty Reliever Problem."
16. Charley Feeney, "Bucs Take a Romo for Extra Relief," *The Sporting News*, December 23, 1978, 46.
17. Feeney.
18. Donovan, "Romo May Solve Bucs' Lefty Reliever Problem"
19. Ibid.
20. Sigler.
21. Dan Donovan, "Man of Many Motions Delivers As Pirate Reliever," *Pittsburgh Press*, June 8, 1979, B-7.
22. Ibid.
23. Ron Cook, "Romo Can't Wait to Leave," *Beaver County* (Pennsylvania) *Times*, August 17, 1979, B-2.
24. Ibid.
25. "Pirate Profiles: Enrique Romo," *Pittsburgh Press*, April 2, 1980, F-3.
26. Joe Starkey, "Tanner perfect for '79 Bucs," *Pittsburgh Tribune-Review*, February 13, 2011.
27. Chraley Feeney, "Pirates Tap Kison For Series Opener Against Flanagan," *Pittsburgh Post-Gazette*, October 8, 1979, 14.
28. Phil Musick, "Tekulve Sinkerball Could Be Key in Big Shootout," *Pittsburgh Post-Gazette*, October 17, 1979, 20.
29. Dan Donovan, "Romo Turns Cold Shoulder To Spring Temperatures Here," *Pittsburgh Press*, April 2, 1980, A-6.
30. Ron Cook, "Fans will see a lot less of slimmed-down Romo," *Beaver County Times*, March 19, 1980, C-2.
31. Cook, "Fans will see a lot less of slimmed-down Romo"
32. Donovan, "Unsung Romo's Saving Grace Guns Down Houston"
33. "Romo provides Pirate relief," Associated Press, September 11, 1980.
34. Dan Donovan, "Romo Pops Montreal, Saves Win," *Pittsburgh Press*, April 13, 1981, B-3.

35 Ron Cook, "Enrique Romo may start," *Beaver County Times*, March 18, 1982, B4.

36 Russ Franke, "Tanner: Don't Want Romo," *Pittsburgh Press*, March 8, 1983, C-1.

37 Franke, "Tanner: Don't Want Romo"

38 Russ Franke, "Berra's New Attitude A Buc Bonus," *Pittsburgh Press*, March 5, 1983, A-10.

39 "Romo won't be back–wife," Associated Press, March 17, 1983. "Extra Innings," *Pirates Gold* (monthly magazine published by the Pittsburgh Pirates), April 1983.

40 John Barker, "Last Word in Sports," *Observer-Reporter*, March 26, 1983, B-8.

41 Franke, "Tanner: Don't Want Romo". "Romo won't be back–wife". Ron Cook, "Buc Bits," *Beaver County Times*, March 27, 1983, C8.

42 For further information on ANABE and this league, see David G. LaFrance, "Labor, the State, and Professional Baseball in Mexico in the 1980s," which forms Chapter 6 of Joseph L. Arbena and David G. LaFrance, editors *Sport in Latin America and the Caribbean* (Wilmington, Delaware: Scholarly Resources Inc., 2002).

43 "Calientan el ambiente ex-Tuzos de Zacatecas," *Imagen de Azacatecas* (Guadalupe, Zacatecas, Mexico), August 21, 2004.

44 Jorge Carlos Menéndez Torre, "'El Huevito' Romo, un ex Ligamayorista que ahora vive de la tornería," Poresto.net, January 1, 2007 (http://www.poresto.net/ver_nota.php?zona=yucatan&idSeccion=19&idTitulo=138860)

45 Bill Ranier and David Finoli, *When the Bucs Won It All: The 1979 World Champion Pittsburgh Pirates* (Jefferson, North Carolina: McFarland & Company, 2005), 155.

46 Claudio Martínez Silva, "Salón de la Fama del Beisbol, a 30 años," *El Siglo de Torreón*, August 21, 2003.

47 Sergio Luis Rosas, "Ex ligamayorista reforzará a Selección Laguna Master," *El Siglo de Torreón*, September 12, 2012. "Laguna conquista la Copa Independencia," *El Siglo de Torreón*, September 19, 2012.

48 Jorge Castillo Morán, "Vivirá Guaymas histórico y fraternal duelo de béisbol," *El Vigia* (Guaymas, Sonora, Mexico), December 4, 2013. Game account with photos, *Deportivas regionales de Jorge Castillo Morán*, the journalist's Facebook page, December 16, 2013.

Jim Rooker

By Rich Shook

JIM ROOKER'S PRO BASEBALL CAREER didn't come right out of left field. Center field is more like it. Rooker, who pitched his first two major-league games for Detroit's 1968 championship team and then never pitched for them again, was not signed as a pitcher out of high school. The Tigers signed him and prep teammate Lindy Kurt out of the same high school in Decatur, Illinois, on June 21, 1960, soon after they graduated. They were scouted and signed by Jack Fournier. Detroit offered $6,000, decent signing money in those predraft days, and Rooker bought "the first real nice car I ever owned — a 1959 Chevy Impala Supersport."

Kurt and Rooker began their pro careers — Kurt as a pitcher and Rooker as the center fielder –later that summer. Rooker, who was born on September 23, 1942, in Lakeview, Oregon, switched full time to pitching in 1966 and two years later was in the big leagues playing a much smaller role as a newcomer than he felt he should have. But at least Rooker found out right off the bat how a championship team conducts itself, an experience that would help him later with the World Series-winning Pittsburgh Pirates.

"It was fantastic being around those guys," Rooker said of his pro baptism with the 1968 Tigers. "Al Kaline, a Hall of Famer; Norm Cash, one of the funniest guys you'd ever meet; Pat Dobson, Mickey Stanley, Jim Northrup. … You did feel comfortable being around them. You felt like you were one of them. They made you feel relaxed. I think it's tougher for some younger players. They weren't as helpful. It was more of holding on to your job and to heck with the other guy."

"Kaline was always nice to me. During spring training it came up there was a possibility he was going to be traded to the [Los Angeles] Dodgers. He asked me what I thought about LA and the Dodgers. I was from that area. I pretty much gave him a glowing report. There was [announcer] Vin Scully. How could you not like him? I thought it was real nice of him to come up and ask me those questions. All those guys treated me real nice. Naturally, in any clubhouse there's always going be a jerk or two. But you find on winning clubs that they all get along and everything goes well."

Rooker didn't pitch his first game in the majors until age 25 and then it was just two relief appearances, making his debut on June 30, 1968. In the two games, he pitched 4⅔ innings and allowed two runs on four hits with a walk and four strikeouts. But his time with Detroit ended before it barely began at the major-league level. He was sent to the New York Yankees as the player to be named later in a late-season deal the Tigers struck to get late-inning relief help in the form of John Wyatt. The veteran was at the end of his career, though, and not helpful enough to be included on the postseason roster. Rooker, meantime, didn't even get to wear pinstripes. He was left unprotected in the expansion draft and taken by Kansas City, where he pitched from 1969 until he was traded to the Pirates after the 1972 season.

"I guess I was surprised," Rooker said. "I was not sure what was going on at that point. To be drafted by an expansion team, it was a lucky thing for me. I got more of an opportunity to still feel my way along and get my feet wet in the big leagues. Which took a while for me to do. I was still learning at the big-league level in K.C. with an inexperienced ballclub." He was traded to Pittsburgh for pitcher Gene Garber.

"It was like walking down the street and finding money," Rooker said of his adjustment to the trade. "From the first day I was around more professional people. You could see it just by the way they went about their work. I was feeling like, 'Where has this been?' I hadn't been around that atmosphere for a long time. I was a little more established. But it was a whole new world. Being there for eight years, taking a big part of winning a World Series, that was the greatest thing that ever happened to me."

Rooker became a successful broadcaster for the Pirates after his career ended with an arm injury during the 1980 season. He worked the team's games from 1981 until he retired from that phase of his life in 1993.

From 1960 through 1964 in the minor leagues, Rooker played the outfield and tried to figure out hitting, clearly without enough success.

Gail Henley was the Lakeland manager in 1963 and his pitching coach was Stubby Overmire. Rooker credited Overmire with his conversion to pitching. Like hitting your first curveball, it was an accident, of course. "I had pitched in a couple of blowouts," he said. "They saw me in batting practice. I was throwing and they asked me to throw harder, throw harder, throw harder. So I said, 'If I throw any harder, you're not going to be able to hit it.' I cut a few loose and he couldn't get the bat on the ball. So Stubby made the comment to me that if things don't work out as an outfielder, I should consider pitching. He was pretty impressed with the velocity I was throwing with."

Trading the known for the unknown can be like deciding whether to run full speed into a brick wall or only half speed. You know it's going to hurt, the question is how much. "I worked my way up to Double A as an outfielder. I just wasn't very consistent as a hitter. After the change they sent me back down to Class-A ball. But there was a period in there of about two, three years of them not knowing what they wanted me to do. … In 1966 is when they let me do nothing but pitch. Things were much more consistent after that. I got called up at the end of the year. Things turned around pretty quickly after that."

Coming up through the Detroit organization in the 1960s placed Rooker on the same fields as some of the Tigers' best players. "Pat Dobson was one. I played with him in Instructional League. I also played with Mickey Stanley, Jim Northrup, Jon Warden, Willie Horton, Denny McLain — Denny and I were roommates in Duluth in Class-C ball one year [1963]. I also played with Daryl Patterson, Fred Scherman, Tommy Matchick, and Dave Campbell. The year I roomed with Denny, I was an outfielder and he was a pitcher. With the team we had, we tore up the league that year.

"I remember McLain, he was afraid of the dark. At night I always used to say I heard these noises. I didn't realize he was terrified of the dark. But at the time it was pretty funny. He used to put pots and pans by the door so they'd make noise if anybody came in. I used to say, 'Did you hear that?' Tried to scare him. I didn't realize at the time how afraid of the dark he was. As great a player as McLain was — and he's a friend of mine — he was a jerk. He's still a friend, but you have to know him and what kind of person he is. But on that '68 team, most of the guys got along real well. Some would rub you the wrong way, but in general they were good guys."

Aside from the comparatively poor playing conditions, terribly long bus rides and low wages, life in the minors is probably like walking barefoot through a room full of bear traps in the dark. The journey takes all of your attention.

Rooker didn't have a breakthrough moment, a time when he went from just trying to get by to the point where he absolutely knew for certain he was destined for the major leagues. "You weren't making any money," Rooker recalled. "You were just trying to survive. Other than Duluth, I can't remember any winning teams I played on. You were trying to survive. Lots of guys have hopes, but I can't say I was loaded with confidence. I wasn't sure what direction I was going in.

"In 1966, my first full year pitching, I was 12-6 for a team in North Carolina, Rocky Mount. That's when I got called up at the end of the year. I kind of saw what was going on. I know the times I would warm up in the bullpen, I would look at the reaction of the guys watching. You kind of had the feeling you had the ability. But mentally for me it took a little time to get my confidence, because I didn't start out as a pitcher. Then I went from Class-A to Double A to Triple A and basically dominated there. There were things you'd hear from other players, coaches and managers, so in the back of your mind you start thinking, 'It's going to happen, I just don't know when.' In 1967-1968 is when I developed some of the confidence. I knew I had the ability. But it was harder to get to the big leagues then than it is now. And in Detroit they had some good players."

THE 1979 PITTSBURGH PIRATES

While not making the club out of the starting gate in 1968 was tough for Rooker to deal with, it also fueled his fire a bit. And he got pushed by his Toledo manager, former Tigers manager Jack Tighe. "He kept telling me, 'You're going to be there.' I'd go up and down, up and down. I kept getting called up every time somebody got injured or had to do [two weeks of] military service, that sort of stuff. I might have been in the category where I didn't get the opportunity."

If that sounds as if Rooker didn't care a whole lot for Mayo Smith (the Tigers skipper in '68) as a manager, he didn't. "He can't defend himself now"—Smith died in 1977—"but I think the ability of the team overshadowed his inability as a manager. I've heard stories since. He was not a great manager, he was not the worst manager. But the one thing he did, the best thing he ever did as a manager, was when he moved Mickey [Stanley] to shortstop for the World Series. He doesn't get enough credit for that. It surprised me there wasn't more made out of it. It was probably one of the gutsiest things ever done—and of all people, him! If you ask anybody about that World Series, probably the first thing they say is, 'Lou Brock.' But I don't think he was any special strategist or anything. Let's make it clear, I didn't like the guy and I don't think I got a shot [from him]. Careerwise, it was proved out by who he kept and who he didn't keep. There are some managers who want to be liked, some want to be respected, and some who want it both ways. I'm not sure guys liked him or respected him. He was in the category of managers who just put the lineup out and stay out of their way."

There was one illustrative incident that stuck in Rooker's mind. There was a game where the pitcher of the moment was struggling, so Smith went out to the mound, probably with the intent of taking the hurler out. "This pitcher [Rooker didn't name him] told Mayo that if he didn't get off the mound, there were going to be some serious repercussions. So finally Mayo just left him in and let the guy get out of his own trouble. Pitchers told him things you really shouldn't say to a manager. But I think the players knew what was going on. Their attitude, I think, was, 'We know what we're doing, just let us do our job.'"

Rooker wasn't on the postseason roster but still retained a vested rooting interest in the team. But something had happened late in the season that would change his life. "They made a trade late in the season. They got John Wyatt from the Yankees for a player to be named later. He was a veteran relief pitcher at the end of his career. I was the player to be named later. So I went to the Yankees on paper that winter and was drafted in the expansion draft by Kansas City." There he joined former teammate Warden, who had beaten him out for a roster spot the previous spring. Another twist of fate: Warden came down with a sore arm and was never the same. Rooker went on to play many more years. Pitching for the Royals was a mixed blessing, however. On the one hand you're a regular starter in the major leagues, the envy of every kid who likes baseball and everybody pitching in the minors. On the other hand, you're playing solitaire with a 50-card deck.

"When you play for a club like that," Rooker said, "you're more playing for yourself than trying to win a ballgame for the organization. Because you know you're not going anywhere. I remember a player who refused to pinch-hit. He wanted to protect his average because he was hitting .300. I'm thinking, 'You gotta be kidding me.' We didn't know how to win, how to play winning baseball. We didn't have the type of leadership you need to teach younger players." Again, Rooker didn't name the player, but the best guess is 1969 AL Rookie of the Year Lou Piniella, who hit .282 that season and was once spotted during one game early in his career taking imaginary swings for nearly a full inning while playing left field.

The '69 Royals were managed by Joe Gordon and actually beat out the Chicago White Sox for fourth place in the AL West by one game and fellow expansionist Seattle by five. The first baseman was Mike Fiore, second baseman was Jerry Adair, and one of the two catchers was Buck Martinez. The pitching staff featured Wally Bunker and Dick Drago plus relievers Moe Drabowsky and Dave Wickersham. Rooker went 4-16 with a 3.75 ERA while logging 158⅓ innings in 28 games (22 of them starts), fifth on the team. His hitting background showed up in a July 7 loss to Jim

Kaat and Minnesota. Rooker became the first Royal to hit two home runs in a game (both off Kaat).

In 1970 Rooker improved to 10-15 with a 3.55 ERA in 38 games, 29 of them starts. His innings rose to 203⅔, third on the staff. One of Rooker's losses came in a 12-inning game on June 4 in which Horace Clarke of the Yankees broke up his bid for a no-hitter with a base hit leading off the ninth. "I won 10," Rooker said, "so I started to think, 'I'm getting the hang of things.' It was hard on everybody." But he went 7-13 over the next two seasons, splitting his time between relief and starting, and was traded to Pittsburgh for the 1973 season.

Those Pirates featured Willie Stargell, Manny Sanguillen in his prime, Al Oliver, Richie Hebner, and Richie Zisk. Pitchers included Nelson Briles, Bob Moose, and Dock Ellis, with a bullpen of Dave Giusti, Bob Johnson, and Ramon Hernandez. Rooker responded to his new environment by going 10-6 in 1973 and 15-11 with a 2.78 ERA in 1974, his best season, as Pittsburgh won the NL East. Rooker started the second game of the NL Championship Series against the Dodgers, giving up two runs in seven innings without a decision.

The Pirates repeated in 1975 as Rooker contributed a 13-11 record and 2.97 ERA. He pitched the second game of the NL Championship Series against Cincinnati, giving up four runs in four innings as the Cincinnati Reds won the series. Rooker was 15-8 and 14-9 the next two years as Philadelphia edged out Pittsburgh for the division title. In 1978 he dipped to 9-11 with a 4.24 ERA and in 1979 Rooker appeared in just 19 games — 17 of them starts, going 4-7.

That Pittsburgh team made the World Series and Rooker was a surprise Game Five starter in a series Baltimore led, 3 games to 1. "I wasn't scheduled to start," Rooker said. "Bruce Kison was. But he had nerve damage to his arm from the first game. It was not a good year for me during the season. But there was one thing: I was very rested for the World Series. I thought I had somewhat of an advantage. I was all charged up and ready to go. Not only was I going to have what I hoped was fun. What a challenge! We were down 3 to 1. If we stink up the joint, we were going home."

Rooker pitched the first five innings and left trailing 1-0. The Pirates rallied for seven runs in the sixth, seventh, and eighth innings to hand the win to Bert Blyleven, who worked four scoreless relief innings. "I honestly thought we had the better team," Rooker said. "The first four games our hitting was limited. But [Baltimore manager] Earl Weaver made a couple of mistakes. He decided to pitch to Bill Madlock. And then we started swinging the bats. Our pitching was pretty consistent. And from that point we took off. All of us still knew we had the ability to beat 'em because we felt we had the better team. I can't remember if it was the sixth or seventh inning [it was the sixth] but Madlock came up with a runner in scoring position and got a base hit to knock in a run or two. Once he did, the hits just kept coming, coming, coming. Once we won that, it was back to Baltimore for the sixth and seventh games. Our bats came alive from that point on." Before Madlock stepped to the plate, Stargell had scored Tim Foli on a sacrifice fly, sending Dave Parker to third base. Then Madlock got his single, scoring Parker.

That marked Rooker's career highlight because the next year, 1980, he hurt his arm throwing a slider in May to Atlanta's Dale Murphy. "At the time I didn't know how serious it was. I waited for it to heal. It never did. Doctors could not find the injury. But I knew I was not going to be able to pitch again. That winter I went on the [press] caravan. As we went to different places, I kind of became a spokesperson for the club. Some of people thought I spoke so well I ought to do more of this."

So his career ended with a 103-109 record and a 3.46 ERA for 1,810⅓ innings. Which brought the left-hander to another career turning point. What to do next? What could be better than playing baseball? Well, for Rooker and many other players, it's extending their association with the game.

"They had fired one of the guys who was going to be one of the broadcasters and I auditioned for the job. I didn't have all the ability in the world, but I think they felt I would get better. And I was terrible — until I started listening to my own tapes. I realized the things I left out. I didn't prepare myself. But I also think I could have had a little more help along the way. But it's a lot like anything else, if you want to work on it, you'll get better. I asked our radio guys to tape the innings and I'd listen to them in my car on the way home. Things got better faster after that.

"I didn't plan ahead to do that. It's different today. You have players listening to broadcasters and they'll tape them for auditions. I thought my job [as a player] was on the field. And I find players don't want to know the truth. When they screw up they don't want to hear it. Had I thought about it, I probably would have gone another route. But what listeners want to know is, 'What's the score and how many outs.' You have to be very descriptive. And that's something you have to work at, especially in radio."

Rooker became a Pittsburgh icon with his ability to combine professional skill as a broadcaster with his propensity to speak his mind and be critical in a nonthreatening manner. No doubt many young Pirates fans don't even know Rooker used to work on the mound instead of the broadcast booth, a professional compliment. His defining moment as a broadcaster came on June 8, 1989, after Pittsburgh scored 10 runs in the top of the first at Philadelphia, capped by a three-run homer by Barry Bonds. "If we lose this game," Rooker said, "I'll walk home."

Naturally, something happened. Von Hayes answered with two-run home runs in the first and third innings. Steve Jeltz hit home runs in the fourth and sixth and the Phillies found by the bottom of the sixth that they trailed only 11-10. The tying run scored in the eighth on a wild pitch, Darren Daulton hit a two-run single, and Philadelphia walked off the field with a 15-11 victory. "I always try to forget that," Rooker said. "We didn't have a good team. Whoever loses 10-0 leads? As long as I've been in baseball, that's never happened. Word spread real quick. The next morning I got a phone call from our radio station. This guy asked if I would go on at noon with him. I thought, 'What's the big deal?' But people were saying, 'Is he going to do it? Is he going to walk from Philadelphia to Pittsburgh? I said I won't do it just for the sake of doing it. Let's get some charities involved, a sponsor. Let's have some reason to do it."

It was billed as "Jim Rooker's Unintentional Walk." It took place that October after the season ended, and the proceeds were to go to Children's Hospital in both Pittsburgh and Philadelphia. "We got people together," he said. With the help of the Pirates and the Phillies, it took me 13 days. And it was hell. You don't realize what it can do to your feet. Day after day. We didn't realize how bad it was going to be. I walked with Carl Dozzi, he was one of those really over-energetic guys. After five days your feet get so bad (blisters). Once you get going for about a half an hour you kind of loosen up. Every five days we went to a half-size bigger shoe, extra socks, and another five days it was another half-size bigger. But we raised $81,000 for Children's Hospital. At least it was something you had to look forward to, a light at the end of the tunnel. There was no way in the world I was going to do it for nothing, no way in the world."

It wasn't his first stunt. During his playing days, there was a time he dived out of a second-floor window at St. Louis's Chase-Park Plaza Hotel and into the swimming pool. "We had played a day game and you get bored. I took a towel, wore it around my neck so it acted like a cape and I just dived in. We weren't even drinking. Just bored."[1]

There were struggles with alcohol later on, and in 1991 Rooker, "who had appeared in a nationally televised beer commercial two years ago, was given an indefinite leave of absence" from his duties as a broadcaster due to three incidents of drunken driving which saddled him with a mandatory 90-day jail term.[2]

Rooker retired from the broadcast booth in 1993 to spend time at home and help out with his restaurant, Just Rook's, located in a suburb about 20 minutes from Pittsburgh. "[In July 2006, my wife and I moved down to Jacksonville [Florida]. My partner and I rotate being at the restaurant. Other than that, I just fish and golf."

In 1996 Rooker contemplated challenging incumbent Congressman Ron Klink (D) in that year's election for the US House of Representatives, and said that his campaign chairman would be Chuck Tanner.[3] Nothing more seems to have come of this.

Later in the decade, Rooker began to write children's books. His first three titles were: *Kitt The Mitt*, *Matt The Bat*, and *Paul The Ball*. "I was flying back to Jacksonville from Pittsburgh one day and it really hit me how much I miss my grandchildren,'" Rooker said. "I started thinking of a way that I might be able to give something to them that would be really lasting. I don't know why exactly it popped into my head, but I thought I'd try to write a book. It's been a very rewarding experience.[4]

SOURCES

For this biography, the author consulted a number of contemporary sources, including *The Sporting News* and clippings from Rooker's Hall of Fame file. The author also is grateful for an interview Rooker gave him on July 11, 2007. All quotations come from this interview, except as noted.

An earlier version of this article originally appeared in the book *Sock It To 'Em Tigers—The Incredible Story of the 1968 Detroit Tigers*, published by Maple Street Press in 2008.

NOTES

1 "Quotable," *Washington Times*, June 23, 1989: 37.

2 "Rooker in Rehab," *State Times Advocate* (Baton Rouge, Louisiana), May 4, 1991: 47.

3 Michael Weisskopf, "Ex-Pirate to Challenge Pa. Representative," *Washington Post*, February 4, 1996: A22.

4 John Perrotto, "Former Pirates Pitcher Rooker Finds Career in Writing Children's Books," *The Intelligencer* (Wheeling, West Virginia), September 27, 2009.

Manny Sanguillen

By Bob Hurte

IN HIS MEMOIR, FORMER PITTSBURGH Pirates pitcher Steve Blass extolled the virtues of the nonverbal communication between a catcher and pitcher. "The reality of a pitcher's relationship with his catcher is that if he is on a roll, he is almost his own decision maker. ... But Manny knew me just as much psychologically as the nuts and bolts of the actual pitch calling. And that is huge. And it comes with time. ..."[1]

To many, Manny Sanguillen was known primarily as an offensive player during his 13 seasons in the majors (1967; 1969-80). The Panamanian swung a big (40 ounces) and potent bat, hitting .296 lifetime with a .398 slugging percentage. "Sangy" did not take a lot of pitches (.326 on-base percentage), so he typically needed a hit to reach first base. For example, he did not walk until his 75th at-bat during the 1969 season. He gave a simple explanation: "When I started, nobody told me what a strike was, they gave me a bat and I swung at the ball!" Indeed, he was also a notorious bad-ball hitter. Former Pirates trainer Tony Bartirome remembered a time when Manny lined a single off a ball that bounced before it reached the plate.[2]

Yet Sanguillen had other dimensions. With his strong arm, he caught 39 percent of the runners who tried to steal against him during his career. He was popular, with a broad, gap-toothed smile, and well-rounded enough as a player to make the National League All-Star team three times. He also received MVP votes in four seasons. Winning the 1971 World Series was the highlight of Manny's career, but he counted catching Bob Moose's no-hitter on September 20, 1969, against the New York Mets as his proudest accomplishment. It was an example of his maturation in calling a game.

Manuel de Jesús Sanguillén Magán was born on March 21, 1944, in Colón, Panama. Colón is the nation's second biggest city, lying near the Atlantic entrance to the Panama Canal. Note that in Spanish, the accent falls on the last syllable of his surname, but in the United States it was typically pronounced "San-GHEE-yen." His father, Helio Sanguillén, was a fisherman. His mother, Zoila Magán, had 12 other children (six boys and six girls). Manny was right in the middle.

Sanguillen began playing baseball late in his youth. Instead, he preferred playing basketball and soccer as a youth. He also boxed, winning five of his seven bouts. When he did play baseball, it was mostly in the infield or outfield. Manny played a little at catcher but it was not his preference.

The man who made a pro baseball player out of Sanguillen was Herb Raybourne. Raybourne was a former pro (1959-61 in the minor leagues) who had grown up in Panama. He was an insider on the local baseball scene —he won the Panamanian batting title in the winter of 1960-61— and went on to become an eminent scout. He became best known for discovering Mariano Rivera, but Sanguillen was the first of several prospects Raybourne found for the Pirates on the isthmus (the other biggest names besides Rivera being Rennie Stennett and Omar Moreno).

Though he kept on playing winter ball in Panama, Raybourne taught and coached baseball at a local high school. During that time he went into scouting. Raybourne had done a little catching himself and after seeing Sanguillen catch, he convinced him he should play behind the plate. Raybourne felt that the young Panamanian had the perfect frame—Manny was built like a bull at 6-feet and 190 pounds.

Raybourne first saw Sanguillen play on a team made up of much older players. When the Pirates scout found out that the Houston Astros were also interested in the young catcher, he wrote to Pete Peterson, the Pirates' director of scouting. Peterson sent Howie Haak, who was considered a "super scout" in the Pittsburgh organization and gained acclaim for opening up all of Latin America to the majors.

When Haak got to Panama, he asked Raybourne to run his prospects, about 10 to 12 players. The crafty scout held Sanguillen back to run last, in an attempt to showcase his exceptional speed for a big man. He ran an impressive 6.6 in the 60-yard dash.

Next, Raybourne had Manny get behind the plate and throw to second. After a few throws, Haak exclaimed, "Wow! We got a player here!"[3]

The young player's baseball career almost ended with a foul popup. Sanguillen got a real kick out of recalling the incident. "I can laugh about it now. It was funny when it happened. I run back and I don't see the ball. Then my head. ... Oh, how it hurt. The people didn't think it was funny."[4]

Although Herb Raybourne thought of Manny as a son, he never met the Sanguillen family. They lived on the Atlantic Ocean side of Panama. But he knew that Manny sent money to them. So Radbourne tried to get the best contract possible for him. This was not an easy task. The Pirates organization was apprehensive about giving a lot of money to raw, unproven talent. Peterson was willing to give Sanguillen an incentive contract. Bonuses were based on how he moved through the minors. For instance, if Sanguillen remained on the Batavia (Class-A) roster for 60 days, he would receive a $500 bonus. If he moved up to Double A and stayed, he could earn an additional $1,000, and if he made it up to Triple A, his bonus increased by another $1,500. Finally, if he played for the Pirates, it meant an additional $5,000.[5]

Sanguillen started at Batavia of the New York-Penn League. Not only was he playing at a higher level of baseball, he had to deal with a language barrier. "I couldn't speak or read much English, I go to a restaurant in Batavia. The waitress, she didn't know that I didn't know English. She would say steak and I'd say 'yeah.' I don't understand, but I like steak."[6]

Sanguillen batted .235 in his first professional season, causing the Pirates to have doubts. Tom Saffell was his manager at Batavia and helped him become a better catcher. Manny felt that he learned how to play baseball in the professional ranks. When he became an established player on the Pirates, he recalled how Saffell did not let him take batting practice. Instead he caught it and also the game. Sanguillen admitted getting really tired and worried about his hitting. Saffell told his young catcher not to worry about batting. "You will hit. Let's make sure you can catch."[7]

After the 1965 season, Sanguillen was making $350 a month but had saved only $500 to take home. He felt it was not enough and decided to quit—he purchased a bus ticket to Panama. Fate stepped in. Danny Murtaugh, who was then a special assistant to general manager Joe Brown, was standing at the door when the young catcher was leaving. Murtaugh let Manny know that the Pirates planned to protect him by putting him on the 40-man roster.[8]

After a brief conversation, Sanguillen calmed down. He read his Bible and prayed. It was the start of a trusting relationship between the catcher and his future manager in Pittsburgh. During the 1971 World Series, Murtaugh sought his opinion on the Orioles batters.

Although the Pirates told him not to be concerned with his batting, Manny worked hard at it with a batting tee during the offseason. He also played winter ball at home in Panama. *The Sporting News* observed, "Catcher Manuel Sanguillen has impressed fans with his great improvement after one season of experience in Organized Baseball."[9] He won the batting title with a .370 mark for Ron Santa Clara.[10]

Sanguillen's hard work paid off. He was the runner-up for the Carolina League batting title with Raleigh in 1966, and he was named to the All-Star team. At the end of the season, Sanguillen was promoted to the Triple-A Columbus Jets, for whom he played in nine games. He played winter ball again in Panama, refusing an offer to play in Nicaragua.[11]

Sanguillen began at Columbus in 1967 but had to be brought up to Pittsburgh in July. The incumbent catcher, Jerry May, fractured his index finger and was placed on the 15-day disabled list on July 21. With May out, the backstop duties fell to Jim Pagliaroni and Sanguillen. Manny's old friend, Danny Murtaugh, had replaced Harry Walker as manager on July 18. Sanguillen reported to the Pirates on July 23 and made his debut at Forbes Field against the Houston Astros. He caught Tommie Sisk as the Pirates won, 15-2. The rookie went 1-for-5 and scored a run. He remained in Pittsburgh, catching in 30 games while batting .271.[12]

The Pirates were pleased with Sanguillen's brief performance. They recommended that he play winter ball again. This time he went to the Dominican Republic, joining Águilas Cibaeñas. Pittsburgh also sold Jim Pagliaroni's contract to Oakland. Then Sanguillen broke a finger, which prevented him from making the Opening Day roster in 1968. Instead, he returned to the Columbus Jets, managed by Johnny Pesky. The injury hampered his hitting early in the season, but he batted .387 over his last 87 games to finish with a .316 average.

A healthy Sanguillen competed with Jerry May for the starting backstop job in 1969. May was coming off a poor season, having batted .219 in 1968. Larry Shepard, the Pirates manager (Murtaugh had returned to the front office), said May needed to beat out Sanguillen to keep his starting job. May was entering his fourth full season, yet he was the same age as Sanguillen. Shepard was confident in Sanguillen defensively, but felt that he had to overcome one main drawback. He was well liked by his teammates, but his English was difficult to understand. Sanguillen had the raw tools — a rifle arm and a quick bat — but his inability to communicate with pitchers was a concern.[13]

Eventually, Sanguillen became the regular behind the plate by virtue of his strengths, which made the young backstop's English tolerable. Pirates reliever Chuck Hartenstein explained, "(E)verybody knows 'in and out' and 'up and down.' That's the primary part of pitching."[14] Shepard did not publicly announce Sanguillen as the starter, but May accepted a supporting role, committing to helping his rival become better.

Fortunately for Sanguillen, he had several Latin friends and role models on the club — players like Matty Alou, Manny Mota, and José Pagán. Roberto Clemente acted like his older brother. Sanguillen also developed a special relationship with trainer Tony Bartirome. Tony, Manny, Pagán, and Alou were all big boxing fans. They regularly went to boxing matches in East McKeesport, a suburb of Pittsburgh.

Sanguillen discussed his peak personal accomplishment — handling Bob Moose's no-hitter — in a

conversation with the author. He proudly explained how they mixed pitches: the knuckleball, sinker, and side-arm delivery. They alternated them for each inning. It was a windy day at New York's Shea Stadium, so the knuckler was especially successful. In the ninth inning, with two outs and Rod Gaspar at second, Art Shamsky bounced a ball to Dave Cash, who flipped to Al Oliver to end it. Moose won 4-0, walking three and striking out six. Clemente made a one-handed grab on a ball hit to the fence.[15] (Three years later, Moose was responsible for Sanguillen's lowest point in his career, a wild pitch that ended the 1972 NL Championship Series on October 11, 1972.)

Sanguillen's maturation continued that December. He married Kathy Swanger of North Versailles, Pennsylvania, a Pittsburgh suburb. "My wife, she is a good baseball fan," said Manny in 1971. "We talk baseball a lot. I don't bring home my baseball problems to her. If I'm not hitting, I don't talk baseball a lot. But we talk about the good things that baseball has given us."[16]

Sanguillen continued to gain respect around the league for his catching, but his ascension was largely overshadowed by that of Johnny Bench. In 1970 Sanguillen's .325 batting average was third best in the National League. The Pirates won a division title, only to lose in the NLCS to the Cincinnati Reds, led by Bench. Sanguillen had a quiet series against the Reds, going 2-for-12.

In March 1971 Pittsburgh played three exhibition games in Panama City against a team of Panamanian all-stars. Joe DiMaggio threw out the first ball. Some 38,000 fans turned out for the series, and Sanguillen went 5-for-11 with a homer in front of his countrymen.[17]

That season Sanguillen finally began to get the reputation as one of the best all-around catchers in baseball. Meanwhile, Bench—the defending NL MVP—had an off-year. Sanguillen was chosen for his first All-Star team in 1971. He did not play; Cincinnati manager Sparky Anderson used Bench for the entire game.

Many of Sanguillen's teammates felt that if not for Johnny Bench, Manny was the best catcher in the National League. They were similar to each other. Each possessed exceptional throwing arms, soft hands, and great agility behind the plate. Both cultivated a rapport with their pitchers.[18]

In some ways they differed. Bench was glamorous, cool, and unflappable. Sanguillen was wildly demonstrative with unabashed enthusiasm. Sometimes his ebullience was misinterpreted as "hot-dogging." Bench had much more power, but Sanguillen hit for a higher average and had unusual speed on the basepaths for a catcher. Bench was one of the foremost defensive catchers of his day, though Sanguillen polished his skills in this area.

Steve Blass answered the charges on hot-dogging: "Manny is not a 'hot dog.' He just enjoys playing and he shows it. … He's deceptive in that he puts more into catching than people realize. You tend to think of him as a hitter who can throw well. But he can spot my own weaknesses before I can. I pitch with a three-quarter delivery. If I drop below that, I'm in trouble. Manny notices my little change."[19]

The 1971 Pirates were a boisterous group that included players like Blass, Dave Giusti, Sanguillen, Bob Veale, Nellie Briles, and Willie Stargell. The clubhouse was diverse, with much good-natured ribbing that saw no color or ethnicity. This was never more evident than in a game against Philadelphia on September 1, 1971. Danny Murtaugh happened to write out an all-black lineup—the first ever in the majors. The Pirates manager said he was simply playing those he felt gave them the best chance of winning. The lineup consisted of Stennett (2B), Gene Clines (CF), Clemente (RF), Stargell (LF), Sanguillen (C), Cash (3B), Oliver (1B), Jackie Hernandez (SS), and Dock Ellis (P). Sanguillen remembered the minority players having a good laugh over it. "We were making fun of everybody and we said, 'We have it now!'"[20]

Pittsburgh repeated in 1971 as winner of the NL's Eastern Division. Sanguillen batted .319, his third consecutive season over .300, with 81 RBIs. The Pirates went on to meet the San Francisco Giants in the NLCS; Sanguillen's 4-for-15 performance was steady, yet unspectacular. He must have been saving his best for the World Series.

One of the more interesting stories of that Series occurred during Game Five, on October 14. Nellie Briles had mastered the Baltimore Orioles up to the seventh inning. To that point, Briles and Sanguillen had blended their pitch selection well, spotting the fastball in and out, mixing speeds, inserting the palmball and slider when needed. The Pirates were leading 4-0 and nine outs away from winning. This is when the two principals had a disagreement. When Manny wanted to continue their game plan, Briles disagreed and wanted to alter it. The result? Sanguillen refused to give signals for the rest of the game! It was a testament to his athleticism. Briles threw a complete-game shutout and put the Pirates ahead for the first time in the World Series.[21]

The seventh and deciding game was played on October 17 at Memorial Stadium in Baltimore. The pitching matchup was the same as in Game Three, Blass against Mike Cuellar. Baltimore trimmed Pittsburgh's lead to 2-1 in the bottom of the eighth and had the tying run on third with two out. Blass and Sanguillen conferred on how to pitch to Davey Johnson, who had seen nothing but sliders all day. They looked to surprise him by setting up for another slider away, then coming with a fastball up and in, but eventually Blass retired Johnson on another slider, not his best. Blass retired Baltimore 1-2-3 in the ninth, and the Pirates were champions. Sanguillen batted .379 in the Series with 11 hits and a 2-for-4 performance in the seventh game. He caught every inning of each of the seven games.[22]

Kathy Sanguillen gave birth to their first child that December: Manuel Jr. They had had a daughter, Sarah, in January 1978.[23]

The Pirates began preparing to replace the aging Roberto Clemente in the outfield during the 1972 season. They eyed Sanguillen as his successor, which would also have paved the way for Milt May to start behind the plate. Sanguillen, who had gained some outfield experience in the Puerto Rican Winter League, was willing to give it a go. The experiment was largely confined to the exhibition season, though; he played just two games in left field during the 1972 season. Clemente, 38 years old, batted .312 in 102 games. The year ended sadly with his untimely death.

In 1972 Sanguillen missed joining the five other catchers in NL history who had posted four consecutive .300 seasons; he batted .298. Once again he was named to the All-Star Game.[24] This time he actually played. Manny replaced Bench in the sixth. He bounced out to second his first at-bat, but his ninth-inning single helped to tie the game, and the National League won in the bottom of the 10th.

Milt May did get more playing time in 1972, reducing Sanguillen's workload—though when the playoffs began (again versus Cincinnati), Sanguillen was back behind the plate full-time. He enjoyed a good series with the bat, going 5-for-16 (.313). He was the hero of Game Three, knocking in the game-winning run in the eighth inning after hitting a homer earlier. But the last pitch of that NLCS was arguably the lowest point of his career. With a 3-2 lead in Game Five and another trip to the World Series just three outs away, Dave Giusti gave up a tying home run to Johnny Bench to lead off the bottom of the ninth, then gave way to Bob Moose after two more singles. Moose got two outs but threw a wild pitch to end a galling loss.[25]

After the season, Clemente invited Sanguillen to Puerto Rico once more to play winter ball for the San Juan Senators. The Senators were coached by Clemente and stocked with several Pirates teammates, including Richie Zisk, Rennie Stennett, and Milt May. It was a great way for Sanguillen to stay in baseball shape, and he worked again on playing the outfield. Clemente had taken the young Panamanian under his wing, acting like an older brother. He enjoyed good-natured teasing.

"Sangy, what position do you play in the winter league?" asked Clemente.

"Right field, I play twenty in right, one in left," replied Manny.

"Sangy, you play left field or go back to catching. You have no chance to take my job!" Roberto smiled.[26]

The mood changed to grave mourning, however, after the tragic crash of Clemente's flight on a mercy mission to Nicaragua on December 31, 1972. Indeed, Sanguillen might have been on the flight too, except that he had misplaced his car keys. Many of the Pirates' management and teammates traveled from the United States to attend a memorial service on the island. Sanguillen chose not to attend; instead, when a search party formed, he showed up ready to do anything to help. A powerful swimmer, he went out with a group of volunteer divers on a rescue boat. They focused on the underground caverns of the coral reefs. A dragging operation brought up the body of Jerry Hall, the pilot. Seeing Hall's body convinced Manny that he would not find his friend alive.[27]

The loss of Clemente led the Pirates to accelerate Sanguillen's move to right field during spring training. No one expected him to be another Clemente, but he showed early signs that he would be an above-average outfielder. He opened the 1973 season in right field. But he had more difficulty adjusting than expected. "Only I wish there was somebody in right field to talk to," he remarked.[28] It soon became obvious that Sanguillen and right field were not a match. The club started off terribly. Sanguillen was moved back to catcher by June 15. He set highs for games played (149), home runs (12), and extra-base hits (45), but his batting average dipped to .282. His defense behind the plate was not as crisp as usual since he played 59 games in the outfield.

Pittsburgh rebounded to win the NL East again in 1974, with much help from Sanguillen, who returned to his form of 1970-72. At the start his batting average floundered around .250, but as the season progressed, he regained the .300 mark, finishing at .287. He caught 151 games in 1974, including the last 53 of the season, but the Pirates lost the NLCS in four games to the Los Angeles Dodgers.[29]

Sanguillen's batting average returned to the .300 level in 1975 –he hit a career-best .328, placing third in the NL. In part this was because he got more rest; the Pirates had obtained Duffy Dyer in the offseason.[30] Batting in the number-2 hole, the free-swinging Panamanian demonstrated more patience at the plate than ever before. He set another career high by walking 48 times. Sanguillen was selected to the All-Star team but once again watched it from the bench. The Pirates won the NL East by 6½ games over Philadelphia but were swept by Cincinnati's Big Red Machine.

In 1976 the Pirates did not win the NL East, for only the second time to that point in the decade. The Philadelphia Phillies were a rising power. Many of the Pirates became old; several of their perennial stars began to fade. Sanguillen batted .290, but he battled a sore shoulder the entire season.

As if the season were not disappointing enough, the team had lost two members of its family during the offseason. Pitcher Bob Moose was killed in a car accident after celebrating his 29th birthday. Then in December, Danny Murtaugh (who had announced his retirement) died. The third blow to Pirates fans came when the club traded fan favorite Sanguillen. Pittsburgh had signed Chuck Tanner as manager from the Oakland A's, and A's owner Charlie O. Finley demanded the catcher as compensation.

Sanguillen spent one year in Oakland. He played in 152 games and batted .275, mediocre for him. He split catching duties with Jeff Newman and was the team's most frequently used designated hitter (the only time he ever served in this role).

Three days before Opening Day 1978, Pittsburgh reacquired Sanguillen. Several of his teammates were happy about reacquiring him—but two catchers were extremely disappointed and made it known. Ed Ott, concerned that Sanguillen would do the majority of the catching, said, "The deal stinks!" Ott added that it was not personal but felt he was back to where he was two years ago. Duffy Dyer was not pleased either. Dyer opened the season on the disabled list and manager Tanner named Ott the number-one catcher. Manny finished the season with a .264 batting average while playing 85 games.[31]

Sanguillen's playing time decreased even more sharply in 1979. He played in just 56 games with the lowest batting average (.230) of his career. Though he was not a major part of the "We Are Family" team, he proved his value in Game Two of the World Series. In the top of the ninth, with two men on, he pinch-hit for Don Robinson and lined a single to right field to bring in Ed Ott with the winning run. Kent Tekulve came in and nailed down the 3-2 win by retiring the Orioles in order. The Pirates went on to win in seven games.[32]

Sanguillen's playing time was limited almost strictly to pinch-hitting in 1980—he did not appear once behind the plate. After the season he was included in a trade that sent Bert Blyleven to the Cleveland Indians. The Indians released Sanguillen during spring training and he retired.

Manny Sanguillen remained a Pirates fan favorite in and around the Pittsburgh community. He stayed active in many of the Pirates' alumni events. Starting in 2002 he hosted a barbecue stand behind center field at PNC Park, regaling fans with stories about the glory days of the team.

As Tony Bartirome said, "If you didn't like Manny, then there was something wrong with you!"[33]

SOURCES

In addition to the sources listed in the Notes, the author consulted the following:

"Injury Bugaboo Finally Catches Up with Pirates," *The Sporting News*, August 5, 1967.

"Jet Set Musicians," *The Sporting News*, May 18, 1968.

"Who Will Be Protected? Here Are Some Good Guesses," *The Sporting News*, October 12, 1968.

THE 1979 PITTSBURGH PIRATES

Feeney, Charley. "Bucs' Hebner a Headache for Hurlers," *The Sporting News*, June 14, 1969.

N. L. flashes, "Brock Rates Arms," *The Sporting News*, July 25, 1970.

Feeney, Charley. "Bucs Touting Manny as a Mighty Fine Catcher," *The Sporting News*, July 3, 1971.

Feeney, Charley. "Job Switch? It's Okay with Bucs' Sanguillen," *The Sporting News*, April 15, 1972.

Feeney, Charley. "Sanguillen in the Outfield? Bucs Ponder Key Shift," *The Sporting News*, February 19, 1972.

Feeney, Charley. "Likeable Manny Draws Bucs Needles," *The Sporting News*, July 15, 1972.

Feeney, Charley. "Manny Willing to Switch, But Not on a Daily Schedule," *The Sporting News*, February 24, 1973.

Feeney, Charley. "Manny Gaining Altitude as a Pirate Hawk," *The Sporting News*, May 19, 1973.

Waddell, Genevieve. "Lost Car Keys Kept Sanguillen Off Clemente Flight," *The Sporting News*, May 19, 1973.

Feeney, Charley. Charley Feeney, "Sanguillen or May? One Is on Bucco Swap List," *The Sporting News*, November 27, 1973.

Feeney, Charley. "Pirates Hot at Home, Cold on Road," *The Sporting News*, July 20, 1974.

Feeney, Charley. "Bucs Give Big Hand to Manny, Their Maskman," *The Sporting News*, August 24, 1974.

Feeney, Charley. "Pirates Puff Out Chests With Duffy on Duty," *The Sporting News*, June 19, 1976.

Feeney, Charley. "Pirates Will Miss Sanguillen's Smile and Bat," *The Sporting News*, December 4, 1976.

Weir, Tom. "A's Grateful for Sanguillen's .300 Bat," *The Sporting News*, March 19, 1977.

Feeney, Charley. "Manny, Rennie Will be Ex-Bucs," *The Sporting News*, October 27, 1979.

Emert, Rich. "Where Are They Now?" *Pittsburgh Post Gazette*, April 10, 2003.

Magazines

Abrams, Al. "Super Stardom Ahead for Sanguillen," *Baseball Digest*, June 1970.

Blount, Roy. "Now Playing Right: Manny Sanguillen," *Sports Illustrated*, March 19, 1973.

Lenoir, Bob. "Manny Sanguillen…Out of Clemente's Shadow," *Baseball Digest*, July 1975.

Books

McHugh, Roy, "Pitching Did It: Manny Believed," in Peterson, Richard (editor) *The Pirates Reader* (Pittsburgh: University of Pittsburgh Press, 2003).

Hronich, Colleen. *The Whistling Irishman: Danny Murtaugh Remembered* (Philadelphia: Sports Challenge Network, 2010).

Telephone interviews with author

Steve Blass, May 15, 2012.

Tony Bartirome, May 24, 2012.

Dave Giusti, June 2, 2012.

Sally O'Leary, June 4, 2012.

Manny Sanguillen, June 14, 2012.

Herb Raybourne, August 13, 2012.

E-mail correspondence with author

Sarah Sanguillen, October 31, 2012.

Chuck Berry, December 23, 2012.

NOTES

1. Steve Blass and Erik Sherman, *Steve Blass: A Pirate for Life* (Chicago: Triumph Books, 2012), 97.
2. Tony Bartirome, telephone interview with author, June 24, 2012.
3. Herb Raybourne, telephone interview with author, August 13, 2012.
4. Charley Feeney, "$5,000 Manny Huge Pirate Treasure," *The Sporting News*, May 1, 1971.
5. Raybourne interview.
6. Feeney, "$5,000 Manny Huge Pirate Treasure."
7. Charley Feeney, "Sanguillen Turns Mistakes Into Profit," *The Sporting News*, August 30, 1969.
8. Manny Sanguillen, telephone interview with author, June 14, 2012.
9. Abdiel A. Flynn, "Rummies Romp to Fast Start, Swing Hot Bats," *The Sporting News*, December 25, 1965: 35.
10. Abdiel A. Flynn, "Buccos Boast Gem in Rough—Sanguillen's Sizzling Warclub," *The Sporting News*, February 5, 1966: 30; Flynn, "Desousa Bat-Title Surge Falls Short," *The Sporting News*, February 12, 1966: 26.
11. Abdiel A. Flynn, "League Officials Nix Plans to Add a Fourth Team," *The Sporting News*, November 5, 1966: 41.
12. "May Put on Disabled List, Bucs Bring Up Sanguillen," *The Sporting News*, August 5, 1967.
13. "May Swinging Torrid Bat, to Remain Bucco Mitt," *The Sporting News*, May 3, 1969.
14. "Sanguillen Smiles, Buc Foes Moan," *The Sporting News*, June 7, 1969.
15. "Moose Makes Lambs Out of the Mets," *The Sporting News*, October 4, 1969.
16. Feeney, "$5,000 Manny Huge Pirate Treasure."
17. Charley Feeney, "38,000 See Bucs in Panama," *The Sporting News*, March 27, 1971: 34; Dave Eisenberg, "Golf Keeps DiMag in Top Condition," *The Sporting News*, March 20, 1971: 55;.

18 Ron Fimrite, "Two Catchers Cut From Royal Cloth," *Sports Illustrated*, June 26, 1972.

19 Ibid.

20 Bruce Markusen, *The Team That Changed Baseball: Roberto Clemente and the 1971 Pirates* (Yardley, Pennsylvania: Westholme Publishing LLC, 2006), 108.

21 Markusen, *The Team That Changed Baseball*, 158.

22 Blass and Sherman, *Steve Blass: A Pirate for Life*, 174.

23 Sarah Sanguillen, e-mail correspondence with the author, October 31, 2012.

24 David Finoli and Bill Ranier, *The Pittsburgh Pirates Encyclopedia* (Champaign, Illinois: Sports Publishing LLC, 2003), 297-299.

25 Willie Stargell and Tom Bird, *Willie Stargell: An Autobiography* (New York: Harper & Row, 1984), 157.

26 David Maraniss, *Clemente: The Passion & Grace of Baseball's Last Hero* (New York: Simon & Schuster, 2006), 305.

27 Maraniss, 347.

28 Bruce Markusen, *Roberto Clemente: The Great One* (Champaign, Illinois: Sports Publishing LLC, 2001), 330.

29 Charley Feeney, "Catching Every Day Is Just Play for Sanguillen," *The Sporting News*, March 1, 1975.

30 Charley Feeney, "Sanguillen's Hefty Bat Key Weapon in Bucco Arsenal," *The Sporting News*, August 16, 1975.

31 Charley Feeney, "Deal for Sanguillen Rocks Pirates' Catcher," *The Sporting News*, April 22, 1978.

32 John McCollister, *Tales From the Pittsburgh Pirates: Remembering "the Fam-A-Lee."* (Champaign, Illinois: Sports Publishing LLC, 2005), 142.

33 Tony Bartirome, telephone interview with author, May 24, 2012.

Willie Stargell

By James Forr

FOLLOWING THE PITTSBURGH PIRATES' loss to the Chicago Cubs on October 1, 2000, 60-year-old Willie Stargell emerged to throw a ceremonial final pitch at the soon-to-be-demolished Three Rivers Stadium. Even though most people who followed the Pirates knew "Pops" was in poor health his frail, spectral appearance that afternoon was shocking. He was almost unrecognizable, barely able to walk on his own, a much-too-large gold Pirate jersey drooping pitifully from his emaciated shoulders. His feeble toss to catcher Jason Kendall barely went 10 feet.

The poignant image of the dying man on the field that afternoon contrasted so dramatically with the mighty and fearsome slugger of an earlier time. It wasn't long ago, with his mile-long home runs and gentle giant persona, that Willie Stargell seemed almost indestructible.

His childhood was not only challenging but also a little bit weird. Wilver Dornel Stargell was born March 6, 1940, in tiny Earlsboro, Oklahoma, the son of William and Gladys Vernell Stargell. (His unusual first name was an amalgamation of his father's first name and his mother's maiden name). But before Willie was born, his dad skipped town. It wasn't until 1960, when Stargell was 19, that the two men finally met. "I accepted my father as he was," Willie insisted later. "I didn't offer judgment on what he had done and eventually I grew to love him for what he was."[1]

Into the breach stepped Will Stargell, Willie's biracial paternal grandfather (Will's own father was a former slave. His mother was Seminole). Will took Gladys and Willie into his home and served as a surrogate father until three years later, when Gladys remarried and took her son with her to California. After Gladys' second marriage ended quickly, she moved in with a relative in the public housing projects of Alameda, just outside of Oakland.

Gladys married again in 1946 but before the newlyweds could get on their feet financially, her older sister Lucy swooped in out of nowhere with an offer she couldn't refuse. The two women agreed Lucy would take Willie back to her home in Orlando and care for him there until Gladys and her new husband got settled.

Stargell's unflattering description of his aunt made her sound like a wicked old crone from a fairy tale. "Lucy [was] large-boned, bowlegged, and with a pinch of snuff tucked loosely inside her lower lip, carried herself awkwardly, almost like a retired cowboy…[T]here was a switch always in sight and a scowl always on her face."[2]

Life in Florida with his aunt was almost a form of incarceration. Lucy, who was divorced and never had children of her own, kept her nephew under strict control, apparently intercepting letters and money that Gladys sent to Willie. He was malnourished and burdened with so many chores that he barely had a chance to be a kid. In the summers, Stargell would sneak out to play baseball while Lucy was at work. Inevitably, he would stay out too long and fail to finish his assigned tasks, which seldom failed to spark Lucy's ire. "Spanking became a permanent part of my late afternoon routine," he recalled.[3]

Gladys finally came to rescue her boy after six long, difficult years. Despite his hard childhood in Orlando, Stargell grew into a strong, athletic teenager after returning to California, learning baseball on the neighborhood fields in and around the projects. "White boys from richer families were given other alternatives such as the Boy Scouts, family vacations, and field trips…Baseball was all we had."[4]

At Encinal High School in Alameda, Stargell was probably only the third-best player on the team. Teammates Tommy Harper and Curt Motton, both of whom also went on to play in the majors, were more polished athletes at that point. Stargell was just a big raw-boned kid still growing into his body. He also wasn't far removed from a fairly serious knee injury suffered while playing football. But Pittsburgh Pirates' scout Bob Zuk spotted a glint of potential underneath Stargell's crude skills and signed him for $1,500 in August 1958.

For 1959 the Pirates assigned Stargell to a Class-D team that represented the towns of Roswell, New Mexico and San Angelo, Texas. Nothing in his background prepared him for life traveling around Eastern New Mexico and West Texas, a region that, for African-Americans, was as inhospitable as anywhere in the Jim Crow South. "People treated me like a dog." he remembered, in a rare moment of open bitterness.[5] According to Pittsburgh sportswriter Roy McHugh, Stargell seldom discussed all he went through that season but the scars remained. "By his manner, you'd never be aware he carried this around with him. But he did."[6]

Many restaurants in the area were white-only. On the road, while the white players dined in relative comfort, Stargell waited outside on the team bus, choking down homemade Spam and salami sandwiches. He and his minority teammates were not welcome at hotels or motels either, so they boarded at the homes of whichever people of color would take them in. The conditions typically were far from luxurious. "I lived on back porches in fold up beds."[7] On one trip, Stargell stayed with a woman who raised bait in her home. The darkness, humidity, and stench were so overwhelming it was like sleeping inside a tackle box.

Stargell said the turning point of his life and career came during a trip to Plainview, Texas that season. As he strolled to the ballpark, a man approached him and put a gun to his head. "Nigger, if you play in that game tonight, I'll blow your brains out." Even though he was terrified, he summoned the courage to take the field that evening. He later claimed that was the moment he became a man, more determined than ever to make it. "I couldn't go back home to the projects where we had prostitutes, pimps, some muggers, and there was no telling what would happen…[Baseball was] an avenue out of the ghetto."[8]

The young outfielder overcame the bigotry, ascended rapidly through the minors, and received the call to join the Pirates in September 1962. He was a little over his head as a rookie in 1963, but he asserted himself the following season, raising his average 30 points, blasting 21 home runs, and appearing as a pinch-hitter in the All-Star Game. The 1965 campaign was even better as he became a much more selective hitter and drove in 100 runs for the first time. Then came one of the best years of Stargell's career in 1966, when he batted .315 with 33 home runs and finished third in the National League in OPS.

That breakout season established an impressive benchmark. So when Stargell fell from that level in 1967 and 1968 reporters, fans, and even some in the Pirate organization began to see him as a bit of an underachiever and focused increased attention on his shortcomings. Although Stargell had put up fine numbers and made three National League all-star teams, it somehow seemed he should have been doing more.

To be sure, Stargell's game was not well-rounded. He was a graceless, plodding left fielder who hurt his team defensively. He had a strong, accurate arm and he did the best he could, but with his rickety knees he just couldn't cover enough ground, especially in a park as spacious as Forbes Field. First base would have been a natural spot for him, and he did play there now and then, but the Pirates were in no hurry to displace their regular first baseman, hard-hitting Donn Clendenon. He also battled numerous minor injuries which kept him out of lineup for short stretches. In his 20-year career, Stargell never played in more than 148 games in a season.

Early in his career Stargell was nearly helpless against left-handed pitching, so much so that his managers often benched him against tougher southpaws. He didn't make too much of a fuss about it, but he unquestionably thought he was getting a raw deal. "I'm the first to know left-handers bother me but if I see enough of them, I'm going hit them. Somebody got the idea I couldn't hit left-handers, so they took me out of the lineup. But if I keep playing against them, I gotta hit 'em."[9] The numbers, however, belie his argument. Through 1968, in nearly 500 career at-bats against lefties, Stargell batted a puny .192 with only 13 home runs.

Furthermore, Stargell's conditioning was an ongoing source of frustration for Pirate management. He regularly came into spring training overweight, but took it to an extreme in the winter of 1966-67, ballooning to a flabby 235 pounds. General manager Joe L. Brown was furious. He fined his rotund left fielder and put him on a crash diet to get him down to a target weight of 215, which Stargell found absurd. "I played at 222 last year and had my best season." At the end of May, he was hitting just .193. "Losing all that weight made me weak when the season started."[10] Eager to avoid a repeat of that debacle, the Bucs ordered Stargell work with a personal trainer the following winter. He reported to camp in the best shape of his life in 1968, but new manager Larry Shepard took one look at him and criticized him for being too muscle-bound. The guy couldn't win. "Pie Traynor [said] if the Pirates left me alone and quit worrying so much about my weight, I'd become the greatest home run hitter in Pirate history," Stargell wrote years later. "Pie was a wise old son of a gun."[11]

But starting in 1969, several important pieces fell into place for Stargell as he transformed himself from merely a very good player into the most prolific power hitter of the 1970s. A dismal .237 season in 1968 persuaded him to take Roberto Clemente's advice and switch to a heftier 38-ounce bat. "Suddenly the holes in his swing were gone," remembered teammate Nellie Briles. "That's when he really got dangerous. He stopped trying to pull everything."[12]

Additionally, the re-hiring of manager Danny Murtaugh in 1970 put Stargell's mind at ease. "When Danny first had to quit after the 1964 season because of his health, I felt like I was losing somebody."[13] He respected Murtaugh's quiet, understated way of running the team, which was a refreshing change for Stargell, who never saw eye-to-eye with Shepard or, especially, Harry Walker, who rode him about his weight incessantly. Walker even picked a fight with Stargell for bringing his dog to spring training. "I needed Danny's presence to re-kindle my confidence," he said.[14]

But perhaps the most critical change came when the Pirates relocated to Three Rivers Stadium. Stargell once claimed he could have hit 600 home runs had he played his entire career somewhere other than gargantuan Forbes Field, which was a daunting 436 feet to center field and 408 feet to right-center. Shepard suggested as much, telling *Baseball Digest* in 1969, "Next year when he gets into the new park with its normal dimensions he'll challenge Ruth, Maris, and all the home run records."[15]

In 1971, his first full season in the new home park, Stargell quieted his doubters and made his mark on the national stage. He served warning early in the year, setting a major league record for the month of April with 11 home runs. Despite constant pain from a knee injury that would require offseason surgery, he went on to lead the majors with 48 home runs and drove in a career-high 125, which helped carry Pittsburgh to a National League East title. Stargell endured a dismal postseason, batting just .132 with one extra-base hit and one RBI. But Roberto Clemente picked up the slack as the Bucs knocked off the Baltimore Orioles to capture their first World Series title since 1960.

Stargell continued his bombardment of National League pitching over the next three seasons, with 33 home runs in 1972 and then a league-leading 44 in 1973. He also led the majors in RBIs (119) in 1973 and topped both leagues in OPS in both 1973 and '74.

His impact, though, goes beyond those superb numbers. Although his statistics made him a star, it was his colorful persona and herculean strength that turned him into a beloved icon all around baseball, and especially in Pittsburgh. At 6-foot-2, Stargell was not a huge man but somehow he *looked* huge. He cut an imposing, swaggering figure and seemed to take perverse joy in messing with pitchers' minds. Everything about him was intimidating. In his later years he took to loosening up in the on deck circle not with a weighted bat but with a sledgehammer. As he stepped into the box he glared out toward the hill, ominously pinwheeling his bat around and around as the pitcher read the signs. Stargell had massive forearms, powerful wrists, and preternaturally quick hands, and as the pitch came home he unleashed a swing that was effortlessly violent, like a man cracking a whip. Even when he came up empty, just the sheer power behind his swing was menacing.

Some players have hit more home runs than Stargell, but perhaps no one has ever been able to hit balls farther with such regularity. He was so strong and generated such tremendous bat speed that when he really laid into one the result was often a blast of absurd, almost cartoonish proportions. In 61 years, only 18 home runs cleared the right field roof at Forbes Field. Stargell did it seven times. Only six homers landed in the upper deck at Three Rivers Stadium. Stargell did it four times. Only four balls have been hit completely out of Dodger Stadium. Stargell did it twice. In 1978, he launched one 535 feet into the shadowy recesses of Montreal's Olympic Stadium. The Expos organization commemorated the event by identifying the seat where the ball landed and painting it gold. As the Dodgers' Don Sutton remarked, "He didn't just hit pitchers. He took away their dignity."[16]

As he emerged as one of the game's great hitters, Stargell began to question whether he was being paid at a level commensurate with his talents. While baseball's biggest earners, Henry Aaron and Dick Allen, raked in salaries in the $200,000 range, the Pirates reportedly paid Stargell less than half that amount. "I don't feel right in their company," he told a reporter in 1973. "I need money to be with Aaron and the others. When I'm in their presence, I know I am not in that class, even though I feel I belong," adding, "You can damn near demand respect or command it if you got the money."[17] Stargell had made himself heard. In February 1974, the Pirates awarded him a new contract that made him one of the five highest-paid men in the game.

Stargell also was keenly aware of the lack of endorsement dollars coming his way. In a revealing interview with *Ebony* magazine in 1971, Stargell observed, "You see a few blacks [with endorsements] but that's tokenism. Clemente has been shaving for years. I eat cereal every morning. [Frank] Robinson drives cars."[18] But yet those opportunities for broader media exposure and extra income were few and far between for Stargell and other black athletes. "[Steelers backup quarterback] Terry Hanratty has a TV show and he's only been in Pittsburgh two years. Clemente has been here for 16 years and has done much more for the city and the first time I even saw Clemente on TV, outside of baseball, was on the *Mike Douglas Show* a year ago… That's a shame."[19]

Although Stargell sensed a lack of respect from society at large, he grew increasingly visible in Pittsburgh's African-American community in the 1970s. "I think the black ballplayer should be responsible to the black community. The people, in many ways, helped put him where he is. He should be visible to the kids in the ghetto."[20] Stargell liked to pass out t-shirts on Halloween and deliver turkeys to poor families on Christmas Eve. On a larger scale, he created a foundation that raised hundreds of thousands of dollars to fight sickle cell anemia, a potentially lethal blood disorder particularly prevalent among African-Americans.

Stargell also opened a popular fried chicken restaurant in Pittsburgh's predominantly African-American Hill District. Customers who were fortunate enough to have an order in when Stargell hit a home run got their meals for free. "You should see the people standing outside the store listening to their radios. They'll all run in and order when Willie's up," marveled the store's assistant manager. "Willie's real popular here. Not just because he gives away chicken when he hits one, but he's a real hero for baseball and for the blacks."[21]

By the late 1970s, it looked like Stargell was almost finished. His decline began in 1975, his first season as a full-time first baseman, when a broken rib limited him to 124 games. The next year he missed significant playing time to care for his wife Delores, who was stricken with a brain aneurysm and spent six weeks in a coma. Statistically, it was one of the worst seasons of his career. "The '76 season was hell. I couldn't concentrate. I could only see Delores with all this equipment strapped on her and my mind drifted quite a bit."[22] By 1977, his wife was out of the hospital and on the path to recovery but his season ended in July when he wrecked his elbow during a bench-clearing brawl with the Phillies.

But then suddenly Stargell revived his career in 1978. He earned National League Comeback Player of the Year honors, batting .295 with 28 home runs and 97 RBIs despite sitting out 40 games. With his expanding paunch and arthritic knees Stargell looked every day of his 38 years—and maybe a day or two beyond that. But he still approached his job with the wide-eyed enthusiasm of a rookie. "When I think of old, I think of 300-year old sheep," he joked. "It's a shame people dwell on age, because they give in to it."[23]

Stargell had acquired the nickname "Pops," which suited him well as the elder statesman and emotional center of a raucous, ethnically diverse Pirate clubhouse. In 1978, he began awarding small stars to his teammates whenever they pitched well, came up with a big hit, or pulled off a brilliant defensive play. By the end of the season in the late '70s and early '80s, players had their black caps festooned with gold Stargell stars. "I don't mind if somebody takes my bat, my glove, or my uniform, but please don't take my stars," said second baseman Phil Garner. "I earned those and I deserve them."[24]

Left fielder Bill Robinson said Stargell became kind of a father figure to his teammates. "Willie was our crutch. Anything you needed, any problems you had personally or in baseball, he took the burden."[25] When Steve Blass was struggling with the inexplicable wildness that eventually ended his career, Stargell was there. "When it was my turn to pitch [in a simulated game], Willie would always say 'I'll be first.' He did it every time. He would go into the cage without a batting helmet. It was almost as if he was saying, 'Go ahead. Hit me in the shoulder. Hit me in the ribs. It doesn't matter. Our relationship is stronger than that'...No one ever stood taller for me than Willie Stargell."[26]

The 1970s had been a frustrating time for the Pirates. Following their 1971 World Championship, they won three more National League East titles only to fall short in the NLCS each time. But in 1979, Stargell led them back to the promised land. His 32 home runs earned him a share of the National League Most Valuable Player Award. And in the postseason, where he had struggled so mightily eight years earlier, Stargell was a monster. He hit .455 in a three-game sweep of Cincinnati in the NLCS, then batted .400 with three home runs against Baltimore in the World Series. Just as they did in 1971, the Bucs rallied from a three-games-to-one deficit to take the Series in seven games. Stargell struck the deciding blow in Game Seven, a two-run homer in the sixth inning off Scott McGregor. For his heroics Stargell captured the World Series MVP award, while the Associated Press named him its Male Athlete of the Year.

The Pirates might have made it back to the postseason in 1980 if Stargell could have stayed in one piece. In just 67 games he homered 11 times and drove in 38 runs. But a July hamstring injury knocked him out for a month, and then recurring knee trouble ended his season prematurely. When he went on the shelf for good in mid-August, the Pirates were in first place; without him they went 16-28 the rest of the way and finished a distant third.

Stargell never played regularly again. He said by the early 1980s, "[m]y life revolved around pain."[27] Manager Chuck Tanner used him almost exclusively as a pinch-hitter the next two seasons. On Labor Day 1982, in the culmination of a season-long farewell tour around the league, the Pirates honored their captain by retiring his No. 8 in an emotional pregame ceremony. Stargell was such a widely respected and adored figure at this point that even President Ronald Reagan called to extend his best wishes.

Stargell's retirement years were difficult ones in many ways. In 1984, he and Delores split after nearly 18 years of marriage. Although she appreciated her husband's humanitarian spirit, she grew resentful of all the obligations he took on. "I said, how about your people at home? Charity begins at home." She said she knew long before their divorce that the marriage was doomed. "Everybody was pulling at him every which way. [It was] awful. He was never around."[28]

The following September at the Pittsburgh drug trials former teammate Dale Berra accused Stargell of providing him with amphetamines—a charge Stargell emphatically denied and which Commissioner Peter Ueberroth dismissed as ludicrous. Not long afterward the Pirates, under new ownership, dismissed Tanner, along with his entire staff, which included Stargell, who had just completed his first year as the team's hitting coach. But Stargell soon re-joined his old boss down south, where Tanner had agreed to manage the Atlanta Braves in 1986.

Stargell endured a couple of awkward homecomings during his two-and-a-half years in a Braves' uniform. Before one game in Pittsburgh a very young and already insolent Barry Bonds began hectoring Stargell with some trash talk. "Get out of here you old man!" Bonds hollered. "They forgot about you in Pittsburgh! I'm what it's all about now!" Bonds meant no harm, really; he was just trying to be funny. But Stargell, who stalked away silently, wasn't in on the joke. As Bonds scurried over muttering an apology, the normally affable Stargell turned and growled, "Boy, you better get some more lines on the back of your baseball card before you talk to me like that." [29]

An even more unpleasant incident occurred in 1988 when Stargell, stung by the Pirates' earlier refusal to consider him for their managerial opening, rejected the organization's plans to hold a Willie Stargell Night to celebrate his first-ballot election to the Baseball Hall of Fame. According to some media reports, Stargell demanded the Pirates buy him an expensive sports car or hand over a percentage of gate receipts if they wanted him to participate. But Stargell insisted compensation wasn't really the issue; his quarrel with Pirate management went deeper than that. "The last dealing I had with these Pirates, the new Pirates, the last thing they said to me was 'You're fired.' I haven't heard a word from the new Pirates since and then I hear they want to honor me."[30] When the Braves came to town a couple weeks later and the public address announcer introduced Stargell as the Braves' third base coach, the crowd of 20,000 reacted viciously, raining down boos on the man who was once a civic treasure. Tanner was appalled. "I wanted to go out there at that moment and pat that guy on the back ten times and gesture to the fans. You don't boo Willie Stargell....I felt so bad for the guy."[31]

Stargell spent nearly a decade in the Atlanta organization, serving as a roving minor-league batting instructor after being dismissed with Tanner and the rest of his staff in May 1988. Then in 1997 Kevin McClatchy, head of the Pirates new ownership group, reached out to Stargell, mended old wounds, and welcomed him back into the Pirate family as an assistant to general manager Cam Bonifay.

But by this time, although Stargell was not yet 60 years old, his health was declining steadily. He was struggling with high blood pressure and since 1996 had suffered kidney problems that required dialysis three times a week. Shortly after rejoining the Pirates he required surgery to remove part of his bowel, a complication of his high blood pressure. "He came very close to not surviving that hospital stay. I consider it a miracle that he survived," said his physician, James McCabe.[32] In the fall of 1999, doctors amputated part of his right index finger after an infection set in.

Stargell entered a hospital near his home in Wilmington, North Carolina to have his gallbladder removed in February 2001. He never recovered, and died at age 61 after suffering a massive stroke on April 9. He was survived by his third wife, Margaret Weller-Stargell and five children. Coincidentally, Stargell died the morning of the first game at Pittsburgh's new PNC Park. People laid flowers at the base of a statue of Stargell, which had been unveiled outside the stadium just days earlier. His death wasn't completely unexpected but it was a body blow for fans and old teammates nonetheless. "When we heard about Clemente's death at four o'clock in the morning, I went to Willie's house," Steve Blass told a reporter. "I'm not sure where to go this morning."33

At the time of his retirement, Stargell's 475 home runs tied him with Stan Musial for 15th on the all-time list. As legendary a power hitter as he was, one is still tempted to ask, "What if?" What if he hadn't played eight-and-a-half years in the home run graveyard of Forbes Field? What if his knees had held up? What if he had been more serious about staying in shape early in his career? Four-hundred-seventy-five home runs, of course, is an extraordinary achievement. But one could imagine how a consistently healthy, consistently fit Stargell shooting at a more inviting right field porch could have boosted that total to well over 500; maybe even, as he suggested himself, close to 600.

But this man was more than a home run total. When 55,000 people embraced an ailing Willie Stargell with a standing ovation on that October afternoon in 2000, it was only partly about statistics and championships. Pirate fans were saying "thank you" for two decades of memories, while also saluting his impact as a leader both in the clubhouse and in the city that adopted him and made him its own.

SOURCES

In addition to the sources cited in the notes, the author also consulted:

Baltimore Afro-American

New York Times

Time

Skirboll, Aaron, *The Pittsburgh Cocaine Seven* (Chicago: Chicago Review Press, 2010).

NOTES

1. Willie Stargell and Tom Bird, *Willie Stargell: An Autobiography* (New York: Harper & Row, 1984), 78.
2. Stargell and Bird, 13.
3. Stargell and Bird, 21.
4. Stargell and Bird, 42.
5. Randy Roberts, *Pittsburgh Sports: Stories From the Steel City* (Pittsburgh: University of Pittsburgh Press, 2002), 198.
6. Dave Kindred, The Sweetheart Called Pops," *The Sporting News*, May 7, 2001.
7. Roberts, 198.
8. *Ellenburg* (Washington) *Daily News*, March 25, 1976.
9. Les Biedermann, "Stargell Startles Bucs' Foes With Cannonading," *The Sporting News*, July 4, 1964.
10. *Pittsburgh Post-Gazette*, June 1, 1967.
11. Stargell and Bird, 118.
12. *USA Today*, April 10, 2001.
13. Bruce Markusen, *The Team That Changed Baseball: Roberto Clemente and the 1971 Pittsburgh Pirates* (Yardley, Pennsylvania: Westholme Publishing, 2006), Kindle DX version, Retrieved from Amazon.com, Chapter 5, para. 39.)
14. Stargell and Bird, 118.
15. *Baseball Digest*, December 1969.
16. *Los Angeles Times*, April 10, 2001.
17. Roberts, 200.
18. Lacy J. Banks, "Big Man, Big Heart, Big Bat," *Ebony*, October 1971.
19. Ibid.
20. Ibid.
21. *St. Petersburg Times*, June 11, 1971.
22. *Sports Illustrated*, August 20, 1979.
23. Ibid.
24. *The Daily Collegian*, September 26, 1979.
25. John McCollister, John, *Tales from the 1979 Pittsburgh Pirates: Remembering "The Fam-A-Lee"* (Champaign, Illinois: Sports Publishing, 2005), 40.
26. McCollister, 39, 42.
27. Stargell and Bird, 237.
28. Jimmy Scott, "The Dee Stargell Interview, Pt. 1, Jimmy Scott's High and Tight," Retrieved June 13, 2011 from http://www.jimmyscottshighandtight.com/node/1035.
29. Jeff Pearlman, *Love Me, Hate Me: Barry Bonds and the Making of an Antihero* (New York: HarperCollins, 2007), 89.
30. *Pittsburgh Press*, May 22, 1988.
31. Ibid.
32. *Pittsburgh Post-Gazette*, April 10, 2001.
33. *Pittsburgh Post-Gazette*, April 10, 2001.

Rennie Stennett

By Joseph Wancho

ON SEPTEMBER 16, 1975, THE PITTSBURGH Pirates were wrapping up a three-game series with the Chicago Cubs at Wrigley Field. They held a six-game lead over Philadelphia in the National League East Division and the season was growing old. With only 12 games remaining on the Pirates' schedule, time was indeed running out on the Phillies.

The drama on the North Side was short-lived as the Pirates sent 14 men to the plate in the first inning, scoring nine runs. Rennie Stennett led off with a double to right field, and singled to right in his next at-bat, later in the frame. He scored both times. He added a single to center in the third inning, and a double to left and single to right in fifth inning when the Pirates batted around again, sending 11 men to bat. The score was 18-0 and the carnage continued. Stennett singled to center in the seventh inning and tripled to right field in the eighth. He was then lifted for pinch-runner Willie Randolph.

The final score was Pirates 22, Cubs 0. It remains the worst defeat suffered by Chicago at Wrigley Field. For Stennett, it was a record-setting day, as he collected seven hits in seven at-bats, scored five runs, and drove in two. His seven hits tied the National League record for hits in a nine-inning game, set by Wilbert Robinson of the Baltimore Orioles in 1892. Stennett also tied a record with the most times getting two hits in one inning. "I got to the ballpark and I wasn't supposed to play that day. I had twisted my ankle and it was badly swollen," recalled Stennett. "But I taped up the ankle and I played. The first time up I hit a ball between (Cubs) first baseman Andre Thornton and the bag, and in my mind that told me that day I was gonna do good because as a right-handed hitter, when I'm hitting the ball to the right side, I know I'm hitting good. That was a shot, and it triggered something. I felt all I had to do was make contact and I was going to get a hit."[1]

Stennett told the team trainer, Tony Bartirome, to tell Pirates manager Danny Murtaugh to remove him from the game because of his ankle. But Murtaugh refused until Stennett made an out. "I came up to bat in the eighth inning for the seventh time and hit a line drive to right-center and they said (outfielder) Champ Summers could have caught it, but he dove and he missed it and I wound up with a triple."[2]

"I heard that when Uncle Robbie (Wilbert Robinson) was managing, whenever any of his players got six hits, he took him out of the game," quipped Murtaugh.[3] But Stennett was not done. The next night, he got three more hits at Philadelphia to set a new mark for most hits (10) in consecutive nine-inning games. The next evening, he collected two more hits, to give him 12 hits in three consecutive nine-inning games, tying a record.

Renaldo Antonio (Porte) Stennett was born on April 5, 1951, in Colon, Panama. He grew up in the same neighborhood as Rod Carew, and attended the same high school, Paraiso, as Carew had. Stennett was a multisport athlete, excelling in volleyball, basketball, and track. He especially excelled on the hardwood; he scored a school-record 45 points in a basketball game. But baseball was his true passion. At age 15, he was a pitcher on a sandlot team; his batterymate was Manny Sanguillen. At 21 Sanguillen was already in the Pirates' minor-league chain. Although both players hailed from Panama, there was a language barrier. Sanguillen was reared in Colon in the Republic of Panama, where Spanish is the dominant language. Stennett was raised in the Canal Zone, then a US possession, and did not speak Spanish. "I remember Rennie well," recalled Sanguillen. "Whenever I wanted to go out to the mound to talk to him, I had to ask the third baseman to come over and translate for us."[4]

At an early age, Stennett was approached by major-league teams about going to the United States. But on the advice of his father, who worked on Canal tugboats, he turned down the offers. "The Yankees, Giants, and Astros talked to me," said Stennett. "They wanted me to come to the States to further my education. But my father wanted me to remain at home and go through high school. I'm glad I did because I don't think I'd ever made it as a pitcher."[5]

After finishing school, Stennett signed a contract with C. Herbert Raybourn, a Pirates scout in the Canal Zone area. At 18, Stennett began his ascent through the Pirates' minor-league chain at Gastonia (North Carolina) of the Class-A Western Carolinas League. He was placed in the outfield, and finished sixth in the league in hitting when he batted .288. Stennett showed a high aptitude for hitting. In 1970 at Salem (Virginia) of the Class-A Carolina League, Stennett led the league in batting (.326), hits (176), and triples (9).

After the 1970 season, Stennett went to Bradenton to play in the Florida Instructional League. The conversion to second base began there, and it was a move he was welcomed. "I always wanted to be in the game and you're in the game at second base," said Stennett.[6] When he reported to Charleston (West Virginia) of the Triple-A International League for the 1971 season, he was inserted as the starter at second base. Manager Joe Morgan was thrilled with Stennett's progress, but wanted the youngster to work on going to his right on grounders up the middle. "He does everything else very well," said Morgan," and he has a whale of an arm."[7]

Stennett was enjoying another terrific season at Charleston in 1971 when he was called up to Pittsburgh. Starting second baseman Dave Cash and third baseman Richie Hebner were to begin back-to-back two-week drills in the military Reserve in July. Stennett made his major-league debut on July 10, 1971, against Atlanta. On August 5, utility infielder Jose Pagan was hit by a pitch in Montreal and suffered a broken left arm. Although it was it an unfortunate circumstance, it opened the door for Stennett to remain in the Steel City for the remainder of the season.

Stennett's defense at the keystone position was shaky at times and he was often replaced in the late innings for defensive purposes. But there was no denying his work with a bat. He put together an 18-game hitting streak from August 22 through September 10. It was the longest streak for a Pirate in two years. Fourteen of the games in the streak were of the multi-hit variety, as his batting average rose from .278 to .405

It was during this streak that Stennett became a part of baseball history. On September 1 Pittsburgh became the first team in major-league history to field an all-minority team to begin the game. The lineup card submitted by Murtaugh read:

Stennett, 2B
Clines, CF
Clemente, RF
Stargell, LF
Sanguillen, C
Cash, 3B
Oliver, 1B
Hernandez, SS
Ellis, P

The Pirates defeated the Phillies that night, 10-7. After the game, Murtaugh was asked about the significance of his lineup. He replied, "I put the best athletes out there. The best nine I put out there happen to be black. No big deal. Next question."[8]

In spite of Stennett's contributions to the Bucs' success, he was left off the 1971 postseason roster. Murtaugh chose to go with the veteran Pagan, who had returned to the team late in the season. The Pirates knocked off the San Francisco Giants in the NLCS, and they capped their year by winning the World Series, defeating Baltimore in seven games. After the Series, Murtaugh was moved to the front office. He had been sidelined during the year with chest pains, and the Pirates were concerned about his health. Bill Virdon, a star center fielder for Pittsburgh in the 1950s and 1960s, and the Pirates' hitting coach since, assumed the manager job.

With Cash entrenched at second base, Stennett seemed to be a player without a position. He put in time at shortstop and at all three spots in the outfield. The 1972 season was his fourth in pro ball, so there was a learning curve for Stennett when he was in the field. But he needed no such excuse when he was at the plate. "He hits everything we throw him," said the Reds' Johnny Bench.[9]

The Bucs captured the NL East Division again in 1972, and this time, Stennett was invited to the party. He led the club with six hits in the NLCS, but the Bucs were ousted by Cincinnati in five games.

However, the Pirates family was devastated when on December 31, 1972, Roberto Clemente lost his life. Clemente was aboard a cargo plane headed from San Juan to Nicaragua to deliver medical and food supplies to earthquake victims in Managua. Shortly after the 9:15 P.M. takeoff, the plane experienced engine problems and tried to return to San Juan International Airport, but it crashed after a series of explosions into the Atlantic Ocean about a mile-and-a-half from shore. There were no survivors.

Stennett recalled: "The only reason I was in Puerto Rico was because Roberto Clemente was supposed to play for San Juan, as he did every year, but after the World Series, he decided to take a rest. So they gave me his contract to take his place. It was my first year in the big leagues and Pittsburgh thought it would be good for me to play in Puerto Rico to gain some experience.

"That night, we went to Bob Johnson's apartment for the New Year's Eve party. Sometime during the night, somebody said, 'Look over the window, there's a ship on fire.' We all looked and we could see flames coming from the water. We all left the party and went home, and at about four o'clock in the morning, we all got a call that woke us up to tell us that Roberto's plane had crashed. Everybody got up and we went over to Clemente's house. It was sad. We just couldn't believe it.

"I'm not saying the flames we saw were Roberto's plane, but when you put everything together, that's what you have to think."[10]

The Pirates' 1973 season was bordered in black as a result of Clemente's death. Virdon was relieved of his duties on September 5, even though the Pirates were in second place, just three games behind the Cardinals. But their record was 67-69 at the time and Murtaugh came down once again from the front office to manage the club. Stennett belted a career-high 10 home runs. But his batting average dropped to a career-low .242. Once again he was in no-man's land as far as an everyday position was concerned. Virdon shuffled Stennett, Jackie Hernandez, and Gene Alley at shortstop until Dal Maxvill was acquired from Oakland in early July to solidify the position. "I wasn't myself," Stennett said of his 1973 batting woes. "Maybe I could blame it on not playing regularly, but I was at fault, too. I got into bad habits. I swung at bad pitches and never stopped."[11] His defense improved; he made only nine errors in 77 starts at the keystone spot. His fielding percentage was .981.

On October 18, 1973, Cash was dealt to Philadelphia for pitcher Ken Brett. The Pirates were looking for a quality starting pitcher, and felt that Cash would bring more quality their way. They also felt that Stennett was a better long-range option at second base, as he demonstrated more range than Cash. "It's a good feeling," said Stennett. "Just going to the ballpark every day and expecting to be in the lineup is something

that is bound to help me."[12] He was correct in his assumption, as his batting average rebounded to a more Stennett-like .291 in 1974. A snowmobile accident in February 1975 hindered Stennett at the start of the '75 season. But he finished strong, batting .367 in August and .330 in September, and batted .286 for the year. Stennett, who batted mostly leadoff in the Pirates batting order, drove in a career-high 62 runs in 1975.

Stennett was playing at a high level, in both the field and at bat for the Pirates. Noted for his hustle and grind-it-out style of play, he was a favorite in the hard-working city of Pittsburgh. "His achievements have gone unnoticed by many people," said Pirates general manager Joe Brown. "There hasn't been a player in baseball, not even Pete Rose, who has hustled more than Stennett this year."[13] Rennie's glove work also was coming around. He put together a streak of 47 errorless games while playing second base in 1974. "I don't worry about errors," said Stennett. "I play as hard as I can and if I make an error, I make an error. There is nothing I can do about it."[14]

Murtaugh was back as the full-time field manager, and the Bucs won the division title in 1974 and 1975. However, they were knocked out in the NLCS both years. Stennett's performance during those two seasons allowed the Pirates to trade one of their prized prospects, Willie Randolph. The Pirates packaged Randolph with Ken Brett and fellow pitcher Dock Ellis and sent them to the New York Yankees for pitcher Doc Medich on December 11, 1975.

The Pirates finished second to Philadelphia in 1976. After the season the Pittsburgh family suffered another major loss, when Murtaugh, who had retired after the season, suffered a stroke and died on December 2.

Under new manager Chuck Tanner, Stennett was enjoying his best offensive year in the majors in 1977. He was batting .336 and batting sixth in the lineup, which was more to his liking. "I am a .300 hitter," said Stennett. "I'll always be aggressive at the plate. That's my style. Maybe I'm not flashy. Mainly, I swing, and I've been getting an awful lot of hits on first pitches."[15] One part of his game was sliding. Stennett had the habit of jumping before sliding, and bruised his right shoulder while sliding into second base. "I had better learn to slide or I am going to break something some day," he said.[16]

Stennett's words were prophetic when on August 21, 1977, anticipating a force play that never occurred; he fractured a bone in his right fibula and dislocated his right ankle sliding into second base against the Giants. He was lost for the year. Phil Garner was moved from third base to second and Dale Berra was called up from Triple-A Columbus to man the hot corner. It was a big blow to the team, which was trailing the Phillies by 6½ games at the time. The Pirates had already lost Willie Stargell on July 8, when he attempted to break up a fight during a game with the Phillies and got a pinched nerve in his left elbow for his trouble. Stargell was waiting for surgery and was out for the season. Stennett was 12 at-bats shy of qualifying for the batting championship. Teammate Dave Parker won the honors with a .338 batting average.

Stennett was back to being a utility infielder in 1978. Because of his injuries, restrictions were placed on the games he would be allowed to play. He would not play both games of a doubleheader, and he would sit if the field was slick, or judged too dangerous to let him play. A bone spur developed over his right ankle, and Stennett was limited to 79 starts at second base and six at third. For the third straight season, the Pirates finished in second place to the Phillies.

The 1979 Pirates won their sixth division title, clearly making Pittsburgh the dominant team of the 1970s. The theme "We Are Family" spread through the Steel City, as they were led by co-league MVP Willie "Pops" Stargell. In retrospect, it may have been best for Stennett to take the 1978 season off in order for his ankle to heal 100 percent. Unfortunately for him, his playing time at second was split with Garner, who was also playing third. That was until a trade with San Francisco brought Bill Madlock to Pittsburgh in late June. While Madlock had been playing second base with the Giants, Tanner immediately returned the two-time batting champion to third base. Garner became the full-time starter at second; while Stennett started only 17 games after the All Star break.

The Pirates swept the Reds in the NLCS, although it was hard-fought; two of the games went into extra innings. Pittsburgh then dug out of a three-games-to-one deficit in the World Series to beat the Orioles. It was the second time in the decade that the Pirates topped Baltimore in the fall classic. But for Stennett, he was merely a benchwarmer in the postseason, totaling one at-bat between both series. "Our mentality with the Pirates was that if we were 0-for-3 and we came up in the ninth inning with the winning run on base and knocked in that run, it was like having a 4-for-4 day," he said. "We felt we couldn't lose."

Stennett sensed he needed a change of scenery. He entered the re-entry draft and was claimed by the limit of 14 teams. San Francisco outbid the competition, and Stennett was the proud owner of a new five-year, $3 million pact. But Stennett never could get untracked in San Francisco. At times he was replaced by Joe Strain, a journeyman infielder, which caused Stennett to seethe. Manager Dave Bristol was not the motivational type of manager "It's very tough to play for Dave Bristol," said Stennett. "He puts too much pressure on players. He just doesn't communicate. He's old-school and you can't depend on him for any motivation."

Many of the other veteran players shared the same sentiment as Stennett, but because of the contract he signed, he carried much of the criticism in the media. Specifically, where did Rennie come off popping off about Bristol after hitting a measly .244?

Bristol was fired after the 1980 season and was replaced by Frank Robinson. But more importantly, two-time MVP Joe Morgan was signed as a free agent. Even though Little Joe was nearly eight years older than Stennett, he was named the Giants' starting second baseman. A good portion of the 1981 season was washed away by a players strike, forcing the leagues to play a split season. San Francisco acquired second baseman Duane Kuiper from the Cleveland Indians after the 1981 season. Kuiper, who played for Robinson when Robby piloted the Tribe, was set to be the backup to Morgan. Stennett was released on April 2, 1982.

Stennett played for Reynosa of the Mexican League in 1982. In 1983, before retiring on July 8, he played in 55 games for Wichita of the Triple-A American Association, a Montreal Expos affiliate managed by Felipe Alou. He moved his family (Gail, his wife, and their two children, Renee and Stevie) to Florida. There he owned a carpet-cleaning business with a friend. The Stennett clan moved to Boca Raton, where he joined Davimos Sports Management in 1986. Sanguillen was a partner in the firm that counseled ballplayers, mostly Latins, on life outside the foul lines.

At 38, Stennett wanted to give baseball one more chance and he signed with the Pirates in 1989. However, he was cut at the end of the spring training. For his career, Stennett batted .274, with 41 home runs, 1,239 hits, and 432 RBIs. His career fielding percentage at second base was .978.

As of 2016 Stennett resided in Boca Raton. He kept in shape by playing tennis and enjoyed his three grandchildren. He has participated in Pirates Fantasy Camp, but also coached baseball back in his native Panama on the professional level.

NOTES

1 Phil Pepe, *Talkin' Baseball: An Oral History of Baseball in the 1970s* (New York: Ballantine Publishing Group, 1998), 190.

2 Pepe, 191.

3 Dave Anderson, "7 for 7-Twice in a Century of Baseball," *New York Times*, September 20, 1975.

4 Charley Feeney, "Rookie Stennett Plugs Hole at Keystone," *The Sporting News* September 18, 1971: 3.

5 Ibid.

6 A.L. Hardman, "Conversions Rimp and Rennie Are Key to Charlies' Success," *The Sporting News,* June 26, 1971: 43.

7 Ibid.

8 George Skornickel, "Characters with Character: Pittsburgh's All Black Lineup," *Baseball Research Journal*, Fall 2011.

9 Charley Feeney, "Bucs' Stennett Earns Reprieve With Hot Bat," *The Sporting News,* May 27, 1972: 13.

10 Pepe, 93-94.

11 Charley Feeney, "Bat Skid Could Give Stennett a Boost," *The Sporting News*, February 2, 1974: 32.

12 Ibid.

13 Charley Feeney, "Pressure Brings Out Star in Stennett, Rooker," *The Sporting News,* "October 12, 1974: 3.

14 Ibid.

15 Charley Feeney, "Steady Stennett—Pirate Keystone Jewel," *The Sporting News*, July 2, 1977: 13.

16 Ibid.

Frank Taveras

By Rory Costello

WHEN THE 2015 SEASON OPENED, Dominicans made up nearly 10 percent of the major leagues' talent pool.[1] They weren't so common in 1971, though, when Frank Taveras made it to the majors for the first time. He was just the 28th of his countrymen to reach the top level—this list has now grown well beyond 600.

Taveras played eight full big-league seasons and parts of three others from 1971 to 1982. He was a type of player who once was archetypal—the light-hitting but speedy shortstop. In 4,399 big-league plate appearances, Taveras hit just two home runs, and his slugging percentage was just .313. But he stole 300 bases, including 70 in 1977, when he led the majors.

With the glove, Taveras was erratic; he made many brilliant plays and muffed easy ones.[2] As a result, the fans in Pittsburgh, where he played most of his big-league career, often booed him. "Every time he made a mistake, everybody was all over him," said Chuck Tanner, his manager with the Pirates from 1977 until April 1979, when Taveras was traded to the New York Mets for Tim Foli. "I think he's always had a tough time in Pittsburgh because the fans thought he couldn't do anything right even the year that he led the league in stolen bases."[3] Taveras was also "an emotional player [who] got extremely upset by criticism and rulings by official scorers."[4]

Franklin Crisóstomo Taveras Fabián was born on December 24, 1949, though at times his year of birth was listed as 1950. Taveras's birthplace was Las Matas de Santa Cruz, though again, while he was an active player, it was sometimes given as Villa Vásquez, a place about half an hour north by bus.[5]

Las Matas de Santa Cruz is the largest city in Monte Cristi province, in the northwestern corner of the Dominican Republic. It's really a town, though; even today its population is less than 20,000. Further information about Frank's parents, Señor Taveras and Señora Fabián, is not presently available. Frank was one of at least five children. He had two brothers (Ramón and Rodrigo) and two sisters (Magalys and Eunice).[6]

The baseball culture runs deep in the Dominican Republic, including Monte Cristi. The local heroes were the Olivo brothers, Diómedes and Chi-Chi, who both made it to the majors as "rookies" in the 1960s, when they were 41 and 35, respectively. It is a rural area; the young Frank Taveras grew up playing ball in the countryside.

It's no surprise that the man who signed Taveras was Howie Haak, the superscout who blazed trails in searching for talent across Latin America. Haak got Taveras for a bonus of $3,500 in January 1968. At the time, the 18-year-old shortstop was playing for the National Police team. He was supposed to be serving police duty at a livestock fair, but he paid a friend 20 Dominican pesos (then officially equal to US$20) to take his place. He then went to Estadio Quisqueya in Santo Domingo, where he met Haak, who took him to the hotel El Embajador. There the signing took place.[7]

Taveras then began his pro career in the spring of 1968. In his first three seasons as a minor leaguer, he played largely at the Class-A level, with five different teams. In the winter of 1968-69, he began to play in his homeland's professional league. He joined Águilas Cibaeñas and spent 10 seasons with that club. There too, his first three years were a learning experience, but mainly from the bench—he played 10 to 20 games per season, about 30 percent of the team's total. He hit .292 in 130 total at-bats.[8] At home, Taveras had two nicknames: *Boroto* (which apparently has no particular meaning) and *Berenjena* ("Eggplant").[9] Their origins are uncertain.

The Pirates invited Taveras to spring training in 1969. It was probably then that the young Dominican first met the great Roberto Clemente, whom he later called "my guide, my mentor, my counselor."[10]

At age 21 in 1971, Taveras began a rapid ascent. He played 87 games in Double A and 48 at Triple A.

According to one report, he "fielded brilliantly" after joining the Pirates' top affiliate, in Charleston, West Virginia. The Charlies' manager, Joe Morgan (who later became skipper of the Boston Red Sox), said, "If I had known Taveras was going to play shortstop the way he did, he would have been in our lineup sooner, and could have meant eight or 10 more victories to us."[11]

When the major-league rosters expanded that September, Taveras got his first call-up to "The Show." He got into one game for the eventual World Series champs, on September 25 at Shea Stadium in New York. That afternoon's contest ran 15 innings. In the top of the 15th, with a runner on second base and one out, Mets-killer Willie Stargell was intentionally walked. Taveras came on as a pinch-runner, but the next batter, Carl Taylor, grounded into a 6-4-3 double play.

In the winter of 1971-72, Taveras became a regular for Águilas Cibaeñas — and a member of a Dominican League champion for the first time. Therefore, he got to play in the Caribbean Series, in which the region's winter-ball champions faced each other in a round-robin tournament. Taveras was on three other Dominican champion teams (in 1975, 1976, and 1978). He recalled with particular satisfaction the battles against the Licey Tigres.[12] Unfortunately for Frank, the Dominican team did not win any of the four Caribbean Series in which he appeared. Overall, he hit .243 in that competition (19-for-78, all singles, in 21 games).[13]

Taveras spent all of the US minor-league season in 1972 with Charleston. That June, Pittsburgh beat writer Charley Feeney noted that the Pirates were keeping a close watch on the young shortstop, saying that he could be called up if Gene Alley's knee problems continued.[14] Soon after, Taveras was the starting shortstop for the International League All-Star Team, which faced the Atlanta Braves at Norfolk, Virginia, on July 10. That September the Pirates called him up again, and he got into four games as a substitute shortstop. He went hitless in his first three big-league at-bats. He also witnessed Clemente's 3,000th hit in the majors.

Taveras returned to Charleston once more, in 1973. The previous November, Pirates manager Bill Virdon had said, "Taveras has to play. I'm not looking at him as a utilityman. I would rather have him playing every day at Charleston than sitting on our bench."[15] Ahead of him in Pittsburgh were veterans Alley and Jackie Hernández, who had been with the Pirates since 1963 and 1971, respectively. Neither man was known for his hitting, yet that July Pittsburgh obtained an even lighter-hitting glove man — Dal Maxvill — to play short.

In the middle of the 1973 season, Charley Feeney wrote that Taveras's stock had slid with the Pittsburgh front office.[16] The Pirates did not call him up after Charleston won the International League pennant. Nonetheless, by the end of the year he was still widely regarded as one of the blue-chip prospects in the IL.[17]

After the 1973 season, the big-league careers of both Alley and Hernández were over. Alley retired and Hernández wound up trading places with Taveras — in 1974, the Cuban went to Charleston and the Dominican made the Pittsburgh roster, never to return to the minors. In search of younger players who could put speed in the lineup, the Pirates released Maxvill on April 20. The Associated Press wrote, "Taveras has long been regarded as the heir apparent to the post. … Pirates' officials feel Taveras has all the tools to become a top-flight infielder — the arm, speed, and range. Only his steadiness is questioned."[18]

"They really surprised me," said Taveras in 1975. "Maxvill was a good player and he'd been around a long time." During the first half of the season, Taveras alternated with Mexican shortstop Mario Mendoza, but Frank carried the load at short during the second half. He committed 31 errors, but credited second baseman Rennie Stennett with helping him to improve in the field. In 126 games (107 starts at shortstop), Taveras hit .246 with no homers and 26 RBIs. Batting coach Bob Skinner encouraged him to choke up on the bat to gain greater control and make better contact.[19]

It's true of athletes in general, but psychology was an especially important factor for Taveras. He said that Danny Murtaugh, the Pirates' outstanding manager, "gave me the confidence to realize my game without pressure."[20]

After missing the playoffs in 1973, Pittsburgh won the National League East again in both 1974 and 1975.

THE 1979 PITTSBURGH PIRATES

The Pirates lost both times in the NL Championship Series, first to Los Angeles and then to Cincinnati. That was the only big-league postseason action for Taveras, who got into five games overall with one hit in nine at-bats. He wept in disappointment over not reaching the World Series.[21]

Taveras (who sported a bushy Afro in those days) remained the Pirates' primary shortstop from 1975 through 1978. Mario Mendoza was also with Pittsburgh throughout that period, but despite his soft hands, Mendoza's notoriously weak hitting kept him in reserve. After the 1976 season, the Pirates traded away another player who became a good major-league shortstop, Craig Reynolds.

During the 1975-78 period, Taveras averaged 146 games, 140 starts at shortstop, and 576 plate appearances per season. He hit .250, with one home run and 114 RBIs. The subject of Taveras's power—or lack thereof—came up in a friendly bet with Willie Stargell. In an April 1976 exhibition game, Taveras hit an inside-the-parker off Al Hrabosky. Stargell said, "Told him last year there ain't no way he can do it [hit a homer]. And I told him if he did I'd pay him 25 bucks during an exhibition game and $100 during the season. ... He's been telling me all spring how he's been lifting weights and how strong he is."[22]

On August 5, 1977, Taveras finally got his first round-tripper in a big-league regular-season game (he'd hit six in the minors). It was an inside-the-park grand slam off Doug Capilla of the Reds at Cincinnati's Riverfront Stadium. It came after Taveras was at the center of a bench-clearing brawl in the opener of that night's doubleheader. Veteran Cincinnati reliever Joe Hoerner plunked Taveras in the ninth inning because he thought that the shortstop had been rubbing it in by stealing a base in the third when the Pirates were already up 7-0. Taveras retaliated by throwing his bat, and in the ensuing melee, Hoerner punched Taveras in the face while Reds catcher Bill Plummer was holding Frank's arms.[23]

Controlling his temper and dealing with the displeasure of fans remained difficult for Taveras. One stretch in early July 1977 captured this. After a tough 14-inning loss on July 1, in which he went 0-for-6 and

was ejected, he reportedly had harsh words for umpire Ed Sudol and was fined by the league. On July 5 he tossed his batting helmet in disgust when the home crowd booed him in each of his four at-bats. He said, "People who watch baseball think bad of me because I'm not hitting the ball like you're supposed to. But you've got to take it because they pay to get in."[24]

Taveras emerged as a major basestealing threat in 1976, when he swiped 58 and got caught just 11 times. "The Pittsburgh Stealer" became his nickname. He credited the tutelage of Maury Wills, one of the all-time greats in this area, whom the Pirates had retained as an instructor during the previous Dominican winter season. The sessions ran for just two weeks but had lasting impact. Wills gave Taveras a variety of technical tips—but perhaps even more important, said Taveras, was how "he taught me not to be afraid."[25]

When Taveras led the majors with 70 steals in 1977, he got caught just 18 times. On September 17, 1977, he stole his 64th base of the year at Montreal's Olympic Stadium. That broke the club record of 63, set by Max Carey in 1916. Omar Moreno set a new Bucs standard in 1978, and topped it in each of the next two seasons.

Yet many years later, Taveras still prized the replica base he was awarded for setting his record.[26]

Among opposing pitchers, Taveras found Steve Carlton and Rick Reuschel the most difficult to steal against. Carlton had a way of lulling runners into moving off first base with a slow motion to the plate; then he would look to trap them. Reuschel had an excellent pickoff move.[27]

In 1978, however, Taveras was much less successful as a basestealer; he stole 46 but opposing catchers nailed him a league-high 25 times. However, he reached a career high with 182 base hits. He thought that curbing his winter-ball play and lifting weights helped him keep up his strength as the season wore on. He was also trying to stay calmer, especially with umpires.[28]

In his last winter with Águilas Cibaeñas, 1977-78, Taveras played just nine regular-season games. He concluded his career at home with a batting average of .265 in 1,349 at-bats across 364 games. He never hit a homer in Dominican play, but he stole 64 bases.[29]

With the glove, Taveras averaged 32 errors a year in the majors from 1975 through 1978. He made three in the first 11 games in 1979. That April 19, Pittsburgh dealt Taveras to the Mets for Foli—who was riding the bench in New York—and minor-league pitcher Greg Field. "The trade came shortly after a home game in which [Taveras] made an error on one ball and then failed to charge one he should have had."[30] The next inning, Dale Berra replaced Taveras. The Pirates announced that Taveras had "an intestinal virus."[31]

When double-play partner Rennie Stennett heard about the trade, he said, "[Taveras] appeared to be playing in a trance for the last few days. I don't know what it was, but I wish him good luck in New York."[32] Chuck Tanner added, "He's a good ballplayer and I think he'll do better in a new location."[33]

Howie Haak opposed the trade. That October, after the Pirates had won the NL pennant, the scout said, "I thought we were giving up too much range in Taveras. I told them my objections. They went ahead and made the trade anyway." As UPI wrote, it turned out to be the best advice the Pirates never took.[34] The fiery Foli was steadier in the field, as expected, and became an important cog in the 1979 World Series champion team. "I doubt if he ever helped any club more than he helped the '79 Pirates," said Joe L. Brown, the team's former general manager, in 1989.[35]

Meanwhile, Taveras upheld Tanner's prediction. Joe Torre, then the Mets' manager, said in May 1979, "In the Taveras we've played against, and the Taveras we're playing with, the reason for complaints hasn't really been seen."[36] Haak also noted that October, "As it turned out, people in New York say that Taveras is playing the best shortstop the Mets have ever seen."[37] That was significant, because for many years the team had a very capable man at the position, Bud Harrelson. The arrival of Taveras also enabled Doug Flynn, a fine glove man, to play at second base, his best spot.

The Mets were then mired in one of the dreariest periods in the history of the franchise. Taveras remained their starting shortstop from the time he arrived through the strike-interrupted season in 1981. Because of scheduling differences in 1979, he played in a league-leading 164 games that year. Only six men have ever reached that mark in a single season.[38]

Taveras cleared a big-league fence for the only time on August 18, 1979. Again the scene was Cincinnati's Riverfront Stadium; he hit a solo shot off Mike LaCoss of the Reds. With the Mets that year, Taveras also had nine triples, which tied a club record, and 42 steals, which was a new mark for the team (whose history to that point was short and marked by anemic offense).

Taveras started 131 games at short for the Mets in 1980, hitting a career-high .279 with no homers, 25 RBIs, and 32 steals—he was caught 18 times. He gave credit to his wife for helping him to hit well after a slow start, saying that she told him to stand up straighter. He also bunted his way on frequently.[39] Taveras formed a good (albeit punchless) double-play combo with Flynn. However, he later said that Shea Stadium had one of the worst infields in the league, "especially after football started."[40] (The New York Jets of the NFL shared the ballpark then.)

In 1981 Taveras started 73 of the team's 105 games. His basic batting line fell off to .230-0-11, and he had just 16 steals. That September New York called up rookie Ron Gardenhire, who became the Mets' new starting shortstop in 1982. Taveras didn't like the way he was used and asked twice to be traded.[41] The Mets obliged, sending him to the Montreal Expos for pitcher Steve Ratzer in December 1981.

With the Expos in 1982, Taveras competed for the shortstop job with Chris Speier. He proclaimed "I'm not a backup player. I expect to play between 80 and 100 games at shortstop."[42] He wound up as a little-used reserve, though he got a brief trial as the starting second baseman. He got into 48 games, including 19 at second—the only time he played a position other than shortstop in the majors.[43] He hit .161-0-4 in 98 plate appearances. Montreal released the 32-year-old in mid-August, and his big-league career came to an end.

In October 1982 the Pirates gave Taveras a minor-league contract and invited him to spring training. He never agreed to terms, though, and general manager Pete Peterson withdrew the offer.[44]

After this retirement without formal notice, Taveras remained in the Dominican Republic. For three years, from 1999 through 2001, he worked for the Pirates organization as Latin American field coordinator. Among other players, he supervised Aramis Ramírez, who emerged as a star in 2001.[45]

Mainly, however, he dedicated himself to religion as a member of the Charismatic Catholic movement. In 2007 he said, "Always in the afternoons I go out to preach. I spent most of my time educating those who seek God." He had one other great passion: fishing. He became a regular at the tournaments held off Cabeza de Toro Beach, in Punta Cana, on the eastern tip of the Dominican Republic. He won the tourney twice.[46]

Taveras and his wife, Sotera Vargas, had two children: Franklin Jr. and Máximo.[47] Franklin Jr. played in the minors and independent leagues from 1993 through 2002. He went on to become a minor-league coach and a scout. Among the numerous players whom he has helped to sign, the most notable to date (as of 2015) was pitcher Michael Pineda.

Among the uniform numbers retired by Águilas Cibaeñas is 10, worn by both Taveras (who was honored in January 1999) and another shortstop, Félix Fermín.[48] In 2007, the Hall of Fame of Dominican Sports inducted Frank Taveras.

NOTES

1 "Opening Day Rosters Feature 230 Players Born Outside the U.S.," MLB.com, April 6, 2015. The pool consisted of 868 players—750 active players on 25-man rosters, plus 118 more on disabled or restricted lists. There were 83 Dominicans.

2 Pohla Smith, United Press International, "Foli Hopes to Make Fans Forget Taveras," May 1, 1979.

3 Associated Press, "Mets Get Taveras for Foli," April 20, 1979.

4 Smith, "Foli Hopes to Make Fans Forget Taveras."

5 This is visible in various editions of *The Sporting News Official Baseball Register*.

6 "Carlton y Reuschel, difíciles de robarle," *Listín Diario* (Santo Domingo, Dominican Republic), September 15, 2007.

7 "Carlton y Reuschel, difíciles de robarle."

8 Cuqui Córdova, "Béisbol de ayer: Franklin Taveras," *Listín Diario*, April 5, 2008. The Águilas played 48 games in 1968-69 and 51 in 1969-70, according to final league standings published in *The Sporting News*, which did not publish that table in the 1970-71 season. The regular-season schedule in 1970-71 was 60 games, as can be determined by the 33-27 record of that year's champion, Licey. However, not all teams played the same number of games each season.

9 Hugo López Morrobel, "Los apodos de peloteros," *El Día* (Santo Domingo, Dominican Republic), February 5, 2014. With regard to the meaning of "Boroto", the answer comes from Dominican native Eddy Olivo Cruz.

10 Bienvenido Rojas, "Franklin Taveras dice Clemente fue su guía," *Diario Libre* (Santo Domingo, Dominican Republic), September 17, 2007.

11 Bill Christine, "Deep 'Snow Job' Convinces Alley, Pirates' Unsigned Reduced to 2," *Pittsburgh Press*, February 20, 1972: D-1.

12 "Carlton y Reuschel, difíciles de robarle."

13 Alfonso Araujo Bojórquez, *Series del Caribe: Narraciones y Estadísticas, 1949-2001, Volume 2*, Colegio de Bachilleres del Estado de Sinaloa (Culiacán, Sianaloa, Mexico), 2002: 117.

14 Charley Feeney, "Bucco Super Subs Building a Fire Under the Regulars," *The Sporting News*, June 17, 1972: 7.

15 Charley Feeney, "Playing Games: Rapping With Bill Virdon," *Pittsburgh Post-Gazette*, November 30, 1972: 23.

16 Feeney, "Playing Games: Some Shorties."

17 A.L. Hardman, "Velez, Taveras Rate as Int's Best," *The Sporting News*, October 13, 1973: 29.

18 Associated Press, "Bucs Cut Dal; Downing 'Catches On,'" April 22, 1974.

19 Ed Rose Jr., "Taveras Never Heard of Sophomore Jinx," *Beaver County* (Pennsylvania) *Times*, March 12, 1975: D-3.

20 Rojas, "Franklin Taveras dice Clemente fue su guía."

21. "Carlton y Reuschel, difíciles de robarle."
22. Ed Rose Jr., "Taveras (honest) hauls out lumber," *Beaver County Times* (Beaver, Pennsylvania), April 7, 1976: D-1.
23. Fred McMane, United Press International, "Taveras Scores Knockout After Decking," August 6, 1977.
24. "Pirate Shortstop Hazy About Sudol Death Wish," Associated Press, July 5, 1977.
25. United Press International, Scott MacLeod, "Pirates' Taveras Credits 'Teacher,'" August 5, 1976.
26. "Carlton y Reuschel, difíciles de robarle."
27. "Carlton y Reuschel, difíciles de robarle."
28. "Self-Control Taveras Goal," Associated Press, March 28, 1978; "Frank Taveras: Pirate Shortstop Has Hot Bat, a New Image," Associated Press, June 23, 1978.
29. Córdova, "Béisbol de ayer: Franklin Taveras."
30. Smith, "Foli Hopes to Make Fans Forget Taveras."
31. Charley Feeney, "Pirates Ship Taveras to Mets, Acquire Foli," *Pittsburgh Post-Gazette*, April 20, 1979: 39.
32. Feeney, "Pirates Ship Taveras to Mets, Acquire Foli."
33. "Mets Get Taveras for Foli."
34. United Press International, "Pirate Scout Opposed Deal for Tim Foli," October 10, 1979.
35. Ed Bouchette, "The Search Goes On: Bucs Still Looking for Shortstop to Replace Alley," *Pittsburgh Post-Gazette*, April 3, 1989: B-4.
36. Jim O'Brien, "Who Got Better of Taveras Trade?," *Pittsburgh Press*, May 15, 1979: B-9.
37. "Pirate Scout Opposed Deal for Tim Foli."
38. In 1962 Maury Wills (Dodgers) played in 165 and José Pagan (Giants) played in 164. That year those two teams faced each other in a three-game playoff. In 1965 Ron Santo and Billy Williams each played in 164 games for the Cubs; César Tovar also played in 164 for the Twins in 1967. Those three men achieved their totals because their teams each played in two games that ended in ties, which were counted in individual statistics but not in the standings.
39. Dan Donovan, "Taveras' New Stance a Big Hit With Mets," *Pittsburgh Press*, June 1, 1980: D-8.
40. Ian MacDonald, "Dogfight for Infield Spots as Taveras Arrives," *Montreal Gazette*, March 8, 1982.
41. Ibid.
42. Ibid.
43. In the minors, he had played some second base and occasionally appeared at third; he had also played second at times in winter ball.
44. Bill Stieg, "Farewell to Frank," *Pittsburgh Post-Gazette*, December 17, 1982: 20. Charley Feeney, "Pittsburgers," *The Sporting News*, December 27, 1982: 40.
45. "Carlton y Reuschel, difíciles de robarle." Newspaper transaction listings show that the Pirates named Taveras Latin American field coordinator in November 1999. John Perrotto, "This Time, Bucs Say Ramirez Is Ready," *Beaver County Times*, March 9, 2000, B1.
46. "Carlton y Reuschel, difíciles de robarle."
47. "Taveras se regocija al ver concretarse un gran sueño," *Listín Diario*, September 15, 2007.
48. Cuqui Córdova, "Béisbol de ayer," *Listín Diario*, April 12, 2008.

Kent Tekulve

By Bob Hurte

AT THE PIRATES' MINOR-LEAGUE PITCH-ing camp in 1970, Harding Peterson, the team's minor-league director, told two pitching prospects to abandon their side-arm pitching delivery. Fortunately neither listened, as each would become a Pirate World Series hero, with Bruce Kison starring in 1971 and Kent Tekulve in 1979 with the "We Are Family" champs. During offseason banquets, Tekulve said, "That's how smart you need to be as the general manager of a World Series champion."[1]

Kenton Charles Tekulve was born on March 5, 1947, in Cincinnati to Edna and Henry Tekulve, and his younger brother Jerry came along a few years later. Kent was named after a used-car dealer his parents patronized and said, "I might be the only major leaguer ever named after a used car dealer!"[2]

Tekulve's father pitched in semipro leagues in Ohio and shared his love of baseball with his son.

The Tekulves lived in Fairfield, a suburb of Cincinnati. His father drove a truck for the Kroger grocery-store chain, and his mother was a purchasing agent for Mercy Hospital in Hamilton, Ohio. Kent began playing in Little League at 9 years old, with Henry as his coach. (Jerry started pitching at 11.) Kent played Little League and Babe Ruth League. He made the high-school team at Hamilton Catholic as a freshman but was cut as a sophomore. Unlike other high-school pitchers, he did not bat cleanup and play another position on the days he was not pitching. Kent always batted ninth and only pitched. He earned a varsity letter in his junior and senior years.

After high school, Tekulve attended Marietta College (1966-69). It was here that his side-arm style began developing into a roundhouse delivery. He recorded a 0.94 ERA during his senior year and was selected to the All-Ohio Athletic Conference second team. (The press box at Don Schaly Stadium was renamed the Kent Tekulve Media Building in 1994.)

No one drafted Tekulve after his college career, although he was invited to a tryout at Forbes Field in Pittsburgh in July 1969. When he got there, he was not asked to pitch. "I just lolled around in the stands and watched," Tekulve said.[3]

Tekulve later learned that the snub was intentional. The coaches found his running inability to be funny. This seemed unfair, since his forte was pitching. Years later, Tekulve commented, "Now that was ridiculous. If I could run, I'd be stealing bases."[4] Eventually, after everybody left, he got a chance to throw. Dick Coury, a Pirates scout, signed him on the spot. Two nights later he was pitching for the Geneva Pirates of the New York-Penn League. The next season, 1970, the Pirates switched Tekulve to relief at Salem, Virginia, of the Carolina League. Tekulve moved on to Sherbrooke of the Double-A Eastern League in 1972, and experimented with what became his trademark submarine delivery. He patterned himself after Ted Abernathy, whom he had watched pitching for the Reds. Pitching exclusively in relief for Sherbrooke in 1973, Tekulve won 12 games, tied for the lead in the Eastern League.

In 1974 Tekulve began the season at Triple-A Charleston, then was called up in May. He made his major-league debut on May 20, 1974, giving up a hit and no runs while pitching one inning of a 4-2 loss to the Montreal Expos. His first win came on May 27, when he gave up a tie-breaking homer to John Grubb of the Padres in the top of the ninth, then the Pirates' Richie Hebner hit a walk-off two-run homer in the bottom of the inning. A few weeks later, Tekulve was sent back to Charleston.

Tekulve was available in the draft after the 1974 season, but all 23 teams passed on him. He began the 1975 season with Charleston, but was recalled in June, and pitched in 34 games for the Pirates. He got his first major-league hit on September 5 off Dale Murray of Montreal using a bat borrowed from first baseman Bob Robertson.

Tekulve got his first playoff exposure in 1975, appearing in two games of the National League Championship Series against the Reds. After the playoffs he went to Aguilas of the Dominican League, where he led the league with an ERA of 1.00.

Tekulve established himself as the top man in the Pirates bullpen during the 1976 season. In 64 games pitched, he went 5-3, with a 2.45 ERA and nine saves. At first, he appeared in mopup situations, but bullpen problems forced manager Danny Murtaugh to call on him when it counted. Tekulve was especially effective in September, posting a 1.64 ERA in 14 games. The Pirates (92-70) finished in second place, nine games behind the Philadelphia Phillies.

After the season, on October 30, Tekulve married Linda Taylor of Washington, Pennsylvania, on October 30. They had met shortly after he joined the Pirates in 1975.

Under new manager Chuck Tanner, many of the Pirates had exceptional seasons in 1977. Right fielder Dave Parker won his first batting title, first baseman Bill Robinson had his only 100-RBI season, and shortstop Frank Taveras set a club record with 70 stolen bases. Tekulve put together an impressive record as Goose Gossage's setup man. He was 10-1 with a 3.06 ERA and seven saves in 72 games. Tekulve was not happy with his secondary role, but he never popped off about how he was used. It was a season of adjustment for him. "I had to adjust to middle-inning relief early, then I had to adjust to when I started getting the call late in the game," he said. "When you're the late man, the game most often is on the line. And I like that challenge."[5] The Pirates went a solid 96-66, but finished second to the Phillies again, five games back.

After the season, Gossage became a free agent and signed with the New York Yankees. The Pirates tried to trade for a dominant closer for 1978, but decided to stay in-house with Tekulve. Chuck Tanner sang his submarine reliever's praises, saying, "Teke made my job easier. Anytime a manager can count on one pitcher to pitch four to five times a week, it makes his job easier."[6] Tekulve regained his closer role in 1978 and never lost his late-inning mentality. He pitched in 91 games and had 31 saves.

For the third season in a row, the Bucs finished behind Philadelphia, this time by 1½ games. Their last four games of the season were against the Phillies, and Tekulve won both games of a doubleheader on September 29 before picking up his 31st save on October 1. He finished second to Rollie Fingers as the Rolaids Fireman of the Year.

Tekulve entered 1979 as the Pirates' closer. The ninth inning with the Pirates leading came to be known as Tekulve Time.[7] The loudspeakers at Three Rivers would blare: "Hey, y'all, prepare yourself, for the Rubber Band Man. ... You're bound to lose control, when the Rubber Band Man starts to jam!"[8]

Seeing Tekulve coming in from the bullpen was a familiar sight to Pirates fans. But seeing him go to left field was not. This happened on September 1, 1979. Pittsburgh was in San Francisco and Chuck Tanner employed an unusual strategy. Tekulve was pitching with two outs in the ninth and left-hander Grant Jackson was warming up in the pen. Darrell Evans, a left-handed power hitter, was due up. It seemed logical for Jackson to come in. What was not logical was for Tanner to send Tekulve to left field. But that is what he did.

Tanner's idea was to keep Tekulve in the game to face the next batter if Jackson did not get Evans out. Tekulve strolled out to left, picked up a few blades of grass, and tossed them into the air to check for velocity and direction of the wind. Evans was a notorious pull hitter, but he got around late on Jackson, and hit a fly ball to Tekulve. The new left fielder did not move and caught the third out.

After three consecutive second-place finishes to the Phillies, the Pirates finally won the NL's Eastern Division title in 1979, clinching on the last day of the season with Tekulve nailing down the save, his 31st of the season. (He pitched in a league-leading 94 games.)

Roger Angell defined the team's character thusly: "All year at Three Rivers Stadium the loudspeakers blasted out the Pirates' theme song during the seventh inning stretch — a thumping, catchy, disco rock number, 'We Are Family' by Sister Sledge!"[9] Willie Stargell appropriated the tune as the team's theme song after hearing it during batting practice in St. Louis.

Pittsburgh squared off against Cincinnati for the National League pennant. In a reversal of their last meeting in the playoffs, in 1975, the Pirates swept the Reds. Tekulve pitched in the first two games, throwing 2⅔ shutout innings.

The World Series started at Memorial Stadium in Baltimore on October 10. Baltimore won the first game, 5-4, scoring five runs in the first inning. The Pirates won the second game, 3-2. Tekulve worked a scoreless ninth for his first World Series save. The Orioles won the third game 8-4.

A rare blown save by Tekulve in Game Four increased the Orioles' lead to three games to one. With one out in the Baltimore eighth, the Pirates leading 6-3 and the bases loaded, Tanner signaled for his bullpen ace. But this was not to be Tekulve's night. He gave up two doubles, a single, and a walk as the Pirates' lead disintegrated into a 9-6 deficit, a lead the Orioles preserved.

The Pirates bounced back in Game Five, winning in a 7-1 romp. In Game Six the successful partnership of John Candelaria and Tekulve resulted in a 4-0 shutout. Tekulve got his second save of the Series, entering in the seventh with the Pirates ahead 2-0 and shutting the door on the Orioles, giving up just one hit in three innings and striking out four.

In Game Seven, at Baltimore, Pittsburgh was up 2-1 when Tanner summoned Tekulve in the bottom of the eighth with two Orioles on and one out. Standing at the plate was Terry Crowley, who had smacked a two-run double off Tekulve in Game Four. Meeting Tekulve at the mound, Willie Stargell told him, "Teke, show the people why you're the best in the National League. And if you don't think you can do that, then play first and I'll pitch!"[10]

Tekulve got Crowley to bounce out to second. Next he intentionally walked Ken Singleton, loading the bases and bringing up Eddie Murray, who was on a 0-for-20 streak. Murray hit a line drive to right field, the kind Dave Parker normally caught easily. Parker slipped a couple of times. "I thought that, 'I hope his legs don't fail him now, but he's made those plays all year and somehow I knew he would get it," Tekulve said after the game.[11] Parker caught the ball, and the threat was over.

In the bottom of the ninth Tekulve struck out Gary Roenicke and Doug DeCinces. Pinch-hitter Pat Kelly batted, with the Pirates one out from the Series victory. "I threw the ball and did not see the catch," Tekulve said. "I was so wrapped up in the game that it didn't hit me until the ball was in the air and Omar [Moreno, Pirates center fielder] caught it. I then thought. world championship; it's ours and nobody can take it away!"[12]

Tekulve's performances during the Series strengthened his celebrity status in the Pittsburgh area. Shortly after the Pirates' victory he went to a department store to buy diapers for his infant son, Jonathan. Bedlam broke out. Tekulve spent over two hours signing everything from pillowcases to sales receipts. Afterward he deadpanned, "By the time I get out of here, my son will be toilet-trained."[13]

Tekulve finished fifth in the Cy Young Award voting, just as he had in 1978, but he took more pride in pitching in nearly 100 games on the season.

Chuck Tanner chose Tekulve for the All-Star squad in 1980, the only time he made it to the midsummer classic. He did not pitch in the National League's 4-2 victory. Tekulve had mechanical difficulties and struggled during the season. His bread-and-butter pitch was his sinker, but it was not sinking, and his slider was hanging. "I wasn't doing the basics," Tekulve recalled. "I wasn't following through. I wasn't driving with my motion. All mechanical."[14] Still, he earned his 100th career save that season.

Tekulve's struggles continued into 1981. He ended a personal 10-game losing streak that dated back to August 29, 1980, with a win on May 26 against Chicago. The Pirates had their first losing season since 1973. They returned to their winning ways in 1982, as Tekulve pitched in 85 games, ending up with a slate of 12-8 and 20 saves. But he was no longer the dominant closer. For instance, he gave up 11 runs during consecutive outings on July 7 and 8.

After a successful 1983 season (18 saves, 1.64 ERA), Tekulve sought a four-year deal from the Pirates. They were far apart in negotiations, and Tekulve became a free agent. Next to Gossage, he was the most coveted reliever on the market. Just before Christmas, Tekulve and the Pirates came to an agreement paying him $900,000 per season for 1984-86.

After the 1984 season Tekulve made it known that he did not like the way he was being used. Chuck Tanner took exception to his comments, saying, "I don't like to hear that Teke is saying such things. It seems that he is making excuses for himself. Sometimes I was confused with the way he pitched. We didn't score many runs last season and we didn't have the luxury of putting Tekulve in with a three- or four-run lead. Sometimes he didn't get the job done but I consider him a quality pitcher and he is always ready to pitch."[15]

Tekulve was traded to the Phillies on April 20, 1985, for reliever Al Holland and a minor leaguer. In Tekulve's first two appearances for the Phillies he allowed just an infield hit in four innings, and the Phillies returned him to the closer role. He won his first game for the Phillies on April 29, when he pitched 2⅔ innings of scoreless relief in a 3-2 win over Montreal. Tekulve finished 1985 as the Phillies closer, but it was the last time he served in that role as a major leaguer. He was 4-10 with 14 saves. He pitched three more years in Philadelphia as a setup man for Steve Bedrosian, who was enjoying his best years during that time, posting 29, 40, and 28 saves, and winning the Cy Young Award in 1987.

Tekulve continued to add to his record by leading the National League with 90 appearances in 1987, a mark that still stood as of 2016 as the Phillies team record for appearances in a season. At the age of 40 he became the oldest pitcher to lead the league in appearances. (Tekulve's Pittsburgh record of 94 appearances in 1979 was tied by Salomon Torres in 2006.) As of 2016 Tekulve's 1,050 pitching appearances placed him ninth in that category.

After the 1988 season the Phillies did not offer Tekulve a contract. Several teams expressed interest, and he decided to go to the Reds' spring training as a nonroster player. He made the team and was signed to a one-year contract. The plan was for him to be a setup man for John Franco. Tekulve was never comfortable with his role. He retired on July 17, 1989, explaining, "After all those years of being in the middle of things, I wasn't enjoying being on the fringe."[16]

Later that season the Pirates honored Tekulve at Three Rivers Stadium. He received an oil painting of himself pitching, a golf cart, a crystal bowl, and a lifetime pass to Pirates games. His wife, Linda, was given a gold necklace with 27 diamonds representing Tekulve's uniform number when a Pirate.

Tekulve could not stay away from baseball. He became a member of the Phillies broadcast team in 1991, and stayed on until 1997. He returned to the Western Pennsylvania area as the general manager and pitching coach of the Washington Wild Things of the Frontier League in 2003, and in 2006 became an advance scout for the Pirates. Later he worked as a postgame analyst for the Pirates games, and was as the president of the Pirates Alumni Association.

In 2008 Tekulve received the William A. "Bill" Shea Distinguished Little League Graduate Award, presented each year to a former Little Leaguer who went on to major-league baseball.

SOURCES

In addition to the sources cited in the notes, the author also consulted:

The Daily Courier, Connellsville, Pennsylvania, May 20, 1974.

THE 1979 PITTSBURGH PIRATES

Fimrite, Ron. "A Series of Ups and Downs," *Sports Illustrated*, October 22, 1979.

Fimrite, Ron. "Rising From the Ashes," *Sports Illustrated*, October 29, 1979.

"Size/On Air: experienced Tekulve has given FSN spot-on analysis," *Pittsburgh Post-Gazette*, May 20, 2008.

Little League On-Line, "Former MLB Relief Pitcher Kent Tekulve to Receive Bill Shea Distinguished Little League Graduate Award,"— Little League Communication Division, August 15, 2008.

Finoli, David, and Bill Ranier. *The Pittsburgh Pirates Encyclopedia*, "The Top 100 Players." (Champaign, Illinois: Sports Publishing, 2003).

Stargell, Willie, and Tom Bird. *Willie Stargell: An Autobiography* (New York: Harper & Row Publishers, 1984).

McCollister, John. *Tales From the 1979 Pittsburgh Pirates* (Champaign, Illinois: Sports Publishing, 2005).

NOTES

1. Kent Tekulve, telephone interview, January 14, 2010. (All quotes otherwise unsourced are taken from this interview.)
2. Ibid.
3. "Here it Comes, Special Delivery," *Sports Illustrated*, May 5, 1980.
4. Kent Tekulve, telephone interview, January 14, 2010.
5. *The Sporting News*, October 8, 1977.
6. *The Sporting News*, October 21, 1978.
7. *The Sporting News*, May 26, 1979.
8. The Spinners, "The Rubber Band Man," 1976.
9. Roger Angell, *Once Around the Park: A Baseball Reader* (Chicago: Ivan R. Dee, 1991), 104.
10. *The Sporting News*, November 3, 1979.
11. *Pittsburgh Press*, "Whew, It's Over! Bucs are Champs!" October 18, 1979.
12. Ibid.
13. *Sports Illustrated*, May 5, 1980.
14. *The Sporting News*, October 4, 1980.
15. *The Sporting News*, December 10, 1984.
16. *The Sporting News*, July 31, 1989.

Ed Whitson

By Mike Huber

A FASTBALL PITCHER WHO SPENT HIS 15-year major-league career playing for five teams, Ed Whitson was an All-Star in 1980 and amassed a 126-123 career record in 2,240 innings pitched. The 6-foot-3 right-hander was a starter for the first half of the Pirates' 1979 championship team, but he might best be remembered for his temper and his rocky tenure with the New York Yankees in the mid-1980s.

Eddie Lee Whitson was born on May 19, 1955, in Johnson City, Tennessee, to Starlin and Anna Mae (Johnson) Whitson. Starlin worked as a logger.

Starlin "took off" when Eddie was 7 years old, leaving a deserted wife and nine children. Eddie's siblings were Bradford, Buford, Eugene, Dennis, Martha, Trula, Randy, and Susan. Anna Mae and Starlin were divorced on June 4, 1981, exactly 16 years after they were married.

Ed Whitson was a star pitcher at Unicoi County High School in Erwin, Tennessee. On June 5, 1974, the right-handed fastball pitcher was drafted by Pittsburgh in the sixth round of the amateur draft. Pirates scout Ken Beardslee signed him to a contract and paid him a $5,000 bonus.[1]

To start his professional career, the 19-year-old Whitson was assigned to the Pirates' rookie-level team in the Gulf Coast League, where he went 1-4 with a 4.30 ERA in eight games. In 1975 he was moved up to Charleston (South Carolina) of the Class-A Western Carolinas League and finished with an 8-15 mark and a 5.07 ERA.

Whitson continued his minor-league career with Salem (Virginia), in the Class-A Carolina League in 1976. By July 4 he was 6-4 with a 1.71 earned-run average and had struck out 78 batters in 84 innings. He finished the season with a mark of 15-9, earning Class-A all-star status.

In 1977 Whitson went to spring training with the Pirates, but by the beginning of April, he was sent to the Columbus (Ohio) Clippers of the Triple-A International League. His strikeouts were down, and by mid-June he had but one victory against five defeats, with a 4.35 ERA. On June 30 he suffered his ninth loss in a row, losing to Charleston, 4-2. *The Sporting News* hinted on August 6, 1977, that Whitson might be superstitious: "After suffering through nine straight losses, he changed his uniform number from 18 to 20 and immediately won his next two starts to up his record to 3-9."[2]

Whitson finished the International League season 8-13 with a 3.84 ERA, and was a September call-up to the Pirates. He made his major-league debut on September 4 at Dodger Stadium in Los Angeles. In 1⅓ innings, he allowed a run on three walks and a sacrifice fly, but recorded his first major-league strikeout.

Whitson's first big-league start (and first victory) came via conditions out of his control on September 17, 1977, in Montreal. First, there was a rain delay of over two hours before the contest started. Then, scheduled starter Jerry Reuss was scratched after developing stiffness in his left shoulder while he was getting ready in the bullpen. Manager Chuck Tanner substituted Whitson as the starter. In his five innings, Whitson gave up five hits and three runs. Goose Gossage pitched four innings of scoreless relief as the Pirates won, 6-3. That was Whitson's only decision in his month with the Pirates.

Whitson started 1978 with Columbus but was called up in late May. Pitching in 43 games, all in relief, he posted a 5-6 record with four saves.

In the Pirates magical 1979 season, Whitson started seven games and relieved in 12 (2-3, 4.37) before being traded on June 28, along with pitchers Fred Breining and Al Holland, to the San Francisco Giants for infielders Bill Madlock and Lenny Randle and pitcher Dave Roberts. After acquiring Madlock, the third-place Pirates, 6½ games behind first-place Montreal, turned their season around and eventually won the pennant and the World Series. On June 30 Whitson, relieving in the ninth inning of a scoreless duel with the Cincinnati Reds, gave up two runs and took the loss.

On August 21, 1979, Whitson duked it out with Giants shortstop Roger Metzger. In batting practice the pitcher was taking some big cuts, and Metzger suggested Whitson concentrate on refining his bunting skills. The players argued, and the spat continued into the clubhouse when Whitson evidently said, "I've had enough," and decked Metzger, knocking him unconscious for about five seconds.[3] Both players downplayed the event, and the Giants snapped a six-game losing streak that night.

Whitson ended 1979 with a 5-8 record for the Giants, posting a 3.95 ERA, and a combined 7-11 record (4.10). He had 17 starts in 18 appearances. When the Pirates players divided their postseason money, they awarded Whitson $7,000.

After the season, on November 24, Whitson and Kathleen A. Mulholland were married in Franklin County, Ohio. In 1980 he was strictly a starter. By June 7 he was just 2-7, both victories shutouts over the Chicago Cubs. By July 1 he had won five straight games and evened his record at 7-7. Two weeks later, Whitson was at the All-Star Game. Vida Blue had been named to the team, but when the Giants placed Blue on the disabled list with a herniated cervical disc, Whitson was named to the National League squad.[4] Shortly after the All-Star Game, Whitson developed a blister on the middle finger of his pitching hand and sat out from July 22 until August 15. He finished the 1980 campaign with a record of 11-13 and an ERA of 3.10 in 34 starts (211⅔ innings pitched).

Whitson had another slow start in the 1981 season, which was interrupted by a players' strike. He was the losing pitcher in his first four decisions. On June 2, pitching against the Cincinnati Reds, Whitson felt some numbness in his right arm. The strike allowed him to rest his arm for two months, but his problems continued after play resumed. In an August 18 start against Pittsburgh, Whitson hyperextended his elbow trying to bunt. After the game, he told reporters, "I twisted my arm trying to bunt. I felt a click on every pitch I threw after that, but I won't miss a turn."[5] Whitson continued to be part of the starting rotation, and he ended the 1981 season with a record of 6-9 and a 4.02 ERA.

After the season Whitson was traded to the Cleveland Indians for second baseman Duane Kuiper. From April through July 1982, Whitson went 1-1 for the Tribe, entirely in relief, but in late July he developed a sore wrist. By August he was placed in the rotation, and he started his last nine games for Cleveland, going 3-1. His season record was 4-2. He had picked up two saves and had pitched a complete game shutout in one of his late-season starts, and he posted a season ERA of 3.26.

For the second offseason in a row, Whitson was traded in 1982, this time to the San Diego Padres, his fourth team in four seasons. The Padres envisioned Whitson as a key to their starting rotation. San Diego traded starting pitcher Juan Eichelberger and first baseman Broderick Perkins to Cleveland for Whitson. The trade stirred some disquiet among Cleveland fans. Pete Franklin, a talk-show host in Cleveland, told his listeners that the Indians were trading away an established right-handed starter for "Pancake" Perkins and "Hamburger" Eichelberger.[6] However, Cleveland general manager Phil Seghi said, "I look at it this way. We are trading a $10 bill for two $5 bills. Whitson and Eichelberger have good arms. But we also get Perkins, who will do a lot for our bench."[7]

Whitson's first season with the Padres also got off to a slow start. He missed the exhibition season with pulled muscles in his rib cage. In a game on April 15 against the Los Angeles Dodgers, Whitson suffered an injured cartilage in his left knee and was placed on the disabled list. He was expected to be gone from the team for three to six weeks, but ended up having knee surgery. When he returned, Whitson became a target for the long ball. A player on another team told him that he was "tipping his pitches,"[8] which had led to 16 home runs in 74 innings pitched. After finding this out, Whitson pitched eight innings in his next start without yielding a home run.

The next season, 1984, brought new success for Whitson. He developed a palmball by accident in the 1983 season. "The palmball developed in the last half of the season, when I couldn't use [my] finger,"[9]

he told reporters. He had cut a finger on his pitching hand opening a soda bottle. This forced him to hold the baseball farther back in his hand.

Although known for having a temper, Whitson was ejected from only one major-league game. That game, on August 12, 1984, in Atlanta's Fulton County Stadium was memorable and deplorable. Whitson was ordered by San Diego manager Dick Williams to hit Braves' pitcher Pascual Perez in retaliation for Perez plunking Alan Wiggins in the first inning. But in the second inning, Whitson's three inside pitches failed to connect with Perez, and both teams were warned. After Whitson fired three more "close ones" at Perez in the fourth, home-plate umpire Steve Rippley ejected both Whitson and Williams. In the end, 13 players, 2 coaches, and 2 managers were ejected.[10]

The Padres had a franchise season in 1984, going to the World Series. Whitson finished the season with a record of 14-8 and posted a 3.24 earned-run average. It was his second winning season. The Padres faced the Chicago Cubs in the National League Championship Series, and Whitson started Game Three, after the Cubs had won the first two games in the then best-of-five NLCS.

Before 58,346 fans in San Diego, Whitson allowed just five hits in eight innings as the Padres won, 7-1. The Padres then rallied for comeback wins in Games Four and Five to secure the NL pennant, and went to their first World Series. Whitson started Game Two against the favored Detroit Tigers at Jack Murphy Stadium, down one game to none, and the Tigers hit him hard. After three pitches, Detroit led, 1-0. After 11 pitches, it was 3-0. After 17 pitches, Whitson was pulled for Andy Hawkins. Whitson had allowed five singles while only retiring two batters. The Padres came back to win this game, 5-3, but the Tigers beat the Padres in three straight games in Detroit to claim the World Series title.

After the Series Whitson became a free agent and was signed by the New York Yankees to a five-year contract for $4.25 million. The fifth starter in the Yankees' 1985 rotation, Whitson had his traditionally slow start. He allowed 13 runs and 16 hits in eight-plus innings in his first two starts. Only five of the runs were earned, as the New Yorkers made five errors behind Whitson.

Whitson was 1-6 with a 6.23 ERA when he started on June 11 against the Toronto Blue Jays at Yankee Stadium. Whitson pitched into the 10th inning and gave up just one run, but the Blue Jays won 4-1 in 11 innings. This night against Toronto seemed special. The fans had been booing Whitson all season, yet in this game, they were chanting, "Ed-die, Ed-die" in the eighth inning. "I didn't know what was going on," said Whitson. "One of the guys told me all the beer vendors here are named Eddie and the fans were just yelling for beer."[11] As the season continued, Whitson was getting verbally abused and heckled by the fans. He even began to receive hate mail. He stopped bringing his wife to the stadium.

Whitson was involved in a notorious incident on September 22, 1985. In a cocktail lounge at the Cross Keys Inn in Baltimore, where the Yankees were staying, Whitson and Yankees manager Billy Martin became involved in a brawl. The "knock-down, drag out battle" began at about 12:20 A.M. and continued into the hotel lobby and then out into the street.[12] Evidently, Whitson was upset about being scratched from a start on September 20. Martin told reporters that Whitson had arm trouble and Ed told reporters he never felt better. The fight became an all-out brawl, with Whitson kicking and punching Martin. At one point, players Dale Berra and Ron Hassey and coach Gene Michael tried to break it up. The peacemakers pushed Whitson outside, but Martin followed. When it was all over, Martin was bleeding from his nose and had suffered a broken right arm. It was the second night in a row that Martin had been involved in an altercation at the hotel bar. Whitson was sent to his home in New Jersey and told to stay away from Martin. The Yankees did not suspend Whitson. Instead, Martin told the press, Whitson would skip his start at Yankee Stadium "to avoid being booed by the fans."[13] Martin was fired after the season ended.

Early the next season, 1986, Whitson was told he would be pitching only on the road—away from Yankee Stadium. Mike Downey, in *The Sporting News*, wrote, "The treatment Whitson gets in New York is rude, crude, and lewd. His own fans treat him like an enemy. Like Khadafy in pinstripes.… All I know is that Ed Whitson is not being allowed to pitch in his home ball park anymore, which is like telling Patrick Ewing he can play anyplace except Madison Square Garden, or like telling Louie Carnesecca he can coach at St. Joe's, St. Jim's, St. Louie's, St. Eva Marie's—anyplace but St. John's."[14] It wasn't quite that bad. In his two seasons with the Yankees, Whitson had a 15-10 record, good enough for a .600 winning percentage. However, it did bother him. "It's like working in an office and your boss comes in and says, 'You suck,' after you've tried your best," Whitson said. "Now multiply that by 50,000 bosses, all of them telling you that you suck, and imagine what that feels like."[15] New York manager Lou Piniella had reduced Whitson to duty as a mop-up pitcher and he did not let him start in Yankee Stadium until after June 2, 1986.[16] He started only a handful of games on the road. In his own defense, Whitson said, "I'm throwing consistent strikes. I'm getting the palmball over. The only reason I haven't been able to use it is I haven't been pitching. I respect Lou Piniella's decision on what he did, but it was hurting me. You can't get your ERA down if you're not being used."[17]

After he pitched to and retired one batter in Yankee Stadium on July 2, Whitson's ERA stood at 7.54 in 14 appearances.

By July 9, 1986, Whitson had had enough. The Padres got him back, trading relief pitcher Tim Stoddard to the Yankees for Whitson, and New York agreed to absorb the remaining 3½ years of Whitson's contract. Whitson was rescued by returning to San Diego.

In four full seasons from 1987 to 1990, Whitson posted double-digit victories (10, 13, 16, and 14). He had been a starter (except for two games at the end of the 1987 season). In 1990 Whitson posted a record of 14-9 with a career-best 2.60 earned-run average. He hit his only major-league home run on April 25, 1990, in a shutout of the Chicago Cubs in San Diego. The 1990 Padres named Whitson as their Pitcher of the Year.

The next season, 1991, was Whitson's last in the major leagues. Again plagued with injuries, he pitched in only 13 games, going 4-6, managing 78⅔ innings in 12 starts and one relief appearance. He gave up 93 hits (13 home runs), and his earned-run average shot up to 5.03, the highest of his career as a starting pitcher. In July he had shoulder surgery. In his final game, on September 29, he allowed five hits and three runs in one-third of an inning in relief against the Reds. The 36-year-old pitcher had a torn ligament in his right elbow. The Padres decided not to renew his contract.

When he retired after the 1991 campaign, Whitson had pitched in the major leagues for 15 seasons. His won-loss record was 126-123, and his ERA was 3.79. He pitched 35 complete games, of which 12 were shutouts. As a batter, he had nine doubles and 27 RBIs, in addition to his round-tripper. As a pitcher, he posted one career postseason victory. One sportswriter commented wryly of Whitson's retirement: "One of the Padres' all-time leading pitchers retired this week, and it hardly made it off page 17 of area newspapers. Newscasts mentioned it after hockey, of all things."[18]

Whitson's elbow did not get better, and he stayed retired, settling in Dublin, Ohio, his offseason home, spending time with his family. The Whitsons have two children. Jennifer A. Whitson was born in 1982 and Andrew M. "Drew" Whitson was born in 1992.

Thanks to Bill Mortell for providing insightful genealogical information and Rod Nelson of SABR's Scouts Committee.

NOTES

1. According to Rod Nelson of SABR's Scouts Committee, Whitson in a SABR questionnaire in 2002 named Beardslee as the scout who signed him.
2. *The Sporting News*, August 6, 1977: 34.
3. *The Sporting News*, September 8, 1979: 32.
4. *The Sporting News*, July 26, 1980: 21.
5. *The Sporting News*, September 5, 1981: 47.
6. *The Sporting News*, December 6, 1982: 50.
7. Ibid.
8. *The Sporting News*, August 22, 1983: 13.
9. *The Sporting News*, July 30, 1984: 5.
10. retrosheet.org/boxesetc/1984/B08120ATL1984.htm and youtube.com/watch?v=HZgw-ujI8UI
11. *The Sporting News*, June 24, 1985: 16.
12. *The Sporting News*, September 30, 1985: 32.
13. William Juliano, "Considering Kuroda; Remembering Ed Whitson," captainsblog.info/2011/12/17/considering-kuroda-remembering-ed-whitson/10534/.
14. *The Sporting News*, April 28, 1986: 5.
15. Ian O'Connor, "Whit's wisdom to Javy: 'I've been there,'" sports.espn.go.com/mlb/columns/story?columnist=oconnor_ian&id=5149683.
16. Whitson had started a game at Yankee Stadium on April 9, 1986, against the Kansas City Royals, but he allowed four runs (three earned) in 2⅔ innings, getting the loss. After that, he pitched three times in April and May in New York, all in relief.
17. *The Sporting News*, July 21, 1986: 14.
18. Dave Distel, "Whitson Always Was a Real Pro," *Los Angeles Times*, November 1, 1992.

Chuck Tanner and the Bullpen

By Rory Costello

"THE BEST CREW I'VE HAD IN MY NINE years as a major-league manager."[1] Chuck Tanner said that in August 1979 about his corps of relief pitchers on the Pittsburgh Pirates, led by Kent Tekulve, Enrique Romo, and Grant Jackson. "Our guys are suited to the situations in which we need them," the skipper said a little less than a year later. "That's why we won all the chips last year."[2]

Having a deep bullpen and seeking the best match-ups in tight spots are the norm today. The conventional notions about how to build and utilize pitching staffs were in a new stage of development in 1979, though—and Chuck Tanner was one of the thinkers who fostered the ongoing evolution.

"Fancy starters and 20-game winners are impressive to some," Tanner told veteran Montreal sportswriter Dink Carroll. "But you can still have a good pitching staff without them."[3] On various occasions over the years, Tanner sounded the same chord: "Give me a five-six-inning pitcher and we'll win."[4] He never won another pennant in his remaining eight-plus seasons as a big-league skipper. Yet his views—and his success with the '79 Pirates—still influenced the game. Tanner also had experimental ideas that were years ahead of their time.

The concept of situational relievers had germinated while Tanner was still an active player. In 2005 Steve Treder wrote a two-part series for *The Hardball Times* about the LOOGY, or (L)eft-handed (O)ne (O)ut (G)u(Y). By Treder's definition, the first major-league pitcher to be used as such was Leo Kiely of the Kansas City A's in 1960. Various others followed in the 1960s, most notably Jack Spring (Los Angeles Angels, 1963) and Bill Henry (San Francisco Giants, 1966). Tanner was not far behind. In his first full season as a big-league manager—1971, with the Chicago White Sox—he had two short-stint lefties in his bullpen. They were 19-year-old rookie Terry Forster and Don Eddy.[5]

The pendulum swung back in the early/mid-1970s, though. As Treder put it, "It was a time of reversing the trends that had been gathering momentum for several decades, of shorter pitching stints and more specialized roles."[6] Here too Tanner played a visible role. In 1972, when he was named AL Manager of the Year, he gave more than 40 starts apiece to three pitchers: Wilbur Wood (49), Stan Bahnsen (41), and Tom Bradley (40). That trio accounted for 64 percent of the innings pitched for the White Sox that year.

Still, an undercurrent was forming. Cincinnati Reds manager Sparky Anderson was earning the nickname "Captain Hook" because he often lifted his starting pitchers early and relied on his bullpen. However, the movement also gained force through Tanner. In January 1973, as the American League was preparing to introduce the designated-hitter rule, he predicted that relief pitching would become even more important as a result. "Under the new rule," he said, "I can bring in a guy like Terry Forster in the sixth inning and not worry about having to lift him for a pinch hitter later."[7]

Tanner was also early to turn pitching prospects into relievers. The prime example is Rich "Goose" Gossage, who'd had a brilliant season as a starter in Class-A ball in 1971 but went to the pen as a rookie with the White Sox in 1972. "Chuck was totally responsible for me being a relief pitcher," said Gossage in 2008, shortly after he had been elected to the Baseball Hall of Fame. He added that in those days the bullpen largely was considered "a junk pile where old starters went."[8]

Both Gossage and Forster made spot starts for Tanner from 1972 through 1974, but in 1975 he focused them on the bullpen. "Tanner might have been ahead of his time, but his decision was rooted in both long-term vision and short-term expediency. He knew it would be a shock to a hitter's system to see Gossage grunting and snorting in 98-mph increments after seven innings of watching Wilbur Wood's knuckleball and Tom Bradley's curve."[9]

The White Sox fired Tanner after the 1975 season. During the one year he spent in Oakland, 1976, he had an excellent righty-lefty relief tandem in veterans Rollie Fingers and Paul Lindblad. He inherited the pair, who had been together with the A's since 1973. It's likely that Tanner was influenced by the Oakland team, Chicago's divisional rival in the American League West. The triple World Series champions of 1972-74 had a very deep and varied bullpen, featuring another lefty in Darold Knowles and (in 1973) a righty with a low side-arm/semi-submarine delivery, Horacio Piña. Piña's style was not too far removed from Kent Tekulve's.

On November 5, 1976, Tanner came to Pittsburgh. A little over a month later, the Pirates got Grant Jackson in a trade with one of the new expansion teams, the Seattle Mariners. Just three days after that, they acquired both Gossage and Forster from the White Sox. Clearly Tanner was behind the latter deal in particular, but he also said, "We came here [to the winter meetings] looking for a left-handed reliever and we landed two."[10] However, Gossage and Forster both spent just one season in Pittsburgh before moving on to other clubs as free agents. As a result, the Pirates didn't have the same depth in their bullpen in 1978, which prompted the acquisition of Enrique Romo (again from Seattle) that December.

Tanner explained his approach to bullpen usage in 1980: "Today managers are reacting more to the immediate situation than the condition of the pitcher. Say, for instance, that my starting pitcher is still looking good, but we face a situation calling for a strikeout. That's when I bring in Enrique Romo. If we want a grounder, setting up a double play, I send for Kent Tekulve. I've removed starters who were leading by as many as five runs."[11] It worked well from the relievers' standpoint, too. In 1985 Tekulve said, "In the old 1979-80 bullpen, Romo, Jackson, and I all knew our roles. It was almost like we didn't need a telephone to the dugout. We knew when to get up."[12]

The peak of Tanner's bullpen management came in the 1979 World Series. The Pirates became the first team ever to win a best-of-seven postseason series by getting more outs from their relievers than from their starters. Since then, only one other club has done it: the St. Louis Cardinals in the 2011 National League Championship Series.[13] Their manager was Tony La Russa, who (for better or worse) took the late-inning chess game to another level.

Getting the hook early didn't sit well with one starter—Bert Blyleven. As Pittsburgh sportswriter Dan Donovan wrote after Pittsburgh beat Baltimore in the '79 Series, Blyleven was "the only Pirate who openly opposed Tanner's revolving-door theory of managing. Blyleven treasures complete games and shutouts, and Tanner believes in the team concept of pitching."[14] The following season, at the end of April, the Dutchman went so far as to jump the club for 10 days and demand a trade to protest the way Tanner handled him. The Pirates dealt "Cryleven" (as Tanner dubbed him in a surprisingly sarcastic moment) to Cleveland that December.[15] But another Pittsburgh pitcher, Jim Rooker, accepted the situation. Looking back in 1988, Rooker (by then a Pirates broadcaster) said, "I think Chuck was tougher to pitch for because Chuck loved to get to his bullpen. You could get mad at him for taking you out of a game, but he was the boss. His job was to manage and win; my job was to get the ball and pitch. I didn't have any problems with that."[16]

"Relief pitchers are the hard core of a team," Tanner said in 1981, emphasizing that bullpen depth was essential.[17] Over the years, he repeated a theme: that pitching staffs were to be built from the bullpen back, rather than from the starting rotation. He echoed something that Sparky Anderson had said—because hitters had become so strong and good, starters had to work much harder and thus were less capable of going the distance.[18] As a result, all he asked of his starters was five or six innings.[19]

A good example of this came during the championship season in 1979. On July 15 Jim Bibby—who always sweated buckets when he pitched—started on a muggy evening in Atlanta. Tanner told Bibby to pitch "as hard as he could as far as he could for we had a lot of pitchers in the bullpen and we would give him rest when he needed it." Bibby was pulled after 6⅓ innings with the Pirates ahead, 4-1, and Tanner said that the big righty "could hardly stand up."[20]

Tanner viewed deep bullpens as a necessity not only within the context of a single game but also over the long haul of a season. In 1983, he said, "In my opinion, the way to look at any pennant race is to divide it into three 54-game seasons; with the second series of 54 games the most important. Because of weather postponements, you almost never need more than a four-man pitching rotation in your first 54 games; your bullpen is still fresh; and the injuries that clubs have to deal with haven't yet begun to take their toll.

"But during those second 54 games, you're often forced to rely on your No. 5 and 6 pitchers; your bullpen becomes overworked; and you begin to have to go to your bench. If you can continue to win while that is happening, then you've got a contender. But if your club falls apart during that period, then your final 54 games aren't going to mean much anyway."[21]

In April 1984, during a spell of postponements, Tanner considered another new wrinkle with the Pirates staff: giving his starter five innings and then giving a second starter the remaining four so both would get some work. He also said that he had considered using three or four pitchers per game during the regular season in somewhat the same way that managers do in exhibition games. "It would give everybody some work," he said, "and who knows, it might be successful. Maybe it would start a trend."[22]

Tanner thought about trying the five-inning/four-inning split again in August 1985, when play resumed after a two-day players' strike. The following spring, by which time he was managing the Atlanta Braves, he said, "I mentioned it to some of my pitchers. They didn't like it. A lot of them had incentives for so many innings pitched, so many victories."[23] Things were different, of course, in the crucial Game Five of the 1979 World Series, when Blyleven willingly relieved Rooker and hurled four shutout innings. "We were in a situation where we couldn't go anywhere but home," Tanner said. "So we used Blyleven."[24]

In a 1986 interview, with Jerome Holtzman of the *Chicago Tribune*, Tanner went into depth about his notion to restructure his staff radically. "The starters would be divided into three three-man squads, A, B, and C. A works on Tuesday, B Wednesday, C Thursday, A Friday, etc. Each pitcher would work three innings on three days of rest. Ideally, there would also be a two-man bullpen, so there would be 11 pitchers in all.

"'Someday, someone's going to do it,' Tanner insisted. 'I'd like to be the guy. But you know what would happen? Everybody would be fighting for the middle three innings. Most of the time, the middle guy would get the win. But just imagine the fun. A guy could start and strike out nine men in a row and he`s taken out for the next guy.'

"Tanner laughed. 'They'd probably have to change the rules. Instead of giving an individual pitcher the win, the win would go to the squad—A, B, or C. Imagine the excitement and the fun we could have.'"[25]

Indeed, two big-league clubs have subsequently conducted such an experiment during the regular season. Oakland—under Tony La Russa—tried it for seven games from July 19 through July 25, 1993. His system had three three-man platoons plus a bullpen, much as Tanner had envisaged.[26] La Russa and pitching coach Dave Duncan limited each hurler to 50 pitches. The scheme ended partway through the seventh game; Duncan said, "We didn't win games. We were 1-6. We didn't accomplish what we wanted."[27] For much of the 2012 season, the Colorado Rockies used a four-man rotation in which the starters were limited to 75 pitches and were followed by an assortment of "piggyback" relievers. That effort ended after about three months for various reasons, but Colorado's assistant general manager, Bill Geivett, said, "The big move that showed courage was to do something that hadn't been tried. We had to try it."[28]

Chuck Tanner had died a little over a year before the Rockies tried their innovation. He would surely have applauded, though. As *Pittsburgh Press* sports editor Pat Livingston wrote in 1981, "Long reliever, short reliever, starter...Tanner rejects such typecasting. 'The way I manage,' chuckled Tanner, 'it doesn't make a difference. I pitch 'em two innings and take 'em out anyway."[29]

WHEN POPS LED THE FAMILY

NOTES

1. "Tanner Getting Relief From Strong Bullpen," Associated Press, August 8, 1979.
2. Dink Carroll, "New Role Charted for Starting Pitchers," *Montreal Gazette*, July 11, 1980: 42.
3. Carroll.
4. "Chuck Tanner Intends to Reverse Braves' Trend," Associated Press, October 11, 1985.
5. Steve Treder, "A History of the LOOGY: Part One," *The Hardball Times*, April 19, 2005 (hardballtimes.com/a-history-of-the-loogy-part-one/).
6. Treder.
7. "New Pinch-Hit Rule Creates New Strategy," Associated Press, January 14, 1973.
8. Robert Dvorchak, "Goose Gossage: Tanner, Allen Had Impacts on Pitching Career," *Pittsburgh Post-Gazette*, July 27, 2008.
9. Jerry Crasnick, "Tanner Backing Gossage." ESPN.com, December 27, 2007.
10. Jim Cour, "Pirates Finally Land Left-Handed Reliever," United Press International, December 8, 1976. "Bucs Get Gossage, Forster for Zisk," United Press International, December 12, 1976.
11. Carroll.
12. "A Tired Tekulve Is Good for Pirates," Associated Press, March 30, 1985.
13. Katie Sharp and Mark Simon, "Bullpens in Focus, Ready for World Series," ESPN.com, October 19, 2011.
14. Dan Donovan, "Blyleven Seals Return with Tanner Embrace," *Pittsburgh Press*, October 19, 1979: B-7.
15. Phil Musick, "Blyleven Returns After Trade Attempt Fails," *Pittsburgh Post-Gazette*, May 10, 1980: 6; "Chuck Tanner Optimistic About Pirates' Chances," Associated Press, February 24, 1981.
16. "Pirates Reflect on Tanner's Firing," *Pittsburgh Post-Gazette*, May 24, 1988: 28.
17. Charley Feeney, "Tanner Finds Relief in Numbers," *The Sporting News*, January 17, 1981: 40.
18. Carroll; "Tanner Talks Pitching Strategy; Cubs Still Fitting Pieces Together," *Christian Science Monitor*, April 25, 1984.
19. Russ Franke, "Tanner Getting Relief from 'Worst' Pitching Staff," *Pittsburgh Press*, July 19, 1983: D-1.
20. "Expos Toss Zeroes at Padres; Bucs Reach Break With Upbeat Note," Associated Press, July 18, 1979.
21. "Dodger Rookies Secure Limelight; Three-Part season," *Christian Science Monitor*, June 1, 1983.
22. Charley Feeney, "Idleness Concerns Tanner," *Pittsburgh Post-Gazette*, April 25, 1984: 13.
23. Jerome Holtzman, "Tanner's 3-Pitcher Plan as Elementary as A-B-C," *Chicago Tribune*, March 25, 1986.
24. Donovan.
25. Holtzman.
26. "La Russa Willing To Experiment—Oakland's Pitchers Divided Into Platoons," *Seattle Times*, July 20, 1993.
27. "La Russa Bags Plan," Associated Press, July 26, 1993.
28. Troy E. Renck, "Rockies to Go With Five-Man Rotation in 2013, but 'Piggybacks' Remain," *Denver Post*, September 14, 2012.
29. Pat Livingston, "Will Tanner Arm Bucs?", *Pittsburgh Press*, February 1, 1981: D-2.

Chuck Tanner

By Dan Fields

SOMETIMES NICE GUYS FINISH FIRST. Chuck Tanner, an eternal optimist who was known as baseball's Mr. Sunshine, managed the Pittsburgh Pirates to a World Series title in 1979. He won more than 1,350 games as a manager of four teams between 1970 and 1988. Tanner also played for eight years in the majors, with the Milwaukee Braves, Chicago Cubs, Cleveland Indians, and Los Angeles Angels. (He spent the first two months of the 1957 season with the Braves before being sent to the Cubs on waivers.) Tanner famously said, "The greatest feeling in the world is to win a major-league game. The second greatest feeling is to lose a major-league game."[1]

Charles William Tanner, Jr. was born in New Castle, Pennsylvania (about 50 miles north of Pittsburgh), on July 4, 1928. Of German-Slovak descent, Tanner was one of three sons of Charles Tanner, Sr., a Pennsylvania Railroad brakeman and conductor, and Anna (Baka) Tanner. He grew up in modest circumstances: "We didn't have electricity until [I was in] tenth grade. No bathroom. We were better off than some because we had a two-holer out back; some people only had one hole. We had a pot-bellied stove, but there were days I'd wake up with snow in my pockets."[2]

As a child Tanner joined a group of older boys in pickup baseball games that would last many hours. He joked that he might have starved if his mother had not shown up every afternoon with peanut-butter sandwiches. His grandfather told him, "You'll be a bum. All you want to do is baseball, baseball, baseball."[3]

Tanner was a ten-letter standout in baseball, basketball, and football while at Shenango High School in New Castle. In June 1946 the Boston Braves signed the 6-foot, 185-pound outfielder, who batted and threw left. In the minors he batted over .300 every year from 1947 through 1954, spending time in Owensboro (Kentucky), Evansville (Indiana), Eau Claire (Wisconsin), Pawtucket (Rhode Island), and Denver. On February 12, 1950, Tanner married Barbara "Babs" Weiss; together, they would have four sons.

In 1954, while playing his fourth year with the Atlanta Crackers in the Double-A Southern Association, Tanner was second in the league in hits (192) and total bases (311). He hit 20 homers and sported a .323 batting average. That year he helped the Crackers win the Southern Association "grand slam": the team won the annual All-Star game, finished first in the regular-season standings, won the league playoffs, and took the Dixie Series over the champions of the Double-A Texas League, the Houston Buffaloes.

In 1955, Tanner's tenth year in professional baseball, he was promoted to the Milwaukee Braves. He made the most of his first appearance: On Opening Day, April 12, he pinch-hit for Warren Spahn in the eighth inning and homered off Gerry Staley on the first major-league pitch he faced to help the Braves defeat the Cincinnati Redlegs, 4-2. Tanner was the seventh player in major-league history to hit a home run on his first pitch and the fifth with a pinch-hit home run in his first at-bat.

In his rookie year, Tanner served as Milwaukee's fourth outfielder. He hit .247, with six home runs and 27 RBIs in 97 games. Tanner was known for his hustle: He would run so hard from left field to the dugout after each inning that he often arrived before the first baseman, Joe Adcock. Tanner saw more limited duty with the Braves in 1956 and 1957, and on June 8, 1957, he was placed on waivers and claimed by the Cubs. In a July 18 game at Forbes Field, both Tanner and Ernie Banks of the Cubs hit inside-the-park home runs, but the Pirates won 6-5. In 95 games with the Cubs that year, Tanner had two four-hit games and six three-hit games. His combined totals for the Braves and Cubs in 1957 were nine home runs and 48 RBIs, with a batting average of .279.

In 1958 with the Cubs, Tanner's 53 pinch-hitting at-bats led the NL. On March 9, 1959, he was traded

to the Boston Red Sox for pitcher Bob Smith. Tanner never saw action with Boston and played 152 games that year with a Red Sox Triple-A team, the Minneapolis Millers. On September 9 he was purchased by the Cleveland Indians. Tanner appeared in 14 games with the Indians that month, and he played in 21 games with Cleveland in 1960. Tanner appeared in 70 games during 1961 with the Indians' Triple-A team, the Toronto Maple Leafs, until he was sold in mid-July to the Los Angeles Angels' Triple-A affiliate, the Dallas-Fort Worth Rangers. After he played in 48 games and batted .300 for the Rangers, his contract was purchased by the Angels on September 8.

Tanner played in seven games with the expansion Angels during that team's inaugural season and another seven games in the spring of 1962. He played his final game in the big leagues on May 8, 1962. He spent the rest of the season with Dallas-Fort Worth. During his major-league career, Tanner compiled a .261 batting average, with 21 home runs and 105 RBIs in 396 games. During his 14-season minor-league career, he collected 1,669 hits in 1,454 games.

After the 1962 season Tanner faced a choice. He could play for another year for $18,000, or he could manage a Single-A team in Davenport, Iowa, for $6,000. Tanner made an investment in the future and headed to Iowa. He managed eight years in the Angels' farm system, leading the Quad Cities Angels (1963-1964), El Paso Sun Kings (1965-1966, 1968), Seattle Angels (1967), and Hawaii Islanders (1969-1970). Tanner had a cumulative record of 561-537 (.511), and he won minor-league Manager of the Year honors in 1968 and 1970.

In September 1970 Tanner took over the last-place Chicago White Sox after Don Gutteridge was fired and managed the team for the final 16 games of the season. As the skipper built his players' confidence and got them believing in themselves, the team's fortunes took an upturn. In 1971 the White Sox finished third in the AL West with a record of 79-83, a 23-game improvement over 1970. Tanner moved Wilbur Wood out of the bullpen, and the knuckleball pitcher responded with a breakout year, with 22 wins, an ERA of 1.91, and 210 strikeouts in 42 starts.

In 1972 the White Sox went 87-67 and finished second in their division, and Tanner won the major-league Manager of the Year award from *The Sporting News* and the AL Manager of the Year Award from the Associated Press. Under Tanner's low-key style of handling ballplayers, moody first baseman Dick Allen thrived, leading the league in home runs (37) and RBIs (113) and winning the MVP award. Wood won 24 games and was named the AL Pitcher of the Year by *The Sporting News*. He started 49 games (still tied for second-most starts in a season in AL history) and pitched 376⅓ innings, the most by an American League hurler since 1912.

In Chicago, Tanner relied heavily on his top pitchers. In 1972, two other White Sox hurlers started at least 40 games, Stan Bahnsen (41) and Tom Bradley (40). In 1973 Wood (48 starts) and Bahnsen (42) again combined for 90 starts; Wood finished with a 24-20 record and again led the majors with 359⅓ innings pitched. On May 28, 1973, Tanner let Wood complete a game that had been suspended two days earlier against the Cleveland Indians. He worked five innings, giving up only one unearned run, and picked up the win. Wood then pitched a four-hit shutout in the regularly scheduled game. On July 20, 1973, Tanner started Wood in both games of a doubleheader against the New York Yankees; the pitcher was pinned with both losses.

Under Tanner the White Sox finished in fifth place in 1973, fourth in 1974, and fifth in 1975. After the 1975 season, the team was sold, and new owner Bill Veeck replaced Tanner with Paul Richards. Tanner signed a three-year contract with the Oakland Athletics, and the team was off to the races: In 1976 the A's stole an AL-record 341 bases in 464 attempts. Eight players had at least 20 steals, including pinch-runners Matt Alexander and Larry Lintz, who combined for 51 steals despite only 34 plate appearances. The A's finished second in the AL West with a record of 87 wins and 74 losses.

On November 5, 1976, Tanner was involved in an unusual trade. When Danny Murtaugh, who had managed the Pirates to 1,115 wins and two World Series championships, retired at the end of the season, the team wanted local boy Tanner to replace him. But Tanner was still under contract with the A's, and owner Charlie Finley wanted to be compensated if he was going to release his manager. The Pirates offered either All-Star catcher Manny Sanguillen or $100,000. Finley demanded both, and to Tanner's surprise, the Pirates agreed. It was one of the few times in baseball history that a player was traded for a manager. Tanner was delighted to be returning home: "I can't wait for spring training. This is such a thrill. It's like a dream come true."[4]

With Tanner at the helm, the Pirates won 96 games in 1977 and finished second in the NL East. The team stole 260 bases (the most in a season by the Pirates in 70 years), giving Tanner's teams a total of 601 steals in 1976 and 1977. Dave Parker led the league with a .338 batting average, and 23-year-old John Candelaria sparkled with a major-league-low 2.34 ERA and a 20-5 record.

In 1978 the Pirates were 11½ games behind the Philadelphia Phillies on August 12 after a miserable 4-17 stretch. Ever the optimist, Tanner told his players, "This may not be the end; it may be the beginning."[5] Over the remainder of the season, the Pirates had a record of 37-12 (.755), including 24 straight wins at home. The Phillies clinched the division on the second-to-last day of the season, and the Pirates finished just 1½ games back with a record of 88-73. It was Tanner's third consecutive second-place finish. Parker was the National League's Most Valuable Player, with a .334 batting average (tops in the majors), 30 home runs, and 117 RBIs. Willie Stargell, who had played in only 63 games the previous year because of a pinched nerve in his left elbow, contributed 28 home runs and 97 RBIs and was named the NL Comeback Player of the Year.

In 1979 Tanner led the Pirates to 98 wins, the most by Pittsburgh since 1908 and good enough to win the National League East by two games over the Montreal Expos. The Pirates adopted the Sister Sledge hit "We Are Family" as its theme song, and their on-field success was a true team effort: No player had as many as 15 wins or 95 RBIs. Tanner was an innovator for using a platoon of relievers, often for an inning each in the same game. Kent Tekulve (94 games), Enrique Romo (84 games), and Grant Jackson (72 games) finished 1-2-3 in games pitched in the NL. The Pirates swept the best-of-five National League Championship Series in three games over the Cincinnati Reds, with Stargell named the series MVP.

In the World Series, Pittsburgh trailed the favored Baltimore Orioles three games to one when Tanner learned that his mother had died. He told his players, "My mother is a great Pirates fan. She knows we're in trouble, so she went upstairs to get some help."[6] The Pirates rallied to win three straight games, including Games Six and Seven on the road. Stargell went 12-for-30, with four doubles and three home runs, and picked up the World Series MVP award. He completed the trifecta by winning the 1979 NL MVP award (along with Keith Hernandez of the St. Louis Cardinals); he was also the third player in eight years to win an MVP award under Tanner. "Having Willie Stargell on your ballclub is like having a diamond ring on your finger," Tanner quipped.[7]

Tanner managed the Pirates for six more years, with winning records in 1980, 1982, and 1983. On May 29, 1983, he became the 35th manager to win 1,000 games in the majors, against 927 losses (.519). Bill Madlock won batting titles in 1981 (.341) and 1983 (.323).

In 1984 the Pirates dropped to sixth place with a 75-87 record, and in 1985, they slid to 57-104. Several players were involved in what became known as the Pittsburgh drug trials of 1985. According to the *Pittsburgh Post-Gazette*: "Seven men—all outside the team—were convicted of selling drugs to baseball players, many of whom testified in exchange for immunity. Mr. Tanner testified he had no more than cursory knowledge of such drug issues, but Dale Berra, a shortstop at the time, contradicted that by testifying that Mr. Tanner warned him to stay away from drug dealers."[8] Tanner was let go by the Pirates and later said, "I would've fired myself."[9] (One bright spot of 1985 was that Tanner's son Bruce pitched ten games for the Chicago White Sox; Tanner's son Mark had pitched in the minor leagues from 1972 through 1975.)

Tanner was hired to manage the Atlanta Braves, who finished last in the NL West in 1986 and fifth in 1987. With a 12-27 record in 1988, Tanner was replaced by Russ Nixon. Tanner had managed a major-league game from September 18, 1970, to May 22, 1988. When he was done, only 18 managers in major-league history had won more games. He finished with a record of 1352-1381 (.495).

But Tanner was not through with baseball. From 1992 to 2002, he served as a special assistant to the general manager of the Milwaukee Brewers. He also scouted for five years for the Cleveland Indians. On July 31, 2004, during the year of the 25th anniversary of the 1979 championship, the baseball field at Shenango High School was dedicated as Chuck Tanner Field. In 2006 Houston Astros manager Phil Garner, an infielder on the 1979 Pirates, honored Tanner by naming him an honorary NL coach in the All-Star Game in Pittsburgh; Tanner also threw out the first pitch. On August 9, 2006, Barbara Tanner, his wife of 56 years, passed away.

In November 2007 the Rotary Club of Pittsburgh presented the first Chuck Tanner Baseball Manager of the Year award to Joe Torre of the Los Angeles Dodgers. Through 2009 the award was given to a major-league manager. In 2010 a second award was presented to the Chuck Tanner Collegiate Baseball Manager of the Year, and the original award was renamed the Chuck Tanner Major League Baseball Manager of the Year award.

In 2008 the Pirates hired Tanner as a senior adviser to the general manager, a job he held until his death on February 11, 2011, in New Castle at the age of 82. He is buried at Castleview Memorial Gardens in New Castle. To honor his passion for teaching baseball, the Pirates created the Chuck Tanner We Are Family Fund, which annually presents an award to the Pirates' minor-league staff person who best exemplifies Tanner's optimism, enthusiasm, work ethic, and leadership. "I've had the greatest life in the world," said Tanner in a 2007 interview. "How many guys can say they won a World Series in their backyard? How can that happen to a kid from Shenango?"[10]

SOURCES

Baseball-Reference.com

Findagrave.com

Pittsburgh.pirates.mlb.com

Pittsburghrotary.org

Retrosheet.org

Feeney, Charley., "Bucs Give Chuck 1,000th, but It's Not All That Pretty," *Pittsburgh Post-Gazette*, May 30, 1983.

Fenster, Kenneth R., "The 1954 Dixie Series," *The National Pastime*, SABR 40 (2010).

Jaffe, Chris, "10 Things I Didn't Know about Chuck Tanner," Hardball Times (hardballtimes.com), February 14, 2011.

Johns, Walter L., "Tanner—With, Without Shoes," *New Castle* (Pennsylvania) *News*, April 8, 1971.

Liska, Jerry (Associated Press), "Chuck Tanner Cons His White Sox Into Stars," *Tuscaloosa* (Alabama) *News*, August 20, 1972, 3B.

McCollister, John, *Tales from the 1979 Pittsburgh Pirates* (Champaign, Illinois: Sports Publishing L.L.C., 2005).

Porter, David L.,, ed., *Biographical Dictionary of American Sports: Baseball* (volume 3) (Westport, Connecticut: Greenwood Press, 2000).

Spatz, Lyle, ed., *The SABR Baseball List & Record Book* (New York: Scribner, 2007).

THE 1979 PITTSBURGH PIRATES

NOTES

1. *The Sporting News,* July 15, 1985, 18.
2. Sharon Robb, "Tanner 'Positive' Braves Can Climb," *Sun Sentinel* (Fort Lauderdale, Florida), October 31, 1985.
3. David Lamb, *Stolen Season: A Journey Through America and Baseball's Minor Leagues* (New York: Random House, 1991), 201.
4. Craig Brown, "Retracing Chuck Tanner's Path to Pirates," ESPN.com, February 13, 2011.
5. Phil Axelrod, "Never-Say-Die Bucs Created Own Miracle," *Pittsburgh Post-Gazette,* September 7, 1978.
6. Dejan Kovacevic, "Chuck Tanner, Popular Pirates Manager, Dies at 82," *Pittsburgh Post-Gazette,* February 11, 2011.
7. "Pops Go the Pirates," *Time,* October 29, 1979.
8. Dejan Kovacevic, 2011.
9. Ibid.
10. Ron Cook, " 'Fam-a-lee' Blessed With Tanner," *Pittsburgh Post-Gazette,* February 12, 2011.

Harvey Haddix

By Mark Miller

WHENEVER THE NAME HARVEY HADDIX is mentioned, there is usually a reference to a 115-pitch game he threw in Milwaukee in 1959. His career in professional baseball, however, was much more—lasting parts of five decades.

Haddix was born on September 18, 1925, the third son of Harvey Haddix, Sr. and Nellie Mae Greider-Haddix. His parents were farmers near Westville, in west central Ohio, but Haddix was born 20 miles away, in Medway, Ohio. "My mother had an aunt who was a midwife who lived there," Haddix explained in a public appearance in 1989.[1]

Life on the farm was typical for the Haddix boys, Harvey, older brothers Ed and Ben, and younger brother Fred. "There on the farm we didn't have any money and there were no kids out there to play ball with, except the neighbor kids, so we played baseball two on a side." His first glove was a first baseman's mitt made from a leather horsecollar.

In 1940, before his freshman year in high school, the family purchased a farm near South Vienna, Ohio. Catawba High School had a successful baseball team loaded with upperclassmen, including brother Ben. Harvey became the team's left-handed shortstop, "I could catch a ground ball," he explained. [2]

Equipment continued to be an issue. Haddix elaborated: "I made the ball team but I didn't have a pair of spikes so I took a pair of my dress shoes and punched holes in the bottom of my dress shoes and riveted cleats on the bottom for my first pair of spikes."[3]

As a senior he began to pitch. "When I became a senior the pitcher had graduated so I took over the pitching chores and we won the county championship." He had an excellent instructor at home in the person of his father, who was a renowned amateur pitcher.[4] Brother Ben, two years older, was playing minor-league baseball for the local Springfield Cardinals, a Class-C Middle Atlantic League club managed by Walter Alston.

In 1943, after Haddix graduated from high school, "I was pitching, semipro, and a scout was there from the Philadelphia Athletics. He comes to me and says, 'I am going to write Connie Mack about you.' I said, 'That would be fine' and I sat around waiting for two weeks and didn't hear anything. One day I picked up the newspaper and there was a little article in the paper that said that there is a Redbird tryout in Columbus.

"I had to go to Columbus, at 9 in the morning until 4 in the afternoon for the tryout camp. They had 350 kids there. … They looked at me and said you will be a pitcher. Pitchers went down to the bullpen, and we sat there until 4. They said: OK warm up and go in and throw nothing but fastballs. They said, 'Can you come back tomorrow?'

"I came back the next day. Now throw what the catcher calls. I probably threw three to four curveballs, and three to four fastballs. As I walked off the mound he says, 'Do you want to sign?' I said no. I am an old country boy, I am thinking about the guy back home that saw me first. I never heard anything more from him and went back over to Columbus and signed with the Cardinals.

"Now (World War II) was going on and I took a two-week trip with the Columbus baseball club. I just turned 18 so I had to leave the trip in Louisville and return to Springfield to register for the draft."[5]

Haddix's next road trip would have to wait three years. As a farmer he received a three-year deferment from military service, which meant his only employment could be the farm.

In 1947, after the war ended, Haddix started his professional baseball career, in Triple A. "I took off for Columbus for spring training. Now I know I can't play with them, I sat there about two weeks and I finally had enough and went up to the office and said, 'Where am I going to go play ball?' He said you are going to Pocatello, Idaho. I looked at him and said, 'No I'm not. That is too far from home. You got something closer to home than that.'"

A couple of days later Haddix was sent to Winston-Salem of the Class-C Carolina League and met the team in Lynchburg, Virginia. "I got there and was setting on the steps waiting for someone to come and here comes a little old school bus with Winston-Salem Cardinals on the side of it. There was one guy on the team that knew me who introduced me to the manager (Zip Payne)." Haddix was 5-feet-6, 175 pounds, and Payne's first impression was not positive. Haddix said he was told the manager said, "Do they expect me to win a pennant sending me something like that down here?"[6]

Haddix's first two appearances were in relief. He did not allow a run in a win and a loss. From then on he was a starter and changed the manager's opinion by winning 19 and losing 5, with 275 strikeouts while also hitting over .300 (including a pinch-hit homer). On August 11 he pitched a seven-inning no-hitter, later threw a nine-inning one-hitter, and had a 19-strikeout game. He was selected a league all-star, the left-handed pitcher of the year, the rookie of the year, and the most valuable player. His 1.90 ERA easily beat out the second-best (3.18).

"The next year I jumped to Triple-A ball. I pitched there for three years, '48, '49, and '50. Now I thought I was good enough to go to spring training with (the Cardinals) but the Cardinals didn't want to see me. They had five good left-handed pitchers (Harry "The Cat" Brecheen, Max Lanier, Howie Pollet, Al Brazle, and Ken Johnson.)"[7]

In Columbus Haddix got the nickname "Kitten." General manager George Sisler, Jr. called him "a second Brecheen," adding, "Won't that be something when he joins the Cards and teams up with Brecheen to pitch a doubleheader? 'The Cat and the Kitten.'"[8]

As Haddix matured he had grown a little and was generously listed at 5-feet-9. In 1948 at Columbus he had 11 wins and a .337 batting average. For a second straight year he was an all-star. Cardinals catcher Joe Garagiola said, "I don't know how far Haddix is away from the majors, but I do know he will be there one of these days."[9]

The 1949 season was more of the same. Haddix won 13 games for the Red Birds and was again selected an all-star. In 1950 he had 18 wins and another all-star selection, as he added a change-up to his repertoire of pitches, which included a fastball and slider. On August 16 for Columbus he retired 28 Milwaukee Brewers batters in a row during an 11-inning game. Retiring more than 27 Milwaukee batters in a row in an extra-inning game might come up again in his future.[10]

On September 9 the playoff-bound Red Birds had Harvey Haddix Day. It was also announced that his contract had been sold to the Cardinals. But a trip to St. Louis would have to wait as he was drafted into the Army and sent to Fort Dix, New Jersey. He got leave to travel to Baltimore to pitch for Columbus in a Junior World Series game. The Orioles were not accommodating, taking the game 8-1.

Haddix served as a Fort Dix athletic director in 1951 and 1952, and managed and pitched for the camp baseball team. In 1952 he led the team to the state semipro championship. In August, his Army service complete, he joined the Cardinals and made his major-league debut on the 20th in St Louis against the Boston

Braves, winning a complete-game five-hitter, 9-2. He finished the season with three complete games, a 2-2 record and a 2.79 ERA. He singled in his first big-league at-bat.

To make up for lost time, Haddix headed to winter ball in San Juan, Puerto Rico. He threw shutouts his first two starts and when the Cardinals shut him down December, he was 6-2. He was so popular that the team threw a banquet in his honor.

Haddix entered spring training in 1953 as the Cardinals' top prospect, coming to camp in great shape and having a great spring. He even won a box of cigars for winning three pitcher's batting awards: collecting the most hits, scoring the most runs, and stealing the most bases.

Haddix opened his rookie season in the starting rotation and shut out the Chicago Cubs on a four-hitter in the Cardinals' home opener. By June 27 Haddix had won 10 games and led the team with 79 strikeouts. He earned a spot on the National League All-Star team, but didn't pitch in the All-Star Game. Returning to action after the game, Haddix threw five straight complete games from July 19 through August 6. The August 6 game was a two-hitter against the Phillies, both Phillies hits coming in the ninth inning. Richie Ashburn, who got the first hit, created controversy by trying to bunt his way on. Haddix's only comment was, "He was only trying to win, that's all."[11] Haddix finished with 20 wins, 19 complete games, six shutouts (leading the league), and a 3.06 ERA, while batting .289. He was second to the Dodgers' Jim Gilliam for Rookie of the Year. Gilliam said he was surprised to have won.[12]

Cardinals manager Eddie Stanky was happy with his southpaw. "What can I say about the guy? He can run, hit, and field better than most pitchers. ... What more can you expect?"[13] Haddix won three new suits from Stanky, who had challenged his pitchers to pitch complete games with no walks.

Haddix again ranked among the elite National League pitchers in 1954. Again selected a National League All-Star, he had to be replaced on the team due after being struck below the right kneecap by a line drive off the bat of someone who would play a significant role in his future, Milwaukee first baseman Joe Adcock. Haddix said the injury bothered him the rest of his life and affected his pitching. "I was never the same after that," said Haddix. "I didn't have the same spring off the mound."[14]

Haddix had won 12 games at the time of the injury. He won only six games the rest of the season but ended on a high note, pitching nine shutout innings against Milwaukee in a no-decision and winning his 18th on September 19 with one inning of relief.

In February Haddix said his injury had healed and was giving him no trouble during the hunting season, but added, "After the leg was hurt I couldn't run well and my conditioning suffered. A pitcher is still only as strong as his legs."[15] And Haddix and the Cardinals got off to rocky starts.

The team began 9-12 start in a rainy spring. Haddix and Brooks Lawrence made 15 appearances as starters or relievers in the first 21, games winning only two. Haddix's ERA was 5.91.

The Cardinals' slow start got manager Stanky fired and replaced by Harry Walker. Haddix's record stood at 2-8, so he spent hours throwing pitches against the outfield wall trying to harness his curveball. Giants coach Frank Shellenback gave him a tip about gripping his curveball. This, plus the fact that he learned he was tipping his pitches helped him turn around his season to some extent.

Despite his poor record (6-9 and a 5.43 ERA), Haddix was selected to the National League All-Star team and for the first time pitched in the game. It would be his sixth and final time as an All-Star. He ended a disappointing season with a 12-16 record and a 4.46 ERA, still good enough for new general manager Frank Lane to call him a Cards untouchable. He would also enter the 1956 season with his new wife, Marcia Williamson. After a honeymoon and a winter of hunting at his South Vienna farm, he entered 1956 spring training ready to go. But on May 11 the "untouchable" was traded to the Philadelphia Phillies with pitchers Stu Miller and Ben Flowers for pitchers Herm Wehmeier and Murry Dickson.

"I didn't want to go to the Phillies," Haddix said in 1989. "But good things come out of bad things. I had a house free of rent there, and with the money I saved the two years in Philadelphia, I bought my first farm."[16]

After pitching coach Whit Wyatt noticed some mechanical flaws in his motion, he regained his form. He had a 12-8 record, and could have been 16-4 if the Phillies bullpen had not blown four leads. Phils manager Mayo Smith listed the acquisition of Haddix as the year's most pleasant surprise.[17]

Haddix was inconsistent in 1957. At times he was the staff ace, but later he was sent to the bullpen. In July he pitched an 11-inning shutout against the Cubs, but in his next game he was knocked out by the Braves in the third inning. He ended the season with a 10-13 record and a 4.06 ERA, and he suffered with a stiff arm for the first time in his career. In the offseason the Phillies, needing hitting, traded Haddix to Cincinnati for slugger Wally Post. "I figured at the end of last season that I would be traded," Haddix said. "I thought I would go to one of any four clubs, but going to the Reds is the best that could have happened. … The Reds have always been my team, even when I was a kid."[18]

For Haddix, 1958 was another season with flashes of greatness and mediocrity. He went to a no-windup delivery to try to stop the recurring problem of tipping his pitches. "I cut down the windup so I could hide the ball from the third base coach," he said.[19] For the season he was 8-7 with a 3.52 ERA and gave up 191 hits in 184 innings, including 28 home runs. On the brighter side, he received his first Gold Glove Award. Then in January he was traded with catcher Smokey Burgess and third baseman Don Hoak to the Pirates for Frank Thomas, Whammy Douglas, Jim Pendleton, and Johnny Powers.

The Pirates were poised to contend. Haddix got off to a hard-luck, start, with poor run support. On May 26 his record was 4-2 with a 2.67 ERA. On that day he was scheduled to pitch against the Milwaukee Braves in Milwaukee. He had the flu, spent most of the chilly, windy, and rainy day in bed and if he hadn't been pitching would not have gone to the ballpark.

In their pregame meeting to go over hitters Don Hoak said, "Harve, if you pitch the way you say you will, you'll have a no-hitter."[20] Matched against the Braves Lew Burdette, he did just that. After 12 innings he hadn't allowed a baserunner. But the run support, lacking all spring, was still lacking this night, and going into the bottom of the 13th inning, the game was still scoreless. The end came quickly for Harvey. In that fateful inning, the Braves' leadoff hitter, Felix Mantilla, reached on a wild throw by Hoak. Eddie Mathews bunted Mantilla to second and Henry Aaron was given an intentional walk, bringing Joe Adcock to the plate, the same Adcock who had smashed a line drive off Haddix's knee in 1954. On a one-ball, no-strike pitch, Adcock hit Haddix's 115th pitch of the night into the right-center-field bleachers. On a base-running blunder, Adcock was called out and credited with a double when Aaron left the basepath and was passed. The final score was 1-0.

Haddix was amazed to find out he had broken the record for consecutive perfect innings to start a game. "Who, me? All I know is we lost. What is so historic about that?"[21] He turned down an opportunity to appear on the television shows *To Tell the Truth* and *The Ed Sullivan Show* feeling it more important to stay with the team. But accolades came from all over the country. National League President Warren Giles presented him with an inscribed silver tea service with 13 cups. Few days would pass the rest of his life when Haddix wasn't asked about the game.

Meanwhile, as the season wore on, Haddix's pitching faltered. He continued to receive little run support and ended the season 12-12 but with a 3.13 ERA. For the second consecutive year, he was recognized for his fielding with the Gold Glove Award. "Haddix really never pitched a bad game for us all year," said manager Danny Murtaugh. "I figured on him for 12 victories but he was consistently good. We just didn't score many runs for him."[22]

The 1960 season began with high expectations for the Pirates, especially if the talented outfielder Roberto Clemente could stay in the lineup. The Pirates were a tight-knit cast of characters. After every win Roy Face would strum his guitar while Fred Green, Bill

Mazeroski, Bill Virdon, Jim Umbricht, Gino Cimoli, and Haddix harmonized. To a man, they would all say it was the best group of players they ever played with. Vern Law said, "Harve was a fun guy—well liked by everyone." [23]

The only question on Haddix's performance was a lack of stamina. His answer: "I've been a seven-inning pitcher at times because I'm a little man and have to work harder out there than some other fellows. I can't afford to coast."[24] Haddix made 28 starts but had only four complete games and finished with an 11-10 record and a 3.97 ERA. Supplemented by midseason acquisition Vinegar Bend Mizell, the Pirates clinched the pennant on September 25.

Going into the World Series against the Yankees, New York first baseman Dale Long, a former Pirate, asked about the Pirates' pitchers: "The one Pittsburgh pitcher who would be likely to make trouble for our team is left-hander Harvey Haddix."[25] Haddix made Long sound like a prophet. He started and won Game Five, pitching into the seventh inning giving up two runs as the Pirates won, 5-2. The victory gave the Pirates a 3-2 lead in the Series. The Yankees won Game Six, and for the seventh game Haddix found himself in the bullpen. In the top of the ninth, with the Pirates leading 9-7, Haddix relieved Bob Friend after the first two Yankees batters got hits. "That was the only time in my life I was really nervous," Haddix said. "The hair stood up on the back of my neck." [26]

Roger Maris was the first batter he faced. "Maris is in there squeezing the sawdust out of the bat and he can't wait to get to me," Haddix recalled. "They were so anxious to hit. I'm talking to myself: 'This is something you have waited for your whole life and now you are going to blow it because of nerves.'" [27]

Haddix got Maris to pop out to the catcher. Then Mickey Mantle singled in a run, and his savvy baserunning on a grounder by Yogi Berra allowed the tying run to score. Haddix retired the side, and when Bill Mazeroski homered in the ninth, Haddix got the victory. He called it his career highlight. Offseason highlights included an $8,400 World Series check and birth of his second child.

The Pirates were favored to win again in 1961, and though Haddix won 10 games and a third Gold Glove, some wondered whether the 34-year-old, nine-year veteran was on the downside of his career. Haddix's innings pitched had dropped to 172⅓ in 1960 and 156 in '61. The team fell to sixth place, a disappointing four games under .500. In September Haddix was moved to the bullpen as manager Murtaugh wanted to see how he reacted to late-inning relief. He was paired with Roy Face to finish games. "I don't find it so bad," he said after the season. "I think I can do the job if that is what they want of me."[28]

In 1962 the plan was for Haddix to stay in the bullpen but an injury to Vern Law changed the plan and Haddix started 20 times in 29 appearances totaling 141 innings, winning nine games and losing six. Although the Pirates won 93 games (in the National League's first 162-game season), they finished in fourth place, behind the Giants, Dodgers, and Reds. Haddix's mother, Nellie, died on June 22. Whether coincidence or not, he struggled for the remainder of the season, which he attributed to losing control of his curveball.

In 1963, the 37-year-old Haddix was the oldest player on the team, and was in the bullpen full time, except for one start. In August teammate Vern Law retired and it appeared the Pirates were preparing to jettison other veterans as they started to rebuild. Haddix pitched 70 innings and ended with three wins, one save, and a 3.34 ERA. The Pirates finished eighth. His relief stint on September 21 turned out to be his last game with the Pirates. On December 14 he was traded conditionally to the Baltimore Orioles for minor-league shortstop Dick Yencha and cash. Although he would always consider himself a Pirate ("A part of me belongs in Pittsburgh"[29]), he said, "It's all right. Wherever there is money I'll go, although this will be my first appearance in the American League."[30]

Haddix's fastball was back in spring training. The Orioles plan was for him to be the left-handed complement to Dick Hall in the bullpen. His career was rejuvenated. For the third-place Orioles in 1964 he pitched 89⅔ innings, all in relief, and had five wins, 10 saves, and a 2.31 ERA. He was the runner-up for the Gold Glove Award. (Haddix's offseason highlights included shooting a 900-pound buffalo owned by a neighbor when it ran wild and attacked their cows.)

After such a strong comeback, few might have imagined that 1965 would be Haddix's last as a pitcher and would end with a trade to the team that had broken his heart six years earlier. Haddix hurt his arm in spring training. "It never got well," he said. "Sometimes it was the shoulder, sometimes the elbow hurt. I didn't pitch much but I used it all the time, hoping work would help, but it didn't."[31] On August 30, Haddix was sold to the Milwaukee Braves, who were fighting for the pennant. Out of sheer honesty, he refused to report and retired instead. "I'd have finished the season if I could have, but there wasn't much sense in changing when I knew I couldn't help a new club the way my arm was feeling," he said at the time. "I wouldn't mind trying again next spring. Or I'd love to catch on with a team looking for a pitching coach."[32] His last big-league appearance was on August 28, 1965.

In November Haddix hired on as the pitching coach of the Vancouver Mounties, the Oakland Athletics' Triple-A team. But on December 29 he resigned and signed as pitching coach of the New York Mets. He would be the first big-league pitching coach for Tug McGraw, Nolan Ryan, Tom Seaver, and Jerry Koosman. In 2009 Ryan said, "Harvey could not have been, from my perspective, more of the right person at the right time for me."[33]

After two ninth-place (out of 10) finishes, Mets manager Wes Westrum was fired near the end of the 1967 season and new manager Gil Hodges replaced the entire coaching staff. Haddix went back to the Pirates' organization in 1968 and coached the Columbus Jets and the Gulf Coast League Pirates. In 1969, he became the Cincinnati Reds' pitching coach. When Reds manager Dave Bristol was fired at the end of the season, it meant back to the minors with Pittsburgh for Haddix. The Boston Red Sox hired him as pitching coach in 1971, but at season's end his wife, Marcia, persuaded him to retire. But when Frank Robinson asked Haddix to join him for his historic managerial tenure in Cleveland, Haddix unretired. From 1975 to 1978, he was the Indians' pitching coach.

In 1979 Haddix joined Chuck Tanner and his beloved "Family"—the Pirates—for the next six seasons, getting his second World Series ring in 1979.

A heavy chain-smoker, who described cigarettes as his best friend, Haddix developed emphysema. This hastened the end of his baseball career and eventually his life. Even though his 1984 Pirates pitchers led the league in ERA, he was fired because thrifty general manager Syd Thrift wanted coaches who could also throw batting practice. Haddix no longer was able. His health continued to deteriorate but he never stopped smoking. He died on January 8, 1994, in Springfield, Ohio. "I loved cigarettes, but they finally got to me," he said a year or so before his death.[34]

In 1999 fans voted Harvey Haddix the left-handed pitcher on the Pirates' All-Century Team to celebrate a career that consisted of much more than the 115 pitches thrown on a rainy night in Milwaukee.

SOURCES

Book

Jim O'Brien, *Maz and the '60 Bucs* (Pittsburgh: James P. O'Brien Publishing Co., 1993).

Newspapers or Magazines:

Dayton (Ohio) *Daily News,* September 9, 1965

Springfield (Ohio) *Daily News,* 1947-1979.

Springfield (Ohio) *Sun,* 1947-1979.

The Sporting News, 1947-1994.

Urbana (Ohio) *Daily Citizen.* May 27, 1992.

Online sources

DVD, *Wright State University Major League Baseball Panel Discussion, April 17, 1989,* produced by Professor Allen Hye, 2009 (Cited as WSU Panel Discussion).

www.baseball-reference.com.

Letters

Letter from Nolan Ryan to Springfield/Clark County Baseball Hall of Fame. May 4, 2009.

Letter from Vern and VaNita Law to Springfield/Clark County Baseball Hall of Fame. January 8, 2009.

Other

Several discussions between the author and Harvey Haddix on numerous occasions in various settings. These were undocumented as both were acquaintances from the same community.

NOTES

1. WSU Panel Discussion.
2. WSU Panel Discussion.
3. WSU Panel Discussion.
4. WSU Panel Discussion.
5. WSU Panel Discussion.
6. WSU Panel Discussion.
7. WSU Panel Discussion.
8. *The Sporting News*, July 21, 1948: 11.
9. *The Sporting News*, September 8, 1948: 21.
10. *The Sporting News*, August 30, 1950: 22.
11. *The Sporting News*, August 18, 1953: 7.
12. *The Sporting News*, January 6, 1954: 8.
13. *The Sporting News*, September 9, 1953: 12.
14. Jim O'Brien, *Maz and the '60 Bucs*, 465.
15. *The Sporting News*, February 16, 1955: 19.
16. WSU Panel Discussion.
17. *The Sporting News*, September 19, 1956.
18. *Springfield Daily News*, December 7, 1957: 2.
19. *The Sporting News*, June 4, 1958: 4.
20. WSU Panel Discussion.
21. O'Brien. *Maz and the '60 Bucs*, 463.
22. *The Sporting News*, November 11, 1959: 16.
23. Vance Law letter.
24. *The Sporting News*, August 31, 1960: 18.
25. *The Sporting News*, September 28, 1960: 10.
26. Quoted in O'Brien, *Maz and the '60 Bucs*, 462.
27. Ibid.
28. *The Sporting News*, January 10, 1962: 23.
29. O'Brien, *Maz and the '60 Bucs*, 468.
30. *The Sporting News*, December 15, 1963: 15.
31. *Dayton Daily News*, September 9, 1965: 22.
32. Ibid.
33. Nolan Ryan letter.
34. O'Brien. *Maz and the '60 Bucs*, 458.

Joe Lonnett

By David E. Skelton

A ONCE-PROMISING PHILADELPHIA Phillies prospect, catcher Joe Lonnett collected fewer than 400 major-league plate appearances yet put in nearly 50 years in professional baseball. An avid fan of the Pie Traynor/Frankie Frisch-led Pirates who played less than 50 miles from his boyhood home, he manned the third-base coaching box during the franchise's famous "We Are Family" 1979 championship season. A devoted family man, Lonnett was nicknamed "Fred Flintstone" for his uncanny resemblance to the cartoon character. Much beloved by teammates and fans alike, he was widely mourned at his 2011 passing.

Born February 7, 1927, in the Rust Belt community of Beaver Falls, Pennsylvania (in the west central part of the state less than 20 miles east of the Ohio border), Joseph Paul Lonnett (pronounced \lon-ETT\) was one of seven children born to Frank Rocco Lonnett and his wife, Rose (Barberio) Lonnett. Around 1910 the Lonnetts (a family of three at the time including Joseph's oldest sister) immigrated to the United States from Italy. Frank found employment in the steel mills while Rose was a stay-at-home mother. Joe, their youngest son, became an accomplished athlete and sports enthusiast. His Beaver Falls High School yearbook cited his prowess on the basketball court above that of his baseball exploits. Graduating in 1944, Lonnett joined the US Navy and served on the battleship Arkansas.

After the war Lonnett was signed by the Cincinnati Reds, but was released in 1947 after batting .221 as an outfielder for Lockport in the Class-D PONY League. In 1948 Lonnett was signed by either Phillies scout Eddie Collins Jr. or George Savino, a scout and minor-league manager. Sent to Bradford in the same Pennsylvania-Ontario-New York League, Lonnett faced release again, and his manager, Savino, suggested a switch behind the plate. The move worked as Lonnett rebounded to place among the league leaders in nearly every offensive category, and Lonnett embarked on a 22-year affiliation with the Phillies in a wide variety of roles—as a player, scout, coach, and minor-league manager.

Lonnett caught the attention of Phillies farm director Joe Reardon and his corps of coaches, the consensus opinion being: "[Lonnett] has a fine arm, is fast, handles himself like a veteran … [and] can hit. … He looks like a 'comer.'"[1] Lonnett was poised to step into the Phillies' catching mix the following spring, but on October 30, 1950, he was drafted by the US Army during the Korean War. Assigned to transportation duties in Newport News, Virginia, Lonnett maintained his catching prowess playing alongside Willie Mays on the Fort Eustis (Virginia) baseball squad while occasionally making the 600-mile round trip to Philadelphia to participate in Phillies workouts. Discharged on October 29, 1952, Lonnett joined the catching competition at spring training in Clearwater, Florida, in 1953. Despite a strong spring, he was optioned to the club's Triple-A affiliate in Baltimore on March 22. "He was as good a receiver or better than either [of our existing catchers] Stan Lopata or Smoky Burgess," explained manager Steve O'Neill. "But he needs a full year's work to put on the finishing touches."[2] But a full year's work was not in the offing. The bulk of catching responsibilities for the International League's Baltimore Orioles went instead to veteran receivers Martin Tabacheck and Al "Moose" Lakeman and, with little use, Lonnett's numbers suffered accordingly.

The season had actually started promisingly for the 26-year-old. Injury and prolonged illness had sidelined the older catchers at the start of the campaign and Lonnett capitalized on the opportunity. A grand slam in his first starting assignment, on April 24, sparked a 6-2 win over the Buffalo Bisons. Six of his first 11 hits were home runs, including a second bases-loaded jolt. But Lonnett suffered a jammed finger on May 23

and a subsequent knee injury, and the healthy return of Tabacheck and Lakeman resulted in less than 200 plate appearances for the season. Despite limited play, he and righty hurler Jack Sanford (an eventual National League Rookie of the Year) were projected to make the jump to the Phillies the following spring, with director of player personnel John Nee reportedly "a big booster for the dark-haired backstop."[3]

After a successful winter league campaign in Colombia, Lonnett batted near .300 in the Grapefruit League. Determined not to lose playing time, he had a fractured finger taped and continued playing. Trade rumors had Lopata or Burgess being sent to Milwaukee for a reserve infielder, but nothing came of this. Despite his inclusion in the list of prized rookies published in April by *The Sporting News*,[4] manager O'Neill reassigned Lonnett to Triple-A Syracuse after having persuaded him to accept a lower-than-sought salary. Excluding a brief promotion in May after Lopata was injured and a September call-up (in neither instance did he get into a game), Lonnett spent the entire 1954 season with Syracuse.

And what a season that would be! The Chiefs became the first team to win the International League playoff championship after a fourth-place finish in the regular season. This success was realized largely on the shoulders of Lonnett. Playing in only 98 games because of the call-ups and time lost to injury, Lonnett still placed among the league leaders in home runs and finished the campaign with a batting line of .268-21-63. A poll of the 16 major-league farm directors rated him one of the league's top prospects. But an advance to the majors was put on hold the following spring when his knee was found to have torn cartilage. Lonnett lost two months when he went under the knife in April 1955, then reinjured the knee on July 13. He ended his second season in Syracuse with just 60 at-bats in 26 games.

Lonnett's long-awaited promotion to the Phillies came in 1956 but not before another injury in spring training, a broken nose from a pitched ball (the injury-prone backstop sustained yet another injury that summer). Under the direction of manager Mayo Smith, who took over the reins the preceding year, the Phillies planned to use Lonnett as a reserve catcher behind 13-year veteran Andy Seminick and move Lopata to first base. This plan worked only until the 35-year-old Seminick demonstrated that his best hitting years were behind him (.146 after May 30). Smith returned Lopata to the starting position behind the plate and designated Seminick as his backup. Relegated to occasional pinch-hit duties, Lonnett made only seven plate appearances after June 5.

No further consideration was given to moving Lopata to first base in 1957 with the advent of powerful left-handed-hitting rookie Ed Bouchee. Meanwhile, Seminick retired, leaving the backup catching responsibilities solely to Lonnett, who had a career-high 160 at-bats. Though he hit only .169, Lonnett's safeties seemed to come in a most timely manner. On June 16 his double in the sixth inning of a scoreless duel between Curt Simmons and Milwaukee's Lew Burdette robbed the Braves righty of a no-hit bid, then Lonnett scored from third base after a sacrifice fly to provide the margin of victory in a 1-0 contest. When Lopata was sidelined by muscle strain beginning in late June, Lonnett flourished in the starting role. On July 4 his first major-league home run (the first of four within a 10-day span) helped the Phillies sweep a doubleheader from the New York Giants. Described as one who would "never win any sprint races,"[5] he managed an inside-the-park four-bagger at Wrigley Field against the Chicago Cubs on July 29 that contributed to a 6-0 win. But Lonnett's real contributions came with the glove. For the second of three consecutive seasons, Lopata placed among the league leaders in errors for a catcher. Meanwhile, Lonnett played error-free until, with only 11 games left in the season he was called for interference. His .997 fielding percentage led NL catchers with 200 or more putouts.

An encouraging start to the 1958 season—.333 in 15 at-bats while still serving as Lopata's backup—succumbed to 29 hitless plate appearances. On June 13, after he started a game in San Francisco, the Phillies traded Lonnett to the Braves for catcher Carl Sawatski. Assigned to Milwaukee's Triple-A affiliate in Wichita, Lonnett didn't resurface in the majors for more than a year.

Fred Haney, manager of the National League champion Milwaukee Braves, sought to enter the 1959 season with three catchers. Among those Lonnett found competing against him that spring was Stan Lopata, traded to the Braves on the last day of March. Failing in his attempt to stick with the Braves, Lonnett was assigned to Triple-A Louisville, where he hit .291 in 86 at-bats. However, on May 28 Lonnett was sent to the Detroit Tigers organization in a multiplayer swap involving minor leaguers. Lonnett refused to report to the Triple-A Charleston (West Virginia) Senators. Perceiving the trade as a means by which the Braves could forgo an agreed-upon restoration of a $3,200 pay cut if he produced well in Louisville, Lonnett instead went home to Beaver Falls and the trade was nullified. The Braves organization sought to have Lonnett placed on the disqualified list, but the Phillies organization stepped back into the picture.

The Phillies' Buffalo affiliate was threatened by a series of injuries. On June 18 the Phillies purchased Lonnett's contract and agreed to pay him about half the money he felt he was due from the Braves. Lonnett picked up at Buffalo where he'd left off in Louisville, then on June 10 was called up to Philadelphia after catcher Valmy Thomas was injured in a home-plate collision. Two days later he swatted a three-run home run during a loss to the Cubs. He got most of the starting assignments over the next 29 games, during which the last-place club was 16-13. Lonnett drew credit for his handling of the pitching staff but when he again lost his hitting stroke—.089 in his final 56 at-bats—he was again relegated to backup duties. On September 26 he had what turned out to be his final three major-league at-bats, against the Braves' Warren Spahn, and was assigned to Triple-A Buffalo at the end of the season.

Never one to escape injury (both on the field and in a car accident in 1959), Lonnett continued in the minors for portions of four seasons, including an all-star campaign in the International League in 1960. His last season was in 1963 with the Arkansas Travelers, where he was teamed briefly with a young slugger whose high-school basketball games he once officiated, Richie "Dick" Allen. "I felt closer to [Lonnett] than anyone," Allen said.[6] Lonnett returned to Beaver Falls, where he scouted for the Phillies in and around western Pennsylvania. In June 1965 he took over the reins of the Huron (South Dakota) Phillies in the short-season Northern League. The next year Lonnett became the first professional manager of another budding slugger, Larry Hisle.

The careers and lives of Lonnett and Chuck Tanner are remarkably similar in many ways. Born 17 months and 23 miles apart, they both spent about the same number of years lingering in the minor leagues. Though Tanner spent twice as many years in the majors, neither player ever attained the level of full-time regular. A lifelong kinship was forged when they were teammates on a barnstorming squad roaming Pennsylvania after the 1957 season. In 1970 Tanner, after taking the reins of the Chicago White Sox, Tanner hired Lonnett as his third-base/catching coach.

From 1971 to 1984, Lonnett and fellow coach Al Monchak accompanied Tanner from Chicago to Oakland to Pittsburgh. The trio won the praise of White Sox general manager Roland Hemond, who told *The Sporting News*, "Tanner has done the best job of managing I've ever seen. With coaches … Joe Lonnett [and] Al Monchak … to help, [they've] molded the talent we've been able to acquire into a high-spirited, enthusiastic and aggressive ballclub."[7] Lonnett was largely credited with shepherding the catching careers of Brian Downing, Ed Ott, and Steve Nicosia, while his humor was oft cited for breaking the monotony of a long season. Assessing the poor playing conditions in Comiskey Park after the White Sox had replaced the AstroTurf infield with natural grass in 1976, Lonnett suggested, "They must have used bumpy blades."[8]

In the spring of 1978 White Sox pitcher Wilbur Wood "turned an extra exhibition game with the Pirates into an eventual farce when he glued down the personal effects of Pittsburgh coach Joe Lonnett. [Joe] had the last laugh when he pinch-hit and, after ducking a Wood lob at his head, singled. He … scored on a single … laugh[ing] all the way home."[9]

Described as a "fellow who takes charge,"[10] Lonnett called on his Roman Catholic upbringing to help maintain a strong sense of right and wrong. As the salary dispute with the Milwaukee Braves indicated, he was no wallflower when it came to expressing his views. In the winter of 1953, while playing in Colombia, he was one of four players protesting for better living arrangements for himself and his teammates. Years later his actions spoke volumes when he left a restaurant that would not serve African-American star Dick Allen. Allen once referred to another as "a good baseball coach, like Joe Lonnett."[11] On this occasion, Lonnett was teaching something more than just baseball.

Lonnett's tenure with the Pirates ended after the 1984 season. He declined an offer to manage the Prince William (Virginia) Pirates in the Class-A Carolina League. He instead spent his later years as a roving minor-league instructor for the Pittsburgh and Toronto organizations. In the 1990s, as he approached his 70th birthday, Lonnett could be found participating in the fan-favorite Legends of Baseball spring exhibitions.

Lonnett was inducted into the Beaver County (Pennsylvania) Sports Hall of Fame in 1980. In 2004 he attended the 25th anniversary celebration of the 1979 championship team at PNC Park. On those few occasions when Lonnett was not attending to baseball-related functions, he enjoyed shooting pool and bowling, sporting a 200 average in the latter while possessing the ability to run the table in the former. "He was good at anything he did both athletically and otherwise," his daughter Barbara remembered. In later years Lonnett battled Alzheimer's disease and was cared for by Alvida, his wife of 56 years. He died on December 5, 2011, two months shy of his 85th birthday. He was survived by Alvida, five daughters, and six grandchildren.

Former pitcher Kent Tekulve said of Lonnett, "He was that universal personality in the clubhouse who would make you happy just looking at him. You would be happy about being a Pittsburgh Pirate. You would be happy about being part of this team and you would be happy about getting to work with Joe Lonnett." Former pitcher and later Pirates broadcaster Jim Rooker said, "There are people with big hearts, but Joe he had a mega-heart. … He was such a wonderful person."

A player who never cracked .200 in his major-league career, Lonnett often quipped that if a kid found his baseball card lying in a ditch he'd keep walking. Lonnett will never be Cooperstown-bound. But should a Hall of Fame be established for beloved and generous human beings Lonnett would undoubtedly be a first-class inductee.

SOURCES

The author wishes to thank Lisa Smith-Curtean, a volunteer at the West Waco (Texas) Library and Genealogy Center, for her helpful support researching the 1940 census. Further thanks to Barbara Lonnett and the extended Lonnett family for their valuable input, and Rod Nelson, chair of the SABR Scouts Committee.

post-gazette.com/stories/local/obituaries/obituary-joe-lonnett-third-base-coach-for-1979-champion-pirates-224526/

triblive.com/x/pittsburghtrib/sports/pirates/s_770986.html#axzz2dvD72XRg youtube.com/watch?v=58C7-7gRSKI

Lonnett, Barbara, email correspondence (from which all unattributed quotes derive), September 2013 to April 2014, and June 22, 2015.

NOTES

1. "Lonnett, Phil Kid Catcher, Called Comer," *The Sporting News*, January 21, 1953: 21.
2. "Kazanski, 80-Grand Kid, Given Shot at Shortstop Job on Phils," *The Sporting News*, April 1, 1953: 20.
3. "Phillies Flash Wide Grin Over Record Harvest," *The Sporting News*, September 9, 1953: 14.
4. "Power, Lynch Tabbed Prize Rookies," *The Sporting News*, April 14, 1954: 2.
5. "Vintage Trio Joins Rookies as Phillies' Surprise Packages," *The Sporting News*, July 24, 1957: 4.
6. "Allen, Fast-Stepping Traveler, Beating Path to Phillies' Door," *The Sporting News*, August 31, 1963: 31.
7. "'Alger' Hemond Major Exec of Year," *The Sporting News*, December 2, 1972: 35.
8. Dick Young, "Young Ideas, *The Sporting News*, June 19, 1976: 18.
9. "White Sox Left With Raw Receivers," *The Sporting News*, April 15, 1978: 20.
10. "'54 Phillies to Be Restyled Into Junior Whiz Kid Model," *The Sporting News*, November 11, 1953: 8.
11. Dick Young, "Young Ideas," *The Sporting News*, June 22, 1974: 14.

Alex Monchak

By Carole J. Olshavsky

WHILE BASEBALL HISTORY IS MOST OFTEN made by winning teams and talented players, there are many less visible people who have had just as profound an impact on the sport. They include Alex Monchak. During his career, he played on 16 baseball teams, managed eight different teams over 13 seasons, coached for four major-league teams over a span of 16 years, and worked for major-league teams for another nine years as a scout and instructor. His baseball career spanned more than 60 years and his enthusiasm for the sport continued long beyond that.

Alex "Al" Monchak was born on March 5, 1917, in Bayonne, New Jersey, the oldest son of George and Matrona Monchak. George (Jurko) Monchak emigrated in 1911 from Turka, (Powiat), Austria-Hungary, a town high in Eastern Europe's Carpathian Mountains. He left home along with three brothers and a sister shortly after the death of their parents. Al's mother, Matrona Marycz, emigrated in 1914 from Galitzia, Poland arriving in America when she was 14. George and Matrona were married in 1916.

The Monchaks settled in Pennsylvania and New Jersey in areas where industrial work was plentiful. George found work as a laborer at a Standard Oil Company refinery in New Jersey and he and Matrona raised three children, Alex, younger brother Edward, and sister Mary. Alex first learned to play baseball in Bayonne and after high school he worked as a laborer when not pursuing his baseball career. His life-long dream was to be involved in major league baseball. In 1937 he played a total of 77 games with middling results for four minor-league teams: 46 games at shortstop for the Clarksdale (Mississippi) Red Sox of the Class-C Cotton States League; one game for the Knoxville (Tennessee) Smokies of the Class-A1 Southern Association); 16 games at third base for the Albany (New York) Senators of the Class-A New York-Pennsylvania League; and 14 games for the Baltimore Orioles of the Double-A International League. In 1938 he moved down to Class-D, as a shortstop in 95 games for the Dover (Delaware) Orioles of the Eastern Shore League, and batted .303 with 10 home runs. Back with Dover in 1939, he batted .337 and hit 15 home runs. Late in the season he played in three games for Baltimore.

In 1940 Monchak started the season with Portsmouth of the Class-B Piedmont League, a Philadelphia Phillies farm team. In June the Phillies called Monchak up and he spent the rest of the season with the National League tail-enders (50-103), though he got into only 19 games, many of them as a late-inning replacement. Monchak made his major-league debut on June 22, in a 10-2 blowout by the Chicago Cubs at Shibe Park. He replaced shortstop Bobby Bragan late in the game and had one at-bat. For the season he was 2-for-14 (.143) He played shortstop in nine games and second base in one. His big-league playing career ended during a doubleheader loss to the Boston Bees on September 1, 1940. Monchak was a pinch-runner in the first game, and started the second game at shortstop (his only major-league start) and went 0-for-4.

In 1941 Monchak played shortstop for the Elmira (New York) Pioneers of the Class-A Eastern League, an affiliate of the Detroit Tigers. With the United States now engaged in World War II, the 6-foot-tall, 180-pound infielder returned to Elmira in 1942, but on June 25 he enlisted in the Army, where he was deployed served in the 11th Armored Division in Europe, and fought under General George Patton in the Battle of the Bulge. Monchak rose to the rank of warrant officer, and acquired the nickname Sarge, which stuck with him for many years.

With the war ended, Monchak returned to baseball in 1946 to play in the Class-A Eastern League with the Hartford Chiefs, an affiliate of the Boston Braves. In midseason Monchak was badly injured in a collision with a first-base umpire that left him unconscious for three days. Monchak suffered from temporary lower-body paralysis, which forced him to the sidelines for the rest of the season and all of the 1947 season. By 1948 Monchak was well enough to join the Austin (Texas) Pioneers of the Class-B Big State League, where the 31-year-old played in 120 games and batted .289.

The next season Monchak started his lengthy coaching career. In 1949 and 1950 he was the player-manager for the Odessa (Texas) Oilers of the Class-D Longhorn League, winning the league championship in 1950. In 1951 the league moved up in classification to Class-C and Monchak spent two years at the helm of the Roswell (New Mexico) Rockets. In 1951 he guided Roswell to the playoffs, where they were beaten by his former Odessa team. As a player he career bests in games played (140), at-bats (565), and hits (176), and batted .312 with 22 home runs.

Late in the 1952 season Monchak was hit in the head while pitching batting practice and was unable to play the rest of the season.[1] The Rockets finished out of the playoffs with a 65-75 record.

In 1953 Monchak managed the Lexington (North Carolina) Indians of the Class-D Tar Heel League to fourth place and the playoff championship. He was able to return as a player and batted .232 in 112 games. He continued as player-manager when he moved for the 1954 season to the Portsmouth Merrimacks of the Piedmont League but was fired in midseason. He caught on for the rest of the season as a player with the Keokuk (Iowa) Kernels, an affiliate of the Cleveland Indians, of the Class-B Illinois-Indiana-Iowa (Three-I) League.

The next three years (1955-1957) were spent managing the Wellsville (New York) Braves of the Class-D Pennsylvania-Ontario-New York (PONY) League, a Milwaukee Braves farm team. His first year he led the team to a fourth-place finish and in 1956 he led Wellsville to first place and the playoff championship. Wellsville finished first again in 1957, but was eliminated in the first round of the playoffs. This was the 40-year-old Monchak's last season as a player, and he appeared in only four games.

For 1958 the Braves made Monchak the manager of Cedar Rapids of the Three-I League. Monchak led the

team to a first-place finish and a league championship, his fourth and final minor-league championship. In 1959 the team plunged to last place. This was apparently no reflection on Monchak, because in 1960 the Braves moved him up to Double-A Austin (Texas League). On his departure from Cedar Rapids with his wife, Audrey, and their children, Alex and Trona, Monchak, in a letter to the *Cedar Rapids Gazette,* captured the depth of his commitment to his sport and his family's value of community:

"There come moments when people find themselves filled with mixed emotion. On the brink of our departure from Cedar Rapids, we find ourselves in that category. ... Our family has enjoyed 2 wonderful years with you. This was made possible by the fine efforts of many and we are thankful and grateful. ... In this friendly, freedom loving land of ours, baseball belongs; enjoy it, but above all support it. We enjoyed your area and fine people. For the Monchaks, each phase of life in Cedar Rapids shall always remain our treasured memories."[2]

For the next season Monchak was assigned to manage the Quad Cities Braves of the Class-D Midwest League. (Quad Cities was the moniker for Davenport and Bettendorf, Iowa, and Moline and Rock Island, Illinois. Monchak managed the 1961 team to a 68-56 record. In 1962 Quad Cities became an affiliate of the expansion Los Angeles Angels, and Monchak went to work for the Angels, as a scout and minor-league instructor. This marked the beginning of a 26-year-long career with Chuck Tanner. Their careers initially overlapped as part of the Milwaukee Braves system when Monchak managed the Wellsville Braves and Tanner played for the team. From 1963 to 1970, Tanner worked his way up the ladder in the Angels organization, then landed his first major-league managing job with the Chicago White Sox. Tanner brought Monchak along as a coach. The *Chicago Tribune* noted that Monchak had "already earned a reputation as one of the best infield tutors around." He was known for teaching the defensive team to attack the ball in the field the way hitters attack the ball at the plate.[3]

Tanner was fired by the White Sox in 1975 and in December of that year he was hired to manage the Oakland Athletics. Monchak became the team's third-base coach. The Oakland stint lasted just one year; in November of 1976 Oakland owner Charlie Finley "traded" Tanner to Pittsburgh in exchange for catcher Manny Sanguillen and $100,000. Tanner's coaching team moved with him to Pittsburgh, Monchak as the first-base coach.

The Pirates in the late 1970s were the stuff of legends with players like Willie Stargell and Bert Blyleven leading the pack. The "We Are Family" team of 1979 won the World Series despite losing three of the first four games to the Baltimore Orioles. The team's success continued until the 1985 season when the glory days faded, and Tanner and his coaching team left the Pirates after a dismal season with 104 losses.

Tanner caught on as manager of the Atlanta Braves in 1986 and Monchak joined him, as the infield coach in Atlanta with Willie Stargell as hitting coach. The team had great expectations after a disappointing season in 1985 when the Braves finished 29 games behind Los Angeles in the NL West. Tanner and his coaching staff continued to lead the Braves through the next two seasons, but finished near the bottom of the division each year. A few weeks into the 1988 season, Tanner and his coaches—Monchak, Stargell, Bob Skinner, and Tony Bartirome—were fired.

While in Atlanta, Braves owner Ted Turner asked a team of Soviet basketball players to come to Atlanta for a series of games against NBA summer teams. The visiting Soviets were welcomed to Atlanta in "spirited Russian" by Monchak, who still spoke his parents' native language.[4]

By this time he left the Braves, Monchak was 71 years old, but not ready to retire. In 1991 he and Ed Napoleon were hired by the Baltimore Orioles to work with Juan Bell and Jeff McKnight in spring training with the goal of increasing their versatility.[5] In 1999 and 2000, he worked again with Tanner as a major-league scout for the Milwaukee Brewers.[6]

In 2004 Al's wife, Audrey Guidry Monchak, died and was buried at Arlington National Cemetery.[7] He had knee-replacement surgery in April of 2012 at the age of 95. After just a few weeks of rehabilitation, he was already looking forward to the all-clear to start dancing and commented, "I enjoy anything with movement in legs, but dancing is one of the better ones."[8] He was one of the oldest living major leaguers.

In 2009 Monchak was honored as the recipient of the Roland Hemond Award at McKechnie Field in Bradenton, Florida, which recognizes the recipients for their leadership and contributions to scouting and coaching. He was inducted into the Cedar Rapids Baseball Hall of Fame on January 17, 2013, specifically for leading the Cedar Rapids Braves to the league championship in 1958. Afterward, blogger Steve Buhr (aka Jim Crikket) posted the following:

"I'm sure most of you have no idea who Monchak is, but this man epitomizes the career baseball man. He had a cup of coffee with the Phillies, but his career was interrupted by World War II. While he never returned to the big leagues as a player, that didn't stop him from spending the rest of his life teaching others to play the game the right way."[9]

Alex Monchak passed away on September 12, 2015, and at the time of his passing he was the third oldest living Major League Baseball Player and the oldest living Philadelphia Phillies player. He is buried alongside his wife, Audrey, in the columbarium at Arlington National Cemetery.

SOURCES

In preparing this biography, the author relied on Baseball-reference.com and Baseball Almanac for chronological baseball information and statistics as well as family documents for personal history.

NOTES

1 Toby Smith, *Bush League Boys: The Postwar Legends of Baseball in the American Southwest*, (Albuquerque: University of Mexico Press, 2014), 173.

2 *Cedar Rapids Gazette*, Letters to the Gazette Sports Department, January 24, 1960.

3 Bob Logan, "Monchak Wants Attack on Defense," *Chicago Tribune*, September 10, 1971: Sect. 3, 1.

4 *New York Times*, August 4, 1987.

5 Peter Schmuck, "Hemond continues talking with Maldonado's agent," *Baltimore Sun*, February 23, 1991.

6 "Where Are They Now," Pittsburgh Sports Report, 1999, and *Baltimore Sun* online.

7 *Bradenton Herald*, September 2, 2004.

8 Press release, "10th Oldest Living MLB Player, Alex Monchak, Receives Knee Replacement," Blake Medical Center, 2013.

9 Jim Crikket, "Kernals Hot Stove & Twins Caravan," Knuckleballsblog, January 18, 2013.

Bob Skinner

By Joseph Wancho

AFTER STAGNATING AT THE BOTTOM OF the National League for much of the 1950s, the Pittsburgh Pirates showed some life toward the end of the decade, finishing in second place in 1958 and in fourth place in 1959.

They began the 1960 season with an Opening Day loss at Milwaukee. They began the home portion of their schedule with a four-game series against Cincinnati starting on April 14. After splitting the first two games, the teams closed out the set with a doubleheader on the 17th, Easter Sunday. Bob Friend pitched a four-hit shutout in the opener as Pittsburgh won, 5-0. In the nightcap, Reds pitchers Don Newcombe and Raul Sanchez pitched their team to a 5-0 lead heading into the ninth inning. But the Pirates battled back in the bottom of the frame. They scratched for a run and after Hal Smith's pinch-hit three-run homer, the deficit was just one run. Then shortstop Dick Groat singled to center field and left-fielder Bob Skinner homered to right off Reds reliever Ted Wieand, giving the Pirates a most improbable victory. Besides providing the winning margin in the second game, Skinner enjoyed a wonderful day at the plate, going 4-for-9 with two runs scored and two runs batted in. Those Pirates fans who remained among the announced Easter Sunday attendance of 16,196 left Forbes Field happy after witnessing a different type of resurrection before their very eyes.

For many baseball fans the arrival of spring brings the promise of warm weather and hopes for a pennant in the autumn for their heroes. But even the most astute Pirates fan could not have imagined how Skinner's game-winning blast would foreshadow how the Bucs' season would end in October.

Robert Ralph Skinner was born to Ralph and Lula Skinner on October 3, 1931, in La Jolla, California. At La Jolla High School he earned two varsity letters in baseball and was named to two all-star teams. Ralph, his father, was a Spanish teacher at the school and coached track and field. After high school, Bob enrolled at San Diego Junior College, where he played basketball as well as baseball.

Pittsburgh scouts Tom Downey and Art Billings signed Skinner to a contract with the Pirates in 1951. Sent to Mayfield, Kentucky, of the Class-D Kitty League, the 19-year-old Skinner played in 29 games and smacked 50 hits in 106 at-bats for an amazing .472 batting average. Moved up to Waco of the Class-B Big State League, he cooled off, batting .283 in 98 games. His combined average was .326 with 87 runs batted in, 107 runs scored, 15 home runs, and 31 doubles. The 6-foot-4, 190-pound left-handed hitting first baseman showed patience at the plate, accumulating 86 walks against 52 strikeouts.

The US was fighting in the Korean War and Skinner was drafted into the Marines. He spent two years at the San Diego Recruiting Depot, where he played for the base team. Toward the end of the 1953 major-league season Pirates general manager Branch Rickey told manager Fred Haney to check Skinner out when he got back home to the West Coast.[1] Haney's report on Skinner prompted Rickey to invite the young player, who was about to be discharged, to the big-league camp the following spring.

On January 4, 1954, Skinner and Joan Phillips were married. The next month he reported to spring training at Jaycee Park in Fort Pierce, Florida. In 1953 the Pirates had finished in last place, 55 games behind pennant-winning Brooklyn. (In '52 they had also finished in last place, 54½ games out.) Whatever the team's goals were, Skinner, in his first spring training camp, hoped to make the Pirates' top farm team. "I hoped to do well enough to be assigned to New Orleans," he said.[2]

The Pirates were high on Skinner's ability. Rickey called him "absolutely the best natural hitter I've seen in many years.... who gets an awful lot of power into his swings. He does not seem to go for too many bad balls. Rickey predicted: "The boy has a tremendous future."[3]

Manager Fred Haney concurred with his boss. "He's destined to be one of the great hitters in baseball," he said. "He has a wonderful attitude too. He doesn't try to be fancy. I asked him the other day how he got so much power in that swing and he said, 'I dunno, I just go up there and swing.'"[4]

Though all he had hoped for in his first big-league camp was to be assigned to Triple A, Skinner performed well enough to make the Pirates roster. On the team's way north he received a call informing him that Joan had been in a head-on car accident in Oklahoma. Bob went to Oklahoma to be with her, and was relieved to find out that she had not been badly injured, and he was able to rejoin the team the day before the season opened.

Skinner started 116 games at first base in his rookie year, hitting .249 with eight home runs and 46 RBIs. Just over a week into the season, on April 22, he got four hits in a 7-4 victory over the New York Giants, the first of several four-hit games in his 12-year major-league career. At season's end the Pirates found themselves in last place for the third season in a row, 44 games off the pace.

In 1955 the Pirates decided Skinner needed more seasoning and sent him to the New Orleans Pelicans of the Double-A Southern Association. After 86 games he was leading the league with a .346 batting average but his season ended when he broke his left wrist. When he reported to spring training in 1956, Bobby Bragan was the manager; he had replaced Haney after another last-place showing by the Bucs in 1955.

Skinner made the team in 1956 but was supplanted at first base by Dale Long. He played only 24 games at first, 36 games in the outfield, bouncing between left field and right field, and even played two innings at third base. Skinner, who had never played in the outfield before, spent the season learning the nuances of being an outfielder. Because of that defensive focus, and as is common with many part-time players, he was unable to establish a smooth flow to his offensive game. He hit .202 for the season as the Pirates left the cellar and moved up to seventh place.

Left-fielder Lee Walls was traded to the Chicago Cubs at the beginning of the 1957 season, and Skinner replaced him against right-handed starters. Although the Pirates were still struggling in the standings, they were forming a good nucleus of ballplayers. Bill Mazeroski and Dick Groat were becoming a terrific keystone combination, Bill Virdon was solid in center field, and Bob Friend and Vern Law were leading a young pitching staff. But the player who brought it all together for the Pirates was Roberto Clemente. He could run, throw, and hit for power and average; the complete player. The Pirates were on the cusp of being a pennant contender.

The 1957 Pirates were 36-67 when Bragan was fired on August 4 and replaced by third-base coach Danny Murtaugh, who would enjoy a long managerial career in Pittsburgh. The new manager informed Skinner, "You're playing left field until you play your way out of it."[5] And 1957 became Skinner's breakout year. Showing he was the hitter Rickey and Haney predicted he would be, Skinner batted .305 and hit 13 home runs. Almost half of his 118 hits came after the patient Murtaugh took the reins of the club.

The Pirates had slipped back to the cellar in 1957 but finished the 1958 season in second place, eight games behind Milwaukee. Skinner led the team in batting average (.321), on-base percentage (.387), and walks (58), and was second to Groat in doubles (33, to Groat's 36). He shined in his left-field position at Forbes Field, leading the league with 17 outfield assists. Skinner was the starter in left field for the National League in the All-Star Game, in Baltimore. He went 1-for-3 with an RBI in a 4-3 loss to the American League.

Skinner was earning respect from his teammates for his hitting. He was being compared to St. Louis Cardinals great Stan Musial as the best left-handed hitter in the league. Teammate Dick Groat rated him the best left-handed hitter in the league after Musial. "And I'm not so sure he isn't about up with Stan," said the Pirates shortstop.[6]

Skinner said his approach at the plate was simple: "My objective is to meet the ball in a level swing. Then it has a chance to go some place whether you hit it in the air or on the ground."[7] Murtaugh, true to his word, penciled Skinner in the lineup and left him there. It didn't matter to Murtaugh which arm the opposing pitcher used to pitch. "He's a hard-working kid," said the manager. "He took up handball to help him get the angle of playing balls hit off the wall and that big scoreboard in left field in Pittsburgh."[8]

The Pirates finished the 1959 campaign in fourth place, nine games behind pennant-winner Los Angeles. Skinner's average dipped some, but he still batted a respectable .280, smacking 13 homers and driving in 61 runs. Both figures were good enough for second on the team behind first baseman Dick Stuart (27 HRs, 78 RBIs). Skinner led the team with 78 runs scored. In a four-game series in Cincinnati in late May he was 7-for-16, with five home runs and 11 RBIs, including a grand slam in the finale. The Pirates stayed in the hunt throughout the season, and as the calendar turned to September they were only five games out of the top spot. An 8-14 record that month, however, sealed their fate, and they finished in fourth place, nine games out of first.

The Pirates brought it all together in 1960, clinching the pennant when the second-place Cardinals lost to the Cubs on September 24. They finished the year with a 95-59-1 record. (The tie was a 7-7 duel with San Francisco on June 28 that was never completed.) Skinner hit for an average of .273, with 15 home runs and 86 RBIs, a career high. He was chosen to start in left field for the National League in both of that year's All-Star Games.

Skinner missed five games of the epic seven-game World Series against the New York Yankees. He went 1-fotr-3 with an RBI and a run scored in Game One, but jammed his thumb when he slid head-first into third base in the fifth inning, then was hit by a pitch in the seventh. After that he was replaced by Gino Cimoli, and didn't return to the Pirates' lineup until the epic seventh game, in Pittsburgh. Down 7-4 to the Yankees in the eighth inning, the Pirates scored five runs to take a 9-7 lead. During the rally, Virdon was on second and Groat on first when Skinner laid down a perfect sacrifice bunt along the third-base line to move the runners up. After the Yankees tied the game with two runs in the top of the ninth inning, Bill Mazeroski won the Series with a dramatic home run off Ralph Terry that gave Pittsburgh its first world championship since 1925.

Success did not last for long. In 1961 the Pirates dropped to sixth place, 18½ games off the pace. They were in third place at the All-Star break, but started the second half with a 3-14 record. For the third straight year, Skinner's average dropped, this time to .268. Virdon and Groat also turned in poor years and no starter won more than 14 games.

In 1962 the National League expanded by two teams, adding Houston and New York. That season Skinner rebounded at the plate with a .302 batting average. He led the team in home runs (20) and walks (76), and ranked second in doubles (29) and RBIs (75). The Pirates improved as well, finishing fourth with a record of 93-68. But in 1963 the team was dismal, finishing ahead of only the two expansion teams. Skinner was not there at the finish, as he became the fourth regular from the 1960 World Series winners to be shipped out of Pittsburgh. Groat, Stuart, and Hoak had all left before the trade that sent Skinner to Cincinnati for pinch-hitter extraordinaire Jerry Lynch

on May 23. The *Dayton Daily News* summarized the trade with the following headline: "Reds Get Regular for Lynch the Pinch." "I've got to like this deal," said Reds Manager Fred Hutchinson. "Skinner can play more for us—he can do more things. Jerry has done a great job for us, but I'd rather have a guy who can play every day. It's nice to have a good bench, but not at the expense of the regular lineup."[9] Skinner had a similar take on the swap: "You always have a soft spot for the first team, but I'm real glad to come to this team. I'd been playing regular, but the last few days Willie Stargell and Ted Savage had been in the lineup for me and Clemente. So I kind of had an inkling that something might be going to happen."[10]

Skinner played regularly at first, but as the season wore on he was sitting on Hutchinson's bench. He was in the starting lineup for only 10 games from July 11 to the end of the season. Skinner hit .253 for the Reds, to end up at .259 for the season. People started to think that perhaps the Pirates were following the adage of trading a player a year too early instead of a year too late. Skinner dismissed these criticisms, instead putting the onus on himself to work hard that winter, and report to spring training in top shape.

Now 32 years old, Skinner was a part-time starter for the Reds as the 1964 opened. Hitting just .220 in 59 at-bats, he was dealt to the Cardinals on June 13, 1964 for a career minor-league catcher, Jim Saul. At first the move proved to be a bit of a rebirth for Skinner. He was inserted into the starting lineup by Cardinals manager Johnny Keane. He was also reunited with Groat, who had come to the Cardinals a year earlier. But on June 15 St. Louis pulled off a blockbuster trade, acquiring Lou Brock from the Cubs in a six-player deal, and by mid-July Brock was getting most of the starts in left field. Skinner was once again relegated to the bench, starting only on occasion for the rest of the season.

The Cardinals won the pennant with a remarkable late-season rush, aided by the Phillies' collapse. In the World Series their opponent was again the New York Yankees, whom Skinner and Groat had faced when they were on the Pirates four years earlier. This Series also went seven games, with the Cardinals winning. Skinner didn't play in the field; in four pinch-hitting appearances he went 2-for-3 with a walk, a double, and an RBI.

In 1965 Skinner was used primarily in a reserve role by new St. Louis skipper Red Schoendienst. He spelled either Brock in left field or Mike Shannon in right. "Bob's still a good hitter—and good hitters are hard to find," Schoendienst said. "He can jump off the bench after a long layoff and do a real good job with the bat. And he's still dangerous as a long-ball threat."[11] In 152 at-bats Skinner hit .309, showing his professionalism by being ready when called on. He also started in 28 games in the outfield. In 1966, though, Skinner was used strictly as a pinch-hitter, 48 times, and not once seeing the field in a defensive position.

Skinner was released by the Cardinals after the season. He managed the San Diego Padres of the Pacific Coast League, the Philadelphia Phillies' Triple-A affiliate, in 1967 and 1968. He led the Padres to the PCL championship in his first season and was named Minor League Manager of the Year by *The Sporting News*. (Skinner was inducted into the San Diego Hall of Fame in 1976.) When Gene Mauch, manager of the Phillies, was fired in mid-June of 1968, Skinner was promoted from San Diego to replace him. When Mauch was fired the Phillies were in fifth place, but only 5½ games out of first place. It was believed that difficulties with Richie Allen, the Phillies' star outfielder and a consistent discipline problem, led to Mauch's sacking. Nevertheless, Skinner was pleased with the promotion: "The organization has been great to me and it's a real thrill and pleasure to be able to manage the team," he said.[12]

The Phillies posted a 48-59 record under Skinner's watch in 1968, finishing 21 games out of first place. The 1969 season was a frustrating one for Bob and the Phillies. Although Skinner said all the right things about being positive and about the team having the proper attitude, it did not take long for the inevitable clash between the manager and the star. Allen skipped a doubleheader in New York on June 24. He was suspended for 26 games and did not play until July 24 in Houston. In addition to the suspension, it was reported that Allen was fined $450 each game he did not play, for a total of $11,700. On August 5, Allen informed Skinner that he had an agreement with Phillies owner Bob Carpenter and that he refused to accompany the team to Reading for an exhibition game against the Phillies' Double-A affiliate. Skinner resigned a few days later.

"Now I know what Gene Mauch went through," said Skinner. "You can fine Allen and he just laughs at you. He negotiates with the front office, makes his own private agreement and it's like handing the money right back to him. I don't want to go on managing this club under the circumstances."[13] The Phillies were 44-64 when Skinner resigned. Bob Carpenter said that Skinner really resigned because the Phillies wouldn't extend his contract past the 1969 season. Carpenter's But his assertion largely fell on deaf ears. An article by New York columnist Jimmy Cannon was headlined, "The Richie Allen Mess—Skinner: Class Guy." Cannon wrote of Skinner: "He isn't working, but he goes voluntarily for matters of pride. He went down with style because he refused to maim his dignity as a man. There aren't many men in baseball who would make this choice. The world is short of them. And that is why there is so much trouble."[14]

Skinner spent the next 30 years in a variety of posts. He coached for the Padres, Angels, Pirates, and Braves from 1970 through 1988. In 1979, he was the hitting coach for the Pirates, who won the World Series that year. One of Skinner's projects in 1979 was Tim Foli, the Pirates' light-hitting shortstop. By getting Foli to hold the bat parallel to the ground and choke up, Skinner helped him raise his batting average that season by 40 points over his career average. Foli proved valuable in the second position of the batting order behind speedster Omar Moreno.

Skinner managed the Tucson Toros, Houston's Triple-A affiliate, in 1989 and 1990. After that he stayed in the Houston organization as a special assignment scout until 2009.

As of 2011 Skinner and his wife, Joan, resided in the San Diego area. They had four sons, Robert, Craig, Andrew, and Joel. In 2002 Bob and Joel became only the second father-and-son combination (George and Dick Sisler were the first) to be major-league managers, when Joel became the Cleveland Indians manager.

SOURCES

Ranier, Bill, and David Finoli. *When the Pirates Won It All* (Jefferson, North Carolina: McFarland and Company, Inc., 2005).

Peterson, Richard. *The Pirates Reader* (Pittsburgh: University of Pittsburgh Press, 2003).

The Pittsburgh Pirate Encyclopedia (Champaign, Illinois: Sports Publishing LLC, 2003).

The Sporting News

1930 United States Census.

http://www.sabr.org/

http://minors.sabrwebs.com/cgi-bin/index.php

http://www.baseballlibrary.com/homepage/

http://www.retrosheet.org/

http://www.sdhoc.com/

NOTES

1 *Pittsburgh Press*, June 1, 1958.
2 *New York Times*, April 19, 1959.
3 Unidentified clipping found in Skinner's player file at the National Baseball Hall of Fame Library.
4 Ibid.
5 *New York Times*, April 19, 1959.
6 *Baseball Digest*, June 1959.
7 Ibid.
8 Ibid.
9 *Dayton Daily News*, May 24, 1963.
10 Ibid.
11 Unidentified clipping found in Skinner's player file at the National Baseball Hall of Fame Library.
12 Ibid.
13 Ibid.
14 Ibid.

Harding "Pete" Peterson

By Richard J. Puerzer

SEVERAL PEOPLE SERVED AS THE ARCHI-tects of the 1979 Pittsburgh Pirates team, but no one had as much influence as general manager Harding "Pete" Peterson. Peterson had been employed by the Pirates organization throughout his entire adult life, serving as a player, minor-league manager, scout, director of scouting, vice president, and general manger. Peterson helped to construct the 1979 team through his years developing talent as a scout and through player acquisitions as the general manager. Peterson even influenced the leadership of the team as he had traded for manager Chuck Tanner. Pete Peterson put together the team that would become known as "the family."

Harding William Peterson was born on October 17, 1929, the eldest child of Lewis and Gladys Peterson. The Petersons lived in Perth Amboy, New Jersey, a town just across the Arthur Kill from Staten Island, New York. Lewis Peterson worked a stationary engineer. As a youth Harding Peterson, then known as Hardy, played several sports, but baseball was always his favorite. His early heroes were Bill Dickey and Joe DiMaggio, and he always chose to emulate DiMaggio in his backyard after attending the occasional Yankees game.[1] After high school, Peterson attended nearby Rutgers University, where he played on the varsity squad as a catcher in the 1948, 1949, and 1950 seasons. In 1950 Peterson was a second team All-America selection by the American Baseball Coaches Association, the first-ever baseball All-America selection at Rutgers. The 1950 Rutgers team, managed by former Washington Senators outfielder George Case, had a fantastic season and finished third in the College World Series, Rutgers' only appearance in the tournament.

After Rutgers, Peterson signed with the Pirates in 1950, beginning a 35-year run with the organization. He began his professional career with the Tallahassee Pirates of the Class-D Georgia-Florida League, where he hit .275 in 45 games. In 1951 he was promoted to the Waco Pirates of the Class-B Big State League. Peterson, then 21 years old, had an excellent season. He caught all 148 games, hit .301, and drove in 122 runs. Beginning in 1952, his baseball career was interrupted by a two-year stint in the US Army during the Korean War. Peterson was stationed for a time in Korea, serving in an observation battalion from the fall of 1952 until July 1953. He was discharged in time to rejoin the Pirates organization during the 1954 season.

Peterson, now 24 years old, was assigned to the New Orleans Pelicans of the Double-A Southern Association, batting .282 in 79 games. In 1955 he began the season with the Williamsport (Pennsylvania) Grays of the Class-A Eastern League, but after only 12 games, he was promoted to the Pirates. He made his major-league debut on Thursday, May 5, grounding out to the pitcher in a pinch-hitting appearance against the Milwaukee Braves at Forbes Field. Peterson stuck with the Pirates, serving mainly as the occasional replacement for the primary catchers, Jack Shepard and Toby Atwell. He played in 32 games, until his season abruptly ended in a game on August 25 in Pittsburgh against the Chicago Cubs. In the fifth inning Cubs center fielder Jim Bolger collided with Peterson while scoring from third base on a fly to left field. Peterson was charged with an error on the play, but worse, he suffered a broken bone in his right forearm.[2] The injury proved to be especially challenging, because it did not heal properly. Peterson eventually had surgery at Johns Hopkins Hospital in Baltimore involving a bone graft and the insertion of a six-inch pin in this arm. He missed the rest of the 1955 season and all of the 1956 season as he recovered from the injury. While rehabbing, Peterson began scouting for the Pirates, beginning his path toward the front office

Having finally recovered, Peterson returned to the playing field in 1957, beginning the season with the Columbus (Ohio) Jets of the Triple-A International League, where he played until he was recalled by the

Pirates in mid-July. Playing in 30 games, he batted .301 and played in the final major-league game at Ebbets Field, against the Brooklyn Dodgers, on September 24, and the New York Giants' final game at the Polo Grounds on September 29. The 1957 season was the apex of Peterson's playing career. In 1958 he split time with three minor-league teams, the Lincoln (Nebraska) Chiefs of the Class-A Western League, the Salt Lake City Bees of the Triple-A Pacific Coast League, and the Triple-A Columbus Jets, along with a two-game appearance with the Pirates in early May. While his playing dreams were fading quickly away, Peterson decided that he would like to pursue managing. In 1959 the 29-year-old was given the reins of the Wilson (North Carolina) Tobs of the Class-B Carolina League as a player-manager. Peterson caught 94 games and hit .261 for the Tobs (short for Tobacconists) but his true impact came in managing the team. The Tobs finished second in the league with a record of 71-58 and won the league championship with a 4-0 series sweep over the Raleigh Capitals, a team that featured 19-year-old second baseman Carl Yastrzemski. He also got back to the Pirates for two more games, his last as a major-league player. In 1960 and 1961, Peterson was the player-manager of the Burlington (Iowa) Bees of the Class-B Three-I League. He led the Bees to finishes in the middle of the league each of the two seasons, and had the opportunity to match wits against Earl Weaver, who managed a Baltimore Orioles farm team, the Fox Cities Foxes. Peterson's last year as a player was in 1961, and he worked solely as a minor-league manager over the next few seasons.

From 1962 to 1967, Peterson managed Pirates farm teams: Kinston of the Class-A Carolina League, (1962-1964); Asheville of the Double-A Southern League (1965-66), and Triple-A Columbus (1967). After the 1967 season, Peterson, then 37 years old and with a family, gave up the idea of becoming a major-league manager, a job he knew would require him to continually move his family. He jumped at the opportunity to become the Pirates' farm director and director of scouting. In these positions Peterson helped to sign and develop a number of future major-league players, including some who would help the Pirates to win the 1971 World Series as well as finish first in the National League East Division in 1970, 1972, 1974, and 1975. Peterson worked closely with Pirates general manager Joe L. Brown, and learned the skills necessary to lead the front office of a major-league baseball team. When Brown retired in 1976, the general manager job was split into the baseball side, assumed by Peterson as he became the head of player personnel, and the business side, taken by Joe O'Toole. Peterson eventually took on both jobs and the title of general manager on January 18, 1979.[3]

Peterson's first task upon taking the job as head of player personnel was to find a manager. Danny Murtaugh retired after the 1976 season and left big shoes to fill. Peterson pursued Chuck Tanner, who managed the Oakland Athletics in 1976 and was still under contract with the A's. In early November, Peterson persuaded A's owner Charlie Finley to trade Tanner to the Pirates for catcher Manny Sanguillen and $100,000. The trade proved very successful; Tanner went on to manage the Pirates for nine seasons.

A major-league manager had not been traded for a player since 1967 (the Washington Senators traded manager Gil Hodges to the New York Mets for pitcher

THE 1979 PITTSBURGH PIRATES

Bill Denehy and $100,000 after that season ended). The deal was the first of many moves Peterson made that would improve the Pirates. He was not afraid to trade away some of the younger players the Pirates had developed for more established talent. Shortly after Tanner was in place as the new manager, Peterson picked up veteran left-handed reliever Grant Jackson from the expansion Seattle Mariners for young infielders Craig Reynolds and Jimmy Sexton. In March of 1977, he traded outfielders Tony Armas and Mitchell Page to Oakland for second baseman Phil Garner. In December of 1977, near the end of the winter meetings in Hawaii, he took part in a four-team trade that brought the Pirates pitcher Bert Blyleven and outfielder-first baseman John Milner. In April of 1978, he traded three players to Oakland in order to get Sanguillen back, and in December of 1978, he acquired reliever Enrique Romo from Seattle in a deal involving five other players. Early in the 1979 season, Peterson made two somewhat controversial trades, one sending pitcher Jerry Reuss to the Los Angeles Dodgers for pitcher Rick Rhoden and another sending shortstop Frank Taveras to the Mets for shortstop Tim Foli. Peterson also ventured into the free-agent market, something his predecessor and mentor Joe Brown did not do. Peterson signed pitcher Jim Bibby and outfielder Lee Lacy as free agents. Perhaps his best deal was made near the trade deadline during the 1979 season, when he acquired third baseman Bill Madlock and left-handed reliever Dave Roberts from the San Francisco Giants for a trio of young pitchers—a move that solidified the Pirates infield and gave them a potent bat and strengthened their bullpen for the pennant and World Series drive.

The many moves made by Peterson clearly positioned the Pirates to contend for and eventually win the World Series in 1979. However, the moves also left the Pirates with a paucity of talent left in the farm system to bring up or to trade. After the 1979 season the Pirates declined in the NL East division. Aside from a third-place finish in 1980 and a second-place finish in 1983, they finished at or near the bottom for the next several seasons. The aging of several players, including future Hall of Famer Willie Stargell, and the departure of other key players did not help. Blyleven, disgruntled over how Tanner managed the pitching staff, demanded a trade after the 1980 season and was sent, along with Sanguillen, to Cleveland for almost no return from the four players received from the Indians. The free-agent signings of first baseman-catcher Gene Tenace for 1983, and former All-Star outfielder Amos Otis for 1984 proved to be huge wastes of money with each player being quickly released. During the 1984 season, pitcher John Candelaria, unhappy with his contract and the team, called Peterson a "bozo" and an "idiot." He was traded to the California Angels in August 1985. Peterson made two especially poor trades for the Pirates in December 1984. On December 12, he sent pitcher John Tudor and catcher Brian Harper to the St. Louis Cardinals for outfielder George Hendrick. Tudor won 21 games for the Cardinals in 1985 and Harper had a solid major-league career, while Hendrick made it clear on and off the field that he did not wish to play in Pittsburgh. Then, on December 20, Peterson traded infielder Dale Berra and two prospects, including outfielder Jay Buhner, to the New York Yankees for shortstop Tim Foli and

outfielder Steve Kemp. Buhner went on to have an excellent career, primarily with the Mariners, while Foli, in his return to Pittsburgh, and Kemp did very little for the Pirates. Peterson did not help his cause after he claimed that he was unaware Kemp had undergone offseason shoulder surgery before he was obtained from New York. After last-place finishes in 1984, a bad start in 1985, and the embarrassment of the drug scandal centered in Pittsburgh and implicating several Pirates, Peterson was fired in May 1985. He remained with the Pirates as a scout for the remainder of the season.

Peterson relocated to Florida and left baseball for four years. But at age 59, he made a comeback. Soon after the 1989 season, Peterson was hired as general manager of the Yankees, replacing Bob Quinn, who left the Yankees to become the general manager of the Cincinnati Reds.[4] During the 1989 season, Peterson had been writing to Yankees owner George Steinbrenner, lobbying for the job of general manager and providing advice on how to bring success to the team. The primary message in these letters was that stability was a key to a successful organization.[5] However, Peterson came to the Yankees in a period when the Yankees were the antithesis of stability. He was actually hired as something of a co-general manager, working in parallel, theoretically, with George Bradley, who was the Yankees' director of player development and scouting. Peterson worked out of the New York City office, and Bradley was to work out of Tampa, Florida, office. Both men were to have an equal say in decision-making, with Steinbrenner overseeing everything. As might be expected, things did not work out well for this management arrangement. In 1990 the Yankees won only 67 games and finished last in the American League East. As a result of the evolving scandal involving Steinbrenner and Yankees outfielder Dave Winfield, Peterson was forced to trade Winfield to the California Angels in May. In June Peterson was tasked with firing manager Bucky Dent and replacing him with Stump Merrill. The ballclub, on and off the field, was in turmoil. On August 20, 1990, Steinbrenner, in his last official move before a supposed lifetime ban from baseball stemming from the Winfield scandal, made Gene Michael general manager and demoted Peterson to Michael's special assistant.[6]

Following his tumultuous time with the Yankees, Peterson went back to scouting, first with the Toronto Blues Jays, and then with the San Diego Padres, who hired him in 1992 to scout Florida spring training, the Florida State League, and the Florida Instructional League.

Peterson's son, Rick Peterson has had a successful career in major-league baseball, working primarily as a pitching coach with the Oakland A's, New York Mets, and Milwaukee Brewers. Harding "Pete" Peterson retired from baseball in 1995, and as of 2016 lived in the Tampa, Florida, area.

SOURCES

In addition to the sources cited in the Notes, the author also consulted:

Finoli, David, and Bill Ranier. *The Pittsburgh Pirates Encyclopedia* (New York: Sports Publishing LLC, 2003).

Ranier, Bill, and David Finoli. *When The Bucs Won It All* (Jefferson, North Carolina: McFarland & Company Inc., 2003).

Sahadi, Lou. *The Pirates: We Are Family* (New York: Times Books, 1980).

NOTES

1. Bob Hertzel, "Sensitive Peterson Tries to Mold Pirates Into Champs," *Pittsburgh Press,* March 25, 1984: C3.
2. Lester J. Biederman, "Bucs Renew Mastery Over Cubs," *Pittsburgh Press,* August 26, 1955: 24.
3. Hertzel.
4. "Peterson to Yankees," *New York Times,* October 14, 1989.
5. Murray Chass, "Yanks Cycle of Change Meets Stabilizing Force," *New York Times,* November 11, 1989.
6. Mark Gallagher, *The Yankee Encyclopedia* (Champaign, Illinois: Sagamore Publishing, 1996), 307.

John W. Galbreath

By Warren Corbett

"HE'S A LITTLE GUY. THINKS HE CAN DO anything. Damn near can." That description of John W. Galbreath came from the longtime manager of his Darby Dan Farm, Olin Gentry.

Galbreath built his Kentucky farm into a world-renowned thoroughbred racing stable. He owned the controlling interest in the Pittsburgh Pirates for 35 years and celebrated three World Series championships. In his business career he reshaped the skylines of cities from his hometown, Columbus, Ohio, to Hong Kong while amassing real estate holdings estimated at $550 million. At his funeral the famed pastor Norman Vincent Peale summed up his life as an "old, traditional American success story."[1]

John Wilmer Galbreath was born in Derby, Ohio, on August 10, 1897, to Francis Galbreath and the former Mary Mitchell, who was called Belle. He grew up on a farm in Mount Sterling as one of six children, and was a 5-foot-6-inch shortstop on his high-school team. He launched his first entrepreneurial venture when he was 10 years old, selling not horses but horseradish. Needing money for college, he worked for a year peddling high-school graduation invitations and pins before he entered Ohio University. He waited tables, repaired bicycles, and played saxophone in a dance band. He set up a darkroom in his dorm room, took photos of his classmates, and sold them to the students' parents.[2] World War I interrupted his education; he served as a lieutenant in the field artillery before returning to graduate in 1920.

Soon afterward he went into the real-estate business with a college fraternity brother, founding John W. Galbreath and Co. in Columbus. His marriage to Helen Mauck produced two children, son Daniel and daughter Joan.

When Galbreath took up polo, he bought a stallion named Tommy Boy and several mares, with the idea of breeding polo ponies. But one of his fillies, Martha Long, won a $400 race at Beulah Park in Columbus in 1935, and that hooked him on racing.[3] He bought a farm near Columbus in Galloway, Ohio, and named it Darby Dan Farm after his son and the Big Darby Creek, which ran across the land.

Galbreath turned the hardship of the Great Depression into an opportunity that laid the foundation for his fortune. He assembled investor groups to buy defaulted real-estate mortgages for as little as 40 cents on the dollar and resell when the market recovered. By one account they bought and sold $7 million worth of property, with Galbreath collecting a 5 percent commission on every transaction. As his prominence grew, he served as president of the local and state real-estate boards.

In 1944 Galbreath was elected president of the National Association of Real Estate Boards. The association credited him with creating a strong nationwide organization by persuading real-estate boards in all 48 states to join what is now the National Association of Realtors. He represented the industry in lobbying for the disposal of surplus government property after World War II and in pushing for government-sponsored low-interest home loans for veterans, a key feature of the G.I. Bill of Rights that enabled millions of American families to become homeowners and transformed vast swaths of the landscape into suburbs.

One of Galbreath's Columbus friends and fellow Ohio State University football boosters was George Trautman, a baseball executive who would become president of the minor leagues' governing body. When Galbreath expressed interest in getting into the game, Trautman tipped him that the Cleveland Indians were for sale. Galbreath decided not to make a bid and Bill Veeck bought the team.

Frank McKinney, a cigar-puffing Indianapolis banker who owned the city's Triple-A team, was seeking investors to buy the Pittsburgh Pirates. On Trautman's recommendation, Galbreath joined McKinney's syndicate as a minority shareholder, along

with singer Bing Crosby and Pittsburgh attorney Thomas Johnson. They closed the deal in August 1946. Despite Organized Baseball's horror at any connection with gambling, new Commissioner Happy Chandler, a former governor and senator from Kentucky, did not share the late Judge Kenesaw M. Landis's distaste for horse racing. Chandler made no effort to block Galbreath and Crosby, who was also involved with racing. Galbreath was named vice president and treasurer of the ballclub.

The Pirates had won six National League pennants early in the century, but none since 1927. The club was in last place on the day the new owners took over and rose only one spot, to seventh, by the end of the 1946 season. In December McKinney made his first big move to upgrade the team by acquiring slugger Hank Greenberg from Detroit. The deal fired up Pittsburgh fans, who rushed to buy season tickets. Just one problem: Greenberg announced his retirement.

Greenberg, a proud man, was disgusted at his treatment by the Tigers, after 16 years with the club (four of them in military service). Detroit had to put him on waivers and all other American League teams had to pass before he could be sent to the National League. The Tigers sold the former MVP to Pittsburgh getting no players in return. Greenberg heard about the sale on the radio, then received only a terse telegram from the Tigers. In his memoirs he wrote that it left "a very harsh, bitter taste in my mouth."[4]

To entice Greenberg to Pittsburgh—and assuage those disappointed ticket buyers—McKinney called on his closer. Galbreath met Greenberg in New York and asked what it would take to bring his bat to the Pirates. Greenberg complained that he was sick of long train trips; Galbreath said he could fly between cities. Greenberg was tired of hotel rooms and roommates; Galbreath guaranteed him a suite to himself. Forbes Field, the Pirates' spacious ballpark, was a graveyard for home runs; Galbreath promised to shorten the fences. He also offered Greenberg's wife, an equestrian, one of Darby Dan's thoroughbreds, but she declined.

At 36, Greenberg didn't have much left. His greatest service to the team was as mentor to the young Ralph Kiner, who hit 51 home runs in 1947 and led the league in homers for seven straight years. But the Pirates still finished seventh. They climbed to fourth in 1948, then fell back to sixth.

As attendance dropped along with the team's place in the standings, McKinney and Galbreath squabbled over the direction of the franchise. Partner Tom Johnson described them as "two prima donnas" who couldn't get along.[5] On July 19, 1950, Galbreath and Johnson bought out McKinney, and Galbreath became president of the Pirates. Although he still lived in Columbus, he had put down some roots in Pittsburgh; his company was building a 35-story tower for U.S. Steel and Mellon Bank, and he had opened an office in the city.

Galbreath knew whom he wanted to run his team. Branch Rickey had turned the nearly bankrupt St. Louis Cardinals into the National League's powerhouse, and then moved on to build another powerhouse in Brooklyn. Twice he had created a baseball revolution, by developing the farm system and by signing Jackie Robinson. In racing terms, Rickey's past performance was unparalleled. Besides, Rickey was another small-town Ohio boy who had to work his way through college and was even a member of

Galbreath's fraternity, Delta Tau Delta. In his lust for Rickey, Galbreath—widely respected for his integrity—engaged in some chicanery to get his man.

Walter O'Malley, who controlled 50 percent of the Dodgers' stock, wanted to rid himself of Rickey and gain complete control of the franchise. O'Malley was out to make money; Rickey liked to spend it. Under an agreement among the team's stockholders, if any of them found a buyer for his shares, the others had the right to match the offered price. Galbreath conjured up a buyer for Rickey's 25 percent: William Zeckendorf, a fellow real-estate deal-maker and Delta Tau Delta brother, offered $1 million—three times what Rickey had paid for his stock.

O'Malley smelled a rat. Why would a canny businessman like Zeckendorf, who was not particularly interested in baseball, want to be a powerless minority partner? But that was the price for O'Malley to be free of Rickey. When the time came to write the check, O'Malley learned that Zeckendorf had included a twist of the knife: He was due an additional $50,000 as payment for tying up his money while his offer was pending. Zeckendorf endorsed that check over to Rickey, adding to the Mahatma's retirement fund and to O'Malley's anger.[6]

When Rickey signed on as the Pirates general manager in November 1950, he was nearly 69 years old. Still, Galbreath gave him a five-year contract for $100,000 a year, plus an additional five years as a consultant at $50,000. Rickey's tenure would be spectacularly unsuccessful in the standings, but he fulfilled his mission. By signing hundreds of young players—applying his dictum, "Out of quantity comes quality"—he built the foundation for Galbreath's first championship. But the victories did not come fast enough, to the frustration of the Pirates' fans and owners. The ever-blabby Tom Johnson later said Galbreath "thought Rickey was the greatest thing since sliced cheese, and the old phony showed up here."[7]

Rickey began his stewardship by paying baseball's first $100,000 bonus to a high-school pitcher, Paul Pettit, who would win only one major-league game. Rickey spent another $400,000 on bonuses to untried amateurs in his first year. He tripled the size of the scouting staff and expanded the farm system. The major-league Pirates might have been able to win in one of those minor leagues, but not in the National. From 1951 through 1955 they lost at least 90 games every year and finished last in four out of five seasons, bottoming out with 112 defeats in 1952. Events conspired against Rickey's youth movement; several of the best prospects, including Dick Groat and Vernon Law, were drafted for two years of military service.

The dreary team was driving away fans and Rickey was feeling pressure. He wanted to get rid of Ralph Kiner, by far the highest-paid Pirate, but Galbreath refused to sell a player to cover his financial losses. Galbreath personally negotiated Kiner's contracts; when the star's salary reached $90,000, the owner was said to be paying a big chunk of it out of his own pocket rather than the Pirates' treasury. Exasperated, Rickey wrote Galbreath a confidential letter before the 1952 season disparaging Kiner: He couldn't run, couldn't throw, and demanded special privileges. After Kiner slumped to a .244 average in 1952, while leading the league in homers, Galbreath stepped aside and assigned Rickey to negotiate a pay cut. When Kiner objected, Rickey told him, "We finished last with you and we can finish last without you."[8] In June 1953 Kiner was swapped to the Chicago Cubs in a four-for-six-player deal (four from the Pirates, six from the Cubs), with the Pirates receiving a reported $100,000.

At the same time he tried to build up the Pirates, Galbreath decided to move into the big leagues of thoroughbred racing. He had acquired a second farm, also renamed Darby Dan, in Lexington, Kentucky. He embarked on a buying spree of unprecedented cost and scope. Thoroughbreds were far more expensive than ballplayers. To strengthen his stable of stallions, he paid a record $2 million for Swaps, a former Horse of the Year. He bought another Horse of the Year, Sword Dancer. In 1959 Galbreath paid a stunning record $1.35 million to lease the stud services of the undefeated "wonder horse of Italy," Ribot. One of the Italian stallion's sons, Graustark, was the leading Kentucky Derby contender in 1966 until he broke down. Although some estimated Galbreath had spent more than $5 million on horses, he demurred: "Frankly,

I never thought about the total investment, and what with all the many transactions going on all the time I wouldn't know where to begin."⁹ The acquisitions secured Darby Dan's position as one of racing's elite stables.

Galbreath married even more thoroughbreds: His wife, Helen, had died in 1946, and in 1955 he wed Dorothy Firestone, a widow. Her horse Summer Tan ran third in the 1955 Kentucky Derby. Galbreath told *The Sporting News* his goal was to win the Derby and the World Series. He was an enthusiastic fan of both his sports teams; he would often drive his convertible around the farm until he found a spot where he could pick up the Pirates broadcasts from Pittsburgh. In 1956 he sat through a nine-hour doubleheader at Forbes Field.¹⁰ He would never say whether he loved baseball or thoroughbreds more; it would have been like a father choosing one child as his favorite.

The baseball franchise was hemorrhaging money, saddled with Rickey's free spending and dwindling attendance. Losses totaled $2.2 million during Rickey's five years. Galbreath said, "I have my hands in several businesses, most of them much bigger than baseball, but none has ever given me the worry and headaches I get from baseball."¹¹

With Rickey's contract as general manager coming to an end in 1955, he made noises about staying. Instead, Galbreath nudged him into a graceful retirement. Galbreath said, "We're not too far away from a contending team and it would be nice if Branch gets some of the credit when we do get going." He told reporters he had turned down four offers to buy the club and insisted he would never give up: "When you have a plan you stick with it. You don't quit until the plan has had a chance to work out."¹²

Rickey left a legacy that would vindicate his plan. As their prospects matured, the Pirates clung to first place early in the 1956 season and attendance doubled, even though the team fell back to finish seventh. In 1958 they climbed to second with the core of the 1960 championship team in place. When the Pirates clinched second place, their owner was on a hunting safari in Africa, but was able to hear the game on Armed Forces Radio. During the trip he survived a charging leopard and water buffalo, killing both along with a rhino and several zebras.

As the Pirates closed in on the long-awaited pennant in September 1960, Galbreath joined the team on a road trip for ten days, waiting to witness the clinching game. The backhanded clincher came in Milwaukee on Sunday, September 25; the game with the Braves was in the seventh inning when the scoreboard flashed news that the Cardinals had lost, assuring Pittsburgh its first pennant in 33 years. Galbreath left his box seat and went under the stands to shed tears in private. Drenched with Champagne in the clubhouse, he hugged manager Danny Murtaugh and called it "the biggest thrill of my life—a dream come true after 14 years of striving and hoping. Nothing can match it."¹³

Three weeks later, in another raucous clubhouse celebration after Bill Mazeroski's dramatic homer gave the Pirates an unbelievable World Series victory, he shouted, "Have we paid our debt to the city of Pittsburgh now? We have. We have. Thank heaven, we certainly have." In a calmer moment he reflected, "There will never be a thrill to match this."¹⁴ But he had not yet won the Kentucky Derby.

Galbreath had little time to savor the triumph. That fall, as a member of the National League's expansion committee, he stepped in as mediator when the two leagues butted heads over expansion plans. He herded the contentious owners to an agreement at a meeting that lasted until 2 a.m.

Characteristically, Galbreath became a leader in baseball circles. In 1951 he negotiated the resignation of Commissioner Chandler. He supported the man who had paved his way into the game, but was overruled by other owners who wanted Chandler out. He served on the pension committee for many years. In 1965 he and Detroit owner John Fetzer headed the search committee to find a successor to retiring Commissioner Ford Frick. The committee approached General Curtis LeMay, chief of staff of the US Air Force, but LeMay, who was overseeing the bombing of North Vietnam, would not leave his post in wartime. He recommended his logistics specialist, retired Lieutenant General William Eckert. When the unknown Eckert was elected commissioner, a juicy though unconfirmed story circulated that the owners had confused his name with that of the former Air Force Secretary Eugene Zuckert.

Racing and baseball made Galbreath famous; he and his family appeared on CBS newsman Edward R. Murrow's interview show, *Person to Person*, in 1955. But it was his real estate deals that made him rich. He managed his three careers by traveling in a private plane, sometimes touching down in four cities in a single day. "He never rested," his grandson, John Phillips, recalled. "He was always on the move. He enjoyed life."[15] Sportswriter Whitney Tower called him a "walking dynamo."[16]

Galbreath operated on a grand scale. He put together syndicates of investors that bought several entire towns—company towns unwanted by their corporate owners—and renovated the houses for resale. He built a planned community, Bramalea, outside Toronto. His office towers and industrial complexes became landmarks in more than two dozen American cities. His most ambitious undertaking was Mei Foo Sun Chuen in Hong Kong, said to be the largest housing project ever built with private funds. When completed after 13 years, it encompassed 100 apartment buildings with 13,000 units and 80,000 residents, on land reclaimed from the sea.[17]

In the tycoon-eat-tycoon world of big-time real estate, where a wheeler-dealer could stand atop his skyscraper one day and descend to bankruptcy court the next, Galbreath was a conservative businessman. He took no ownership stake in many of his most famous projects, limiting his risk while he profited by collecting large management fees. He would not break ground until he had lined up an anchor tenant, a large corporation that pre-leased much of the space.[18] *The Wall Street Journal* described him as "ironfisted."[19]

Galbreath didn't smoke or drink, but there was showmanship in his soul; he loved to recite poetry and once signed his name on $100 bills and passed them out to employees to celebrate his birthday. He chartered buses to bring 900 residents of his childhood hometown, Mount Sterling, to see a Pirates game. Women from Mount Sterling catered parties at his Ohio farm in return for a donation to their church.[20] Guests at Darby Dan in Kentucky included President Gerald Ford and Britain's Queen Elizabeth II, who boarded some of her racehorses there.

While entertaining royalty and millionaires, Galbreath regularly attended local Rotary Club meetings in Columbus. As a leading booster of the Ohio State Buckeyes, he recruited Heisman Trophy winner Vic Janowicz (who later signed with the Pirates) and basketball all-American Jerry Lucas. He remained true to his rural roots; he enjoyed talking to other farmers about crop yields and the price of corn.

Galbreath achieved his second sporting goal when his horse Chateaugay, a son of Swaps, carried Darby Dan's fawn-and-brown silks to victory in the 1963 Kentucky Derby. A 30-to-1 longshot, Proud Clarion, gave Galbreath a second Derby victory four years later. Darby Dan's Little Current won the other two legs of racing's Triple Crown, the Preakness and the Belmont Stakes, in 1974. Galbreath became the first owner to win the premier races on both sides of the Atlantic when Roberto (yes, named for Clemente) edged Rheingold by a head in Britain's Epsom Derby in 1972. "You haven't lived until you've crossed over the track to the infield to get a plate or a trophy," Galbreath said. "There isn't any sport like it."[21]

Galbreath served as chairman of the board of Churchill Downs, the storied Louisville track that is home to the Kentucky Derby. While chairman of the Greater New York Association, he supervised construction of the new Aqueduct race track and the rebuilding of Belmont Park in the 1950s.

When the Pirates claimed their next World Series championship, in 1971, Galbreath chartered two planes and took more than 200 club employees and their spouses—including office personnel, scouts, minor-league managers, and batboys—to the games in Baltimore. In the 1970s he turned day-to-day management of the club and his real-estate company over to his son, Dan. But when Pete Rose crisscrossed North America auctioning his talent to the highest bidder after the 1978 season, John Galbreath invited the free agent to his farm and promised him two mares with good bloodlines, plus the services of Darby Dan's stallions to breed them. Rose preferred the cash offered by the Philadelphia Phillies, but the Pirates won the 1979 World Series without him. After the Series, baseball owners presented the 82-year-old Galbreath with an award for meritorious service to the game.

Just two years after the '79 championship, Pittsburgh's attendance fell to the lowest in the league. By 1984 the Pirates had sunk to last place in the National League East while losing $6 million. Allegations surfaced of cocaine use in the clubhouse, with the team's mascot serving as the players' drug courier. At an emotional press conference in November 1984, Dan Galbreath said the club was for sale, but no buyers emerged. Rumors swirled that the team would leave town until a group of Pittsburgh business and civic leaders stepped up to buy it in October 1985.

John Galbreath's life of striving and succeeding ended on July 20, 1988, three weeks short of his 91st birthday. Within a few years a severe real-estate downturn brought the Galbreath Company, and Dan Galbreath, close to bankruptcy. In 1998 Lizanne Galbreath, the third-generation CEO of the family business, merged the company with Jones Lang LaSalle. The founder's legacy lives on at Darby Dan Farm, now operated by his grandson, John Phillips.

NOTES

1. Edward L. Bowen, *Legacies of the Turf: A Century of Great Thoroughbred Breeders*, Vol. 2 (Lexington, Kentucky: Eclipse Press, 2004), 49, 51.
2. *The Sporting News*, December 7, 1960: 7.
3. Bowen, *Legacies of the Turf*, 50.
4. Hank Greenberg, with Ira Berkow, ed., *The Story of My Life* (New York: Times Books, 1989), 177.
5. Andrew O'Toole, *Branch Rickey in Pittsburgh* (Jefferson, North Carolina: McFarland & Company, Inc., 2000), 12.
6. Lee Lowenfish, *Branch Rickey, Baseball's Ferocious Gentleman* (Lincoln: University of Nebraska Press, 2007), 488-492, 495-496.
7. O'Toole, *Branch Rickey in Pittsburgh*, 14.
8. Lowenfish, *Branch Rickey*, 519.
9. Whitney Tower, "The Man, the Horse and the Deal that Made History," *Sports Illustrated*, June 1, 1959, online archive.
10. Rick Cushing, *1960 Pittsburgh Pirates: Day by Day* (Philadelphia: Dorrance Press, 2010), 85; *The Sporting News*, November 30, 1955: 13.
11. O'Toole, *Branch Rickey in Pittsburgh*, 112.
12. *The Sporting News*, November 30, 1955: 13; and June 27, 1956: 2.
13. *The Sporting News*, October 5, 1960: 8.
14. *The Sporting News*, December 21, 1960: 7.
15. John Phillips interview, September 30, 2011. Information about Galbreath's personality and family life comes from this interview.
16. Whitney Tower, "The Derby Victory Prance," *Sports Illustrated*, May 13, 1963, online archive.
17. National Association of Realtors, "Presidents of the National Association of Realtors: 1944—John W. Galbreath," http://www.tourthenewrealtor.com/library/virtual_library/president1944?tourthenewrealtor. Accessed August 14, 2011; "Dan Galbreath 1928-1995," *National Real Estate Investor*, October 1, 1995, online archive.
18. *Wall Street Journal*, February 19, 1991: B1.
19. *Wall Street Journal*, February 19, 1991: B3.
20. *The Sporting News*, July 31, 1957: 20.
21. Associated Press, *New York Times*, "John Galbreath, 90, a Sportsman and Real Estate Developer, Dies," July 21, 1988.

1979 Pittsburgh Pirates Regular Season Summary

By Richard Riis

APRIL 6. MONTREAL 3, PITTSBURGH 2. Five errors by the Pirates, including two in the 10th inning, erased a solid start by Bert Blyleven and handed the game to the Expos on a cold and windy Opening Day at Three Rivers Stadium. Dave Parker, the beneficiary of professional sports' first million-dollar-per-year contract during the offseason, was roundly booed when he dropped a fly ball in the sixth.

APRIL 7. PITTSBURGH 7, MONTREAL 6. The Pirates pulled out a win with two outs in the bottom of the ninth when a wild throw to first by reliever Elias Sosa and a dropped throw by Gary Carter at the plate allowed Matt Alexander and Dave Parker to score the tying and winning runs. Bucs catcher Steve Nicosia's second-inning homer was his first ML hit.

APRIL 8. MONTREAL 5, PITTSBURGH 4. Willie Stargell's first homer of the season was the 430th of his career, but it wasn't enough to defeat the Expos. Starter Bruce Kison struck out 10 in 6⅓ innings, but an ineffective bullpen proved the Pirates' undoing. Off the field, the Pirates shipped Jerry Reuss, disgruntled at a demotion to the bullpen, to the Dodgers for starter/reliever Rick Rhoden.

APRIL 10. PHILADELPHIA 7, PITTSBURGH 3. Reliever Enrique Romo lost his second game in a row as the Phillies scored four runs in the seventh to break a 3-3 tie. Pete Rose, who moved into eighth place past Tris Speaker in career at-bats at the end of the 1978 season, hit two doubles for Philadelphia to tie Charlie Gehringer for eighth place on the career doubles list.

APRIL 11. PHILADELPHIA 5, PITTSBURGH 4. Mike Schmidt's three RBIs, including a tie-breaking solo homer in the seventh, clinched the game for Steve Carlton and the Phillies. Defending batting champion Dave Parker, 0-for-3 and hitting .176 after five games, told reporters, "I'm doing a lot of things wrong, but there's no sense getting worried until I've got 350 at-bats anyhow."[1]

APRIL 12. PITTSBURGH 3, ST. LOUIS 1. Dave Parker and John Milner each drove in a run with an extra-base hit in the sixth as the Pirates snapped a three-game losing streak and gave St Louis its first loss of the season. Don Robinson pitched a seven-hit, nine-strikeout complete game for Pittsburgh. Willie Stargell sat out the game with a bruised hip.

APRIL 13. PITTSBURGH 7, ST. LOUIS 6. Playing his second game in place of Stargell, John Milner clubbed a pair of two-run homers. The first capped a five-run Pirates outburst in the third; the second, in the seventh, proved the game-winner. Jim Bibby pitched 4⅓ innings of two-hit ball in relief of a roughed-up Bruce Kison to get the win.

APRIL 14. PITTSBURGH 7, ST. LOUIS 4. Ed Ott drove in four runs with a home run and a triple, and John Milner continued on a tear with seven hits and seven RBIs in his last 10 at-bats. Minor-league umpires worked the game as major-league umpires in a labor dispute took advantage of a nationally televised game to picket at Three Rivers Stadium.

APRIL 15. ST. LOUIS 9, PITTSBURGH 4. On a rainy Easter Sunday, the Cardinals scored five runs off Kent Tekulve in the 10th inning to win. John Milner left the stadium on crutches after he was hit on the knee by a grounder that skipped off the wet surface; he would return to the lineup on April 20. Shortstop Frank Taveras raised a few eyebrows by removing himself from the game after three innings claiming to be sick; on April 19 Taveras was shipped to the Mets.

APRIL 17. PHILADELPHIA 13, PITTSBURGH 2. Garry Maddox greeted reliever Enrique Romo with a grand slam, and Bake McBride added two homers and five RBIs as the Phillies racked up 13 runs on 17 hits. Bucs starter Bert Blyleven was tagged for seven runs in 2⅔ innings. Willie Stargell, back in the lineup, hit a double and a single in four at-bats.

APRIL 18. PHILADELPHIA 3, PITTSBURGH 2. Stargell homered and Dave Parker, on a .391 tear over the last six games, collected two hits to raise his batting average to .300, but a two-run blast into the fifth level at Three Rivers Stadium by Greg Luzinski in the sixth inning off loser Don Robinson was the difference as the Pirates dropped to 4-7.

APRIL 20. HOUSTON 5, PITTSBURGH 4. Third baseman Phil Garner snared Craig Reynolds's 10th-inning grounder, then threw the ball into right field, allowing Reynolds to reach third. Moments later Reynolds scored on Jeff Leonard's sacrifice fly to secure Houston's walk-off win. Shortstop Tim Foli, acquired from the Mets for Frank Taveras, went 0-for-3 in his Pirates debut, and both Bruce Kison (ankle sprain) and Enrique Romo (groin pull) went down with short-term injuries.

APRIL 21. HOUSTON 5, PITTSBURGH 4. The Pirates dropped their fifth in a row, and second straight in 10 innings at the Astrodome, as Jose Cruz singled off Kent Tekulve (0-3) with the bases loaded and one out to drive in the winning run. Bert Blyleven suffered his second straight ineffective outing, surrendering hits and four runs in 5⅔ innings.

APRIL 22. HOUSTON 3, PITTSBURGH 2. Craig Reynolds scored to break an eighth-inning tie when Tim Foli let Bob Watson's grounder get by him into left field for an error. Joe Niekro held the Pirates to only three hits in seven innings, as NL West-leading Houston swept the three-game series. The loss dropped Pittsburgh to 4-10 and into last place in the NL East.

APRIL 24. PITTSBURGH 9, CINCINNATI 2. Taking advantage of Tom Seaver's back spasms, the Pirates teed off on last-minute replacement Frank Pastore, making his first major-league start, for 10 hits and 6 runs in 3⅔ innings. Red-hot John Milner went 3-for-5, boosting his batting average to .484. Don Robinson (2-1, 2.16) went the distance for the Pirates.

APRIL 25. PITTSBURGH 3, CINCINNATI 2. Three and one-third innings of hitless pitching by Kent Tekulve helped the Pirates win their first extra-inning game of the season. A double by Dave Parker, a groundout by Bill Robinson, and a sacrifice fly by Lee Lacy produced the winning run in the 11th. Bert Blyleven started and pitched a strong 6⅔ innings, giving up five hits and two runs.

APRIL 27. HOUSTON 9, PITTSBURGH 8. Art Howe drove in four runs with four hits, including a tiebreaking RBI single in the 11th inning, to lead the Astros to victory. The Pirates, down by six runs early in the game, trailed 8-6 in the bottom of the ninth when Dave Parker and Willie Stargell hit back-to-back homers to send the game into extra innings.

APRIL 29. PITTSBURGH 10, HOUSTON 5. Omar Moreno, Tim Foli, and Dave Parker each had three hits, and Moreno and Willie Stargell collected three RBIs each in toppling the Astros. Bruce Kison pitched 7⅓ innings in relief to earn the win. Don Robinson left with cramps in his pitching shoulder after serving up a leadoff homer to Terry Puhl.

NATIONAL LEAGUE STANDINGS

East Division	Won	Lost	Pct.	GB
Montreal	14	5	.737	-
Philadelphia	14	5	.737	-
St. Louis	9	10	.474	5
Chicago	8	9	.471	5
New York	8	10	.444	5.5
Pittsburgh	7	11	.389	6.5

West Division	Won	Lost	Pct.	GB
Houston	15	6	.714	-
Cincinnati	11	10	.524	4
Los Angeles	10	14	.417	6.5
San Diego	9	14	.391	7
San Francisco	9	14	.391	7
Atlanta	7	13	.350	7.5

THE 1979 PITTSBURGH PIRATES

MAY 1. ATLANTA 5, PITTSBURGH 2. Gary Matthews' second homer of the game was an inside-the-park drive off Kent Tekulve (1-4) that broke a 2-2 tie in the top of the ninth. Phil Niekro held on, despite a cramped pitching hand, to finish the game and register his 200th career victory for the Braves. Bert Blyleven pitched eight innings of two-hit, two-run ball but came up empty.

MAY 2. PITTSBURGH 10, ATLANTA 2. Bill Robinson, who had lost his left-field job to Milner's hot bat, started at first base in place of Willie Stargell and blasted a pair of two-run homers in a romp. Milner, for his part, sat out the game with the flu. John Candelaria, who contributed a two-run double, went the distance for the first time since June 21, 1978.

MAY 4. ST. LOUIS 4, PITTSBURGH 3. Tony Scott drove in two runs on three hits and Ken Reitz drove in the other two to edge the Pirates. Lou Brock added three hits of his own plus his 919th career stolen base. Losses by the Mets on May 3 and 4, though, allowed the Pirates to move into a tie with New York for fifth place.

MAY 5. PITTSBURGH 6, ST. LOUIS 5. Willie Stargell's two-out, two-run, pinch-hit single in the top of the ninth capped a three-run rally for a come-from-behind victory. All three runs were unearned after an error by shortstop Garry Templeton. Bert Blyleven was chased in the fourth after staking St. Louis to a 4-0 lead on Ted Simmons's home run and a two-run triple by pitcher Bob Forsch.

MAY 6. ST. LOUIS 4, PITTSBURGH 2. After another lackluster effort by the Pirates, manager Chuck Tanner expressed confidence in the hot-and-cold Pirates: "Some teams start off well, then taper off and maybe have a poor finish. Other teams start slowly, build momentum, and come on strong at the end. This has been our story the last two seasons and it looks like we may be doing it again this year."[2] Regardless, team captain Willie Stargell called a team meeting after the game.

MAY 7. PITTSBURGH 4, ATLANTA 2. Bill Robinson broke a 2-2 tie in the sixth in Atlanta with a solo home run, and Kent Tekulve got the final two outs with two runners on for his first save of the season. John Candelaria (2-1) went six innings for the win, and Omar Moreno stroked three hits and stole his third base in two games, giving him a league-leading 14.

MAY 8. ATLANTA 4, PITTSBURGH 1. Rick Rhoden made his first—and, as it turned out, only—start and appearance of this season for the Pirates, giving up four runs in five innings in a game twice delayed by rain. On May 17 Rhoden went on the disabled list with a sore shoulder. He underwent surgery in July for removal of a bone spur and missed the rest of the season.

MAY 9. PITTSBURGH 17, ATLANTA 9. Two homers by Bill Robinson and a grand slam by John Milner led the Pirates' biggest offensive output of the season and highlighted a bitter contest that featured 10 unearned runs, five errors, four hit batsmen, three passed balls, two bench-clearing melees, and five ejections. Chuck Tanner, who was tossed in the fifth inning, called it "the wildest game I've ever been involved in,"[3] while Ed Ott put the blame on the continuing umpires' strike. "The regular NL umps," said Ott, "would never have let things get that far out of hand."[4]

MAY 11. CINCINNATI 8, PITTSBURGH 4. After an hour's rain delay at the outset, Dave Concepcion (4 hits, 4 RBIs) and Junior Kennedy (4 hits, 4 runs scored) led the Reds to their eighth victory in 11 games, and dropped the fifth-place Pirates to a season-high nine games out of first place. Ed Whitson lost in relief of Bert Blyleven.

MAY 12. PITTSBURGH 3, CINCINNATI 2. Willie Stargell and Omar Moreno each drove in a run with consecutive clutch singles after a disputed call on a checked swing by Stargell kept a seventh-inning rally alive. Bruce Kison yielded only one hit in five innings but Jim Bibby got the win in relief after allowing the Reds to tie the game in the sixth and go up one run in the seventh.

MAY 13. CINCINNATI 7, PITTSBURGH 3. Thirty-five-year-old Paul Blair, released by the Yankees in April and signed as a free agent by the Reds, made his first NL hit count, belting a two-run homer off John Candelaria that broke a 1-1 tie in the sixth inning and put the Reds on top to stay. Phil Garner stroked three hits and scored twice for the Pirates.

MAY 15. NEW YORK 3, PITTSBURGH 0. A six-hit combined shutout by Craig Swan and Skip Lockwood dropped the Pirates to six games under .500, their deepest hole of the season. Despite some good hitting—four Pirates were batting over .300—the Pirates continued to be dogged by inconsistent pitching, as exemplified by Don Robinson's nine walks in seven innings in picking up his third loss.

MAY 16. PITTSBURGH 4, NEW YORK 3. The Pirates triumphed in 13 innings on pinch-hitter Mike Easler's walk-off homer off Skip Lockwood. Three innings earlier, Chuck Tanner lodged a protest when the Mets' Steve Henderson was ejected—then reinstated—by strike-replacement umpire Ron Hutson for slamming his bat to the ground after striking out. Enrique Romo pitched three scoreless innings for his first win.

MAY 17. PITTSBURGH 6, NEW YORK 5. Willie Stargell's second homer of the game, a two-run shot with two outs in the eighth inning off first-year reliever Jesse Orosco, powered the Pirates to victory. Despite missing 12 of the season's first 32 games with an ailing hip, Stargell is hitting a team-leading .333 with seven home runs. Kent Tekulve pitched two scoreless innings for the win.

MAY 18. PITTSBURGH 9, CHICAGO 5. At Wrigley Field, Stargell hit his fourth home run in three games as the Pirates won their third straight. Dave Kingman clubbed his 13th homer for the Cubs. Despite yielding 13 hits and nine runs, Ken Holtzman pitched all nine innings for Chicago. John Candelaria also went the distance for Pittsburgh for his third win.

MAY 19. PITTSBURGH 3, CHICAGO 0. Jim Rooker, making his first appearance of the season after injuring his elbow in a spring-training game, was touched for only three hits before yielding to the bullpen in the ninth. Grant Jackson got Bill Buckner to ground out with the bases loaded to end the game, and the Pirates moved into a fourth-place tie with the Cubs. The major-league umpiring crew, returning from the settled strike, received a rousing ovation as they took the field.

MAY 20. PITTSBURGH 6, CHICAGO 5. Omar Moreno and Dale Berra each homered and starred defensively for Pittsburgh and the Pirates handed the Cubs their fifth straight defeat. Shortstop Berra made a barehanded stab of a bouncer by Steve Ontiveros, throwing to second for an inning-ending force out to snuff a Cubs rally in the seventh, and center fielder Moreno made a leaping, one-handed catch at the wall of Bill Buckner's leadoff drive in the ninth.

MAY 21. PITTSBURGH 4, MONTREAL 2. At Montreal's Olympic Stadium, Omar Moreno and Willie Stargell homered as Bert Blyleven earned his first win of the season and the first decision in his last seven starts to put the Pirates at .500 for the first time since April 14. Blyleven, who retired 13 in a row at one point, scattered six hits over 8⅓ innings. "If Bert just keeps plugging away," said Chuck Tanner, "with all the starts he'll get, he'll have lots of wins."[5]

MAY 22. MONTREAL 6, PITTSBURGH 3. The Expos scored four runs in the third then held on to snap the Pirates' six-game winning streak. Montreal nearly blew a 5-1 lead with a pair of errors in the seventh that handed the Pirates two unearned runs. Bucs starter Ed Whitson failed to make it out of the third inning.

MAY 23. MONTREAL 3, PITTSBURGH 0. Steve Rogers tossed an eight-hit shutout with a big assist from Pittsburgh batters, who went 0-for-12 with runners in scoring position. John Candelaria, who gave up one run in six innings, was the hard-luck loser. Omar Moreno collected three of the Bucs' hits, and added his 18th stolen base.

THE 1979 PITTSBURGH PIRATES

MAY 25. PITTSBURGH 3, NEW YORK 3. The Pirates and Mets played to a fog-shrouded tie at New York's Shea Stadium. Play was halted with none out in the bottom of the 11th after left fielder Bill Robinson lost sight of Joel Youngblood's fly ball, allowing Youngblood to reach third with a triple. After an hour and 18 minute delay, the game was called. The game would be replayed a month later, with the expansion of a June 25 night game into a twi-night doubleheader.

MAY 26. NEW YORK 10, PITTSBURGH 8. The lead changed hands five times before a two-run homer by Steve Henderson in the seventh put the Mets on top to stay. Omar Moreno drove in a career-high four runs for the Pirates, who left 15 men on base. Mets reliever Skip Lockwood got the win, ending a 14-game personal losing streak dating back to June 13, 1978.

MAY 27. PITTSBURGH 2, NEW YORK 1. A leadoff homer by Bill Robinson in the ninth and clutch relief pitching by Grant Jackson, who struck out two Mets with the bases loaded in the eighth and the game tied, was the difference in a close contest. Reliever Kent Tekulve was not with the club, having been sent back to Pittsburgh for an orthopedic exam of a knotted right shoulder which proved negative.

MAY 28. PITTSBURGH 6, NEW YORK 1. Bill Robinson stroked three hits, including a tiebreaking home run, and drove in three runs. The Pirates scored three insurance runs in the ninth after a 90-minute rain delay at the start of the inning. John Candelaria pitched 7⅔ innings, limiting the Mets to one run on six hits while striking out seven. Candelaria's reliever, Ed Whitson, walked two to load the bases, but Grant Jackson induced Lee Mazzilli to ground to third to end the threat.

MAY 29. PITTSBURGH 8, CHICAGO 0. Back in Pittsburgh for the start of a 12-game homestand, Don Robinson and Grant Jackson combined on a five-hit shutout to return the Pirates to the .500 mark. Dave Parker contributed two doubles, a homer, and three RBIs. "It's about time for me to put something together," said Parker, who'd gone eight games since his last home run. "I consider it a slump when I get only one hit a day."[6]

MAY 30. PITTSBURGH 9, CHICAGO 2. Jim Rooker tossed a two-hitter to give the Pirates their 10th victory in 13 games. After three starts, Rooker has a 2-0 record with a 0.74 ERA and a 0.53 WHIP. Willie Stargell and Bill Robinson each connected for his 10th homer, while the Cubs' Dave Kingman hit his 15th to tie Philadelphia's Mike Schmidt for the NL lead.

MAY 31. PITTSBURGH 4, CHICAGO 3. The Pirates continued on a roll, tagging Bruce Sutter for four singles in the 10th to earn a walk-off win. Enrique Romo's failure to hold a 3-2 lead in the eighth left Bert Blyleven with his ninth no-decision in 12 starts. A slumping John Milner, hitting .469 as the month began, went 0-for-4 to see his batting average dip to .266.

After a dismal 7-11 April, the Pirates improved to 16-10 (with one tie) in May.

NATIONAL LEAGUE STANDINGS

East Division	W	L	Pct.	GB
Montreal	29	15	.659	-
Philadelphia	27	20	.574	3.5
St. Louis	24	20	.545	5
Pittsburgh	23	21	.523	6
Chicago	20	25	.444	9.5
New York	16	28	.364	13

West Division	W	L	Pct.	GB
Houston	29	23	.558	-
Cincinnati	26	23	.531	1.5
Los Angeles	26	26	.500	3
San Francisco	25	26	.490	3.5
San Diego	24	29	.453	5.5
Atlanta	18	31	.367	9.5

JUNE 1. PITTSBURGH 9, SAN DIEGO 8. The Pirates entered the bottom of the ninth behind 8-5, but a three-run homer by Dave Parker with one out tied the score. A two-out single by Stargell, a double by Phil Garner, and a walk to Ed Ott, followed by a full-count walk to pinch-hitter Lee Lacy by veteran reliever Rollie Fingers forced in the winning run. Kent

Tekulve, back from a sore shoulder, gave up three runs in three innings, but got the win.

JUNE 2. SAN DIEGO 3, PITTSBURGH 1.
Gaylord Perry pitched a four-hitter and Fred Kendall and Gene Tenace homered off losing pitcher John Candelaria to snap Pittsburgh's six-game winning streak. The Pirates' only run came in the sixth when pinch-hitter Manny Sanguillen singled, advanced to second on a single by Omar Moreno, took third on a wild pitch, and scored on a grounder to short by Tim Foli.

JUNE 3. PITTSBURGH 7, SAN DIEGO 0.
Only an eighth-inning grounder by rookie Barry Evans that skipped off the glove of Phil Garner at third and was ruled a double kept Bruce Kison from hurling a no-hitter. Kison, given the start after Don Robinson developed shoulder stiffness during his pregame bullpen warmup, was supported by two home runs and four RBIs by Bill Robinson and solo shots by Dave Parker, Omar Moreno, and Lee Lacy.

JUNE 4. LOS ANGELES 4, PITTSBURGH 2.
A two-run homer by Joe Ferguson in the second off Jim Rooker gave Los Angeles a lead they never relinquished, and rookie Rick Sutcliffe scattered four hits in picking up his sixth win. Both Pittsburgh runs came on Dave Parker's inside-the-park home run, his second such clout of the season. Omar Moreno went 0-for-4 to snap his 15-game hitting streak, the Pirates' longest of the season.

JUNE 5. PITTSBURGH 3, LOS ANGELES 1.
Dave Parker's home run off Don Sutton in the first inning staked the Pirates to a two-run lead that held up until the end. Parker's shot to right, his third home run in as many games, hit the second tier at Three Rivers Stadium. Bert Blyleven won his second game against two losses, and Kent Tekulve notched his fifth save.

JUNE 6. PITTSBURGH 5, LOS ANGELES 4.
Bill Robinson's second home run of the game highlighted a four-run eighth-inning rally that carried the Pirates to victory and moved them into third place in the NL East. Robinson's fourth two-homer game of the season raised his total to 14, matching his output for all of 1978, and tying him for third in the NL.

JUNE 8. PITTSBURGH 3, SAN FRANCISCO 2.
Down 2-0 with two outs after Omar Moreno singled, the Pirates struck again in the eighth inning as Willie Stargell, coming off the bench, and Dave Parker hit back-to-back homers off lefty starter John Curtis to put three runs on the scoreboard and beat the Giants. A pain-free Don Robinson pitched six innings of one-run ball, but Tim Foli sprained his ankle in the first inning and missed the next three games.

JUNE 9. SAN FRANCISCO 6, PITTSBURGH 2.
Willie McCovey's pinch-hit, three-run homer off Grant Jackson made him the NL's all-time left-handed home-run hitter and capped a four-run eighth inning that propelled the Giants to victory. McCovey's home run gave him 512 for his career, surpassing Mel Ott among NL left-handers, and put him in a tie with Ernie Banks and Eddie Mathews for ninth on the all-time list.

JUNE 10. SAN FRANCISCO 7, PITTSBURGH 4.
San Francisco's Gary Lavelle, 7-0 lifetime against the Pirates, pitched three innings of one-hit relief to earn the win. Bert Blyleven got another no-decision, leaving with the score tied and two on in the sixth. The loss eventually went to Enrique Romo, who walked in the go-ahead run two batters later, and was driven from the mound in the seventh after the Pirates had scored twice in the sixth to take a short-lived 4-3 lead.

JUNE 12. SAN DIEGO 6, PITTSBURGH 3.
The Pirates began their first West Coast trip of the season with a loss and a drop into fourth place. Gaylord Perry went the distance, striking out 10, in notching his 273rd career victory and moving into a 17th-place tie with Red Ruffing. All of Pittsburgh's runs came on Dave Parker's three-run homer with two outs in the ninth inning.

JUNE 13. SAN DIEGO 3, PITTSBURGH 2.
Former Pirate Fernando Gonzales clubbed a two-run homer as one of his four hits while Bob Owchinko and Rollie Fingers combined on a seven-hitter to

send the Pirates to their fourth consecutive loss. In early All-Star voting, Dave Parker, on the strength of 13 homers and a .312 batting average, moved into second place among NL outfielders behind the Phillies' Greg Luzinski.

JUNE 14. SAN DIEGO 2, PITTSBURGH 1.
John Candelaria, called in to relieve in the 13th, suffered the loss when Tim Foli's two-out error in the 14th allowed Ozzie Smith to reach first. A walk to Dave Winfield and a single by Barry Evans produced the winning run. Lee Lacy, 0-for-1 as a pinch-hitter, could be forgiven if his mind was elsewhere. Lacy and his longtime sweetheart, Suzanne Weeks, were married earlier in the day in San Diego with Dave Parker serving as best man.

JUNE 15. PITTSBURGH 6, LOS ANGELES 2.
Bert Blyleven pitched 7⅔ scoreless innings to put the Pirates a game over .500. The pitcher, who had been pouting about "infrequent" starts, met with Chuck Tanner, who pointed out that Blyleven had started 15 of the Bucs' first 59 games. "That's one in four," the skipper explained. "I can't control the weather or the offdays. Blyleven has had more starts than anyone on the staff." Blyleven was not satisfied. "I'm more than a once-a-week pitcher," he sulked.[7]

JUNE 16. PITTSBURGH 6, LOS ANGELES 3.
Omar Moreno put on a one-man show in the fifth inning after Gary Thomasson misplayed his fly ball to center field. Moreno reached second on the error, stole third, then sprinted home when catcher Joe Ferguson's throw went into left field. Moreno's two runs scored and three RBIs, coupled with Don Robinson's five-hit complete game, sealed the game for Pittsburgh.

JUNE 17. PITTSBURGH 5, LOS ANGELES 1.
Ed Whitson held the Dodgers to two hits and a single tally, while Kent Tekulve picked up his eighth save in sending the defending NL champions to their 11th loss in 15 games). The Bucs' sweep of the Dodgers was their first in Los Angeles since 1971. At a press conference, Willie Stargell announced the launch of a nationwide fundraising drive by the Willie Stargell Foundation for Sickle Cell Anemia to aid research.

JUNE 19. PITTSBURGH 9, SAN FRANCISCO 4.
Phil Garner went 5-for-5 with four singles and a triple, and Willie Stargell added his 12th homer to return the Pirates to third place. With two outs, two-run doubles by Ed Ott and starting pitcher John Candelaria sparked a five-run rally in the third inning. Enrique Romo pitched three innings of one-hit ball to earn his first save.

JUNE 20. PITTSBURGH 8, SAN FRANCISCO 5.
The Pirates won their fifth straight to move into second place. A pair of Pirates errors allowed the Giants to tie the game, 5-5, in the sixth, but a triple by Rennie Stennett and a sacrifice fly by Manny Sanguillen put them back on top in the eighth. The loser was Gary Lavelle, his first to Pittsburgh in eight career decisions.

JUNE 22. PITTSBURGH 7, CHICAGO 2.
To begin a brief three-game homestand, Bert Blyleven improved to 4-2 with the help of Bill Robinson's three hits and two RBIs. Phil Garner also chipped in with two RBIs, and six different Pirates scored at least one run. Dave Kingman hit his 25th home run, and his fifth in the last six games, for the Cubs and raised his league-leading RBI total to 57.

JUNE 23. CHICAGO 4, PITTSBURGH 3.
Bill Buckner hit a two-run home run and light-hitting Tim Blackwell drove in what proved to be the winning run with a single against Don Robinson as the Cubs won for the first time in eight games this season against the Pirates. The loss also ended Pittsburgh's six-game winning streak. Bruce Sutter recorded his 17th save for the Cubs.

JUNE 24. CHICAGO 5, PITTSBURGH 0.
The Pirates drew 43,402 fans to Three Rivers Stadium on Bat Day, one of whom was arrested for hurling his bat at Dave Parker in right field in the ninth inning. "It's a scary thing," Parker told reporters. "Something like that could end my career."[8] Home runs by Bill Buckner and Jerry Martin and the five-hit pitching of Rick Reuschel shut down the Pirates and sent the fans home disappointed.

JUNE 25 (FIRST GAME). PITTSBURGH 8, NEW YORK 1.
The rescheduling of the May 25 game called due to heavy fog and ending as a tie created an unusual Monday doubleheader at Shea Stadium. In the 5:35 P.M. opener, the Pirates jumped on Mets reliever Wayne Twitchell for five runs in the eighth and John Candelaria retired 16 of the first 17 Mets on the way to tossing a five-hit complete game.

JUNE 25 (SECOND GAME). NEW YORK 4, PITTSBURGH 0.
The Pirates could muster only five singles in the regularly scheduled night game, as Pete Falcone pitched his first complete game and first shutout in two years. Jim Rooker was the loser. Pittsburgh's split, coupled with Chicago's win over Philadelphia, put the Pirates and Cubs in a tie for second place, six games behind the Expos. Sizing up his division rivals, Expos manager Dick Williams said, "I respect all of them, but I respect Pittsburgh the most. I think they've got the best balance."[9]

JUNE 26. PITTSBURGH 2, NEW YORK 1.
Bill Robinson celebrated his 36th birthday by breaking a 1-1 tie in the seventh with a homer into the left-field bullpen, then preserving the win in the eighth inning with a running, backhanded catch of Joel Youngblood's drive to the wall in left-center with a runner on second. Bert Blyleven allowed only four hits in eight innings to win his fifth game against two losses. Grant Jackson earned his eighth save after a wild ninth inning that included former Pirate shortstop Frank Taveras being called out for interference on an attempted bunt. Mets manager Joe Torre and coach Chuck Cottier were ejected for disputing the call.

JUNE 27. NEW YORK 12, PITTSBURGH 9.
After three games in New York, the Pirates and Mets traveled to Pittsburgh for two more. Willie Montanez and Steve Henderson hit back-to-back solo home runs in the ninth to start a five-run rally to beat the Pirates. Ed Whitson went six innings, leaving with the score tied 3-3, but Romo, Tekulve, and Jackson were dreadful, allowing 10 hits, five walks, and nine runs (six earned) between them in three innings.

JUNE 28. NEW YORK 3, PITTSBURGH 2.
The big news on this day was not the Pirates second straight loss to the last-place Mets, but an unexpected trade with the San Francisco Giants. In exchange for pitcher Ed Whitson and a pair of minor-league hurlers, the Bucs acquired former (and future) batting champion Bill Madlock, reliever Dave Roberts, and veteran infielder Lenny Randle. Randle was assigned to Triple-A Portland. Chuck Tanner suggested that Madlock, hitting just .261 but with 41 RBIs while playing second base for San Francisco, would alternate with third baseman Phil Garner and second baseman Rennie Stennett. "Madlock's an established hitter and he will help us," said Garner. "But I don't know how I'm going to feel if I stop hitting and find myself on the bench."[10]

JUNE 29. PITTSBURGH 6, MONTREAL 5.
The division-leading Expos arrived in Pittsburgh 6½ games ahead of the third-place Pirates, who jumped on Bill Lee for three runs in the first, including back-to-back homers by Bill Robinson and Lee Lacy. Enrique Romo relieved a shaky Bruce Kison in the sixth, and Kent Tekulve pitched the final 2⅔ innings to notch his 10th save. In All-Star voting, Dave Parker moved into first place among outfielders, while Stargell polled fourth among first basemen.

JUNE 30. MONTREAL 5, PITTSBURGH 3.
Three home runs powered the Expos to an easy victory. New Pirate Dave Roberts pitched two scoreless innings. Bill Madlock's arrival was postponed until July 1 to allow him to attend the funeral of his grandmother in Tennessee. To make room for Madlock, the Pirates optioned infielder Dale Berra to Triple-A Portland.

The Pirates posted a 14-13 mark for the month of June.

NATIONAL LEAGUE STANDINGS

East Division	Won	Lost	Pct.	GB
Montreal	43	27	.614	-
Chicago	36	33	.522	6.5
Pittsburgh	37	34	.521	6.5
Philadelphia	39	36	.520	6.5
St. Louis	36	34	.514	7
New York	31	39	.443	12

THE 1979 PITTSBURGH PIRATES

West Division	Won	Lost	Pct.	GB
Houston	49	31	.613	–
Cincinnati	41	37	.526	7
San Francisco	38	39	.494	9.5
San Diego	35	46	.432	14.5
Los Angeles	33	46	.418	15.5
Atlanta	31	47	.397	17

JULY 2. PITTSBURGH 5, ST. LOUIS 4. Heavy rain in Pittsburgh washed out a Sunday doubleheader with the Expos scheduled for July 1, and Bill Madlock found himself surrounded in the clubhouse by the press. "We were loose in San Francisco," Madlock told reporters, comparing his old and new teams. "But the Pirates are in a Class-All by themselves. Loose? That's an understatement."[11] Madlock finally made his Pirates debut the following evening in St. Louis. With Phil Garner shifted to second, Madlock played third base and went 2-for-4 at the plate. The Cardinals chased Don Robinson with four runs in the sixth to erase a 4-0 deficit, but Tim Foli's RBI single in the seventh proved to be the game-winner.

JULY 3. PITTSBURGH 4, ST. LOUIS 1. Tony Scott broke up John Candelaria's no-hit bid with a game-tying home run in the fifth, but a run-scoring double by Dave Parker an inning later put the Pirates back on top to stay. Parker also collected his 14th homer. Enrique Romo picked up his second save and chipped in with an RBI single.

JULY 4. PITTSBURGH 6, ST. LOUIS 4. Willie Stargell's 14th homer and second of the game dented a seat 510 feet away in Busch Stadium's right-center-field upper deck. "I was kidding with Candelaria when we came out here today," recalled Stargell. "He said there was no way you could hit a pitch over the scoreboard. I guess now he knows that there is."[12] Chuck Tanner, who was celebrating his 51st birthday, said of Stargell's clout, "It was the best birthday gift I could receive. What a hit! He is going to walk into the Hall of Fame when he's done playing."[13]

JULY 5. ST. LOUIS 2, PITTSBURGH 0. The Cardinals' John Fulgham, making his fourth major-league start, blanked the Pirates on nine hits, three by Bill Madlock. The shutout, and likely the game, was preserved for St. Louis when right fielder George Hendrick crashed into the wall hauling in a drive by pinch-hitter John Milner for the final out with runners on second and third.

JULY 6. CINCINNATI 2, PITTSBURGH 1. George Foster's two-out, pinch-hit single in the bottom of the ninth drove in Dan Driessen from second for the winning run. The Pirates squandered a fine start by Bruce Kison, who allowed only four hits and struck out seven in seven innings. Madlock, hitting a robust .474 (9-for-19) since joining the club, accounted for two of Pittsburgh's seven hits.

JULY 7. CINCINNATI 6, PITTSBURGH 2. The Pirates dropped another to the Reds, and also dropped into a third-place tie with the Cubs in the tightly contested NL East. Don Robinson was driven from the mound in the second inning, while Paul Moskau went all the way for Cincinnati. Robinson developed soreness in his pitching arm and would not pitch again for two weeks.

JULY 8 (FIRST GAME). CINCINNATI 4, PITTSBURGH 2. A three-run homer by Dan Driessen in the fourth inning and an RBI single by winning pitcher Fred Norman was all the Reds needed to serve the Pirates their fourth straight loss. Dave Parker accounted for three of the Pirates' eight hits with a single, a double, and his 15th home run, and added his 13th stolen base.

JULY 8 (SECOND GAME). PITTSBURGH 2, CINCINNATI 1. Strong pitching by Blyleven, Jackson, and Tekulve held the Reds to a lone run, and a towering home run by Willie Stargell in the ninth gave the Pirates a split for the day. The final results of fan balloting for the NL All-Star team were announced, with Dave Parker finishing third behind San Diego's Dave Winfield and Cincinnati's George Foster to earn a starting spot in the outfield. Stargell came in third among first basemen.

JULY 10. PITTSBURGH 4, HOUSTON 3. Omar Moreno had a double and a triple, and Dave Parker had two RBI as the Pirates nipped the Astros in the

Astrodome. Houston made it close in the ninth when Enrique Romo balked in one run and Denny Walling singled in another before Kent Tekulve came in to get the final out with the bases loaded.

JULY 11. PITTSBURGH 5, HOUSTON 1.
Back-to-back home runs by Parker and Stargell in a four-run seventh inning powered the Pirates to victory. Dave Parker, who had agreed to terms on his $5 million contract in January, finally signed the deal after a variety of tax-related issues had been resolved. The details were newsworthy: a signing bonus of $625,000, $650,000 in annual salary, plus $350,000 annually in deferred salary at 8.5 percent interest. The last of the deferred payments was made in 2007.

JULY 12. PITTSBURGH 5, HOUSTON 3.
Bill Madlock and Willie Stargell slugged homers and Bert Blyleven and Kent Tekulve combined on a seven-hitter to beat the slumping Astros, losers of their last six games. Houston would extend that streak to seven games, win one, then lose the next five, yet retain its hold on first place over the Cincinnati Reds in the NL West.

JULY 13. ATLANTA 13, PITTSBURGH 4.
The Braves and Pirates each got eight hits at Atlanta, but the Braves got the better ones, including a grand slam by Jeff Burroughs, two home runs for three RBI from Bob Horner, and a three-run blast by Mike Lum. Atlanta scored 10 runs in four innings off Jim Rooker, while Phil Niekro earned his 12th win against 11 losses.

JULY 14. PITTSBURGH 5. ATLANTA 1.
The Pirates won with a big assist from Braves third baseman Bob Horner, whose three errors supplied Pittsburgh with three unearned runs. John Candelaria won his eighth game, limiting the Braves to five hits and walking none, although Horner's homer in the seventh robbed Candelaria of a shutout.

JULY 15. PITTSBURGH 7, ATLANTA 3.
Jim Bibby allowed only two hits in 6⅓ innings and Willie Stargell and Bill Robinson hit back-to-back home runs in the sixth to top the Braves. At the All-Star break, the Pirates found themselves with a 46–39 record, fourth in the NL East, but only a game behind the third-place Phillies and 1½ behind the second-place Cubs.

JULY 17. NATIONAL LEAGUE 7, AMERICAN LEAGUE 6.
Dave Parker batted second and played right field as the Pirates' only representative at the 1979 All-Star Game at Seattle's Kingdome. Parker went 1-for-3 with a sacrifice fly, but it was throwing out Jim Rice trying to stretch a double into a triple in the seventh, and a perfect strike to Gary Carter at the plate to prevent Brian Downing from scoring the go-ahead run in the eighth that won Parker the game's MVP award.

JULY 19 (FIRST GAME). PITTSBURGH 9, HOUSTON 5.
A two-run homer by Willie Stargell—his fifth in seven games—and another by Phil Garner combined to sink the Astros in the first game of a twi-night doubleheader in Pittsburgh. Dave Roberts won his first game as a Pirate in relief of Bert Blyleven, who failed to make it out of the fourth inning.

JULY 19 (SECOND GAME). PITTSBURGH 4, HOUSTON 2.
Bruce Kison allowed the Astros only four hits and no walks in eight innings, and John Milner ended a long dry spell by clubbing his first home run since May 20, a span of 42 games and 83 at-bats. With the sweep of the twin bill, the Pirates moved into a second-place tie with the Cubs, 2½ games behind the Expos.

JULY 20. PITTSBURGH 9, HOUSTON 3.
Phil Garner drove in three runs with a homer and a single as Pittsburgh won its fifth in a row and ninth of the last 10, and Houston lost its fourth straight and 11th of the last 12. Moreno stole his 40th base.

JULY 21. PITTSBURGH 6, HOUSTON 5.
Dave Roberts's first start for Pittsburgh was a five-inning no-decision. Bill Robinson slugged his 20th homer and Phil Garner hit his third in three days to lead the surging Pirates. Both homers came in the eighth inning off Joe Sambito, the first earned runs off the Astros relief ace since May 1, a span of 40⅔ consecutive

innings. The Pirates, losers of their first four match-ups with the Astros this season, swept the final eight.

JULY 22 (FIRST GAME). PITTSBURGH 5, ATLANTA 4.
The Pirates won the first game of a doubleheader on pinch-hitter Mike Easler's two-run single in a sixth inning twice interrupted by rain delays totaling nearly four hours. Pitcher Don Robinson chipped in a single for two RBIs, and Kent Tekulve hurled three scoreless innings for his 15th save.

JULY 22 (SECOND GAME). PITTSBURGH 3, ATLANTA 2.
The pitcher with the big hit in the second game was starter Jim Bibby, who hit a two-run home run, the second of his major-league career. Kent Tekulve pitched another scoreless inning to pick up his 16th save. "Everybody's contributing," said Chuck Tanner. "That's why we're winning."[14] After the doubleheader sweep, the Pirates were a half-game back of the first-place Expos.

JULY 23 (FIRST GAME). PITTSBURGH 7, ATLANTA 1.
After a two-month homer drought, John Milner socked his third in four games. Tim Foli had three hits and four RBIs, and the red-hot Pirates won their ninth in a row in the first game of another doubleheader. Bert Blyleven recorded his first complete-game win of the season.

JULY 23 (SECOND GAME). ATLANTA 8, PITTSBURGH 0.
A two-hitter by Phil Niekro in the nightcap ended the Pirates' winning streak. The Bucs, however, pulled off their first triple play since July 9, 1971, when, with runners at first and second in the second inning, Niekro faked a bunt and slapped a grounder to Madlock, who stepped on third and fired to Garner for the force at second. Garner's relay to Stargell at first beat Niekro by a step.

JULY 24. CINCINNATI 6, PITTSBURGH 5.
A Pirates rally was snuffed out, not by the Reds but by umpire Dick Stello. With Pittsburgh down 4-3 in the fourth and runners on first and third, Omar Moreno took a 3-and-1 pitch as Lee Lacy broke from first. The pitch was ball four, but Bench fired the ball to Concepcion who tagged Lacy, who was called out by Stello. Seeing Moreno moving toward first, Lacy attempted to return to second, but was tagged again by Concepcion for what was determined to be the third out, setting off an argument between the Pirates and all four umpires that lasted 34 minutes and led to the game being played under protest. The protest was turned down by NL President Chub Feeney, who said, "Since Lacy left second base of his own volition and should have been aware of the possibilities of Moreno receiving a base on balls, and because there was no rules misinterpretation by the umpires, the protest is disallowed."[15]

JULY 25. CINCINNATI 6, PITTSBURGH 5.
Doubles by Dave Collins and Hector "Heity" Cruz in the 10th inning gave Cincinnati the win in a game played amid rain delays. Milner, Stargell, and Garner each had three hits, while Johnny Bench belted two homers for the Reds.

JULY 26. CINCINNATI 9, PITTSBURGH 7.
Bench's third homer in two games highlighted the Reds' victory and sweep of the series. Dave Roberts made his second start for the Pirates, surrendering six runs in two innings for the loss. Willie Stargell collected his 20th home run and Bill Robertson his 21st in the losing effort.

JULY 27 (FIRST GAME). PITTSBURGH 5, MONTREAL 4.
Phil Garner was 3-for-4, including a homer and two RBIs, to lead the Pirates to victory in the first game of a twi-nighter before the season's largest crowd, 59,260, in Montreal's Olympic Stadium.

JULY 27 (SECOND GAME). PITTSBURGH 9, MONTREAL 1.
Phil Garner was 3-for-4 again with four runs scored, and John Milner drove in four runs to back the five-hit pitching of Bert Blyleven, who won his ninth game against three losses. With the doubleheader sweep, the Pirates moved to with a half-game of the first-place Expos.

JULY 28. PITTSBURGH 5, MONTREAL 3.
Dave Parker's 499th and 500th career RBIs, coming on his 17th homer of the season, helped the Pirates supplant the Expos atop the NL East. Montreal had

been in sole possession of first place in the East since June 13, with a 6½-game lead over Pittsburgh and Chicago as recently as July 2. Jim Bibby improved his record to 7-2, and Kent Tekulve registered his 17th save.

JULY 29. MONTREAL 5, PITTSBURGH 3.

The Expos reclaimed first place on the arm of Steve Rogers, who held the Pirates to three runs on eight hits to score his 10th win. "This is the toughest division I've been in since I've been managing," observed Chuck Tanner. "It's going to be fun all the way down the line."[16] Willie Stargell hit his 450th career home run in the ninth inning.

JULY 30. PITTSBURGH 8, NEW YORK 5.

Ed Ott's RBI single broke a 5-5 tie and sparked a three-run eighth inning to carry the Pirates over the Mets at Three Rivers Stadium. Tim Foli collected four hits as the Pirates returned to first place again for a single day. Starter John Candelaria completed five innings, but was ineffective for the first three frames before Enrique Romo took over for him. Grant Jackson eventually won in relief, and Kent Tekulve notched his 18th save.

JULY 31. NEW YORK 2, PITTSBURGH 1.

Candelaria was treated at a hospital for a sprained back following a two-car crash on a rain-slicked highway in Meadville, Pennsylvania, about 90 miles north of Pittsburgh, but, to the Pirates' great relief, would not miss a start. In that night's game, three Mets pitchers combined on a four-hitter, and Bert Blyleven, who had won nine of his last 10 decisions, took the loss.

The surging Pirates went 20-11, a .645 percentage, in July, to end the month one game behind the division-leading Expos.

NATIONAL LEAGUE STANDINGS

East Division	Won	Lost	Pct.	GB
Montreal	57	43	.570	-
Pittsburgh	57	45	.559	1
Chicago	54	46	.540	3
Philadelphia	54	49	.524	4.5
St. Louis	51	49	.510	6
New York	44	56	.440	13

West Division	Won	Lost	Pct.	GB
Houston	61	47	.565	-
Cincinnati	58	51	.532	3.5
San Francisco	52	55	.486	8.5
San Diego	49	59	.454	12
Los Angeles	45	61	.425	15
Atlanta	43	64	.402	17.5

AUGUST 1. PITTSBURGH 4, ST. LOUIS 3.

Pinch-hit triples by Manny Sanguillen leading off the sixth and Mike Easler with two outs in the seventh keyed a late-game comeback from a 3-0 deficit, and Dave Parker's eighth-inning run-scoring double won it. Four Pirates relievers held the Cardinals scoreless over the last three innings. "That's why they call it a team," said Parker. "We're a club that more or less puts things together from the fifth inning on."[17]

AUGUST 2. ST. LOUIS 5, PITTSBURGH 4.

Jim Rooker was frustrated in his the ninth straight start trying for his 100th career victory. Rooker, winless since May 30, carried a 4-1 lead into the eighth before a four-run St. Louis rally turned the game around. Bill Robinson, who connected for his 22nd homer, was philosophical. "All St. Louis did was halt our pennant express a little bit," he shrugged.[18]

AUGUST 3 (FIRST GAME). PITTSBURGH 6, PHILADELPHIA 3.

Dave Parker's 18th home run, a three-run shot off Tug McGraw in the seventh, broke a 3-3 tie and gave the Pirates a win in the first game of a twi-night doubleheader. Enrique Romo pitched three hitless innings in relief for his seventh win in 10 decisions.

AUGUST 3 (SECOND GAME). PITTSBURGH 5, PHILADELPHIA 1.

Bill Robinson and Bill Madlock had two RBIs each to back the five-hit pitching of Jim Bibby and give the Pirates a doubleheader sweep. Bibby went the distance in recording his eighth win against two losses.

AUGUST 4. PITTSBURGH 4, PHILADELPHIA 0.

Before the largest Saturday afternoon crowd—34,754—in Three Rivers Stadium history, John Candelaria and Kent Tekulve combined on a six-hit shutout to move the Pirates within a half-game of the first-place Expos. The Phillies' Pete Rose singled in the fifth inning to tie Honus Wagner's NL record of 2,426 career singles.

AUGUST 5 (FIRST GAME). PITTSBURGH 12, PHILADELPHIA 8.
John Milner hit a pinch-hit grand slam off Tug McGraw in the ninth to power the Pirates to a come-from-behind victory. Pete Rose hit a bases-loaded single in the fifth to become the career NL singles leader and move into fourth place in hits behind Ty Cobb, Eddie Collins, and Willie Keeler. A crowd of 46,006 gave the Pirates their largest home attendance of the season to date.

AUGUST 5 (SECOND GAME). PITTSBURGH 5, PHILADELPHIA 2.
The Pirates moved into first place, a half-game ahead of the Expos, by defeating the three-time defending NL East champs for the fifth time in three days. Winner Enrique Romo pitched 3⅔ scoreless innings in relief of Don Robinson, whose arm had tightened up during a 51-minute rain delay in the fifth inning. Kent Tekulve, who won the first game, earned his 20th save in the nightcap.

AUGUST 7. CHICAGO 15, PITTSBURGH 2.
At Wrigley Field, Steve Ontiveros, Jerry Martin, and Ivan De Jesus each had three hits for Chicago and pitcher Rick Reuschel contributed two hits of his own and scored two runs in handing the Pirates their biggest defeat of the season. Veteran hurler Joe Coleman, signed by the Pirates as a free agent in May, relieved Jim Rooker in the third and pitched the rest of the way, giving up 13 hits and nine runs in 5⅓ innings, to give the Pirates bullpen a rest.

AUGUST 8. PITTSBURGH 5, CHICAGO 2.
Phil Garner's three-run home run off Dick Tidrow in the 10th inning gave the Pirates their sixth win in seven games. Pittsburgh left fielder Bill Robinson was the game's defensive star, throwing out the potential winning run at home in the ninth and making a game-ending sliding catch with two Cubs on base in the 10th.

AUGUST 9. CHICAGO 11, PITTSBURGH 3.
Dennis Lamp held Pittsburgh scoreless until the ninth when the Pirates scored three runs, two of them on Bill Madlock's 11th home run, but 17 Chicago hits—four each by Bill Buckner and Mike Vail—and two homers and four RBIs by Steve Dillard put the Cubs on top.

AUGUST 10 (FIRST GAME). PHILADELPHIA 4, PITTSBURGH 3.
The biggest crowd in the majors this season, 63,346, the largest regular-season crowd in Phillies history, packed Veterans Stadium for a twi-night doubleheader. Bud Harrelson's single off Grant Jackson with two out in the 12th inning drove in the winning run in the first game, three times delayed by rain. Phil Garner and Dave Parker homered for the Pirates.

AUGUST 10 (SECOND GAME). PITTSBURGH 3, PHILADELPHIA 2.
Bill Robinson tripled home two runs in support of the three-hit pitching of Bruce Kison to earn the Pirates a split on a soggy night that didn't end until 2:03 A.M. Second baseman Rennie Stennett snared a grounder with the tying run at third to start a 4-6-3 double play that ended the eighth, and threw out Bake McBride at first with the tying run on second to end the game. "They threw some leather at us tonight," said Pete Rose.[19]

AUGUST 11. PITTSBURGH 14, PHILADELPHIA 11.
Ed Ott had four hits, including a grand slam, as the Pirates rallied from an 8-0 deficit after just four innings to beat the Phillies. The Pirates banged out 23 hits, and scored five runs in the fifth, four in the seventh, four more in the eighth, and one in the ninth. The Phillies rallied for three runs in the ninth before Kent Tekulve came in to nail down his 22nd save.

AUGUST 13. PITTSBURGH 9, PHILADELPHIA 1.
A rainout in Philadelphia on August 12 failed to cool off the red-hot Pirates. "If there was one team I would not want to face right now, it is the Pittsburgh Pirates," said Jim Bibby, who posted his sixth straight victory to raise his record to 9-2. "This is a hot ballclub."[20] John Milner, hitting .389 with 9 homers and 25 RBIs since the All-Star break, drove in four runs.

The rained-out game will be made up as part of a twi-night doubleheader on September 19.

AUGUST 14. PITTSBURGH 7, SAN DIEGO 1.
Back in Pittsburgh, the Pirates won their fourth straight and 15th of their last 21 games, sending 11 batters to the plate in a five-run second inning highlighted by a homer and an RBI single by Ed Ott. John Candelaria improved his record to 11-8 while hurling his sixth complete game of the season.

AUGUST 15. PITTSBURGH 5, SAN DIEGO 1.
The Pirates are in a pennant race but they remain loose. "I can't lift my arm," Kent Tekulve told Chuck Tanner before the game. "My gosh, what happened?" Tanner said, stunned. "Don't worry, Skip," the right-hander laughed. "It's my left arm. I must have slept on it and it is stiff."[21] In the game, Bill Robinson and Dave Parker homered to propel the Pirates to their fifth straight victory. Bert Blyleven pitched a four-hitter to notch his 10th win against four losses.

AUGUST 16. PITTSBURGH 5, SAN DIEGO 4.
Omar Moreno's two-run single capped a three-run fourth inning as the Pirates won their sixth straight to increase their division lead to four games—their largest margin of the season—over second-place Montreal. The Padres ended Enrique Romo's string of 22⅔ innings without yielding an earned run when Jay Johnstone tripled in a run with two out in the seventh.

AUGUST 17. LOS ANGELES 7, PITTSBURGH 6.
The Dodgers arrived in Pittsburgh on a tear of their own, having taken six of their last seven games, and snapped the Pirates' winning streak at six games. Gary Thomasson drove in five runs with a homer and a double to pace the Dodgers. Ed Ott collected four singles in a losing cause.

AUGUST 18. LOS ANGELES 5, PITTSBURGH 1.
The Dodgers stayed hot, with former Buc lefty Jerry Reuss defeating the Pirates on the strength of a combined five RBIs by Dusty Baker and Gary Thomasson, to win their 21st of 29 games since the All-Star break. The Expos, meanwhile, defeated Atlanta to move within two games of the Pirates.

AUGUST 19. PITTSBURGH 2, LOS ANGELES 0.
Bill Madlock homered with two out and one on in the bottom of the ninth to give the Pirates a walk-off victory. John Candelaria scattered four hits over eight innings and Kent Tekulve pitched one scoreless inning for the win. Burt Hooton held Pittsburgh scoreless on five hits through eight innings before hanging up his first loss to the Pirates since July 10, 1975.

AUGUST 20. PITTSBURGH 6, SAN FRANCISCO 5.
Pinch-runner Alberto Lois scored on a passed ball with two outs in the eighth inning to give the Pirates the victory in a game temporarily halted by rain in the sixth for 3 hours and 42 minutes. In 11 games for the Pirates in 1979, Lois scored six runs and stole one base without registering a single plate appearance. An eye injury sustained in an auto accident during the offseason ended Lois's career in professional baseball.

AUGUST 21. SAN FRANCISCO 6, PITTSBURGH 1.
Fortunes changed quickly for Bruce Kison when, working on a 1-0 one-hitter in the sixth, he surrendered a one-out single to opposing pitcher Bob Knepper and a double to Bill North, Bill Madlock booted a grounder that scored Knepper, and Jack Clark slugged a three-run home run.

AUGUST 22. PITTSBURGH 8, SAN FRANCISCO 6.
With the game tied 6-6 in the bottom of the eighth, Ed Ott drew a walk and was sacrificed to second by Phil Garner. Pinch-hitter Bill Robinson was given a pass. Ott and Robinson advanced on a groundout by Omar Moreno. Tim Foli then lined a single to deep center to drive in two runs and give the Pirates an 8-6 victory. Dave Parker collected his 1,000th career hit on a leadoff single to center in the fifth inning.

AUGUST 24. SAN DIEGO 3, PITTSBURGH 2.
The Padres overcame a 2-1 Pirates lead by scoring twice with two outs in the eighth at San Diego. The Pirates put a runner on in the ninth, but Willie Stargell grounded into a game-ending double play. Dave Parker drove in both Pittsburgh runs with his 23rd homer and a sacrifice fly.

AUGUST 25. PITTSBURGH 4, SAN DIEGO 3.
Gaylord Perry lost a 2-0 shutout when the Pirates tied the game in the ninth inning. Each team scored a run in the 12th, and the Bucs scratched out a run in the 19th to win. Dave Roberts pitched four scoreless innings to earn the victory. The Padres left 26 men on base, one shy of the major-league record, in what turned out to be the season's longest game by innings for both clubs.

AUGUST 26. PITTSBURGH 9, SAN DIEGO 2.
Bruce Kison hit a grand slam in a five-run second inning and Bill Madlock drilled four hits, including a two run homer. Kison's grand slam was the first of his career and the first by a Pirates pitcher since Al McBean on July 28, 1968. By winning 11 of their last 15 games and 22 of 32, the Pirates surged to the NL East lead with 75 victories and a .586 winning percentage. In Atlanta, the Expos, now three games back of the Pirates, were rained out for the second day in a row. Should it be necessary, those games will have to be made up in late September.

AUGUST 27. LOS ANGELES 4, PITTSBURGH 2.
Starter Jim Bibby staked himself to a 1-0 lead with his second homer of the season and pitched hitless ball into the fourth inning, but Dusty Baker's three-run homer off Enrique Romo with two out in the ninth gave the Dodgers the win.

AUGUST 28. PITTSBURGH 4, LOS ANGELES 1.
John Candelaria pitched a four-hitter and Willie Stargell hit his 24th home run to lead the Pirates over the Dodgers. Candelaria won his 12th game against eight losses, but lost an opportunity for his first shutout of the season when Davey Lopes homered in the sixth. In Philadelphia, Cincinnati won its seventh straight game to slip a half-game ahead of Houston atop the NL West.

AUGUST 29. PITTSBURGH 4, LOS ANGELES 1.
After being held to three hits over the first seven innings, the Pirates erupted for four runs in the eighth to give Bert Blyleven his 11th victory against four losses. Kent Tekulve came in with two on and one out in the eighth to shut down the Dodgers and earn his 24th save.

AUGUST 31. PITTSBURGH 6, SAN FRANCISCO 4.
In relief of winner Don Robinson, Enrique Romo snuffed out a San Francisco rally in the sixth inning by retiring pinch-hitter Willie McCovey on a fly ball to right field with two on and two outs to preserve a 6-4 victory. The red-hot Pirates went 21-9 in August, their winningest month of the season, and remained three games ahead of the Expos. The slumping Phillies, NL East champs the past three seasons, fired manager Danny Ozark.

After a sluggish start, the Pirates enter the final month of the season with the best record in the National League.

NATIONAL LEAGUE STANDINGS

East Division	Won	Lost	Pct.	GB
Pittsburgh	78	54	.591	-
Montreal	72	54	.571	3
Chicago	71	60	.542	6.5
St. Louis	70	61	.534	7.5
Philadelphia	66	67	.496	12.5
New York	52	78	.400	25

West Division	Won	Lost	Pct.	GB
Cincinnati	77	58	.570	-
Houston	76	58	.567	.5
Los Angeles	62	72	.463	14.5
San Francisco	60	74	.448	16.5
San Diego	57	78	.422	20
Atlanta	53	80	.398	23

SEPTEMBER 1. PITTSBURGH 5, SAN FRANCISCO 3 (FIRST GAME).
Willie Stargell hammered a pair of homers, his 25th and 26th, to help erase a 3-0 deficit and enable the Pirates to take their 34th come-from-behind victory this season in the first game of a Saturday-afternoon doubleheader. The home runs gave Stargell 22 lifetime at Candlestick Park, the most ever for a visiting player. Grant Jackson notched his 13th save in unusual fashion: With a runner on first and two out in the ninth, Chuck Tanner pulled left fielder John Milner, sent reliever Kent Tekulve from the mound to left field, and brought in the lefty Jackson

in to face the left-handed batter Darrell Evans. Evans flied out to Tekulve for the final out.

SEPTEMBER 1. PITTSBURGH 7, SAN FRANCISCO 2 (SECOND GAME). Lee Lacy's three hits, including a two-run homer, paced the Pirates as they swept the twin bill and captured their 16th win in their last 21 games. Jim Bibby went the distance to raise his record to 10-3. Bibby's .769 winning percentage tops the NL.

SEPTEMBER 2. PITTSBURGH 5, SAN FRANCISCO 3. The torrid Pirates won their sixth in a row behind a 10-strikeout performance by John Candelaria. Backup receiver Steve Nicosia drove in two runs with a pair of doubles, as the Pirates became the first visiting team to go 6-0 in a season in San Francisco since the Giants relocated in 1958.

SEPTEMBER 3. PHILADELPHIA 2, PITTSBURGH 0 (FIRST GAME). Steve Carlton and Tug McGraw combined on a one-hitter to snap the Pirates' winning streak during the first game of a Labor Day doubleheader at Pittsburgh. Carlton held the Pirates hitless through five innings and led 1-0 through seven before leaving the game with a leg muscle strain. The lone Pirate hit was a leadoff double down the third-base line by Steve Nicosia in the sixth.

SEPTEMBER 3. PITTSBURGH 7, PHILADELPHIA 3 (SECOND GAME). Jim Rooker won his 100th career game in the nightcap. Rooker, who had spent the last two weeks of August on the disabled list with a sore elbow, hadn't won a game since May 30, going 0-6 in his last 11 starts. Dale Berra, recalled from the minors on September 1, drove in three runs for the Bucs.

SEPTEMBER 5. PITTSBURGH 7, ST. LOUIS 5. With the score knotted at 5-5 in the 11th at Busch Stadium, the Pirates loaded the bases against Roy Thomas on a double by Omar Moreno, an intentional walk to Dave Parker, and an infield single by Bill Robinson. With two outs, Darold Knowles was brought in to face John Milner, but instead threw the ball past Keith Hernandez at first attempting to pick off Robinson, allowing Moreno and Parker to score the go-ahead runs.

SEPTEMBER 6. ST. LOUIS 8, PITTSBURGH 6. Pittsburgh jumped out to a 3-0 lead in the second, but the Cardinals capitalized on some defensive lapses by the Pirates and chased starter Jim Bibby in the third to win. Earlier in the afternoon at Chicago, the Expos nipped the Cubs 1-0 to move to within a game of first place. "I've thought all along it could go down to the wire with two or three clubs," said Chuck Tanner. "I still think it will."[22]

SEPTEMBER 7. PITTSBURGH 6, NEW YORK 4. Dave Parker's bad-hop infield single drove home the tiebreaking run as the Pirates scored twice in the 14th inning to win at New York. Grant Jackson won his seventh game, pitching 3⅔ innings of one-hit relief. Starter Craig Swan pitched 10 innings and loser Neil Allen went the last four in relief for the Mets, striking out 14 Pirates between them.

SEPTEMBER 8. NEW YORK 3, PITTSBURGH 2. The following day brought another marathon. Mets starter Kevin Kobel retired the first 10 batters and held the Bucs to one hit through seven innings, while the Mets took a 2-0 lead on Ed Kranepool's sixth-inning home run, the last of his 18-year career, off Bert Blyleven. Pittsburgh tied it in the eighth on three singles and a sacrifice fly. In the bottom of the 15th, Lee Mazzilli doubled off Jim Rooker and advanced to third on an infield out. Jim Bibby, the Pirates' seventh pitcher of the game, intentionally walked Joel Youngblood, then yielded a single to John Stearns to score Mazzilli with the winning run. Ex-Buc Dock Ellis's three innings of scoreless relief to earn the win must have impressed the Pirates front office; on September 21 Pittsburgh purchased Ellis from the Mets.

SEPTEMBER 9. PITTSBURGH 6, NEW YORK 5. Willie Stargell doubled home Dave Parker with one out in the ninth to snap a 5-5 tie and enable the Pirates to maintain a one-game lead over the hard-charging Expos. In the NL West, the Astros and Reds are see-sawing for first place, with Houston now a half-game ahead.

SEPTEMBER 11. PITTSBURGH 7, ST. LOUIS 3.
Willie Stargell's 28th home run and four innings of scoreless relief by Dave Roberts, celebrating his 35th birthday with his 100th career win, gave the Pirates an important victory over the Cardinals at Pittsburgh. The Expos, winners of 14 of their last 15, swept a doubleheader from the Cubs to take the lead in the NL East by six one-hundred-thousandths of a percentage point, .60145 to .60139. "We're two games behind in the loss column, and you don't like to be in a situation like that," said Phil Garner. "But I still think the pressure's on them. They have to continue to win as long as we keep winning."[23]

SEPTEMBER 12. PITTSBURGH 2, ST. LOUIS 0.
Pittsburgh won again behind the six-hit pitching of John Candelaria (14-8) and Kent Tekulve's 27th save, but the Expos downed the Cubs 6-3 to maintain a razor-thin edge over the Pirates.

SEPTEMBER 15. PITTSBURGH 5, NEW YORK 4.
Heavy rain from Hurricane Frederic washed out a Cardinals-Bucs tilt scheduled for September 13, allowing the Expos, who rallied late to beat Chicago, to edge .003 ahead of the Pirates. Both the Pirates and Expos were idle on the 14th, but Bill Robinson's two-out single in the seventh the following day broke a 4-4 tie to put Pittsburgh back on top, .607 to .606, as the Expos split a twilight-night doubleheader with St. Louis. Despite pain from being hit on the shoulder blade by a pitch by Kevin Kobel, Willie Stargell remained in the game and will not miss an inning of play the rest of the season.

SEPTEMBER 16. NEW YORK 3, PITTSBURGH 0.
The Mets' Pete Falcone and Neil Allen combined to shut out the Pirates, while the Expos split another doubleheader with the Cardinals, creating a virtual dead heat atop the NL East, with Montreal at 87-57, Pittsburgh at 88-58, and the Pirates on their way to Montreal for a two-game matchup.

SEPTEMBER 17. PITTSBURGH 2, MONTREAL 1.
The Pirates took a 1-0 lead in the third at Montreal against Expos ace Steve Rogers as Dave Parker singled in Omar Moreno, who had singled, stolen second, and advanced to third on a sacrifice bunt by Tim Foli. Bucs starter Don Robinson scored what proved to be the winning run in the fifth when he singled, moved to second on a single by Foli, and scored on Parker's second RBI single. The Expos narrowed the gap in their fifth when Moreno bobbled a single to center field, permitting a run to score, but Robinson allowed only one hit over the final four innings to give Pittsburgh a clutch victory. "That's the best I've seen Robinson pitch all year," said Chuck Tanner. "It's gratifying to get the first win of this two-game series, but this is just the start."[24]

SEPTEMBER 18. PITTSBURGH 5, MONTREAL 3.
Willie Stargell launched a 2-2 pitch from Dale Murray over the wall for a two-run homer in the 11th inning to sink the Expos again. Rain-soaked play between two delays in the fifth inning, the second one lasting 2 hours 54 minutes, caused Montreal's Dick Williams to play the game under protest, eventually disallowed. The Expos, now two games out, have 16 games left to play, 13 of them on the road, where they've played under .500. The Pirates have 14 to go, eight at home.

SEPTEMBER 19. PITTSBURGH 9, PHILADELPHIA 6 (FIRST GAME).
The Pirates rallied for eight runs in the last two innings to take the makeup opening game of a twi-night doubleheader at Veterans Stadium, coming from behind for the 40th time in 91 victories. "You guys are unreal," said a reporter to Dave Parker after the game. "We're real," Parker replied. "We've just got a darn good ballclub." Pete Rose scored three runs for the Phillies to move past Willie Mays into fifth place for career runs scored, and Omar Moreno stole two bases, his 71st and 72nd, to break his own club record of 71 set the season before.

SEPTEMBER 19. PHILADELPHIA 6, PITTSBURGH 5 (SECOND GAME).
The Phillies turned the tables on the Pirates by rallying

for a 6-5 win after falling behind 5-1 in the top of the sixth inning. Meanwhile the Expos took a pair from the Mets to shave the Pirates' division lead back down to one game.

SEPTEMBER 20. PHILADELPHIA 2, PITTSBURGH 1.
The Pirates benefited from a reversed call in the sixth when a drive into the left-field corner by Philadelphia's Keith Moreland, at first ruled a three-run home run, was changed to a foul ball. It went for naught, though, as Pete Rose, batting .536 in an 18-game hitting streak that would extend to 23 games, collected two hits and helped topple Pittsburgh for the second consecutive game. The Expos swept another doubleheader from the Mets to retake first place by a half-game.

SEPTEMBER 21. CHICAGO 2, PITTSBURGH 0.
Lynn McGlothen pitched a four-hit shutout at Wrigley Field as the slumping Pirates dropped their third in a row, falling a game behind the Expos, idle due to a rainout in Philadelphia. Pittsburgh purchased former Buc Dock Ellis from the Mets to bolster the pitching staff.

SEPTEMBER 22. PITTSBURGH 4, CHICAGO 1.
Bruce Kison allowed just four hits in 6⅔ innings while Kent Tekulve finished up for his 29th save. Bill Madlock homered to halt the Pirates' skid and pare the Expos' lead to a half-game as Montreal split a doubleheader against the Phillies.

SEPTEMBER 23. PITTSBURGH 6, CHICAGO 0.
Willie Stargell's two-run double capped a five-run second inning, and Jim Bibby went the distance in hurling a three-hit shutout. The Pirates, whose eight remaining games are all at home, finished 50-31 (.617) on the road for the season. They remained a half-game behind division-leading Montreal as the Expos arrived in Pittsburgh for a four-game series.

SEPTEMBER 24. PITTSBURGH 5, MONTREAL 2 (FIRST GAME).
A noon rally drew thousands of fans as Pittsburgh Mayor Richard Caligiuri proclaimed "Back the Bucs Day." In the first game of a twilight-night doubleheader before a crowd of 47,268, Bill Robinson knocked in three runs with a homer and a triple as the Pirates replaced the Expos atop the NL East. The Expos made three errors and hit into four double plays to squelch any chance of pulling out a victory.

SEPTEMBER 24. MONTREAL 7, PITTSBURGH 6 (SECOND GAME).
The Expos scored three runs in the eighth inning of the nightcap to tie the game at 6-6, and a two-out run-scoring single off loser Grant Jackson by Ellis Valentine in the ninth put the Expos back into first place. After notching his 30th save in the opener, Kent Tekulve came up short in the second game, allowing the tying runs to score. "Nobody ever said it was going to be easy," said Chuck Tanner. "You just have to keep grinding it out. The reason the Expos are where they are is because they never give up, and the reason the Pirates are where they are is because they never give up."[25]

SEPTEMBER 25. PITTSBURGH 10, MONTREAL 4.
Willie Stargell hit a homer in the first to put Pittsburgh up 2-0, then, striding to the plate to a standing ovation as he led off in the fourth, belted another to break a 2-2 tie. Ed Ott matched Stargell by driving in three runs, Omar Moreno broke out of an 0-for-29 slump with two hits, and Enrique Romo pitched four innings of scoreless relief as the Pirates recaptured first place by a half-game. Stargell's 30th and 31st home runs put him over the 30-homer mark for the sixth time in his career. After the game, Stargell told reporters that, pennant or no, this season had been the most emotionally satisfying of his career. "I guess it's because I've gone out there prepared to go to war every day," the Pirates' leader reflected. "People say I'm 38 years old, so if I don't do the job it's understandable. But I'm not a complacent individual. I'm never satisfied with what I do."[26]

SEPTEMBER 26. PITTSBURGH 10, MONTREAL 1.
The Pirates erupted for 10 runs for the second straight game. Tim Foli and Phil Garner each drove in three runs, with Garner also scoring three. Bruce Kison went the distance in boosting Pittsburgh to a 1½-game lead over Montreal. Kison's victory was his 22nd of 28 career decisions in

THE 1979 PITTSBURGH PIRATES

September. "If I knew why," Kison answered when asked to account for his late-season clutch pitching, "I'd apply it in April, May, June, July, and August."

SEPTEMBER 27. ST. LOUIS 9, PITTSBURGH 5.

In an afternoon rain-makeup game, infrequent starter Dave Roberts lasted only three innings as he and five other Bucs hurlers surrendered 17 hits. John Candelaria made a rare relief appearance and lasted only a third of an inning, giving up two runs on three hits. Bullpen ace Kent Tekulve, pitching his club-record 92nd game of the season, had a similarly bad outing, hitting one batter, tossing a wild pitch, and yielding two runs on two hits. With Montreal unable to play any part of a makeup doubleheader in Atlanta due to rain, the Pirates' lead was trimmed to one game.

SEPTEMBER 28. PITTSBURGH 6, CHICAGO 1.

Dave Parker hit a two-run homer, his 25th, and Jim Bibby pitched a four-hitter. The rain-interrupted victory, coupled with the Expos' 3-2, 11-inning loss to the Phillies, gave the Pirates a two-game lead with two to play. In the event of a tie, the league announced plans for a one-game divisional playoff on Monday, October 2, at Montreal.

SEPTEMBER 29. CHICAGO 7, PITTSBURGH 6.

Dave Parker got five hits, but the Bucs came up short when Willie Stargell's throwing error allowed a run to score in the 13th. Starter Bert Blyleven, pulled with the score tied 3-3 in the sixth, set a record for most no-decisions in a season, with a 12-5 won-lost record and 20 no-decisions in 37 starts. The Expos beat the Phillies 3-2 to move within a single game of the Pirates.

SEPTEMBER 30. PITTSBURGH 5, CHICAGO 3.

With news of the Expos' 2-0 loss to the Phillies flashing on the scoreboard in the eighth inning, the Pirates—having now clinched the NL East title—beating the Cubs for their 25th victory in their last 36 games was merely icing on the cake. Willie Stargell drove in two runs with a sacrifice fly and his 32nd home run to pass Honus Wagner as the Pirates' all-time career RBI leader with 1,476. Starter Bruce Kison was removed after six innings with a blister on his pitching hand, and Kent Tekulve, making his club record 94th appearance, pitched the final three innings to earn his 31st save, tying his own year-old team record. After the game, the Pirates sprayed champagne and superlatives. "A thing of beauty," mused Stargell. "This was the best of 'em. No comparison. We did today what we did all year—whatever it takes."[27] "Phenomenal," Dave Parker smiled. "I think we're going to be in the World Series."[28]

With a 20-10 (.667) record in September, the Pirates won their sixth NL East title of the 1970s. The 98 wins were the most for the franchise since 1909, and tied for the club's third best overall.

In the NL West, the Cincinnati Reds claimed the title by 1½ games over the Houston Astros, and will face the Pirates in a best-of-five League Championship Series to decide the NL pennant. The Reds had an 8-4 edge over the Pirates in the regular season.

NATIONAL LEAGUE STANDINGS

East Division	Won	Lost	Pct.	GB
Pittsburgh	98	64	.605	-
Montreal	95	65	.594	2
St. Louis	86	76	.531	12
Philadelphia	84	78	.519	14
Chicago	80	82	.494	18
New York	63	99	.389	35

West Division	Won	Lost	Pct.	GB
Cincinnati	90	71	.559	-
Houston	89	73	.549	1.5
Los Angeles	79	83	.488	11.5
San Francisco	71	91	.438	19.5
San Diego	68	93	.422	22
Atlanta	66	94	.413	23.5

SOURCES

Pittsburgh Post-Gazette

Pittsburgh Press

The Sporting News

NOTES

1 "Schmidt Paces Phillies Over Pirates," *Gettysburg* (Pennsylvania) *Times*, April 12, 1979: 15.

WHEN POPS LED THE FAMILY

2 "Brock, Bucs Go Separate Ways," *Beaver County* (Pennsylvania) *Times,* May 7, 1979: B1.

3 "Pirates Beat Braves in a Wild One, 17-9," *San Bernardino County*(California) *Sun,* May 10, 1979: D2.

4 "Umps Unload 10 Baseballers," *The Daily News* (Huntingdon, Pennsylvania), May 10, 1979: 5.

5 "Long Way to Go Says Tanner," *The Sporting News,* June 9, 1979: 28.

6 "Parker Starting to Shake Slump," *Gettysburg Times,* May 30, 1979: 15.

7 "Major Flashes," *The Sporting News,* July 14, 1979: 27.

8 "Pirates Draw Season-High Crowd," *Gettysburg Times,* June 25, 1979: 11.

9 "Expos Manager Williams Crows," *The Pantagraph* (Bloomington, Illinois), June 26, 1979: A-11.

10 "Pirates Acquire Bill Madlock," *Gettysburg Times,* June 29, 1979: 13.

11 "Madlock Greeted by a Wild and Crazy Group," *Gettysburg Times,* July 2, 1979: 15.

12 "Stargell Gives Skipper King-Size Present," *Southern Illinoisan* (Carbondale, Illinois), July 5, 1979: 9.

13 Ibid.

14 "Bucs Rely on Every Player," *The Daily News* (Huntingdon, Pennsylvania), July 23, 1979: 5.

15 Charley Feeney, "Stennett's Last Year as a Buc? He's Unhappy Riding the Bench," *The Sporting News,* August 11, 1979: 6.

16 "Expos Regain Lead in Eastern Scramble," *Tyrone* (Pennsylvania) *Daily Herald,* July 30, 1979: 6.

17 "Teamwork Helps Bucs Trim Cards," *Southern Illinoisan,* August 2, 1979: 13.

18 "Cards Steal Pirates' Lightning, Game," *Southern Illinoisan,* August 3, 1979: 15.

19 "Phils' Try for Sweep Foiled by Pirates," *Gettysburg Times,* August 11, 1979: 10.

20 "Pirates Pound Phillies Again," *Gettysburg Times,* August 14, 1979: 9.

21 Charley Feeney,"Pirates Sweep the Decks Looking for MVB," *The Sporting News,* September 1, 1979: 27.

22 "Pirates Can't Always Be Perfect—and Cards Are Glad," *Southern Illinoisan,* September 7, 1979: 14.

23 "Pirates Triumph, But Drop Behind," *The Pantagraph,* September 12, 1979: 15.

24 "Round One to Pirates; Expo Bats Silent," *Ottawa* (Ontario) *Journal,* September 18, 1979: 21.

25 Pohla Smith,"Pirates Split in Crucial Meeting," *The Daily News* (Huntingdon, Pemmsylvania), September 25, 1979: 5.

26 Skip Wachter,"Stargell Says '79 Tops List," *The Daily News* (Huntingdon, Pennsylvania), September 26, 1979: 5.

27 "Pirates Capture N.L. East Crown," *Asbury Park* (New Jersey) *Press,* October 1, 1979: D1.

28 "Pirates Head for Cincinnati," *Poughkeepsie* (New York) *Journal,* October 1, 1979: 11.

Wham, Bam, and a Grand Slam: Bucs Conquer Braves in Spite of Substitute Umps

May 9, 1979: Pittsburgh Pirates 17, Atlanta Braves 9, at Atlanta-Fulton County Stadium

By Frederick C. Bush

THE PITTSBURGH PIRATES OUTLASTED THE Atlanta Braves 17-9 in the rubber match of a three-game series at Atlanta-Fulton County Stadium on May 9, 1979, a game in which the 26 hits, 10 walks, and 26 runs scored (10 unearned) were not the only notable numbers. The sloppy, beanball-marred slugfest also included five errors, three passed balls that resulted in as many runs, five ejections, four players hit by pitches, two near-brawls, and two protests. Substitute umpires, used by the major leagues during the ongoing umpires' strike, turned the game into a fiasco through questionable calls and poor game management. In fact, things became so bad in the fifth inning that the game devolved from a tightly contested struggle into an all-out war between the Pirates, Braves, and umpires.

The high-scoring tone of the game was set immediately as the Pirates jumped on Braves knuckleballer Phil Niekro for three runs in the first inning, the last of which came on a solo home run by former Brave Bill Robinson. The Braves returned the favor with a three-run frame of their own off Pirates starter Don Robinson in the bottom of the second inning and captured their first lead with another run in the third inning. Bill Robinson responded with his second solo home run off Niekro to lead off the top of the fourth. That tied the game at 4-4. Atlanta took a 5-4 lead in the bottom of the fourth, but then the Pirates scored three in the top of the fifth to continue the pattern of lead changes and ties that the game would follow into the seventh inning. It was not long, however, before the number of runs scored was not the only aspect of the game to create excitement among the players and the 6,855 fans.

The chaos began in the bottom of the fifth inning as the Pirates were clinging to a 7-5 lead. Pirates reliever Ed Whitson wrapped two walks around one out before the next batter, Niekro, swung at a pitch that hit him on the right shoulder. After a trainer tended to Niekro, home-plate umpire Hank Rountree — an obstetrician turned substitute umpire — awarded him first base because he thought Niekro had been squaring around to bunt when the pitch hit him.

Pirates manager Chuck Tanner stormed out of the dugout and began a fray that lasted more than six minutes during which arguments broke out all over the field. Tanner disputed with Rountree; shortstop Tim Foli argued with first-base umpire Dick Tremblay, the only professional umpire on the crew, and Pirates coach Joe Lonnett took up the issue with third-base umpire Ed Norris. Tanner went into a complete conniption after Tremblay affirmed Rountree's call and was ejected by Rountree while Norris threw out Lonnett simultaneously.

In his postgame conference, Tanner asked, "If he didn't swing, how could the ball hit a right-handed hitter on the right shoulder?" He also declared the call a "disgrace" and asserted of Rountree, "He needs glasses."[1]

After the tumult over Rountree's decision had died down, but before the next batter could hit, Lonnett jogged back out to Rountree to inform him that the Pirates were playing the remainder of the game under protest. Two batters later, Gary Matthews hit a grand slam off Whitson that gave the Braves a 9-7 lead.

Once the chaos had begun, it continued apace with the number of runs scored in the game. In the top of the sixth, with one out, Craig Skok walked Phil Garner and pinch-hitter Lee Lacy and surrendered an RBI single to Omar Moreno. Skok then plunked Foli, who had scored runs on passed balls in both the first and fifth innings, to load the bases. The Pirates tied the game when pitcher Bruce Kison, pinch-running for Lacy, scored on a groundball force out at second base. At the same time, Braves manager Bobby Cox lodged a protest of his own after he claimed to have seen both Tanner and Lonnett still standing in the back of the Pirates' dugout even though they had been ejected.

Both the scoring and bickering continued in the seventh inning. The Pirates retook the lead in the top half of the frame when Robinson scored his third run of the night on Garner's single off Gene Garber. In the bottom of the inning, second-base umpire Andy Anderson ruled that second baseman Rennie Stennett's foot had been off the bag on the front end of what would have been a double play and called the runner safe at second. Stennett jumped in front of Anderson to argue the call but accidentally stepped on the umpire's foot, an unfortunate mishap for which he was ejected. Anderson explained later, "He didn't have to say anything. He put a hole in my shoe."

The Pirates held a 10-9 advantage entering the ninth inning when the game spiraled even further into chaos. After Garber recorded a quick out, Ed Ott and Dale Berra reached base on a pair of Braves infield errors. Garber then hit Garner with a pitch to load the bases, and an unlikely single by stringbean Pirates reliever Kent Tekulve scored Ott. Berra was forced out at home on Moreno's grounder to first, but Foli followed with a two-RBI base hit that extended the lead to 13-9.

Garber's frustration became apparent when he hit Dave Parker, the eighth Pirates batter of the inning, and again loaded the bases. An incensed Parker charged at Garber and later admitted, "When I started out there I wanted to punch his lights out, but as I got closer I cooled down." Parker explained that he and Garber had been teammates in winter ball one year and that was why he had just grabbed him and asked, "What's the matter with you?" Though both benches cleared, a brawl was avoided, but Rountree still ejected Parker. After Matt Alexander entered the game as Parker's pinch-runner, Atlanta-born John Milner stepped to the plate and hit a grand slam.

Milner's homer capped the scoring and gave the Pirates a 17-9 lead that belied how tight the game had been up to the final inning, but the hostilities were not yet at an end. In the bottom of the ninth, the Braves' Barry Bonnell was on second with two outs when a Tekulve pitch brushed back pinch-hitter Rowland Office, who threw off his batting helmet and walked toward the mound as both benches cleared. Once again, a brawl was avoided, and once again a player—Office—was ejected. After walking pinch-hitter Charlie Spikes, who was now batting for the just-ejected Office, Tekulve struck out Jerry Royster to end the 3-hour 42-minute game and its shenanigans.

The "Battlin' Bucs" had certainly lived up to their nickname on this night. Pirates vice president Harding Peterson approved of the message Tekulve had sent to Office via his ninth-inning brushback pitch, saying, "I was glad to see it. You can't let other teams throw at our guys and let them get away with it. I was glad to see Tekulve pitch that way."

After a game that "lacked only sanity," the consensus among the Pirates was that the umpires had lost control of the game. Stennett remarked, "I wish [Commissioner] Bowie Kuhn [who had been in attendance early in the game] would have stayed and watched that," and Ott asserted that "It was the worst example of umpiring I ever saw." Everybody from both the Pirates and Braves may well have concurred with Parker, who said, "I want to donate to help get the professional umpires back."

SOURCES

MLB.com.

Pittsburgh Post-Gazette.

Pittsburgh Press.

The Sporting News.

Youtube.com; the bottom part of the fifth inning can be seen at: youtube.com/watch?v=wTscNRd2g3E.

NOTES

1. All direct quotations used in this article were taken from Dan Donovan, "Pirates Conquer Braves, Beanballs, Umps," *Pittsburgh Press*, May 10, 1979.

Flushing Fog Out

May 25, 1979: Pittsburgh Pirates 3, New York Mets 3, at Shea Stadium

By Matthew Silverman

THE LONG HISTORY BETWEEN THE NEW York Mets and Pittsburgh Pirates saw the teams play the first home game in Mets history in 1962 at the Polo Grounds and the first game ever at Shea Stadium. The Pirates won both, though for the record the Mets won the first game between the teams at Citi Field, in 2009. That, however, came 30 years after one of the strangest games between the two teams that never properly ended.

The Mets hadn't won the season series at home against the Pirates since 1973, when they vaulted from last place to first in the last month of the season. The "Ya Gotta Believe" touchstone moment occurred when a seemingly sure Pirates home run hit the top of the wall, caromed to left fielder Cleon Jones, and turned into an out at the plate by the Mets on their way to a division title and NL pennant. That was the distant past as the 1970s drew to a close. The 1979 Mets were terrible, run into the ground by management, and within a year were sold by the husband of original Mets owner Joan Payson, dead since 1975. Drawing the fewest fans at home for a season in their history (788,905), manager Joe Torre's moribund Mets had to win their last six games of '79 just to avoid 100 losses. (Yet they still fetched a record price that winter from Nelson Doubleday of the Doubleday publishing empire with local developer Fred Wilpon ponying up 3 percent of the record $21.1 million price.)

Still, the 1979 Mets were feisty against the Pirates. When the teams first met, in mid-May, the last-place Mets came to Three Rivers Stadium with a record of 10-20 and promptly shut out the fifth-place Pirates, who fell to 12-18. The next night the Mets tied Pittsburgh in the ninth on a Gil Flores RBI and pulled it out in the 13th inning on Mike Easler's pinch-hit home run. The next night the Pirates trailed by a run in the eighth when Willie Stargell, with more homers against the Mets than any other player, launched a two-out, two-run shot off rookie left-hander Jesse Orosco that stood up for a 6-5 Pittsburgh triumph. From that point on, the Pirates had the best record in baseball at 86-46.

Despite a six-game winning streak begun by Easler's home run, the Pirates were still under .500 when they arrived at Shea Stadium on Memorial Day weekend. The crowd of 6,611 for the opener, on Friday, May 25, would have been laughable if it hadn't been larger than two of the crowds in Pittsburgh the previous week against the Mets. And the weather had been just about as lousy as the Mets. May had more days with measured precipitation than any other month in New York in 1979. The mist lingered.[1]

Former Pirate Richie Hebner, acquired before the season, had made it clear he did not like playing in New York. But he still had just about the most productive bat on a bad team. The cleanup hitter singled home Lee Mazzilli for the first run of the game off lefty Jim Rooker, making his second start of the year after beginning the year on the disabled list.[2]

Craig Swan, the 1978 league ERA leader, who had tossed a combined shutout with Skip Lockwood for the Mets in Pittsburgh a week earlier, was perfect for four innings. Stargell broke up the early no-hit bid with a leadoff double in the fifth. Pops was promptly picked off second base by catcher John Stearns. Stargell's double and Dale Berra's infield single were the only two hits for the Pirates through seven innings.

The game moved along with little action, but in the stands it was a disturbingly different story. Sitting in a front-row box seat along the first-base line, not far from the Mets dugout, Jennifer Davidoff of Manhattan, a 14-year-old ninth-grader at Horace

Mann School, was struck in the face by a line drive by the Mets' Steve Henderson. Ensconced in box seats held by American Express, where her uncle was an executive, the girl was looking at the right-field scoreboard when the ball hit her face. The blow struck her with such force that the stitches on the baseball left impressions on her skin. It shattered her cheekbone, causing a concussion and leaving her legally blind in her left eye. Mets owner and president Lorinda de Roulet, Joan Payson's daughter, accompanied her to the first-aid station. The girl spent one night at the nearby Booth Memorial Medical Center and 10 at Mount Sinai Hospital.[3] The Davidoff family lost a $2.75 million suit against the city and the team's insurance carrier in the state Court of Appeals in 1984.[4]

Henderson later said the incident "scared the hell out of me; I thought I killed her."[5] Regardless of how it affected the players who witnessed the scene, there was minimal action until the eighth inning. Lee Lacy singled to begin the top of the inning for Pittsburgh's third hit of the game, and was still on first with two outs when Easler pinch-hit for Rooker. Easler had spent parts of five seasons in the big leagues and his biggest moment to date in 69 major-league games had been his game-winning home run nine days earlier against the Mets. He had not played the field yet in 1979 and would start just three times all year before becoming a regular. Easler hit Swan's pitch over the right-field wall and into the growing mist. Omar Moreno followed with a triple to right field and scored when first baseman Willie Montanez threw wild on the relay.

The Pirates had a chance to improve on their 3-1 lead, but they stranded two runners when pitcher Dale Murray snagged Ed Ott's lineout to end the top of the ninth. Against the '79 Mets a two-run lead was plenty—one-run was generally a big enough lead as the Mets went 24-35 in those situations. (The '79 Pirates were 30-26.) But there was something about the '79 Mets when they faced the Pirates in their pillbox hats and garish uniform combinations.

The Mets' Joel Youngblood singled to left field to start the bottom of the ninth. Frank Taveras, traded by the Pirates to the Mets for Tim Foli in a swap of shortstops in April, made the first out by flying out to Moreno. But Mazzilli doubled home Youngblood and took third on Moreno's error. With the tying run 90 feet away, lefty-swinging Hebner did not come through against a southpaw in the ninth as he had in the first. Grant Jackson got him to fly to Bill Robinson in left, too shallow to bring in the tying run. Then came a surprise. Chuck Tanner popped out of the dugout and motioned to the bullpen. The Pirates had already used Kent Tekulve. Enrique Romo was available, but Tanner opted for right-handed starter Bruce Kison, whose last save had come in 1976. Stearns foiled Tanner's strategy with a single to left to tie the score. It was the third straight Pirates-Mets game in which one of the teams had come from behind in the eighth inning or later.

The night grew murkier, but Henderson was able to catch a fly ball without difficulty in left field the top of the 10th. Dave Parker did the same in the bottom of the inning in right field. Youngblood, who had been moved to second base two innings earlier, caught an infield popup in the top of the 11th. But those watching on TV saw mostly gray as the bottom of the 11th began. The fog had taken over. Robinson complained to umpire Billy Williams, but was sent on his way out to left field.[6] His complaint quickly gained merit.

Youngblood's leadoff fly ball to left off Enrique Romo was routine on any other night, or at any time earlier in the game. It was simply lost in the fog. Youngblood made it to third base as Robinson located the baseball on the outfield grass. Robinson followed close behind his throw, arguing with the umpires he'd warned about the fog just minutes earlier. The umpires pulled the players off the field for a fog delay. One hour and 18 minutes later, with Shea Stadium still shrouded in pea soup, the game was called.[7]

Exactly one month later the Mets and Pirates replayed the game from the start, as was the long-standing rule for ties then. On June 25 the teams played a twi-night doubleheader at Shea Stadium with the Pirates winning the first game and the Mets the second. Sounds like an amicable way to settle a tie unless you figure that with a runner on third and no one out, the chances of the run scoring and the home team winning are very high — even for the 1979 Mets. And the Mets' 8-10 record was as good as that of any other National League East team against the Pirates. (The Phillies matched that mark.) Every win was needed in a race that came down to the wire. If the fog had lifted on May 25 and the game resumed, the outcome at Shea could have led to a whole different ending in an NL East race decided the last weekend.

Perhaps October would have had different heroes entirely if not for a foggy night in May.

NOTES

1. [1] "Historical Weather for 1979 in New York, USA." weatherspark.com/history/31081/1979/New-York-United-States.
2. [2] Bill Rainer and David Finoli, *When the Pirates Won It All: The 1979 World Champion Pittsburgh Pirates* (Jefferson, North Carolina: McFarland and Co., 2005), 22.
3. [3] David Margolick, "Girl Hurt at Shea Seeks $2.7 Million and Fan Safety," *New York Times*, July 31, 1982.
4. [4] "Girl Hit by Ball at Shea Loses Suit," *New York Times*, March 28, 1984.
5. [5] Ibid.
6. Rainer and Finoli.
7. Ibid.

A Comeback Victory and the Beginning of the "We Are Family" Pirates

June 1, 1979: Pittsburgh Pirates 9, San Diego Padres 8, at Three Rivers Stadium

By Eric Robinson

AS MAY TURNED TO JUNE THE PITTSBURGH Pirates found themselves sitting in an unremarkable fourth place in the National League East. Their current five-game win streak had improved their record to 23-21 but as recently as May 20 they had a losing record and had been as far as nine games behind the division-leading Montreal Expos. With the fifth-place San Diego Padres of the NL West visiting, the streaking Bucs hosted 12,928 fans at Three Rivers Stadium on a Friday evening whose weather caused the opening pitch to be delayed 39 minutes by rain.[1]

By that same spring Sister Sledge, a band of four sisters, had released two albums that had marginal success but still lost money for its record label, Cotillion.[2]

After a quiet first inning, a flurry of activity began in the second inning. Pirates starter Ed Whitson, retired the first two batters. An error by third baseman Dale Berra allowed Padres catcher Fred Kendall to reach base. Pitcher Randy Jones singled and Gene Richards walked to load the bases. Ozzie Smith singled to right field, driving in two unearned runs, and right fielder Dave Parker's error on Smith's hit allowed the speedy Richards to race home for the third unearned San Diego run. Dave Winfield grounded out to second to end the inning. Enjoying his team's 3-0 advantage, Jones retired the first two Pirates batters in the bottom of the inning, but Phil Garner tripled to center field, and Steve Nicosia drove him in with a double. Berra flied out to end the inning and San Diego led, 3-1.

The third inning was quiet for the Padres, but the Pirates made it 3-2 when Omar Moreno singled, swiped second, and scored on Tim Foli's single to left field. Richards hit a two-out single for the Padres in the fourth but was thrown out by Nicosia trying to steal second. In the bottom of the inning an error by Winfield on a fly ball allowed Garner to score, tying the game, 3-3.

In the fifth inning Winfield hit a solo home run to give the Padres the lead again but the Pirates quickly matched it as Moreno walked, stole second again, and scored when Foli singled to center. San Diego manager Roger Craig pulled Jones and replaced him with Dennis Kinney; two batters later Kinney gave up a double to Bill Robinson that scored Foli. After Kinney retired Willie Stargell on a groundout, he was replaced by John D'Acquisto, who got Garner to line out to center. As the teams returned to their dugouts the Pirates had the lead for the first time in the game at 5-4. In the top of the sixth, Pirates skipper Chuck Tanner summoned Enrique Romo to replace Whitson with one out and a runner on first. Romo gave up a single to Broderick Perkins, sending pinch-runner Bill Almon to third, and Richards drove in Almon with a fly ball to right field.

The Pirates were scoreless in the sixth. Star reliever Kent Tekulve took the mound in the Padres seventh and promptly gave the visitors a 6-5 lead with his second home run of the game. The Pirates failed to score in the bottom of the inning.

Neither team scored in the eighth inning. The Padres padded their lead in the ninth inning when

Ozzie Smith singled and then scored from first base on a two-out double by Jerry Turner. Tanner and catcher Ed Ott argued with home-plate umpire Jerry Dale that Ott's sweep tag had connected with Smith. Their arguments failed to convince Dale.[3] Turner then scored on a single to center by Kurt Bevacqua. With three outs left in the game, San Diego was leading 8-5, putting the hometown Pirates in a difficult position.

The song "We Are Family" was sung by Kathy Sledge and was about "people leaning on each other for help."[4] It had a big chorus and catchy beat but after some success on the dance and soul charts, by the end of May 1979 it began to stall on the pop charts.

The Pirates needed three runs to tie the game, four runs for another victory to run their winning streak to six games. Pinch-hitter John Milner led off against Padres pitcher John D'Acquisto and flied out to center field. Omar Moreno and Tim Foli both singled and there were runners on first and second. Dave Parker, next up, had been booed by the small crowd twice during the game, after making his error in the second inning and again after he struck out in the fifth.[5] Parker quickly turned the boos into cheers, swinging at a first-pitch fastball and sending the ball over the center-field fence. The game was tied. Parker had popped up to short off D'Acquisto in the bottom of the seventh so he was sitting on the pitch in the ninth. "You can't tell me the balls aren't juiced up this year," D'Acquisto said after the game. "I kept waiting for Richards to catch Parker's ball and it just kept going."[6]

After Robinson popped out, manager Craig replaced D'Acquisto with Bob Shirley to face Willie Stargell, who singled to center field. The Padres then brought in star reliever Rollie Fingers. Garner doubled to left for his fourth hit of the contest, moving Stargell to third. Ed Ott was intentionally walked with the intention of having Fingers face Berra, who was batting .195. Manager Tanner countered, sending in Lee Lacy to pinch-hit for Berra. Fingers got two strikes on Lacy, but then missed with four straight balls, forcing Stargell home and giving the Pirates a 9-8 victory.

It was "the fourth disaster Fingers has suffered in the last seven games the Padres have played at Three Rivers Stadium," wrote the *San Diego Union's* Phil Collier.[7]

The come-from-behind victory was one of 25 Pirates comeback victories that season[8] and after the game Willie Stargell celebrated the victory by singing the song "We Are Family" by Sister Sledge. The team latched onto the song and soon "The Family" was seen stenciled on the dugout roof, T-shirts, and street signs in the area. The song was played multiple times throughout the games at Three Rivers Stadium. At times the players' wives even disco-danced on the dugout roof during the seventh-inning stretch.[9] Years later, when asked about the team being identified with "We Are Family," manager Chuck Tanner replied, "That's what we really were. They all fed off one another. ... I loved it. That's what you want—a family. They argued all day in the clubhouse and then went out there like a family and they played to win. That's what we were like."[10]

Kathy Sledge said after the season, "It's a miracle. We thought the song had made as much noise as it ever would. Then the Pirates came along."[11] Both the album and the single sold over a million copies before the end of the year and it finished as the number-two pop song on the *Billboard* charts for 1979. However, the Pirates using the song was somewhat bittersweet for the Sledges. The sisters were third-generation Philadelphians and Kim Sledge was quick to say, "We appreciate our Phillies. They should have used our song."[12]

NOTES

1. Charley Feeney, "Bucs' Late Rally Beats San Diego," *Pittsburgh Post-Gazette*, June 2, 1979: 9.
2. Richard K. Rein, "When the Pirates Hustled to Sister Sledge's 'We Are Family,' the Steel City Went Platinum," *People*, November 5, 1979.
3. Ibid.
4. Ibid.
5. Feeney.
6. Phil Collier, "Pirates Cut Padre String, 9-8," *San Diego Union*, June 2, 1979: C1.
7. Ibid.
8. Frank Garland, *Willie Stargell: A Life in Baseball* (Jefferson, North Carolina: McFarland Publishers, 2013), 129.

THE 1979 PITTSBURGH PIRATES

9   Rein.
10 Garland, 129.
11 Rein.
12 Ibid.

Kison Throws One-Hitter; Upset with Official Scorer

June 3, 1979: Pittsburgh Pirates 7, San Diego Padres 0, at Three Rivers Stadium

By Gregory H. Wolf

AS SHORTSTOP TIM FOLI CAUGHT DAVE Winfield's popup to secure Bruce Kison's sparkling one-hit shutout against the San Diego Padres, the rail-thin right-handed hurler with a wicked slider raised his hand in what might have looked like a sign of accomplishment or relief. But it wasn't. Kison was angrily pointing to the press box, where sat the official scorer, who in the eighth inning had ruled a tough-hop grounder to third base a hit and not an error. "It was a once-in-a-lifetime thing for me," said Kison, still fuming after the game. "Of course, I wanted it [a no-hitter] bad. Real bad. I thought under the circumstances, he could have called it an error."[1]

As the Pirates warmed up before the contest at Three Rivers Stadium on Sunday, June 3, 1979, to play the rubber match of a three-game set with the Padres, manager Chuck Tanner's squad had been playing good ball recently. The Bucs had won six straight games before 40-year-old ageless wonder Gaylord Perry stopped them on four hits in a 3-1 loss the night before. At 24-22, Pittsburgh was in fourth place in the NL East, five games behind Montreal. The 25-30 Padres, perennial also-rans who had recorded the first winning campaign in the franchise's 10-year history (84-78) the year before under rookie skipper Roger Craig, occupied fifth place in the NL West, trailing Houston by 6½ games.

Scheduled to start for the Pirates was right-hander Don Robinson. Just minutes before the game, the second-year hurler informed Tanner that he couldn't get loose. The affable Tanner turned to Kison as an emergency starter. "He was rested the most," said Tanner, who also explained his game plan. "I hoped he could give us a few innings. ... [starter] Bert Blyleven volunteered to pitch two or three innings in the middle, and then I would use Kent Tekulve as long as I could and finish up with Grant Jackson or Enrique Romo."[2]

Affectionately called Buster by his teammates, Kison started the season in the rotation, but two dismal outings in April, coupled with chronic blisters on the middle finger of his pitching hand prohibiting him from pitching deep in the game, sent him to the bullpen. The ultra-competitive Kison, who was known for his brushback pitches, was no stranger to big games. As a rookie in 1971, he blanked the Baltimore Orioles on one hit in a 6⅓-inning relief appearance to win Game Four of the World Series. Along with his stellar 4-0 postseason record, the 29-year-old right-hander owned a 70-57 record in parts of nine big-league seasons, but had not achieved the success or stardom some had predicted.

The start of the game was delayed by about 10 minutes as Kison rushed to warm up. On a balmy late-spring day with temperatures reaching the 80s in the Steel City, the game drew a scant crowd of 13,370 to Three Rivers Stadium.

After Kison got through the first inning, yielding only a two-out walk to Winfield, who subsequently stole second base, the Pirates wasted no time attacking Padres left-hander Bob Owchinko, who came into the game with a 21-28 record in parts of four seasons. With Foli and Dave Parker on base, courtesy of one-out singles, Bill Robinson spanked a three-run home run to get the Pirates on the board. Seeing action at first base in place of Willie Stargell, the right-hand-hitting Robinson was normally part of Tanner's platoon system with John Milner in left field.

THE 1979 PITTSBURGH PIRATES

The offensive fireworks continued for the Pirates in the third. Omar Moreno, better known for his feet than his bat (he led the NL with 71 and 77 stolen bases in 1978 and 1979, respectively), led off with a solo shot to left-center to improve his hitting streak to 15 games. Two batters later, Parker launched one over the fence in right field for his ninth homer and a 5-0 Pirates lead. The next batter, cleanup hitter Robinson, connected for his second blast and his team-high 12th homer of the season to send Owchinko to the showers. "Robinson is having a great year," said Tanner.[3] Reliever Bob Shirley set down eight of the nine Pirates he faced, yielding only a single to Rennie Stennett. Pittsburgh picked up its final run on Lee Lacy's leadoff homer in the sixth to make it 7-0.

Kison, who had not tossed a complete game since he defeated Montreal 10-2 on June 25, 1977, looked sharp. He whiffed the side in the second, and cruised along, scrapping Tanner's plan to use Blyleven in the middle innings. "[Kison's] slider was outstanding," said batterymate Steve Nicosia. "It was on the outside corner 85 or 90 percent of the time. He threw about 70 percent sliders."[4]

Dan Briggs hit what turned out to be the Padres' only hard-hit ball of the game with one out in the seventh. Parker, en route to winning his third straight Gold Glove Award in right field, made a nice leaping catch to preserve the no-hitter. "I thought that ball was gone," admitted Kison after the game. "Dave made it look easy, but my heart was pounding."[5]

Kison was just four outs away from the sixth no-hitter in Pirates history and the first since teammate John Candelaria held the Los Angeles Dodgers hitless on August 9, 1976, when third baseman Barry Evans, a befreckled 22-year-old batting a miserable .197, stepped to the plate. He did not "fit the spoiler mold," wrote Phil Axelrod of the *Pittsburgh Post-Gazette*, but Evans hit a tricky shot to third base.[6] According to Charley Feeney, also of the *Post-Gazette*, third sacker Phil Garner was "playing about eight feet wide of the bag, moved a step, maybe two, and then tried to backhand the ball."[7] The ball hit the tip of his glove and rolled into left field. According to Dan Donovan, the official scorer for the game, all four accredited scorers in the press box, two from each team, agreed unanimously that it was a hit, eliciting moans of disapproval from the spectators.[8] Evans reached second base on the play and was credited with a double.

"I thought I had it," said the versatile Garner, who started games at third, second, and short for the Bucs in '79. "Then it hit the dirt and kicked off down the line. It just touched the very end of my glove."[9] He also admitted that had the game been close, he would have played closer to the line and would have probably fielded the ball cleanly.[10] Evans disagreed. "Even if [Garner] gets the ball," he said, "he probably has to eat it. I don't think he would have thrown me out."[11] The Padres third-base coach, Doug Rader, a five-time Gold Glove winner at the hot corner, was emphatic in his evaluation: "A base hit all the way."[12] Bucs backstop Nicosia was less convinced: "It could have gone either way."[13]

Visibly upset by the official ruling, Kison regained composure to retire Bill Almon on a fly ball to left for the final out in the eighth and then polished off the Padres in a 1-2-3 ninth to record his third victory of the season.

After Kison's remonstrations on the mound, he and his teammates retired to the clubhouse. The normally congenial hurler refused to speak to reporters for about 40 minutes, though Tanner was quick to offer praise. "That was the finest I've ever seen him pitch," said the skipper of Kison's first of two career one-hitters."[14] Tanner, always with the big picture in mind, viewed Kison's excellent performance in the context of the pitcher's future. "The no-hitter would have been great," opined Tanner, "but the big thing is that Bruce didn't have any problems with his pitching hand."[15]

Some members of the Pittsburgh media, upset with the way Kison vilified them, excoriated him in the press. "Instead of being happy, Kison was angry," wrote *Pittsburgh Press* correspondent Dan Donovan. "Instead of an extraordinary one-hitter, Kison thought he should have had one of the most remarkable no-hitters in baseball history." Ultimately the brouhaha led to a significant change. Feeney and Donovan resigned as official scorers and the local press initiated a new policy that prohibited Pittsburgh sportswriters from serving as scorers.

NOTES

1. Charley Feeney, "Bucs Breeze, 7-0, on Kison's One-Hitter," *Pittsburgh Post-Gazette*, June 4, 1979: 9.
2. Dan Donovan, "Donovan No-Hit With Kison After 1-Hitter," *Pittsburgh Press*, June 4, 1979: B-5.
3. Ibid.
4. Ibid.
5. Ibid.
6. Phil Axelrod, "Evans Plays Spoiler Role," *Pittsburgh Post-Gazette*, June 4, 1979: 9.
7. Feeney.
8. Donovan, the official scorer, reported that there were four writers in the press box at the time who were accredited scorers (himself, Charley Feeney of the *Pittsburgh Post-Gazette*, and two from the Padres). It would have been highly unusual if there had been more than one "official" scorer.
9. Ibid.
10. Feeney.
11. Donovan.
12. Axelrod.
13. Ibid.
14. Donovan.
15. Feeney.

The Pirates Stage a Comeback Win Using the Long Ball

July 21, 1979: Pittsburgh Pirates 6, Houston Astros 5, at Three Rivers Stadium

By Rock Hoffman

"THIS WAS A HELL OF A WIN FOR US," said Pirates manager Chuck Tanner after his team rallied in the eighth inning with a pair of solo home runs to beat the Houston Astros 6-5 on July 21 at Three Rivers Stadium. The win was the Pirates' sixth in a row and 10th in 11 games, a stretch that began before the All-Star Game on July 17. The winning streak eventually reached a season-high nine games and it finally allowed the Pirates to put behind them a slow start to the 1979 season. (They were 7-11 in April and reached their lowest point on May 15, when they were six games under .500 at 12-18. They immediately evened their record with a six-game winning streak, but didn't hit the .500 mark to stay until their 43rd game.) After a 9-3 win over Houston on July 20 Tanner's team was 49-39, tied with the Chicago Cubs for second place in the National League East, 1½ games behind the Montreal Expos.

As hot as the Pirates were, the Astros were just the opposite. They had completed a 20-8 month in June, but had won just five times in 17 tries in July, and had lost four of five before coming into Pittsburgh and losing the first three of a four-game set. But Astros manager Bill Virdon, a former Pirates skipper, still had his team leading the NL West by 3½ games over the Cincinnati Reds.

All the Pirates needed to do to continue their winning ways and extend the Astros misery was get the best of Houston's All-Star relief pitcher, Joe Sambito, who entered the game with a 0.95 ERA. Since allowing four runs at St. Louis on May 1, Sambito hadn't allowed an earned run to score (and only two unearned runs) in a stretch that covered 27 appearances and 40⅔ innings.

It was 84 degrees with light drizzle when the teams took the field that Saturday afternoon. The Pirates were sending veteran left-handed pitcher Dave Roberts, a one-time Astro, to the mound for his first starting assignment since joining the Pirates on June 28. Two days earlier, Roberts won the first game of the series when he pitched 2⅔ innings of scoreless relief in the first game of a twi-night doubleheader. The Pirates had acquired Roberts and Bill Madlock in a six-player trade with the San Francisco Giants. Roberts was expected to add more flexibility to the bullpen, where the only left-handed reliever had been Grant Jackson.

However, the Pirates' schedule got in the way. Three scheduled doubleheaders and four that were needed to make up for postponements meant the Pirates had to play 29 games in 23 days after the All-Star break (July 19 through August 10). That forced Tanner to start reliever Roberts twice. (He had been mainly a starter up to the 1979 season.)

Against Roberts, the Astros got their leadoff man on in each of the first two innings and he scored both times. In the first inning, second baseman Julio Gonzalez tripled to center field and scored on a single to center by shortstop Craig Reynolds. An inning later, Enos Cabell doubled to left field and José Cruz knocked him home with a single to right. For the Pirates, Tim Foli had a one-out single in the first but went no farther. With one out in the second, Madlock walked and went to second when catcher Ed Ott singled. They advanced on a groundout by Phil Garner but were left on base when Roberts grounded out to end the inning.

After stranding three runners in the first two innings, Pittsburgh broke through in the third when right fielder Dave Parker drove in Omar Moreno with a grounder and first baseman John Milner hit a two-run homer, his eighth of the season, to right-center off Joaquin Andujar.

The Pirates' 3-2 advantage did not last long. José Cruz led off the fourth with an infield single and stole second. Art Howe walked and, after Roberts got two outs, Gonzalez who knocked Cruz home with a single to center.

The Pirates immediately grabbed the lead back. With two outs, Moreno singled to center, then stole second, his 41st swipe of the season. Foli sent him home with a double to right field.

Pitcher Enrique Romo took over for the Pirates in the sixth inning and gave up the tying run on doubles by Bruce Bochy and Gonzalez. Romo was also shaky in the top of the seventh but kept the Astros off the scoreboard as catcher Ott gunned down two Houston runners attempting to steal. In the eighth Cruz got his third hit, a single to shortstop, went to second when Romo threw a wild pitch, then stole third, his second stolen base of the game and his 25th of the season. Howe walked and Bochy struck out. Denny Walling pinch-hit for Astros starter Andujar and singled to left, plating Cruz. Left fielder Bill Robinson fielded Walling's hit and threw it to relay man Madlock, who fired it to Phil Garner to get Walling at second. Romo got Gonzalez on a foul fly to left field for the third out, but the Astros were up 5-4.

The stage was set for heroics by the Pirates. Joe Sambito entered the game in the bottom of the eighth and Bill Robinson greeted him by hitting a two-strike pitch over the wall in right-center field for his 20th home run of the season. Sambito got Madlock and Ott, but with two outs, Garner hit his third homer of the series and sixth of the year.

The Pirates weren't out of it yet. Grant Jackson came on in the top of the ninth to close out the game and pinch-hitter Jesus Alou, leading off, got aboard on a hit to shortstop. Pinch-runner Jimmy Sexton went to second on a groundout by Terry Puhl. Enter Kent Tekulve, who got the final two outs, striking out Jeffrey Leonard and getting Enos Cabell to ground back to him. It was Tekulve's 14th save of the season. Up to this point he and Jackson had split the closer role. However, for the rest of the season, Tanner made Tekulve the primary closer. Jackson had 11 saves coming into the game but got just three more the rest of the season while Tekulve finished with 31. As for Enrique Romo, despite throwing a wild pitch, committing a balk, walking one batter, and giving up two runs on six hits while facing 13 batters during his three innings of work, he got the win and his record improved to 5-3.

Sambito's record fell to 4-3 with the loss and the two runs he surrendered pushed his ERA up from 0.95 to 1.24. (At season's end it was 1.77.) Philosophical about it all, he said, "When I lose, I lose in style."[2]

NOTES

1 Ron Cook, "Confident Pirates Eyeing First Place," *Beaver County* (Pennsylvania) *Times*, July 22, 1979.

2 Ron Cook, "Astros' Honeymoon is Over," *Beaver County Times*, July 22, 1979.

No Doggin' It. "Mad Dog" Belts Two-Run Walk-Off Homer

August 19, 1979: Pittsburgh Pirates 2, Los Angeles Dodgers 0, at Three Rivers Stadium

By Gregory H. Wolf

THE PITTSBURGH PIRATES SPENT MOST of the first 2½ months of the 1979 season struggling to play at the .500 level before they engineered a blockbuster trade that beat reporter Charley Feeney considered "too good to be true."[1] On June 28 the Pirates sent three pitching prospects (Fred Breining, Al Holland, and Ed Whitson) to the San Francisco Giants for infielder (and former two-time NL batting champion) Bill Madlock, utilityman Lenny Randle, and left-handed reliever Dave Roberts. Madlock was unhappy hitting in Candlestick Park, and had been switched from playing third base to second in 1978, and remained there, so far, in '79. Manager Chuck Tanner immediately penciled in Madlock for a return to the "hot corner." In arguably Pittsburgh's most successful in-season trade ever, Madlock provided a spark to a dormant Pirates offense, brought stability to the Bucs' infield, and enabled Phil Garner to move from third to second base, his natural position. "In one fell swoop," opined Dan Donovan of the *Pittsburgh Press*, "the Pirates became potentially their best hitting team in years and turned an undermanned infield into an overmanned infield."[2]

As the Pirates took the field at Three Rivers Stadium on Sunday, August 19, 1979, they had many reasons to be excited. Since Madlock's first game, on July 2, they had transformed a 6½- game deficit into a two-game lead over the Montreal Expos in the tense NL East Division race, and had won 17 of their previous 25 games. They also had cause for concern. They had just lost the first two games of a three-game set with the Los Angeles Dodgers, and their inspirational leader, Willie Stargell, would miss his third consecutive start with an infected finger.

The two-time reigning NL pennant-winning Los Angeles Dodgers were in an unaccustomed position. At 57-65 (and en route to their first losing season since 1968), they were in third place, 12½ games behind the Houston Astros in the NL West. However, they were playing their best ball of the season, riding a five-game winning streak.

The pitching matchup featured two of the NL's top starting pitchers. Pittsburgh's 25-year-old southpaw John Candelaria had won 20 games and led the NL with a 2.34 ERA in 1977, and entered the game with a sparkling 67-37 record in five seasons. At 6-feet-7, he relied on pinpoint control and movement instead of a power game for his success. Los Angeles's 29-year-old hurler, right-hander Burt Hooton, was noted for his mesmerizing knuckle curve. He had enjoyed a career year in 1978, winning 19 games, and had amassed a 105-91 record since his debut with the Chicago Cubs in 1971. Both of these veteran starters had a no-hitter on their impressive major-league résumés. Hooton in 1972, and Candelaria in 1976.

A crowd of 28,382 at Three Rivers Stadium witnessed one of the best pitched and most exciting games of the year. Candelaria held the Dodgers scoreless on just four hits through eight innings. His only trouble was in the fourth inning when shortstop Bill Russell led off with a single. A walk to third sacker Ron Cey and a wild pitch put runners on second and third with one out, but "Candy" induced left fielder Dusty Baker to pop out to Omar Moreno in short center with Russell holding at third, and catcher Joe Ferguson to fly out to right.

On the heels of an impressive two-hit shutout against the St. Louis Cardinals in his previous outing,

Hooton increased his scoreless streak to 17⅓ innings by blanking the Pirates through eight innings. He permitted as many as two baserunners only in the sixth inning, when right fielder Dave Parker lined a two-out double to center field and John Milner, subbing for Stargell at first base, walked. Hooton then fanned left fielder Bill Robinson to end the threat.

"The Pirates may win the National League East pennant," wrote Pittsburgh sportswriter Phil Musick, because "the Pirate bullpen is in toto the game's best."[3] Bucs skipper Chuck Tanner leaned on his relievers more than any other manager in the club's history. A trio of 30-somethings, Grant Jackson, Enrique Romo, and Kent Tekulve, would appear collectively in more than 250 games. The affable manager had no second thoughts when he interrupted Candelaria's shutout bid by sending Mike Easler to pinch-hit for him to lead off the bottom of the eighth in a scoreless game. "I wasn't at all anxious about that [decision]," said Tanner. "You're trying to win a ballgame. You have to have faith in other guys."[4] Rail-thin closer Tekulve, en route to a franchise-record 94 appearances, pitched a 1-2-3 ninth. "If we can stay even for seven, we have the advantage because of our bullpen," said "Teke." "We have a lot of money players. They just don't press, get tight in a game like this."[5]

Parker, who had captured the last two NL batting titles, led off the ninth with what Tanner called the "hardest ball hit this season."[6] According to Charley Feeney, Parker "crushed a line drive toward the mound. In self defense, Hooton speared the ball with his glove hand against his left shoulder."[7] After Milner doubled and Robinson struck out, Madlock came to the plate with the game on the line.

"I've always hit well against the Dodgers,' said "Mad Dog" after the game. "I've had pretty good success against Hooton. I was surprised they pitched to me."[8] Madlock swung at Hooton's first pitch and connected for his third hit of the day, a game-winning two-run home run to center field. "It was a fastball up and away," he said of his first career walk-off round-tripper.[9] "Why didn't I walk Madlock?" rhetorically asked a dejected Tommy Lasorda, wondering why he did not choose to face the next batter, catcher Ed Ott, in that situation. Ott had been 0-for-3 with a strikeout, and had not hit the ball out of the infield during his at-bats.

As an elated Madlock rounded third base in his home-run trot, Hooton gave him a friendly pat on the back. "Burt and I have been friends for a long time," he said. "We went through some struggling times together [in Chicago] and we're pretty close."[10] Madlock relished competing in the first pennant race of his career, and batted a team-high .328 in 85 games after his trade to the Pirates. He fit in seamlessly with the "We are Family" team. "It is easy to be loose around here," he said.[11]

With the victory, the Pirates improved their record to 71-51 and maintained a two-game lead over the Expos in the NL East while the Dodgers fell to 57-66, still in third place, 12½ games behind the Astros.

SOURCES

Pittsburgh Post-Gazette.

Pittsburgh Press.

SABR.org.

The Sporting News.

NOTES

1 *The Sporting News*, July 14, 1979: 40.

2 Dan Donovan, "Madlock Provides Another Good Bat," *Pittsburgh Press*, June 29, 1979: B-6.

3 Phil Musick, "Tekulve's Job Isn't That Easy," *Pittsburgh Post-Gazette*, August 20, 1979: 11.

4 Ibid.

5 Ibid.

6 Charley Feeney, "Ninth-Inning Blast Lifts Bucs to 2-0 Win," *Pittsburgh Post-Gazette*, August 20, 1979: 11.

7 Ibid.

8 Ibid.

9 Phil Axelrod, "Madlock's Home Run Saves Pirates' Day," *Pittsburgh Post-Gazette*, August 20, 1979: 11.

10 Associated Press, "Dodgers' Winning Streak Axed at 5," *San Bernardino County* (California) *Sun*, August 20, 1979: 20.

11 Ibid.

Pirates Tiredly Raise the Jolly Roger

August 25, 1979: Pittsburgh Pirates 4, San Diego Padres 3, at San Diego Stadium

By Nick Waddell

THE STORYLINES HEADING INTO THE Saturday, August 25, 1979, night game between the San Diego Padres and Pittsburgh Pirates were intriguing. The last time the Pirates had won the NL East Division was four years earlier. The team had then spent three seasons trying to get past their in-state rivals, the Philadelphia Phillies. Heading into this contest, the Pirates were the best team in the National League with a record of 73-53. Their division rival, the Montreal Expos, were only two games behind thanks to a win the night before and a Pirates loss. The Pirates were still hot, though, having won 20 of the previous 30 games.

The Padres were heading in the opposite direction. Hopes were high after the 1978 season, when San Diego posted its first winning record ever. But 1979 was disappointing. Going into tonight's game, the Padres, at 55-74, were in fifth place, 17½ games behind the first-place Houston Astros in the NL West. The day before, Padres owner Ray Kroc gave up his control of the team to his son-in-law, executive vice president Ballard Smith. "Baseball can go to hell. ... There's a lot more future in hamburgers than baseball," said Kroc, the architect behind the rise of the McDonald's fast-food chain.[1]

The game featured a matchup of two of the season's best pitchers. For the Pirates, it was 28-year-old ace Bert Blyleven, 10-4 with a 3.71 ERA. His mound opponent was reigning NL Cy Young Award winner Gaylord Perry, three weeks from his 41st birthday, 10-11 with a 3.29 ERA, and the loser of his last five starts.

At just after 7 P.M. under clear skies, with the temperature in San Diego 75 degrees and a crowd of 14,607 on hand, the Pirates' Omar Moreno led off by grounding out to second baseman Bill Almon, who was getting another start over regular second baseman and former Pirate Fernando Gonzalez. Perry then gave up singles to Tim Foli and Dave Parker (the only Pirate on the '79 All-Star squad) before getting Willie Stargell to ground into a 4-6-3 double play.

Blyleven got his first two outs quickly, a strikeout of Gene Richards and a groundout by shortstop Ozzie Smith, before giving up an infield single to Paul Dade and walking Gene Tenace. He struck out Jay Johnstone to end the threat.

In the second inning John Milner reached Perry for a leadoff single, but Bill Madlock hit into a 6-4-3 double play and Ed Ott flied out. Blyleven gave up a leadoff triple to rookie center fielder Jim Wilhelm in the bottom of the second. After a groundout and a walk to Bill Almon, Perry bunted. Almon went to second but Wilhelm could not score as Stargell charged in to field the bunt and tagged Perry out. Richards' groundout to second retired the side.

Blyleven yielded two runs in the bottom of the third inning. He gave up a leadoff double to Ozzie Smith, who continued to third base when left fielder Milner misplayed the ball in the corner. With Dade up, a wild pitch by Blyleven allowed Smith to scamper home for a 1-0 Padres lead. After Dade struck out, Tenace smacked a double to left and advanced to third on another error when Milner fell down at the warning track.[2] He scored when second baseman Phil Garner bobbled Johnstone's grounder. Almon flied out to right to end the inning with a 2-0 Padres lead after the three defensive miscues by the Pirates.

Perry continued his mastery, while Blyleven settled down. Perry did not give up another hit until the top of the seventh, when Stargell led off with a single, but the Pirates couldn't score. In the top of the eighth, Perry surrendered another leadoff single, to Ed Ott, but retired the next three batters. Blyleven, meanwhile, yielded only two hits from the third to the seventh before being lifted for pinch-hitter Mike Easler in the top of the eighth.

In the bottom of the eighth, Enrique Romo held the Padres scoreless. If Perry could hold the Pirates in the ninth, Pittsburgh would be 0-5 in San Diego for the season. But Parker smacked a one-out double and advanced when Stargell grounded to second. Perry walked Milner, placing runners at the corners with two out. Madlock singled to left to score Parker and advanced to second on the throw as pinch-runner Matt Alexander went to third. Padres closer Rollie Fingers, who had a career-high 37 saves in 1978, relieved Perry. With Ed Ott batting, Padres catcher Bill Fahey, had one of his three passed balls that season, and Alexander scored the tying run. Ott was intentionally walked and Fingers gave up another walk, to Phil Garner, loading the bases. Padres manager Roger Craig pulled Fingers for reliever Mark Lee, who struck out pinch-hitter Bill Robinson to end the inning. The blown save for Fingers, who was struggling with a sore right elbow, was his 10th of the 1979 season, and his pitching appearance was his last of the season.

Neither team scored in the 10th or 11th. In the Pirates' 11th, manager Chuck Tanner and Bill Madlock were both ejected. Madlock had struck out looking and tossed his helmet, earning him a trip to the showers. Tanner then charged out to defend his player, and he too was tossed by home-plate umpire Dave Pallone. Coach Bob Skinner managed the rest of the game, although Roger Craig accused Tanner of managing from the dugout runway.[34]

In the top of the 12th, Padres reliever Eric Rasmussen gave up a double to Garner, walked Bill Robinson, and yielded an RBI single by Moreno to give Pittsburgh the lead. Foli grounded into a double play to end the inning. In the bottom of the inning, Don Robinson, normally a starter, pitched his second inning of relief. Robinson got leadoff batter Jerry Turner to ground out, but gave up a single to Fahey and walked Dave Winfield. Pinch-hitter Fred Kendall (father of future Pirates catcher Jason Kendall) grounded into a force out. With the Padres down to their last out, Dan Briggs singled home Winfield from second to tie the score. Robinson got Ozzie Smith to fly out, ending the inning.

The story of the rest of the game was Pirates reliever Dave Roberts. Roberts, who was with San Diego from 1969 to 1971, pitched the final four innings and earned the win after getting out of bases-loaded jams in the 16th and 17th.

In the bottom of the 16th, the bases were full on a single by Jay Johnstone and two intentional walks. Pitcher John D'Acquisto, batting because the Padres were out of bench players, ran the count to 3-and-0 before taking three straight strikes. Winfield tried to rattle Roberts from second base by taunting him and making the "choke" sign. "I won't forget what he was saying to me," Roberts said after the game.[5]

The bottom of the 17th was even more for Roberts and the Pirates. A bunt single by Smith, a hit by Dade and an intentional walk to Gonzalez loaded the bases with no outs. Roberts got Jay Johnstone on a called third strike that Johnstone argued was not a strike. "It was a curveball across my eyes. I just didn't think it was a strike," Johnstone said later. Manager Craig had to tackle Johnstone to keep the center fielder from being ejected. Craig's bench was only two pitchers, so he could not afford to lose a position player.[6] The next Padres batter, Jerry Turner, hit a grounder that forced Smith out at home. Fahey then grounded out to end the threat.

The top of the 19th inning started off uneventfully as Ott struck out and Garner flied to right. Then Bill Robinson, who had entered the game as a pinch-hitter in the ninth, doubled and Moreno was intentionally walked. Foli, 1-for-6 to this point, rapped a single to center, scoring Robinson. The Pirates had the run they needed. Smith led off the Padres' 19th with a single and was sacrificed to second, but Roberts got two fly balls to end the game. The Pirates had outlasted the Padres, 4-3. About 1,000 fans were still there when the game ended at 1:20 Sunday morning Pacific Time (4:20 in Pittsburgh).[7]

THE 1979 PITTSBURGH PIRATES

Each team had used 21 players. Other notable statistics from the combined 161 plate appearances: The teams combined to leave 40 runners on base; the 26 left on by San Diego were one short of the major-league record. The Pirates made four errors and hit into six double plays, but and still managed to win. The two teams batted .111 (4-for-36) with runners in scoring position. Nine of the game's 24 walks were intentional.

Bill Fahey, who caught all 19 innings for the Padres, said "[t]he game was always on the line … real exciting." Ed Ott also caught the entire game for the Pirates, as Manny Sanguillen and Steve Nicosia were used as pinch-hitters. At 6 hours 12 minutes, the game set a Padres record that was broken a year later, when they lost to the Houston Astros, 3-1, in 6:17 on August 15, 1980, during a 20-inning affair. For the Pirates, the game was the longest until they were beaten by the Braves 4-3 in 19 innings in 6:39 on July 26, 2011, in Atlanta. The Pirates finished the 1979 season at a 24-11 clip, including a convincing win the afternoon after the 19-inning marathon.

NOTES

1 John Schumacher, "Kroc Gives Himself a Break—From Baseball," *Los Angeles Times*, August 25, 1979.

2 John Schumacher, "Padres and Pirates Go Into 14th Inning in a 3-3 tie," *Los Angeles Times*, August 26, 1979.

3 Charles Feeney, "Kison Rips Grand Slam, Bucs Win," *Pittsburgh Post-Gazette*, August 27, 1979.

4 There is discrepancy regarding Madlock's ejection. *The Post-Gazette* said he was ejected after a third strike, but some records of the game do not indicate that he struck out in the game. Retrosheet's David Smith said, "[w]e have three scoresheets for that game. Two say that Madlock popped out to first in the 11th and one says he flied out to left. Our account chose the fly to left because that scorer proved to be more reliable over the season. However, none of these showed him with a strikeout. In fact, the official records on microfilm at the Hall of Fame (we have a copy) show Madlock with no strikeouts. The newspaper story was clear that he threw his helmet after a called strikeout. … I am very confident that Madlock did not strike out in this game and I cannot explain the newspaper story." Smith indicated that one scoresheet indicates Madlock and Tanner were both ejected, but there is no authoritative record that this occurred in the 11th as the *Post-Gazette* article indicated.

5 Ibid.

6 Associated Press, "San Diego Strands 26 in 19-Inning Defeat," August 27, 1979.

7 John Schumacher, "This Time the Pirates Don't Need 19 Innings," *Los Angeles Times*, August 27, 1979.

Bibby Tosses Three-Hit Shutout in Pirates' Stretch-Run for Division Crown

September 23, 1979: Pittsburgh Pirates 6, Chicago 0, at Wrigley Field

By Gregory H. Wolf

"IT'S SHOW TIME IN THE NATIONAL League East," wrote Charley Feeney of the *Pittsburgh Post-Gazette* after the Pirates downed the Chicago Cubs in a "must-win" game to stay hot on the trail of the division-leading Montreal Expos.[1] The season was coming down to the wire with nine more games to play. While the Pirates were fighting for a title, the Cubs were on the verge of mutiny.

As the Pirates prepared to play the Cubs on Sunday, September 23, manager Chuck Tanner might not have shown any outward concern for his "We Are Family" ballclub, but he must have been nervous. Three days earlier, the Pirates lost their second straight game to the Philadelphia Phillies to fall out of first place for the first time since they claimed sole possession of the top spot after winning a doubleheader on August 5. A third consecutive loss followed—a four-hit, 2-0 shutout at the hands of Lynn McGlothen in the first game of a three-game set at Wrigley Field to drop the Pirates a full game behind the Expos. Pittsburgh finally stopped its longest losing streak since dropping four straight July 23-26, when Bruce Kison scattered four hits while Kent Tekulve closed out to subdue the Cubs, 4-1, to pull within a half-game of Montreal (92-61). The Pirates had their work cut out for them. The Expos, the hottest team in baseball, having won 28 of their last 36 games, seemed destined to capture their first-ever division crown since the expansion franchise started play in 1969 in the newly formed National League East.

Fireworks began even before the game started. The Cubs, who were a half-game out of first place on July 27, had lost 22 of their last 33 games and had fallen to fifth place in the NL East (78-76). Manager Herman Franks, a baseball lifer, had had enough. With rumors about his eventual firing at the end of the season, Franks lambasted the front office and his club to the AP's Joe Mooshil in the clubhouse. "I know it and they know it," said Franks of his fate. "I don't know what they are waiting for. I've had it up to here [his hand going to this throat]. Some of these players are crazy."[2] Franks whipped out his wallet and showed a check for $24,000 made out to a country club in his offseason home in Salt Lake City to prove he was serious. As can be expected, Cubs players did not react warmly to their skipper's comments. "If we're crazy, what does this make him," said an unnamed player. "He's 65, worth millions of bucks, but he wants to waste the last three years being a lousy manager on a lousy team."[3] Cubs reliever Dick Tidrow, known for his own antics, mused, "Crazy? I don't think we're crazy enough."[4]

The pitching match-up featured two big, rugged right-handers. Eight-year veteran Jim Bibby, a 34-year-old journeyman with his fourth team, signed with the Bucs as a free agent in 1978 spring training. Serving as a swingman that season, Bibby had been used primarily in relief in 1979 until he was moved into the starting rotation on July 10, winning his first six decisions. Despite a nifty 10-4 record and 3.16 ERA, the stout North Carolinian had been clobbered in his last two starts, surrendering nine runs in 7⅓ innings. Rick "Big Daddy" Reuschel toed the rubber for the North Siders. Since breaking in as a 23-year-old rookie in 1972, Reuschel had proved to be one of the NL's most consistent workhorses, averaging 14 wins and 244 innings for mainly poor Cubs teams over the previous six years. With a record of 18-10 and two starts remaining, Reuschel was aiming to reach the 20-win plateau for the second time in his career.

Before many in the afternoon crowd of 24,571 spectators at Wrigley Field on Fan Appreciation Day had a chance to settle in their seats and sip their Old Style, the Pirates got on the board in the first inning. Tim Foli was hit by a pitch, moved to second on Dave Parker's single, and then scampered home on John Milner's single to left. Little did the Pirates know that that was the only run they would need.

Ed Ott, Phil Garner, and Bibby led off the second with consecutive singles, the last of which made the game 2-0. Omar Moreno, who entered the game mired in a 2-for-21 slump in his last five games, hit a grounder to third base, but according to Charley Feeney, third sacker Steve Ontiveros failed to tag Garner as he slid back into third on a fielder's choice, filling the bases. (No error was charged.) Foli followed with a sacrifice fly deep enough to center field to drive in Garner, who barreled over catcher Barry Foote. Center fielder Scot Thompson's throw home enabled Bibby and Moreno to each move up a base. Playing the percentages, the Cubs had Parker intentionally walked to load the bases and play for a twin killing with the slow-footed Willie "Pops" Stargell at the plate. The 39-year-old charismatic leader of the club derailed that plan by smacking a double to deep right, knocking in Bibby and Moreno. Reuschel intentionally walked Milner (who had managed only three hits in his last 20 at-bats entering the game) to face former Cub and two-time NL batting champ Bill Madlock and again hope for a double play. "Mad Dog" Madlock, whose acquisition from the San Francisco Giants in a blockbuster trade on June 28 stabilized the infield and added yet another dangerous bat to the lineup, chopped a grounder to third for what appeared to be an easy inning-ending double play. Ontiveros booted the ball, allowing Parker to score the Pirates' fifth run of the inning. Reuschel's worst outing of the season (1⅓ innings, six hits, six runs, all earned) was over. Left-hander Dave Geisel, a mid-September call-up, retired Ott and Garner to end the frame.

While the Pirates cruised the rest of the game, and connected for only four more hits in the final seven innings off Geisel and Doug Capilla, Bibby mesmerized the Cubs with an assortment of fastballs, curves, and sliders. He yielded only three hits and issued a walk; only one batter advanced as far as second base (Ivan De Jesus doubled in the third.) Bibby whiffed Thompson to record his seventh punchout and complete the game in 2 hours and 22 minutes.

Bibby's shutout, the 16th of 19 in his career, evened his record at 80-80. But more important than personal accomplishments, Bibby's complete game allowed Tanner to rest his overworked bullpen. While Pirates starters completed only 24 games and hurled only two shutouts in '79, a trio of relievers led by Kent Tekulve, Enrique Romo, and Grant Jackson made a collective 250 appearances and logged 345⅔ innings.

The mood in the Pirates clubhouse was reserved after the victory. The players had no time to savor the crucial victory and recognized that a four-game set with Montreal beginning the next evening at Three Rivers Stadium would probably determine their season. "The potential is there," opined beat writer Charley Feeney. "Many Pirates, including their manager, Chuck Tanner, say they are entering the most exciting week of their career."[5] The club often looked to Willie Stargell to provide some levity to the situation, but even he revealed that this coming series got him anxious. "I get butterflies and goose bumps just like anybody else," said Pops. "It's just that if things don't develop like we want, I'm not going to jump off the Hancock building."[6] But Stargell, en route to sharing the NL MVP with Keith Hernandez of the St. Louis Cardinals, also exuded the confidence that the Pirates felt as a team. "We'll be ready for the [Expos]," he said. "It's a thrill just to be out there. We're doing something that a lot of clubs wanted to be doing back in spring training. Now we have to meet the challenge."[7]

The situation in the Cubs locker room was equally tense, but for all the wrong reasons. Still smarting from their manager's comments before the game, many players wondered if Franks would be their skipper the next game. They didn't have to wait long. The Cubs fired him the following morning and named bench coach Joey Amalfitano interim skipper.

NOTES

1. Charley Feeney, "Bucs Tops Cubs, 6-0, Face Expos Tonight," *Pittsburgh Post-Gazette*, September 24, 1979: 11.
2. Bob Verdi, "Frank cries foul after saying 'I quit'," *Chicago Tribune*, September 24, 1979: C1.
3. Ibid.
4. Ibid.
5. Feeney.
6. Ibid.
7. United Press International, "Pirates, Expos to Clash," *Pharos Tribune* (Logansport, Indiana), September 24, 1979: 9.

The Bucs Hold Off the Expos to Take the NL East Crown

September 30, 1979: Pittsburgh Pirates 5, Chicago Cubs 3, at Three Rivers Stadium

By Gregory H. Wolf

"THIS IS THE GREATEST DAY OF MY LIFE," said the champagne-drenched Chuck Tanner, manager of the Pittsburgh Pirates, in the clubhouse after his team defeated the Chicago Cubs, 5-3, to capture a hard-fought NL East title on the last day of the 1979 season.[1] The victory concluded a fairy-tale, emotional journey for the Bucs, who survived a furious challenge from the Montreal Expos. "This may or may not be the most talented Pirate team ever," wrote Dan Donovan of the *Pittsburgh Press*, "but it is the gutsiest."[2]

Ten weeks earlier, struggling to play .500 ball in early July, the Pirates seemed like unlikely candidates for a division crown. But propelled by timely hitting, boosted by the late-June acquisition of third baseman Bill Madlock, and supported by the league's deepest pitching staff, the Pirates went on a 23-8 run that transformed a seven-game deficit into a half-game lead on August 5. Pittsburgh increased its cushion to four games on August 16, but could not pull away from Montreal. Expos skipper Dick Williams, seemingly destined for another "Impossible Dream" performance like the one when he piloted the 1967 Boston Red Sox in dramatic fashion to their first AL pennant in 21 years, led the Expos on a 30-9 surge to take first place by a half-game on the eve of a dramatic four-game series with the Pirates in the last week of the season. The Pirates took three of four from the Expos in Pittsburgh, and then had the chance to clinch the division title in the next to last game of the season. But the Pirates' inspirational leader, Willie Stargell, made a costly throwing error in the 13th inning of a tied game to allow the Cubs to score and win the game, 7-6. A dramatic stage was set for September 30, the final day of the season.

Three Rivers Stadium was packed with 42,176 spectators who were all anxiously watching the scoreboard—not just because their beloved Steelers were en route to an expected loss at the hands of the Philadelphia Eagles, but rather to see the results of the Expos-Philadelphia Phillies game taking place at the same time in Montreal. The Pirates needed a victory and a loss by the Expos to capture the title outright.[3] "We were upset with the guy operating the scoreboard because he was making us stop the game when we were going," said "Mad Dog" Madlock. "We called upstairs and told him not to do it."[4] The operator obliged, and in the days before cell phones, the lack of knowledge about the Expos-Phillies game only increased the dramatic tension at the park.

Bruce Kison got the start for the Pirates. The 29-year-old righty was best known for his spectacular outing in Game Four of the 1971 World Series against the Baltimore Orioles as a rookie (6⅓ innings of scoreless relief to pick up the win), and had quietly carved out a reputation as excellent late-season pitcher, picking up 23 of his 81 career wins in September. Lacking his best stuff in this game, Kison gave up two singles in the first, third, and fourth innings. But the Pirates infield, underrated defensively, squelched each scoring opportunity with inning-ending double plays. Pittsburgh turned its fourth double play in the fifth inning, erasing a leadoff walk. With two outs in the sixth inning, Kison surrendered his first and only run on Dave Kingman's league-leading 48th round-tripper.

The Pirates struck quickly against the Cubs starter, 29-year-old Lynn McGlothen. With one out in the first inning, Tim Foli walked, moved to third on Dave Parker's single, and then scored on Stargell's sacrifice fly to center field. The Pirates increased their lead to 2-0 in the fourth inning when second baseman Phil Garner singled just beyond Cubs second baseman Steve Dillard to drive in left fielder John Milner from third base. The Pirates tacked on another run the following inning when Stargell connected for a solo shot, his 32nd home run of the year, off McGlothen. He also moved past Pittsburgh Hall of Famer Honus Wagner to become the Pirates' all-time leader with 1,476 RBIs.

Nursing a precarious 3-1 lead, Kison had developed blisters on his middle finger (a chronic problem) making it difficult to throw his slider, and yielded to the Pirates bullpen, by far the busiest in the major leagues, to begin the seventh inning. Dependable sidearm closer Kent Tekulve, appearing in his 19th game of the month and league-leading 94th for the season, hurled the final three frames to earn his 31st save, but not before testing everyone's resolve by surrendering a run in both the seventh and eighth innings.

The "decisive hit" of the game, according to Jim Naughton of the *New York Times*, occurred in the bottom of the seventh with the Pirates leading, 3-2.[5] With two outs and the bases full, left fielder Bill Robinson lined a single to right field off reliever Dick Tidrow to drive in center fielder Omar Moreno and Foli and give the Pirates a commanding 5-2 lead. "[That hit] was the ballgame," said Madlock after the game.[6]

In a 1-2-3 ninth inning, Tekulve induced the final batter, catcher Bruce Kimm, to pop up to Madlock. "A soon as it went up," said shortstop Foli, "I knew it was over."[7] Just about 15 minutes earlier, the raucous crowd had learned from the PA announcer that the Expos had lost to the Phillies, 2-0. The victory gave the Pirates their sixth NL East crown in the decade.

As the Pirates celebration moved from the field to the clubhouse, players and coaches were overcome by a combination of excitement, emotion, and relief. Willie Stargell, a goat the day before but one of the heroes this day, was moved to tears. "We don't have many .300 hitters and we don't have any 20-game winners; what we have is 25 guys who play hard," said the team captain. "What we have is a lot of junkyard dogs."[8] The close-knit, racially integrated "We Are Family" Pirates, whom Bob Verdi of the *Chicago Tribune* called "as much machine as it is a melting pot," was noted as much for its competitive and team-oriented approach to the game as it was for its down-home and relaxed nature.[9] "We aren't very pretty, we make a lot of noise, and we make fun of one another," said "Scrap Iron" Garner. "But when we go out on that field, we're all business."[10]

NOTES

1. Charley Feeney, "Pirates Climax Tense Finish—NL East Champs," *Pittsburgh Post-Gazette*, October 1, 1979: 1.

2. Dan Donovan, "'79 Pirates Gave It Their All and Then Some," *Pittsburgh Press*, October 1, 1979: B1.

3. While the Pirates were playing their 162nd game, the Expos were playing their 160th due to rainouts. Had the Expos beaten the Phillies, they would have played a doubleheader in Atlanta. If they had won those two games, they would have forced a one-game playoff with the Pirates in Pittsburgh. Pittsburgh won the season series with the Expos, 11-7.

4. John Clayton, " 'Ganghouse' Pirates Play It Cool," *Pittsburgh Press*, October 1, 1979: B4.

5. Jim Naughton, "Pirates Win Division By Defeating Cubs, 5-3," *New York Times*, October 1, 1979: C1.

6. Dan Donovan, "NL East Title Only the Beginning for Bucs," *Pittsburgh Press*, October 1, 1979: B3.

7. Naughton.

8. Phil Musick, "Stargell's Brilliance Drives Pirates to Top," *Pittsburgh Post-Gazette*, October 1, 1979: 9.

9. Bob Verdi, "Pirates Win the Title with a Loaded Deck," *Chicago Tribune*, October 1, 1979: E1.

10. Ibid.

Pops Puts Bucs on Top in 11

October 2, 1979: Pittsburgh Pirates 5, Cincinnati Reds 2, at Riverfront Stadium

1979 NLCS—Game One

By Thomas E. Schott

IT WAS A FAMILIAR SCENARIO FOR THE Pirates and their fans, and one not likely to foster a bunch of fond memories. Pittsburgh had fielded some pretty good baseball teams in the 1970s, and five of the previous ones had been good enough to win the National League's Eastern Division. Three of those times in the first half-dozen years of the decade, Fate decreed that they play the Cincinnati Reds for the pennant. First the fledgling Big Red Machine in 1970, the maturing engine in 1972, and then the full-grown monster in 1975. In those three best-of-five series, the Pirates had managed to win two of 11 games. Meanwhile, the Reds had roared through the decade, winning the National League's Western Division crown six times, finishing second three times, and winning two World Series. They were a team comfortable with dominance.[1]

But this year, 1979, when Cincinnati finished 90-71, it had spent only 45 days in first place, latching onto it to stay in mid-September and finishing only a game and a half ahead of the Houston Astros. The Pirates won their division by two games over the Montreal Expos, winning 98 games in the process, but they had not clinched the NL East title until the final day of the season.

For the playoffs, the Pirates figured to display a little more prowess at the plate than their opponents. They had hit more home runs during the season as a team and scored more runs, garnered more hits, and hit for a higher average. And they stole more bases, too—77 by leadoff hitter Omar Moreno alone. But both teams sported 99+ OPS. Pirates pitching also appeared slightly superior on paper: better ERA+, WHIP, slightly fewer runs allowed per game, and the league's best bullpen. One writer suggested that submarining right-handed reliever Kent Tekulve alone accounted for the eight-game difference between the teams in total wins. But one significant fact mitigated this advantage: The Pirates and their playoff opponents had met fully a dozen times in regular league play and the Reds had won eight of those contests, the only team to achieve a positive record against the Bucs that year. And the then best-of-five Championship Series would begin in Cincinnati's home park, Riverfront Stadium. But playoff baseball is a different kind of animal, and seasonal numbers and comparisons, as inevitable as they are, more often than not can all be thrown out the window in the postseason. And so it was with this series.[2]

Bucs manager Chuck Tanner chose towering (6-feet-7) southpaw John Candelaria as his starter for Game One, something of a surprise. Although he led the Pirates staff in wins (14) as well as losses (9) and complete games (9) with a respectable 3.22 ERA, he'd been plagued most of the season with rib and back problems. Candelaria had not started since mid-September. And on his last outing, in relief on September 27 against the Cardinals, he faced four batters and gave up three hits. During the season he had started three times against the Reds, who beat him up twice, while the third game was a no-decision. But, said Tanner, "Candy is a money pitcher, and he said he's ready. So he's our man."[3] Joe Morgan, the future Hall of Fame second-sacker for the Reds, thought Tanner's choice gave Cincinnati the advantage.[4]

As well he might, for John McNamara, the Reds' skipper, had designated veteran righty Tom Seaver, another future Hall of Famer, 11-time All-Star, and three-time NL Cy Young Award winner, as his starter. Seaver had legitimate ace credentials. He had gone 16-6 during the season.—winning 14 of his last 15 decisions — with a sparkling 3.14 ERA, and he led the staff in every pitching stat category that mattered. And he would be pitching at home. Only the weather mottled the picture. Although with the temperature in the mid-60s and only the barest whisper of a breeze, the outfield was treacherous; the game had been delayed 45 minutes by rain.[5]

Neither pitcher would be facing exactly creampuff lineups. The Pirates had a passel of formidable bats: Six out of their eight starting position players sported batting averages over .280, led by midseason acquisition Bill Madlock (.328) and 1978 NL MVP right fielder Dave Parker (.310). And Parker, who was among the league leaders that year with a 6.7 WAR, along with first baseman Willie "Pops" Stargell combined for 57 home runs, 176 RBIs, and a .904 OPS, power not to be trifled with. Not that the Reds were slackers at the plate. They had four .300 hitters, including left fielder George Foster, who led the team in homers with 30. (The others were 26-year-old Ray Knight, who hit .318 to lead the team, and outfielders Dave Collins and Ken Griffey Sr.[6])

The 55,006 fans jamming Riverfront that Tuesday evening got treated to a splendid game that went 3 hours and 14 minutes. Both starting pitchers lived up to their hype. Supposedly shaky Candelaria delivered seven strong innings, gave up only five hits and a pair of runs before leaving with a sore rib cage. Seaver went Candy one better, also giving up five hits, but going eight strong innings, retiring the last 10 Bucs he faced. But he too had surrendered two runs. So with the Reds coming to bat in the bottom of the eighth, the game was knotted at two runs apiece.[7]

The Pirates had drawn first blood in their half of the third inning. Leading off, on a 2-and-0 count, second baseman Phil Garner, who had hit only 11 homers during the season, drilled an opposite-field round-tripper into the right-field stands, his first and only postseason dinger. After Candelaria struck out, speedy Omar Moreno stroked a low liner to right that Collins misplayed; the ball rolled to the wall, and Moreno ended up with a triple. Shortstop Tim Foli's fly ball to medium right-center easily plated Moreno, and the Pirates had a two-run lead. Which lasted all of one inning. In the bottom of the fourth, the Reds got to Candelaria for two runs themselves. Shortstop Dave Concepcion led off the inning with a single, and then George Foster muscled the first pitch he saw from Candelaria over the wall in left.[8]

The game remained tied for the next six innings. Cincinnati mounted a serious threat in the bottom of the eighth inning. Long-haired, black-bearded right-hander Enrique Romo started the inning in relief of Candelaria and quickly got into trouble, surrendering a one-out single to Collins, who stole second. After Romo walked Morgan on four pitches, Tanner, as he had done 94 times that season, called on Kent Tekulve to quell the flames. Which he did, inducing Concepcion to hit into an around-the-horn double play.[9]

In the top of the 11th inning, old man Willie Stargell, 38, put the game on ice for the Pirates. After Foli singled to left and Parker followed with a sharp single through the infield, Stargell sent reliever Tom Hume's first pitch to him out of the park in right-center for a three-run homer. Not to be outdone so easily, the Reds scared the daylights out of Pittsburgh fans by loading the bases with two out in the bottom of the inning against relievers Grant Jackson and Don Robinson. But the big right-hander Robinson, normally a starter, saved the game by getting Ray Knight to whiff.

The Pirates were in the catbird seat. All they had to do now was play .500 ball the rest of the NLCS, and the pennant would be theirs.

NOTES

1 All statistical data in this article derived from baseball-reference.com.

2 Jim Naughton, "Pirates Rely on Candelaria," *New York Times*, October 2, 1979.

3 Charlie Feeney, "Tanner Names Candelaria Surprise Starter," *Pittsburgh Post-Gazette*, October 2, 1979.

4 Ibid.

5 Ibid.; retrosheet.org/boxesetc/1979/B10020CIN1979.htm. The Pirates had hit Seaver hard during the one start he had against them during the year, but he did not figure in the decision.

6 Knight in 1979, at least, turned out to be a more-than-suitable replacement for Pete Rose, who had left the Reds for the Phillies in the offseason.

7 Joseph Durso, "Pirates Win in 11 on Stargell Homer," *New York Times*, October 3, 1979.

8 Ibid.

9 nerdbaseball.com/2010/04/enrique-romo/.

Another Nail-biter Pirated Away

October 3, 1979: Pittsburgh Pirates 3, Cincinnati Reds 2, at Riverfront Stadium

1979 NLCS—Game Two

By Thomas E. Schott

GAME TWO OF THE NLCS WAS ANOTHER extra-inning nail-biter, with the Pirates again prevailing in extra innings by a narrow margin. Only for drama, this game outdid its predecessor on several counts. Clutch hitting, controversy, terrible baserunning, heroics: it had it all. Chuck Tanner selected Jim Bibby, a strapping, intimidating right-hander, as his starter. The veteran had enjoyed a good year in a dual starter-reliever role, winning 12 games and losing 4, with an ERA of 2.81 and WHIP of 1.140. Cincinnati manager John McNamara's selection, by contrast, was odd: he chose to pitch Frank Pastore, a 22-year-old right-handed rookie, who had not had a sterling year (6-7 with a 4.25 ERA) in this pressure-cooker game before this Wednesday afternoon crowd of 55,000. This was a must-win for the Reds, for the series moved to Pittsburgh after this. And this was not the same Big Red Machine that had dominated the NL throughout the 1970s.[1]

Indeed, the Reds were amid a significant transition. Popular manager Sparky Anderson had paid with his job for the sin of finishing second to the Los Angeles Dodgers in 1977-78, and third baseman Pete Rose had been lost to free agency in the offseason. Although Ray Knight picked up the slack well at third, the Reds didn't hit too many homers or for notable average, but they took walks and hit the alleys at Riverfront well. Overall, their pitching was pretty good, the NL's fourth-best ERA. The sturdy rotation—Seaver, Mike LaCoss, Fred Norman, Bill Bonham, and Paul Moskau—all had ERAs in the 3's. Pastore had turned in some key starts, but the bullpen was anchored by another hybrid, Tom Hume, who started a dozen games and came in to relieve in 45.[2]

After a fairly consistent start, the Reds spent most of the season chasing the Houston Astros for the division lead, and at one point were as many as 10½ games back. They clawed their way back to the top after the All Star break, and after a two-game sweep against their nemeses at Riverfront in Cincinnati on September 11-12, took the divisional lead, but they went on to drop two of three to the Astros in Houston on September 21-23. They nursed a 1½-game lead through the season's final week and did not clinch the title until Friday. Pastore delivered two victories during that week, including the road win against Houston.[3]

So perhaps this is what prompted McNamara to trust this crucial game to his rookie. In fact, his instincts had been spot-on: Pastore pitched seven solid innings and gave up only two runs, and one of those, anybody from Cincy would tell you, was bogus. The home team had gotten on the board first in the bottom of the second inning, when none other than Pastore hit a sacrifice fly to center after singles by Dan Driessen and Knight. The Pirates tied the game in the top of the fourth, but it could have been much worse for the Reds. Shortstop Tim Foli led off the inning with a single. Parker also singled, and Foli stopped at second. This brought Stargell to the plate, and he stroked a fly to deep left. George Foster looked as though he was going to make the catch, but the ball sailed over his head, bounced against the base of the wall, and right back into Foster's glove. Both runners advanced a base, but Stargell had not been watching the runner ahead of him and was almost to second when he had to make a desperate U-turn. A head-first dive back into first base couldn't beat the relay throw from Morgan; he was out. The Pirates managed later to scratch over a run on a groundout by Bill Madlock, but that was it.[4]

The Bucs grabbed the lead in the top of the next inning. The leadoff hitter, Phil "Scrap Iron" Garner, laced a sharp, sinking liner to right-center. Reds right fielder Dave Collins bolted toward the ball, stretched way out, nabbed it, and then lost his balance and fell. He slid and tumbled before jumping up to show everyone the ball in his glove. It had been a highlight-reel catch, but second-base umpire Frank Pulli begged to differ. He signaled "safe," meaning that Collins had trapped the ball. McNamara stormed out of the dugout; Collins and other Reds screamed and hollered. Joe Morgan had to act as a demilitarized zone between Collins and Pulli. After a heated exchange, Pulli of course did not change his call, and the next batter, pitcher Bibby, laid down a perfect sacrifice bunt and moved Garner into scoring position. After Moreno flied to center, Foli slammed a line-hugging double past Knight at third and Garner scored. Pirates 2, Reds 1.[5]

And there the game stood until the bottom of the ninth inning. With their backs to the wall, the Reds managed to tie it up. They almost did in their half of the eighth. Southpaw Grant Jackson in relief of Bibby got lefty-hitting Morgan to ground out. At this point Tanner, playing the percentages, brought in righty Enrique Romo to pitch to right-handed Dave Concepción, who promptly singled. As did right-handed Foster. So much for percentages. As ever in such situations, it was Tekulve time, and the stringbean submarine hurler did indeed strike the dangerous Johnny Bench out … but it was on a wild pitch that moved the runners to second and third. After Romo intentionally put Driessen on, Knight flied out lazily to center.

Which set the stage for the dramatic bottom of the ninth. The Bucs could do nothing in their half. So the Reds had three outs left. After striking out César Gerónimo, Tekulve gave up back-to-back doubles to pinch-hitter Hector Cruz and Collins. With the score tied now, Tanner waved in left-hander Dave Roberts, who issued an "unintentional" intentional walk to Morgan. Tanner then lifted Roberts for Don Robinson, who had saved the bacon for him in Game One. Robinson retired Concepción on a swinging strikeout and Foster on a roller to second. For the second consecutive game, these teams were going into extra innings.

The Pirates lost no time in putting the Reds back in the hole in the top of the 10th. Against the new Reds pitcher, Doug Bair, it required only three batters. Omar Moreno singled, Foli bunted him to second, and then Parker singled Moreno home. Wanting nothing to do with Stargell, the Reds put him on and got the next two batters out. Down a run, Cincinnati went quietly. Robinson struck out Bench, and got Driessen and Knight to fly out. Robinson got the win to go with his previous evening's save, and the jubilant Bucs were headed home to the "Family," only a win away from glory.[6]

NOTES

1. All statistical data and play-by-play information in this article derived from baseball-reference.com.
2. thesportsnotebook.com/2014/09/1979-cincinnati-reds-sports-history-articles/.
3. Ibid.
4. John McCollister, *Tales From the 1979 Pittsburgh Pirates Dugout: Remembering "The Fam-A-Lee"* (New York: Sports Publishing, 2005), 84.
5. McCollister, 84-85.
6. A tragic sidelight to the 1979 "Family" Pirates is that two members of their pitching staff who played prominent roles in the NLCS later lost sons in tragic accidents. In 1985 John Candelaria's two-year-old boy fell into the family swimming pool on Christmas Day and never woke up from a coma that lasted six months. articles.chicagotribune.com/1985-04-25/sports/8501250206_1_john-candelaria-hands-christmas-morning. And Don Robinson's 30-year-old son was killed, along with his wife and three others, in an automobile accident in Kentucky on Christmas Eve in 2012. wsaz.com/home/headlines/Don-Robinsons-Son-Killed-in-Kentucky-Crash-184923501.html.

A Family Celebration

October 5, 1979: Pittsburgh Pirates 7, Cincinnati Reds 1, at Three Rivers Stadium, 1979 NLCS—Game Three

By Thomas E. Schott

IT WAS, IN A WORD, ANTICLIMACTIC. On the basis of the performance of the two playoff teams in this final game of the 1979 NLCS, one could strongly argue that Cincinnati was a beaten team even before the third game was played on Friday afternoon. It would have been little short of a miracle for them to have rallied from an 0-2 deficit in a best-of-five-game series anyway. But after two heartbreaking extra-inning losses in their own ballyard, a reversal of their ultimate fate would have required direct divine intervention, several times.[1]

Which would not be forthcoming—not in this electrically charged atmosphere, not before 42,000-plus rabid members of the partisan Pirates "Family." Even with a short rain delay before the first pitch, the smell of sweet revenge for their decade-long humiliations at the hands of these Cincinnati guys wafted about the stadium. Early on in the season, the Pirates had adopted as their theme song the catchy, thumping disco tune "We Are Family" by the group Sister Sledge. It was now blaring from everywhere. And almost like grandpa among a bunch of kids who looked to him for leadership, Willie "Pops" Stargell had then adopted the song as a suitable metaphor for the team. The joyful unity in the stands mirrored that of a loose, confident clubhouse. Hirsute, swaggering, and even a bit scruffy, the Pirates embodied almost perfectly their rough-edged, working-class hometown. "We took a back seat to nobody," manager Chuck Tanner proclaimed proudly. "We were a 'dirty shirt' ball club.... We weren't afraid to try anything.... (A) blue-collar club in a blue-collar town."[2]

And the heart if not the soul of that club was Stargell. He had broken in with the Pirates in the fall of 1962 and by 1979 at age 39 was nearing the end of a sterling career. A seven-time All Star and 11-time MVP candidate, Stargell, expanding paunch and arthritic knees aside, actually enjoyed two of his best years in 1978 and 1979, averaging 30 home runs and 90 RBIs. Of course, he had posted prodigious numbers for years, and the distance he powered some balls out of NL parks became legend. "He was so strong and generated such tremendous bat speed," his biographer wrote, "that when he really laid into one the result was often a blast of absurd, almost cartoonish proportions."[3]

But sparkling numbers aside, Pops was special: the "elder statesman" and emotional center of the team. The gold "Stargell stars" he awarded teammates for extraordinary feats on the field proudly adorned the caps of honored Bucs. Tekulve had a galaxy on his. Outfielder Bill Robinson described Pops as "kind of a father figure" to the team, "our crutch" who took on all their problems, personal or professional.[4]

So it was more than fitting that as he had played a key role in Game One of the series, Stargell did likewise in Game Three. He hit his second home run of the NLCS, off lefty Fred Norman, to open the Bucs' half of the third inning, a shot high into the second deck in right field. After a joyous welcome from his teammates, Pops took a curtain call and blew a kiss to the ecstatic crowd. But even before Stargell's blast the Reds already trailed by two. Pittsburgh scored a run in the first when Moreno sprinted home on a fly ball to left by Parker and another the next inning when Phil Garner, who had tripled, scored on a second sacrifice fly by Tim Foli. That had been enough to chase the Reds' starter, Mike LaCoss. Bill Madlock added a solo homer of his own later in the third inning, and at the end of three the Pirates led 4-0. And they continued to pile it on the hapless Norman in the fourth inning. Pirates starter Bert Blyleven singled and Moreno bunted him to second. After a fly out, Parker walked. Which brought Stargell to the plate again to a deafening welcome from the crowd. Pops obliged them once more by smashing a vicious grounder past first baseman Dan Driessen down the line in right for a double and scoring two more runs. The Pirates led by six.[5]

The rest is easily told. Blyleven, a future Hall of Fame pitcher whom naysayers branded as a guy who couldn't win the big games, went the distance and surrendered only one run, a solo homer by Johnny Bench in the sixth. Blyleven scattered eight hits and struck out nine in his first career postseason win. The Pirates added another run in the eighth on an ugly misplayed fly ball to left-center for an error by four-time Gold Glove center fielder César Gerónimo. The game ended with the score 7-1, Pirates. As Roger Angell observed, the Reds "looked corpselike at the end."[6]

But Three Rivers went crazy. A harbinger of the end-of-game frenzy had already occurred during the seventh-inning stretch, when the Pirates wives seated just behind the screen began dancing to "We Are Family" blasting from the stadium's loudspeakers. Now they had "clambered up onto a low, curving shelf that rims the field around home plate."[7] First a few, then many more young women ran down the aisles and joined them. "They were all dancing together there arm in arm, jiving and boogieing and high-kicking in rhythm, in their slacks and black-and-gold scarves and long, ballplayer-wife's fur coats, all waving and laughing and hugging and shaking their banners in time to the loud music. It was terrific."[8]

Indeed it was. Little did anyone in Steel Town realize that raucous evening that it would be 11 more years before a string of NLCS losses from 1990-92, and then well into the next century before the Pirates could even think about going to the World Series again. The MVP for the NLCS was obvious: Willie Stargell hit .455, 5-for-11, with three walks, two doubles, two homers, and six RBIs. Garner and Parker deserved honorable mentions. The three-game Pirates sweep in the 1979 NLCS sounds a lot more dominating than it actually was. But *these* Pirates were bound for glory. There would be no stopping them even after they were down three games to one in the ensuing World Series with the Orioles. They had a date with Destiny.

NOTES

1. All statistical data and play-by-play information in this article derived from baseball-reference.com.
2. "Revisit the 'Family's' 1979 NLCS," pittsburgh.pirates.mlb.com/content/printer_friendly/pit/y2004/m10/d12/c891911.jsp; John McCollister, *Tales from the 1979 Pittsburgh Pirates Dugout: Remembering "The Fam-A-Lee"* (New York: Sports Publishing, 2005), 1.
3. James Forr, "Willie Stargell," SABR Baseball Biography Project, sabr.org/bioproj/person/27e0c01a.
4. Ibid.
5. Joseph Durso, "Pirates Win National League Pennant in Sweep of Reds," *New York Times*, October 6, 1979. See also, youtube.com/watch?v=VaG6T_XOC3M.
6. Roger Angell, *Late Innings: A Baseball Companion* (New York: Simon and Schuster, 1982), 211.
7. Ibid.
8. Ibid.

The 1979 Baltimore Orioles: Young Birds Take Flight

By Gordon Gattie

THE BALTIMORE ORIOLES ENTERED THE 1979 campaign with high expectations. The Orioles had finished the 1978 season with a 90-71 record, ending an up-and-down year in fourth place in the American League East. Although they had won at least 88 games for the sixth consecutive season, they finished a distant nine games behind the AL East champion New York Yankees. Their fourth-place finish ended a streak of three consecutive second-place finishes. Baltimore had reason for optimism; during the offseason, right fielder Ken Singleton rebounded from surgery on his sore right elbow,[1] and 1973 AL Rookie of the Year Al Bumbry, who tested the free agent re-entry draft and signed a new three-year contract with the Orioles,[2] returned after breaking his left fibula and dislocating his left ankle while sliding back into second base during a May 1978 game.[3] In addition, John Lowenstein was selected off waivers from the Texas Rangers to improve the outfield while Steve Stone was signed as a free agent to join the solid Baltimore pitching staff.

The Orioles were projected to remain a force in the AL East, but their focus on pitching and defense was not anticipated to keep pace with the Yankees and the Boston Red Sox for the division crown. The Yankees were back-to-back World Series champions. Bob Lemon, who succeeded Billy Martin as manager in midseason 1978, was back. The Yankees' veteran-laden clubhouse was led by catcher and 1976 MVP Thurman Munson. The Red Sox boasted the league's best offense behind 1978 Most Valuable Player (and future Hall of Famer) Jim Rice, Cooperstown-bound Carl Yastrzemski, and perennial All-Star center fielder and 1975 MVP Fred Lynn. While Baltimore was expected to compete with the Milwaukee Brewers and Detroit Tigers for third place, Orioles manager Earl Weaver commented in *Sports Illustrated*, "We've got the best pitching in the league, and I predict we'll hit more homers than the Yankees."[4] *Baseball Digest* selected the Orioles to finish second in the AL East, behind the Yankees and ahead of the Red Sox. Although the Orioles had a "good young pitching staff, fine power at the corners, with solid infield defense," they wouldn't outperform the Yankees' "enormous pitching depth in starters, strong bullpen, good infield defense, great power."[5]

Baltimore left spring training in Miami with an underwhelming 10-15 record. Organizational changes were on the horizon; after 10 years with the Orioles, catcher Elrod Hendricks had been released as a player and named a coach,[6] and the club was about to be sold by Jerold C. Hoffberger's Baltimore Baseball Group to Washington lawyer Edward Bennett Williams. Attendance at Baltimore's Memorial Stadium had been relatively flat for two decades, and Hoffberger was under pressure to sell the family-owned franchise. The uncertainty surrounding the transfer and the lack of name recognition on the roster placed additional emphasis on the solid pitching and defense that had defined the team in the 1970s.

On a wintry Opening Day, Friday, April 6, the Orioles hosted the Chicago White Sox. Orioles ace Jim Palmer and the White Sox' Ken Kravec were the pitchers. Chicago scored two runs in the second inning on two singles, two stolen bases, a passed ball, and a walk. Baltimore responded with three runs in the bottom of the frame, sparked by a two-run single by second baseman Rich Dauer. The single was especially significant for Dauer, who had begun the previous two seasons by hitting 1-for-41 and 3-for-31. The Orioles scored single runs in the fifth and seventh innings and held on, winning 5-3 on Palmer's three-hitter. While Palmer benefited from a solid defense, Kravec was victimized by three errors and two wind-blown fly balls that dropped for hits.[7]

Even more noteworthy was Baltimore manager Earl Weaver winning his 1,000th game as a major-league manager, the 31st manager to reach the milestone. The combination of a balanced offensive attack, effective pitching, and good defense would serve Weaver and the Orioles well all season.

Weaver, in his 12th year managing the Orioles, experienced consistent success guiding the team. After the Orioles won three consecutive AL pennants and a World Series during his first four years as manager, the team hadn't advanced past the AL Championship Series since 1971. During the mid- to late 1970s, the Orioles did not sign any big-name free agents, and they lost several key players to free agency, including slugging outfielder Reggie Jackson and defensive standout infielder Bobby Grich in 1976, and starting pitcher Ross Grimsley in 1977.[8] With several younger players still maturing, Weaver was impatient with his less-experienced stars at times, but still developed excellent players like first baseman Eddie Murray and third baseman Doug DeCinces, as well as platoon players like John Lowenstein and Pat Kelly.[9] Weaver valued power over speed, using the entire roster with defined roles for everyone, and did not use the running game or sacrifice bunts. His managerial style perfectly suited the 1979 Orioles: Veteran players provided leadership and productivity, a five-man rotation made 154 of 159 starts, platoon players were relied upon throughout the season, and defensive specialists were valued during the late innings.

In the second game of the opening series, on April 7, Chicago scored first, on a fourth-inning sacrifice fly. Baltimore responded with two runs in the fifth. In the top of the sixth, the White Sox scored two runs to retake the lead. In the bottom of the inning, left fielder Gary Roenicke was hit with the bases loaded to knot the game, and catcher Rick Dempsey delivered a two-run double that highlighted the Orioles' four-run inning.[10] Reliever Sammy Stewart quieted the Chicago bats, pitching three hitless innings to earn the save. After starting the season 2-0, the Orioles then followed the pattern of previous years and went 1-8 over the next nine games to fall into the AL East basement with a 3-8 record.

Heading into Yankee Stadium to face the Yankees on April 19, Baltimore was playing the final game of a six-game road trip. They had lost six straight—blanked by the Yankees at home, swept three games by the Milwaukee Brewers, and lost the first two of this series in New York. Their foes, the two-time defending world champion Yankees, were riding a four-game winning streak, and were a half-game behind the Brewers for the division lead. Weaver sent Palmer to the mound against Luis Tiant, who was pitching in his second game wearing a Yankee uniform. Palmer was 1-1 with a 3.46 ERA after three games, while Tiant had been shelled in his season debut, allowing six runs (three earned) to the White Sox in two-plus innings. Against Palmer, the Yankees scored a run in the first inning. Doug DeCinces' home run tied the score in the top of the second. But in the bottom of the inning Palmer allowed three singles, the Orioles made two errors, and New York took a 3-1 lead. The deficit could have been larger for Baltimore, but Reggie Jackson grounded into a 6-4-3 double play to end the inning. The Orioles came back in the third, as a two-run single by Ken Singleton tied the score again. Palmer settled down, allowing only three hits the rest of game, while the Orioles scored a run in the fifth and two in the seventh to end their six-game losing streak with a 6-3 victory, earning their first road win of the season. Said Palmer, "We should start winning when we do turn things around. We've had good pitching in this series, but no hitting until today."[11] Palmer was prophetic, as the Orioles won their next eight games, averaging 5.8 runs scored a game.

After dropping an 8-5 decision to the Athletics in Oakland on April 28, Baltimore answered with a 13-1 rout of the A's the following evening. The victory, highlighted by three home runs during a 10-run seventh inning, initiated another six-game winning streak. In the final game of the streak, Orioles starter Dennis Martinez fired a two-hit shutout against the California Angels, taking a no-hitter into the seventh inning. Martinez didn't start strong, as his first six pitches were balls. Pitching coach Ray Miller went to the mound after the sixth pitch. "I told Dennis to start throwing the ball and stop aiming it," said Miller.[12] Both Murray and Roenicke homered for the Orioles, who started adding more power to their offense. Baltimore had won 15 of 16 games, and took sole possession of first place with an 18-9 record, one game ahead of Boston.

Over the next two weeks, Baltimore and Boston fought vigorously for the division lead, with neither team having more than a 1½-game lead. On May 18 the Orioles defeated the Toronto Blue Jays 7-6 in 11 innings; from that day forward, there was only one day—June 5—when they did not have first place in the AL East all to themselves. After steadily climbing the ladder in convincing fashion during April and May, the Orioles took flight in June. Their 23-6 record was their best record during a single month since the club moved from St. Louis in 1954. Eleven of the 23 victories came on rallies in the eighth inning or later, and four of the wins were walk-offs.[13] In a *Sports Illustrated* article that month, general manager Hank Peters stressed the club's emphasis on using homegrown talent: On the 25-man roster, 14 came up through the Orioles' organization while only three were free agents. "We don't need free agents as long as we have good players. We can't afford them," Peters said. "We can't send a player a contract and say, 'Fill in the figures,' like some of these teams."[14]

Winning 23 games in a month likely provides significant excitement for fans; one specific victory in June stands out. On the 22nd, "Orioles Magic" was born.[15] The Orioles entered the day three games ahead of the Red Sox, and were hosting the Detroit Tigers. (The Tigers' first-year manager, Sparky Anderson, had last visited to Memorial Stadium on October 15, 1970, when the Orioles defeated his Cincinnati Reds 9-3 to win their second World Series title.) Anderson sent Pat Underwood to the mound while Weaver called on Mike Flanagan. At the end of three innings, the Tigers were ahead 5-3, and both starting pitchers were gone. Detroit's Kip Young and Baltimore's Sammy Stewart quieted both offenses, and no more runs were scored through the eighth inning. In the ninth inning against Detroit reliever Dave Tobik, Ken Singleton hit his 15th home run of the season with one out to bring the Orioles within one run. Eddie Murray singled to right but Gary Roenicke popped to second. With two outs, Doug DeCinces socked a two-run blast over the left-field fence.[16] The crowd of 35,456 was ecstatic. The next day the *Detroit Free Press* wrote about the fans' excitement over the Orioles, especially in view of a possible move out of Baltimore, expectations from the national press, and the team's relative anonymity. Weaver was quoted as saying, "We're in first place because we have a damn good ballclub. It's just a shame that people are over the country are unfamiliar with our names."[17] The next day, Eddie Murray's three-run walk-off blast produced an 8-6 Orioles victory in the first game of a doubleheader, then the Orioles won the nightcap, 6-5, with still another late-inning comeback, and sent an even larger crowd of 45,814 home excited as well.

After a July swoon that reduced Baltimore's lead to 1½ games after the first game of a doubleheader on July 19, the Orioles went 14-2 from July 20 through August 4 to extend their lead to eight games. Despite losing Jim Palmer for nearly six weeks from early in July to mid-August with right arm soreness[18] and Scott McGregor for most of May with a faulty left elbow and shoulder stiffness,[19] the pitching staff remained steadfast as the offense began producing. Baltimore clinched the AL East Division title on September 22. At the end of the regular season the Orioles were 102-57, finishing eight games ahead of Milwaukee. The Orioles' .642 winning percentage was the best in the major leagues. Their home attendance of 1,681,009 was a club record, surpassing the previous high mark of 1,203,366 in 1966 by nearly 480,000 patrons.[20]

Ken Singleton led the hitters with a .938 OPS (sixth in the AL), .295 batting average, 35 home runs, and 111 RBIs. Singleton tied for eighth in the league with 5.7 offensive Wins Above Replacement (WAR). He finished second in the vote for the American League Most Valuable Player Award behind California's Don Baylor. Team statistics demonstrated the power-focused nature of the offense: The Orioles finished 11th in the 14-team American League in batting average (.261) but third in home runs. True to Earl Weaver's preseason prediction, Baltimore (181) outhomered

THE 1979 PITTSBURGH PIRATES

the Yankees (150). Mike Flanagan won the AL Cy Young Award with a 23-9 record and 3.08 ERA; he finished sixth in the MVP voting. The pitching staff led the American League with a 3.26 ERA, far ahead of the Yankees' second-lowest 3.83. The mound staff allowed the lowest opponents' batting average (.241) and tied with Milwaukee for the most shutouts (10). The defense was strong, with catcher Rick Dempsey earning a 2.0 WAR rating and second baseman Rich Dauer 1.9. Reliever Don Stanhouse earned his lone All-Star Game appearance, saving 21 games with a 7-3 record and a 2.85 ERA.

Baltimore faced the California Angels in the best-of-five American League Championship Series. The Orioles had dominated the Angels during the season (9-3), outscoring them 56-33, with a stress on pitching and defense compared with the Angels' emphasis on hitting. In Game One, at Memorial Stadium, John Lowenstein continued the late-game heroics for Baltimore, delivering a two-out, three-run pinch-hit homer in the 10th inning for a 6-3 walk-off victory. In Game Two Baltimore jumped out to a 9-1 lead after three innings, but held on as the Angels scored seven unanswered runs. With the bases loaded in the ninth, Stanhouse induced Brian Downing into a force-play grounder and preserved the 9-8 win. In Game Three, at Anaheim, the Angels flipped roles and rallied for two runs with one out in the ninth for a 4-3 victory. In Game Four Scott McGregor fired a six-hit, 8-0 shutout as a five-run seventh inning by the Orioles put the game out of reach for the Angels. The victory gave the Orioles their fifth pennant. If an ALCS MVP award had been selected (that didn't begin until 1980), Eddie Murray arguably would have been voted series MVP after his stellar performance (5-for-12, 5 RBIs).

Game One of the World Series, scheduled for October 9 at Memorial Stadium, was postponed because of heavy rain.[21] Baltimore experienced its earliest recorded snowfall on October 10, but the postponed game proceeded. The Orioles struck quickly, scoring five runs in the first inning and escaping with a 5-4 victory. In Game Two, the Pirates created the late-inning heroics when Manny Sanguillen delivered a two-out pinch-hit single in the top of the ninth to drive in the go-ahead run in a 3-2 win. Pittsburgh jumped out to a 3-0 lead in Game Three, but the Orioles responded with two runs in the third on a home run by Benny Ayala and followed with a five-run fourth inning after a 67-minute rain delay[22] as McGregor pitched the distance in an 8-4 decision. In Game Four, the Pirates scored four runs in the second inning, but the Orioles rallied for three runs in the third inning and exploded for six runs in the eighth for a 9-6 win and a three-games-to-one Series lead. The Pirates responded with a dominating performance in Game Five, scoring seven runs in the sixth, seventh, and eighth innings and winning 7-1. In Game Six, John Candelaria and Kent Tekulve combined on a seven-hit shutout to even the Series. In the deciding Game Seven, the Orioles scored first when Rich Dauer homered in the third inning. In the sixth, Willie Stargell delivered the pivotal hit, a two-run homer, as the Pirates won, 4-1, and captured the World Series in seven games.[23]

The 1979 Baltimore Orioles should be remembered for their team depth and tenacity, transitioning from 1970s stars to a new generation, and increasing excitement for the Orioles fans.

SOURCES

In addition to the sources cited in the Notes, the author also consulted:

1978 Baltimore Orioles Media Guide.

Baseball-Almanac.com.

thebaseballcube.com.

NOTES

1 Ken Nigro, "Orioles Need to Teach Flyhawks How to Talk," *The Sporting News,* March 3, 1979: 31.

2 Jim Henneman, "Orioles Discover a Homing Pigeon in Bumbry," *The Sporting News,* February 17, 1979: 43.

3 "Alonza (Al) Benjamin Bumbry," *1980 Baltimore Orioles Media Guide,* 91.

4 Jim Kaplan, "American League East," *Sports Illustrated,* April 9, 1979: 64.

5 George Vass, "How the '79 Major League Pennant Races Shape Up," *Baseball Digest,* April 1979: 32.

6 "Manager and Coaches," *1980 Baltimore Orioles Media Guide,* 76.

7. Associated Press, "Palmer, Dauer Lift Orioles in Opener," *Rochester (New York) Democrat and Chronicle,* April 7, 1979: 36.
8. "1977 Baltimore Orioles transactions," baseball-reference.com/teams/BAL/1977-transactions.shtml.
9. Bill James, "Earl Weaver in a Box," *The Bill James Guide to Baseball Managers* (New York: Scribner, 1997): 242-249.
10. United Press International, "Orioles Beat Sox Again," *Logansport (Indiana) Pharos-Tribune,* April 8, 1979: 17.
11. Al Mari, "Palmer Had Yanks Swinging at the Air," *Poughkeepsie (New York) Journal,* April 20, 1979: 13.
12. Associated Press, "Martinez responds to advice," *Poughkeepsie Journal,* May 7, 1979: 15.
13. "A Summary of the 1979 Season," *1980 Baltimore Orioles Media Guide:* 40.
14. Douglas S. Looney, "Smile for the Birdies," *Sports Illustrated,* June 18, 1979: 20-21.
15. Pete Kerzel, "Thirty-Four Years Ago Tonight, Orioles Magic Was Born," masnsports.com/orioles-buzz/2013/06/thirty-four-years-ago-tonight-orioles-magic-was-born.html; Orioles Magic, "The Birth of Orioles Magic," orioles-magic.blogspot.com/.
16. Associated Press, "Singleton and DeCinces Homer as Orioles Escape," *Rochester Democrat and Chronicle,* June 23, 1979: 48.
17. Jim Hawkins, "Fans Flocking to Watch No-Name Orioles," *Detroit Free Press,* June 23, 1979: 31.
18. Mark Armour, "Jim Palmer", sabr.org/bioproj/person/3c239cfa.
19. "Scott Houston McGregor," *1980 Baltimore Orioles Media Guide,* 128.
20. "Orioles Attendance Information," *1980 Baltimore Orioles Media Guide:* 6.
21. Steve Tracton, "Snow in October?" voices.washingtonpost.com/capitalweathergang/2008/10/snow_in_october.html.
22. Call To The Pen, "A Look to the Past: 1979 World Series," callto-thepen.com/2011/06/20/a-look-to-the-past-1979-world-series/.
23. "1979 World Series Review," *1980 Baltimore Orioles Media Guide*: 61-64.

For One Night, Bucs' Theme Song Changed to "Slip Slidin' Away"

October 10, 1979: Baltimore Orioles 5, Pittsburgh Pirates 4, at Memorial Stadium

Game One of the World Series

By Frederick C. Bush

THE 76TH WORLD SERIES IN 1979 FEA-
tured the two teams with the best records in their respective leagues; however, before this clash between the Pirates and Orioles could begin, the weather first took center stage. Game One was to have been played on Tuesday, October 9, in Baltimore, but a torrential downpour resulted in the first-ever Game One postponement in Series history.[1] The field situation was made worse by the fact that the NFL's Baltimore Colts and New York Jets had trampled the surface during their October 7 game. Thus, over the course of 12 hours on October 10, Memorial Stadium's head groundskeeper, Pat Santarone, had to enlist the aid of 25 men to use hand pumps to drain the water and wheelbarrows to distribute a ton of sand in order to improve the playing conditions in the outfield.[2] Baseball Commissioner Bowie Kuhn put up a façade of warmth by trying to ignore the frigid conditions, and "[h]e saw to it that players kept up appearances as well, forbidding the wearing of woolen ski caps during batting practice and on the bench."[3] Frank Robinson, the former slugger and future Hall of Famer, who had been a player on the Orioles team that had faced the Pirates in the 1971 Series and was now an Orioles coach, quipped, "They always said it would be a cold day in hell before the Orioles ever got in another World Series."[4]

Once the grounds crew finished its work, Santarone, noting that they had used the full ton of sand, asserted that "nobody should slip and slide too much. ... It will be safe."[5] Then the veracity of his words was put to the test. The 53,735 fans who braved the opening game's start-time temperature of 41 degrees represented the third largest crowd in Memorial Stadium history.[6] The Orioles faithful were whipped into a pregame frenzy by the antics of local fan personality Wild Bill Hagy, who contorted his body atop the home team's dugout to spell out the letters O-R-I-O-L-E-S, and by the ceremonial first pitch from legendary Orioles third baseman and future Hall of Famer Brooks Robinson to his successor at third base, Doug DeCinces.[7]

Orioles left-hander Mike Flanagan, a 23-game winner and soon to be the recipient of the AL Cy Young Award, worked around a Dave Parker double in the first inning before his teammates gave him all the support he needed on this night against the Bucs' starter, Bruce Kison. Kison entered the game at 4-0 with a 0.41 ERA in his postseason career, but the 1979 World Series would not be a triumphal moment as he yielded five runs (four earned) in only one-third of an inning, a disastrous start that turned out to be his only appearance in this Series due to numbness in his pitching arm.

Orioles center fielder Al Bumbry started the bottom half of the first with a single to short left field and advanced to second when Kison walked weak-hitting shortstop Mark Belanger. Ken Singleton followed with what should have been a double-play grounder back to the mound, but Kison bobbled the ball and was only able to throw Singleton out at first. A clearly out-of-sync Kison then walked Eddie Murray to load the bases. The next play resulted in the second "double play that should have been" of the inning when John Lowenstein hit a grounder to second but Phil Garner sailed his throw to shortstop Tim Foli into left field, allowing Bumbry and Belanger to score the first runs of the Series. Garner later asserted, "I was shivering, my fingers were numb. When I fielded the ball, it was soaking wet. It was like throwing a bar of soap."[8] Murray and Lowenstein were at the corners when Kison uncorked a wild pitch that brought Murray home for the third run of the inning. Doug DeCinces then became the 15th player to homer in his first World Series at-bat when he pulled a Kison fastball to left field to make the score 5-0 with only one out in the inning.[9]

Second baseman Billy Smith ended Kison's night with a sharp line-drive hit to right field. Dave Parker slipped in the morass and tore a hole into the playing surface but still managed to hold Smith to a single. Manager Chuck Tanner hurriedly went to the mound and brought in left-hander Jim Rooker to relieve Kison. Catcher Rick Dempsey then hit a liner to Foli, who threw wide of first base when he tried to double off Smith on the play; Smith picked himself up and raced to second base. Fortunately for the Pirates, their second error of the inning did not lead to another run as Flanagan hit a tapper in front of the plate and was thrown out by catcher Steve Nicosia. The damage had been done, though, as the Orioles had set a Series record for most runs in a first inning by any team and held an early five-run advantage.[10]

After the marathon first inning, things calmed down for a time and the most important event of the third inning involved members of the grounds crew using towels to soak up water from right field and shoveling more sand onto the area where Parker had slipped and which he afterward deemed to have been "wet, sloppy, slippery and dangerous."[11]

The Pirates scored their first run in the top of the fourth inning when, after leadoff singles by Foli and Parker, Stargell picked up his first RBI of the Series on a one-out grounder to second that made the score 5-1. That score held for a time as Rooker finished his night with 3⅔ scoreless innings, and Enrique Romo contributed another scoreless inning by a Pirates reliever in the fifth.

In the top of the sixth, Parker and Bill Robinson led off with singles, and the Pirates closed the gap to 5-3 when Orioles third baseman DeCinces booted Nicosia's two-out grounder to load the bases and Phil Garner grounded a two-RBI single through the hole to left field. The next batter, Lee Lacy, who was pinch-hitting for Romo, reached first on DeCinces' second error of the inning—which tied a Series record—and the bases were again filled with Pirates, but Omar Moreno followed with a weak pop fly to center field that left the Bucs to lament another lost opportunity.[12] Don Robinson, the fourth Pirates pitcher of the game, took the mound in the bottom of the frame and held the Orioles without a run for two innings.

Pirates captain Willie Stargell, who would be named the 1979 NL Co-MVP (together with the St. Louis Cardinals' Keith Hernandez), made the score 5-4 in the top of the eighth with a leadoff homer to deep right field that turned out to be the final run of the game.

After Grant Jackson held the Orioles at bay for another inning, Parker garnered his World Series-record-tying fourth hit of the game in the ninth with a one-out single, but he was quickly picked off of first base by Flanagan.[13] Parker bolted for second base and slid hard enough to kick first baseman Eddie Murray's throw out of shortstop Belanger's glove, a play that was ruled an error on Belanger. Bill Robinson's grounder to second moved Parker to third with two outs, but even the mighty "Pops" could not bring him home this time. Stargell's popup to Belanger in short left field summed up the Pirates' futile hitting effort in what turned out to be, at 3 hours and 18 minutes, the longest nine-inning night game in World Series history.[14]

The Orioles escaped with a 5-4 victory and a 1-0 Series lead, but the Pirates had reason to be upbeat. The fact was that they had wasted several scoring opportunities due to an inability to string hits together for a rally. Even though they ended up outhitting the Orioles 11 to 6, they were only 1-for-16 with runners in scoring position. Game One had turned out to be a tale of two games: The first game lasted one inning and resulted in a 5-0 Orioles lead, while the second game featured seven innings of three-hit shutout ball by four Pirates relievers and a four-run Pirates advantage. Bucs third baseman Bill Madlock said, "We outplayed them eight out of nine innings. In fact, after the first inning it was all us."[15] Surely the weather, the field conditions, and the Pirates' clutch hitting would all improve in Game Two.

NOTES

1. Lowell Reidenbaugh, " 'My Kind of Weather'—Flanagan," *The Sporting News*, October 27, 1979: 6.
2. Joseph Durso, "Groundskeeper Wins the Battle," *New York Times*, October 11, 1979.
3. "Pops' Go the Pirates," *Time*, October 29, 1979: 106-108.
4. Ken Nigro, "No DH Hampers AL in Series, Earl Says," *The Sporting News*, October 27, 1979: 3.
5. Durso, "Groundskeeper Wins the Battle."
6. Dan Donovan, "Parker's 4 Hits Shatter Righty-Lefty Theory," *Pittsburgh Press*, October 11, 1979.
7. David Ginsburg, "O-R-I-O-L-E-S fan 'Wild Bill' Hagy dead at 68," *USA Today*, August 20, 2007, usatoday30.usatoday.com/sports/baseball/al/orioles/2007-08-20-hagy-obit_N.htm, accessed May 20, 2014.
8. Reidenbaugh, "'My Kind of Weather'—Flanagan."
9. Ibid.
10. Donovan, "Parker's 4 Hits Shatter Righty-Lefty Theory."
11. Ibid.
12. Reidenbaugh, "'My Kind of Weather'—Flanagan."
13. Ibid.
14. Donovan, "Parker's 4 Hits Shatter Righty-Lefty Theory."
15. Dan Donovan, "Pirates Confident Despite 5-4 Loss," *Pittsburgh Press*, October 11, 1979.

Shades of 1971 as Sanguillen Comes Through in 9th

October 11, 1979: Pittsburgh Pirates 3, Baltimore Orioles 2, at Memorial Stadium

Game Two of the World Series

By Frederick C. Bush

GAME TWO OF THE FALL CLASSIC PROM- ised a potential pitchers' duel between the Orioles' Jim Palmer, a three-time AL Cy Young Award winner, and the Pirates' curveball specialist Bert Blyleven. Palmer was a four-time World Series participant and two-time champion with a 7-2 postseason record, who had had returned in July from tendinitis in his right elbow to help the Orioles reach their fifth Series. Prior to Game Two, he acknowledged the Pirates' hitting prowess but also exuded both confidence and cockiness as he discussed his strategy for pitching to Dave Parker: "He'll get fastballs on the outside corner. He shouldn't be able to pull them for homers. He'll get them until he proves to me that he's smart enough to accept the singles I'm offering him."[1] The Pirates were equally confident, with Omar Moreno stating his belief that the Montreal Expos—whom the Pirates had fought to the last day of the season for the NL East championship—were a better team than the Orioles and Bill Madlock making the prophetic comment that "They [Orioles] can't stay with us for an entire Series."[2]

Once the talking was over and play began, not much seemed different from the night before. The attendance was an almost identical 53,739, the game-time temperature was 45 degrees, and the Pirates couldn't escape the first inning without committing a blunder. Moreno began the game with a single up the middle for his first hit of the Series, but any good feeling did not last long as he bungled a hit-and-run attempt that resulted in an easy double play for the Orioles. Moreno was running at full speed and had rounded second base when he lost track of the ball Tim Foli had hit for a foul popup. Eddie Murray caught the ball and tossed it to Palmer, who was covering first base, for the twin killing. The bottom of the first inning was certainly different from Game One, however, as Blyleven set the Orioles down in order.

Willie Stargell, John Milner, and Madlock led off the second inning with consecutive singles to plate the first run, and Ed Ott followed with a sacrifice fly that scored Milner to give the Pirates a 2-0 lead. The Orioles struck back immediately on Eddie Murray's leadoff home run in the bottom of the inning, but Blyleven avoided further trouble and preserved the 2-1 lead by striking out Palmer with two out to end the frame.

Both pitchers held opposing batters in check until Ken Singleton led off the bottom of the sixth inning with a looping single to left field and scored on Murray's long double to left-center field to tie the game, 2-2. Murray advanced to third on Doug DeCinces' hopper to Foli and attempted to score on Lowenstein's line out to Parker. The strong-armed Parker rifled a perfect throw to catcher Ott, who moved forward to tag Murray out before he ever got near home plate in what Ott termed "an instance [...] of 'Mohammed coming to the mountain.'"[3] Parker's throw preserved the 2-2 tie for the Pirates, and it was reminiscent of the two throws he had made in that summer's All-Star Game that had garnered him the MVP award for the midsummer classic.

The decision to send Murray home on the play was defended by the managers on both sides after the game. Orioles manager Earl Weaver explained, "Cal [third-base coach Cal Ripken Sr.] sent him. We were trying to force the play […] When you shoot craps and gamble, sometimes you lose."4 Bucs skipper Chuck Tanner concurred: "If I or my coach had to make that decision, we would have sent him in. It had to be a perfect throw and a good tag. If you're scared to make that play, then you shouldn't be here."5

A heavy rain began to fall in the top of the seventh inning, and its effects were noticeable as both the field and the play became reminiscent of Game One. In the top of the inning, Madlock hit a one-out infield single and advanced to second base when DeCinces threw the ball over first baseman Murray's head for his third error in two games. After Palmer struck out Ott, he intentionally walked Phil Garner to set up a force play at any base as the pitcher Blyleven was due to bat next. Mike Easler pinch-hit for Blyleven and worked a walk to load the bases, but Omar Moreno struck out on three pitches to end the inning. Don Robinson took the mound for the Bucs in the bottom of the seventh and walked the bases loaded before escaping his jam by striking out Singleton for the final out of the inning.

The Orioles mounted another scoring threat in the bottom of the eighth inning. Murray led off the frame with a blooper to center field for a single. DeCinces then bunted the ball toward the mound, but Foli couldn't handle Robinson's throw—which was to the wrong side of the base—and was charged with an error that resulted in runners on first and second with no outs, Weaver allowed John Lowenstein to swing away, and he hit a sharp grounder to Foli, who missed the tag on Murray but kept his wits about him and threw to Garner for the force on DeCinces. Garner relayed the ball to third base, where Madlock now had Murray in a rundown. Once Garner made the tag on Murray, the Orioles were left in a two-out situation with only Lowenstein on first base, after which Billy Smith grounded out to end the inning. Later, when Orioles manager Weaver was asked if he regretted not having Lowenstein bunt on that play, he replied, "No way. That's our style of play."6

Though Weaver expressed no regrets after the game, the Orioles' lost scoring opportunities in the late innings of Game Two came back to haunt them in the end. Bill Robinson, pinch-hitting for Milner, led off the top of the ninth with a single. Weaver pulled Tippy Martinez from the game in favor of his closer, Don Stanhouse, while Tanner inserted basestealing specialist Matt Alexander as a pinch-runner for Robinson. After Alexander was thrown out at second on a steal attempt and Madlock flied out, Ott singled on a bad-hop bouncer off second baseman Smith's chest and reached scoring position when Garner drew a four-pitch walk.

The next batter was grizzled veteran Manny Sanguillen, who stepped to the plate to pinch-hit in the pitcher's spot. "Sangy," as his teammates called him, fouled off a pair of pitches before lining a single to right field. As Ott chugged around third base toward home plate, Singleton fielded the ball and made a throw that looked to be the equal of Parker's throw in the sixth inning, but Murray cut the ball off and threw a relay to catcher Rick Dempsey that was a split-second too late. Ott made a great hook slide around Dempsey's attempted tag to give the Pirates the lead. After Moreno lined out to Smith at second to end the top half of the inning, Bucs relief ace Kent Tekulve closed out the game with a one-two-three bottom of the ninth that included strikeouts of Dempsey and Kiko Garcia to seal the 3-2 victory for the Bucs.

After the game, opinion was split over Murray's decision to cut off Singleton's throw. Ott might have been out if Murray had let the throw through, but Orioles catcher Dempsey put the issue into proper perspective when he said, "You'll never know."7 Right or wrong, Murray would not be the same player for the rest of the Series. Through Game Two, he batted .800 with a double and a home run, drew three walks, scored two runs, and had two RBIs, but through the last five games he would draw one walk and score one run while going 0-for-21 with the bat.

In the Pirates' locker room, the attention centered on pinch-hitting hero Sanguillen, whose history with the club included 11 hits in the 1971 World Series against the Orioles. Sangy, who had been the most grief-stricken of all the Pirates after the legendary Roberto Clemente died in a plane crash on December 31, 1972, invoked the memory of his dear friend as he said, "I have him in my heart. Anything we do, we're going to do for him. … And tonight, what happened tonight, I give it to the great No. 21, Roberto Clemente."[8]

Thanks to Sanguillen's clutch single, the Pirates had taken a game from the Orioles at Memorial Stadium, thus negating Baltimore's home-field advantage. The Series, tied at one game apiece, would now shift to Pittsburgh's Three Rivers Stadium for Game Three.

NOTES

1. Marino Parascenzo, "Palmer Was Prepared for Pirates," *Pittsburgh Post-Gazette*, October 12, 1979.
2. Phil Musick, "Parker Fixes His Name on World Series," *Pittsburgh Post-Gazette*, October 12, 1979.
3. Ron Fimrite, "A Series of Ups and Downs, *Sports Illustrated*, October 22, 1979: 24-31.
4. Lowell Reidenbaugh, "Manny is the Most Jubilant for Bucs," *The Sporting News*, October 27, 1979: 8.
5. Ibid.
6. Ibid.
7. Fimrite, "A Series of Ups and Downs."
8. Joseph Durso, "Pirates Dedicated to Clemente," *New York Times*, October 12, 1979.

Pirates Succumb to Orioles' McGregor after Rain Delay

October 12, 1979: Baltimore Orioles 8, Pittsburgh Pirates 4, at Three Rivers Stadium

Game Three of the World Series

By Frederick C. Bush

GAME THREE BROUGHT A CHANGE OF scenery to the World Series as play shifted to Pittsburgh's Three Rivers Stadium, but the cold, rainy weather of Baltimore had followed along and would again affect the outcome of events. In spite of the conditions, 50,848 fans packed the nine-year-old ballpark for the Pirates' homecoming in the hopes of getting to sing the Bucs' theme song—"We are Family" by Sister Sledge—as a victory anthem at the end of the evening. Pirates fans who recalled the 1971 Series between these same two teams no doubt hoped that the hometown nine could duplicate the feat of that earlier squad and win all three games to be played in Pittsburgh, which would result in a quick Series victory for the 1979 Pirates. John Candelaria, the Pirates' 6-foot-7 left-hander, took the mound against fellow lefty Scott McGregor, but he soon found out that he would not be facing the same Orioles lineup that had been held to a mere six hits in each of the first two games.

To counter Candelaria, Orioles manager Earl Weaver brought in a new middle infield of shortstop Kiko Garcia and second baseman Rich Dauer and inserted Gary Roenicke in center field alongside Benny Ayala in left field, which gave him an all right-handed-hitting lineup for the game, since switch-hitters Ken Singleton and Eddie Murray would turn around to hit from the right side; even the left-handed pitcher McGregor was a natural right-handed batter. When asked about his strategy, Weaver stated, "It's designed to score runs. Nothing unusual, we did it [lineup changes] all summer."[1] Garcia and Ayala, two of Weaver's new starters, led off the game with a double and single respectively before Candelaria set down the next three batters to quell the immediate scoring threat.

In the Pirates' half of the first, Omar Moreno began to shake off his hitting funk by drilling a leadoff double to center field. With Tim Foli at the plate, first-base umpire Terry Tata called McGregor for a balk and Moreno advanced to third. Weaver had a surprisingly calm debate with Tata over the call, which Orioles catcher Rick Dempsey afterward validated: "I saw (McGregor) move. I called for a changeup and he signaled for me to go around again (with the sign sequence) and then I saw him move."[2] After Foli popped out foul to Dempsey, Dave Parker hit a sacrifice fly that scored Moreno for a quick 1-0 lead.

In the second inning, the Bucs set to work on extending that lead. Willie Stargell led off with a sharp single and, two batters later, catcher Steve Nicosia advanced him to second base with a single of his own. Phil Garner then lined a two-run double to the wall in left-center, but he was caught in a rundown and eventually tagged out at third base when he tried to advance on an anticipated relay throw by Garcia to the plate instead of to third. Candelaria followed with what would have been an RBI single to left field had Garner been safe on the previous play; nonetheless, after Moreno's groundout ended the inning, the Pirates still led 3-0.

The Garcia-and-Ayala tandem that had led off the game for the Orioles struck again to greater effect in the top of the third when Garcia drew a one-out walk that Ayala followed with a home run over the wall in left-center to narrow the gap to 3-2. As the two-run blast left the park, an agitated Candelaria—who thought he had fanned Ayala on the previous pitch—complained briefly to home-plate umpire Russ Goetz. After Ken Singleton stroked a base hit, Candelaria issued his second walk of the inning to Eddie Murray. With two outs, another of Weaver's new lineup additions, Gary Roenicke, grounded a single past a diving Madlock into left field. Bill Robinson scooped it up and quickly threw to Nicosia, who took the throw in front of the plate and lunged to his left to tag out the sliding Singleton. After this play, both teams had time to reflect and to strategize as a steady downpour caused the game to be delayed for 67 minutes.

Once play resumed, it soon appeared as though an entirely different ballgame was being played. McGregor posted his first scoreless inning of the game in the bottom of the third, and then the Orioles' bats broke out for their second five-run inning of the World Series—the first having come in the first inning of Game One—although not without some help from an error and inconsistent pitching by the Pirates. The Orioles' Rich Dauer led off the frame with a double to left-center that skipped by Moreno on the wet turf, and advanced to third on a single by Dempsey. Then Tim Foli lost the handle on a high hop off McGregor's grounder for an error that loaded the bases. Garcia, who turned out to be a super substitute for usual shortstop Mark Belanger on this night, cleared the bases on a 1-and-2 count with a triple to right-center that gave the Orioles a 5-3 advantage. Candelaria, who was ineffective after the rain delay, was replaced by Enrique Romo at this point.

Weaver elected to play the percentages and sent in left-handed-hitting Al Bumbry to pinch-hit for Ayala against the right-handed Romo. Romo hit Bumbry square in the back with his first pitch to put Orioles runners at the corners, and Singleton drove in Garcia with his second base hit of the game, past a diving Garner. Bumbry scored two batters later on a

grounder by Doug DeCinces that forced Singleton at second base after Garner made an errant throw on his attempt at a double play, and the Orioles now led 7-3.

While Candelaria was unable to record a single out after the game had been delayed, McGregor became stronger and more effective as the game continued. His only concerns with Pirates batters after the rain delay came in the bottom of the fifth inning as Parker's long drive with a man on was hauled in by Singleton to retire the side, and in the sixth when Stargell belted a one-out double and scored on Bill Madlock's single to make the score 7-4. Other than those two hiccups, McGregor retired the side in order in the fourth, seventh, eighth, and ninth innings and allowed one hit — Moreno's second double of the game — in the fifth. After the game Dempsey said of McGregor, "Thank God for the rain delay. He was a little tired afterward and his ball sinks better when he's tired."[3] McGregor offered his own theory as to why he was more effective later in the game: "We've had quite a few delays like that the past few years. I don't know why I'm usually better after the interruption. Maybe it's the second warm-up."[4] Whatever the reason, the Pirates were unable to mount any real threat against McGregor after the rain-delayed third inning.

As for the Orioles, after their five-run outburst in the top of the fourth inning, they added only one additional run through the rest of the game. Romo gave up a one-out double to Dempsey in the seventh inning, and Dempsey scored two batters later on Garcia's looping single to center field. Garcia's base hit gave him a four-hit game, the 38th in World Series history [Dave Parker had registered the 37th in Game One], and led to an odd sequence of events that included the second Pirates error of the night.[5] Moreno knew he could not throw out Dempsey at home plate, so he fired the ball to Stargell at first base, who was behind Garcia and had him caught in a rundown. Stargell's throw to second base hit Garcia in the back for an error that enabled Garcia to reach the base safely. Bucs manager Chuck Tanner sent Grant Jackson to the mound to relieve Romo, and Jackson retired Bumbry to end the scoring threat.

McGregor and Kent Tekulve, who took the mound for the Pirates in the top of the eighth inning, did not allow any further baserunners for the remainder of the game, and the Orioles took the home-field advantage back from the Pirates with an 8-4 victory that gave them a 2-1 lead in the Series.

After his rough first two innings, McGregor had settled down to pitch a dominant complete-game victory in which he threw only 95 pitches, an amazing 78 of which were strikes.[6] Weaver's modified lineup also paid great dividends at the top: Leadoff hitter Garcia was 4-for 4, drew a walk, scored two runs and drove in another four; number-two batter Ayala was 2-for-2 with a home run and two RBIs. Garcia, the Orioles' hitting star of Game Three, turned out to be the "second most celebrated player born in Martinez, California," after Joe DiMaggio.[7] For one night at least, Garcia, who would finish his career with an anemic .239 batting average, had hit like DiMaggio as well.

NOTES

1 Joseph Durso, "Orioles Win, 8-4, and Lead Series, 2-1," *New York Times*, October 13, 1979.

2 Lowell Reidenbaugh, "Kiko's Bat a Lethal Weapon, Stunned Pirates Concede," *The Sporting News*, October 27, 1979: 9.

3 Ibid.

4 Ibid.

5 Ibid.

6 Ibid.

7 Dave Anderson, "Kiko Moves Into the Spotlight," *New York Times*, October 14, 1979.

Bucs Pushed to Brink After 8th-Inning Implosion

October 13, 1979: Baltimore Orioles 9, Pittsburgh Pirates 6, at Three Rivers Stadium

Game Four of the World Series

By Frederick C. Bush

GAME FOUR WAS THE FIRST DAY GAME of the 1979 World Series, but the 42-degree game-time temperature was no warmer than it had been for any of the previous games. The crowd of 50,883 cheered as the Pirates summoned up a bit of their glorious past in the person of former general manager Joe L. Brown to throw out the ceremonial first pitch. During his tenure with Pittsburgh, from 1955 through 1976, Brown had presided over World Series championship squads in 1960 and 1971. The Bucs sent Jim Bibby to the mound to oppose Baltimore's Dennis Martinez at the start of what turned into a 3 hour and 48-minute marathon, which was the "longest nine-inning game in World Series history and, therefore, joined the opening game of this Series, which … was the longest Series night game, in the record book."[1]

Willie Stargell started the scoring for the Bucs in the bottom of the second with a leadoff home run, his second of the Series, to the deepest part of center field. After John Milner singled, Bill Madlock hit a ground-rule double down the left-field line that bounced into the Pirates' bullpen. Ed Ott followed with another ground-rule double, which bounced over the center-field wall and scored both Milner and Madlock, for a 3-0 lead.

Phil Garner drilled a single to center field, but the Pirates missed out on another run when Ott was tagged out in a rundown between home and third base. Third-base coach Joe Lonnett said afterward, "(Ott) didn't go through a stop sign. I challenged Bumbry and I'd challenge him again tomorrow."[2] Ott, who had hesitated as he rounded third, explained, "I thought of not running, and all of a sudden (Lonnett) said go. I took about four steps and looked up and there was the ball waiting for me."[3] Earl Weaver brought in reliever Sammy Stewart, and Garner scored on Omar Moreno's single. Stewart picked Moreno off first base to end the inning, but the Pirates had amassed an early 4-0 lead.

The Orioles proved themselves to be a resilient bunch and came right back with three runs of their own in the top of the third inning. Once again they had assistance from a Pirates error as third baseman Madlock fielded Dave Skaggs's grounder on a high hop and threw the ball wide of first base. After Al Bumbry singled, Game Three hitting star Kiko Garcia and Ken Singleton hit consecutive doubles to cut the Orioles' deficit to 4-3.

After Steve Stone replaced Stewart in the bottom of the fifth inning, the Pirates began to increase their lead. After a leadoff walk to Tim Foli and a single by Dave Parker, Milner knocked a one-out double down the right-field line that scored Foli for a 5-3 lead. In the bottom of the sixth inning, Foli singled with two outs and scored again on Dave Parker's double to extend Pittsburgh's advantage to 6-3.

In the top of the eighth inning, as the Pirates appeared to be on their way to evening up the Series at two games apiece, the bottom fell out just as it had done the night before. Garcia, who had become a considerable thorn in the Bucs' side, led off with a single to right field that was misplayed by Parker. Parker later confessed, "It was catchable. But as the ball got in the gray sky, I lost it. I didn't want it to get over my head."4 Three batters later, an ineffective Don Robinson ceded the mound to Kent Tekulve with the bases full of Orioles, and the two opposing managers — Chuck Tanner and Earl Weaver — then engaged in the baseball equivalent of a championship chess match.

Weaver had prepared for the likelihood of the Orioles facing Tekulve again in Game Four, saying, "We figured early that Tekulve would be the guy in there once the game got on the line. So we saved our left-handed pinch-hitters. We had three of them sitting there on the bench."5 Weaver believed that left-handed batters had a decided advantage against Tekulve because they would get a "long … look at his side-arm pitches."6 The first of these lefty pinch-hitters was John Lowenstein — hitting for Gary Roenicke — whose double to the right-field corner scored Garcia and Eddie Murray and advanced DeCinces to third.

The second left-handed pinch-hitter, Billy Smith — batting for Rich Dauer — was intentionally walked to load the bases because, as Tanner said, "We wanted a force out at any base. We were looking for the double play."7 Tanner's gamble did not work out well for the Pirates. Instead of a double play, the Pirates watched as Weaver's third consecutive left-handed pinch-hitter, Terry Crowley — batting for Skaggs — hit a double deep down the right-field line that scored DeCinces and Lowenstein and gave the Orioles a 7-6 lead.

Such an implosion was rare for Tekulve; catcher Ed Ott later said, "All I know is he didn't make the pitches he's made for the last month or two." But he was to suffer an additional ignominy as the Orioles' rally continued.8 Weaver sent pitcher Tim Stoddard to bat for himself and advised him, "If you don't feel comfortable, take two strikes, then try it."9 Stoddard, who had not hit in a game since his days as a minor leaguer, did not allow himself enough time to get uncomfortable as he bounced a single past Madlock into left field on the first pitch he saw and drove in Smith for the Orioles' fifth run of the inning.

When Weaver was asked why he had Stoddard hit, rather than sending up a fourth consecutive pinch-hitter, he replied, "By then we were ahead and I wanted him pitching."10 Rick Dempsey entered the game as a pinch-runner for Crowley and scored on Bumbry's fielder's-choice grounder to make the score 9-6, which would be the final tally for the game. This six-run outburst in the eighth "equaled a record for that inning set by the Chicago Cubs against the Detroit Tigers [on] October 11, 1908."11

The Orioles had pulled off two straight comeback victories on the Pirates' home field and put the Bucs at a three-games-to-one disadvantage in the World Series. Weaver, who later was named *The Sporting News*'s Manager of the Year for 1979, was hailed as a genius for the way he had used his pinch-hitters in Game Four, and the Orioles had to be confident about their ability to win at least one more game to finish off a World Series championship.12 Weaver himself later crowed, "They might say on television that I-do-strange-things-but-I-don't-think-I-do-strange-things [in a tone that mocked ABC television announcer Howard Cosell's vocal style]. I say I'm logical because I don't think I ever made a move that was illogical."13

The Pirates' clubhouse was understandably subdued. When Bucs players were reminded that three teams — the 1925 Pirates, 1958 Yankees, and 1968 Tigers — had overcome a 3-1 deficit in a seven-game World Series, Phil Garner said, "That has nothing to do with us."14 As for opinions of their opponents, the Orioles, Garner added, "They're kicking our butts," and Madlock reversed course from his comments after Game One as he conceded, "They've got a great ballclub."15

Still, the Series was not over yet, and Tanner would continue his managerial chess match against Weaver the next day with what would be considered an unconventional move: He would open the game with a "Rook," Jim Rooker, as his starting pitcher. When Rooker was informed that he would be the Pirates' Game Five starter, he prophetically stated, "If the guys on our team do the job they haven't been doing, we'll be all right."16

NOTES

1   Ron Fimrite, "A Series of Ups and Downs," *Sports Illustrated*, October 22, 1979: 24-31.

WHEN POPS LED THE FAMILY

2 Lowell Reidenbaugh, "Rallies? Orioles Own the Patent," *The Sporting News*, October 27, 1979: 11.

3 Malcolm Moran, "In Losing Clubhouse, a Helpless Feeling," *New York Times*, October 14, 1979.

4 Lowell Reidenbaugh, "Game 4 Notes," *The Sporting News*, October 27, 1979: 11.

5 Joseph Durso, "Orioles Rally to Defeat Pirates, 9-6, for 3-1 Edge," *New York Times*, October 14, 1979.

6 Fimrite, "A Series of Ups and Downs."

7 Reidenbaugh, "Rallies? Orioles Own the Patent."

8 Moran, "In Losing Clubhouse, a Helpless Feeling."

9 Murray Chass, "Stoddard Succeeds on Mound and at Bat," *New York Times*, October 14, 1979.

10 Reidenbaugh, "Rallies? Orioles Own the Patent."

11 Ibid.

12 Ken Nigro, "Peers Pick Weaver as Manager of Year," *The Sporting News*, October 27, 1979: 3.

13 Murray Chass, "Series Managers: Contrast of Styles," *New York Times*, October 15, 1979.

14 Reidenbaugh, "Game 4 Notes."

15 Ibid.

16 Moran, "In Losing Clubhouse, a Helpless Feeling."

The "Family" Unites to Extend the Series Back to Baltimore

October 14, 1979: Pittsburgh Pirates 7, Baltimore Orioles 1, at Three Rivers Stadium

Game Five of the World Series

By Frederick C. Bush

AS THE DAY OF GAME FIVE DAWNED, tragedy struck the Bucs' extended family. Manager Chuck Tanner, a native son who had been born and raised 50 miles northwest of Pittsburgh in the town of New Castle, called to check on his ailing mother and was told, "I'm sorry, Mr. Tanner. Your mother died at 7:40."[1] Tanner decided to manage the Bucs in Game Five after both his father and sister reminded him that it was what his mother would have wanted him to do, and the Pirates players rallied around their grief-stricken skipper.[2] Bill Mazeroski, the Pirates' former second baseman and the hero of the 1960 World Series, provided further inspiration as he threw out the ceremonial first pitch.

Game Five was the second lefty-versus-lefty matchup of this Series as Mike Flanagan opposed Tanner's surprise starter, Jim Rooker. Rooker had suffered through an injury-plagued season that had included two stints on the disabled list — first for elbow and then for back problems — which had resulted in a 4-7 record with a 4.59 ERA for the year, and he had been on the DL as recently as September 2.[3] Tanner, however, did not consider his decision to be shocking and explained, "He's a great competitor, and when he's healthy, he's as good as anybody."[4] With that endorsement from his manager, Rooker took the mound and set about turning around the Pirates' World Series fortunes.

Rooker turned in a clutch five-inning performance in which he allowed the Orioles only one run. He retired the Orioles in order in each of the first three innings and surrendered only a one-out walk to Benny Ayala in the fourth. Trouble started in the fifth inning when Gary Roenicke led off with a double to left-center and Doug DeCinces followed with a line-drive single to right-center just over a leaping Phil Garner to put runners at the corners. Rooker induced a 4-6-3 groundball double play by Rich Dauer that allowed Roenicke to score for a 1-0 Orioles lead, but he escaped the inning without further damage.

If anything kept the 50,920 fans in attendance from fully appreciating Rooker's effort, it was the fact that his mound opponent, Flanagan, had allowed only four hits — three of which were singles — and had kept the Pirates off the scoreboard for five full innings. The Bucs finally broke through for two runs against Flanagan in the sixth inning. Tim Foli drew a leadoff walk which Dave Parker followed with a single, and they both advanced on Bill Robinson's sacrifice bunt. A sacrifice fly by Willie Stargell scored Foli to tie the game, and Bill Madlock's bloop single to center scored Parker for a 2-1 Pirates edge.

Bert Blyleven had come into the game in relief in the top of the sixth inning, and he had picked up where Rooker had left off. Blyleven was slated to be the Game Six starter, but Tanner knew that there would not be a sixth game if the Pirates did not win now.[5] Even though Blyleven had made only six relief appearances in his career — the last one in 1972 — he embraced the role and said afterward, "When it comes down to the final games and millions of people are watching, it doesn't matter when you come into a game."[6]

Over the final four innings, Blyleven surrendered only three hits and one walk and held the Orioles without another run to become the winning pitcher. Second baseman Phil Garner supported Blyleven with an outstanding defensive play in the top of the eighth inning. After Blyleven deflected Ken Singleton's grounder, Garner scooped it up and made a backhanded flip of the ball to shortstop Foli as part of a 1-4-6-3 double play that ended the inning.

As the Bucs worked their pitching and fielding magic, their bats began to come alive again and close plays began to go their way. In the bottom of the seventh inning, with Tim Stoddard now pitching for the Orioles, Omar Moreno was at first base with two outs. Sammy Stewart had picked Moreno off first in the previous game, and it looked as though Stoddard had him dead to rights now as well, but Stoddard's throw hit Moreno and bounced away. Eddie Murray recovered the ball quickly and almost nabbed Moreno at second, but his throw was too late. Foli's triple to right-center scored Moreno and, after Tippy Martinez relieved Stoddard, Dave Parker's double to left-center plated Foli and made the score 4-1 in favor of the Pirates.

Stargell led off the bottom of the eighth with a single that chased Martinez from the game, but the Bucs continued to score against Don Stanhouse. After a single by Madlock, Garner brought Stargell home for the fifth Pirates run with a single of his own. Blyleven helped his own cause with a sacrifice bunt that advanced Madlock and Garner, and Moreno was intentionally walked, loading the bases. With the table set for him, Foli grounded a single to center and drove in two more runs to increase the lead to 7-1, which ended up being the final score.

The Orioles tried to mount a threat in the ninth inning with consecutive two-out singles by DeCinces and pinch-hitter John Lowenstein, but pinch-hitter Terry Crowley ended the game with a fly ball to Bill Robinson in left field. The Pirates had won Game Five, closed their deficit in games to 3-2, and sent the Series back to Baltimore, where Game Six was scheduled to be played on Tuesday, October 16.

Game Five showed that in baseball nothing is certain, circumstances change quickly, and genius can be fleeting. The strategies that had worked so well for Earl Weaver and his Orioles in previous games were implemented to no positive effect this time. Facing a left-hander in Rooker, Weaver once again used an all right-handed-hitting lineup (except for his pitcher Flanagan) but they managed only a paltry three hits, two walks, and one run against the Bucs' starter. The Orioles' pinch-hitters, "who after four games stood at four hits, three walks, and a hit batsman in nine tries" and who had devastated the Pirates in Game Four, were 1-for-4 in Game Five with the lone hit being Lowenstein's single.[7] The use of the intentional walk to try to induce a double play had quelled a Pirates threat in Game Four but had backfired on the Orioles in Game Five. Even the pickoff attempts by Orioles pitchers, one of which had nabbed Moreno one night earlier, had resulted in nothing but failure for the Orioles now.

Baltimore still had to win only one game (of a potential two) at home to win the World Series, and the Orioles tried to project all due confidence. Rick Dempsey said, "Now we go back home with a definite advantage because we get that ninth-inning chance," while reliever Tim Stoddard pointed out, "It gives us a chance to win the World Series at home."[8] When asked if Game Five had brought about a change in momentum in the Series, Weaver said, "If [Game Six starter] Palmer goes out and pitches a good game, then there is no such thing as momentum."[9]

To the careful observer, all of the Orioles' talk of chances and the "ifs" contained in their statements made those remarks sound more like doubt-filled false bravado. After all, the Orioles were well aware that through Game Four the Pirates had hit well but had been "squandering their hits in meaningless situations. This time they [had] made them count."[10] If the Pirates' clutch hitting continued and their pitching and fielding remained of the caliber of Game Five, then the Orioles were in trouble.

The atmosphere in the Pirates' locker room was, of course, the exact opposite of what it had been after Game Four. Rooker exulted, "The *real* Pirates played today. The first four games, we had some no-shows. Today we rose to the occasion."[11] Indeed, the Pirates had come together as the "family" they touted themselves to be through their Sister Sledge theme song. Stargell said of the grieving Tanner after the game, "He walked very tall today. I really saw something in that man. It was a very touching performance on his part."[12] The same things were true of the entire Pirates team in Game Five.

NOTES

1. Dave Anderson, "'Your Mother Died at 7:40,'" *New York Times*, October 15, 1979.
2. Ibid.
3. Malcolm Moran, "The Real Pirates Stand Up and Win," *New York Times*, October 15, 1979.
4. Lowell Reidenbaugh, "Madlock Mauls Oriole Hurlers," *The Sporting News*, October 27, 1979: 12-14.
5. Joseph Durso, "Pirates Win, 7-1, and Send Series Into 6th Game," *New York Times*, October 15, 1979.
6. Ron Fimrite, "A Series of Ups and Downs," *Sports Illustrated*, October 22, 1979: 24-31.
7. Lowell Reidenbaugh, "Rallies? Orioles Own the Patent," *The Sporting News*, October 27, 1979: 11.
8. Lowell Reidenbaugh, "Game 5 Notes," *The Sporting News*, October 27, 1979: 14.
9. Phil Musick, "World Series Notebook," *Pittsburgh Post-Gazette*, October 15, 1979.
10. Fimrite, "A Series of Ups and Downs."
11. Phil Musick, "Rooker Survives on Guts," *Pittsburgh Post-Gazette*, October 15, 1979.
12. Reidenbaugh, "Game 5 Notes."

"Candy Man" and "Teke" Find World Series Redemption in Game Six Shutout

October 16, 1979: Pittsburgh Pirates 4, Baltimore Orioles 0, at Memorial Stadium

Game Six of the World Series

By Frederick C. Bush

THE PIRATES AND ORIOLES FINALLY GOT their second travel break in World Series action on Monday, October 15, as both teams made the trip back to Baltimore for Game Six. As the media analyzed the Series, even the opinions of Yankees slugger Reggie Jackson, the hero of the previous two World Series, were solicited. Jackson believed that the Orioles would win Game Six but astutely observed, "But the pressure is really on the Orioles in the sixth game. If they don't win, then they know they can blow it all after being ahead 3-1, and they don't want that."[1] The Orioles most certainly did not want that, and, with Jim Palmer taking the mound, they had reason for confidence in their ability to win the game and the Series on this Tuesday night.

Palmer had held the Pirates to two runs over seven innings in Game Two but had not factored in the decision in that contest, which the Pirates had won in the ninth inning. The Pirates countered Palmer with John "The Candy Man" Candelaria, who had not only had a disastrous start—giving up six runs (five earned) in only three innings—in the rain-delayed Game Three but was also suffering from a muscle tear in his rib cage.[2] This time the Pirates' wounded hurler would contribute an even more thrilling performance than Jim Rooker had in Game Five.

As had been the case in Game Two, 53,739 fans packed Memorial Stadium, but now the weather was better and the game-time temperature was an almost spring-training-like 61 degrees. Omar Moreno, who had been derisively dubbed "Omar the Outmaker" after his ineffective 1-for-10 hitting effort in the first two games, had become one of the hottest hitters in the Series and led off the game by bouncing a single up the middle, which Tim Foli followed with a bouncing double off DeCinces' glove that immediately put Pirates runners at second and third.[3]

When the next batter, Dave Parker, smashed a smoking grounder to third base, Doug DeCinces evoked memories of his predecessor Brooks Robinson—the 16-time Gold Glove winner and 1970 World Series MVP—as he backhanded the ball, held Moreno at third, and fired the ball to Eddie Murray to nip Parker on a close play at first. After Palmer retired Willie Stargell on a pop foul to third and John Milner on a groundball to the pitcher unassisted to escape danger, he and Candelaria—who had escaped a two-on-with-one-out jam in the first inning—settled into a classic pitchers' duel in which they both hung up zeros for six full innings.

The Pirates finally broke the scoreless tie in the top of the seventh inning. After Lee Lacy, pinch-hitting for Candelaria, struck out to start the frame, the next three batters—Moreno, Foli, and Parker—hit consecutive singles, the latter two of which were magnified by questionable fielding by the Orioles' middle infield. Moreno broke for second as Foli hit a ball that Palmer deflected ever so slightly. The ball was still headed straight for shortstop Kiko Garcia, who was standing on second base and inexplicably stayed back only to have the ball take a bad hop and go under his glove. Second baseman Rich Dauer backed up the play deftly, but his throw to first base was not in time to retire Foli. Though the play was ruled a hit, Palmer later asserted, "I think that Kiko didn't catch it because he was trying to get two outs. He was trying to catch the ball and step on second base all at the same time. Nothing against Kiko, he's had a good year, but Mark Belanger's had more experience at shortstop."[4] Garcia contradicted Palmer as he explained, "I wasn't going for a double play. I think I took my eye off it and it hit in front of me."[5]

Parker's base hit was a smash to the right side that Dauer tried to turn into a double play, but he too had trouble fielding the ball, and it went past him for an RBI single with Foli racing to third. Dauer said of Parker's sharp grounder, "The ball behaved like a knuckleball. I saw it in front of me and the next thing I knew, it was in right field."[6] After Parker's hit knocked in Moreno for the first run of the game, Stargell hit a sacrifice fly to deep left that plated Foli and gave the Bucs a 2-0 lead.

The Pirates doubled their lead in the eighth inning through timely hitting and additional adventures in fielding on the part of the Orioles. After Ed Ott's one-out single, Garner hit a line drive to deep left field that Benny Ayala misjudged. Ayala initially came in on the ball and, when he saw that the ball had been hit harder than he had thought, could not get back in time to make the catch; all he could do was watch as the ball sailed over his head and bounced over the outfield wall for a ground-rule double. Palmer, "who (…)had talked earlier in the Series about how Weaver's use of Ayala in left was a gamble because of his questionable fielding ability," was forthright, if also less than gracious, about his teammate's play when he stated, "I think most people think (Garner's double) should have been caught."[7] Once again, Palmer's teammate disagreed. Ayala defended his play and said, "I thought Garner was jammed. … When a batter is jammed, it's tough for an outfielder to adjust. I don't think I wasted that much time going back on the ball. Even if I had turned around immediately, I doubt that I would have caught the ball."[8] Bill Robinson hit a sacrifice fly to left, scoring Ott, and Moreno singled Garner home to extend the Bucs lead to 4-0.

Kent Tekulve had taken the mound in the bottom of the seventh inning—his first appearance since being shelled for three runs and taking the loss in Game Four—and he became the second Pirates pitcher of the night to find redemption. Tekulve held the Orioles without a run for the final three innings, thus combining with Candelaria for the first World Series shutout since Luis Tiant of the Boston Red Sox blanked the Cincinnati Reds in Game One of the 1975 Series.[9]

As he had done in Game Four, Orioles manager Earl Weaver sent left-handed batters to the plate to hit against Tekulve, but Weaver's strategy failed this time as Tekulve allowed only Billy Smith's single to the five lefty pinch-hitters who faced him in the seventh and eighth innings. Tekulve placed an exclamation point on the victory that drew the Bucs even in the Series by striking out two of the final three batters, including DeCinces to end the game.

The Pirates were firing on all cylinders at just the right time. Most of the Bucs had been batting well throughout the Series, but they were now stringing their hits together to score runs. Both the starting and relief pitching had been outstanding in the past two games, allowing the Orioles only one run in Game Five and shutting them out in Game Six. As the weather had improved so had their glove work and Game Six was their first errorless game of the Series. Manager Chuck Tanner said afterward, "This is the most excited I've ever seen this club since I came here three years ago"[10] He also related how Dave Parker had encouraged the team as they were losing late in Game Four: "He came along and told (the dejected Bucs): 'What are you guys sitting on the bench for? Don't you know this is a seven-game World Series?'"[11]

The Orioles, on the other hand, appeared to be coming apart at the seams. Palmer, whose expressed disappointment in his teammates' fielding abilities was thinly disguised finger-pointing, accurately summed up the Orioles' dilemma when he said, "You can't win when we don't score."[12] Weaver also understood the situation, saying, "We've got one more shot. Maybe we'll bust loose tomorrow. I really don't know what's wrong with our hitting."¹³ It was not a good omen for the Orioles that their manager seemingly had run out of answers.

NOTES

1. Dave Anderson, "Mr. October Says: Birds Win in Six," *New York Times*, October 16, 1979.
2. Lowell Reidenbaugh, "Candy Sweet Pitching in Pain," *The Sporting News*, November 3, 1979: 41.
3. Murray Chass, "Pirates Triumph, 4-0, and Tie Series," *New York Times*, October 17, 1979.
4. Joseph Durso, "Parker's Hit a Key Pirate Break," *New York Times*, October 17, 1979.
5. Chass, "Pirates Triumph, 4-0, and Tie Series."
6. Reidenbaugh, "Candy Sweet Pitching in Pain."
7. Chass, "Pirates Triumph, 4-0, and Tie Series."
8. Reidenbaugh, "Candy Sweet Pitching in Pain."
9. Ibid.
10. Durso, "Parker's Hit a Key Pirate Break."
11. Ibid.
12. Lowell Reidenbaugh, "Game 6 Sidelights," *The Sporting News*, November 3, 1979: 41.
13. Durso, "Parker's Hit a Key Pirate Break."

"Pops" Named MVP as Pirates Complete Comeback to Win World Series

October 17, 1979: Pittsburgh Pirates 4, Baltimore Orioles 1, at Memorial Stadium

Game Seven of the World Series

By Frederick C. Bush

AS THE PIRATES AND ORIOLES PREPARED to meet in the winner-take-all Game Seven of the 76th World Series, there arose a commotion over a column written by Baltimore sports editor John Steadman. The Pittsburgh media provided the Pirates and their fans with the gist of Steadman's opinion, which was that the Bucs calling their team a family was "a cheap grandstand play, a sickening put-on, a bad pun. The Orioles haven't been gagging themselves to keep from ridiculing 'The Family' reference, but it must be amusing."[1] The Orioles probably wished that Steadman had not given the Bucs such "bulletin-board material" to provide extra motivation, especially after Game Seven when the only gagging the Orioles would be accused of doing was choking away what had seemed to be a certain Series victory after Game Four. Such an outlook, however, would sell "The Family's" efforts short as "(i)n truth, the Pirates won the world championship more than the Orioles lost it, beating Baltimore's best pitchers and holding its hitters to only two runs in the final three games."[2]

The atmosphere was electric as 53,733 fans packed Memorial Stadium one more time on a pleasant 65-degree evening. One of the fans in attendance was incumbent President Jimmy Carter, who threw out the ceremonial first pitch to Orioles catcher Rick Dempsey. Carter was the first president to attend a World Series game since Dwight Eisenhower visited Brooklyn's Ebbets Field during the 1956 World Series between the Dodgers and New York Yankees.[3]

Once the game was under way, it appeared as though Baltimore's Scott McGregor and Pittsburgh's Jim Bibby were going to duplicate the previous game's pitching duel. Neither team mounted any threat in the first two innings, but second baseman Rich Dauer hit a line-drive home run to left field to lead off the bottom of the third that put the Orioles up 1-0. It was the only run Bibby and the Bucs relievers who followed him—Don Robinson, Grant Jackson and Kent Tekulve—would allow in Game Seven.

The Pirates began to take over the game in the sixth inning. Bill Robinson hit a one-out, bad-hop grounder that was just out of shortstop Kiko Garcia's reach for a single. Stargell batted next and delivered a two-run home run to right-center, giving the Pirates a lead they never relinquished. Stargell's ball was also just out of reach, this time of Orioles right fielder Ken Singleton, who briefly hung on the outfield wall as he watched the ball land in the Pirates' bullpen. In a twist of fate, exactly eight years to the day after he had scored the winning run in Game Seven of the 1971 World Series against the Orioles, Stargell scored the winning run in Game Seven of the 1979 Series against the same team.[4]

The Pirates were in danger of surrendering their 2-1 lead in the bottom of the eighth inning when Jackson gave up one-out walks to pinch-hitter Lee May and Al Bumbry. After the second walk, Tekulve entered the game and retired pinch-hitter Terry Crowley on a groundball to second base that allowed both runners to move up. Singleton was intentionally walked to load the bases, after which Murray hit a fly ball to deep right field. Dave Parker stumbled but made an over-the-shoulder catch of Murray's ball to end the inning, a play about which Tekulve later said, "I thought, 'I hope his legs don't fail him now,' but he's made those plays all year and somehow I knew he'd get it."[5]

After Phil Garner doubled to lead off the ninth inning, Orioles manager Earl Weaver "paraded a record five pitchers to the mound in a futile bid to stem the inevitable."[6] Mike Flanagan replaced Tim Stoddard with one out and gave up a single to Omar Moreno that scored Garner. Weaver then brought in Don Stanhouse, who surrendered a base hit to left-center by Tim Foli that advanced Moreno to third. Tippy Martinez took the mound next and loaded the bases by hitting Parker with a pitch. Finally, Dennis Martinez, the fifth Orioles pitcher of the inning, hit Bill Robinson with a pitch that brought Moreno home with the Pirates' final run of the game. It did not take an astute spectator to sense the desperation behind Weaver's procession of relievers, all of whom were ineffective and—as a group—gave up the last two runs that resulted in the final 4-1 score.

In the bottom of the ninth, Tekulve struck out Gary Roenicke and Doug DeCinces before getting pinch-hitter Pat Kelly to fly to Moreno in center field for the final out. For their efforts, Jackson got the win, Tekulve got his third save of the Series, and the Pirates got their fifth world championship. As Tekulve said, "(I)t's ours and nobody can take it away."[7]

The Pirates had pounded out 81 hits against the Orioles over the course of the seven-game Series and had compiled a team batting average of .323, which was a record for a winning team in the World Series and second only to the 1960 New York Yankees' .338.; The 81 hits were also second only to the same 1960 Yankees squad's 91 hits.[8]

Five Pirates accumulated double-digit hit totals: Willie Stargell (.400) and Phil Garner (.500) led the way with 12 each, Omar Moreno (.333) tallied 11, and Dave Parker (.345) and Tim Foli (.333) had 10 apiece. Foli also set a record for the most at-bats (30) without a strikeout.[9] Bill Madlock batted .375 while rapping out nine hits and drawing five walks and, in Game Five, became one of three Pirates batters—along with Parker (Game One) and Stargell (Game Seven)—to tie the Series record of four hits in one game. The Orioles' inability to stop the Pirates in the top of the ninth inning of Game Seven was simply a microcosm of the entire World Series, especially those games in which the Pirates bunched their hits together to score more runs.

Stargell's performance stood out above all, and he was the unanimous choice of the nine-man committee as the Most Valuable Player of the World Series.[10] In addition to batting .400 with 7 RBIs, Stargell set a World Series record with seven extra-base hits—four doubles and three home runs (the Pirates' only home runs in the seven games)—and tied Reggie Jackson's 1977 record of 25 total bases.[11] The award made Stargell the first player player to win the regular-season, League Championship Series, and World Series MVPs in the same season. For that matter, the Pirates made a clean sweep of all MVP awards in 1979 as Parker had been voted MVP of the All-Star Game that summer.

President Carter visited the jubilant Pirates' locker room after the game to offer his congratulations and watched the team accept the championship trophy. Manager Chuck Tanner could not remember what Carter said to him because he was so excited, while a jovial Stargell joked, "I wanted to ask him if he had any peanuts on him. But there were too many Secret Service men around, and I was afraid to ask."[12]

Stargell turned serious for a moment when he was asked about Steadman's column that had denigrated the Pirates' use of the word "family" to describe their team. "Pops" Stargell, the Bucs' inspirational father figure, said, "I thought that was unfair. That man didn't live with us all year. He didn't understand that we depend on closeness, that we are a family. No words can express what we've done. We've overcome. We've worked hard. We've scratched and clawed. We took that song 'We Are Family' and identified with it. We weren't trying to be sassy or fancy. We're just a ballclub that is a family in our clubhouse. And that's why we won the World Series, that's why we came from behind."¹³ Stargell's response was a fitting summary of the 1979 Pittsburgh Pirates.

NOTES

1. Pat Livingston, "Stand-Up Pirates Set Down Birds," *Pittsburgh Press*, October 18, 1979.
2. Ron Fimrite, "Rising From the Ashes," *Sports Illustrated*, October 29, 1979: 61-64.
3. Murray Chass, "Pirates Capture World Series With 4-1 Triumph," *New York Times*, October 18, 1979.
4. Lowell Reidenbaugh, "Stargell's Bat? Just Plain Poison!," *The Sporting News* November 3, 1979: 43-44.
5. Dan Donovan, "Whew, It's Over! Bucs Are Champs," *Pittsburgh Press*, October 18, 1979.
6. Reidenbaugh, "Stargell's Bat? Just Plain Poison!"
7. Donovan, "Whew, It's Over! Bucs Are Champs."
8. "World Series Notes: Garner Won the Hard Fight," *Pittsburgh Press*, October 18, 1979.
9. Lowell Reidenbaugh, "Room at Top Just for Bucs," *The Sporting News*, November 3, 1979: 40.
10. Reidenbaugh, "Stargell's Bat? Just Plain Poison!"
11. "World Series Notes: Garner Won the Hard Fight."
12. Ibid.
13. Dave Anderson, "Pops Hit One for 'The Family,'" *New York Times*, October 18, 1979.

We Are Family

By David E. Skelton

3:35 MINUTES OF VINYL FROM 1979 have found boundless expression from R-rated movies to Disney Channel specials, providing resonance and delight decades after its release. At the height of the disco era the single climbed the R&B, soul, and pop charts worldwide while forging a bond among teammates in sports everywhere. But it was the Pittsburgh Pirates who became most closely identified with "We Are Family," a tune that provided the inspiration and additional spur to hoist the 1979 Bucs to a world championship.

The song was written by Nile Rodgers and Bernard Edwards[1] especially for the Philadelphia-based four-sister group called Sister Sledge. The identically named album *We Are Family* was released in December 1978 and went double platinum (more than 1.5 million copies sold). In April 1979 it placed among the top five songs in the United States only to rebound six months later in Pittsburgh after the Pirates adopted it as their theme song. Record store outlets in Western Pennsylvania could not keep the single or the album on their shelves. Meanwhile the sisters—Debbie, 25; Joni, 23; Kim, 22; and Kathy, 20—had no inkling that the "song had become baseball's first disco battle hymn until the World Series was almost over. 'It was so ironic the way we found out about it,' said Kim Sledge shortly after a 26-day European fall tour. 'We did a TV show in Hamburg, Germany, and we were on our way back to the hotel listening to the international news. The announcer was talking about the fifth game of the World Series. We couldn't believe it when he said there were 50,000 at the World Series screaming "We Are Family." … We feel like it's been a gift from God.'"[2] The young women considered jetting to the United States to add their support in person but were committed to a taping session in Brussels. Instead they sent yellow chrysanthemums with black ribbons and a banner saying, "Good Luck from Sister Sledge."[3]

The Pirates had once made the National League East flag their recurrent possession by winning the division five of six seasons starting in in 1970. (In 1973 they finished third.) But from 1976 to 1978 they had yielded the title to their cross-state rival Philadelphia Phillies. A sluggish start to the 1979 campaign seemingly telegraphed another exit from postseason play. But on July 8 Pittsburgh initiated a surge of 13 wins in 14 contests that thrust the club to within one game of first. It was during this time that "We Are Family" became a staple in the Pirates clubhouse. Hall of Famer Willie "Pops" Stargell's veteran leadership is largely credited for tying the notion of team-as-family to the inspirational song. But in his typically humble fashion, the National League's 1979 co-Most Valuable Player yielded the credit to former general manager Joe Brown: "Joe always stressed that the ballclub was a family."[4]

Over the last three months of the '79 season the enlivened club played at a .670 pace to squeak by the Montreal Expos and capture the division championship by two games. They brushed aside the Cincinnati Reds in the League Championship Series (then best-of-five) in a three-game sweep and were pitted against the Baltimore Orioles in the World Series. Pittsburgh dug itself a deep hole after dropping three of the first four games to the O's. A Game Five trouncing of American League Cy Young Award winner Mike Flanagan and three Baltimore relievers closed the margin but the Pirates still faced the daunting task of needing two consecutive wins on the Orioles' turf. As the Pirates exited the field in Three Rivers Stadium, management pulled out all the stops, broadcasting "We Are Family" for the benefit of the team and its "more than 50,000 wild adherents."[5] At a minimum, the song worked wonders for the Pirates' pitching staff, which surrendered only one run in the final two games to capture the world title.

THE 1979 PITTSBURGH PIRATES

Over the years scores of inspirational songs have served sports teams through the generations, often at ear-splitting volumes. Queen's "We Are the Champions" and Survivor's "Eye of the Tiger" are but two of many. But in 1979 no song held sway in the athletic world more than "We Are Family."

NOTES

1 Members of the funk/disco group Chic.
2 "Pittsburgh's Theme Song Surprise to Sister Sledge," *Gettysburg (Pennsylvania) Times*, October 31, 1979: 21.
3 Ibid.
4 "Tale of the Tapes in Bucs' Clubhouse: No Punk Rock," *The Sporting News*, August 16, 1982: 12.
5 "Madlock Mauls Oriole Hurlers," *The Sporting News*, October 27, 1979: 12.

1979 Pittsburgh Pirates
By the Numbers
By Dan Fields

1

Hit allowed by Bruce Kison in a shutout of the San Diego Padres on June 3. Rookie Barry Evans bounced a double into left field that glanced off third baseman Phil Garner's glove with two outs in the eighth.

1

Pittsburgh player at the 1979 All-Star Game: Dave Parker, who started in right field. The game was played on July 17 at the Kingdome in Seattle, Washington. Parker put on a defensive show, throwing out Jim Rice at third base in the seventh inning and Brian Downing at home plate to end the eighth. He also drove in a run with a sacrifice fly and hit a single. The NL beat the AL 7-6 for its eighth straight win, and Parker was named the game's Most Valuable Player.

1-2-3

Order in which Kent Tekulve, Enrique Romo, and Grant Jackson finished in games played among NL pitchers in 1979. Tekulve appeared in 94 games (most in the majors and a franchise record), Romo in 84, and Jackson in 72.

1.169

WHIP of John Candelaria, sixth in the NL. Bruce Kison (1.172) was seventh in the league.

1.783

Walks per nine innings pitched by John Candelaria, second lowest in the NL.

2nd

Consecutive year in which Dave Parker had at least 25 home runs and 20 stolen bases.

3

Doubles by Tim Foli in consecutive plate appearances against Phil Niekro of the Atlanta Braves on May 1.

3rd

Consecutive Gold Glove Award as outfielder by Dave Parker.

4

Runs scored by Phil Garner in the second game of a July 27 doubleheader against the Montreal Expos. He got on base with a single, a double, a triple, and a walk. In the first game, he also had three hits (including a home run).

5

Hits in five at-bats by Phil Garner in a June 19 game against the San Francisco Giants. Dave Parker had five hits in six at-bats on September 29 against the Chicago Cubs (13 innings).

6

Pitchers on the 1979 Pirates who won at least 10 games: John Candelaria (14), Bruce Kison (13), Jim Bibby (12), Bert Blyleven (12), Enrique Romo (10), and Kent Tekulve (10). No pitcher on the team lost 10 games.

8-0

Score by which the Pirates trailed the Philadelphia Phillies after three innings on August 11. The Pirates rallied to win 14-11.

12

Triples by Omar Moreno, tied for second in the NL.

15

Errors by right fielder Dave Parker, the most by any outfielder in the majors.

THE 1979 PITTSBURGH PIRATES

19
Innings in an August 25 game against the Padres. The Pirates won 4-3. Shortstop Ozzie Smith was involved in each of the six double plays turned by San Diego.

31
Saves by Kent Tekulve, second in the NL.

37
Games started by Bert Blyleven, tied for fifth in the NL. With a record of 12-5, he set a single-season record for starting pitchers with 20 no-decisions.

37.5
At-bats per strikeout by Tim Foli with the 1979 Pirates. HIs mark of 38.0 for the entire season (included three games with the New York Mets) was best in the majors and has not been topped since then (through 2015).

39 1/2
Age in years of Willie Stargell when he and Keith Hernandez of the St. Louis Cardinals were named co-winners of the NL MVP Award. Stargell became the oldest player to win an MVP award in either league. He hit 32 home runs (fifth in the NL) and drove in 82 runs in only 126 games, and his fielding percentage of .997 was the highest of any first baseman in the majors.

45
Doubles by Dave Parker, third in the majors in 1979 and the most by a Pirate since Paul Waner hit 53 doubles in 1936.

67
Games finished by Kent Tekulve, most in the NL and a new franchise record.

77
Extra-base hits by Dave Parker, most in the NL.

77
Stolen bases by Omar Moreno, most in the NL and a new franchise record.

94
RBIs by Dave Parker, eighth in the NL.

98
Wins by the 1979 Pirates, against 64 losses (.605). It was the most wins by the team since 1909.

102
Intentional walks drawn by the 1979 Pirates, a new major-league record.

110
Runs scored by Omar Moreno, second in the NL. Dave Parker was tied for third with 109 runs; it was the third consecutive season in which he scored at least 100 runs.

162
Games played by Omar Moreno.

172
Strikeouts by Bert Blyleven, fourth in the NL.

196
Hits by Omar Moreno, fifth in the NL. Dave Parker was sixth in the league with 193 hits.

296
Home runs by Willie Stargell during the 1970s, the most by any major-league player.

.310
Batting average of Dave Parker, seventh in the NL. It was the fifth consecutive season in which he hit at least .300. Bill Madlock (acquired by the Pirates on June 28) had a .328 batting average in 85 games with Pittsburgh.

327
Total bases by Dave Parker, second in the NL. It was his third consecutive year with at least 325 total bases.

.416
Slugging average of the 1979 Pirates, highest in the NL.

490
Putouts as outfielder by Omar Moreno, most in the majors in 1979 and the most by an NL outfielder since 1958.

.675
Winning percentage of the Pirates after the All-Star break, with a record of 52-25.

695
At-bats by Omar Moreno, most in the majors.

.746
OPS of the 1979 Pirates, highest in the NL.

.750
Winning percentage of Jim Bibby, highest in the NL. He had 12 wins and 4 losses. Bert Blyleven (.706) was third in the league, and Bruce Kison (.650) was seventh.

757
Plate appearances by Omar Moreno, most in the majors and a new franchise record. Dave Parker was sixth in the NL with 707 plate appearances.

775
Runs scored by the 1979 Pirates, most in the NL.

.906
OPS of Dave Parker, seventh in the NL. It was his third consecutive season with an OPS of at least .900.

NL Championship Series: Pittsburgh Pirates over Cincinnati Reds (3-0)

2
Home runs by Willie Stargell. He hit a three-run homer in the 11th inning of Game One and a solo homer in Game Three. Stargell had six RBIs during the NLCS and was named the MVP.

4
Runs by Phil Garner, who scored in all three games.

5
Runs scored by the Reds in the three-game series. The Pirates had 15 runs.

6
Hits by Dave Concepcion of the Reds (two hits in each game). Phil Garner and Willie Stargell led the Pirates with five hits each.

26
Strikeouts thrown by Pittsburgh pitchers, including nine in a complete game by Bert Blyleven in Game Three. Cincinnati pitchers threw 13 strikeouts during the series.

World Series: Pittsburgh Pirates over Baltimore Orioles (4-3)

1st
Player to sweep the MVP awards for the regular season, League Championship Series, and World Series: Willie Stargell. He batted .400 (12-for-30) in the World Series, with three home runs, seven runs scored, and seven RBIs. Stargell tied Reggie Jackson's 1977 record of 25 total bases.

1st
World Series at-bat in which Doug DeCinces of the Orioles hit a home run.

2nd
World Series in which the Pirates overcame a deficit of three games to one. The other was in 1925 against the Washington Senators.

3
Players who remained from the 1971 Pirates team that also beat the Orioles in the World Series in seven games: Bruce Kison, Manny Sanguillen, and Willie Stargell. Mark Belanger, Jim Palmer, and manager Earl Weaver remained from the 1971 Orioles. Grant Jackson played for the 1971 Orioles and 1979 Pirates.

THE 1979 PITTSBURGH PIRATES

3
Saves by Kent Tekulve (in Game Two, Game Six, and Game Seven).

3.34
ERA of the Pirates. The Orioles had an ERA of 4.35.

.323
Batting average of the Pirates. The Orioles batted .232; Ken Singleton (10-for-28) led the team in hits.

.500
Batting average of Phil Garner (12-for-24). During the 1979 postseason, he batted .472 (17-for-36).

Around the Majors in 1979

0
Hits allowed by Ken Forsch of the Houston Astros in an April 7 shutout against the Braves. He and his younger brother Bob (who threw a no-hitter the year before) became the first brothers with no-hitters.

1st
Career game by Jesse Orosco of the Mets, on April 5; he was 21 years old. His 1,252nd and final game (with the Minnesota Twins) was on September 27, 2003; he was 46 years old.

1st
Game as manager of the Detroit Tigers by Sparky Anderson, on June 14. He had won four pennants and two World Series titles as manager of the Reds. He would win 1,331 games (and the 1984 World Series title) with the Tigers over 17 years.

1st
Game as a major-league manager by Tony La Russa, on August 3. He replaced Don Kessinger as manager of the Chicago White Sox; Kessinger played in 56 games and batted .200 while compiling a 46-60 record as manager in 1979. La Russa managed the White Sox, Oakland Athletics, and Cardinals during his 33-year managerial career, collecting 2,728 wins, six pennants, and three World Series titles.

1.069
WHIP of Ken Forsch, lowest in the majors. Scott McGregor of the Orioles had the lowest in the AL (1.076).

2
Consecutive games in which Willie Aikens of the California Angels hit a grand slam, on June 13 (second game of doubleheader) and June 14 against the Toronto Blue Jays.

2-9
Record of Catfish Hunter of the New York Yankees in 1979. He retired after the season, at the age of 33, owing to arm problems and the effects of diabetes. Hunter won at least 21 games for five consecutive years (1971 to 1975).

2.71
ERA of J.R. Richard of the Astros, lowest in the majors. Ron Guidry of the Yankees had the lowest in the AL (2.78), and teammate Tommy John finished second (2.96).

3
Consecutive home runs as a pinch-hitter by Del Unser of the Phillies on June 30, July 5, and July 10.

3
Grand slams each by Joe Rudi of the Angels and Andre Thornton of the Cleveland Indians in 1979.

4
Home runs in four consecutive plate appearances by Mike Schmidt of the Phillies on July 6 (one home run) and July 7 (three home runs) against the Giants.

4
Bases stolen by Ron LeFlore of the Tigers in the second game of a September 23 doubleheader against the Boston Red Sox. After stealing second in the 10th inning, he scored the deciding run as the Tigers won 3-2.

4

Grand slams given up by veteran southpaw Tug McGraw of the Phillies in 1979, a new NL record. All were hit by left-handed batters.

4

Players who hit for the cycle in 1979: George Brett of the Kansas City Royals on May 28 (16-inning game), Dan Ford of the Angels on August 10 (14-inning game), Bob Watson of the Red Sox on September 15, and Frank White of the Royals on September 26. Watson's cycle was in "natural" order, with a single in the second inning, a double in the fourth, a triple in the eighth, and a home run in the ninth. Having previously hit for the cycle with the Astros in 1977, he became the first player to accomplish the feat in both leagues.

5

Home runs by the Braves (two) and the Giants (three) in the fourth inning on May 25.

5

Walks drawn by Johnny Bench of the Reds in the first game of a July 22 doubleheader against the Cubs. He also singled.

5

Runs scored by Lee Mazzilli of the Mets on August 14 against the Braves. The Mets won 18-5.

5

Inside-the-park home runs by Willie Wilson of the Royals in 1979, the most in a season since Kiki Cuyler hit nine in 1925.

6

Wild pitches thrown by J.R. Richard on April 10 against the Los Angeles Dodgers and by Phil Niekro on August 4 against the Astros (second game of doubleheader). Niekro threw four wild pitches in the fifth inning alone to set an NL record for most in one inning.

8

RBIs by Don Baylor of the Angels on August 25 against the Blue Jays. He hit a grand slam in the first inning, doubled in the third to drive in a run, and hit a three-run homer in the sixth. The Angels won 24-2.

9-0

Score by which the Tigers won a forfeited game against the White Sox on Disco Demolition Night at Comiskey Park on July 12. Admission to a scheduled twi-night doubleheader was 98 cents if you brought a disco record to be destroyed between the two games. During the first game, the crowd of nearly 50,000 took to throwing records from the stands, and the Tigers donned batting helmets in the field to protect themselves. After the Tigers won 4-1, a bin filled with records was detonated in center field, sending vinyl shards all over the outfield. Fans swarmed onto the field, and the police were unable to control the partying crowd. Eventually, the umpires postponed the second game. The next day, the Tigers were awarded a victory via forfeit by AL President Lee MacPhail.

10

Triple plays in the AL during 1979. The only triple play in the NL was by the Pirates against the Braves on July 23 (second game of doubleheader).

10th

Season with at least 200 hits by Pete Rose of the Phillies, to break Ty Cobb's record.

11

Consecutive errorless games by the Dodgers from May 5 to 16.

11

Runs scored in the 11th inning by the Mets (six runs) and Cubs (five runs) on June 30. The Mets won 9-8.

14

Consecutive losses by Matt Keough of the Athletics to start the season. He lost the last four games that he pitched in 1978, giving him a total of 18 consecutive losses.

THE 1979 PITTSBURGH PIRATES

15
Runs scored in the sixth inning by the Mets (10 runs) and Reds (five runs) on June 12. The Mets won 12-6.

16
Strikeouts thrown by Nolan Ryan of the Angels on June 9 against the Tigers.

16
Games lost in relief by Gene Garber of the Braves to set a major-league record. Mike Marshall of the Twins lost 14 games in relief to tie an AL record.

17
Wins by NL Rookie of the Year Rick Sutcliffe of the Dodgers, against 10 losses.

18
Losses by Phil Huffman of the Blue Jays, most in the AL. He won six games.

18
Seasons played with the Mets by Ed Kranepool from 1962 (the team's first year) through 1979. He played in 1,853 games, which remains a Mets record (through 2015).

20
Triples by George Brett, most in the majors. He was the first player since Willie Mays in 1957 to have at least 20 doubles, 20 triples, and 20 home runs in a season. Garry Templeton of the Cardinals led the NL with 19 triples; it was the third consecutive year that he led the league.

20
Age in years of Danny Ainge in his major-league debut with the Blue Jays on May 21. From 1979 through 1981 with Toronto, he played in 211 games and batted .220. Ainge was chosen in the 1981 NBA draft by the Boston Celtics, and later became Celtics GM.

20th
Consecutive year with at least one win by Jim Kaat. In 1979, he had a 1-0 record with the Phillies and a 2-3 record with the Yankees.

21-20
Record of Phil Niekro. He tied his younger brother Joe Niekro of the Astros for most wins in the NL; they became the second pair of brothers (after Gaylord and Jim Perry in 1970) with at least 20 wins in a season. Phil Niekro also led the majors in losses. He became the first NL pitcher since 1905 with at least 20 wins and 20 losses in the same season.

23
Consecutive games with a hit by Pete Rose from September 3 (first game of doubleheader) through September 25. During the streak, he had 42 hits in 91 at-bats (.462)

23
Wins by AL Cy Young Award winner Mike Flanagan of the Orioles, most in the majors. He had only nine losses.

23-22
Score by which the Phillies beat the Cubs in 10 innings on May 17 at Wrigley Field. The game featured 11 home runs (including three by Dave Kingman of the Cubs and two by Mike Schmidt), to tie a major-league record for homers in a game. It was the highest scoring game since August 25, 1922, when the Cubs beat the Phillies 26-23.

28 and 11
Homers hit at home and on the road, respectively, by Fred Lynn of the Red Sox in 1979. In contrast, Gene Tenace of the Padres hit only two homers at home and 18 on the road.

32
Age in years of seven-time All-Star catcher Thurman Munson of the Yankees when he died on August 2, after a plane that he was piloting crashed at the Akron-Canton Regional Airport.

WHEN POPS LED THE FAMILY

34
Sacrifice hits by Craig Reynolds of the Astros, most in the majors in 1979 and the most in the NL since 1943.

37
Saves by Bruce Sutter of the Cubs, most in the majors. He tied the NL record for saves in a season and won the league's Cy Young Award in 1979. Mike Marshall led the AL with 32 saves.

40 2/3
Consecutive innings in which reliever Joe Sambito of the Astros did not allow an earned run, from May 3 to July 21.

41
Home runs allowed by Phil Niekro, most in the majors. Ferguson Jenkins of the Texas Rangers led the AL with 40.

45
Days that major-league umpires were on strike, from Opening Day until May 18. Replacement umps were criticized by players and managers for missing calls.

48
Doubles by Keith Hernandez, most in the majors. Cecil Cooper of the Milwaukee Brewers and Chet Lemon of the White Sox tied for most in the AL with 44 doubles.

48
Home runs by Dave Kingman, most in the majors. He had more homers than walks (45). Gorman Thomas of the Brewers led the AL with 45 home runs.

49
Home runs by the Astros in 1979, including only 15 in the pitcher-friendly Astrodome. The Astros hit more triples (52) than home runs during the season.

50th
Career shutout by Tom Seaver of the Reds, on July 20, and Don Sutton of the Dodgers, on August 10.

83
Stolen bases by Willie Wilson, most in the majors in 1979 and the most in the AL since Ty Cobb stole 96 bases in 1915.

84
Games finished by Mike Marshall, a major-league record that still stands (through 2015).

85
Extra-base hits by George Brett, most in the majors.

90
Games played by Mike Marshall, most in the AL and a new league record.

106
RBIs by designated hitter Willie Horton of the Seattle Mariners, tied for eighth in the AL. His most-recent season with 100 RBIs was in 1966 — 13 years earlier while playing left field for the Detroit Tigers.

120 and 139
Runs scored and RBIs, respectively, by AL MVP Don Baylor, both tops in the majors. Keith Hernandez led the NL in runs (116), and Dave Winfield of the Padres led in RBIs (118).

121
Walks drawn by Darrell Porter of the Royals, most in the majors. He became the second catcher (after Mickey Cochrane in 1932) with at least 100 walks, 100 runs, and 100 RBIs in one season. Mike Schmidt led the NL with 120 walks.

121
Walks allowed by Mike Torrez of the Red Sox, most in the majors. Phil Niekro led the NL with 113 walks.

144
Double plays as shortstop by Roy Smalley of the Twins, a new major-league record.

THE 1979 PITTSBURGH PIRATES

146th
Career pinch-hit by Manny Mota of the Dodgers on September 29, to break the major-league record set by Smoky Burgess.

164
Games played by Frank Taveras in 1979. He played 11 games with the Pirates before being traded on April 19 to the Mets, with whom he played 153 games.

175
Strikeouts by Gorman Thomas, most in the majors. He tied the AL record set by Dave Nicholson of the White Sox in 1963. Dave Kingman led the NL with 131 strikeouts.

212
Hits by George Brett, most in the majors. Garry Templeton led the NL with 211 hits, and teammate Keith Hernandez finished second with 210.

.285 and .287
Batting average of John Castino of the Twins and Alfredo Griffin of the Blue Jays, respectively, who tied for AL Rookie of the Year.

.299
Batting average of Buddy Bell of the Rangers. He was the first player in AL history to have 200 hits with a batting average under .300.

300th
Career home run by Bobby Bonds of the Indians, on May 2, and by Willie Horton of the Mariners on June 6. Bonds became the second player (after Willie Mays) with 300 home runs and 300 stolen bases.

313
Strikeouts by J.R. Richard, most in the majors and a new NL record for right-handed pitchers. He had exactly 100 more strikeouts than the NL runner-up in 1979, Steve Carlton of the Phillies. Nolan Ryan led the AL with 223 strikeouts.

342
Innings pitched by Phil Niekro, most in the majors. He also led the majors in games started (44, the most in the NL since 1917) and complete games (23). Dennis Martinez of the Orioles led the AL with 292 1/3 innings pitched, 39 games started, and 18 complete games.

.344
Batting average of Keith Hernandez, highest in the majors. Fred Lynn led the AL with a .333 average.

369
Total bases by Jim Rice of the Red Sox, most in the majors. It was the third consecutive year that he led the AL in total bases. Dave Winfield led the NL with 333 total bases.

400th
Career home run by Carl Yastrzemski of the Red Sox, on July 24 off Mike Morgan of the Athletics.

.423 / .637 / 1.059
On-base percentage, slugging average, and OPS, respectively, of Fred Lynn, all tops in the majors. Pete Rose led the NL in on-base percentage (.418). Dave Kingman led the NL in slugging average (.613) and OPS (.956).

670
At-bats by Buddy Bell, most in the AL.

729
Plate appearances by Roy Smalley, most in the AL.

.875
Winning percentage of Ron Davis of the Yankees, highest in the majors. He had 14 wins against only two losses.

938th
And final stolen base by Lou Brock of the Cardinals, on September 23. Brock was recognized for breaking Billy Hamilton's record of 937 stolen bases, but Hamilton's total from 1888 through 1901 has since been

lowered to 914 (Brock stole his 915th base on August 4, 1978). Brock's record of 938 steals was broken by Rickey Henderson on May 1, 1991; Henderson stole a base in his major-league debut with the Athletics on June 24, 1979.

.991
Fielding percentage as shortstop by Larry Bowa of the Phillies, a new single-season major-league record.

1.000
Fielding percentage as outfielder by Terry Puhl of the Astros. He handled 359 chances without a miscue.

1,000th
Career win by Baltimore manager Earl Weaver, on Opening Day, April 6.

1,053
Career RBIs by Willie Davis, who played 43 games (mostly as a pinch-hitter) with the Angels in his final season. The closest he got to amassing 100 RBIs in a season was 93 in 1970.

2,832
Career strikeouts by Mickey Lolich, who spent his final two seasons with the Padres. When he retired in 1979, he was the all-time leader among left-handed pitchers.

3,000th
Career hit by Lou Brock on August 13 and by Carl Yastrzemski on September 12. Yastrzemski became the first AL player with 3,000 hits and 400 home runs.

SOURCES

Charlton, James, ed. *The Baseball Chronology*. (New York: Macmillan, 1991).

Nemec, David, ed. *The Baseball Chronicle: Year-by-Year History of Major League Baseball* (Lincolnwood, Illinois: Publications International, 2003).

Society for American Baseball Research. *The SABR Baseball List and Record Book* (New York: Scribner, 2007).

Solomon, Burt. *The Baseball Timeline* (New York: DK Publishing, 2001).

Sugar, Burt Randolph, ed. *The Baseball Maniac's Almanac* (third edition) (New York: Skyhorse Publishing, 2012).

baseball-almanac.com

baseball-reference.com

retrosheet.org

thisgreatgame.com/1979-baseball-history.html

Contributors

PHILLIP BOLDA was born in Milwaukee, growing up within walking distance of Milwaukee County Stadium. A graduate of Ripon College, he spent his career on university campuses as a fundraiser and now lives in Tempe, Arizona. He first joined SABR in 1979 and currently serves as Chair of the Fund Raising and Development Committee.

FREDERICK C. (RICK) BUSH, his wife Michelle, and their three sons Michael, Andrew, and Daniel live in the Houston area, and he teaches English at Wharton County Junior College in Sugar Land, Texas. Throughout his vagabond youth as an "Army brat," baseball was a constant, and it still is today. As a SABR member, he has contributed articles to both the Biography and Games Projects and to numerous books. Currently, he is an associate editor and contributing author for a book about the Houston Astrodome and is co-editor for a book about the 1948 Birmingham Black Barons and Homestead Grays, the two teams that competed for the last Negro League World Series championship.

ALAN COHEN has been a SABR member since 2011, and serves as Vice-President/Treasurer of the Connecticut Smoky Joe Wood Chapter of SABR. He has written over 30 biographies for SABR's bio-project, and has contributed to 15 SABR books, the first being *Sweet 60: The 1960 Pittsburgh Pirates*. He is expanding his research into the Hearst Sandlot Classic (1946-1965), an annual youth All-Star game which launched the careers of 88 major-league players. His research on the subject first appeared in the Fall 2013 edition of the *Baseball Research Journal*, and was followed with a poster presentation at the SABR Convention in Chicago. He is currently expanding his research and is looking forward to having a book published. He is the datacaster (stringer) for the Hartford Yard Goats of the Class-AA Eastern League. He lives in Connecticut with his wife Frances, two cats, and two dogs.

WARREN CORBETT is the author of *The Wizard of Waxahachie: Paul Richards and the End of Baseball as We Knew It*, and a contributor to SABR's BioProject. He lives in Bethesda, Maryland.

RORY COSTELLO remembers that while Pittsburgh held off Montreal to win the 1979 NL East, the New York Mets (Rory's team since childhood) won their last six games and avoided a 100-loss season. Rory has contributed to many of SABR's team biography books, often with Latino and African-American players in mind. He lives in Brooklyn, New York with his wife Noriko and son Kai.

TOM CRIST is an energy policy analyst for the Government of Canada with a budding interest in baseball history. He is a lifelong Pirates fan, even though he is too young to have witnessed the team's last World Series championship in 1979. He holds a Bachelor of Arts degree from Western University and a Master of Public Administration from the University of Victoria. He currently resides in Ottawa, Ontario with his wife Deryn and their children Edan and Emme.

DAN FIELDS is a senior manuscript editor at the *New England Journal of Medicine*. He loves baseball trivia, and he attends Boston Red Sox and Pawtucket (Rhode Island) Red Sox games with this teenage son whenever he can. Dan lives in Framingham, Massachusetts, and can be reached at dfields820@gmail.com.

JAMES FORR is past winner of the McFarland-SABR Baseball Research Award and the co-author (along with David Proctor) of *Pie Traynor: A Baseball Biography*, which was a finalist for the 2010 CASEY Award. He lives in Columbia, Missouri.

GORDON J. GATTIE serves as a human-systems integration engineer for the US Navy in Virginia. His baseball research interests involve ballparks, baseball records, and statistical analysis. A SABR member since 1998, Gordon earned his Ph.D. from State University of New York at Buffalo, where he used baseball to investigate judgment/decision-making performance in complex dynamic environments. Originally from Buffalo, Gordon learned early the hardships associated with rooting for Buffalo sports teams. Ever the optimist, he now roots for the Cleveland Indians and Washington Nationals. Meanwhile, Lisa, his lovely bride, who also enjoys baseball, continues to challenge him by supporting the Yankees.

PAUL GEISLER serves as pastor of Christ Lutheran Church in Lake Jackson, Texas, where he lives with his wife and their three children. For his entire life, Paul has enjoyed all aspects of baseball - playing, watching, coaching, researching, and writing.

CHIP GREENE, the grandson of former major leaguer Nelson Greene, joined SABR in 2006. He is a regular contributor to SABR's Biography Project and edited the SABR book *Mustaches and Mayhem: Charlie O's Three-Time Champions*. Chip lives in Waynesboro, Pennsylvania, with his wife, Elaine, and daughters Anna and Haley.

PAUL HOFMANN is the Associate Vice President for International Programs and Global Engagement at California State University - Sacramento. A native of Detroit, Michigan, Paul is a lifelong Detroit sports fan and avid baseball card collector. His research interests include 19th century and pre-World War II Japanese baseball. Paul currently resides in Folsom, California with his wife and two children.

ROCK HOFFMAN has been a SABR member since 1995, he co-hosts *Sports Page*, a sports talk radio show Saturday at 10 PM on WRDV-FM (WRDV.org) in suburban Philadelphia. He's active in the Connie Mack Chapter by helping at local meetings and running the chapter Facebook site. He was a member of the local organizing committee for the 2013 SABR National Convention in Philadelphia and volunteers to judge oral and poster presentations at the national conventions. He enjoys disc golf and American Civil War history. His home in Ardsley, Pennsylvania is a Ruthian clout from the final resting place of Hall of Fame pitcher Charles Albert "Chief" Bender. This is his first attempt at writing for a SABR publication.

MIKE HUBER is Professor of Mathematics at Muhlenberg College in Allentown, Pennsylvania. He has been a SABR member for 20 years and was fortunate to attend a playoff game in 1979. He enjoys researching and modeling rare baseball events, such as hitting for the cycle and pitching no-hitters.

BOB HURTE, of Stewartsville, New Jersey has been a member of SABR since 1998. He is one of the early writers for its Baseball Biography Project. Over his tenure he has authored 16 bios for the BioProject website, and has contributed five others to appear in future publications. He has been active in youth sports in his town, serving as its vice president for 10 years, and coaching baseball and soccer for fourteen. To say that he is a Pittsburgh Pirates fan would be an understatement; he lives and dies with them. Bob enjoys interviewing former players and has developed a friendship with many of them. He has been married to Barbara for 26 years and they have raised three children; Matthew (deceased), Tegan (21) and Samuel (18). He considers it an honor to be a part of this book project.

MICHAEL JAFFE is from Mesa, Arizona where he is an Assistant Professor of Small Animal Surgery at Midwestern University College of Veterinary Medicine. He is a life-long Mets fan stemming from his father›s love of baseball as a former sportswriter for the *Newark Star-Ledger* in New Jersey. Michael has previously contributed to SABR team biography books, and resides in Mesa with his wife Tracy and their three children and four dogs.

MAXWELL KATES is a chartered accountant who lives and works in midtown Toronto. His involvement with SABR publications dates back to 2002 when his article about Red Sox yearbooks appeared in *The Northern Game and Beyond*. He has attended baseball games in 21 of the 30 current big-league stadiums, including PNC Park in Pittsburgh on the eve of the 2008 SABR convention. The visiting Yankees sought revenge for Game Seven of the 1960 World Series with a 10-0 victory while the Bucs featured a young third baseman named Jose Bautista in the starting lineup.

THOMAS E. KERN was born and raised in Southwest Pennsylvania. Listening to the mellifluous voices of Bob Prince and Jim Woods, how could one not become a lifelong Pirates fan. He now lives in Washington, DC, and sees the Nationals and Orioles as often as possible. He is a SABR member dating back to the mid-1980s. With a love and appreciation for Negro League Baseball, he has written a bio of Leon Day (having met him at a baseball card show in the early 1990s) as well a short history of the Homestead Grays, both published by SABR. Tom's day job is in the field of transportation technology.

NORM KING lives in Ottawa, Ontario, and has been a SABR member since 2010. He has contributed to a number of SABR books, including, *"Thar's Joy in Braveland" — The 1957 Milwaukee Braves* (2014), *Winning on the North Side. The 1929 Chicago Cubs* (2015), and *A Pennant for the Twins Cities: The 1965 Minnesota Twins* (2015). He was also the senior editor and main writer for: *Au jeu/Play Ball: The 50 Greatest Games in the History of the Montreal Expos* (2016). He thought he was crazy to miss his beloved Expos after all these years until he met people from Brooklyn.

RUSS LAKE lives in Champaign, Illinois, and is a retired college professor emeritus. The 1964 St. Louis Cardinals remain his favorite team, and he was distressed to see Sportsman's Park (aka Busch Stadium I) being demolished not long after he had attended the last game there on May 8, 1966. His wife, Carol, deserves an MVP award for watching all of a 13-inning ballgame in Cincinnati with Russ in 1971—during their honeymoon. In 1994, he was an editor for David Halberstam's baseball book, *October 1964*.

LEN LEVIN is an ardent Red Sox fan but has always admired the Pirates. A retired newspaper editor in Providence, Rhode Island, he edits the decisions of the Rhode Island Supreme Court and also spends a lot of time editing articles for SABR books and for BioProject.

MARK MILLER is a retired recreation department director in Springfield, Ohio, where he lives with his wife, Connie. Also a high-school baseball coach for 22 years, he is currently president of the Springfield/Clark County Baseball Hall of Fame. His research, speaking, and writing are related to local baseball topics.

ROD NELSON is the Chair of the SABR Scouts Committee and maintains the Who-Signed-Whom database which is the foundation of the *Diamond Mines* exhibit on the Baseball Hall of Fame website. He was SABR's first Research Services Manager (2006-2007) and the founder and moderator of the BaseballNecrology Yahoogroup, as well as Managing Editor of the *Emerald Guide to Baseball* from its first edition in 2008 through 2014. He makes his home in Saint Clair Shores, Michigan.

BILL NOWLIN, HOF 2016 (the International Bluegrass Music Hall of Fame), also researches and writes about baseball. His most fervent rooting for the Pirates came during the 1960 World Series. He considers PNC Park in Pittsburgh one of the nicest ones in the majors.

CAROLE OLSHAVSKY, a licensed architect in Columbus, Ohio, is currently a Vice President of the Pizzuti Companies. Her career has included serving as Ohio's State Architect and as Senior Executive in charge of a major capital improvements program for Columbus City Schools. Her interest in 19th century baseball stems from her family history research and to date she has identified over 10 family members who have been involved in professional baseball going as far back as the 1860's. Al Monchak is a second cousin of her husband who will always be a Pirates fan.

J.G. PRESTON lives in Benicia, California, and is press secretary for Consumer Attorneys of California. He previously served as editor of the Minnesota Twins program magazine, wrote feature articles for the Twins' program and yearbook, and wrote the script for a video biography of Kirby Puckett narrated by Bob

Costas. He writes about baseball history at prestonjg.wordpress.com.

RICHARD J. PUERZER is an associate professor and chairperson of the Department of Engineering at Hofstra University in Hempstead, New York. His previous research and writings on baseball have appeared in *Nine: A Journal of Baseball History and Culture*, *Black Ball*, *The National Pastime*, *The Cooperstown Symposium on Baseball and American Culture* proceedings, *FAN*, and *Spitball*. He was co-director of The 50th Anniversary of the New York Mets Conference, held at Hofstra University in April, 2012.

RICHARD RIIS is a writer, researcher, and professional genealogist. On the subject of baseball he has written for *Vintage and Classic Baseball Collector* and been a contributor to SABR books on the New York Yankees, Detroit Tigers, Milwaukee Braves and Brewers, and Houston Astros. He is currently collaborating with a notable television and film actress on her memoirs, with an anticipated publication date in 2017. He resides in South Setauket, New York.

ERIC ROBINSON is an educator in the North Texas area. He has presented his research on Central Texas negro league history and other topics to groups ranging from the SABR National Conference, regional SABR conferences, elementary schools, Nerd Nite, and on Central Texas NPR. His website is www.lyndonbaseballjohnson.com and can be contacted at ericrobinson1776@gmail.com.

THOMAS E. SCHOTT, Tom, is a professional historian, holder of a Ph.D. in American history from LSU, retired historian for the DoD, free-lance editor, Texas Ranger fan, nephew of SABR co-founder the late Arthur O. Schott, writer/editor of numerous books and articles on the American Civil War, baseball, and American biography. Erstwhile poet. All of these and more. Lives in Norman, Oklahoma, with wife of 49 years, Susan. Daughter, two sons in Florida, two grandchildren.

RICHARD L. SHOOK is a free-lance writer who has covered baseball out of Detroit since 1967. He has covered several World Series, but sadly not Pittsburgh's, although he did sit next to Willie Stargell in the auxiliary pressbox for one game while the Detroit Tigers were playing the San Diego Padres in 1984. He lives in Plymouth, Michigan.

MATTHEW SILVERMAN went to Shea Stadium the night *before* the Mets/Pirates 1979 fog out. At age 14, he watched the next night on TV as the fog rolled in and he still feels the 99-loss Mets were ripped off of a win. He got over it and later became associate publisher at Total Sports Publishing and oversaw the sixth and seventh editions of *Total Baseball* and was managing editor of baseball and football encyclopedias branded by ESPN. He is author of *One-Year Dynasty: Inside the Rise and Fall of the 1986 Mets, Baseball's Impossible One-and-Done Champions*, *Swinging '73: Baseball's Wildest Season*, *100 Things Mets Fans Should Know and Do Before They Die*, and *New York Mets: The Complete Illustrated History*. He co-authored *Mets by the Numbers*, *Cubs by the Numbers*, and *Red Sox by the Numbers*. He co-edited *The Miracle Has Landed: The Amazin' Story of How the 1969 Mets Shocked the World* for SABR. He lives in High Falls, New York.

From an early age **DAVID E. SKELTON** developed a lifelong love of baseball when the lights from Philadelphia's Connie Mack Stadium shone through his bedroom window. Long removed from Philly, he resides with his family in central Texas where he is employed in the oil & gas industry. An avid collector, he joined SABR in 2012.

GEORGE SKORNICKEL has been a die-hard Pirates fan for over 60 years. A retired educator, he and his daughter collect memorabilia from the 1960 season. Chairman of the Forbes Field Chapter of SABR, he has written numerous articles and is the author of *Beat 'em Bucs: the 1960 Pittsburgh Pirates*. He lives with his wife, Kathy, and his two Labs, Maz, and Dexter.

While laid up with a ruptured Achilles tendon in 1998, **JON SPRINGER** began a research project to chronicle every uniform number in Mets history. That project became the acclaimed Mets By The Numbers website (mbtn.net), and book of the same name (Skyhorse Publishing 2008, 2016). A graduate of the University of Delaware, Jon is an editor at a business publication in New York, a SABR member since 2003, and a former daily newspaper sports writer. He lives in Brooklyn, New York with his family.

WAYNE STRUMPFER is the Chief Counsel at the California State Auditor's Office. He became a life-long San Francisco Giants fan at the age of 7 when Gaylord Perry tossed him a baseball at Candlestick Park. He also coaches the high school mock trial team at Sacramento Country Day School.

CLAYTON TRUTOR is a lecturer in Northeastern University's College of Professional Studies. He is also a PhD candidate in US History at Boston College. He is finishing a dissertation that examines the political and cultural history of Atlanta's emergence as a "Major League City" in the 1960s and 1970s. Additionally, he writes about college football for SB Nation. You can follow him on Twitter: @ClaytonTrutor

NICK WADDELL has contributed as both an author and an editor to SABR's BioProject. He is a lifelong Tigers fan, and proudly wears the Old English D every chance he gets. He currently resides in Chicago, Illinois.

JOSEPH WANCHO is a lifelong Cleveland Indians fan who resides in Westlake, Ohio. He has been a SABR member since 2005. He serves as the chair for the organizations Minor League Research Committee.

STEVE WEST is a math nerd, a history nerd, and a wannabe writer. Combine these with his love of baseball and the SABR BioProject is right in his wheelhouse. Steve works as a data analyst in the energy industry, messing around with computers and numbers all day long, and comes home and does the same with baseball stats while watching Rangers games at night. Steve (a SABR member since 2006), his wife Marian, and son Joshua are die-hard Rangers fans, which is one reason why Steve is now editor of a BioProject book on the 1972 Texas Rangers.

A lifelong Pirates fan, **GREGORY H. WOLF** was born in Pittsburgh, but now resides in the Chicagoland area with his wife, Margaret, and daughter, Gabriela. He remembers vividly listening to a 45 of Sister Sledge's "We Are Family" before attending a few games at Three Rivers in 1979, decked out in black and gold and topped off with a Pirates pill box cap. A professor of German studies and holder of the Dennis and Jean Bauman Endowed Chair in the Humanities at North Central College in Naperville, Illinois, he has edited five SABR books, most recently *From the Braves to the Brewers: Great Games and Exciting History at Milwaukee's County Stadium* (2016). He is currently working on projects about the Houston Astrodome and Sportsman's Park in St. Louis

SABR BioProject Team Books

In 2002, the Society for American Baseball Research launched an effort to write and publish biographies of every player, manager, and individual who has made a contribution to baseball. Over the past decade, the BioProject Committee has produced over 6,000 biographical articles. Many have been part of efforts to create theme- or team-oriented books, spearheaded by chapters or other committees of SABR.

THE 1986 BOSTON RED SOX:
THERE WAS MORE THAN GAME SIX
One of a two-book series on the rivals that met in the 1986 World Series, the Boston Red Sox and the New York Mets, including biographies of every player, coach, broadcaster, and other important figures in the top organizations in baseball that year. .
Edited by Leslie Heaphy and Bill Nowlin
$19.95 paperback (ISBN 978-1-943816-19-4)
$9.99 ebook (ISBN 978-1-943816-18-7)
8.5"X11", 420 pages, over 200 photos

THE MIRACLE BRAVES OF 1914
BOSTON'S ORIGINAL WORST-TO-FIRST CHAMPIONS
The other book in the "rivalry" set from the 1986 World Series. This book re-tells the story of that year's classic World Series and this is the story of each of the players, coaches, managers, and broadcasters, their lives in baseball and the way the 1986 season fit into their lives.
Edited by Leslie Heaphy and Bill Nowlin
$19.95 paperback (ISBN 978-1-943816-13-2)
$9.99 ebook (ISBN 978-1-943816-12-5)
8.5"X11", 392 pages, over 100 photos

SCANDAL ON THE SOUTH SIDE:
THE 1919 CHICAGO WHITE SOX
The Black Sox Scandal isn't the only story worth telling about the 1919 Chicago White Sox. The team roster included three future Hall of Famers, a 20-year-old spitballer who would win 300 games in the minors, and even a batboy who later became a celebrity with the "Murderers' Row" New York Yankees. All of their stories are included in Scandal on the South Side with a timeline of the 1919 season.
Edited by Jacob Pomrenke
$19.95 paperback (ISBN 978-1-933599-95-3)
$9.99 ebook (ISBN 978-1-933599-94-6)
8.5"x11", 324 pages, 55 historic photos

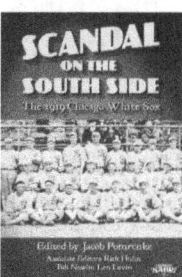

WINNING ON THE NORTH SIDE
THE 1929 CHICAGO CUBS
Celebrate the 1929 Chicago Cubs, one of the most exciting teams in baseball history. Future Hall of Famers Hack Wilson, '29 NL MVP Rogers Hornsby, and Kiki Cuyler, along with Riggs Stephenson formed one of the most potent quartets in baseball history. The magical season came to an ignominious end in the World Series and helped craft the future "lovable loser" image of the team.
Edited by Gregory H. Wolf
$19.95 paperback (ISBN 978-1-933599-89-2)
$9.99 ebook (ISBN 978-1-933599-88-5)
8.5"x11", 314 pages, 59 photos

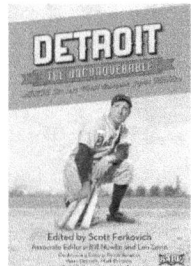

DETROIT THE UNCONQUERABLE:
THE 1935 WORLD CHAMPION TIGERS
Biographies of every player, coach, and broadcaster involved with the 1935 World Champion Detroit Tigers baseball team, written by members of the Society for American Baseball Research. Also includes a season in review and other articles about the 1935 team. Hank Greenberg, Mickey Cochrane, Charlie Gehringer, Schoolboy Rowe, and more.
Edited by Scott Ferkovich
$19.95 paperback (ISBN 9978-1-933599-78-6)
$9.99 ebook (ISBN 978-1-933599-79-3)
8.5"X11", 230 pages, 52 photos

THE TEAM THAT TIME WON'T FORGET:
THE 1951 NEW YORK GIANTS
Because of Bobby Thomson's dramatic "Shot Heard 'Round the World" in the bottom of the ninth of the decisive playoff game against the Brooklyn Dodgers, the team will forever be in baseball public's consciousness. Includes a foreword by Giants outfielder Monte Irvin.
Edited by Bill Nowlin and C. Paul Rogers III
$19.95 paperback (ISBN 978-1-933599-99-1)
$9.99 ebook (ISBN 978-1-933599-98-4)
8.5"X11", 282 pages, 47 photos

A PENNANT FOR THE TWIN CITIES:
THE 1965 MINNESOTA TWINS
This volume celebrates the 1965 Minnesota Twins, who captured the American League pennant in just their fifth season in the Twin Cities. Led by an All-Star cast, from Harmon Killebrew, Tony Oliva, Zoilo Versalles, and Mudcat Grant to Bob Allison, Jim Kaat, Earl Battey, and Jim Perry, the Twins won 102 games, but bowed to the Los Angeles Dodgers and Sandy Koufax in Game Seven.
Edited by Gregory H. Wolf
$19.95 paperback (ISBN 978-1-943816-09-5)
$9.99 ebook (ISBN 978-1-943816-08-8)
8.5"X11", 405 pages, over 80 photos

MUSTACHES AND MAYHEM: CHARLIE O'S THREE TIME CHAMPIONS:
THE OAKLAND ATHLETICS: 1972-74
The Oakland Athletics captured major league baseball's crown each year from 1972 through 1974. Led by future Hall of Famers Reggie Jackson, Catfish Hunter and Rollie Fingers, the Athletics were a largely homegrown group who came of age together. Biographies of every player, coach, manager, and broadcaster (and mascot) from 1972 through 1974 are included, along with season recaps.
Edited by Chip Greene
$29.95 paperback (ISBN 978-1-943816-07-1)
$9.99 ebook (ISBN 978-1-943816-06-4)
8.5"X11", 600 pages, almost 100 photos

SABR Members can purchase each book at a significant discount (often 50% off) and receive the ebook edtions free as a member benefit. Each book is available in a trade paperback edition as well as ebooks suitable for reading on a home computer or Nook, Kindle, or iPad/tablet.
To learn more about becoming a member of SABR, visit the website: sabr.org/join

SABR BioProject Team Books

In 2002, the Society for American Baseball Research launched an effort to write and publish biographies of every player, manager, and individual who has made a contribution to baseball. Over the past decade, the BioProject Committee has produced over 6,000 biographical articles. Many have been part of efforts to create theme- or team-oriented books, spearheaded by chapters or other committees of SABR.

THE 1986 BOSTON RED SOX:
THERE WAS MORE THAN GAME SIX
One of a two-book series on the rivals that met in the 1986 World Series, the Boston Red Sox and the New York Mets, including biographies of every player, coach, broadcaster, and other important figures in the top organizations in baseball that year. .
Edited by Leslie Heaphy and Bill Nowlin
$19.95 paperback (ISBN 978-1-943816-19-4)
$9.99 ebook (ISBN 978-1-943816-18-7)
8.5"X11", 420 pages, over 200 photos

THE MIRACLE BRAVES OF 1914
BOSTON'S ORIGINAL WORST-TO-FIRST CHAMPIONS
The other book in the "rivalry" set from the 1986 World Series. This book re-tells the story of that year's classic World Series and this is the story of each of the players, coaches, managers, and broadcasters, their lives in baseball and the way the 1986 season fit into their lives.
Edited by Leslie Heaphy and Bill Nowlin
$19.95 paperback (ISBN 978-1-943816-13-2)
$9.99 ebook (ISBN 978-1-943816-12-5)
8.5"X11", 392 pages, over 100 photos

SCANDAL ON THE SOUTH SIDE:
THE 1919 CHICAGO WHITE SOX
The Black Sox Scandal isn't the only story worth telling about the 1919 Chicago White Sox. The team roster included three future Hall of Famers, a 20-year-old spitballer who would win 300 games in the minors, and even a batboy who later became a celebrity with the "Murderers' Row" New York Yankees. All of their stories are included in Scandal on the South Side with a timeline of the 1919 season.
Edited by Jacob Pomrenke
$19.95 paperback (ISBN 978-1-933599-95-3)
$9.99 ebook (ISBN 978-1-933599-94-6)
8.5"x11", 324 pages, 55 historic photos

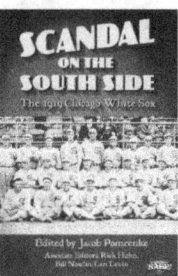

WINNING ON THE NORTH SIDE
THE 1929 CHICAGO CUBS
Celebrate the 1929 Chicago Cubs, one of the most exciting teams in baseball history. Future Hall of Famers Hack Wilson, '29 NL MVP Rogers Hornsby, and Kiki Cuyler, along with Riggs Stephenson formed one of the most potent quartets in baseball history. The magical season came to an ignominious end in the World Series and helped craft the future "lovable loser" image of the team.
Edited by Gregory H. Wolf
$19.95 paperback (ISBN 978-1-933599-89-2)
$9.99 ebook (ISBN 978-1-933599-88-5)
8.5"x11", 314 pages, 59 photos

DETROIT THE UNCONQUERABLE:
THE 1935 WORLD CHAMPION TIGERS
Biographies of every player, coach, and broadcaster involved with the 1935 World Champion Detroit Tigers baseball team, written by members of the Society for American Baseball Research. Also includes a season in review and other articles about the 1935 team. Hank Greenberg, Mickey Cochrane, Charlie Gehringer, Schoolboy Rowe, and more.
Edited by Scott Ferkovich
$19.95 paperback (ISBN 9978-1-933599-78-6)
$9.99 ebook (ISBN 978-1-933599-79-3)
8.5"X11", 230 pages, 52 photos

THE TEAM THAT TIME WON'T FORGET:
THE 1951 NEW YORK GIANTS
Because of Bobby Thomson's dramatic "Shot Heard 'Round the World" in the bottom of the ninth of the decisive playoff game against the Brooklyn Dodgers, the team will forever be in baseball public's consciousness. Includes a foreword by Giants outfielder Monte Irvin.
Edited by Bill Nowlin and C. Paul Rogers III
$19.95 paperback (ISBN 978-1-933599-99-1)
$9.99 ebook (ISBN 978-1-933599-98-4)
8.5"X11", 282 pages, 47 photos

A PENNANT FOR THE TWIN CITIES:
THE 1965 MINNESOTA TWINS
This volume celebrates the 1965 Minnesota Twins, who captured the American League pennant in just their fifth season in the Twin Cities. Led by an All-Star cast, from Harmon Killebrew, Tony Oliva, Zoilo Versalles, and Mudcat Grant to Bob Allison, Jim Kaat, Earl Battey, and Jim Perry, the Twins won 102 games, but bowed to the Los Angeles Dodgers and Sandy Koufax in Game Seven
Edited by Gregory H. Wolf
$19.95 paperback (ISBN 978-1-943816-09-5)
$9.99 ebook (ISBN 978-1-943816-08-8)
8.5"X11", 405 pages, over 80 photos

MUSTACHES AND MAYHEM: CHARLIE O'S THREE TIME CHAMPIONS:
THE OAKLAND ATHLETICS: 1972-74
The Oakland Athletics captured major league baseball's crown each year from 1972 through 1974. Led by future Hall of Famers Reggie Jackson, Catfish Hunter and Rollie Fingers, the Athletics were a largely homegrown group who came of age together. Biographies of every player, coach, manager, and broadcaster (and mascot) from 1972 through 1974 are included, along with season recaps.
Edited by Chip Greene
$29.95 paperback (ISBN 978-1-943816-07-1)
$9.99 ebook (ISBN 978-1-943816-06-4)
8.5"X11", 600 pages, almost 100 photos

SABR Members can purchase each book at a significant discount (often 50% off) and receive the ebook edtions free as a member benefit. Each book is available in a trade paperback edition as well as ebooks suitable for reading on a home computer or Nook, Kindle, or iPad/tablet.
To learn more about becoming a member of SABR, visit the website: sabr.org/join

The SABR Digital Library

The Society for American Baseball Research, the top baseball research organization in the world, disseminates some of the best in baseball history, analysis, and biography through our publishing programs. The SABR Digital Library contains a mix of books old and new, and focuses on a tandem program of paperback and ebook publication, making these materials widely available for both on digital devices and as traditional printed books.

Greatest Games Books

TIGERS BY THE TALE:
GREAT GAMES AT MICHIGAN AND TRUMBULL
For over 100 years, Michigan and Trumbull was the scene of some of the most exciting baseball ever. This book portrays 50 classic games at the corner, spanning the earliest days of Bennett Park until Tiger Stadium's final closing act. From Ty Cobb to Mickey Cochrane, Hank Greenberg to Al Kaline, and Willie Horton to Alan Trammell.
Edited by Scott Ferkovich
$12.95 paperback (ISBN 978-1-943816-21-7)
$6.99 ebook (ISBN 978-1-943816-20-0)
8.5"x11", 160 pages, 22 photos

FROM THE BRAVES TO THE BREWERS: GREAT GAMES
AND HISTORY AT MILWAUKEE'S COUNTY STADIUM
The National Pastime provides in-depth articles focused on the geographic region where the national SABR convention is taking place annually. The SABR 45 convention took place in Chicago, and here are 45 articles on baseball in and around the bat-and-ball crazed Windy City: 25 that appeared in the souvenir book of the convention plus another 20 articles available in ebook only.
Edited by Gregory H. Wolf
$19.95 paperback (ISBN 978-1-943816-23-1)
$9.99 ebook (ISBN 978-1-943816-22-4)
8.5"X11", 290 pages, 58 photos

BRAVES FIELD:
MEMORABLE MOMENTS AT BOSTON'S LOST DIAMOND
From its opening on August 18, 1915, to the sudden departure of the Boston Braves to Milwaukee before the 1953 baseball season, Braves Field was home to Boston's National League baseball club and also hosted many other events: from NFL football to championship boxing. The most memorable moments to occur in Braves Field history are portrayed here.
Edited by Bill Nowlin and Bob Brady
$19.95 paperback (ISBN 978-1-933599-93-9)
$9.99 ebook (ISBN 978-1-933599-92-2)
8.5"X11", 282 pages, 182 photos

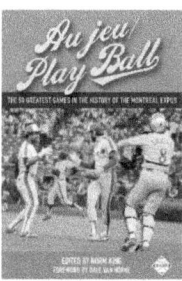

AU JEU/PLAY BALL: THE 50 GREATEST GAMES IN THE
HISTORY OF THE MONTREAL EXPOS
The 50 greatest games in Montreal Expos history. The games described here recount the exploits of the many great players who wore Expos uniforms over the years—Bill Stoneman, Gary Carter, Andre Dawson, Steve Rogers, Pedro Martinez, from the earliest days of the franchise, to the glory years of 1979-1981, the what-might-have-been years of the early 1990s, and the sad, final days.and others.
Edited by Norm King
$12.95 paperback (ISBN 978-1-943816-15-6)
$5.99 ebook (ISBN978-1-943816-14-9)
8.5"x11", 162 pages, 50 photos

Original SABR Research

CALLING THE GAME:
BASEBALL BROADCASTING FROM 1920 TO THE PRESENT
An exhaustive, meticulously researched history of bringing the national pastime out of the ballparks and into living rooms via the airwaves. Every play-by-play announcer, color commentator, and ex-ballplayer, every broadcast deal, radio station, and TV network. Plus a foreword by "Voice of the Chicago Cubs" Pat Hughes, and an afterword by Jacques Doucet, the "Voice of the Montreal Expos" 1972-2004.
by Stuart Shea
$24.95 paperback (ISBN 978-1-933599-40-3)
$9.99 ebook (ISBN 978-1-933599-41-0)
7"X10", 712 pages, 40 photos

BioProject Books

WHO'S ON FIRST:
REPLACEMENT PLAYERS IN WORLD WAR II
During World War II, 533 players made the major league debuts. More than 60% of the players in the 1941 Opening Day lineups departed for the service and were replaced by first-timers and oldsters. Hod Lisenbee was 46. POW Bert Shepard had an artificial leg, and Pete Gray had only one arm. The 1944 St. Louis Browns had 13 players classified 4-F. These are their stories.
Edited by Marc Z Aaron and Bill Nowlin
$19.95 paperback (ISBN 978-1-933599-91-5)
$9.99 ebook (ISBN 978-1-933599-90-8)
8.5"X11", 422 pages, 67 photos

VAN LINGLE MUNGO:
THE MAN, THE SONG, THE PLAYERS
40 baseball players with intriguing names have been named in renditions of Dave Frishberg's classic 1969 song, Van Lingle Mungo. This book presents biographies of all 40 players and additional information about one of the greatest baseball novelty songs of all time.
Edited by Bill Nowlin
$19.95 paperback (ISBN 978-1-933599-76-2)
$9.99 ebook (ISBN 978-1-933599-77-9)
8.5"X11", 278 pages, 46 photos

NUCLEAR POWERED BASEBALL
Nuclear Powered Baseball tells the stories of each player—past and present—featured in the classic Simpsons episode "Homer at the Bat." Wade Boggs, Ken Griffey Jr., Ozzie Smith, Nap Lajoie, Don Mattingly, and many more. We've also included a few very entertaining takes on the now-famous episode from prominent baseball writers Jonah Keri, Joe Posnanski, Erik Malinowski, and Bradley Woodrum.
Edited by Emily Hawks and Bill Nowlin
$19.95 paperback (ISBN 978-1-943816-11-8)
$9.99 ebook (ISBN 978-1-943816-10-1)
8.5"X11", 250 pages

SABR Members can purchase each book at a significant discount (often 50% off) and receive the ebook edtions free as a member benefit. Each book is available in a trade paperback edition as well as ebooks suitable for reading on a home computer or Nook, Kindle, or iPad/tablet.
To learn more about becoming a member of SABR, visit the website: sabr.org/join

Society for American Baseball Research
Cronkite School at ASU
555 N. Central Ave. #416, Phoenix, AZ 85004
602.496.1460 (phone)
SABR.org

Become a SABR member today!

If you're interested in baseball — writing about it, reading about it, talking about it — there's a place for you in the Society for American Baseball Research. Our members include everyone from academics to professional sportswriters to amateur historians and statisticians to students and casual fans who enjoy reading about baseball and occasionally gathering with other members to talk baseball. What unites all SABR members is an interest in the game and joy in learning more about it.

SABR membership is open to any baseball fan; we offer 1-year and 3-year memberships. Here's a list of some of the key benefits you'll receive as a SABR member:

- Receive two editions (spring and fall) of the *Baseball Research Journal*, our flagship publication
- Receive expanded e-book edition of *The National Pastime*, our annual convention journal
- 8-10 new e-books published by the SABR Digital Library, all FREE to members
- "This Week in SABR" e-newsletter, sent to members every Friday
- Join dozens of research committees, from Statistical Analysis to Women in Baseball.
- Join one of 70 regional chapters in the U.S., Canada, Latin America, and abroad
- Participate in online discussion groups
- Ask and answer baseball research questions on the SABR-L e-mail listserv
- Complete archives of *The Sporting News* dating back to 1886 and other research resources
- Promote your research in "This Week in SABR"
- Diamond Dollars Case Competition
- Yoseloff Scholarships

- Discounts on SABR national conferences, including the SABR National Convention, the SABR Analytics Conference, Jerry Malloy Negro League Conference, Frederick Ivor-Campbell 19th Century Conference
- Publish your research in peer-reviewed SABR journals
- Collaborate with SABR researchers and experts
- Contribute to Baseball Biography Project or the SABR Games Project
- List your new book in the SABR Bookshelf
- Lead a SABR research committee or chapter
- Networking opportunities at SABR Analytics Conference
- Meet baseball authors and historians at SABR events and chapter meetings
- 50% discounts on paperback versions of SABR e-books
- 20% discount on MLB.TV and MiLB.TV subscriptions
- Discounts with other partners in the baseball community
- SABR research awards

We hope you'll join the most passionate international community of baseball fans at SABR! Check us out online at SABR.org/join.

SABR MEMBERSHIP FORM

	Annual	3-year	Senior	3-yr Sr.	Under 30
U.S.:	☐ $65	☐ $175	☐ $45	☐ $129	☐ $45
Canada/Mexico:	☐ $75	☐ $205	☐ $55	☐ $159	☐ $55
Overseas:	☐ $84	☐ $232	☐ $64	☐ $186	☐ $55

Add a Family Member: $15 each family member at same address (list names on back)
Senior: 65 or older before 12/31 of the current year
All dues amounts in U.S. dollars or equivalent

Participate in Our Donor Program!
Support the preservation of baseball research. Designate your gift toward:
☐ General Fund   ☐ Endowment Fund   ☐ Research Resources   ☐ _____
☐ I want to maximize the impact of my gift; do not send any donor premiums
☐ I would like this gift to remain anonymous.

Note: Any donation not designated will be placed in the General Fund.
SABR is a 501 (c) (3) not-for-profit organization & donations are tax-deductible to the extent allowed by law.

Name _____

E-mail* _____

Address _____

City _____ ST _____ ZIP _____

Phone _____ Birthday _____

*Your e-mail address on file ensures you will receive the most recent SABR news.

Dues $_____
Donation $_____
Amount Enclosed $_____

Do you work for a matching grant corporation? Call (602) 496-1460 for details.

If you wish to pay by credit card, please contact the SABR office at (602) 496-1460 or visit the SABR Store online at SABR.org/join. We accept Visa, Mastercard & Discover.

Do you wish to receive the *Baseball Research Journal* electronically?: ☐ Yes   ☐ No
Our e-books are available in PDF, Kindle, or EPUB (iBooks, iPad, Nook) formats.

Mail to: SABR, Cronkite School at ASU, 555 N. Central Ave. #416, Phoenix, AZ 85004